From the days of Richard Sears to now —

90 Years of Service to the American Consumer

I t all began in 1886, with a jewelry company's error. A Chicago company had shipped some watches to a jeweler in Redwood Falls, Minnesota. The jeweler didn't want them. But the railroad station agent in nearby North Redwood, with spare time and a keen eye for a chance to do some business, did. He bought the watches, and sold them to other station agents at a handsome profit.

The agent's name was Richard W. Sears. And the R. W. Sears Watch Company was the beginning of one of America's greatest business success stories. As his business grew, some of his customers needed their watches repaired. So in 1887, Sears hired a watch repairman from Indiana named Alvah C. Roebuck.

In 1893, the firm, now in Chicago, became Sears, Roebuck and Co. Originally, it offered only watches and other jewelry. The first catalog, issued in 1888, featured no other products. But Richard Sears, once called a "showman of the calibre of P.T. Barnum," recognized the tremendous potential market for general merchandise at reasonable prices. In those days of difficult transportation, farmers were rarely able to buy anywhere but at the small (and high-priced) rural stores near them.

But, with the growth of railroads and later the introduction of parcel post and rural free delivery, Sears was able to offer substantial savings to the farmers. For the first time, in 1894, the Sears catalog offered almost everything: from men's clothing and musical instruments to sewing machines and firearms. This first "complete" catalog of 322 pages is the one you are now about to enjoy.

Richard Sears also recognized that customers of that day felt it was risky to order and pay for merchandise before it had been examined. So, as an assurance of the company's integrity, Sears established the now-famous policy of "Satisfaction Guaranteed or Your Money Back." This policy has been expanded to include not only the customer's opportunity to examine his purchase, but to use it before making up his mind. For 90 years Sears has continued its promise to customers of "Satisfaction Guaranteed or Your Money Back."

Another innovative Sears approach was the establishment of a testing laboratory. It was started in 1911 to test food products sold by Sears. The "food" laboratory soon expanded to become the Sears Merchandise and Testing Laboratory — the "watchdog of the catalog." To Sears customers it meant a new approach to mail order selling: he or she no longer had to guess about quality. Customers could rely on testing — and can to this day.

Sears expansion was immediate and continuous. In 1906 the Company built on a 40-acre site, a $5 million Chicago mail order plant and office which was then the world's largest business building, and is still in use. In the same year a Dallas branch office was opened; six years later it blossomed into a new mail order plant. Today Sears operates a total of twelve Catalog Merchandise Distribution Centers. Their location throughout the country made possible the savings of lower freight rates, faster delivery, and reduced merchandise damage.

When General Robert E. Wood joined Sears in 1924, he recognized a new American era. New and better automobiles and roads had released the farmer from his isolation. Now he could drive into town to shop — even to the big city. General Wood opened Sears first retail store adjoining the Chicago mail order plant. An immediate success, it was followed by seven more retail stores in 1925. And by 1927, there were 27 Sears retail stores.

Since 1906 Sears, Roebuck and Co. has been a publicly owned corporation listed on the N.Y. Stock Exchange. It operates 3600 stores throughout the United States with over 400,000 employees.

Sears is proud of its beginnings and of the many services and innovations it has been able to bring to American consumers. This 1894 Sears catalog is just one chapter from our past — and we know you'll find it interesting and enjoyable reading.

Our Combined Catalogue.

PRESERVE THIS BOOK. ●●●●● ◄●◄► ●●●●● **IT'S A MONEY SAVER.**

TO OUR PATRONS:

Again we come to you, and we honestly believe, with the grandest collection of Bargains ever printed in one volume. **This is a Book of Bargains; a Money Saver for Everyone.** It is not our aim to include in this book and confuse you with a great variety of goods on which we can save you no money, but it has been our aim to include goods on which you can make a great saving. By a comparison of our prices with those of any thoroughly reliable house, you will see at once **you can save money** on everything you buy from us. It would be useless for us to include in this book a lot of goods at prices which with transportation charges added would cost you as much as you could buy the same article for in your local market. **We have studied to avoid this** by offering you only such goods as we are in a position to buy from the manufacturers direct and in such quantities as enables us to deliver them to you for as little or less money than they would cost your local dealer.

OUR OLD FRIENDS AND PATRONS

Will remember us as originally **an Exclusive Watch House, and later, Watches, Diamonds, Jewelry and Silverware,** and we believe we can modestly claim what is universally conceded that we honestly earned and have since maintained the reputation of being The LARGEST WATCH and JEWELRY HOUSE in the WORLD selling goods direct to the consumer. **Our daily average sales of Watches have been over 400, Jewelry and Silverware in proportion,** while in the **Diamond** business our sales have almost from the very start **exceeded that of any firm in America** selling direct to the consumer.

WE HAVE ADDED MANY NEW LINES

And we shall hope for the same support in our new departure that has been so liberally accorded us in the past. **We have studied** to carefully and honestly represent every article so that when it reaches you, its appearance will almost universally be **better** than the description we give.

ABOUT OUR RELIABILITY.

We are authorized and incorporated under the laws of the State of Minnesota, with a cash capital paid in full of **$75,000.00.** We refer you to The Union National Bank of Minneapolis, and you are at liberty, if you choose, to send your money to them with instructions not to turn it over to us unless they know us to be perfectly reliable. We refer to any Express Company doing business in Minneapolis or Chicago—Adams, American, United States, Great Northern or Northern Pacific, or you can very likely find people in your own locality who know of us. **Ask your nearest Express Agent** about us; most any Express Agent can tell you about us. **Every Express Agent** in the United States knows of our reputation, as they have delivered our goods, and must, in most cases, know what our customers think of us.

WHERE WE SELL GOODS.

Almost Everywhere! There isn't a town in the Union where we haven't sold goods, our goods go into every city, town and hamlet in every state, as well as most every country on the globe. **Don't think** you live too far away. Our biggest trade is in Pennsylvania; 2d, New York; 3d, Illinois; 4th, Ohio, and so on, according to the population of the several states. **Distance cuts no figure. We can serve you anywhere, anytime. Freight rates are low. Express rates are low.** We have **Special facilities for Shipping** and in many cases **Special rates.**

WE AIM TO MAKE CUSTOMERS

Of Everyone by treating every customer in such a manner as to insure their always remaining a customer. **WE CAN'T AFFORD TO LOSE A CUSTOMER,** and by instructing our employes to treat every customer at a distance exactly as they would like to be treated were they in a customer's place, and rigidly enforcing this rule, we have grown into one of the first institutions of the country and our patrons far and near are talking in our favor and thus adding new customers daily.

WHO WE SELL.

We sell the consumer, by that we mean we deal direct with the party who buys for his own use, thus saving you the middle man's profit. Anyone can buy from us; there is no restriction. Our terms and conditions are the most liberal ever offered. We make it very easy to buy of us.

Read our Terms, Conditions, etc., on next page. Very truly,

SEARS, ROEBUCK & CO.,

Globe Building, Minneapolis, Minn.   149 West Van Buren Street, Chicago, Ills.

◄ ADDRESS US AT EITHER PLACE. ◄

4

TERMS, CONDITIONS OF SHIPMENT, ETC.

The terms and conditions of Shipment will usually be found under each description, but in all cases, unless otherwise specified, CASH IN FULL MUST ACCOMPANY YOUR ORDER. We have tried in all cases to make our terms as liberal as possible, and by comparison you will find we offer terms not given by any other house in existence. On account of weight and bulk some goods can not be sent by express or C. O. D., but so far as we can, we send C. O. D., subject to examination to anyone.

Our Watches, Diamonds and Jewelry we continue sending C. O. D. to any one anywhere, subject to exam- ination. **NO MONEY IN ADVANCE. Prepay all Express Charges on Watches,** excepting a few special cheap watches on which we require cash in full and do not pay charges as explained under each description. ☞ UNDERSTAND, Diamonds, Watches and Jewelry will be sent to anyone, **NO MONEY IN ADVANCE.** No other House on Earth handling the fine line we do give such liberal terms.

Pianos and Organs we will send to anyone and allow **TEN DAYS TRIAL FREE,** subject to the conditions fully explained in Catalogue pages.

Guns and Revolvers we will send to anyone anywhere C. O. D., subject to examina- tion, on receipt of 50c to $3.00 as a guarantee of good faith. For full particulars read **GUN PAGES.**

Harness. We send Harness C. O. D., subject to examination to any one, on receipt of $1.00 as a Guarantee. For particulars read **HARNESS PAGES.**

Silverware. Some Silverware we send C. O. D., subject to examination, **No Money in Advance.** For particulars see **SILVERWARE PAGES.**

Clothing. We send Clothing C. O. D., subject to examination on **VERY LIBERAL TERMS.** For particulars see **CLOTHING DEPARTMENT.**

Bicycles. C. O. D.; subject to examination on receipt of **ONE DOLLAR.**

Baby Carriages. C. O. D., subject to examination on receipt of **TWO DOLLARS.**

FULL PARTICULARS as to **TERMS OF SALE, CONDITION OF SHIPMENT,** Etc., will be found under the General Descriptions throughout this Book, and in most cases will be found more liberal than is offered by any other concern.

YOU TAKE NO RISK in ordering of us whether you send part or full amount of cash with your order, as we **ALWAYS REFUND MONEY** where goods are not found perfectly satisfactory.

HOW TO ORDER.

ALWAYS WRITE YOUR ORDERS PLAINLY; Order Everything by Number; Always sign your Name plainly and in full; Always give the Name of your nearest Express Office or Railroad Station to which you wish goods shipped. If goods are to be sent by Express, give Name of Express company, or Name of Railroad company if to be sent by freight. **GOODS CAN NOT BE SENT BY MAIL C. O. D.** Anything to be sent by mail must be paid for in Advance.

IF YOU DON'T FIND WHAT YOU WANT in this Book, write us. We may have the very thing in stock; if we haven't, we can no doubt get it for you at a great saving. Don't hesitate to write us at any time. We are always at your service. Your obedient servants,

SEARS, ROEBUCK & CO.,

Globe Building, MINNEAPOLIS, MINN.   149 West Van Buren St., CHICAGO, ILL.

◆ ADDRESS US AT EITHER PLACE. ◆

OUR WATCH DEPARTMENT

$1.15

We Don't Think We Have a Competitor
IN THE WATCH BUSINESS.

☞ We honestly believe our prices are Below all others. ☜

☞ We consider ourselves Headquarters in this LINE. ☜

☞ Look this catalogue over and say What you Think. ☜

ONE DOLLAR and FIFTEEN CENTS

Buys our Victoria Patent Wind, Nickel Watch.

The cheapest watch in the market—sometimes called a clock watch. It is made by the *New Haven Clock Co.* on the same principle as Nickel Alarm Clocks are made. They are very strong and durable and particularly adapted to those who want a time piece for a **VERY SMALL SUM.**

No. 8000.

We furnish these watches in three styles: **In nickel case, $1.15; Electro gold plated case, $1.28; Fancy silver plated case, $1.39. Cash in full** must accompany all orders for this watch. If you want the watch sent by mail, postage paid, enclose 6 cents extra to pay postage, if by registered mail 14 cents. ☞ **We do not pay Express Charges** on this watch, we have made the price on this watch **BELOW** all competitors, and at the price we can not pay charges and must have cash in full with your order.

A Stem-wind Watch for $1.68!

Other Houses Sell the Same Watch at $3.00 to $5.00.

All Express or Postage Charges Paid by Us.

CASH IN FULL Must Accompany all orders for this Watch. We cannot afford to send it C. O. D. **WE MAKE NOTHING** on the watch. **THIS IS A LEADER.** The actual cost to manufacture in Switzerland, duty and transportation makes **$1.68,** and that is our price to everyone everywhere.

☞ **Description of Watch!** A Regular $5.00 Watch $1.68. This case is stem-wind and patent setting, **Solid German Silver,** warranted to wear and retain its color a lifetime; extra heavy flat crystal, solid enameled **Arabic Dial,** finest steel hour, minute and second hands. The movements are carefully tested and will keep good time.

The Watch is Called the Wonder!

And it really is a wonder. **Send us $1.68** by registered mail, or by postal note, or by express, or postal money order, and we will send it to you by mail securely packed and **guarantee it to reach you safely and prove satisfactory.** If you don't find it equal to any watch sold by other houses at $3.00 to $5.00 return it and we will **refund your money.**

No. 8001.

Cash Only Will Secure this Watch at $1.68!

YOU CAN MAKE MONEY

Every month selling our watches. Many are selling our watches and writing us from every state in the Union that they make more money than at anything else they ever did. Railroad and express agents write us that their profits from our watches amount to more than their salaries. Merchants write that at our incomparably low prices they make more selling our watches than on all other goods they handle. But it isn't confined to Jewelers, Merchants and Railroad Men. Traveling men selling goods of various kinds on the road, buy our watches and carry them as a side line and sell them from town to town. Peddlers, Clerks, Farmers, Traders, Laboring Men, YES, ALL CLASSES SELL OUR WATCHES, and from all classes in all parts comes daily by the hundreds the one universal report: —— Grandest Success Ever Attained.

BEST watches in the market.
TERMS most liberal ever offered.
PRICES far the lowest in the market.
TREATMENT fair, honorable and just.

You need not take our word alone, for further along in this price list will be found testimonials taken from a few of the many **THOUSANDS WE HAVE RECEIVED.** They have (on account of the satisfactory treatment received) of their own free will taken this way of expressing themselves.

We don't want to take all your time telling you what we can and are doing. But if you don't want a watch yourself, we know you can sell some. Give us a chance to prove our statements by actions.

LET US SEND YOU A WATCH.

OUR SPECIAL PRICE, $2.75!

◦ ◦ FREE ◦ ◦ ◦ FREE ◦ ◦

To see and thoroughly examine at the express office, then if found to be all we claim for it and entirely satisfactory, pay the express agent $2.75 and the watch is yours, otherwise it will be returned at AT OUR EXPENSE and you will not be out one cent.

This watch is warranted A GENUINE, 3½ ounce, DUEBER silverine, guaranteed by the Manufacturer to wear and retain its color (which is equal in appearance to pure silver) for a life-time. Case is highly polished, full bassine pattern, double thick beveled edge, flat genuine French crystal (will stand 200 pounds pressure). **MOVEMENT** is a fine full jeweled, full plate, quick train, warranted an accurate time-keeper.

We bought just **2,000** of these watches at less than half-price and will sell them at less than half-price. When they are gone you will have to pay $5.00 for the same watch.

No. 6029.

REMEMBER, ALL EXPRESS CHARGES WE PAY.

YOU PAY $2.75, NO MORE, NO LESS.

A BLOW AT HIGH PRICES!

A Dueber Stem Wind Silverine Case, and an 11 Jeweled Nickel or Gilt Stem Wind Movement for $2.95. It's Our NO SPECIAL 5. Order by Number.

IS OUR PRICE BELOW ALL OTHERS?

Just look at a comparison of prices from the catalogues of five of the largest concerns with some reputation for low prices on this watch. We find they make the following prices:

One Concern makes a Price of	$7 75
One Concern makes a Price of	6 50
One Concern makes a Price of	5 95
One Concern makes a Price of	5 00
WE MAKE THE PRICE	2 95

MAKE THE COMPARISON

Yourself, with any prices you ever see quoted, and see if we have exagerated.

The same difference will apply on all our goods.

NO SPECIAL 5. Order by Number.
This is a picture of the Case, engraved from a photograph.

This is a picture of the Movement, engraved from a photograph.

DESCRIPTION OF OUR No SPECIAL 5.

THIS CASE is a genuine Dueber Silverine. See copy of Dueber's own guarantee at bottom of page, which goes with every case. 3½ ounce **Stem Wind** and **Stem Set** open face flat beveled edge French crystal, tested to 300 pounds, dead weight pressure, to insure their never breaking, solid inside cap, all beautifully polished and finished, equal in appearance and finish to **Coin Silver,** and guaranteed by The Great Dueber Watch Co. to wear and retain their color a lifetime.

MOVEMENT comes in either **Nickel** or **Gilt.** It is 11 Jeweled, **Stem Wind and Stem Set,** quick train, patent pinion and escapement, and a movement that will give satisfaction.

OUR TERMS CASH IN FULL must accompany all orders for this, our **Special No. 5** watch. **WE CAN'T SEND IT C. O. D.** There is but a **very few cents** profit on it, and as we have made the price so low, we don't think it unfair to ask for cash with your order for this watch. **YOU TAKE NO RISK.** If you are not perfectly satisfied, return it and we will refund your money. If you want it sent by mail, **postpaid,** send 6 cents extra to pay postage; if by registered mail, 14 cents extra.

REMEMBER....

Our price for this complete watch is **$2.95.** Wholesale houses ask from $5.00 upwards. Retail houses ask from $8.00 to $12.00.

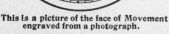

This is a picture of the face of Movement engraved from a photograph.

This is a picture of Dueber's own guarantee, which goes with every case.

CASH IN FULL MUST ACCOMPANY YOUR ORDER FOR THIS WATCH.

GENUINE DUEBER SILVERINE!

ON THIS Watch we have no COMPETITORS

A $9.00 Watch for $4.50
A $12.00 Watch for 5.50

All Retail Stores Sell These ====
==== **Watches at from $9.00 to $12.00**

WE MAKE IT A LEADER!

No. Special 1.
ORDER BY NUMBER.

It's Our Special No. 1.
Order It By Number.
Call For Special No. 1.

This case is warranted to wear and retain its perfect color a lifetime! ☞ Read the manufacturer's guarantee at bottom of page. This guarantee goes with every case, it is signed by John C. Dueber, President of the great Dueber Watch Co.

BEWARE OF IMITATIONS!

There are many imitations on the market under various misleading names, such as silveroid, ore-silver, silverus, etc. **BEWARE OF ANY SUCH!**

This is the only Genuine Silverine Case made. This case cannot in appearance be told from coin silver, in fact, it is in appearance, finish and every way except in intrinsic value **the equal of coin silver** and it will remain so as long as you live.

☞**DESCRIPTION!** This case is 3½ ounce, stem-wind and stem-set, open face, jointed back and inside cap, tripple strength, flat beveled edge, French crystal, tested to 300 pounds dead weight pressure to insure its never breaking. It is gent's regulation 18 size.

⮞ COMPARE OUR PRICES! ⮜

We fit in this case a solid nickel, stem-wind and
    stem-set 7 jeweled Trenton movement $4.50
    7 jeweled Waltham, Hampden or Elgin . . 5.50
11   "   "   "   " . . 7.00
15   " patent regulator, Waltham Hamp-
    den or Elgin 8.50

YOU KNOW OUR TERMS!

THEY COULDN'T BE EASIER.

We will send this watch to any address anywhere by express, *all express charges paid by us.* You can examine it at the express office and if found perfectly satisfactory pay the express agent our special price, **no more**, and the watch is yours. Don't forget our Guarantee. It goes with every watch and it is the most binding guarantee ever issued. Guarantees every movement for 5 years and every gold filled case for 20 years.

DUBBER'S GUARANTEE.
THIS IS A PICTURE OF THE MANUFACTURER'S
OWN GUARANTEE WHICH GOES WITH
EVERY SILVERINE CASE.

DUEBER HUNTING SILVERINE!

Look where you may! Read all the watch catalogues issued, and where can you buy such a watch as this for **$4.95**

AND REMEMBER **We Pay All The Express Charges!**

Don't forget the price we quote to you is just what the watch will cost you, **not one cent more.** You have no express charges to pay on the package going, nothing to pay for returning the money to us. **We pay it all.** We name the amount the watch will cost you, delivered to any place in the **United States. You will be disappointed** if you order from a concern that does not pay the charges; for the agent will require you to pay in addition to the price advertised, the regular local rate of express on the watch going to you and and on the return of money for same.

WE SAVE YOU THIS and that is not all; notwithstanding we pay all the express charges, our prices will be found far below all other dealers.

YOU NEEDN'T TAKE OUR WORD Send for any watch we advertise, compare it with any watch you ever saw offered for the same money, and **YOU BE THE JUDGE.**

No. 8012. ORDER BY NUMBER.

DESCRIPTION OF THIS WATCH:

This is a genuine **DUEBER SILVERINE HUNTING CASE,** made by the great Dueber Watch Case Co. Every case is warranted to wear and retain its color a life-time, and a binding guarantee (as illustrated) signed by **Jno. C. Dueber** accompanies every case. **THESE CASES** are in appearance, finish and every way except in intrinsic value, the equal of **Coin Silver.** They are 3½ ounce, stem-wind and stem-set, **Hunting,** full bassine, beautifully finished.

COMPARE OUR PRICES!

We fit in this case a solid nickel, stem-wind and
stem-set 7 jeweled Trenton movement at   - $4.95
With 7 jeweled Waltham, Hampden, or Elgin, -   5.95
 " 11   "   "   "   "   "   -   7.20
 " 15   " patent regulator, Waltham, Hampden, or Elgin,   -   -   -   -   9.45

EVERYTHING IS MADE EASY!

We will send the watch to you by express C. O. D. subject to examination.

NO MONEY IN ADVANCE!

You can examine it at the express office, and if perfectly satisfactory, pay the express agent our price and the watch is yours; otherwise, **PAY NOTHING,** and the agent will return it our expense.

DUEBER'S GUARANTEE.
THIS IS A PICTURE OF THE MANUFACTURER'S OWN GUARANTEE WHICH GOES WITH EVERY SILVERINE CASE.

DUEBER SILVERINE—GOLD INLAID!

OUR PRICE IS
$4.95!
Take Your Choice of Either Locomotive or Deer, The Price is the Same, $4.95

OTHER HOUSES ASK 8, 10 and 12 Dollars.

No. 8010.
ORDER BY NUMBER.

No. 8011.
ORDER BY NUMBER.

☞ Our price is alike to all **$4.95**, and we prepay all express charges. When you get the watch you pay the express agent $4.95, no more. There can be no misunderstanding, no disappointment when you order from us. **We always do the same.** Everyone knows our terms, you know just what to expect and you get just what you are looking for.

~ ENORMOUS ~

Sales on these watches the last year has enabled us to buy them in such quantities that we can offer them to you at prices **never before heard of**, prices that other dealers cannot understand, prices that will enable you to sell them at a handsome profit.

You Can Make MONEY

From the day you start selling these watches. You ought to sell them rapidly at $10.00. **JUST THINK OF IT!** A Genuine Dueber Silverine Case, Inlaid with 14 Karet Gold, Complete with a 7 Jeweled Trenton Movement for **$4.95.**

☞**DESCRIPTION!** These cases are Genuine Dueber Silverine, 3½ ounce, open face, stem-wind and stem-set, inlaid with **14 Karet Solid Gold** as shown in cuts. The raised solid gold ornamentations on these cases are the same class of work as put on the very best class of gold and gold filled cases. No one would believe such a watch could be had for less than $10.00 to $15.00, and no retailer can sell them for less than $8.00 to $10.00. **These cases are the only Genuine Dueber** silverine case made, and are warranted by the Dueber Watch Case Co. A special guarantee signed by John C. Dueber, President, is sent with each case.

DUBBER'S GUARANTEE.
THIS IS A PICTURE OF THE MANUFACTURER'S OWN GUARANTEE WHICH GOES WITH EVERY SILVERINE CASE.

We fit in these Cases Complete:

7 Jeweled Trenton Movement		$4.95
7 " Waltham, Hampden or Elgin		5.95
11 " " " "		7.20
15 " Patent Regulator, Waltham, Hampden or Elgin		9.45

SENT C. O. D. SUBJECT TO EXAMINATION.
NO MONEY IN ADVANCE.   ALL CHARGES PAID.

$3.25 FOR A $6.00 WATCH!

C.O.D. TO ANYONE, ANYWHERE, No Money in Advance.

BEST SWISS NICKEL WATCH MADE!

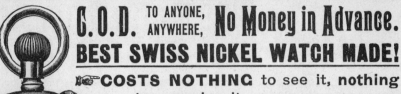

COSTS NOTHING to see it, nothing to examine it.

WE PAY EVERYTHING.

You pay nothing unless you are satisfied and wish to keep the watch; but then, **you know those are our TERMS** on all Good Watches.

DESCRIPTION! This is one of the best nickel watches imported. **Case** is made of SOLID NICKEL, beautifully finished, stem-wind and stem-set. **Movement** is SOLID NICKEL, nicely jeweled, stem-wind and stem-set, accurately regulated and guaranteed in every respect.

IT PAYS TO BUY A GOOD WATCH!

No. 8029.

Order by Number.　Open Face Only.　☞You can make no better investment than to add a few cents to the price you intend paying for a watch, you will get a better movement, better case, in fact in every way you will be far better satisfied.

OUR $5.75 HORSE TIMER!

☞Our price is about one=half the price charged by retail dealers, in fact $3.00 be=low what we have ever seen it advertised.

This watch will cost you just

$5.75

UNDERSTAND, we pay all the express charges, the prices we quote on watches are the prices at which we will deliver them to any point in the United States.

DESCRIPTION OF HORSE TIMER!

Solid Nickel, Open Face, Stem-wind and Stem-set, Jeweled Nickel Movement, Start, Stop and Fly Back Attachment, Beats Quarter Seconds, Registers **Minutes, Seconds and Fractions of Seconds.**

C. O. D. TO ANYONE.
ON MONEY IN ADVANCE.

No. 8030.

Order by Number.　Open Face Only.

WHERE ARE OUR COMPETITORS!
GOLD PLATED WATCH FOR $2.75!

Again we ask, WHERE ARE OUR COMPETITORS!

This is the same watch that is being so extensively advertised in papers and by circulars by many **cheap John** — shoddy goods houses. **Beware of some** of the representations you may see them make: they will describe it as a **very fine** heavy gold plated, gold filled, aluminum gold, goldentine, etc.; tell you it can't be told from a $100 solid gold watch. **DON'T BE DECEIVED!** We have put this class of goods in our catalogue for **just what they are** and at the **proper price** to save any of our customers from being taken in by any of these howlers. **As a matter of fact,** these watches are in no way as they represent them. We guarantee this watch to be the same as they are praising so high.

THIS CASE is **electro gold plated** over brass, not **guaranteed to wear,** imitation **hand engraved** and fitted with **a cheap imitation** American movement, not guaranteed as a time keeper.

Our Price, open face, key-wind, - -	$2.75
Our Price, open face, stem-wind, - -	3.55

NO. 8004.

UNDERSTAND we do not guarantee or recommend these watches, and **we do not send them C. O. D.** Cash in full must accompany all orders for this class of goods. We don't pay express charges on this watch; if you want it sent by mail, **post paid,** send 6 cents to pay postage; if by registered mail, send 14 cents.

WHERE ARE OUR COMPETITORS!
GOLD PLATED WATCH FOR $2.80

AGAIN WE ASK
WHERE ARE OUR COMPETITORS!

This is the same watch that is being so extensively advertised in papers and circulars at various prices ranging from $3.98 to $10.00, and represented as a wonderful watch, etc. **Don't let them deceive you!** It's no such thing.

THIS CASE is electro gold plated over brass, imitation hand engraved, not guaranteed to wear.

MOVEMENT is a Swiss imitation American, not recommended as a time keeper.

Our Price, hunting case, key-wind, - -	$2.80
Our Price, hunting case, stem-wind, - -	3.65

UNDERSTAND, we do not recommend these watches, and we do not send them C. O. D. **CASH IN FULL** must accompany all orders for this class of goods. We don't pay express charges on this watch. If you want it sent by mail, post paid, send 6 cents to pay postage; if by registered mail, send 14 cents.

NO. 8005.

WHERE ARE OUR COMPETITORS!

Ladie's Gold Plated Watch

$2.80

☞ **Again we Ask, Where are our Competitors?** This is the same watch that is being so extensively advertised in papers and circulars by these loud, cheap, trashy dealers as the **Greatest Wonder of the Age, etc. WE WILL NOT LET THEM FOOL YOU!**

☞ Read our description and know the truth.

This Case is electro gold plated over brass, imitation hand engraved, *not guaranteed to wear*.

Movement is a Swiss, imitation American and not recommended as a timekeeper.

No. 8006.

Our Price, Hunting Case, Key-wind $2.80
Our Price, Hunting Case, Stem-wind 3.95

UNDERSTAND, we do not guarantee or recommend these watches, and we do not send them C. O. D. **Cash in Full** must accompany all orders for this class of goods. If you want it sent by mail *post paid* send **6** cents extra to pay postage, if by registered mail **14** cents.

WHERE ARE OUR COMPETITORS!

Gent's Box Joint, Gold Plated Watch.
OUR PRICE, $3.90

Others ask from 7 to 12 Dollars.

☞ **Again we Ask, Where are our Competitors?** THE VERY SAME watch you hear so much about in many papers, *fake* circulars, *fake* catalogues, etc., advertised as finest gold plated, or gold filled, cannot be told from a $100.00 solid gold watch and all such trash. **Read this** catalogue and you will not be fooled. *We will tell you all about it.*

☞ **This is the Honest Description.** This case is **BRASS,** *electro gold plated,* imitation hand engraved, will not hold its color long and is not guaranteed, hunting case, stem-wind and stem-set, fitted with an imported imitation American movement not guaranteed as a timekeeper.

☞ **We don't like to sell this class of goods,** but in order that our customers may know just what they are, and just what they are worth, we offer them for the first time.

Cash in Full must Accompany all orders for this grade of goods.

No. 8007.

YOUR CHOICE FOR $3.95!

☞ Open Face or Hunting Case. ☜

CASH IN FULL MUST accompany ALL ORDERS FOR THESE WATCHES. We don't Guarantee them.

READ CAREFULLY! We don't like to sell this grade of goods, for the reason heretofore we never have handled anything of a cheaper quality than genuine, 20 year gold filled cases, but we have had so much call for a **cheap trading watch** that we have finally been persuaded to add them to our catalogue. While many houses advertise them in glowing colors as **fine gold filled, extra quality gold plated,** warranted to wear 20 years, equal to solid gold, and many other such misleading representations, **we do not.**

The Truth is these cases are brass, electro gold plated, imitation hand engraved, stem-wind and stem-set, and while we do not guarantee these watches to wear **we do guarantee them in every way equal** to watches that are being advertised by many so-called large watch houses as **fine gold filled** and at prices ranging from $5.00 to $10.00.

No. 8027.

Order by Number.   Open Face Only.

These Movements are stem-wind and stem-set, and while not guaranteed as time-keepers, many of them will keep excellent time, and for trading purposes these watches are often very desirable as they present a very showy appearance and yet the price is very low. **In fact, these watches will always appear far better** than our representation would lead you to believe, for the reason we prefer to sell nothing cheaper **than a good gold filled case,** one **that we know will give satisfaction, a watch we can guarantee,** and one we will be pleased to send C. O. D. Subject to Examination. So, in our eagerness to sell a better watch, we do not do justice to these unguaranteed watches in our description.

∿ WE ARE PLAIN. ∿

All guaranteed watches, unless otherwise specified, will be sent to anyone, anywhere,

C. O. D. Subject to Examination.

No Money in Advance. - - -

BUT THESE WATCHES,

Like all Watches we do not Guarantee,

Will not be sent C. O. D.

CASH IN FULL must accompany your order, when we will ship by registered mail postage paid.

No. 8028.

Order by Number.   Hunting Case Only.

Genuine American Gold Plated Watch

Sold Everywhere at 10, 15 and 20 Dollars.

Our Price, $5.45

Movement is Warranted. ❀ Case is not Warranted.

While this case is generally sold as a gold filled case warranted to wear for 5, 10, 15 or 20 years it is *not a genuine gold filled case*, and the manufacturers do not guarantee it.

Thoroughly reliable houses will not misrepresent goods, but we regret there are many unreliable houses that do.

This is the Best Gold Plated Case Made, it is heavy electro plated over brass and many cases will wear for some time, they are imitation hand engraved and can not be told from genuine hand work, and the cases can not be told from a genuine gold filled case. Our price for this hunting case with:

7 Jeweled Trenton Movement, *warranted*	$5.45
7 " Waltham or Elgin Movement, *warranted*	6.70

CASH IN FULL must accompany all ordes for these watches.

ALL WARRANTED watches are sent C. O. D. subject to examination.

No. 8008.

For Our Guaranteed Goods See Following Pages.

WHERE ARE OUR COMPETITORS!

We Have None! ❀ There are None!

Some claim to compete with us, but they don't!
Many houses advertise this a High Grade Gold Filled Watch!

☞**BEWARE OF ANY SUCH!** This is not a Gold Filled Watch, but is the **BEST GOLD PLATED WATCH MADE!**☜

OUR PRICE IS $5.95

Sold by others at 10, 15 and 20 Dollars.

☞*This is a genuine American watch.* **You can't possibly tell it** from a Genuine Gold Filled Watch. This case is *heavy electro gold plated* over brass, imitation hand engraved, cannot be told from hand engraving. Understand, we do not guarantee or recommend this case as it is impossible to say how long it will wear, some will wear for several months, some a year or more.

☞*MOVEMENT* is a genuine **Solid Nickel**, seven jeweled, stem-wind Trenton, guaranteed a good timekeeper.

No. 8009.

Our price for watch complete with 7 jeweled Trenton movement	**$5.95**
" " " " " " 7 " Waltham or Elgin Movement	**7.45**

☞**UNDERSTAND,** we don't guarantee this watch and would not recommend our customers to buy this class of goods. ☞**CASH IN FULL MUST ACCOMPANY** all orders for this watch. *It will not be sent C. O. D.*

About our Eight Departments

Watches, Diamonds and Chains
have been our entire line, but now from our eight separate departments **We Handle Everything** in the jewelry line, including WATCHES, DIAMONDS, CHAINS, RINGS, JEWELRY, SILVERWARE, CLOCKS, OPTICAL GOODS, Etc., Etc.

You may ask, When we sold 80,000 annually, why did we confine ourselves to **watches** alone, and later **watches** and **diamonds**, and still later **watches, diamonds and chains**, why didn't we handle a full line. You may say most every other catalogue house advertises a full line of jewelry. **We will answer:**

OUR REPUTATION IS AT STAKE!

We have always enjoyed and mean to maintain our reputation as the **CHEAPEST WATCH HOUSE ON EARTH.** Few people can comprehend what is necessary to keep our prices below all others. We must be able to buy in very large quantities **FOR CASH.** We must contract with factories by the year, often taking their entire product. To handle such immense quantities it requires endless preparation in order to move the goods. In adding our **Diamond Department** we realized in order to **maintain our reputation,** (the lowest prices on earth) we had many things to overcome, many arrangements to make; the same with our **Chain Department** and every department we have added from time to time, and now we can honestly say **"WE ARE HEADQUARTERS"** for everything in the jewelry line. **Headquarters** because we can sell you a watch, diamond, chain or any piece of jewelry or silverware for less money than you can possibly buy it elsewhere. **WE POSITIVELY GUARANTEE** every article in our catalogue is from *20 per cent to 100 per cent cheaper* for same quality than in any other catalogue published in America.

This is a catalogue of bargains. We never have, and if possible, never shall offer a single article for sale until **we know** the price is below all others. **Everything** in this catalogue is a bargain; something on which we have special advantage, and we give you the benefit of our advantage.

Boys' Best Silver Watch Made!!

Warranted Solid Coin Silver!

Our Price, $5.25--Regular Retail Price, $10.00

No. 6031.

This coin silver watch is open face, stem-wind and stem-set, beautifully engraved by hand. Every piece and part, including back, centre, cap, crown, bow and bezel, is *Warranted Solid Coin Silver*. **Movement** is a solid nickel, nicely jeweled, stem-wind and stem-set Swiss, warranted an accurate time-keeper.

A Boy's Watch, yet large enough and good enough for any man to own

WHAT WE DO! Warrant every watch we sell! Pay all express charges! Send to anyone C. O. D. subject to examination! Require no money in advance! *Can anyone ask more?*

WHO BUY WATCHES!

We make no Distinction but sell to the JEWELRY STORE, MERCHANT, PEDDLER, MECHANIC, FARMER AND LABORER AS WELL, *all at the same price* and *all on the same terms,* viz: By express C. O. D., subject to examination (all express charges prepaid by us). The Jeweler, Merchant and Peddler buy and sell again as a business.

The Farmer or Laborer buys a watch for his own use or to trade or sell, and we often find that although they may commence by buying ONE of our cheapest watches, in time they make our best customers, and in some cases finally engage in the watch business exclusively.

Some of our very best customers are started in this manner. They send for a watch for their own use. The day they get it their friends see it and are delighted with its appearance; and, say it is one of our gold filled watches costing about $12.00, some one OFFERS YOU $20.00 CASH for it, and, knowing you can get another one just like it from us in a very few days for $12.00, you sell it, CLEAR $8.00 and immediately you send for another and another, selling them as fast as you get them, until finally you get them IN DOZEN LOTS.

Now you may only have a few dollars, possibly barely enough to buy one of our cheapest watches, IF SO, that is quite enough; it may lead in a very short time to your selling a dozen watches each month and even more. So you see the POOREST customers often become the BEST and EVERYBODY BUYS WATCHES.

IMPORTANT! Do not order unless in good faith.

We take it for granted when we receive your order that it is in good faith and that you want the watch, and if found upon examination at the express office to be as represented, you will immediately take it and pay the express agent our price. Now, if you do not mean to do this we don't want your order; (no gentleman will *impose* upon *such liberality* as we give.)

DON'T WRITE FOR ANY SPECIAL PRICES ON ANYTHING.

Our prices and terms are alike to one and all, and under no circumstances will we deviate from them.

WONDER OF THE 19th CENTURY!

We furnish this Watch in either Solid Coin Silver Cases, or 14 Karet Gold Filled, as desired.

THE GREATEST CALENDAR WATCH EVER MADE!

25 PER CENT BELOW ANY OTHER HOUSE IN AMERICA!

Solid Coin Silver, $14.95.
14 Karet Gold Filled, 19.85.

Works automatically; gives the time of day to the second; gives the day of the week; gives the day of the month; gives the year; gives the changes of the moon; all as accurately as a $500.00 CALENDAR WATCH.

THE COIN SILVER CASES are Solid Coin Silver, 900 fine, open face, stem-wind and stem-set, beautifully engraved by hand and warranted in every respect.

THE GOLD FILLED CASES are 14 Karet Gold Filled, made of two plates of Solid Gold over composition metal and warranted to wear for 15 YEARS. *A Guarantee is sent with each watch.* The case is open face, stem-wind and stem-set, beautifully engraved by hand.

THE MOVEMENT is one of the very finest imported movements made, in fact it is one of the finest pieces of mechanical ingenuity yet produced. SOLID NICKEL, full ruby jeweled, quick train, patent escapement, patent day, week, month, year and moon calendar, accurately regulated and adjusted and warranted for 5 YEARS.

Our Same Liberal Terms on this Watch!

We will send this watch to any one C. O. D. subject to examination, you can examine it at the express office and if found perfectly satisfactory pay the agent our price and take the watch, but if not perfectly satisfactory REFUSE IT AND DON'T PAY A CENT.

No. 6444.

Be sure to say whether you wish the Silver or Gold Filled Watch.

COIN SILVER—OPEN FACE!

Our Special Price is $6.25

NOTHING Like it Ever Offered for the MONEY!

This Watch Is one of the finest **Open Face, COIN SILVER** watches ever advertised. In this line of gents' silver watches we are offering a grade of goods which cannot be found in any other watch catalogue. Heretofore these goods have only been found in first-class jewelry stores, and always at prices fully double what we ask. **This Case** is warranted coin silver, 900 fine, with coin silver cap, stem-wind and stem-set. **The Movement** is solid nickel, nicely jeweled, quick train, stem-wind and stem-set, and warranted an accurate time-keeper.

We are anxious for you to see this watch, we know it will please yr „ we know you can sell them to your neighbors at nice profit.

A' ,D YOU CAN SEE IT!

We send to anyone C. O. D. subject to examination, no money in advance, take all the risk ourselves.

No. 8032.

Order by Number.   Open Face Only.

WE ARE ADVERTISERS!

WE DON'T DEPEND much on newspapers to advertise us.

WE DON'T DEPEND very much on printed matter to advertise us.

BUT WE DO DEPEND ON YOU!

AND YOU WILL ADVERTISE US.

If you buy a watch from us and the watch pleases you, you will be almost sure to speak a kind word for us to a friend, and that kind of advertising is **better than newspapers, better than printed matter**, its the strongest, most binding advertising we can get, its the kind of advertising we are after, we can't get too much of it. We can't afford to send out a watch that don't give satisfaction, every watch must satisfy our customers and thus lead to more sales.

☞ **This Beautiful Watch** is the finest imported coin silver watch we handle, and we believe the best watch of the kind in the market.

OUR SPECIAL PRICE $7.85!

Retails Everywhere at $15.00

No. 8033.

Order by Number.   Open Face Only.

DESCRIPTION! Case is coin silver, 900 fine, stem-wind and stem-set, beautifully engraved by hand, coin silver inside cap. **Movement** is of very fine quality, nicely jeweled, solid nickel imported, quick train, stem-wind and stem-set, with very fancy dial as shown in cut, **Solid Gold** hands, in fact in every way a thing of beauty.

BEST SILVER WATCH MADE!

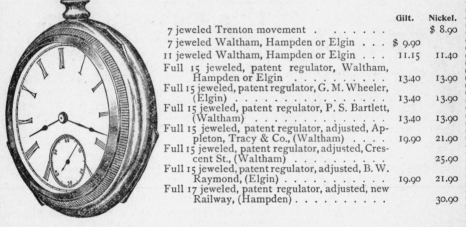

We warrant this to be the **BEST SOLID COIN SILVER WATCH MADE,** 3 ounce, stem-wind and stem-set, open face or hunting case, screw back and bezel, or regular jointed, as desired.

～ SOLID GOLD JOINTS ～

We furnish this case complete with:

	Gilt.	Nickel.
7 jeweled Trenton movement		$ 8.90
7 jeweled Waltham, Hampden or Elgin . . .	$ 9.90	
11 jeweled Waltham, Hampden or Elgin . . .	11.15	11.40
Full 15 jeweled, patent regulator, Waltham, Hampden or Elgin	13.40	13.90
Full 15 jeweled, patent regulator, G. M. Wheeler, (Elgin)	13.40	13.90
Full 15 jeweled, patent regulator, P. S. Bartlett, (Waltham)	13.40	13.90
Full 15 jeweled, patent regulator, adjusted, Appleton, Tracy & Co., (Waltham)	19.90	21.90
Full 15 jeweled, patent regulator, adjusted, Crescent St., (Waltham)		25.90
Full 15 jeweled, patent regulator, adjusted, B. W. Raymond, (Elgin)	19.90	21.90
Full 17 jeweled, patent regulator, adjusted, new Railway, (Hampden)		30.90

No. 6034. **NO MONEY REQUIRED IN ADVANCE.**

Our Hand Engraved Silver Watch!

Open face or hunting case, *warranted the best Solid Coin Silver case made.* Engraved, decorated and finished by hand. Weighs 3½ ounces. Stem-wind and Stem-set. *Solid Gold Joints, Solid Silver Cap.*

We furnish this case complete with:

	Gilt.	Nickel.
7 jeweled Trenton movement		$ 9.40
7 jeweled Waltham, Hampden or Elgin .	$10.40	
11 jeweled Waltham, Hampden or Elgin .	11.65	11.90
Full 15 jeweled, patent regulator, Waltham, Hampden or Elgin	13.90	14.40
Full 15 jeweled, patent regulator, G. M. Wheeler (Elgin)	13.90	14.40
Full 15 jeweled, patent regulator, P. S. Bartlett (Waltham)	13.90	14.40
Full 15 jeweled, patent regulator, adjusted, Appleton, Tracy & Co., (Waltham)	20.40	22.40
Full 15 jeweled, patent regulator, adjusted, Crescent St., (Waltham)		26.40
Full 15 jeweled, patent regulator, adjusted, B. W. Raymond, (Elgin)	20.40	22.40
Full 17 jeweled, patent regulator, adjusted, new Railway, (Hampden)		31.40

No. 6035.

WHAT ᴛʜᴇ PEOPLE SAY!

St. Paul, Minnesota.

Gents.—Your manner of doing business and the magnificent bargains you actually give are so commendable in any house and so different from the course of some firms that I have taken upon myself the privilege of bearing testimony to your fairness and business integrity. I can only account for your giving so much for the money upon the fact that you purchase in such large quantities. I feel to assure anybody dealing, or who contemplates dealing with you, that they will not only get *full value* but in fact *a bargain!* This letter is not written for publication, but you may use it thus if you wish. Respectfully yours,

G. E. McALLISTER,
Mem. Minn. Legislature, 31st Dist.

Toledo, Ohio.

Gents.—I received my watch, and simply to say that I am well pleased, will not describe how well satisfied I am. I will require a gold watch for my wife, before the holidays, and I will not forget your firm when I order. Wishing you success for your fair dealing.

Very truly, Thos. H. Price.

Laredo, Texas.

Gents.—I received the watch you sent me and am very much pleased with it. The jewelers say it is all it is represented to be and even more. Now gentlemen, if I can be of any service to you, I will only be to glad to do what I can in helping you in any way.

Yours truly, R. C. Jarvis.

Norwood, Georgia.

Gents.—Watch received and am well pleased. I had it tested with nitric acid and it proved to be gold. This day I express to you $18.50, your price for it. May order more in the near future. Yours respectfully, W. H. Harris.

La Crosse, Kansas.

Gents.—Goods received all right. Am well pleased with them. It is a great bargain. You can recommend them to anybody as they are first-class. Hoping to again order some goods in the near future. I am, Yours respectfully, Chas. W. Talbott.

Our Special Price, $9.90 TO $31.60!

Others Ask From $15.00 to $50.00

We prepay all express charges. You pay nothing until after you see and examine the watch. **It's free** to examine at your nearest express office. Solid Silver, Gold Inlaid, Screw Back and Bezel. Dust proof, water proof, and weighs 3½ ounces. THE BEST COIN SILVER WATCH MADE! This stem-wind and stem-set, *COIN SILVER, GOLD INLAID CASE* is acknowledged the highest perfection attained in silver case making, and in offering it at about two-thirds the price of other dealers we feel confident we will be favored with your order if you are in a position to use one or more of them.

We furnish this case complete with:

	Gilt.	Nickel.
7 jeweled Trenton movement		$ 9.90
7 jeweled Waltham, Hampden or Elgin .	$10.90	
11 jeweled Waltham, Hampden or Elgin .	12.15	12.40
Full 15 jeweled, patent regulator, Waltham, Hampden or Elgin	14.40	14.90
Full 15 jeweled, patent regulator, G. M. Wheeler (Elgin)	14.40	14.90
Full 15 jeweled, patent regulator, P. S. Bartlett (Waltham)	14.40	14.90
Full 15 jeweled, patent regulator, adjusted, Appleton, Tracy & Co., (Waltham)	20.90	22.90
Full 15 jeweled, patent regulator, adjusted, Crescent St., (Waltham)		26.90
Full 15 jeweled, patent regulator, adjusted, B. W. Raymond, (Elgin)	20.90	22.90
Full 17 jeweled, patent regulator, adjusted, new Railway, (Hampden)		31.60

Open face only, this is back view.
No. 6036.

Our Special Price, $9.90 TO $31.60!

We prepay all express charges. You pay nothing until after you see and examine the watch. **It's free** to examine at your nearest express office. Solid Silver, Gold Inlaid, Screw Back and Bezel. Dust proof, water proof, and weighs 3½ ounces. **THE BEST COIN SILVER WATCH MADE!** This stem-wind and stem-set, *COIN SILVER, GOLD INLAID CASE* is acknowledged the highest perfection attained in silver case making, and in offering it at about two-thirds the price of other dealers we feel confident we will be favored with your order if you are in a position to use one or more of them.

Others Ask From $15.00 to $50.00

We furnish this case complete with :

	Gilt.	Nickel.
7 jeweled Trenton movement		$ 9.90
7 jeweled Waltham, Hampden or Elgin .	$10.90	
11 jeweled Waltham, Hampden or Elgin .	12.15	12.40
Full 15 jeweled, patent regulator, Waltham, Hampden or Elgin	14.40	14.90
Full 15 jeweled, patent regulator, G. M. Wheeler (Elgin)	14.40	14.90
Full 15 jeweled, patent regulator, P. S. Bartlett (Waltham)	14.40	14.90
Full 15 jeweled, patent regulator, adjusted, Appleton, Tracy & Co., (Waltham)	20.90	22.90
Full 15 jeweled, patent regulator, adjusted, Crescent St., (Waltham)		26.90
Full 15 jeweled, patent regulator, adjusted, B. W. Raymond, (Elgin)	20.90	22.90
Full 17 jeweled, patent regulator, adjusted, new Railway, (Hampden)		31.60

Open face only, this is back view.
No. 6037.

Prices Slaughtered!

Open Face.

No. 6038.

We have bought the entire stock from the manufacturers and with **ONE DEEP CUT**

We Make the Price $7.95,
ALL EXPRESS PAID.

Never before was a genuine (all American) gold filled watch sold for **$7.95.** No money required until you have examined the watch at the express office and found it to be all we claim for it. *Warranted* genuine **Solid Gold Filled**—not gold plate but **Gold Filled.** Such a gold filled watch was never sold before for less than $15.00 and many retail stores ask $25.00. **On this watch we defy competition.** *WARRANTED SOLID GOLD FILLED.*

Warranted to wear and retain its color for 20 years. **Warranted superior to any watch now in the market for $15.00.** A $25.00 **$7.95** watch for $7.95, *all express charges paid.* This is our great leader. You can trade it even up for a horse or you can sell it the day you get it at a handsome profit. Between us it is the bargain of bargains. Order it now and be convinced. Case is open face, stem-wind and stem-set, made of two heavy plates of **Solid Gold** over composition metal and warranted to wear for **20 years.** *A written guarantee is sent with each watch.* The cases are beautifully engraved, decorated and polished by hand. The movement is a fine Trenton, stem-wind and stem-set, richly jeweled, full plate, quick train and warranted an accurate time-keeper.

Remember, this watch, like any other, will be sent to any address, C. O. D. subject to examination, (all express charges paid by us) and if not found perfectly satisfactory, **don't pay a cent,** but if found perfectly satisfactory pay the express agent our special price, $7.95, and the watch is yours.

OUR SPECIAL PRICE, $7.45!

WE PAY ALL CHARGES.　　COSTS NOTHING TO EXAMINE.
MOST WONDERFUL BARGAIN EVER OFFERED.
HIGHEST GRADE SCREW BEZEL GOLD FILLED.

$7.45

Warranted Best Gold Filled.

Warranted Dust Proof.

$7.45

FRONT OF CASE.
No. SPECIAL 2.
ORDER BY NUMBER.

This cut shows case open with front and back unscrewed, showing just how the case is made and put together.

BACK OF CASE.
No. SPECIAL 2.
ORDER BY NUMBER.

Read This Page Carefully.　Nothing Like it Ever Offered Before.

READ DESCRIPTION! This is one of the very finest **screw back** and bezel gold filled cases made made under the latest patents and **warranted absolutely dust proof**, highest grade gold filled, made from two plates of **solid gold** over composition metal and *warranted to wear for* **20 years**. These cases are beautifully engraved by hand in the most elaborate and pleasing designs, stem-wind and stem-set, with **Solid Gold Bows**. They of course are open face and are fitted with the very best grade French tripple strength flat crystals.

WE MAKE THE PRICE A Stem-wind, Solid Nickel, 7 Jeweled Trenton Movement **$7.45**
on this watch Same Case with a 7 Jeweled Waltham, Hampden or Elgin Movement **8.45**
complete with: " " " 11 " " " " " " " . **9.70**
" " " 15 " Patent Regulator, Waltham, Hampden or Elgin Mvt. . **11.95**

YOU KNOW OUR TERMS! We send any of these watches to any address, any where in the United States, by express C. O. D. subject to examination. **We prepay all express charges**, you can examine the watch at the express office and if found perfectly satisfactory pay the express agent **JUST OUR PRICE, NO MORE, and the watch is yours.**

REMEMBER OUR GUARANTEE! It is the longest, strongest and most binding guarantee given by any concern. We send with every gold filled watch, in addition to the guarantee in the back of every case, another special contract guarantee warranting the case for 20 years and the movement for 5 years. **We make everything easy for you, we make everything secure, BECAUSE we want to get hold and merit your trade.**

YOU MAY WONDER how we can make such low prices. We are not surprised that you should for at a glance you will see this is by far the cheapest genuine gold filled, screw back and bezel watch you have ever seen advertised, but the reason we can sell this watch for so little money will apply to nearly every watch we handle.

We are the Largest Watch House in the World

And we contract with the factories for such large quantities of cases and movements that we are enabled to not only make you an extremely low price, **BUT A PRICE** far below that made by any other house.

COMPARE OUR PRICES

With those of any reliable house and decide for yourself. If you conclude our prices are below all others, if you conclude we are the cheapest give us a trial. **IT WILL cost you NOTHING to order, NOTHING to see and examine this watch.**

CERTIFICATE OF GUARANTEE
No.
TRADE MARK
THIS CASE IS MADE OF
TWO PLATES OF SOLID GOLD
OVER A COMPOSITION OF FINE METAL
GUARANTEED TO WEAR
20 YEARS
"SEARS, ROEBUCK & CO."

THIS IS A PICTURE OF OUR SPECIAL GUARANTEE WHICH GOES WITH EVERY WATCH.

Something Very Fine!

$16.65 FOR A $35.00 WATCH

Do you want the Best?

Are you willing to pay

$16.65?

If so, Order

THIS WATCH!

IT'S THE BEST IN THE WORLD FOR THE MONEY!

This page should interest you. You should read every word.

THIS IS A PICTURE OF THE MOVEMENT ENGRAVED FROM A PHOTOGRAPH.

THIS IS A PICTURE OF THE CASE ENGRAVED FROM A PHOTOGRAPH.

No. SPECIAL 3. ORDER BY NUMBER.

☞ THIS IS ONE OF OUR LEADERS!

In fact, it is the **finest watch ever offered** for anything like the price. **It pays to buy a good watch,** and that is the reason we recommend this so highly because in this we are able to offer you **A REGULAR $35.00 WATCH FOR $16.65!** We say a regular $35.00 watch, *honestly believing* it can not be duplicated in any market for less than $35.00 spot cash. **THESE MOVEMENTS** were made for us under contract by a very large manufacturer and under instructions to spare nothing to make them equal to the very finest movements made. We are glad to be able to say the manufacturer carried out his part of the contract to the letter and has delivered us a lot of movements which we do not hesitate to match with any movement made, and yet our contract was at such a price that we are enabled to offer the complete watch for **less money** than any other concern can sell you a movement of the same grade.

DESCRIPTION OF MOVEMENT:

The movement is one of the finest we ever sold: 16 size, three quarter plate, the very best Micrometer regulator, full jeweled with extra fine Ruby jewels, in solid gold settings, jeweled centre and barrel arbor, beveled head gilt screws, expansion balance, Breguit hair spring, patent centre pinion, finest escapement, patent back main spring, plates elegantly finished and ornamented, enameled dial, Fleur de Lis Lands, accurately regulated and adjusted to heat, cold, position and isochronism. With this movement we send the *most binding 5 year guarantee*.

THIS MOVEMENT WILL LAST A LIFE-TIME!

DESCRIPTION OF CASE:

This is one of the finest quality gold filled cases made. Made from **two plates of 14 KARET SOLID GOLD** over composition metal and is *guaranteed to wear for 20 years*. Latest style, 16 size, **extra thin**, extended centre, solid gold bow. crown and thumb pieces, either **Open Face** or **Hunting Case, Antique** or regular bow, as desired.

THIS IS A PICTURE OF OUR SPECIAL GUARANTEE WHICH GOES WITH EVERY WATCH.

READ OUR OFFER!

We will send this watch in either open face or hunting case, gent's 16 size, antique or regular style bow, or Ladies' size, to any address any where in the United States, C. O. D. subject to examination. **NO MONEY IN ADVANCE! You needn't pay one cent. WE WILL PAY ALL EXPRESS CHARGES!** You can go to the express office and examine it thoroughly, call any of your friends to examine it, and if it is found exactly as represented, **A REGULAR $35.00 WATCH FOR $16.65**, and you are in every way perfectly satisfied, pay the express agent our special price, $16.65, and the watch is yours. Otherwise **don't pay a cent** and the agent will return the watch at our expense.

COULD WE OFFER MORE? When we offer to send you any watch C. O. D. subject to examination, require no money in advance, pay all express charges ourselves, place the watch before you at our own expense, allow you and your friends to make your own decision, **WE THINK WE HAVE DONE OUR PART! DON'T YOU?**

WE LEAD ON CHRONOGRAPH WATCHES!

OUR PRICE, $15.75 TO $39.75.

With Silverine *Case*	$ 15 75
With Coin Silver *Case*	19 75
With GOLD FILLED *Case* . . .	19 95
With 14 Karet Solid Gold *Case* . .	38 75

Our Leader A 14 karet Gold Filled Case, with BEST TRENTON CHRONOGRAPH, for **$19.95**

SPECIAL No. 6.
ORDER BY NUMBER.

This is a picture of our Special Guarantee, which goes with every Watch.

· TERMS ·

ON ALL CHRONOGRAPH WATCHES, we require at least **one dollar** to accompany your order, when we will ship C. O. D., subject to examination, for the balance.

DESCRIPTION OF THIS, OUR LEADER, AT $19.95.

CASE 14 Karet Gold Filled, open face, made of two plates of solid gold rolled down over composition metal, and warranted to wear for 20 years. A guarantee goes with every case. (See guarantee above.) These cases are beautifully engraved, decorated and finished by hand. **Solid Gold** bow, crown and thumb pieces, gold filled inside caps, and all warranted.

MOVEMENT The latest genuine American Chronograph, made by the Trenton Watch Co., and fully warranted by the company and ourselves for **five years.** A written guarantee goes with every watch. Movement is a gilt fifth-second chronograph, with start, stop and flyback, working from the pendent. Nine jewels, cut expansion balance. Plain or very fancy dial, as desired. Guaranteed as a time keeper, and **the best horse timer in the world for the money.**

DON'T FORGET $1.00 must accompany all orders for these Chronographs.

Picture of Movement, engraved from a Photograph.

WE CARRY a full line of fine Swiss Chronographs, manufactured by Henri Tandoz, of Locle, Switzerland, and ranging in price from $110.00 to $2,500.00, according to grade of movement and ornamentation of case. **For particulars,** see Swiss Chronographs, in this catalogue.

Picture of Face of Movement, engraved from a Photograph.

On Watches We Are Headquarters!

Read this catalogue carefully and we believe you will agree we are about as near headquarters as you can get.

We Are General Selling Agents for **HAMPDEN MOVEMENTS** and **DUEBER CASES** and we honestly believe they are the best movements and cases in the market. There are more Hampden movements in use on railroads than any other make made, they are being adopted by the railroads generally where it is necessary to have the variation in time reduced to a few seconds per month. **There is no Question** but the **Dueber is the Best Gold Filled Case Made,** more pure gold used in its construction, better made and better finished than any other case made.

We Have Many Advantages in handling these goods. **As General Selling Agents** we make a lower price than any other concern in existance, but owing to our restrictions as Selling Agents on these goods **we are compelled to** require $1.00 in advance with every order as a guarantee before we can ship C. O. D. subject to examination. The dollar paid will always be deducted from price of watch. We quote price of movements and cases separately; to get the price of complete watch add the price of any movement wanted to the price of case wanted.

REMEMBER, in ordering these goods always send $1.00 with your order. Our arrangements with the manufacturers compell us to require this. We can make no exception.

HAMPDEN MOVEMENTS AND DUEBER CASES.

Gladiator.
9 jeweled, gilt, patent regulator . . . . **Price, $4.95**
11 jeweled, nickel, patent regulator . . . . . " 5.95

Dueber Watch Co. Movement **$5.70**
Gilt, 11 jewels in composition settings, compensation balance, patent regulator and patent safety pinion.

The Dueber Watch Co., No. 45 . . . . **$6.95**
Nickel, 11 jewels in composition settings, patent regulator, Roman circular dial, spade hands.

Dueber Movement **$7.95**
Nickel, 16 ruby jewels in composition settings, sunk second and circle dial, Roman figures and seconds, Breguet hair spring, compensation balance, patent regulator.

To get price of complete watch add price of movement to price of case.

☞We will sell you one of these Hampden Movements or any Dueber Case separately or the complete watch, but in every case **$1.00** must accompany your order.
☞We do not prepay charges on these watches, express charges must be paid by party receiving the goods.

Down with Monopoly! Down with Watch Trusts!
DOWN WITH PRICES!

For Best Goods at Lowest Prices READ THIS CATALOGUE.

HAMPDEN MOVEMENTS AND DUEBER CASES.

To get the price of complete watch add the price of movement to the price of case.

No. 49 . . . . **$9.45**
Gilt, 15 jewels, adjusted, patent regulator, double sunk dial, red marginal figures.

John C. Dueber Movement **$11.95**
Nickel, 17 ruby jewels in composition settings, adjusted to heat and cold, sunk second and circle dial, Roman and Arabic figures and seconds, Breguet hair spring, compensation balance, patent regulator.

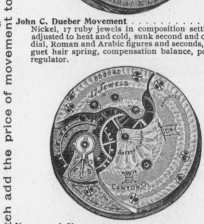

No. 108, 16 Size **$9.95**
Nickel, 17 jewels in composition settings, ruby pallets, patent center pinion, micrometer regulator, S. S. and imitation double sunk dials.

No. 107, 16 Size **$11.95**
Nickel, 17 ruby jewels in composition settings, ruby pallets, blue bevel head screws, Breguet hair spring, micrometer regulator, D. S. dial, red marginal figures, patent center pinion, adjusted.

No. 106, 16 Size **$14.95**
Nickel, 17 fine ruby jewels in gold settings, ruby pallets, gilt screws, Breguet hair spring, micrometer regulator, D. S. hard enamel dial, red marginal figures, adjusted.

No. 104, 16 Size **$34.95**
Nickel, 17 extra fine ruby jewels in gold settings, ruby pallets, gilt bevel head screws, magnificent gilt damaskened, Breguet hair spring, highly finished steel work, micrometer regulator, D. S. glass enamel dial, accurately compensated and timed to position and isochronism.

On Hampden Movements and Dueber Cases we do not pay express charges and we require **$1.00 with every order.**

ARE PRICES ANY OBJECT?

If so, read this catalogue carefully. We are positively **below all others. DO YOU WANT EASY TERMS?** If so, read this catalogue carefully. Our terms are more liberal than any other house. **On cheap imported watches** we require cash in advance, on Hampden movements and Dueber cases we are compelled to require $1.00 to accompany your order, **but on all other watches** we require no money in advance, send C. O. D. subject to examination to any one any where and we pay all charges.

HAMPDEN MOVEMENTS AND DUEBER CASES.

John C. Dueber Special Movement **$14.95**
Nickel, 17 ruby jewels in composition settings, Breguet hair spring, adjusted compensation balance, gilded patent regulator, gilt screws double sun k dial with marginal figures, specially guaranteed to be the best time-keeper in the world for the price and superior in appearance and finish to any other full plate watch made outside of THE DUEBER HAMPDEN FACTORIES.

Anchor Movement **$19.95**
Nickel, 17 extra fine ruby jewels in solid gold settings, patent regulator, compensation balance, accurately adjusted to temperature, isochronism and position.

To get the price of complete watch add the price of movement to the price of case.

New Railway Movement **$24.95**
Nickel, 17 extra fine ruby jewels in solid gold settings, 14 karet gold patent regulator, compensation balance, accurately adjusted to temperature, isochronism and six positions; particularly desirable and especially recommended to meet the requirements of the railway service.

Railway Special Movement **$34.95**
Nickel, 17 extra fine ruby jewels in solid gold settings, jeweled center, magnificently damaskened and finished, bevel head gilt screws, 14 karet gold patent regulator, expansion balance, perfectly compensated and accurately timed to all positions and isochronism, double sunk glass, enamel dial with red marginal figures, Breguet hair spring.

No. 110, 16 Size **$5.70**
Gilt, 11 jewels in composition settings, expansion balance, patent center pinion, S. S. dial.

No. 109, 16 Size **$7.95**
Nickel, 13 jewels in composition settings, jeweled center, (upper and lower) S. S. dial, patent center pinion.

On Hampden Movements and Dueber Cases
We do not pay express charges and We require $1.00 with every order.

WE SELL THE BEST

At Prices BELOW all Others.

Read this catalogue carefully and we believe you will agree we are selling cheaper than any other house in existance.

Ladies' 6 Size, Hampden Movements.

No. 200 . . . . $4.45
Fine gilded movement, 7 jewels, compensation balance, flat hair spring, patent centre pinion, sunk second dial, spade hands, elegantly engraved and gilded, and regular Hampden main spring.

No. 206 . . . . $6.20
Fine nickel movement, 11 jewels in composition settings, compensation balance, flat hair spring, patent center pinion, sunk second dial, elegantly engraved and damaskened, fine moon hands and regular Hampden main spring.

No. 213 . . . . $7.95
Nickel, 15 fine ruby jewels, elegantly engraved and damaskened, compensation balance, flat hair spring, blue bevel screws, patent center pinion, fine Roman or Arabic figures, double sunk dial, red marginal figures, morning glory hands, composition jewel settings, Hampden back action main spring and accurately timed.

To get price of complete watch add price of movement to price of case wanted.

No. 215 . . . . $9.95
Nickel, 16 fine ruby jewels, raised gold center, jewel settings, Arabic double sunk glass enamel dial, red marginal figures, neat gold border on dial, delicate blue spade hands, flat hair spring, gilt bevel screws, gilt regulator, patent center pinion, compensation balance, Hampden back action main spring and accurately timed.

No. 220 . . . . $14.95
Nickel, 17 jewels, raised gold center and train settings, highly polished center and escape wheels, flat hair spring. Hampden back action main spring, gilt bevel screws throughout, fine gilt spade hands, double sunk glass enamel dial, elegantly painted neat, gilt marginal figures, adjusted to heat and cold and five positions, and very accurately timed. The best 6 size watch on the market.

☞ We will sell you one of these Hampden Movements or any Dueber Case separately or the complete watch, but in every case **$1.00** must accompany your order.

☞ We do not prepay charges on these watches, express charges must be paid by party receiving the goods.

WE SELL BEST GOODS AT LOWEST PRICES.

REMEMBER, In ordering these goods always send $1.00 with your order. Our arrangements with the manufacturers compel us to require this. We can make no exception.

From Manufacturer to Consumer!

No retailers profit, no jobbers profit, no brokers profit, no traveling salesmen to pay, no bad debts.
☞**When you buy from us** all this middle class is avoided.
☞**Compare our prices and become convinced.**

We are General Agents for *Hampden Movements and Dueber Cases* by the American route **from the factory to the home.** We are not always able to match the engravings illustrated exactly as there may be none of the exact pattern in stock when your order is received, but we will match them as closely as possible. The illustrations will give you a good idea of the variety we handle and how they look. Cases illustrated on this page are Dueber's 10 karet, warranted to wear for 20 years. All guarantees are signed by JNO. C. DUEBER, President.

To get price of a complete watch add price of case to price of movement.

Always send one dollar with your order.

A—18 size, fancy engraved case.
10 karet, warranted 20 years, hunting case . . **$8.45**
10 karet, warranted 20 years, open face 7.95

B—18 size, full engraved case.
10 karet, warranted 20 years, hunting case . . **$8.95**
10 karet, warranted 20 years, open face 8.45

Order Hampden Movements by name or number.

Order Dueber Cases by letter.

C—18 size, full engraved case.
10 karet, warranted 20 years, hunting case . . **$8.95**
10 karet, warranted 20 years, open face 8.45

D—18 size, full engraved case.
10 karet, warranted 20 years, hunting case . . **$8.95**
10 karet, warranted 20 years, open face 8.45

Dueber-Hampden Watches Below all Others

THE DUEBER CASES
are acknowledged everywhere as the Best Gold Filled Cases Made. They are the oldest and most reliable case in the market. Every case Guaranteed by Special Certificate to **wear 20 and 25 years.** The regular quality guaranteed for 20 years, the special quality for 25 years. All guarantees are signed by Jno. C. Dueber, President.

Cases illustrated on this page are all 14 karet gold filled, warranted 20 years. It is often impossible to furnish engravings to match illustrations exact, as there are so many patterns; when we cannot match exactly we send as near as possible to the engraving you select. The illustrations will give you a good idea of how the assortment runs.

To get the price of a complete watch add price of case to price of movement.

Don't Forget, on these watches **YOU PAY EXPRESS CHARGES,** and send $1.00 with your order.

E—18 size, fancy corrugated case.
14 karet, warranted 20 years, hunting case, . . $9.95
14 karet, warranted 20 years, open face, ... 9.45

F—18 size, engine turned case.
14 karet, warranted 20 years, hunting case . . . $9.95
14 karet, warranted 20 years, open face 9.45

Order Hampden Movements by name or number.

Order Dueber Cases by letter.

G—18 size, fancy engraved case.
14 karet, warranted 20 years, hunting case . . . **$9.95**
14 karet, warranted 20 years, open face 9.45

H—18 size, fancy engraved case.
14 karet, warranted 20 years, hunting case . . . **$9.95**
14 karet, warranted 20 years, open face 9.45

THE ONLY RAILROAD WATCH!

We say the only Railroad Watch for the reason everywhere that railroad companies are requiring employes to provide themselves with watches that will pass a regular inspection and maintain a certain rate **THE HAMPDEN LEADS THEM ALL.** No other movement will compare with the Hampden, and the **Dueber Cases** are generally acknowledged the **Best Gold Filled Cases Made.**

OUR PRICES ARE BELOW ALL OTHERS.

COMPARE CAREFULLY OUR PRICES.

☞Cases illustrated on this page are 14 karet Dueber, warranted to wear for 20 years.☜

☞ To get price of complete watch add price of case to price of movement wanted.☜

Order Hampden Movements by name or number.

Order Dueber Cases by letter.

I—18 size, full engraved case.
14 karet, warranted 20 years, hunting case . . **$10.95**
14 karet, warranted 20 years, open face 10.45

J—18 size, full engraved case.
14 karet, warranted 20 years, hunting case . . **$10.95**
14 karet, warranted 20 years, open face 10.45

Be sure to send One Dollar with your order in

ordering Dueber Cases and Hampden Movements.

K—18 size, full engraved case.
14 karet, warranted 20 years, hunting case . . **$10.95**
14 karet, warranted 20 years, open face 10.45

L—18 size, full engraved case.
14 karet, warranted 20 years, hunting case . . **$10.95**
14 karet, warranted 20 years, open face 10.45

DUEBER 14 KARET SPECIAL!

The best gold filled case made. Warranted by special certificate to wear for 25 years.

READ WHAT Mr. Dueber, the Manufacturer, says about these special cases.

"These cases are made to meet the requirements of the finest retail trade and are equal in appearance and finish to the solid gold watch cases made by us. They are made in our unrivaled **Juergensen, Full Bassine, Engraved** and other desirable styles suitable for the above trade, richly ornamented and decorated and in every respect are superior to all other filled cases. The Backs, Caps, Centers, and Bezels of these Cases are made from 14 Karet Gold Bars, rolled down over composition metal. The Pendant Bow, Joints, Joint Plugs and Thumb Pieces are Solid Gold. Contains more Gold than any other so-called Filled Case on the market, and combines in its construction all the latest improvements of any value in the art of Watch Case making."

To get the price of a complete watch add price of case to price of movement.

Order Hampden Movements by name or number.

Order Dueber Cases by letter.

M—18 size, engine turned case.
14 karet, warranted 25 years, hunting case . . **$12.45**
14 karet, warranted 25 years, open face 11.95

N—18 size, full engraved case.
14 karet, warranted 25 years, hunting case . . **$12.45**
14 karet, warranted 25 years, open face 11.95

WE WILL send Hampden Movements and Dueber Cases to anyone anywhere C. O. D. subject to examination, but One Dollar must always accompany your order.

O—18 size, full engraved case.
14 karet, warranted 25 years, hunting case . . **$12.45**
14 karet, warranted 25 years, open face 11.95

P—18 size, full engraved case.
14 karet, warranted 25 years, hunting case . . **$12.45**
14 karet, warranted 25 years, open face 11.95

DUEBER 20 AND 25 YEAR CASES!

Gents 16 Size, Hunting Case or Open Face.

To get the price of a complete watch add price of case to price of movement wanted.

These cases are 16 size, and will take nothing but 16 size movements.

Order Hampden Movements by name or number.

Order Dueber Cases by letter.

Q—16 size, full engraved case.
14 karet, warranted 20 years, hunting case . . **$10.95**
14 karet, warranted 20 years, open face 10.45

R—16 size, full engraved case.
14 karet, warranted 20 years, hunting case . . . **$10.95**
14 karet, warranted 20 years, open face 10.45

IN ORDERING Dueber Cases and Hampden Movements be sure to enclose ONE DOLLAR with your order when the watch will be sent C. O. D. subject to examination.

S—16 size, full engraved case.
14 karet, warranted 25 years, hunting case . . **$12.45**
14 karet, warranted 25 years, open face 11.95

T—16 size, full engraved case.
14 karet, warranted 25 years, hunting case . . **$12.45**
14 karet, warranted 25 years, open face 11.95

Buy Dueber Cases and Hampden Movements from us.
WE ARE HEADQUARTERS.

HAMPDEN WATCHES SLAUGHTERED.

We say slaughtered because we are offering **Hampden Movements and Dueber Cases** for less money than any other wholesale house in America. **COMPARE OUR PRICES** with those of other houses, then decide!

☞In ordering Hampden movements and Dueber cases be sure to send one dollar with your order.☜
☞To get price of complete watch add price of case to price of movement wanted.☜

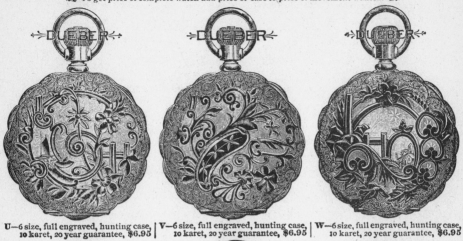

U—6 size, full engraved, hunting case, 10 karet, 20 year guarantee, **$6.95** | V—6 size, full engraved, hunting case, 10 karet, 20 year guarantee, **$6.95** | W—6 size, full engraved, hunting case, 10 karet, 20 year guarantee, **$6.95**

X—6 size, full engraved, hunting case, 14 karet, 20 year guarantee, **$7.95** | Y—6 size, full engraved, hunting case, 14 karet, 20 year guarantee, **$7.95** | Z—6 size, full engraved, hunting case, 14 karet, 20 year guarantee, **$7.95**

A A—6 size, plain, hunting case, 14 karet, 25 year guarantee, **$7.95** | B B—6 size, full engraved, h'nt'g case, 14 karet, 25 year guarantee, **$8.95** | C C—6 size, full engraved, h'nt'g case, 14 karet, 25 year guarantee, **$8.95**

We Sell the Best and Our Price is

$8.50 TO $30.50

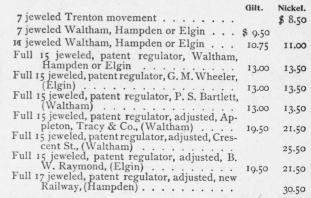

This is the best **Screw Back and Bezel** case made. Made by the great and only **Jos. Fahys Watch Case Co.** Made as good as a **GOLD FILLED** case can be made, **cannot be told from SOLID GOLD.** *WILL WEAR A LIFE-TIME.*

DESCRIPTION! It's an open face, stem-wind and stem-set, extra finished in **every** respect, **GOLD FILLED**, made of two heavy plates of solid gold over fine composition metal, *and warranted to wear* **20 years,** (it will wear a lifetime) beautifully engraved and decorated. For a screw back and bezel gold filled case **IT'S THE GRANDEST SUCCESS EVER ATTAINED.**

We furnish this case complete with:

	Gilt.	Nickel.
7 jeweled Trenton movement		$ 8.50
7 jeweled Waltham, Hampden or Elgin . . .	$ 9.50	
11 jeweled Waltham, Hampden or Elgin . . .	10.75	11.00
Full 15 jeweled, patent regulator, Waltham, Hampden or Elgin	13.00	13.50
Full 15 jeweled, patent regulator, G. M. Wheeler, (Elgin)	13.00	13.50
Full 15 jeweled, patent regulator, P. S. Bartlett, (Waltham)	13.00	13.50
Full 15 jeweled, patent regulator, adjusted, Appleton, Tracy & Co., (Waltham)	19.50	21.50
Full 15 jeweled, patent regulator, adjusted, Crescent St., (Waltham)		25.50
Full 15 jeweled, patent regulator, adjusted, B. W. Raymond, (Elgin)	19.50	21.50
Full 17 jeweled, patent regulator, adjusted, new Railway, (Hampden)		30.50

No. 6040.

NO MONEY REQUIRED IN ADVANCE. WE PAY THE EXPRESS.

Don't Pay to Much for a Watch!

FIRST satisfy yourself the watch you intend ordering is **thoroughly reliable**, some **standard make**, like for example, the **old time tested, original and reliable HAMPDEN.**

If it's a *High Grade, Gold Filled Case* like this one, and a *Hampden, Columbus, Springfield, Rockford, Elgin or Waltham,* **THAT SETTLES THE QUESTION OF QUALITY.** **What About the PRICE?** Well, the average retail dealers would ask for such a watch about $25.00, you might possibly buy it for a little less money.

BUT SUPPOSE YOU COULD BUY THE WATCH FOR $9.95!

There is only one place where it can be had at any such a **LOW PRICE** and that is **DIRECT FROM US.** We will send it to any address, by express C. O. D. subject to examination, **all express charges paid by us.** You can examine it at the express office and if found perfectly satisfactory, pay the agent Eleven dollars and fifty-five cents.

DESCRIPTION! Case is high grade, beautifully

engraved, stem-wind and stem-set and open face case, **warranted to wear 20 years.** *A written guarantee goes with each watch.* **MOVEMENT** is a genuine **Hampden, Columbus, Springfield, Rockford, Elgin or Waltham,** stem-wind and stem-set, quick train, patent pinion, patent escapement, dust proof protected, patent pendant setting, and **FULLY WARRANTED.**

No. 6041.

DOWN! DOWN!

WE REFER TO PRICES. ★ ★ ★

We have been able to buy such large quantities of American watches this season that we are now able to make such unheard-of **LOW PRICES** that every one who sees this list **WILL BE ASTONISHED!**

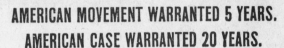

$9.00! | GOLD FILLED ★ GOLD FILLED
GOLD FILLED
GOLD FILLED ★ GOLD FILLED | **$9.00!**

AMERICAN MOVEMENT WARRANTED 5 YEARS.
AMERICAN CASE WARRANTED 20 YEARS.

Hunting case, full engraved, stem-wind, stem-set, made of two plates of solid gold over composition metal, and warranted to wear 20 YEARS! Movement made for us under contract and known as the Madison. An American movement, solid nickel, 7 jeweled, expansion balance, quick train, stem-wind and stem-set, warranted an accurate time-keeper. You can sell it the day you get it for $20.00. NOTHING LIKE IT EVER OFFERED before for less than $16.00. Sent to any address C. O. D. subject to examination, all express charges paid.

No. 6043. ★ ★ ★ COSTS YOU NOTHING TO SEE IT!

DOWN GOES PRICE TO $8.95!

We are always at work with every leverage we can bring to bear to get the **PRICES DOWN.** When we can buy a watch cheaper— **DOWN GOES THE PRICE!** We are now able to sell you THIS WATCH FOR MUCH LESS THAN IT COST us a few months ago. **A FINE, GOLD FILLED WATCH,** made of two plates of **solid gold** over composition metal, and *warranted to wear for 20 years.* Hunting case, stem-wind and stem-set, beautifully engraved.

This gold filled case complete with:

	Gilt.	Nickel.
7 jeweled Trenton movement		$ 8.95
7 jeweled Waltham, Hampden or Elgin	$ 9.95	
11 jeweled Waltham, Hampden or Elgin	11.20	11.45
Full 15 jeweled, patent regulator, Waltham, Hampden or Elgin	13.45	13.95
Full 15 jeweled, patent regulator, G. M. Wheeler, (Elgin)	13.45	13.95
Full 15 jeweled, patent regulator, P. S. Bartlett, (Waltham)	13.45	13.95
Full 15 jeweled, patent regulator, adjusted, Appleton, Tracy & Co., (Waltham)	19.95	21.95
Full 15 jeweled, patent regulator, adjusted, Crescent St., (Waltham)		25.95
Full 15 jeweled, patent regulator, adjusted, B. W. Raymond, (Elgin)	19.95	21.95
Full 17 jeweled, patent regulator, adjusted, new Railway, (Hampden)		30.95

Open Face $1.00 Less. WE ARE ALWAYS IN THE LEAD.

No. 6044.

We Want Your Trade!

If Low Prices and Good Goods will attract you
We shall have your trade.

Our Price, $8.95 Others Ask, $15.00

BUY THIS WATCH AND YOU WILL THEN SAY OURS IS

The Cheapest House on Earth.

We pay the express charges on this and all watches.
Send it anywhere C. O. D. subject to examination.
If you **DON'T WANT IT** when you see it **DON'T TAKE IT.**

DESCRIPTION! Solid Gold Filled, open face, stem-wind and stem-set, full engraved, screw back and bezel, dust proof, damp proof, double thick French crystal.

Warranted to wear 20 years.

MOVEMENT—**Trenton,** solid nickel, damaskened, 7 jeweled, cut expansion balance, patent pinion, quick train, stem-wind and stem-set, and warranted an accurate time-keeper. *A written guarantee goes with each watch.* BEAR IN MIND, this is the house that sends ANY WATCH, to ANY ONE, ANY WHERE, ANY TIME, C. O. D., all express charges paid, no money in advance.

No. 6039.

What the People Say!

CALDWELL, KANSAS.

Gents.—I received your watch about ten days ago. Has given perfect satisfaction. Was much better than I expected. Will gladly recommend your firm to any one wanting to buy a good watch for the same money they would have to pay for an inferior one. Please send me at once, by Adams Express, lady's solid gold watch No. 5021 in catalogue.

Yours very truly, E. O. LEVERBY.

ALLENDALE, ILLINOIS.

Gents.—The watch which I ordered of you came to me in good order, and I can only say that I am highly pleased with it. I sold it in a few days, and thus far it has given complete satisfaction. I shall favor you with another order in the near future, for I believe what you say, in regard to your watches, to be reliable. Yours, &c., DR. F. S. GRAY.

HILLS, MINNESOTA.

Gents.—Your card received this A. M., and am quite surprised. As regards to the watch sent me about three weeks ago I took from the office same day as it came, and allow me to say right here, that I am more than satisfied with it, and wonder how you could afford to give such goods for so little money. I have repeatedly refused three times what it cost me, fearing I could not duplicate it. Very respectfully yours, CHAS. P. BISSELL, M. D.

KANOPOLIS, KANSAS.

Gents.—I have compared the Nos. 5041 and 5056 watches purchased of you with others selling at from $25.00 to $30.00, and find them equal, and in fact better, in many respects. I am well pleased and will use every occasion to recommend your watches to my friends.

I remain respectfully, etc., FRANK WATTS,
Sec'y Watts & Co. Loan and Investment Association.

SANTA ANNA, TEXAS.

Gents.—Your watch has been received, and am perfectly satisfied with it, believing it to be just what is represented. It is a beauty and as a time-keeper it is unsurpassed, having given it a thorough test. Would recommend it to any body. Yours truly, T. W. HUNTER,
Pub. Santa Anna *News.*

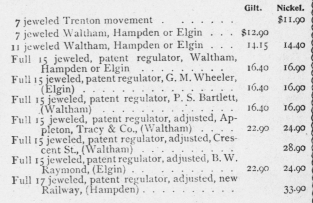

DOWN GOES PRICE TO $11.90!

Warranted BEST GOLD FILLED. ➤ **Warranted to wear for 20 years.**

Full Box Joint. We have succeeded in buying a large lot of these cases at a **greatly reduced price** and we give you the benefit. **Jos. Fahys & Co.'s** best screw back and bezel, box joint, stem-wind and stem-set, fully engraved, open face case, warranted to wear for **20 years.** *A written guarantee is sent with each case.*

We furnish this case complete with:

	Gilt.	Nickel.
7 jeweled Trenton movement		$11.90
7 jeweled Waltham, Hampden or Elgin . . .	$12.90	
11 jeweled Waltham, Hampden or Elgin . . .	14.15	14.40
Full 15 jeweled, patent regulator, Waltham, Hampden or Elgin	16.40	16.90
Full 15 jeweled, patent regulator, G. M. Wheeler, (Elgin)	16.40	16.90
Full 15 jeweled, patent regulator, P. S. Bartlett, (Waltham)	16.40	16.90
Full 15 jeweled, patent regulator, adjusted, Appleton, Tracy & Co., (Waltham)	22.90	24.90
Full 15 jeweled, patent regulator, adjusted, Crescent St., (Waltham)		28.90
Full 15 jeweled, patent regulator, adjusted, B. W. Raymond, (Elgin)	22.90	24.90
Full 17 jeweled, patent regulator, adjusted, new Railway, (Hampden)		33.90

No. 6042. Costs you nothing to see and examine it.

WE PAY THE EXPRESS

On all watches—both on the watch going to you and for the return of the money to us, and if you don't take the watch (but we feel sure you will) we always pay the express both ways, so you only pay the price quoted in our price list—**NO MORE.**

How we Ship C. O. D.
We send any watch by express, to any address, C. O. D., subject to examination (all express charges paid). You can examine it at the express office and if **perfectly satisfactory,** pay the agent our price.

IMPORTANT! Goods can only be sent by express C. O. D. to points on railroads where there is an express office. ☞ **IF YOU WISH US TO SHIP BY MAIL, Cash in Full must accompany each order,** when we will send the watch to your post office (postage paid).

How to Order.
WRITE YOUR ORDERS PLAINLY. (Order watches by their numbers). Always sign name plainly and in full. Always give the name of your nearest express office to which you wish goods shipped, and if possible give name of express company doing busines at that express office. Watches must be sent to your nearest express office, (they cannot be sent by mail C. O. D.) Be sure to comply with these instructions and thus insure receiving the goods promptly and in good order.

READ THIS!
We will ship the watch the day we receive your order. It will go by express C. O. D. to your nearest express office, and we will, the same day, send you a notice by mail to your post office. **IT IS IMPORTANT** that you go to the express office without delay (as the agent may otherwise return the watch to us). Show the agent your notice from us and ask to examine the watch. If for any reason it has not arrived at the express office, ask the agent to send you a notice by mail when it arrives and then hold the watch until you come to examine it. Address all orders plainly to

SEARS, ROEBUCK & CO.,   CHICAGO, ILL. and MINNEAPOLIS, MINN.

CAN'T YOU DECIDE?

Open Face $1.00 Less.

Regular Gents' 18 Size.

WELL WE KNOW IT'S HARD. We know every watch we offer in this list is A GREAT BARGAIN selected from all the standard makes of American manufacturers and not one will we buy, or offer for sale, until we are able to put the price **BELOW ALL OTHERS!** So any watch you may order from this price list you may be sure you are getting **FOR LESS MONEY** than you could possibly get it elsewhere. **This is** one of the LATEST and BEST Gold Filled Cases out, hunting case, stem-wind and stem-set, beautifully engraved, and **warranted to wear twenty years.**

We furnish this case complete with:

	Gilt.	Nickel.
7 jeweled Trenton movement		$13.75
7 jeweled Waltham, Hampden or Elgin	$14.75	
11 jeweled Waltham, Hampden or Elgin	16.00	16.25
Full 15 jeweled, patent regulator, Waltham, Hampden or Elgin	18.25	18.75
Full 15 jeweled, patent regulator, G. M. Wheeler (Elgin)	18.25	18.75
Full 15 jeweled, patent regulator, P. S. Bartlett (Waltham)	18.25	18.75
Full 15 jeweled, patent regulator, adjusted, Appleton, Tracy & Co., (Waltham)	24.75	26.75
Full 15 jeweled, patent regulator, adjusted, Crescent St., (Waltham)		30.75
Full 15 jeweled, patent regulator, adjusted, B. W. Raymond, (Elgin)	24.75	26.75
Full 17 jeweled, patent regulator, adjusted, new Railway, (Hampden)		35.75

No. 6045.   Examination Free.   All Express Charges Paid by Us.

WHAT THE PEOPLE SAY!

ENOREE, SOUTH CAROLINA.

Gents.—Of the several watches I have ordered from you I am free to say every one has come fully up to your description and beyond my expectations. The first watch I bought of you I sold for three times its original cost to me, and it can't be bought from its owner at that to-day.

Respectfully,   HUGH TOLAND, M. D.

SPRINGVALE, KANSAS.

Gents.—I received watch and am well pleased with it. Sold it to a friend and it gives entire satisfaction. Hope to be able to order again in the near future. I have been carrying one of your watches for over six months, do not want a better time-keeper.

Yours truly,   H. E. THARP, Grocer.

SAN FRANCISCO, CALIFORNIA.

Gents.—Yours at hand. I am not in need of a watch of any description at present, but you can say over my signature, the watch forwarded to my address, some time ago, has given satisfaction beyond my expectation, am satisfied it was of better value than same could be had for on this coast for one hundred per cent more money. Cheerfully recommend your house for fair and honest dealing.   Respectfully yours,   EZRA WASHBURN,
Bailiff Supreme Court, State of California.

LAKE GENEVA, WISCONSIN.

Gents.—Watch arrived O. K. in good time. Have delayed writing you in order to test its time keeping qualities. As in looks it more than met my expectations. Am well pleased and no one has a closer time-keeper than this one. Will send you orders, if possible, soon.

Respectfully,   F. W. SMITH,
Supt. South Park Stock Farm.

BRIDGEWATER, SOUTH DAKOTA.

Gents.—Your favor of the 8th inst. came duly to hand. I bought a watch from you and received it December 31, 1891. It 's gold filled, Waltham works, price $12.65. I started it and have carried it ever since and it has not lost one minute. I consider it a daisy. Please send two catalogues, as I wish to give them to friends to show them what value you give in your line for the ready money.   Respectfully yours,   D. A. SMITH, M. D.

NOTHING LIKE IT FOR THE MONEY

EVER OFFERED! MADE FOR US UNDER CONTRACT. ONE OF OUR SPECIAL BARGAINS.

Gent's
Regular
18 Size.

☞Cut
From a
Photograph.

No. 6046.

There is no better GOLD FILLED case made. This case is made from two plates of **SOLID GOLD** over composition metal and is warranted to wear for **20 YEARS.** *A special certificate of guarantee goes with every watch.* They are hunting style, beautifully engraved by hand, stem-wind and stem-set, **SOLID GOLD** bow, crown and thumb pieces. **Open Face $1.00 Less.**

We fit in this case:

	Gilt.	Nickel.
7 jeweled Trenton movement		$11.00
7 jeweled Waltham, Hampden or Elgin . . .	$12.00	
11 jeweled Waltham, Hampden or Elgin . . .	13.25	13.50
Full 15 jeweled, patent regulator, Waltham, Hampden or Elgin	15.50	16.00
Full 15 jeweled, patent regulator, G. M. Wheeler, (Elgin)	15.50	16.00
Full 15 jeweled, patent regulator, P. S. Bartlett, (Waltham)	15.50	16.00
Full 15 jeweled, patent regulator, adjusted, Appleton, Tracy & Co., (Waltham)	22.00	24.00
Full 15 jeweled, patent regulator, adjusted, Crescent St., (Waltham)		28.00
Full 15 jeweled, patent regulator, adjusted, B. W. Raymond, (Elgin)	22.00	24.00
Full 17 jeweled, patent regulator, adjusted, new Railway, (Hampden)		33.00

With every watch we sell we issue a binding guarantee which protects our customers in every way all the time.

COSTS NOTHING TO SEE OUR WATCHES. ★ NOTHING TO EXAMINE THEM.

What the People Say!

JORDAN VALLEY, OREGON.

Gents.—I received the watch some time ago, and it is far better than I expected. I like your way of doing business. If I can assist you I will gladly do so. Respectfully yours,
D. A. CONNORS.

GREENVALE, IOWA.

Gents.—The gold watch I bought of you recently for $19.75 I can say is just as you represented it to be, and I am perfectly satisfied with it. It keeps the best of time and I couldn't duplicate it here for twice the money. Yours truly, LORENZO WORTHING.

AUBURN, TEXAS.

Gents.—I received the watch, find it in good order and just as you represented it to be. I had a jeweler examine it who said it was well worth the money you claimed it to be. I find the watch to be a splendid time-piece. Yours truly, JNO. H. FOSTER.

RANSON, ILLINOIS.

Gents.—I am in possession of the watch purchased of you December 5, 1891, and am in no hurry to dispose of it. It has proven everything that you recommended and a great deal more. It is the most beautiful watch I ever saw and you may feel assured I will do all I can for you, for such a bargain is not obtainable in Illinois. Yours truly, R. F. HERBERT.

VIRGINIA CITY, MONTANA.

Gents.—I received the watch last Sunday and was well pleased with it as it was just as represented. I paid the price, $12.65, for it the day I received it. Send me three (3) of the same kind and under like conditions. They are for friends of mine. Yours very truly, GEO. E. GOHN.

HAZLE PATCH, KENTUCKY.

Gents.—I received the watch you sent me and I found it just as you said I would. The watch gives me good satisfaction and I will have orders for three or four more watches from others. I was never so well satisfied in the watch line before. I think the boys will have me order them all one. Yours &c., LOGAN REIMER.

WE ARE SLAUGHTERING PRICES!

YES, DOWN GOES THE PRICE TO $11.90!

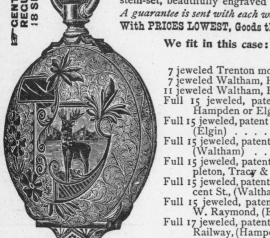

GENT'S REGULAR 18 SIZE.

This is a fine, gold filled hunting case, **box joint**, stem-wind and stem-set, beautifully engraved and **warranted to wear 20 YEARS.** *A guarantee is sent with each watch.* With PRICES LOWEST, Goods the Best, **WE WANT YOUR TRADE.**

We fit in this case:

	Gilt.	Nickel.
7 jeweled Trenton movement		$11.90
7 jeweled Waltham, Hampden or Elgin	$12.90	
11 jeweled Waltham, Hampden or Elgin	14.15	14.40
Full 15 jeweled, patent regulator, Waltham, Hampden or Elgin	16.40	16.90
Full 15 jeweled, patent regulator, G. M. Wheeler, (Elgin)	16.40	16.90
Full 15 jeweled, patent regulator, P. S. Bartlett, (Waltham)	16.40	16.90
Full 15 jeweled, patent regulator, adjusted, Appleton, Tracy & Co., (Waltham)	22.90	24.90
Full 15 jeweled, patent regulator, adjusted, Crescent St., (Waltham)		28.90
Full 15 jeweled, patent regulator, adjusted, B. W. Raymond, (Elgin)	22.90	24.90
Full 17 jeweled, patent regulator, adjusted, new Railway, (Hampden)		33.90

No. 6047.

BEST BOX JOINT HUNTING GOLD FILLED CASE MADE.

Sent C. O. D. subject to examination. ✢ ✢ **NO MONEY REQUIRED IN ADVANCE.**

DUEBER or BOSS! 14 KARET GOLD FILLED.

WARRANTED THE BEST GOLD FILLED CASE MADE.

YOUR CHOICE, the Genuine JNO. C. DUEBER or JAS. BOSS. This is the best case, **DUEBER or BOSS** make, made from two extra heavy plates of **SOLID GOLD** over composition metal and **warranted to wear 20 YEARS.** While no case is guaranteed to wear longer than 20 years, these cases will wear a life-time, in fact many are now in use which have been worn for 30 years. DUEBER'S BEST never have been known to wear through.

Open Face $1.00 Less, Regular 18 Size.

We fit in this case:

	Gilt.	Nickel.
7 jeweled Trenton movement		$14.50
7 jeweled Waltham, Hampden or Elgin	$15.50	
11 jeweled Waltham, Hampden or Elgin	16.75	17.00
Full 15 jeweled, patent regulator, Waltham, Hampden or Elgin	19.00	19.50
Full 15 jeweled, patent regulator, G. M. Wheeler (Elgin)	19.00	19.50
Full 15 jeweled, patent regulator, P. S. Bartlett (Waltham)	19.00	19.50
Full 15 jeweled, patent regulator, adjusted, Appleton, Tracy & Co., (Waltham)	25.50	27.50
Full 15 jeweled, patent regulator, adjusted, Crescent St., (Waltham)		31.50
Full 15 jeweled, patent regulator, adjusted, B. W. Raymond, (Elgin)	25.50	27.50
Full 17 jeweled, patent regulator, adjusted, new Railway, (Hampden)		36.50

No. 6048.

Any watch will be sent anywhere C. O. D. subject to examination.

NO MONEY IN ADVANCE.

BOX JOINT DUEBER OR BOSS!

14 KARET GOLD FILLED. THE BEST GOLD FILLED CASE MADE.

Gent's Regular 18 Size, Open Face, $1.00 Less.

YOU TAKE NO RISK in placing your orders in our hands, as we issue a binding guarantee with every watch we sell, send you any watch by express C. O. D. subject to examination, and require **NO MONEY IN ADVANCE.**

We fit in this case:

	Gilt.	Nickel.
7 jeweled Trenton movement		$20.95
7 jeweled Waltham, Hampden or Elgin . . .	$21.95	
11 jeweled Waltham, Hampden or Elgin . . .	23.20	23.45
Full 15 jeweled, patent regulator, Waltham, Hampden or Elgin	25.45	25.95
Full 15 jeweled, patent regulator, G. M. Wheeler, (Elgin)	25.45	25.95
Full 15 jeweled, patent regulator, P. S. Bartlett, (Waltham)	25.45	25.95
Full 15 jeweled, patent regulator, adjusted, Appleton, Tracy & Co., (Waltham)	31.95	33.95
Full 15 jeweled, patent regulator, adjusted, Crescent St., (Waltham)		37.95
Full 15 jeweled, patent regulator, adjusted, B. W. Raymond, (Elgin)	31.95	33.95
Full 17 jeweled, patent regulator, adjusted, new Railway, (Hampden)		42.95

No. 6051.

REMEMBER, we ask no money from any one until after
✛ **they have seen and examined the goods.** ✛

WHAT THE PEOPLE SAY!

BLOOMSBURG, PENNSYLVANIA.

Gents.—I received the watch the 15th ult. and it is a dandy. I don't see how you can sell as good a watch as that is for the small amount of money. I have been offered twice what I paid for it. I like your way of doing business and will help you all I can to make sales in this locality. Very thankfully yours, OTTO A. WOLF.

ELK PARK.

Gents.—I received the watch you shipped to me and was well pleased with the same. It was all that you advertised and far better than I expected. I think I made about $10 more than if I had bought it in any town around here. If this is of any use to you, you are at liberty to use it. GUST CARLSON.

MAIDEN, NORTH CAROLINA.

Gents.—I received the watch. I am well pleased with it; it is a good timekeeper, and has done well so far. If you want an agent in this locality, I would like to have your catalogue and terms. Respectfully, A. S. MARTIN.

DURHAM, NORTH CAROLINA.

Gents.—I received the watch yesterday in good order, and will say it is the best watch in the world for the money. I will order another watch soon of the same style. Yours truly, L. PEAKS.

SOUTHBOROUGH.

Gents.—This will inform you that I received the watch in good order, and that I am very well satisfied. Please inform me of the different prices and styles of ladies' watches. I may want one or perhaps two of them. I will do the best I can for your house. Yours truly, S. F. FLAGG.

MILLEDGEVILLE, OHIO.

Gents.—My watch came safe to hand. I am much pleased with the watch and I will do all I can to get customers for you. I paid $10.00 to the agent at Milledgeville, O., for you. Would like to have your large catalogue. F. L. HARRISON.

Dueber or Boss 14 Karet Gold Filled!

WARRANTED THE BEST GOLD FILLED CASE MADE.

Your choice, the genuine **JNO. C. DUEBER** or **JAS. BOSS.** There is little left to say about a **Dueber or Boss 20 Year 14 Karet, Full Engraved Case: EVERY ONE KNOWS THEY ARE THE BEST!**

Made from two plates of **Solid Gold** over composition metal and **warranted to wear 20 YEARS.** Beautifully engraved by hand, stem-wind and stem-set.

We fit in this case:

	Gilt.	Nickel.
7 jeweled Trenton movement		$17.95
7 jeweled Waltham, Hampden or Elgin . . .	$18.95	
11 jeweled Waltham, Hampden or Elgin . . .	20.20	20.45
Full 15 jeweled, patent regulator, Waltham, Hampden or Elgin	22.45	22.95
Full 15 jeweled, patent regulator, G. M. Wheeler, (Elgin)	22.45	22.95
Full 15 jeweled, patent regulator, P. S. Bartlett, (Waltham)	22.45	22.95
Full 15 jeweled, patent regulator, adjusted, Appleton, Tracy & Co., (Waltham)	28.95	30.95
Full 15 jeweled, patent regulator, adjusted, Crescent St., (Waltham)		34.95
Full 15 jeweled, patent regulator, adjusted, B. W. Raymond, (Elgin)	28.95	30.95
Full 17 jeweled, patent regulator, adjusted, new Railway, (Hampden)		39.95

No. 6049.
Open Face $1.00 Less.
Regular 18 Size.

REMEMBER, we ask no money from any one until after they have seen and examined the goods.

Dueber or Boss 14 Karet Gold Filled!

WARRANTED THE BEST GOLD FILLED ★ CASE MADE! ★

Your choice, the genuine **JNO. C. DUEBER or JAS. BOSS.** There is little left to say about a Dueber or Boss 20 Year, 14 Karet, Full Engraved Case:

EVERY ONE KNOWS THEY ARE THE BEST!

Made from two plates of **SOLID GOLD** over composition metal, and **warranted to wear 20 YEARS.** Beautifully engraved by hand, stem-wind and stem-set.

We fit in this case:

	Gilt.	Nickel.
7 jeweled Trenton movement		$17.95
7 jeweled Waltham, Hampden or Elgin . . .	$18.95	
11 jeweled Waltham, Hampden or Elgin . . .	20.20	20.45
Full 15 jeweled, patent regulator, Waltham, Hampden or Elgin	22.45	22.95
Full 15 jeweled, patent regulator, G. M. Wheeler, (Elgin)	22.45	22.95
Full 15 jeweled, patent regulator, P. S. Bartlett, (Waltham)	22.45	22.95
Full 15 jeweled, patent regulator, adjusted, Appleton, Tracy & Co., (Waltham)	28.95	30.95
Full 15 jeweled, patent regulator, adjusted, Crescent St., (Waltham)		34.95
Full 15 jeweled, patent regulator, adjusted, B. W. Raymond, (Elgin)	28.95	30.95
Full 17 jeweled, patent regulator, adjusted, new Railway, (Hampden)		39.95

No. 6050.
Open Face $1.00 Less.
Regular 18 Size.

REMEMBER, WE ASK NO MONEY FROM ANY ONE UNTIL AFTER THEY ★ HAVE SEEN AND EXAMINED THE GOODS. ★

Your Choice for $16.95

Is the best good enough?   THEN READ!

If you have read the description of our ladies' watches, Nos. 8042 and 8043, you have got the description of these; what applies to one applies to both. These cases are a special grade **25 Year Gold Filled**, made for the finest trade, a... are handled almost exclusively by the best retail stores in the large cities. We believe **our customers are entitled to the best service we** are able to give, and we would not feel we had performed our part unless we offered you your choice from a thoroughly complete line; but when we offer you everything **there is made, from the cheapest to the very best,** and put the price below all competitors we believe we have performed our part faithfully.

WE CHALLENGE ANYONE

To meet our prices. We dr w no lines, be they wholesale or retail dealers, manufacturer or otherwise, **until our prices have been meet** we shall boldly assert our claim, **THE CHEAPEST WATCH HOUSE ON EARTH.** While every watch in this catalogue tends to confirm our claim, there is none more forcible than those illustrated on this page.

No. 8044 — ORDER BY NUMBER. HUNTING CASE ONLY.

WE FIT IN THESE CASES:

				Gilt.	Nickel.
7 jeweled Trenton movement					$16.95
7 " Waltham, Hampden or Elgin				$17.95	
11 " " "				19.20	19.45
Full 15 " patent regulator, Waltham, Hampden or Elgin			21.45	21.95
" 15 " " " G. M. Wheeler (Elgin)			21.45	21.95
" 15 " " " P. S. Bartlett (Waltham)			21.45	21.95
" 15 " " " adjusted, Appleton, Tracy & Co. (Waltham)		27.95	29.95
" 15 " " " Crescent Street (Waltham)			33.95
" 15 " " " B. W. Raymond (Elgin)		27.95	29.95
" 17 " " " New Railway (Hampden)			38.95

THESE CASES

Are made from two heavy plates of **14 Karet Solid Gold,** rolled down over composition metal and are **GUARANTEED TO WEAR FOR 25 YEARS.** The manufacturers guarantee and ours accompany each case. They are all elaborately engraved in Solid Gold Patterns and can not be told from **SOLID GOLD.** They have Solid Gold crown, bow and thumb pieces, full escaloped with hand finished edges, In fact they are in ev ry way the finest possible to make in Gold Filled.

LET US KNOW

What you want. Any watch will be sent
C. O. D. Subject to Examination to Anyone.
NO MONEY IN ADVANCE.
WE PAY ALL CHARGES.

No. 8045 — ORDER BY NUMBER. HUNTING CASE ONLY.

Dueber or Crown 14 Karet Gold Filled!

Warranted to wear for 20 Years. ⊹ FINE RAISED GOLD ORNAMENTED.

No. 6052.
Open Face $1.00 Less.
Regular 18 Size.

FEW PEOPLE have ever seen such a watch as this—such a work of art, no words or description can give you any idea of its beauty. We don't suppose there are ten jewelry stores in the Union, outside of the larger cities, that carry in stock such a beautiful case. They can only be found in the very finest jewelry stores in the largest cities. No one could imagine such a watch could possibly be gotten up for less than $100.00 and very few have any idea such a beautiful watch is being made at all. It's **the Best Gold Filled Case Possible to Make**, in the first place, then it is most beautifully ornamented and decorated with different colors and designs of raised gold work so that it most certainly is a thing of beauty, and to the owner must be **A JOY FOREVER.**

We fit in this case:

	Gilt.	Nickel.
7 jeweled Trenton movement		$24.00
7 jeweled Waltham, Hampden or Elgin . . .	$25.00	
11 jeweled Waltham, Hampden or Elgin . . .	26.25	26.50
Full 15 jeweled, patent regulator, Waltham, Hampden or Elgin	28.50	29.00
Full 15 jeweled, patent regulator, G. M. Wheeler, (Elgin)	28.50	29.00
Full 15 jeweled, patent regulator, P. S. Bartlett, (Waltham)	28.50	29.00
Full 15 jeweled, patent regulator, adjusted, Appleton, Tracy & Co., (Waltham)	35.00	37.00
Full 15 jeweled, patent regulator, adjusted, Crescent St., (Waltham)		41.00
Full 15 jeweled, patent regulator, adjusted, B. W. Raymond, (Elgin)	35.00	37.00
Full 17 jeweled, patent regulator, adjusted, new Railway, (Hampden)		46.00

REMEMBER, we ask no money from any one until after
⊹ they have seen and examined the goods. ⊹

GENUINE DIAMOND SETTING!

THIS is as **Fine 14 Karet, Gold Filled Case** as can be made, is set with a very fine **GENUINE DIAMOND.** So large is the **Diamond** that it cuts clear through the case. Description of the case is otherwise the same as Watch described above.

MONEY CAN NOT BUY BETTER!

Warranted 14 Karet Fine,
U. S. Mint Assay.

We fit in this case:

	Gilt.	Nickel.
7 jeweled Trenton movement		$35.00
7 jeweled Waltham, Hampden or Elgin	$36.00	
11 jeweled Waltham, Hampden or Elgin	37.25	37.50
Full 15 jeweled, patent regulator, Waltham, Hampden or Elgin	39.50	40.00
Full 15 jeweled, patent regulator, G. M. Wheeler, (Elgin)	39.50	40.00
Full 15 jeweled, patent regulator, P. S. Bartlett, (Waltham)	39.50	40.00
Full 15 jeweled, patent regulator, adjusted, Appleton, Tracy & Co., (Waltham)	46.00	48.00
Full 15 jeweled, patent regulator, adjusted, Crescent St., (Waltham)		52.00
Full 15 jeweled, patent regulator, adjusted, B. W. Raymond, (Elgin) .	46.00	48.00
Full 17 jeweled, patent regulator, adjusted, New Railway, (Hampden) .		57.00

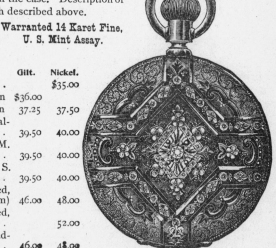

No. 6053.

GENTS' REGULAR 18 SIZE.

⊹ **EXAMINATION FREE.** ⊹ **EXPRESS PAID.** ⊹

WHAT THE PEOPLE SAY!

GREAT WORKS, MAINE.

Gents.—I received my watch on the 17th of last month, and find the watch to be just as you represented it in your price list. I am well pleased with it. It keeps good time.

Yours truly, N. PELKEY.

LINCOLN, NEBRASKA.

Gents.—I received the watch, and I am very much pleased with it. The watch is exactly what you represented it to be. I will do all I can for you. Yours truly, H. TAYLOR.

BAYOU GOULA, LOUISIANA.

Gents.—I am more than pleased with the watch which I received from your house about ten days ago. The watch arrived in good order, and is keeping good time. You will hear from me again in a short time. I will do all I can to advertise your house. Very Respectfully,

JOSEPH JONES.

McCOLL, SOUTH CAROLINA.

Gents.—I received the watch a few days ago, and I am well pleased with it. I found the watch to be as you recommended it. Will be pleased to act as your agent. Yours truly,

H. T. GROOMS.

CATAWBA, SOUTH CAROLINA.

Gents.—I received the watch a few days since. I am surprised that you can sell such a watch for so small a sum of money. I may in a few days order another watch. Yours truly,

R. L. SWETT.

PAINTSVILLE, KENTUCKY.

Gents.—I received the watch yesterday, and was very well pleased with it. I can recommend you to all my friends who want a good watch at a fair price. I wish you great success.

Yours truly, JOHN R. AKERS.

ARLINGTON, GEORGIA.

Gents.— I received the watch, and I am well pleased with it. The watch is nice enough for anybody. Yours truly, J. G. PARK.

GENUINE DIAMOND SETTING!

EXAMINATION FREE.
EXPRESS PAID.

No. 6054.

GENTS' REGULAR 18 SIZE.

THIS is as **Fine 14 Karet, Gold Filled Case** as can be made, is set with a very fine **GENUINE DIAMOND.** So large is the **Diamond** that it cuts clear through the case. Description of the case is otherwise the same as Watch on preceding page.

MONEY CAN NOT BUY BETTER!

Warranted 14 Karet Fine, U. S. Mint Assay.

We fit in this case:	Gilt.	Nickel.
7 jeweled Trenton movement		$35.00
7 jeweled Waltham, Hampden or Elgin	$36.00	
11 jeweled Waltham, Hampden or Elgin	37.25	37.50
Full 15 jeweled, patent regulator, Waltham, Hampden or Elgin	39.50	40.00
Full 15 jeweled, patent regulator, G. M. Wheeler, (Elgin)	39.50	40.00
Full 15 jeweled, patent regulator, P. S. Bartlett, (Waltham)	39.50	40.00
Full 15 jeweled, patent regulator, adjusted, Appleton, Tracy & Co., (Waltham)	46.00	48.00
Full 15 jeweled, patent regulator, adjusted, Crescent St., (Waltham)		52.00
Full 15 jeweled, patent regulator, adjusted, B. W. Raymond, (Elgin) .	46.00	48.00
Full 17 jeweled, patent regulator, adjusted, New Railway, (Hampden) .		57.00

Jas. Boss 14 Karet Gold Filled!

BOSS-14 K Thinest ❖ Latest ❖ Best ❖ 16 Size.

This is the finest thing in the market. At present they can only be found in big retail stores in cities where they are having wonderful sale. 16 size, very thin, antique bow, patent rounded edge crystal, open face, made of two plates of solid gold over composition metal and *warranted to wear* 20 years. Finished in Engine Turned, Plain Polished or Satin Finished, as desired.

We fit in this case:

	Jlt.	Nickel.
7 jeweled Springfield or Elgin	6.50	
11 jeweled Hampden, Columbus, Springfield or Elgin . . .	17.75	
13 jeweled, patent regulator, adjusted, Hampden, Columbus, Springfield or Elgin	20.00	
Full 15 jeweled, patent regulator, adjusted, Hampden, Columbus, Springfield or Elgin	25.00	$31.00

WE ASK FOR NO MONEY in advance. Any one can order a watch from us. We take all the risk; send it anywhere by express C. O. D. Subject to examination.

No. 6055.

Open Face. ◊ Plain Polished. ◊ Engine Turned. ◊ Satin Finished.

Jas. Boss 14 Karet Hunting Case!

LATEST THING OUT!   16 SIZE.

BOSS-14 K

THINEST WATCH CASE MADE!
HANDSOMEST IN THE MARKET!

Antique or regular style bow **Engine Turned, Plain Polished** or Satin Finished. Made of two plates of **solid gold** over composition metal and warranted for **20 Years.**

We are selling these cases **BY THE HUNDRED** from our retail department to city trade.

We fit in this case:

	Gilt.	Nickel.
7 jeweled Springfield or Elgin, ...	$17.50	
11 jeweled Hampden, Columbus, Springfield or Elgin, ...	18.75	
13 jeweled patent regulator, Hampden, Columbus, Springfield or Elgin, ...	21.00	
Full 15 jeweled patent regulator, adjusted, Hampden, Columbus Springfield or Elgin, ...	26.00	$32.00

FREE! FOR YOUR EXAMINATION FREE!

No. 6056.

OUR CHRONOGRAPH WATCH

IS THE

Best Horse Timer Made for the Money.

A Perfect (all American) Watch, an Accurate Time Keeper and a Perfect Horse Timer Combined.

Beats Quarter Seconds, Starts, Stops and Flies Back.

A Marvel of Perfection. We have had many calls for a reliable horse timer and watch combined, but heretofore the prices have been so very high for anything of the kind which could be guaranteed as thoroughly reliable that we have not handled them. We have recently arranged for the manufacture of a large number of CHRONOGRAPH WATCHES which, although perfect in every respect, we can sell at about one-half the price usually asked for them. They are open face, stem-wind and stem-set, accurately regulated and adjusted, and warranted in every respect.

Price complete with Coin Silver Case $23.50
"   "   "   14 Karet Gold Filled Case,
        warranted 20 years 28.50
Price complete with 14 Karet Solid Gold Case . 45.50

No. 6058.

Sent to any address by Express,
C. O. D. subject to examination, all express Charges Paid.

WHAT THE PEOPLE SAY!

ENOREE, SOUTH CAROLINA.

Gents.—The gold watch, No. 5061, arrived in good order and is satisfactory. The lady says she would not take $35.00 for it. The Paillard and Dueber both are in Express office and will be taken by the 12th or 15th, as that is pay day at the factory, and the parties for whom I sent will have the money. Don't be uneasy about them. I do not send for a watch from curiosity, but always for a bona fide order. Money will be forthcoming in a very few day.
Respectfully, DR. H. TOLAND.

NEWPORT, GILES COUNTY, VIRGINIA.

Gents.—A few days since I bought three watches from you. It affords me pleasure to say that they give entire satisfaction, and are even better than you represented them to be. Have sold two of the watches at a nice profit. Please accept thanks for your fair dealing and for giving me good watches for the price you have. Yours very truly, GEO. H. ECHOLS.

MILNOR, NORTH DAKOTA.

Gents.—I received the two watches you sent me in good condition, and am pleased to say that they are not to be excelled as time-keepers by watches costing twice the price paid. I readily sold one for what both cost, and am too well satisfied with the other to part with it even at double its cost. If in need of anything in your line in the future, I shall know just where to get fair dealing. Yours respectfully, ALLISON M. BLYTHE,
Agent for New Home Sewing Machine.

HOLMESVILLE, OHIO.

Gents.—Your card received, in reply will say that I cannot use one of your watches at present, but think I can get an order for a watch before long. The $12.65 watch purchased of you some time ago is a dandy, and cannot be excelled for keeping time. Case is wearing the best kind and I can recommend the watch to any person wishing to purchase a watch. Ever person that has seen the watch thinks there is something wrong with it or you could not sell them so cheap, as the same style of watch here in our jewelry stores will cost $30.00. I took the watch to one of our jewelers and he pronounced it a good watch and said it was as cheap as dirt at the money paid for it. Yours truly, J. E. McCLELLAND.

Our Solid Gold Watch Department!

Last year was our banner year in **SOLID GOLD** watches. We sold more 14 karet solid gold cases than any other concern in America. This year we are trying to double last year's sales, and, in order that we may double our previous, remarkable record, **we have a great inducement to offer—IT'S THE PRICE—***we have purchased an interest in a gold case factory* and this year we offer gold cases at the intrinsic value of the gold, with $1.62 added for making the case and the cost of engraving, ornamenting and diamond setting added. *No concern in America* pretend to meet our prices on **SOLID GOLD WATCHES.** *They can't do it—*Fourteen (14) Karet Solid Gold, United States Mint Assay, is the grade we handle. **Nothing but the Best—** No. 8, 10 or 12 karet—Only U. S. Mint Assay, Full 14 Karet. **THE BEST THAT'S MADE** and yet cheaper than any other house sells 10 karet. *WHY?* Because you pay for the gold, pay $1.62 for making the case, pay for engraving it, **THAT'S ALL, NOTHING MORE.**

BUY A GOLD WATCH

and you will always be satisfied. Gold filled watches are getting to be very common, nearly every one wears a gold filled watch. They are very nice if you can't afford **solid gold**; but as nice as a gold filled case can be made **you can** tell the difference; *a gold filled watch is nothing but a gold filled watch*, while **a solid gold watch is a solid gold watch once, always and forever.** Besides, at our prices **you can afford it.** We will sell you the finest, 14 karet solid gold watch ever made for as little money as the average dealer asks for a good gold filled watch.

To urge you to order a 14 karet solid gold watch, and thus **AN EXTRA INDUCEMENT!** get the best, and push work at the case factory, we shall give away, **ABSOLUTELY FREE, a nice, valuable present with every solid gold watch sold.** We will during the year **SEND FREE** as presents a number of fine $100.00 organs, $100.00 top carriages, fine silverware table sets, gold, gold filled and gold plated chains, etc. *Everyone cannot* get a $100.00 present, but a certain percentage will be such valuable presents, and everyone will get some nice present. **Not until the watch is paid for** will we send the present. If cash in full accompanies the order we will send the present the same day we send the watch. If watch is sent C. O. D. subject to examination, we will send the present the day we receive the money from the express company.

YOU GET A PRESENT with every gold watch, whether paid cash in advance or C. O. D., as soon as we get the money. **We Will Sacrifice Our Profit** this year on **Gold Cases** to boom the gold case business, and enlarge the factory, by dividing our gold case profits among our customers, sending a present to everyone who buys a gold watch, the presents ranging from a nice gold plated chain up to a $100.00 parlor organ or top carriage.

YOU UNDERSTAND—We will send any watch **C. O. D. SUBJECT TO EXAMINATION.**

EXAMINATION IS FREE. ★ ★ ★ **NO MONEY IN ADVANCE.**

Warranted 14 Karet Solid Gold!

We do not handle anything in SOLID GOLD CASES but the Very Finest (14) Karet Solid Gold, United States Mint Assay. Every case is plainly stamped in the back by the manufacturers and warranted **14 Karet Solid Gold, U. S. Mint Assay.** *We issue a Binding Guarantee with every Solid Gold Case we Sell*, guaranteeing it to be solid 14 karet gold of **U. S. Mint Assay, and to** wear and retain its color a life-time.

THIS SOLID GOLD CASE

is the latest style and best made engine turned case in the market, with ornamented shield and hand finished centre, **18 Size, Hunting Case.**

We fit in this case:

	Gilt.	Nickel.
7 jeweled Trenton movement		$28.50
7 jeweled Waltham, Hampden or Elgin .	$29.50	
11 jeweled Waltham, Hampden or Elgin .	30.75	31.00
Full 15 jeweled, patent regulator, Waltham, Hampden or Elgin	33.00	33.50
Full 15 jeweled, patent regulator, G. M. Wheeler (Elgin)	33.00	33.50
Full 15 jeweled, patent regulator, P. S. Bartlett (Waltham)	33.00	33.50
Full 15 jeweled, patent regulator, adjusted, Appleton, Tracy & Co., (Waltham)	39.50	41.50
Full 15 jeweled, patent regulator, adjusted, Crescent St., (Waltham)		45.50
Full 15 jeweled, patent regulator, adjusted, B. W. Raymond, (Elgin)	39.50	41.50
Full 17 jeweled, patent regulator, adjusted, new Railway, (Hampden)		50.50

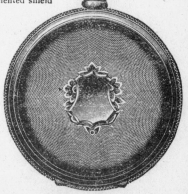

No. 6059.

14 KARAT SOLID GOLD.

WEIGHT, 40 DWTS.

WHAT THE PEOPLE SAY!

CINCINNATI, OHIO.

Gents.—Received the watch and was surprised to see it. I am very well satisfied with it. As long as I have had it it suits me all right, for I wanted a good timekeeper and I think I have got one now that does keep time. Thanking you kindly for your promptness, you will hear from me again soon. Respectfully, HENRY JAPSE.

LONDON, WISCONSIN.

Gents.—I received the watch and have it now. I am very much pleased with it and others are as well pleased with it as I myself. I got the watch as soon as it came to the office and paid the agent the price. Hope the money has been sent safely to you. Yours truly,
EDITH L. McCOURT.

CHUALAR, CALIFORNIA.

Gents.—The watch came in splendid order and I am more than pleased with it. It is a splendid watch and keeps fine time. So far it is a watch that will sell here quick. Will you let any more go at the same price? If you will write and let me know, I will do all I can for you. Send me a catalogue and price list. Yours truly, JOHN W. KIFFE.

McCRACKEN, KANSAS.

Gents.—I have this day received watch shipped to me by you in perfect condition, and am well satisfied, and can say that I do not know a more fair, strong and reliable firm. I am glad to find I can get what is advertised. I will favor you with my future orders as I can get just what I want. Yours truly, M. D. GAZZELL.

ANN ARBOR, MICHIGAN.

Gents.—I received the watch you sent me, and think the watch is a good one. It is as you claim, and has kept good time ever since I started it. You may send me another one as soon as possible, the same as the one you sent me. I think you will have several orders from this place before long. Please send me a catalogue. I will help to sell all I can for you.
Yours Respectfully, CHRIST. WICKS.

NEVER BEFORE ADVERTISED!

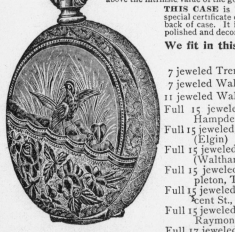

We say **NEVER BEFORE ADVERTISED,** for the reason that until we purchased an interest in the gold case factory, they only made gold cases for the finest retail stores in large cities. The factory built up a reputation for the finest gold cases made and found market for them direct to the fine retail stores in New York, Philadelphia, Chicago, and other large cities where something extra fine was appreciated. They never sold to wholesale houses, catalogue houses, small or ordinary retail dealers, and not until we purchased an interest in the factory have we been able to get such goods.

BUT NOW WE OFFER YOU the finest gold cases made at a very small percentage above the intrinsic value of the gold and the actual cost of labor to make and engrave them.

THIS CASE is 14 Karat Solid Gold, U. S. Mint Assay, and so warranted by a special certificate of guarantee and the manufacturer's registered stamp in back of case. It is stem-wind and stem-set, beautifully engraved, finished, polished and decorated by hand.

We fit in this case:

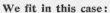

	Gilt.	Nickel.
7 jeweled Trenton movement		$29.75
7 jeweled Waltham, Hampden or Elgin . . .	$30.75	
11 jeweled Waltham, Hampden or Elgin . . .	32.00	32.25
Full 15 jeweled, patent regulator, Waltham, Hampden or Elgin	34.25	34.75
Full 15 jeweled, patent regulator, G. M. Wheeler, (Elgin)	34.25	34.75
Full 15 jeweled, patent regulator, P. S. Bartlett, (Waltham)	34.25	34.75
Full 15 jeweled, patent regulator, adjusted, Appleton, Tracy & Co., (Waltham)	40.75	42.75
Full 15 jeweled, patent regulator, adjusted, Crescent St., (Waltham)		46.75
Full 15 jeweled, patent regulator, adjusted, B. W. Raymond, (Elgin)	40.75	42.75
Full 17 jeweled, patent regulator, adjusted, new Railway, (Hampden)		51.75

No. 6060.

★ **14 KARAT SOLID GOLD.** ★ **WEIGHT, 43 DWTS.** ★

14 KARET SOLID GOLD!

★ UNITED STATES GOVERNMENT MINT ASSAY. ★

A BINDING LIFE CERTIFICATE of guarantee goes with each case.
OUR GOLD CASES are the very HIGHEST GRADE MADE.

THIS GOLD CASE weighs 43 pennyweights, it is hunting style, solid 14 karet gold through and through, including cap, crown, bow, front, back and all. It is beautifully engraved by hand by expert engravers and we guarantee for finish, style, quality and general appearance they are unexcelled.

We fit in this case:

	Gilt.	Nickel.
7 jeweled Trenton movement		$31.75
7 jeweled Waltham, Hampden or Elgin	$32.75	
11 jeweled Waltham, Hampden or Elgin	34.00	34.25
Full 15 jeweled, patent regulator, Waltham, Hampden or Elgin	36.25	36.75.
Full 15 jeweled, patent regulator, G. M. Wheeler, (Elgin)	36.25	36.75
Full 15 jeweled, patent regulator, P. S. Bartlett, (Waltham)	36.25	36.75
Full 15 jeweled, patent regulator, adjusted, Appleton, Tracy & Co., (Waltham)	42.75	44.75
Full 15 jeweled, patent regulator, adjusted, Crescent St., (Waltham)		48.75
Full 15 jeweled, patent regulator, adjusted, B. W. Raymond, (Elgin) .	42.75	44.75
Full 17 jeweled, patent regulator, adjusted, New Railway, (Hampden) .		53.75

No. 6062.

14 Karet Solid Gold,

Weight 43 dwts.

HOW GOOD! ‖ HOW NICE! ‖ HOW CHEAP!

CAN A 14 KARET SOLID GOLD CASE BE MADE AND SOLD!
We have made them the nicest, we have made them the best, and we sell them the cheapest of any concern in existence. **We sell a 14 karet Solid Gold Watch SO CHEAP** that every one should order Solid Gold.

BUY THE BEST! A trifle more invested at first and you have a watch that will be a source of pleasure as long as you live. **AT OUR PRICES** you get a 14 Karet Solid Gold Watch for the same price a retail dealer will ask you for a gold filled watch.

REMEMBER! We issue a binding guarantee that the case is 14 Karet Solid Gold, United States Mint Assay, and every case is so stamped by the manufacturer.

DESCRIPTION OF THIS CASE: Case is regular Gents' 18 size, hunting, stem-wind and stem-set, solid 14 karet gold, U. S. Mint Assay, engraved, polished, decorated and finished by hand, and by the most skilled artists. You will not find a case to compare with it outside of the very finest retail stores in cities.

We fit in this case:

	Gilt	Nickel.
7 jeweled Trenton movement		$31.75
7 jeweled Waltham, Hampden or Elgin	$32.75	
11 jeweled Waltham, Hampden or Elgin	34.00	34.25
Full 15 jeweled, patent regulator, Waltham, Hampden or Elgin	36.25	36.75
Full 15 jeweled, patent regulator, G. M. Wheeler, (Elgin)	36.25	36.75
Full 15 jeweled, patent regulator, P. S. Bartlett, (Waltham)	36.25	36.75
Full 15 jeweled, patent regulator, adjusted, Appleton, Tracy & Co., (Waltham)	42.75	44.75
Full 15 jeweled, patent regulator, adjusted, Crescent St., (Waltham)		48.75
Full 15 jeweled, patent regulator, adjusted, B. W. Raymond, (Elgin) .	42.75	44.75
Full 17 jeweled, patent regulator, adjusted, New Railway, (Hampden) .		53.75

No. 6063.

14 Karet Solid Gold, Weight, 43 dwts.

Warranted 14 Karet Solid Gold!

THIS CASE WE GUARANTEE 14 KARET SOLID GOLD U. S. MINT ASSAY.

HUNTING CASE, extra heavy (about 6o dwts.), beautifully engraved by hand, **EXACTLY LIKE CUT**, full box joint, stem-wind and stem-set.

No. 6066.

Gent's Regular 18 Size, Box Joint, Hunting Case.

We fit in this case:

	Gilt.	Nickel.
7 jeweled Trenton movement		$42.75
7 jeweled Waltham, Hampden or Elgin	$43.75	
11 jeweled Waltham, Hampden or Elgin	45.00	45.25
Full 15 jeweled, patent regulator, Waltham, Hampden or Elgin	47.50	48.00
Full 15 jeweled, patent regulator, G. M. Wheeler, (Elgin)	47.50	48.00
Full 15 jeweled, patent regulator, P. S. Bartlett, (Waltham)	47.50	48.00
Full 15 jeweled, patent regulator, adjusted, Appleton, Tracy & Co., (Waltham)	53.75	55.75
Full 15 jeweled, patent regulator, adjusted, Crescent St., (Waltham)		59.75
Full 15 jeweled, patent regulator, adjusted, B. W. Raymond, (Elgin) .	53.75	55.75
Full 17 jeweled, patent regulator, adjusted, New Railway, (Hampden) .		64.75

SENT TO ANY ADDRESS BY EXPRESS, C. O. D. SUBJECT TO EXAMINATION.

Set With a Genuine Diamond!

CASE MADE OF 14 KARET SOLID GOLD. We Doubt if one out of a hundred who receive our catalogue have ever seen a watch case such as we describe here, there are very few carried in the stocks of the largest retail stores in the country, and if they have such a case it is used as a show and advertisement, they can seldom sell one on account of **THE PRICE. Look in some fine retail store** and if you find such a case, ask the price and for the case alone, they will tell you $100 to $150. **NO WONDER THEY DON'T SELL THEM! We do different!!** We figure the intrinsic value of 45 dwts. of 14 Karet Solid Gold, a pure white and perfect one-quarter carat Genuine Diamond, add to this the actual cost to make and engrave the case, and then to this add the smallest percentage of profit possible and then offer the complete watch, diamond set case, movement and all for less money than other dealers ask for an ordinary gold case alone. **THIS WATCH CASE** is made of 14 Karet Solid Gold, and set with a Genuine Diamond weighing one-quarter of a carat. The diamonds in our diamond set cases are all carefully selected stones, perfectly cut, pure white and free from any flaws, and in setting are cut clear through the case. The case in hunting style, stem-wind and stem-set, beautifully engraved and decorated by hand.

We fit in this case:

	Gilt.	Nickel.
7 jeweled Trenton movement		$59.75
7 jeweled Waltham, Hampden or Elgin .	$60.75	
11 jeweled Waltham, Hampden or Elgin .	62.00	62.25
Full 15 jeweled, patent regulator, Waltham, Hampden or Elgin	64.25	64.75
Full 15 jeweled, patent regulator, G. M. Wheeler (Elgin)	64.25	64.75
Full 15 jeweled, patent regulator, P. S. Bartlett (Waltham)	64.25	64.75
Full 15 jeweled, patent regulator, adjusted, Appleton, Tracy & Co., (Waltham)	70.75	72.75
Full 15 jeweled, patent regulator, adjusted, Crescent St., (Waltham)		76.75
Full 15 jeweled, patent regulator, adjusted, B. W. Raymond, (Elgin)	70.75	72.75
Full 17 jeweled, patent regulator, adjusted, new Railway, (Hampden)		81.75

No. 6067.

14 Karet Solid Gold, Weight 45 dwts.

Warranted 14 Karet Solid Gold!

THIS CASE WE GUARANTEE 14 KARET SOLID GOLD, U. S. MINT ASSAY!

HUNTING CASE, extra heavy (about 60 dwts.), beautifully engraved by hand, **EXACTLY LIKE CUT,** full box joint, stem-wind and stem-set.

We fit in this case:

	Gilt.	Nickel.
7 jeweled Trenton movement		$42.75
7 jeweled Waltham, Hampden or Elgin	$43.75	
11 jeweled Waltham, Hampden or Elgin	45.00	45.25
Full 15 jeweled, patent regulator, Waltham, Hampden or Elgin . . .	47.25	47.75
Full 15 jeweled, patent regulator, G. M. Wheeler, (Elgin)	47.25	47.75
Full 15 jeweled, patent regulator, P. S. Bartlett, (Waltham)	47.25	47.75
Full 15 jeweled, patent regulator, adjusted, Appleton, Tracy & Co., (Waltham)	53.75	55.75
Full 15 jeweled, patent regulator, adjusted, Crescent St., (Waltham)		59.75
Full 15 jeweled, patent regulator, adjusted, B. W. Raymond, (Elgin) .	53.75	55.75
Full 17 jeweled, patent regulator, adjusted, New Railway, (Hampden) .		64.75

No. 6064.
Gents' Regular 18 Size,   Box Joint, Hunting Case.

SENT TO ANY ADDRESS BY EXPRESS, C. O. D. SUBJECT TO EXAMINATION.

Warranted 14 Karet Solid Gold!

THIS CASE WE GUARANTEE 14 KARET SOLID GOLD U. S. MINT ASSAY.

HUNTING CASE, extra heavy (about 60 dwts.), beautifully engraved by hand, **EXACTLY LIKE CUT,** full box joint, stem-wind and stem-set.

We fit in this case:

	Gilt.	Nickel.
7 jeweled Trenton movement		$42.75
7 jeweled Waltham, Hampden or Elgin	$43.75	
11 jeweled Waltham, Hampden or Elgin	45.00	45.25
Full 15 jeweled, patent regulator, Waltham, Hampden or Elgin . . .	47.25	47.75
Full 15 jeweled, patent regulator, G. M. Wheeler, (Elgin)	47.25	47.75
Full 15 jeweled, patent regulator, P. S. Bartlett, (Waltham)	47.25	47.75
Full 15 jeweled, patent regulator, adjusted, Appleton, Tracy & Co., (Waltham)	53.75	55.75
Full 15 jeweled, patent regulator, adjusted, Crescent St., (Waltham)		59.75
Full 15 jeweled, patent regulator, adjusted, B. W. Raymond, (Elgin) .	53.75	55.75
Full 17 jeweled, patent regulator, adjusted, New Railway, (Hampden) .		64.75

SENT TO ANY ADDRESS BY EXPRESS, C. O. D. SUBJECT TO EXAMINATION.

No. 6065.
Gent's Regular 18 Size,   Box Joint, Hunting Case.

Set With a Genuine Diamond!

14 Karet Solid Gold, Weight, 45 dwts.

CASE MADE OF 14 KARET SOLID GOLD. We Doubt if one out of a hundred who receive our catalogue have ever seen a watch case such as we describe here, there are very few carried in the stocks of the largest retail stores in the country, and if they have such a case it is used as a show and advertisement, they can seldom sell one on account of **THE PRICE. Look in some fine retail store** and if you find such a case, ask the price and for the case alone, they will tell you $100 to $150. **NO WONDER THEY DON'T SELL THEM! We do different!!** We figure the intrinsic value of 45 dwts. of 14 Karet Solid Gold, a pure white and perfect one-quarter carat Genuine Diamond, add to this the actual cost to make and engrave the case, and then to this add the smallest percentage of profit possible and then offer the complete watch, diamond set case, movement and all for less money than other dealers ask for an ordinary gold case alone. **THIS WATCH CASE** is made of 14 Karat Solid Gold, and set with a Genuine Diamond weighing one-quarter of a carat. The diamonds in our diamond set cases are all carefully selected stones, perfectly cut, pure white and free from any flaws, and in setting are cut clear through the case. The case in hunting style, stem-wind and stem-set, beautifully engraved and decorated by hand.

No. 6068.

We fit in this case:

	Gilt.	Nickel.
7 jeweled Trenton movement		$59.75
7 jeweled Waltham, Hampden or Elgin .	$60.75	
11 jeweled Waltham, Hampden or Elgin .	62.00	62.25
Full 15 jeweled, patent regulator, Waltham, Hampden or Elgin	64.25	64.75
Full 15 jeweled, patent regulator, G. M. Wheeler (Elgin)	64.25	64.75
Full 15 jeweled, patent regulator, P. S. Bartlett (Waltham)	64.25	64.75
Full 15 jeweled, patent regulator, adjusted, Appleton, Tracy & Co., (Waltham)	70.75	72.75
Full 15 jeweled, patent regulator, adjusted, Crescent St., (Waltham)		76.75
Full 15 jeweled, patent regulator, adjusted, B. W. Raymond, (Elgin)	70.75	72.75
Full 17 jeweled, patent regulator, adjusted, new Railway, (Hampden)		81.75

SOLID SILVER CHATELAINE!

PRICE, $4.90.

The Best Ladies Silver Watch

Made for the Money!

CASE Warranted Solid Coin Silver.

Movement Warranted an Accurate Time-keeper.

Open Face, Stem-wind and Stem-set.

No. 6069.

Sent to Any Address C. O. D. Subject to Examination!

All Express Charges Paid by Us!

SOLID SILVER CHATELAINE!

PRICE, $5.75.

The Best Ladies Silver Watch
Made for the Money!

CASE Warranted Solid Coin Silver.

Movement Warranted an Accurate Time-keeper.

Hunting Case, Stem-wind and Stem-set.

No. 6070.

Sent to Any Address C. O. D. Subject to Examination!

All Express Charges Paid by Us!

Solid Gold Chatelaine!

➤ Price, $12.75! ◄

The Best Ladies' Solid Gold
Watch Made for the Money.

Case Warranted Solid Gold.

Movement Warranted

an accurate time-keeper.

No. 6071.

Open Face, Stem-wind and Stem-set.

Sent to Any Address C. O. D. Subject to Examination!

ALL EXPRESS CHARGES PAID BY US!

Solid Gold Chatelaine!

Price, $14.75

The Best Ladies' Solid Gold

Watch Made for the Money.

Case Warranted Solid Gold.

Movement Warranted an Accurate Time-keeper.

Hunting Case, Stem-wind and Stem-set.

No. 6072.

Sent to Any Address C. O. D. Subject to Examination!

All Express Charges Paid by Us!

Require no Money in Advance!

Smallest Genuine American Watch in the Market!

Open Face, Stem-wind and Stem-set.

Your Choice:
{ Solid Silveroid, $6.25
Solid Coin Silver, 7.50
Silver, Gold Inlaid, 8.75 }
Elgin or Waltham Movement.

These Cases are Genuine American Stem-wind and Stem-set.

The **Silveroid** cases are beautifully finished and in every way, except in intrinsic value, the equal of coin silver. Warranted to wear and retain their perfect coin silver color a life-time.

The **Coin Silver** cases are the best solid coin silver cases made. They are beautifully polished and finished by hand.

The **Gold Inlaid** cases are solid coin silver, beautifully inlaid and decorated with **solid gold.**

Ladies' O Size, Open Face.
Front of Watch.
No. 6073.

Ladies' O Size, Open Face.
Back of Watch.
No. 6073.

Our price complete with:	For Silveroid Case.	For Solid Coin Silver Case.	For Gold Inlaid Silver Case.
7 jeweled, Elgin or Waltham movement	$6.25	$7.50	$8.75
11 " " " "	7.75	9.00	10.25

Sent C. O. D. Subject to Examination.   No Money Required in Advance.

LADIES' CHATELAINE WATCHES!

YOU WILL FIND
WE ARE HEADQUARTERS ON THESE GOODS.

$3.68 BUYS OUR
Ladies' Nickel
Chatelaine.

No. 8034 — Order by Number.

C. O. D. to Anyone.

No Money in Advance.

All Express Charges Paid.

⚜ DESCRIPTION ⚜

☞ **Solid Nickel Case**, Highly Polished, Beautifully Finished, *warranted to wear* and retain its color a **lifetime**, stem-wind and stem-set. **Movement** is a nicely jeweled, quick train stem-wind and stem-set, **warranted** an accurate time-keeper.

OUR PRICE $6.20
Retails Everywhere
for $12.00

No. 8035 — Order by Number.

☞ There is a certain demand for something extraordinary in a ladies' open face, silver chatelaine, and to supply this demand we offer you here one of the finest silver chatelaines made.

☞ **DESCRIPTION!** This case is Solid Coin Silver **900 Fine** including inside cap, beautifully engraved, decorated and finished by hand. **MOVEMENT** is one of the finest imported chatelaine movements made, **Solid Nickel**, full ruby jeweled, quick train, patent pinion and escapements, stem-wind and stem-set, and **warranted an accurate** time-keeper.

Our $6.98 CHATE-LAINE!

No. 8036 — Order by Number.

To meet the demand of all classes we have added to our line a complete assortment of open face and hunting case Solid Gold and Coin Silver Chatelaines.

This is one of our

BEST
Coin Silver, Hunting Case Chatelaines.

OUR SPECIAL PRICE
$6.98
Retails Everywhere at $15.00.

DESCRIPTION ! **Coin Silver, 900 Fine**, hunting case, beautifully engraved, ornamented and decorated by hand, stem-wind and stem-set. **Movement** is a very fine **Solid Nickel**, stem-wind and stem-set, richly jeweled with patent pinion and escapement, best French enameled dial with fancy hands.

C. O. D. TO ANYONE !

Examination Free.   No Money in Advance.

Our Best $7.45!
Other concerns sell the
same watch for $15.00

No. 8037 — Order by Number.

☞ We have always conducted our business on what we consider a somewhat original plan, viz: By furnishing **OUR CUSTOMERS** standard goods, always exactly as represented, and at prices as low as possible consistent with a safe and honest business. As a **CONSEQUENCE** our prices are invariably **very much lower** than the same goods are sold by other houses, while our terms are far more liberal. From a strict adherence to these rules our business has grown until we are without a peer in the watch business. ☞ Our customers have appreciated our business methods, they have patronized us liberally, would it be policy for us to abandon the ship which has carried us **TRIUMPHANTLY** to the front rank? **"NO."** We appreciate your patronage, we have won your confidence honestly, and we consider it our sacred duty to maintain it. **This Watch** is the **Best** hunting case, full hand engraved, stem-wind Chatelaine we handle. **Movement** is one of the very finest **Solid Nickel**, stem-wind, full jeweled, accurately regulated, and *guaranteed*.

LADIES'
GOLD AND SILVER CHATELAINES

COSTS YOU NOTHING

to See and Examine this Watch, THE FINEST Coin Silver Chatelaine made.

OUR SPECIAL PRICE,

$5.95

RETAILS AT $12.00 AND UPWARDS.

No. 8050.
Front of Watch.
This is a picture of the front of the watch, engraved from a photograph.

CASES are fine Coin Silver, beautifully engraved, as shown in cut; a finish only put on the FINEST watches; SOLID COIN SILVER, inside cap, best beveled edge, flat French crystal.

No. 8050.
Back of Watch.
This is a picture of the back of the watch, engraved from a photograph.

MOVEMENT is a very fine solid Nickel stem-wind and stem-set, full jeweled, quick train, **warranted an accurate time-keeper.**

A BINDING GUARANTEE

Goes with every watch; Warranting case **Solid Coin Silver** and Movement an accurate time-keeper **for 5 years.**

WARRANTED 14-KARAT SOLID GOLD.

Stamped by the Swiss Government as an absolute Guarantee of its Fineness.

$15.90 BUYS ..A.. $30.00
WATCH.

READ DESCRIPTION.

These pictures are engraved from photographs, but will give you a faint idea of how the watch looks.

No. 8051.
Front of Watch.
This is a picture of the front of the watch, engraved from a photograph.

NOTHING COULD BE NICER. The cases are the finest corrugated pattern, with plain polished circle in back to admit monogram or name being engraved on, dial is VERY FANCY, a most beautiful production, you can get some idea from picture. It is enameled in fancy

No. 8051.
Back of Watch.
This is a picture of the back of the watch, engraved from a photograph,

colors, with raised white enameled circles for figures; figures in black enamel and all ornamented in gold, beveled edge, flat French crystal, modern style patent ANTIQUE BOW, with antique winding crown, all 14-karat Solid Gold, including inside cap and all. MOVEMENT is one of the finest Ladies' Solid Nickel Stem Wind and Stem Set Swiss Chatelains, full ruby jeweled, quick train, accurately regulated and WARRANTED, 14-karat SOLID GOLD, fancy hands, perfect timekeeper. **A BINDING GUARANTEE goes with Every Watch.**

OUR TERMS always easy. We want you to see our goods and we know you will buy.

WE WILL SEND YOU THIS WATCH, all Express Charges Paid. You can examine it at the Express office, and if found perfectly satisfactory, pay the agent **$15.90** and it is yours. OTHERWISE, pay nothing, and the agent will return it AT OUR EXPENSE.

Ladies' Gold and Silver Chatelaines!

Ladies' Hunting Case, Coin Silver Chatelaine.

Our Price $6.75!

Retails at $15.00 and Upwards.

◀ ◆ ● ◆ ▶

No. 8052.

Case Is hunting style, as shown in cut, fancy corrugated, stem-wind and stem-set.

Movement Is one of the best Swiss chatelaines made, **Solid Nickel,** full jeweled, quick train, warranted an accurate time-keeper.

TERMS: { C. O. D. to Anyone Anywhere. All Express Charges Prepaid. No Money in Advance.

Ladies' 14k Solid Gold, Hunting Case Chatelaine.

Our Price $18.90

Every Case Stamped by the Swiss Government as an absolute guarantee of its fineness.

No. 8053.

Case Is **Finest Solid Gold** (14 Karet) fancy corrugated as shown in cut, plain polished circle on front and back to admit of monogram or name being engraved, *14 Karet Solid Gold* inside cap, fancy antique bow and fancy antique winding crown.

Movement Is a very fine Swiss chatelaine, **Solid Nickel,** full jeweled, quick train, stem-wind, very fancy dial, **14 Karet Solid Gold** fancy hands.

Terms: C. O. D. TO ANYONE; No Money in Advance; All Express Charges Paid by Us.

Ladies' Solid Gold, Hunting Case Chatelaine

Our Price $19.95!

No. 8054.

You can't Buy this watch in any retail store for less than double our price.

WE ARE Offering you the very finest goods at **PRICES** never before heard of.

This Case Is 14 Karet Solid Gold throughout, including inside cap, crown, bow and all beautifully engraved by hand, stem-wind and stem-set. ☞**MOVEMENT** is a full jeweled, quick train, stem-wind and stem-set, *warranted* an accurate time-keeper.

C. O. D. TO ANYONE ANYWHERE.

No Money in Advance.   We Pay all Express.

BEST WE HANDLE!

Our Price $23.95

Nothing Better Made!
A Thing of Beauty!

No Picture, No Description can do it Justice.

☞YOU MUST SEE IT to appreciate it and YOU CAN SEE IT without one cent of cost to yourself.

No. 8055.

Ladies' Fancy Chatelaine, 14 Karet Solid Sold, Guaranteed and stamped with the stamp of the Swiss Government. Everything Fancy and Fine.

☞**DESCRIPTION!** Case is *14 Karet Solid Gold*, plain polished and burnished, **Solid Gold** inside cap, Fancy antique crown and bow, very fancy **Colored** enameled dial, very fancy **Gold** enameled figures, **14k Solid Gold** fancy hands. Movement is finest solid nickel, full ruby jeweled, quick train, stem-wind, the finest chatelaine movement. Of our chatelaines this is the **BEST,** the **HANDSOMEST** and the **GRANDEST BARGAIN.**
☞**TERMS!** C. O. D. to Anyone; No Money in Advance; All Express Charges Paid by Us.

SOLID GOLD CHATELAINES!

BEST AND CHEAPEST EVER OFFERED

14 Karet Solid Gold

Chatelaine Watch for

$13.90

No. 8038 — Order by Number.

We honestly believe we for the first time in the history of the watch business offer you a **14 Karet Solid Gold** watch for $13.90.

We warrant this case **14 KARET SOLID GOLD**, and every case is stamped with the **Swiss Government Stamp** as an absolute guarantee it is plump **14 Karet.** They are beautifully engraved by hand, nicely finished and polished. **MOVEMENT** is of superior quality Swiss, Solid Nickel, full jeweled stemwind and stem-set, accurately regulated and **fully warranted.**

You All Know Our Terms:

C. O. D. Subject to Examination to Anyone.
No Money in Advance.
All Express Charges Paid by Us.

14 Karet Solid Gold

Hunting Case,
Stem-wind,
Stem-set.

Our Price is

$15.90

READ DESCRIPTION!

No. 8039 — Order by Number.

☞**THIS CASE** is warranted **14 Karet Solid Gold**, stamped with the **Swiss Government Stamp** as an absolute guarantee. It is 14 Karet, hunting case, beautifully engraved and decorated by hand, stem-wind and stem-set. **MOVEMENT** is one of the finest **Solid Nickel, Quick Train, Full Jeweled, Swiss** make, warranted an accurate timekeeper.

14 Karet Solid Gold

Our Special Price is

$15.60

Retails at from $25.00 to $30.00

No. 8040 — Order by Number.

We offer this as the finest we handle and the best goods made.

If you get the best you can't buy better!

☞**DESCRIPTION!** This watch is very similar to our No. 8039, the case is a little heavier and both case and movement a little finer finish. **CASE** is warranted 1 4 **Karet Solid Gold** and bears the Swiss government stamp as a guarantee. **MOVEMENT** is one of the very finest and guaranteed in every respect.

Tell us what you want, that's all you have to do, a 1 cent postal card or a 2 cent stamped envelope addressed to **Sears, Roebuck & Co.**, Chicago, Ills., or Minneapolis, Minn., is all you have to do. Then the duty falls on us, we will acknowledge receipt of your order the day it is received, the watch will be shipped the following day **Subject to Examination**, a notice of shipment and our binding guarantee will be mailed you, the express agent will allow you to examine the watch without asking a cent, if it don't suit you, you are under no obligation to take it, it will be returned at our expense.

14 Karet Solid Gold

Our Special Price is

$17.25

Just Think

14 Karet
Solid Gold
Warranted.

Case the BEST,

No. 8041 — Order by Number.

Movement the BEST, and all for **$17.25**

Retails at Double Our Price.

☞Hand Engraved, Hunting Case, Stem-wind and Stem-set. Case extra heavy. Movement our very finest Stem-wind, Nickel Chalelaine **WARRANTED.** You should see the guarantee we send. GUARANTEE **ABSOLUTE.**☜

TERMS EASY. PRICES BOTTOM.
CAN WE HAVE BUT A TRIAL ORDER?

LADIES' BARGAIN PAGE.

A $20.00 WATCH FOR $9.95

C. O. D. to Anyone. No money in Advance.

We pay all Express Charges,

You pay $9.95. Nothing More.

WE HONESTLY believe we give you Greater Value for your Money in this Watch than in any other Ladies' Watch we illustrate in this Catalogue. **.   .   .   .   .**

SPECIAL No. 6.

Order by Number.

This is a picture of our Special Guarantee which goes with every watch.

You Can Only Get Them From Us. We have bought them all. No one else can furnish you this Watch. We never take advantage of our customers because we monopolize any particular grade or product. Everything always figured as low as possible, which means **far below all others. We endeavor to increase our sales** by cutting the price down, and this we have done on everything until we have got the selling price as near the cost price as it is safe for any business to run.

Description of our Special No. 6 at $9.95.

This is one of the finest Gold Filled Cases made. **REGULAR LADIES' 6 SIZE,** Hunting, Full Engraved, Decorated and Finished by Hand, Solid Gold Bow, Crown and Thumb Pieces, Gold Filled Inside Cap, **Warranted to wear for 20 Years,** a Certificate of Guarantee accompanies each case. See copy of Guarantee at top.

MOVEMENT is a **SPECIAL HIGH GRADE,** Full Jeweled, Stem Wind and Stem Set, Quick Train, Warranted an accurate time-keeper for five years, a Guarantee is sent with each movement. The movement alone would sell by others at far more than we ask for the complete watch, and anyone would consider this watch a BARGAIN at even DOUBLE our price. **You can see for yourself.** It will cost you nothing to see and examine the watch ; we will send it to any address, C. O. D., subject to examination. **NO MONEY** in advance. **Pay all the Express Charges** ourselves ; you can examine it, and if not found perfectly satisfactory and exactly as represented, **YOU REFUSE IT, PAY NOTHING,** and the Agent will RETURN IT AT OUR EXPENSE.

We offer Many Bargains but among them all, there is no such Bargain offered in a LADIES' GOLD FILLED WATCH as this OUR SPECIAL NO. 6 at **$9.95.**

IF YOU HAVE EVER DEALT WITH US

You know how our goods compare with our representations ; you know what values we give, and **we are doing better** all the time, **constantly working** to improve our goods, constantly working the prices down, **our old customers** know this, our new customers are fast learning it, and if you have never dealt with us, **give us one chance, please,** ALL at OUR RISK, ALL at OUR EXPENSE. If you want a LADIES' WATCH, let us send you SPECIAL No. 6, at **$9.95** to Examine.

This is a picture of the Movement which goes in our Special No. 6.

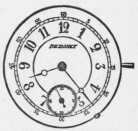

This is a picture of the face of movement which goes in Special No. 6.

YOUR CHOICE $12.95!

No. 8042.
Order by Number. ❊ Ladies' 6 Size.

W̤E WANT TO OFFER you the finest goods made as well as the cheapest, and we believe you will agree with us we have left nothing undone. While it is true we offer an American watch for **$1.15,** less money than a watch was ever sold before, it is equally true that we offer the highest grade goods made at less money than they were ever offered before, and in reference to high grade goods, **too much can not be said about**

The Wadsworth 25 Year
Gold Filled Cases!

The Wadsworth Watch Case Co. make a general line of watch cases, but they also make a few extra fine **25 year** cases for fine retail trade, the sale of which is confined exclusively to the finest retail jewelry stores in large cities.

We Think There is Nothing too Good

for our trade, and accordingly, we take pleasure in presenting for your kind consideration the two handsomest, high grade, 25 year gold filled cases they make, one in ladies' regular 6 size and one in o size. ☞ **IN REGARD TO PRICE!** ☜ We believe you will not question our statement when we tell you we are not only offering you these watches for less money then they were ever advertised before, but we are offering them to you for less money than any retailer on earth has ever bought them.

We fit in these cases the following movements:

		Gilt.	Nickel.
7 Jeweled, Solid Nickel, Trenton			$12.95
7 " Waltham, Hampden or Elgin		$13.95	
11 " " " "		15.20	15.70
Full 15 " " " "			19.45
Full 15 " " - " " extra fine solid nickel, raised gold settings, adjusted to heat, cold, position and isochronism			29.45

No. 8043 furnished with Waltham, Hampden or Elgin movements only. Trenton movements are not made in O size.

━ Description of Cases ━

These cases are not to be told from **SOLID GOLD,** they are in appearance, finish, and every way except in intrinsic value, the equal to solid gold, made from two very heavy plates of 14 karet solid gold rolled down over composition metal, and are **guaranteed to wear for 25 years.** The manufacturers guarantee and ours accompany every case. They are beautifully engraved by hand by the most skilled artists, and every case is indeed a work of art. They come in the exact patterns as shown in the illustrations, full escaloped edges, hand burnished and finished, **Warranted 14 Karet Fine U. S. Mint Assay,** with 14 Karet Solid Gold bow, joints and thumb pieces.

Sent C. O. D. to Anyone.

No Money in Advance.

No. 8043.
Order by Number. ❊ Ladies' O Size.

Address Your Orders to Us at { OR **CHICAGO, ILLS.**
MINNEAPOLIS, MIN

THE WORLD IS OURS ON WATCHES!

NEVER BEFORE was a Ladies' genuine Gold Filled Watch sold for $9.00!

WE WILL ACCEPT YOUR JUDGMENT and send this watch to you all charges prepaid. You examine it, call any expert to examine it, and if it is not found the greatest bargain ever seen in a ladies' watch, don't pay a cent and the agent will return it at our expense. We are compelled to give more value than any other firm in existence.

REASON FOR YOURSELF.

There is no other concern that will send a watch out unless they first receive a deposit of from 50 cts. to $2.00. *WHY?* They know it is doubtful if their customers will take the watch and pay the charges, it is likely to be returned at their expense, their customer may be able to buy cheaper elsewhere.

WE ASK NO MONEY IN ADVANCE! WE TAKE ALL THE RISK!

Consequently we can't afford to be undersold. You send us no money when you order a watch and therefore we know our price must be below all others or the watch will be returned at our expense.

We don't allow our watches to be returned, we make the price so low they are always taken. When you see the greatest bargain you ever saw you take it, and not only the one watch, but we will sell you more.

No. 6074.

THIS, OUR LADIES' $9.00 WATCH, is the cheapest ladies' genuine Gold Filled watch we have. Made of two plates of Solid Gold over composition metal and warranted to wear 20 YEARS. Beautifully engraved by hand, hunting case, stem-wind and stem-set. (*A special 20 year certificate of guarantee goes with each watch*). We fit in this case a fine, solid nickel, quick train, stem-wind, genuine American Movement.

YOU HAVE NO EXPRESS CHARGES TO PAY, you pay NINE DOLLARS after examination, nothing more.

ONE OF THE BEST ➤ SOLID GOLD FILLED CASES MADE!

OUR $10.00 LEADER! Nothing like it in the Market for less than $18.00. For a Ladies' Watch, THE GREATEST BARGAIN EVER OFFERED!

WE FEEL CONFIDENT when you order this watch you get as we advertise, THE GREATEST BARGAIN EVER OFFERED! CASE is Gold Filled, hunting, beautifully engraved by hand and warranted to wear for 20 YEARS.

We fit in this case:

			Gilt.	Nickel.
7 jeweled Trenton movement			$10.00	
7 " Elgin, Waltham or Hampden . . . $12.00				
11 " " " " . . . 13.25				14.25
15 " " " " . . .				17.50

IF YOU WANT A WATCH let us send you one by express to your nearest express office; it won't cost you anything to see and examine it. We know if we sell you one watch we will sell many more in your neighborhood. Our Motto is,

MAKE A WATCH SELL A WATCH.

No. 6075.

IT'S NO TROUBLE to see our watches; just select the watch you want, write us, giving number of watch and movement wanted (that's all). We do the rest, send the watch to your express office and so advise you by mail. The express agent will also send you a notice by mail the day it arrives, you go and examine it, allow your friends to examine it. **YOU DECIDE** if it is a bargain, we are not there to speak. We must depend upon the quality of our goods.

➤ CAN WE BE MORE FAIR? ◄

Jno. C. Dueber or Jas. Boss Best 14 Karet Gold Filled!

LATEST, NICEST AND BEST THING OUT!
ALL THE RAGE IN CITIES.
FIRST INTRODUCED IN NEW YORK where there are more sold than any other case ever made!

WHAT THEY ARE! Perfectly plain polished, satin finished or engine turned, as desired, very thin, latest model and the most beautiful case made. *Warranted 14 Karet Gold Filled*, made of two plates of solid gold over composition metal and *warranted to wear for 20 years.*

THE RESULT OF LOW PRICES.

We sell more watches to the consumer than any other concern in existence. Ask any express agent anywhere, if he knows of our business, ask him if he does not receive more packages from us than all other watch houses combined, ask him if he ever saw a poor watch come from our house. Write to any reputable business house in this city and learn for yourself something about the magnitude of our business. **NOTHING LIKE IT IN AMERICA!** Prices, quality and terms no other house can match.

No. 6076.

LADIES' 6 SIZE, REGULAR STYLE BOW.

No. 6077.

LADIES' 6 SIZE, ANTIQUE BOW.

We fit in these cases:

	Gilt.	Nickel.
7 jeweled, solid nickel Trenton movement		$12.00
7 " Waltham, Hampden or Elgin	$13.00	
11 " " " "	14.25	14.75
Full 15 " " " "		18.50
Full 15 " " " " extra fine solid nickel, raised gold settings, adjusted to heat, cold, position and isochronism		28.50

Jno. C. Dueber or Jas. Boss Best 14 Karet Gold Filled!

Full Engraved by Hand.   Nothing Better Ever Made.

Not only guaranteed to wear 20 years—**BUT THEY HAVE STOOD.** Their reputation long since established, **DUEBER** and **BOSS** cases are worn everywhere today that have stood even 30 to 40 years constant wear. **NEVER WORN THROUGH.** Dueber's or Boss' best cases have never worn through. **MORE GOLD in Dueber's or Boss' Best 14 Karet** cases than in any other cases made. Made of two plates of Solid Gold over composition metal and warranted to wear for **20 YEARS!**

FIRST SALE THE HARDEST! It often requires a great deal of advertising and soliciting to make the first single sale. **AFTERWARDS** we can sell many with little soliciting; make the first watch give such satisfaction that it will influence the sale of more.

"Make a Watch Sell a Watch"
That's Our Motto.

OUR BINDING GUARANTEE! Every movement is warranted for **5 years.** Every gold filled case is warranted for **20 years.** Our *binding guarantee* is sent with each watch; we always fulfill our guarantee to the letter. **WE DEFY** anyone to point to a single instance where we ever deviated in the least from the word and letter of our guarantee and our description of goods.

No. 6078.

No. 6079.

We fit in these cases:

	Gilt.	Nickel.
7 jeweled, solid nickel Trenton movement		$13.00
7 " Waltham, Hampden or Elgin	$14.00	
11 " " " "	15.25	15.75
Full 15 " " " "		19.50
Full 15 " " " " extra fine solid nickel, raised gold settings, adjusted to heat, cold, position and isochronism		29.50

Jno. C. Dueber or Jas. Boss Best 14 Karet Gold Filled!

SOLID GOLD CASE PATTERN.

JUST PLACED ON THE MARKET.

No. 6080.

THERE IS NOTHING TOO GOOD FOR OUR TRADE! We are offering the very latest novelties in high standard grade goods; the very same goods as you will find in the very finest stores on Broadway in New York, and yet at unheard of low prices, half retail price; less than any wholesale price.

THIS NEW CASE has the very latest style escaloped centre, full engraved, decorated and ornamented by hand, made of two plates of **SOLID GOLD** over composition metal, and *warranted to wear for 20 Years.*

You need not take our word alone: READ what others say through this catalogue, people who have bought our watches and who have of their own free will written us expressing their entire satisfaction.

Write to any express company in **You need not take their word alone:** this city, or the Union National Bank in this city, and ask what they know about us (be sure to enclose a 2 cent stamp for answer).

You need not take their word alone: We have sold watches everywhere, and at your request we will gladly give you the name of some one in your own county or town who has bought goods of us.

Let us send you a watch to examine **You need not take any one's word,** for yourself. **USE YOUR OWN JUDGMENT!**

We fit in these cases:

	Gilt.	Nickel.
7 jeweled, solid nickel Trenton movement		$14.00
7 " Waltham, Hampden or Elgin	$15.00	
11 " " " "	16.25	16.75
Full 15 " " " "		20.50
Full 15 " " " " extra fine solid nickel, raised gold settings, adjusted to heat, cold, position and isochronism		30.50

Raised Colored Gold Ornamented!

JNO. C. DUEBER, JAS. BOSS, CROWN OR FAHYS
BEST 14 KARET GOLD FILLED CASE!

No. 6081.

NOTHING LEFT UNDONE to make this case a BEAUTY! In quality, finish, style and beauty **IT'S PERFECT.** It is made of two plates of **SOLID GOLD** over composition metal and *warranted to wear 20 years.* Raised and colored solid gold ornamentations and decorations, beautifully finished, ornamented and decorated by hand, hunting case, stem-wind and stem-set.

OUR BEST GOLD CASES! Not only have the most gold of any case made, not only guaranteed to wear for 20 years, but they are in every way the best, **14 KARET GOLD FILLED** bezel and cap, **SOLID GOLD** bow, crown and thumb pieces, best case and lift springs, strongest and best winding crown, all hand engraved by the most skilled engravers.

We fit in this case:

	Gilt.	Nickel.
7 jeweled, solid nickel Trenton movement		$15.00
7 " Waltham, Hampden or Elgin	$16.00	
11 " " " "	17.25	17.75
Full 15 " " " "		21.50
Full 15 " " " " extra fine solid nickel, raised gold settings, adjusted to heat, cold, position and isochronism		31.50

14 Karet Solid Gold!

We will sell you any kind of a 14 Karet Solid Gold Watch for less money than any retail dealer can buy them for. No dealer can buy a watch like this for

~~≈$19.95!≈~~

WE ARE HEADQUARTERS FOR SOLID GOLD WATCHES!

We guarantee our prices below all others. THESE CASES are warranted SOLID GOLD, 14 Karet Fine, U. S. Mint Assay, beautifully engraved and decorated by hand. Extra heavy and warranted in every respect. Our Solid Gold Cases are without comparison. BEST QUALITY MADE.

A binding certificate of guarantee is sent with every gold watch we sell.

No. 6091.
Ladies' Regular 6 Size, Hunting Case.

No. 6092.
Ladies' Regular 6 Size, Hunting Case.

We fit in these cases:

	Gilt.	Nickel.
7 jeweled, solid nickel Trenton movement		$19.95
7 " Waltham, Hampden or Elgin	$20.95	
11 " " " "	22.20	22.70
Full 15 " " " "		26.45
Full 15 " " " " extra fine solid nickel, raised gold settings, adjusted to heat, cold, position and isochronism		36.45

OUR BEST 14 KARET SOLID GOLD!

Warranted 14 Karet Solid Gold, United States Government Mint Assay, Beautifully Engraved by Hand.

We make the price on gold cases so low, that every one should order Solid Gold. Nothing so nice in a ladies' watch as 14 KARET SOLID GOLD!

Write to any one whose testimonial appears in this catalogue and learn what they know of us (enclose 2c. stamp for reply). We refer you to the Union National Bank or any express company doing business in this city.

No. 6093.
LADIES' REGULAR 6 SIZE.
Hunting Case.

No. 6094.
LADIES' REGULAR 6 SIZE.
Hunting Case.

We fit in these cases:

	Gilt.	Nickel.
7 jeweled, solid nickel Trenton movement		$19.95
7 " Waltham, Hampden or Elgin	$20.95	
11 " " " "	22.20	22.70
Full 15 " " " "		26.45
Full 15 " " " " extra fine solid nickel, raised gold settings, adjusted to heat, cold, position and isochronism		36.45

Nothing Better Made!

Our Very Best 14 Karet Solid Gold!

Warranted Solid Gold 14 Karet Fine United States Mint Assay.

These are the finest Solid Gold cases made, they are extra heavy, beautifully engraved, *decorated and finished by hand*. They were first made for our city trade, but the demand from the country for extra fine goods has been such that we illustrate in this catalogue the *very finest goods we carry* and the

FINEST MADE.

No. 6095.
Ladies' Regular 6 Size, Hunting Case.

<u>Costs Nothing to See Our Watches.</u>

No. 6096.
Ladies' Regular 6 Size, Hunting Case.

We fit in these cases:

	Gilt.	Nickel.
7 jeweled, solid nickel Trenton movement		$21.95
7 " Waltham, Hampden or Elgin	$22.95	
11 " " " "	24.20	24.70
Full 15 " " " "		28.45
Full 15 " " " " extra fine solid nickel, raised gold settings, adjusted to heat, cold, position and isochronism		38.45

---

14 Karet Solid Gold Box Joint!

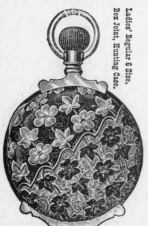

Ladies' Regular 6 Size, Box Joint, Hunting Case.

This Case is Extra Heavy 14 Karet Solid Gold, United States Government Mint Assay, Beautifully Engraved by Hand.

If you will compare our prices with those of any other thoroughly reliable house, you will find other wholesale dealers ask from $30.00 to $40.00 for this case alone.

We offer Case and Movement Complete for $24.95!!

And in consideration of our extremely low prices we shall hope for your trade.

A $50.00 Watch for $24.95!

No. 6097.

Examine it and be Convinced.

We fit in this case:

	Gilt.	Nickel.
7 jeweled, solid nickel Trenton movement		$24.95
7 " Waltham, Hampden or Elgin	$25.95	
11 " " " "	27.45	27.95
Full 15 " " " "		31.45
Full 15 " " " " extra fine solid nickel, raised gold settings, adjusted to heat, cold, position and isochronism		41.45

FINEST DIAMOND SET CASE!

THIS IS OUR VERY FINEST DIAMOND SET CASE, 14 Karet Solid Gold, Extra Heavy, Beautifully Engraved by Hand and set with **GENUINE DIAMONDS!**

OUR DIAMONDS used in our **Diamond Set Cases** are all carefully selected stones, pure white and perfect in every respect and so warranted.

OUR GOLD CASES are all 14 karet fine, of United States Government Assay, and so warranted. *A certificate of guarantee is sent with each watch.*

We fit in these cases:

	Gilt.	Nickel.
7 jeweled, solid nickel, Trenton movement		$29.50
7 jeweled Waltham, Hampden or Elgin	$30.50	
11 jeweled Waltham, Hampden or Elgin	31.75	32.25
Full 15 jeweled Waltham, Hampden or Elgin . . .		36.00
Full 15 jeweled Waltham, Hampden or Elgin, extra fine solid nickel, raised gold settings, adjusted to heat, cold, position and isochronisn		46.00

No. 6100.

LADIES' REGULAR 6 SIZE.

Diamond Set, Hunting Case.

FIVE GENUINE DIAMONDS.

No. 6101.

LADIES' REGULAR 6 SIZE.

Diamond Set, Hunting Case.

FOUR GENUINE DIAMONDS.

No Money Required in Advanee!

What the People Say!

FINE CHRONOGRAPHS AND MINUTE REPEATERS!

THE FINEST MADE!

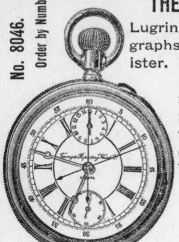
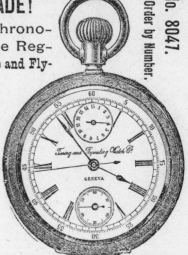

Gold Filled Diamond Set Watches!

Your Choice for $28.50

Retails at $50.00 === Wholesales at $35.00

OUR SPECIAL PRICE $28.50

Description of Case No. Special 37 is 14 Karet Gold Filled, Warranted to Wear 20 Years, Hunting Case, Stem-wind and Stem-set. **Very Fancy** corrugated, regular solid gold pattern, can't be told from solid gold, escalloped edge, fancy patent antique bow, raised fancy gold centre set with a **Large Genuine Diamond.**

Description of Case No. Special 38 is 14 Karet Gold Filled, Warranted to Wear 20 Years, Hunting Case, Stem-wind and Stem-set. **Very Fancy** raised and colored gold ornamentations which are 22 Karet Solid Gold. Case is set with a **Large Genuine Diamond.**

No. Special 37—Order by Number.
This is a picture of the case engraved from a photograph.

We fit in these cases the following movements:

				Gilt.	Nickel.
7 jeweled Trenton movement					$28.50
7 " Waltham, Hampden or Elgin				$29.50	
11 " " " "				30.75	31.00
Full 15 " patent regulator, Waltham Hampden or Elgin				33.00	33.50
" 15 " " " G. M. Wheeler (Elgin)				33.00	33.50
" 15 " " " P. S. Bartlett (Waltham)				33.00	33.50
" 15 " " " Appleton, Tracy & Co. (Waltham) adjusted				39.50	41.50
" 15 " " " B. W. Raymond (Elgin) "				39.50	41.50
" 15 " " " Crescent Street (Waltham) "					45.50
" 17 " " " New Railway (Hampden) "					50.50

UNDERSTAND, the above prices include your choice of cases with movement complete.

OUR TERMS

☞All orders for these watches must be accompanied by **one dollar** as a guarantee of good faith, when they will be sent to anyone, anywhere by express, C. O. D. Subject to Examination, *all express charges paid by us.* You can examine them at the express office and if found perfectly satisfactory pay the agent our price less the **$1.00** sent in advance.

☞**On Receipt of ONE DOLLAR** we will ship to anyone, anywhere, C. O. D. Subject to Examination, all express charges paid by us.

No. Special 38—Order by Number.
This is a picture of the case engraved from a photograph.

DIAMOND SET, Raised Colored Gold Ornamented Gold Filled Cases.
A Ladies' Diamond Gold Filled Watch.

Your Choice
FOR
$19.95

No. Special 33, Order by Number
This is a picture of the case engraved
from a photograph.

No. Special 34, Order by Number
This is a picture of the case engraved
from a photograph.

OUR TERMS

These are special watches at special prices, and, as a protection to ourselves, we require all orders to be accompanied by **one dollar.** We will then ship C.O.D. Subject to Examination, you can examine the watch at the express office and if found perfectly satisfactory pay our price less the one dollar.

OUR PRICE, for your choice of cases, complete with following movements:

	Gilt.	Nickel.
7 jeweled Trenton movement		$19.95
7 " Waltham, Hampden or Elgin $20.95		
11 " " " " 22.20		22.70
Full 15 " " " "		26.45
Full 15 " " " " extra fine solid nickel, raised gold settings, adjusted to heat, cold, position and isochronism		36.45

UNDERSTAND, the above prices include your choice of cases with movement complete. **OUR TERMS** are C.O.D. to anyone on receipt of one dollar.

What these Cases Are!

They are the finest gold filled cases made, **Cannot be told from 14 Karet Solid Gold,** all the raised and colored gold ornamentations are **22 Karet Solid Gold,** the cases are warranted **20 YEARS** and will wear a lifetime.

No. Special 35, Order by Number
This is a picture of the case engraved
from a photograph.

No. Special 36, Order by Number
This is a picture of the case engraved
from a photograph.

14 Karet Gold Filled Hunting Cases, Warranted to Wear for 20 Years, Raised and Colored Solid Gold Ornamentations, Set with a Large Genuine Diamond.

Diamond Department.

OUR TERMS, CONDITIONS, ETC.

We Sell Diamonds **Exactly as we Sell Watches,** viz: Select any diamond you want and we will send it to any address and place in the United States, by express C. O. D., subject to examination. You can examine it at the express office and, if perfectly satisfactory, pay the express agent our price and take it; otherwise let the agent return it at our expense. **You Need Not Pay One Cent in Advance.**

OUR BINDING GUARANTEE AND REFUND CERTIFICATE.

With every diamond sold we send the following Guarantee and Refund Certificate:

We guarantee the diamond this day sold to Mr._____for

_____Dollars, to be a genuine diamond and perfectly cut and finished; and we hereby bargain and agree to take back the diamond any time within one year and refund the purchase price, less ten per cent.

Sears, Roebuck & Co.

We Are Slaughtering the Price of Diamonds as we have slaughtered the price of watches. *Diamonds* are as good an investment as government bonds if bought at the right price. *We will redeem them* any time at ten per cent. discount. *Don't pay the retail* price for diamonds. At our prices the goods are always as good as the money. *They never wear out,* never change, always the same; but heretofore they have been sold at such unreasonable profits that few people could afford to wear them.

WE CHANGE ALL THIS, Everyone Can Wear Diamonds.

we Are Acknowledged Headquarters in this line. We import our own loose stones, buy our mountings by contract, and do our own mounting. *No One Can Meet Our Prices! No One Can Meet Our Terms!*

DON'T FORGET We send *any diamond to anyone, anywhere,* C. O. D., subject to examination. *No Money in Advance.* Examine it at the express office and if found satisfactory pay the express agent our price and express charges and it is yours; *otherwise* pay nothing and it will be returned at our expense.

SEE OUR GRAND ARRAY OF BARGAINS.

DIAMOND RINGS AT EUROPEAN PRICES!!

ALL OUR MOUNTINGS ARE HAND MADE AND WARRANTED 14 KARAT SOLID GOLD.

No. D 700.
Small genuine diamond, exact size of illustration, beautifully engraved, solid gold mounting.
Price $3.85.

No. D 701.
Small genuine diamond, exact size of illustration, beautifully engraved by hand.
Price $4.60.

No. D 702.
Beautifully cut genuine diamond, hand made solid gold mounting.
Price $5.75.

No. D 703.
Beautifully cut genuine diamond, exact size of illustration, solid gold hand engraved mounting.
A very nice ring.
Price $7.65.

No. D 704.
Weight, 1/8 Carat.
Price $9.50

No. D 705.
Weight, 1/8 Carat.
Price $9.50.

No. D 706.
Weight, 1/4 Carat.
Price $15.95.

No. D 707.
Weight, 3/8 Carat.
Price $22.50.

No. D 708.
Weight, 3/8 Carat.
Price $22.50.

No. D 709.
Weight, 1/2 Carat.
Price 29.75.

No. D 710.
Weight, 5/8 Carat.
Price $38.95.

No. D 711.
Weight, 3/4 Carat.
Price $51.10.

No. D 712.
Weight, 1 Carat.
Price $74.00.

No. D 713.
Weight, 1¼ Carat.
Price $92.00.

No. D 714.
Weight, 1½ Carat.
Price $111.00.

No. D 717.
2 diamonds, beautiful hand made mounting.
Price $11.95.

Select any style mounting you wish. We will furnish any style mounting shown in Nos. D 704 to D 714, inclusive, with any size diamond without extra charge. We can furnish any special stone or special size up to 5 carats. Prices furnished on application.

DIAMOND RINGS AT EUROPEAN PRICES!!

ALL OUR MOUNTINGS ARE HAND MADE AND WARRANTED 14 KARET SOLID GOLD.

No. D 718.
2 diamonds and 1 Ruby,
sapphire or emerald.

Price $15.90.

No. D 719.
1 diamond and 1 Ruby,
sapphire or emerald.

Price $14.60.

No. D 720.
2 diamonds, 2 sapphires,
emeralds or rubies.

Price $15.20.

No. D 721.
3 diamonds,

Price $15.90.

No. D 715.
4 diamonds, 1 emerald,
ruby or sapphire.

Price $5.95.

No. D 716.
12 pearls, 1 large emerald,
ruby or sapphire.

Price $6.65.

No. D 722.
1 diamond, 1 ruby,
sapphire or emerald.

Price $26.30.

No. D 723.
Marquis ring, 26 diamonds,
4 rubies, sapphires or emer'lds

Price $27.50.

No. D 724.
8 diamonds, 1 sapphire,
emerald or ruby.

Price $29.75.

No. D 725.
7 diamonds,
STAR.

Price $28.10.

No. D 726.
20 diamonds, 5 opals
(very fine).

Price $30.45.

No. D 727.
2 diamonds, 1 ruby,
sapphire or emerald.

Price $34.60.

No. D 728.
10 diamonds,
1 ruby, opal, sapphire or
emerald.

Price $35.00.

No. D 729.
Marquis ring.
24 Diamonds, 1 ruby,
Very fine ring.

Price $69.00.

No. D 699.
Child's ring.
Genuine rose diamond.
Size, 0 to 5.

Price $1.35.

No. D 698.
Genuine diamond,
beautifully cut, fancy
engraved mounting.

Price, $8.15.

Diamond Rings at European Prices!

No. D 697.
Genuine diamond,
beautifully cut,
fancy engraved.
PRICE $8.50.

No. D 696.
Genuine diamond,
beautifully cut,
fancy engraved.
PRICE $8.90.

No. D 695.
Genuine diamond,
plain band,
fancy star.
PRICE $6.75.

No. D 694.
Genuine diamond,
beautifully cut,
fancy engraved.
PRICE $9.05.

No. D 693.
6 Rose diamonds, 1 ruby doublet.
PRICE $11.50.

No. D 692.
Marquis Ring, 16 diamonds,
turquoise or opal centre
as desired.
PRICE $17.50.

No. D 691.
8 diamonds, ruby, sapphire or
emerald doublet centre
as desired.
PRICE $17.65.

No. D 690.
5 diamonds,
PRICE $29.75.

No. D 689.
5 diamonds.
PRICE $24.95.
With Real Pearls $12.00.

No. D 688.
1 diamond, 1 ruby,
genuine sapphire or emerald
as desired.
PRICE $38.00.

ALWAYS SAY SIZE WANTED, USING OUR SCALE FOR SIZE, AS DESCRIBED ON ANOTHER PAGE.

TESTIMONIALS.

Diamonds at European Prices!

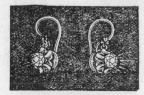

DIAMONDS AT EUROPEAN PRICES.

GENTS' DIAMOND SCARF PINS.

No. D 733.
Solid gold, Diamond set
Price $2.50.

No. D 734.
Solid gold, Diamond set.
Price $2.95.

No. D 735.
Solid gold, Diamond set.
Price $3.10.

No. D 736.
Solid gold, Diamond set.
Price $3.25.

No. D 737.
Solid gold, Diamond set
Price $3.50.

No. D 738.
Solid gold, Diamond set.
Price $4.00.

No. D 739.
Solid gold, Diamond set.
Price $4.95.

No. D 739½.
12 Diamonds, 1 large
Opal, Ruby, Sapphire or
Emerald
Price $38.00.

DIAMOND STUDS.

No. D 740.

Price $5.95.

No. D 741.
Weight ⅛ carat.
Price $9.00.

No. D 742.
Weight ¼ carat.
Price $15.75.

No. D 743.
Weight ⅜ carat.
Price $22.00.

No. D 744.
Weight ½ carat.
Price $29.50.

No. D 745.
Weight ¾ carat.
Price $51.00.

No. D 746.
Weight 1 carat.
Price $73.00.

Diamonds at European Prices!

• DIAMOND BAR PINS. •

No. D 758.—Solid gold, diamond set.
Price $2.75.

No. D 759.—Solid gold, diamond set.
Price $2.95.

No. D 760.—Solid gold, diamond set.
Price $3.25.

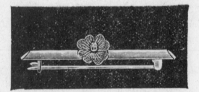

No. D 761.—Solid gold, diamond set.
Price $3.95.

No. D 762.—Solid gold, diamond set.
Price $4.95.

No. D 763.—Solid gold, diamond set.
Price $5.50.

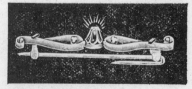

No. D 764.—Weight, ⅛ Carat.
Price $12.90.

No. D 765.—2 diamonds, ¼ Carat.
Price $19.50.

BEST QUALITY GOLD PLATED VEST CHAINS!

All full length with bar and charm attachments.

These are the Best Quality Gold Plated Chains made and are warranted to wear 5 years.

No. 6430.
Price each, $1.45

No. 6431.
Price each, $1.60

No. 6431¼.
Price each, $1.70

No. 6431½.
Price each, $1.75

No. 6432.
Price each, $1.85

No. 6433.
Price each, $2.20

No. 6433¼.
Price each, $2.25

No. 6433½.
Price each, $2.40

No. 6434.
Price each, $2.45

No. 6435.
Price each, $2.75

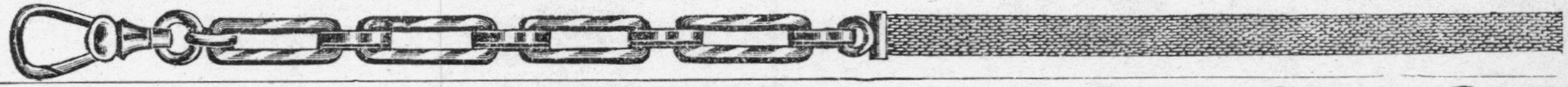

No. 6436.
Price each, $2.85

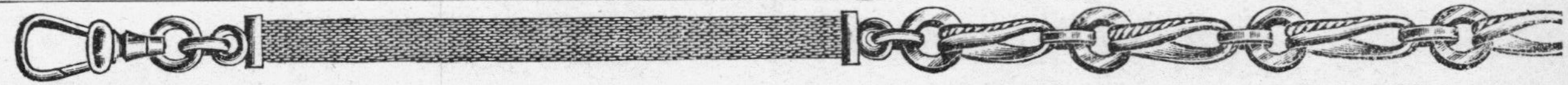

Any of these Chains will be sent C. O. D. subject to examination. NO MONEY IN ADVANCE!

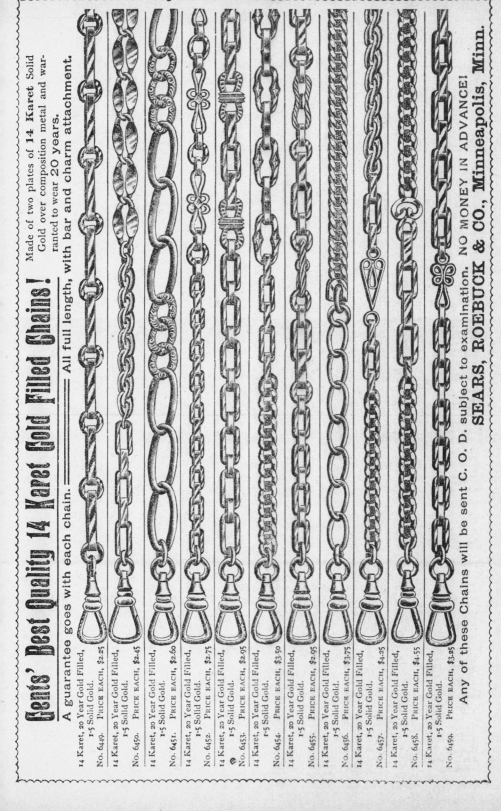

Gents' Best Quality 14 Karat Gold Filled Chains!

Made of two plates of **14 Karat** Solid Gold over composition metal and warranted to wear 20 years.

A guarantee goes with each chain. —— All full length, with bar and charm attachment.

14 Karet, 20 Year Gold Filled, 1-5 Solid Gold. No. 6449. PRICE EACH, $2.25

14 Karet, 20 Year Gold Filled, 1-5 Solid Gold. No. 6450. PRICE EACH, $2.45

14 Karet, 20 Year Gold Filled, 1-5 Solid Gold. No. 6451. PRICE EACH, $2.60

14 Karet, 20 Year Gold Filled, 1-5 Solid Gold. No. 6452. PRICE EACH, $2.75

14 Karet, 20 Year Gold Filled, 1-5 Solid Gold. No. 6453. PRICE EACH, $2.95

14 Karet, 20 Year Gold Filled, 1-5 Solid Gold. No. 6454. PRICE EACH, $3.50

14 Karet, 20 Year Gold Filled, 1-5 Solid Gold. No. 6455. PRICE EACH, $2.95

14 Karet, 20 Year Gold Filled, 1-5 Solid Gold. No. 6456. PRICE EACH, $3.75

14 Karet, 20 Year Gold Filled, 1-5 Solid Gold. No. 6457. PRICE EACH, $4.25

14 Karet, 20 Year Gold Filled, 1-5 Solid Gold. No. 6458. PRICE EACH, $4.55

14 Karet, 20 Year Gold Filled, 1-5 Solid Gold. No. 6459. PRICE EACH, $3.25

Any of these Chains will be sent C. O. D. subject to examination. NO MONEY IN ADVANCE!

SEARS, ROEBUCK & CO., Minneapolis, Minn.

Gent's Best Quality 14 Karat Gold Filled Chains!

Made of two plates of **14 Karat** Solid Gold over composition metal and warranted to wear **20 Years.**

A guarantee goes with each chain.

All full length, with bar and charm attachment.

Gents', Ladies' or Boys' Chain. 14 Karet; 20 years. gold filled, 1-5 solid gold.
No. 9000.   Price, each, $1.55

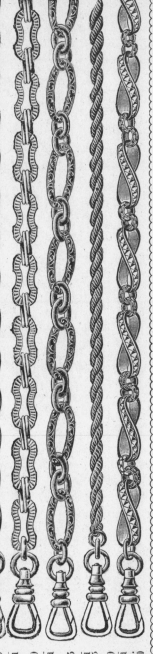

14 Karet, 20 year gold filled, 1-5 solid gold.
No. 9001.   Price, each, $1.65

14 Karet, 20 year gold filled, 1-5 solid gold.
No. 9002.   Price, each, $1.70

14 Karet, 20 year gold, filled 1-5 solid gold.
No. 9003.   Price, each, $1.75

14 Karet, 20 year gold filled. 1-5 solid gold.
No. 9004.   Price, each, $1.80

14 Karet, 20 year gold filled. 1-5 solid gold.
No. 9005.   Price, each, $1.85

14 Karet, 20 year gold filled. 1-5 solid gold.
No. 9006.   Price, each, $1.90

14 Karet, 20 year gold filled, 1-5 solid gold.
No. 9007.   Price, each, $2.55

14 Karet, 20 year gold filled, Rope chain, 1-5 solid gold.
No. 9008.   Price, each, $2.20

14 Karet, 20 year gold filled chain, 1-5 solid gold.
No. 9009.   Price, each, $2.60

Gents' Best Quality 14 Karet Gold Filled Chains!

Made of two plates of **14 Karet** Solid Gold over composition metal and warranted to wear **20 years**. A guarantee goes with each chain. All full length, with bar and charm attachments.

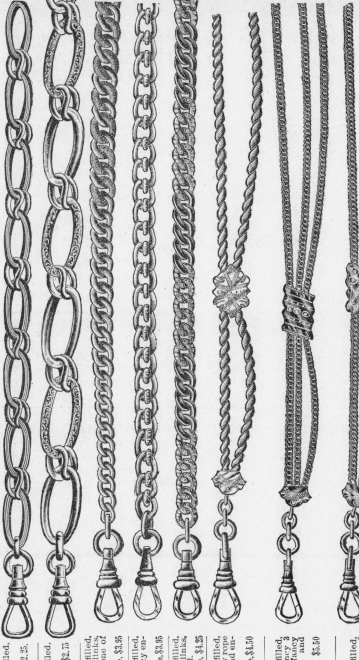

14 Karet, 20 year gold filled, 1-5 solid gold. No. 9010. Price, each, $2.25.

14 Karet, 20 year gold filled, 1-5 solid gold. No. 9011. Price, each, $2.75.

14 Karet, 20 year gold filled, 1-5 solid gold, graduated links, very fancy engraved; one of the finest chains made. No. 9012. Retails at $7. Our price, $3.95.

14 Karet, 20 year gold filled, 1-5 solid gold, very fancy engraved coil links. No. 9013. Retails at $7. Our price, $3.95.

14 Karet, 20 year gold filled, 1-5 solid gold, very fancy links, engraved and decorated. No. 9014. Retails at $7. Our price, $4.25.

14 Karet, 20 year gold filled, 1-5 solid gold, very fancy rope pattern, solid gold hand engraved tips and slide. No. 9015. Retails at $8. Our price, $4.50.

14 Karet, 20 year gold filled, 1-5 solid gold, very fancy 3 strand curb, solid gold fancy band engraved slide and tips. Retails at $10.00. No. 9016. Our price, $5.50.

14 Karet, 20 year gold filled, 1-5 solid gold, very fancy 2 curb strands, 1 rope strand, solid gold fancy hand engraved slides and tips. Retails at $12.00. No. 9017. Our price, $5.95.

Gents' Best Quality 14 Karet Gold Filled Chains!

Made of two plates of 14 Karet Solid Gold over composition metal and warranted to wear 20 years. A guarantee goes with each chain. All full length, with bar and charm attachments.

14 Karet, 20 Year Gold Filled, 15 Solid Gold.
No. 6165. PRICE EACH, $2.20

14 Karet, 20 Year Gold Filled, 15 Solid Gold.
No. 6166. PRICE EACH, $2.70

14 Karet, 20 Year Gold Filled, 15 Solid Gold.
No. 6166½. PRICE EACH, $2.95

14 Karet, 20 Year Gold Filled, 15 Solid Gold.
No. 6167½. PRICE EACH, $3.95

Flat Link Solid Gold Pattern.

14 Karet, 20 Year Gold Filled, 15 Solid Gold.
No. 6168. PRICE EACH, $4.20

Warranted by the Manufacturer equal to Solid Gold.

14 Karet, 20 Year Gold Filled, Best 20 Year, Gold Filled, 3 Strand Chain Made.
No. 6169. PRICE EACH, $4.95

Flat Link Solid Gold Pattern.

14 Karet, 20 Year Gold Filled, 15 Solid Gold.
No. 6170. PRICE EACH, $3.95

14 Karet, 20 Year Gold Filled, 15 Solid Gold.
No. 6171. PRICE EACH, $4.20

Warranted by the Manufacturer equal to Solid Gold.

14 Karet, 20 Year Gold Filled, 15 Solid Gold.
No. 6172. PRICE EACH, $5.35

Warranted by the Manufacturer equal to Solid Gold.

14 Karet, 20 Year Gold Filled, Double Strand Chain Made.
No. 6175½. PRICE EACH, $3.95

Any of these Chains will be sent C. O. D. subject to examination. NO MONEY IN ADVANCE!

BEST SOLID GOLD CHAINS MADE!

Warranted 10 and 14 Karet Solid Gold U. S. Mint Assay.

All Full Length with Bar and Charm Attachments.

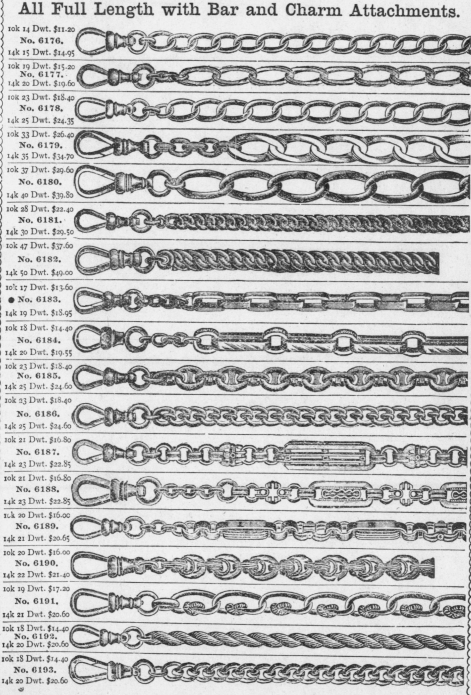

10k 14 Dwt. $11.20
No. 6176.
14k 15 Dwt. $14.95

10k 19 Dwt. $15.20
No. 6177.
14k 20 Dwt. $19.60

10k 23 Dwt. $18.40
No. 6178.
14k 25 Dwt. $24.35

10k 33 Dwt. $26.40
No. 6179.
14k 35 Dwt. $34.70

10k 37 Dwt. $29.60
No. 6180.
14k 40 Dwt. $39.80

10k 28 Dwt. $22.40
No. 6181.
14k 30 Dwt. $29.50

10k 47 Dwt. $37.60
No. 6182.
14k 50 Dwt. $49.00

10k 17 Dwt. $13.60
● **No. 6183.**
14k 19 Dwt. $18.95

10k 18 Dwt. $14.40
No. 6184.
14k 20 Dwt. $19.55

10k 23 Dwt. $18.40
No. 6185.
14k 25 Dwt. $24.60

10k 23 Dwt. $18.40
No. 6186.
14k 25 Dwt. $24.60

10k 21 Dwt. $16.80
No. 6187.
14k 23 Dwt. $22.85

10k 21 Dwt. $16.80
No. 6188.
14k 23 Dwt. $22.85

10k 20 Dwt. $16.00
No. 6189.
14k 21 Dwt. $20.65

10k 20 Dwt. $16.00
No. 6190.
14k 22 Dwt. $21.40

10k 19 Dwt. $17.20
No. 6191.
14k 21 Dwt. $20.60

10k 18 Dwt. $14.40
No. 6192.
14k 20 Dwt. $20.60

10k 18 Dwt. $14.40
No. 6193.
14k 20 Dwt. $20.60

LADIES' GOLD PLATED VICTORIA VEST CHAINS.

These Chains are the **very best quality gold plated made**. Guaranteed to wear ten years. Every chain **guaranteed by the manufacturer**. Beautifully engraved and ornamented by hand. **We do not handle cheap or low grade chains of any kind**. **Best 14 Karet 5 year rolled gold plated and best 14 Karet 20 year gold filled** are all we handle, and only those made by manufacturers of established reputation.

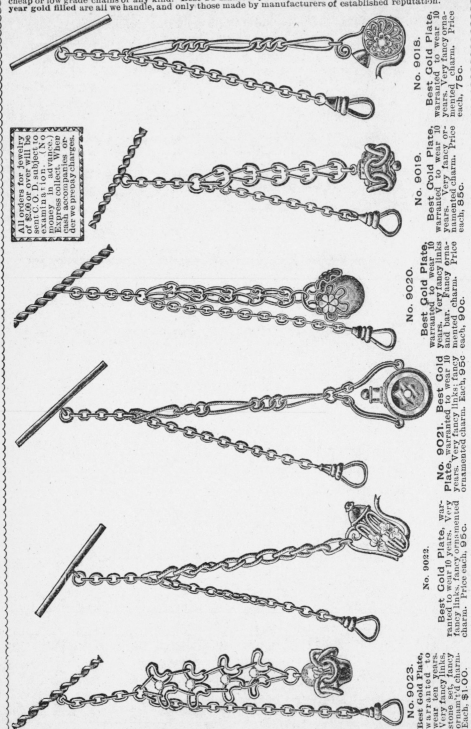

All orders for jewelry of $2.00 or over will be sent C. O. D. subject to examination. (No money in advance.) Express collect. When cash accompanies order we prepay charges.

No. 9018. Best Gold Plate, warranted to wear 10 years. Very fancy ornamented charm. Price each, 75c.

No. 9019. Best Gold Plate, warranted to wear 10 years. Very fancy ornamented charm. Price each, 85c.

No. 9020. Best Gold Plate, warranted to wear 10 years. Very fancy links and bar. Fancy ornamented charm. Price each, 90c.

No. 9021. Best Gold Plate, warranted to wear 10 years. Very fancy links; fancy ornamented charm. Each, 95c.

No. 9022. Best Gold Plate, warranted to wear 10 years. Very fancy links, fancy ornamented charm. Price each, 95c.

No. 9023. Best Gold Plate, warranted to wear ten years. Very fancy links, stone set, fancy ornam't'd charm. Each, $1.00.

Ladies' Gold Plated Victoria Vest Chains!

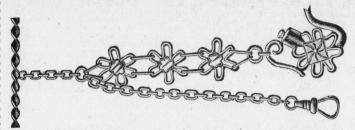

These chains are the very best quality gold plated made; guaranteed to wear for ten years. Every chain guaranteed by the manufacturer, beautifully engraved and ornamented by hand. We do not handle cheap or low grade chains of any kind. Best 14 Karet 5 year rolled gold plated and best 14 Karet 20 year gold filled are all we handle and only those made by manufacturers of established reputation.

All orders for jewelry of $2.00 or more will be sent C. O. D., subject to examination. (No money in advance) express collect. When cash accompanies order we prepay charges

Best gold plate, warranted to wear 10 years. Very fancy links, stone set. Fancy ornamented charm. No. 9024. Price, each, $1.00.

Best gold plate, warranted to wear 10 years, fancy links and bar, very fancy charm. No. 9025. Price, each, 95c.

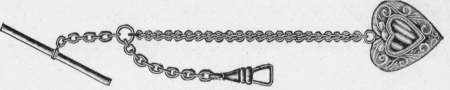

Best gold plate, warranted to wear 10 years, hand engraved charm, fancy links. No. 9026. Price, each, $1.10.

Best gold Plate warranted to wear 10 years, hand engraved charm, fancy links. No. 9027. rice, , $1.15.

Best gold plate, warranted to ... ears, hand engraved charm, fancy links. No. 23. rice, each, $1.25

Best gold plate, warranted to wear 10 years, hand engraved charm, fancy links. No. 9029. Price, each, $1.25.

Ladies' Gold Plated Victoria Vest Chains.

These chains are the very best quality gold plated made, guaranteed to wear for ten years. Every chain guaranteed by the manufacturer. Beautifully engraved and ornamented by hand. We do not handle cheap or low grade chains of any kind. Best 14 Karet 5 year rolled gold plated and best 14 Karet 20 year gold filled are all we handle, and only those made by manufacturers of established reputation. Orders for jewelry of $2.00 or more sent C. O. D. subject to examination. No money in advance; express collect. When cash accompanies order we prepay charges.

Best Gold Plate, warranted to wear 10 years, hand engraved charm, fancy links.
No. 9030. Price each, $1.25.

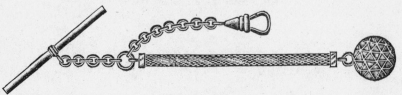

Best Gold Plate, warranted to wear 10 years, hand engraved charm, very fancy woven links.
No. 9031. Price each, $1.35.

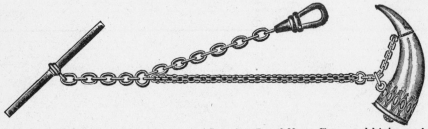

Best Gold Plate, warranted to wear 10 years. Genuine Pearl Horn Charm, gold trimmed,
Fancy links. No. 9032. Price each, $1.40.

Best Gold Plate, warranted to wear 10 years. Genuine Crystal Pot Charm, gold trimmed,
fancy links. No. 9033. Price each, $1.45.

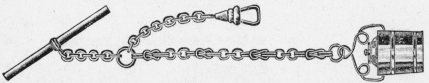

Best Gold Plate, warranted to wear 10 years, Genuine Pearl Pail Charm, colored pail staves,
gold hoop, bail and ornaments, fancy links. No. 9034. Price each, $1.90.

Best Gold Plate, warranted to wear 10 years. Genuine Pearl Urn Charm, gold trimmed, very
fancy links, with solid gold ornamentations. No. 9035. Price each, $2.00.

LADIES' GOLD FILLED VICTORIA CHAINS!

These chains are the very BEST QUALITY GOLD FILLED MADE!

Made of two plates of **14 KARET SOLID GOLD** over composition metal and warranted to wear **20 YEARS!** *Every chain guaranteed by the manufacturers.* All the raised color work and ornamentation are **SOLID GOLD.** All engraving done by hand. **WE DO NOT HANDLE** cheap or low grade chains of any kind. *Best 14 Karet, 5 year, rolled gold plated and Best 14 Karet, 20 year, gold filled,* are all we handle, and only those made by manufacturers of established reputation.

★ All Orders for Jewelry of over $2.00 will be sent C. O. D. subject to examination. (NO MONEY IN ADVANCE.) ★
Express Collect. Where Cash Accompanies Order WE PREPAY CHARGES.

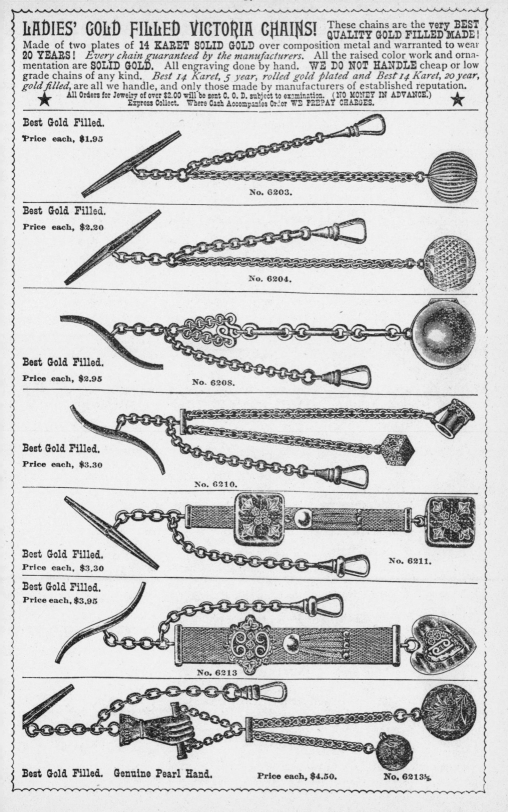

Best Gold Filled. Price each, $1.95 — No. 6203.

Best Gold Filled. Price each, $2.20 — No. 6204.

Best Gold Filled. Price each, $2.95 — No. 6208.

Best Gold Filled. Price each, $3.30 — No. 6210.

Best Gold Filled. Price each, $3.30 — No. 6211.

Best Gold Filled. Price each, $3.95 — No. 6213

Best Gold Filled. Genuine Pearl Hand. Price each, $4.50. No. 6213½.

Ladies' Gold Plated Victoria Vest Chains!

These chains are the very best quality gold plated made; guaranteed to wear for ten years. **Every chain guaranteed by the manufacturer,** beautifully engraved and ornamented by hand. **We do not handle cheap or low grade chains of any kind. Best 14 Karet 5 year rolled gold plated and best 14 Karet 20 year gold filled** are all we handle and only those made by manufacturers of established reputation.

All orders for jewelry of $2.00 or more will be sent C. O. D., subject to examination. (No money in advance). Express collect. When cash accompanies order **we prepay charges.**

Best Gold Plate, warranted to wear 10 years, very fancy pod charm, with raised colored gold and enameled ornamentations, four Borneo diamonds, fancy woven chain, fancy bar. **NO. 9036.** Price each, **$2.10.**

Best Gold Plate, warranted to wear 10 years, colored pearl and gold plated links, fancy gold and pearl adjustable fan. **NO. 9037.** Price, each, **$2.15.**

Best Gold Plate, warranted to wear 10 years, very fancy links, Satin finished, gold heart charm, 1 genuine pearl charm, gold ornamented. **NO. 9038.** Price, each, **$2.25.**

Best Plate Gold, warranted to wear 10 years, very fancy links, fancy pitcher charm with raised solid gold ornamentations. **NO. 9039.** Price, each, **$2.50.**

Ladies' Gold Filled Victoria Chains!

These chains are the very best quality gold filled made. Made of two plates of **14 Karet Solid Gold** over composition metal and warranted to wear **20 years.** Every chain guaranteed by the manufacturers. All the raised color work and ornamentation are solid gold. All engraving done by hand. **We do not handle** cheap or low grade chains of any kind. Best 14 Karet, 5 year, rolled gold plated and best 14 Karet, 20 year, gold filled, are all we handle, and only those made by manufacturers of established reputation.

All orders for jewelry of over $2.00 will be sent C. O. D. subject to examination. (No money in advance). Express collect   When cash accompanies order we we prepay charges.

Best Gold Filled, warranted to wear 20 years, fancy links, ornamented gold center set with one Ruby Doublet and 21 Pearls, very fancy charm set with 8 stones. **No. 9040. Price, each, $2.75.**

Best Gold Filled, warranted to wear 20 years, very fancy gold front heart charm, beautifully enameled. No. 9041.   Price each, $2.80.

Best Gold Filled, warranted to wear 20 years, fancy links, very fancy gold front charm, ornamented with solid gold raised ornamentations, set with six ruby doublets. No. 9042. Price each, $2.95.

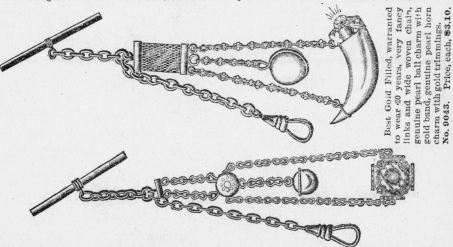

Best Gold Filled, warranted to wear 20 years, very fancy links and wide woven chain, genuine pearl ball charm with gold band, genuine pearl horn charm with gold trimmings. No. 9043. Price, each, $3.10.

Best Gold Filled, warranted to wear 20 years, fancy links, 3 gold front satin finished charms, one with eight ruby doublets. No. 9044. Price each, $3.05.

LADIES' GOLD FILLED VICTORIA CHAINS!

These chains are the **very best quality gold filled made**. Made of two plates of **14 Karet Solid Gold** over composition metal and warranted to wear **20 years**. Every chain guaranteed by the manufacturers. All the raised color work and ornamentation are **Solid Gold**. All engraving done by hand. **We do not handle** cheap or low grade chains of any kind. Best 14 Karet, 5 year, rolled gold plated and Best 14 Karet, 20 year, gold filled, are all we handle, and only those made by manufacturers of established reputation.

All orders for jewelry of over $2.00 will be sent C. O. D. subject to examination. No money in advance. Express collect. Where cash accompanies order we prepay charges.

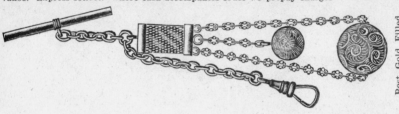

Best Gold Filled, warranted to wear 20 years. Fancy links and woven chain, two gold front hand engraved ball charms. No. 9045. Price each $3.25.

Best Gold Filled, warranted to wear 20 years. Fancy links three Roman gold charms, four Borneo diamonds. No. 9046. Price each $3.25.

Best Gold Filled, warranted to wear 20 years. Fancy links, one plain polished gold front heart charm, two Roman gold charms, two ruby doublets. No. 9047. Price each $3.50.

Best Gold Filled, warranted to wear 20 years. Very fancy links, with one genuine pearl link, three very fancy gold ornamented charms. No. 9048. Price each $3.75.

Best Gold Filled, warranted to wear 20 years. Very fancy links and woven chain, three very fancy gold finished charms. No. 9049. Price each $3.95.

LADIES' GOLD FILLED VICTORIA CHAINS.

These chains are the **Best Quality Gold Filled made.** Made of two plates of **14 Karet Solid Gold** over composition metal and warranted to wear **20 years.** Every chain guaranteed by the manufacturers. All raised color work and ornamentation are **solid gold.** All engraving done by hand. **We do not handle** cheap or low grade chains of any kind. **Best 14 Karet 5 year rolled gold plated, and best 14 Karet 20 year gold filled,** are all we handle, and only those made by manufacturers of established reputation.

All orders for jewelry of over $2.00 will be sent C. O. D. subject to examination. (No money in advance.) Express collect. When cash accompanies order **we prepay charges.**

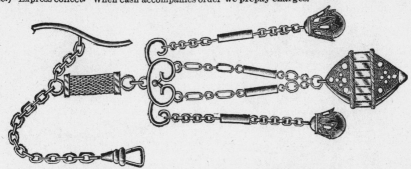

Best gold filled, warranted to wear 20 years. Very fancy gold filled pearl and woven chain, three very fancy gold ornamented charms. **No. 9050. Price each, $4.60.**

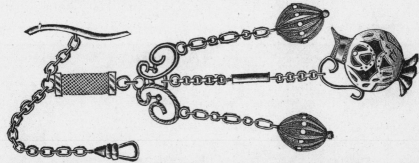

Best gold filled, warranted to wear 20 years. Very fancy gold filled, pearl and woven chain, three very fancy gold ornamented charms. **No. 9051. Price each, $4.40.**

Best gold filled, warranted to wear 20 years. **The handsomest chain made.** Very fancy pearl and gold link chain, three very fancy gold ornamented charms. **No. 9052. Price each, $4.95.**

Best gold filled, warranted to wear 20 years. **The best we handle and the best made.** Four very fancy gold ornamented stone set charms, handsomely engraved, a work of art. **No. 9053. Price, $5.25.**

LADIES' GOLD FILLED VICTORIA CHAINS!

These chains are the very **best quality gold filled made!** Made of two plates of 14 Karet Solid Gold over composition metal and warranted to wear **20 years.** Every chain guaranteed by the manufacturers. All the raised color work and ornamentation are solid gold. All engraving done by hand. **We do not handle cheap or low grade chains of any kind.** Best 14 Karet, 5 year, rolled gold plated and best 14 Karet, 20 year, gold filled, are all we handle, and only those made by manufacturers of established reputation.

☞All orders for jewelry of over $2.00 will be sent C. O. D. subject to examination. (No money in advance.) Express collect. When cash accompanies order **we prepay charges.**

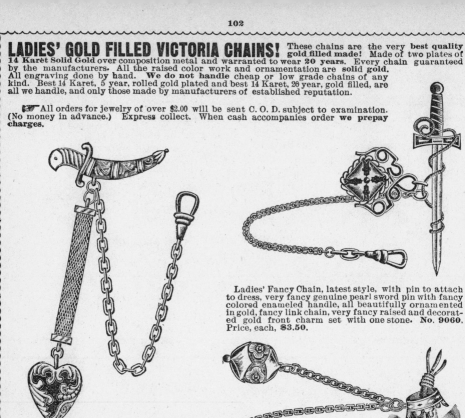

Ladies' Fancy Chain, latest style, with pin to attach to dress, very fancy genuine pearl sword pin with fancy colored enameled handle, all beautifully ornamented in gold, fancy link chain, very fancy raised and decorated gold front charm set with one stone. No. 9060. Price, each, **$3.50.**

Ladies' Fancy Chain, latest style with pin to attach to dress. Fancy engraved sword pin, very fancy woven wire chain, Roman gold finished heart charm, beautifully finished and enameled. **No. 9064.** Price each, **$2.85.**

Ladies' Fancy Chain, latest style, with pin to attach to dress, very fancy hand engraved, bright cut pin of crown and plumes, fancy chain, fancy gold ornamented charm, ruby settings. No. 9062. Price each, **$3.75.**

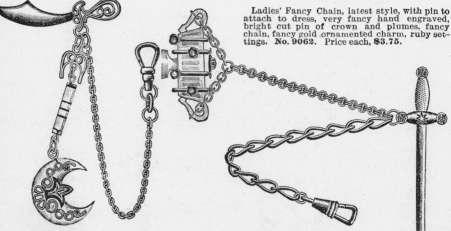

Ladies' Fancy Chain, latest style with pin to attach to dress, fancy sword pin plain polished blade, fancy handle, real pearl gold trimmed and fancy gold link chain, real pearl crescent charm, fancy gold trimmed, reversible. No. 9061. Price, each, **$3.50.**

Ladies' Fancy Chain, latest style, with **pin to attach** to dress, fancy finished sword pin with 3 stone setting, fancy link, very fancy pearl vase charm with gold ornamentations set with three beautiful stones. No. 9065. Price each, **$3.20.**

LADIES' GOLD FILLED VICTORIA CHAINS

These chains are the **VERY BEST QUALITY GOLD FILLED MADE.** Made of two plates of **14-KARET SOLID GOLD** over composition metal and warranted to wear **20 Years.** Every chain guaranteed by the manufacturers. All the raised color work and ornamentation are **SOLID GOLD.** All engraving done by hand. **WE DO NOT HANDLE** cheap or low grade chains of any kind. Best **14-karet, 5 year, rolled gold plated** and best **14-karet, 20 year, gold filled,** are all we handle, and only those made by manufacturers of established reputation.

☞ All orders for jewelry of over **$2.00** will be sent **C. O. D.** subject to examination. No money in advance; express collect. Where cash accompanies order **WE PREPAY CHARGES.**

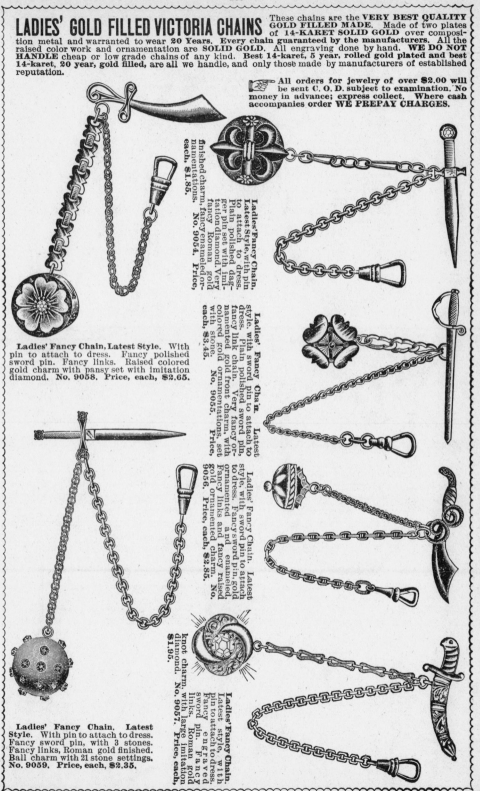

Ladies'Fancy Chain. Latest Style, with pin to attach to dress. Plain polished dagger pin set with imitation diamond. Very fancy Roman gold finished charm, fancy enameled ornamentations. No. 9054. Price, each, $1.35.

Ladies' Fancy Chain. Latest style, with pin to attach to dress. Plain polished sword pin. Fancy link chain. Very fancy ornamented gold front charm, with colored gold ornamentations, set with stone. No. 9055. Price, each, $3.45.

Ladies' Fancy Chain, Latest Style. With pin to attach to dress. Fancy polished sword pin. Fancy links. Raised colored gold charm with pansy set with imitation diamond. No. 9058. Price, each, $2.65.

Ladies' Fancy Chain. Latest style, with sword pin to attach to dress. Fancy sword pin, gold ornamented and enameled. Fancy links and fancy raised gold ornamented charm. No. 9056. Price, each, $2.85.

Ladies' Fancy Chain. Latest style, with pin to attach to dress. Fancy enraved sword pin. Fancy links, Roman Gold finished, with large imitation knot charm, diamond. No. 9057. Price, each, $1.95.

Ladies' Fancy Chain. Latest Style. With pin to attach to dress. Fancy sword pin, with 3 stones. Fancy links, Roman gold finished. Ball charm with 21 stone settings. No. 9059. Price, each, $2.35.

LADIES' GOLD FILLED VICTORIA CHAINS

These chains are the **VERY BEST QUALITY GOLD FILLED MADE.** Made of two plates of **14-KARET SOLID GOLD** over composition metal and warranted to wear 20 years. Every chain guaranteed by the manufacturers. All the raised color work and ornamentation are **SOLID GOLD.** All engraving done by hand. **WE DO NOT HANDLE** cheap or low grade chains of any kind. **Best 14-karet, 5 year, rolled gold plated and best 14-karet, 20 year, gold filled, are all we handle,** and only those made by manufacturers of established reputation.

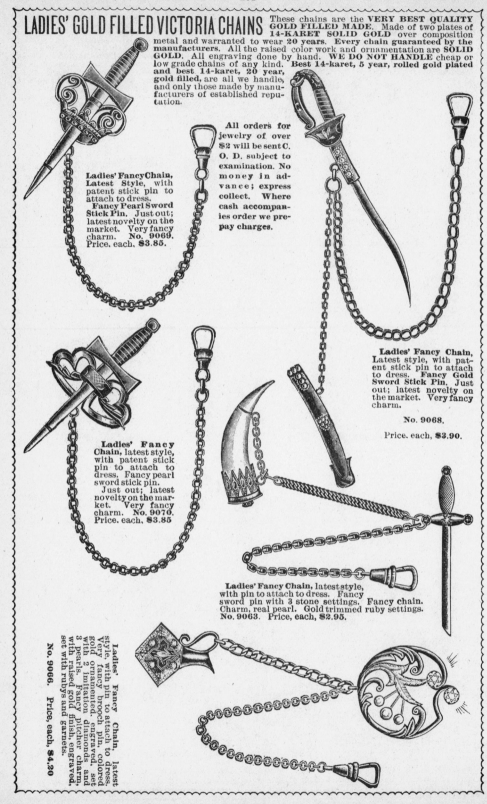

All orders for jewelry of over $2 will be sent C. O. D. subject to examination. No money in advance; express collect. Where cash accompanies order we prepay charges.

Ladies' Fancy Chain, Latest Style, with patent stick pin to attach to dress. Fancy Pearl Sword Stick Pin. Just out; latest novelty on the market. Very fancy charm. No. 9069. Price, each, $3.85.

Ladies' Fancy Chain, Latest style, with patent stick pin to attach to dress. Fancy Gold Sword Stick Pin. Just out; latest novelty on the market. Very fancy charm.

No. 9068.

Price, each, $3.90.

Ladies' Fancy Chain, latest style, with patent stick pin to attach to dress. Fancy pearl sword stick pin. Just out; latest novelty on the market. Very fancy charm. No. 9070. Price, each, $3.85.

Ladies' Fancy Chain, latest style, with pin to attach to dress. Fancy sword pin with 3 stone settings. Fancy chain. Charm, real pearl. Gold trimmed ruby settings. No. 9063. Price, each, $2.95.

No. 9066. Price, each, $4.20.

Ladies' Fancy Chain, latest style, with pin to attach to dress. Very fancy brooch pin, colored gold ornamented, engraved, set with 2 imitation diamonds and 3 pearls. Fancy pitcher charm, with raised gold finish, engraved, set with rubys and garnets.

LADIES' GOLD FILLED VEST CHAINS.

These chains are the very Best Quality Gold Filled made. Made of two plates of 14 KARET SOLID

GOLD over composition metal and warranted to wear 20 YEARS. Every chain guaranteed by the manufacturers. All the raised color work and ornamentation are SOLID GOLD. All engraving done by hand. WE DO NOT HANDLE cheap or low grade chains of any kind. Best 14 Karet, 5 year rolled gold plated, and Best 14 Karet, 20 year gold filled, are all we handle, and only those made by manufacturers of established reputation.

All orders for Jewelry of over $2.00 will be sent C. O. D. subject to examination. No Money in Advance. Express Collect. Where Cash Accompanies Order WE PREPAY CHARGES.

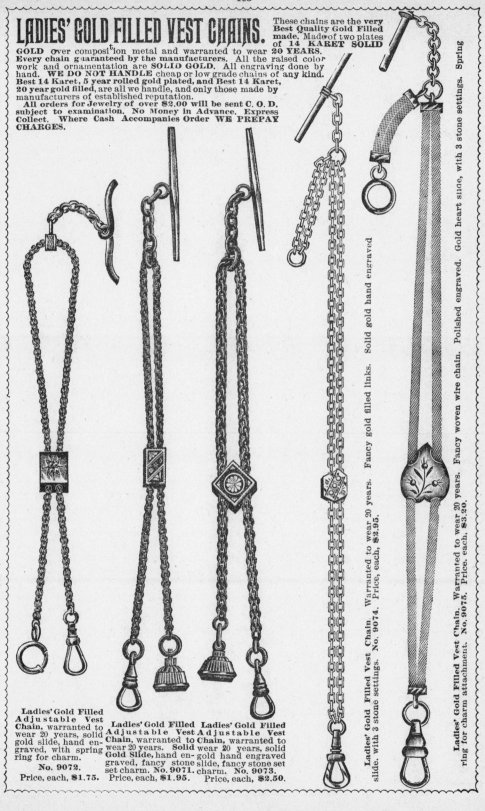

Ladies' Gold Filled Adjustable Vest Chain, warranted to wear 20 years, solid gold slide, hand engraved, with spring ring for charm.
No. 9072.
Price, each, $1.75.

Ladies' Gold Filled Adjustable Vest Chain, warranted to wear 20 years. Solid Gold Slide, hand engraved, fancy stone slide, set charm. No. 9071.
Price, each, $1.95.

Ladies' Gold Filled Adjustable Vest Chain, warranted to wear 20 years, solid gold hand engraved fancy stone set charm. No. 9073.
Price, each, $2.50.

Ladies' Gold Filled Vest Chain. Warranted to wear 20 years. Fancy gold filled links. Solid gold hand engraved slide, with 3 stone settings. No. 9074. Price, each, $2.95.

Ladies' Gold Filled Vest Chain. Warranted to wear 20 years. Fancy woven wire chain. Polished engraved. Gold heart slide, with 3 stone settings. Spring ring for charm attachment. No. 9075. Price, each, $3.20.

Ladies' Gold Filled Vest Chains!

These chains are the very best quality gold filled made. Made of two plates of 14 Karet Solid Gold over composition metal and warranted to wear 20 years. Every chain guaranteed by the manufacturers. All the raised color work and ornamentation are solid gold. All engraving done by hand. We do not handle cheap or low grade chains of any kind. Best 14 Karet, 5 year, rolled gold plated and best 14 Karet, 20 year, gold filled, are all we handle, and only those made by manufacturers of established reputation. When cash accompanies order we prepay charges. All orders for jewelry of over $2.00 will be sent C. O. D. subject to examination. (No money in advance.) Express collect.

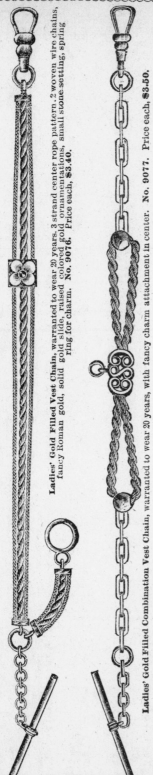

Ladies' Gold Filled Vest Chain, warranted to wear 20 years, 3 strand center rope pattern. 2 woven wire chains, fancy Roman gold, solid gold slide, raised colored gold ornamentations, small stone setting, spring ring for charm. No. 9076. Price each, $3.40.

Ladies' Gold Filled Combination Vest Chain, warranted to wear 20 years, with fancy charm attachment in center. No. 9077. Price each, $3.50.

Ladies' Gold Filled Combination Vest Chain, warranted to wear 20 years, solid gold engraved slide with pearl settings. No. 9078. Price each, $3.75.

Ladies' Gold Filled Combination Vest Chain, warranted to wear 20 years, fancy woven wire chain, fancy real pearl knot center with fancy horseshoe charm, set with pearls and turquois. No. 9079. Price each, $3.95.

Ladies' Gold Filled Guard AND Vest Chains

These Chains are the **very best quality gold filled made.** Made of two plates of **14 Karet Solid Gold** over composition metal and warranted to wear **20 YEARS!** Every chain guaranteed by the manufacturer. All the raised color work and ornamentation are **SOLID GOLD.** All engraving done by hand. **We do not handle** cheap or low grade chains of any kind. **Best 14 Karet, 5 year, rolled gold plated and best 14 Karet, 20 year, gold filled, are all we handle,** and only those made by manufacturers of established reputation.

All orders for jewelry of over $2.00 will be sent C. O. D. subject to examination. (No money in advance.) Express Collect. Where Cash accompanies order **WE PREPAY CHARGES.**

Ladies' **Gold Filled Guard Chain,** warranted to wear 20 years; **38 inches long, to go around neck. Fancy** double link, **very strong.** These chains are again becoming very popular. **No. 9080.** Each, **$3.25.**

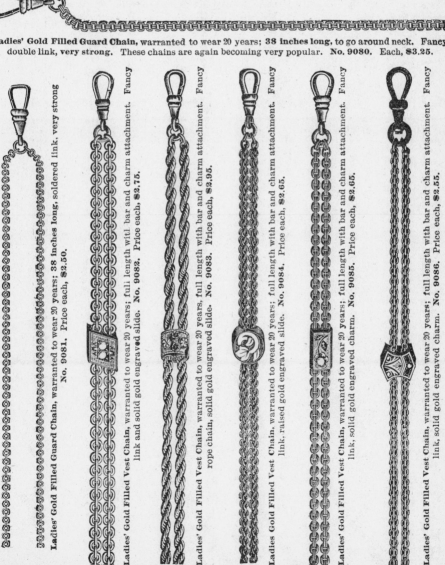

Ladies' Gold Filled Guard Chain, warranted to wear 20 years; 38 inches long, soldered link, very strong. No. 9081. Price each, $2.50.

Ladies' Gold Filled Vest Chain, warranted to wear 20 years; full length with bar and charm attachment. Fancy link and solid gold engraved slide. No. 9082. Price each, $2.75.

Ladies' Gold Filled Vest Chain, warranted to wear 20 years, full length with bar and charm attachment. Fancy rope chain, solid gold engraved slide. No. 9083. Price each, $2.95.

Ladies' Gold Filled Vest Chain, warranted to wear 20 years; full length with bar and charm attachment. Fancy link, raised gold engraved slide. No. 9084. Price each, $2.65.

Ladies' Gold Filled Vest Chain, warranted to wear 20 years; full length with bar and charm attachment. Fancy link, solid gold engraved charm. No. 9085. Price each, $2.65.

Ladies' Gold Filled Vest Chain, warranted to wear 20 years; full length with bar and charm attachment. Fancy link, solid gold engraved charm. No. 9086. Price each, $2.55.

BEST QUALITY SOLID GOLD CHAINS.

Warranted 10 & 14 Karet Fine, U. S. Mint Assay.

We guarantee our Gold Chains the finest grade made. All orders for jewelry of over $2.00 will be sent C. O. D., subject to examination. No Money in Advance. Express collect. When cash in full accompanies order we prepay charges.

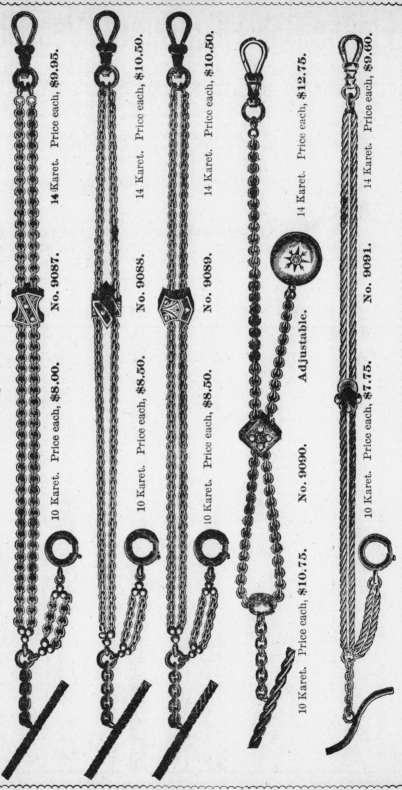

14 Karet. Price each, $9.95.
No. 9087.
10 Karet. Price each, $8.00.

14 Karet. Price each, $10.50.
No. 9088.
10 Karet. Price each, $8.50.

14 Karet. Price each, $10.50.
No. 9089.
10 Karet. Price each, $8.50.

14 Karet. Price each, $12.75.
Adjustable.
No. 9090.
10 Karet. Price each, $10.75.

14 Karet. Price each, $9.60.
No. 9091.
10 Karet. Price each, $7.75.

LADIES' 14 Karet Solid Gold Victoria Chains. Full length, 5 7-8 inches, with Chain and Swivel.

Diamond Set, Hand Engraved, Enameled, Etc., Etc. Guaranteed the Best Goods Made.

TERMS—C. O. D to anyone. No Money in Advance, Express Collect. When Cash in full accompanies order we prepay all charges.

Warranted 14 Karet Solid Gold, Roman finish, hand engraved Chain and Charm. No. 9098 Price, each, $8.95

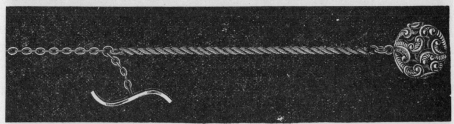

Warranted 14 Karet Solid Gold, Roman finish, hand engraved Ball Charm. No. 9099. Price, each, $9.30.

Warranted 14 Karet Solid Gold; Roman finish, fancy chased Heart Charm. No. 9100. Price, each, $10.75.

Warranted 14 Karet Solid Gold, Roman finish, fancy chased Ball Charm. No. 9101. Price, each, $8.75.

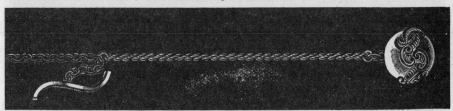

Warranted 14 Karet, Solid Gold, Roman finish, fancy chased Ball Charm. No. 9102. Price, each, $7.90.

Warranted 14 Karet Solid Gold, Roman finish, fancy chased Ball Charm. No. 9103. Price, each, $8.90.

Ladies' 14 Karet Solid Gold Victoria Chains.

Diamond Set, Hand Engraved, Enameled, Etc., Etc. Guaranteed the Best Goods Made.

TERMS C. O. D. to anyone. No Money in Advance, Express Collect. When cash in full accompanies order we prepay all charges.

Full length, 5 7-8 inches with Chain and Swivel.

Warranted 14 Karet Solid Gold, Roman finish, hand engraved, Chain and Charm fancy ornamented.
No. 9092. Price, each, $9.75.

Warranted 14 Karet Solid Gold, Roman finish, hand engraved Chain and Charm.
No. 9093. Price, each, $10.75.

Warranted 10 Karet Solid Gold. Plain polished, fancy corrugated Charm.
No. 9094. Price, each, $6.95.

Warranted 14 Karet Solid Gold, Roman finish, fancy engraved Chain and Charm.
No. 9095. Price, each, $8.95.

Warranted 14 Karet Solid Gold, Roman finish, hand engraved. Very fancy Charm of Solid Gold Wreath and Bow Knot, with swinging Roman gold ball in center, set with genuine Diamond.
No. 9096. Price, each, $13.50.

Warranted 14 Karet Solid Gold, Roman finish, hand engraved Chain and Charm, Charm set with Genuine Diamond. No. 9097. Price, each, $15.75.

GOLD FILLED NECK CHAINS

Made of two plates of Solid Gold over composition metal and warranted to wear 20 years.
Every Chain Full Length, 13 Inches.

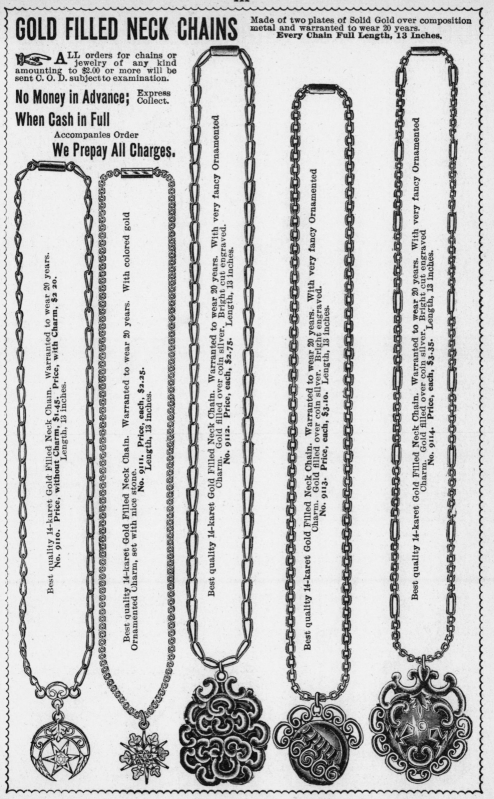

ALL orders for chains or jewelry of any kind amounting to $2.00 or more will be sent C. O. D. subject to examination.

No Money in Advance; Express Collect.

When Cash in Full

Accompanies Order

We Prepay All Charges.

Best quality 14-karet Gold Filled Neck Chain. Warranted to wear 20 years. No. 9110. Price, without Charm, $1.45. Price, with Charm, $2 20. Length, 13 inches.

Best quality 14-karet Gold Filled Neck Chain. Warranted to wear 20 years. With colored gold Ornamented Charm, set with nice stone. No. 9111. Price, each, $2.25. Length, 13 inches.

Best quality 14-karet Gold Filled Neck Chain. Warranted to wear 20 years. With very fancy Ornamented Charm. Gold filled over coin silver. Bright cut engraved. No. 9112. Price, each, $2.75. Length, 13 inches.

Best quality 14-karet Gold Filled Neck Chain. Warranted to wear 20 years. With very fancy Ornamented Charm. Gold filled over coin silver. Bright engraved. No. 9113. Price, each, $3.10. Length, 13 inches.

Best quality 14-karet Gold Filled Neck Chain. Warranted to wear 20 years. With very fancy Ornamented Charm. Gold filled over coin silver. Bright cut engraved. No. 9114. Price, each, $3.35. Length, 13 inches.

LADIES' GOLD FILLED and COIN SILVER CHAINS and PINS

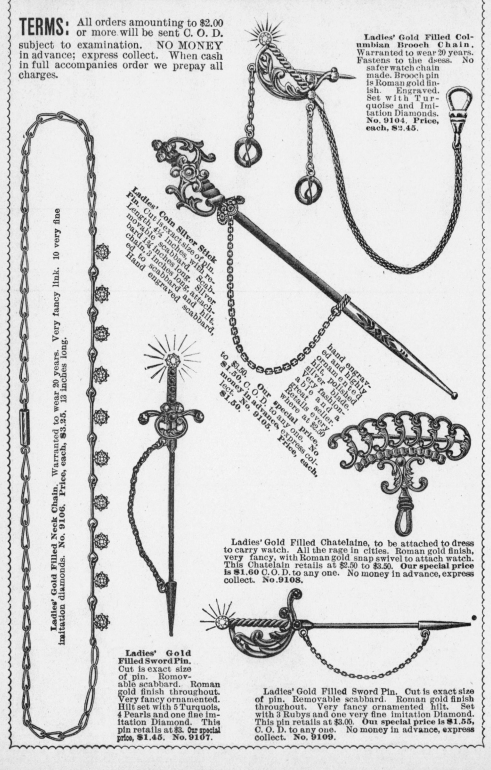

TERMS: All orders amounting to $2.00 or more will be sent C. O. D. subject to examination. NO MONEY in advance; express collect. When cash in full accompanies order we prepay all charges.

Ladies' Gold Filled Columbian Brooch Chain. Warranted to wear 20 years. Fastens to the dress. No safer watch chain made. Brooch pin is Roman gold finish. Engraved. Set with Turquoise and Imitation Diamonds. **No. 9104. Price, each, $2.45.**

Ladies' Coin Silver Stick Pin. Cut is exact size of pin. Length, 4¾ inches, with removable scabbard. Scabbard 1¾ inches long. Silver chain, 3 inches long, attached to scabbard and hilt. Hand engraved scabbard, hand engraved and highly ornamented hilt, polished silver blade. Very fashionable and a great seller. Retails everywhere at $2.50. Our special price, $1.50, C. O. D. to any one. No money in advance, express collect. **No. 9105. Price, each, $1.50.**

Ladies' Gold Filled Neck Chain. Warranted to wear 20 years. Very fancy link. 10 very fine imitation diamonds. **No. 9106. Price, each, $3.25.** 13 inches long.

Ladies' Gold Filled Chatelaine, to be attached to dress to carry watch. All the rage in cities. Roman gold finish, very fancy, with Roman gold snap swivel to attach watch. This Chatelain retails at $2.50 to $3.50. **Our special price is $1.60** C. O. D. to any one. No money in advance, express collect. **No. 9108.**

Ladies' Gold Filled Sword Pin. Cut is exact size of pin. Removable scabbard. Roman gold finish throughout. Very fancy ornamented. Hilt set with 5 Turquois, 4 Pearls and one fine imitation Diamond. This pin retails at $3. Our special price, $1.45. **No. 9107.**

Ladies' Gold Filled Sword Pin. Cut is exact size of pin. Removable scabbard. Roman gold finish throughout. Very fancy ornamented hilt. Set with 3 Rubys and one very fine imitation Diamond. This pin retails at $3.00. **Our special price is $1.55,** C. O. D. to any one. No money in advance, express collect. **No. 9109.**

LADIES' 14-Karet Solid Gold NECK CHAINS

Warranted 14-karet Solid Gold U. S. mint assay. We handle nothing but the highest grade in Solid Gold.

TERMS: All orders for Jewelry amounting to $2.00 or more will be sent to any address C. O. D. subject to examination.

NO MONEY IN ADVANCE. Express collect. When cash in full accompanies order WE PREPAY ALL CHARGES.

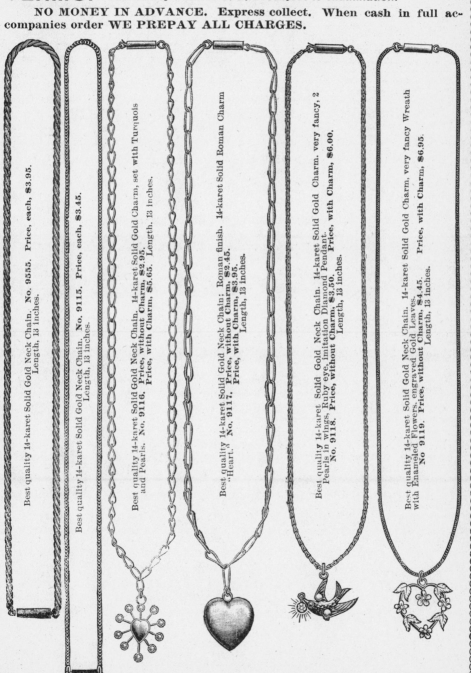

Best quality 14-karet Solid Gold Neck Chain. No. 9555. Price, each, $3.95. Length, 13 inches.

Best quality 14-karet Solid Gold Neck Chain. No. 9115. Price, each, $3.45. Length, 13 inches.

Best quality 14-karet Solid Gold Neck Chain. 14-karet Solid Gold Charm, set with Turquois and Pearls. No. 9116. Price, without Charm, $2.95. Price, with Charm, $5.65. Length, 13 inches.

Best quality 14-karet Solid Gold Neck Chain; Roman finish. 14-karet Solid Gold Roman Charm "Heart." No. 9117. Price, without Charm, $2.45. Price, with Charm, $3.95. Length, 13 inches.

Best quality 14-karet Solid Gold Neck Chain. 14-karet Solid Gold Charm, very fancy, 2 Pearls in wings, Ruby eye, imitation Diamond Pendant. No. 9118. Price, without Charm, $3.50. Price, with Charm, $6.00. Length, 13 inches.

Best quality 14-karet Solid Gold Neck Chain. 14-karet Solid Gold Charm, very fancy Wreath with Enamelled Flowers, engraved Gold Leaves. No 9119. Price, without Charm, $4.45. Price, with Charm, $6.95. Length, 13 inches.

Gold, Gold Filled and Composition Gold Rings.

•————— **RULES FOR MEASUREMENT** —————•

MEASURES SHOWING SIZES OF RINGS.

Take narrow slip of paper and measure around the finger, making sure that when both ends meet it will fit exactly as ring should. To get number of size, measure slip in spaces below. When ordering, always write number of size as slip is sometimes lost and order delayed until another is procured.

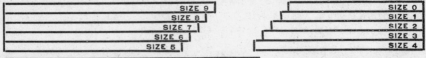

SIZE 9   SIZE 0
SIZE 8   SIZE 1
SIZE 7   SIZE 2
SIZE 6   SIZE 3
SIZE 5   SIZE 4

SIZE 14
SIZE 13
SIZE 12
SIZE 11
SIZE 10

BE SURE TO FOLLOW THESE INSTRUCTIONS in ordering rings, whether Diamond, Gold Filled or Solid Gold, we must know the size from this table.

BEST QUALITY GOLD FILLED RINGS.

We handle only the Best Gold Filled Rings Made. There are many cheaper grades, but they are dear at any price. Our rings are all the best and made exactly the same as Dueber or Boss filled cases, from two plates of solid gold, our composition metal and are warranted to wear 20 years.

THIS ILLUSTRATION SHOWS JUST HOW THE RING IS MADE.

14 K SOLID GOLD
COMPOSITION METAL
14 K SOLID GOLD

This illustration is designed to show just how our gold filled rings are made. It shows one of our **14 karet gold filled rings** cut in two and enlarged, showing thickness of gold and inside composition metal, **equal in appearance and finish to 14 Karet Solid Gold and will wear a lifetime,**

No. 9208.	No. 9209.	No. 9210.	No. 9211.	No. 9212.
Coin Silver Initial Rings. Initials set with nice stones.	20 year gold filled.	20 year gold filled.	20 year gold filled.	20 year gold filled.
Price Each, 25c. Any initial.	Any size. Price Each, 75c.	Any size. Price Each, 78c.	Any size. Price Each, 90c.	Any size. Price Each, $1.05

No. 9213.	No. 9214.	No. 9215.	No. 9216.	No. 9217.
20 years gold filled. Any size.	20 year gold filled. Any size.	20 year gold filled. Any size.	20 year gold filled. Any size.	20 year gold filled. Any size.
Price Each, $1.25.	Price Each, 80c.	Price Each, $1.40.	Price Each, $1.05.	Price Each, $1.75.

No. 9218.	No. 9219.	No. 9220.	No. 9221.	No.9222.
20 year gold filled. Any size.	20 year gold filled. Any size.	20 year gold filled. Any size	20 year gold filled. Any size.	20 year gold filled. Any size.
Price Each, $2.45.	Price Each, $1.75.	Price Each, $1.95.	Price Each, $1.95.	Price Each, $2.35.

No. 9223.	No. 9224.	No. 9225.	No. 9226.
20 year gold filled. Any size.	20 year gold filled. Hand engraved. Any size.	20 year gold filled. Hand engraved. Any size.	20 year gold filled. Hand engraved. Any size.
Price Each, $2.15.	Price Each, $1.95.	Price Each, $2.15.	Price Each, $2.50.

ALL ORDERS FOR RINGS amounting to $2.00 or more, will be sent to anyone, anywhere, C. O. D., subject to examination; less than **$2.00 cash must accompany your order. No money in advance. Express collect.** Compare our prices with those of other houses.

COMPOSITION GOLD RINGS. CAN NOT BE TOLD FROM 14 KARET SOLID GOLD.

GUARANTEED TO WEAR FOR 15 YEARS.

LOOKS LIKE SOLID GOLD—SOUNDS LIKE SOLID GOLD—WEARS LIKE SOLID GOLD
Guaranteed to Stand a Gold Acid Test.

THE MANUFACTURERS of these rings have a secret process by which the ring is made of the one metal which will never tarnish and can not be told by any test except weight from 14 karet solid gold. Always say size wanted, using our scale for size, as described on another page.

No. 9227.
Composition gold, warranted 15 yrs. Child's ring, hand engraved, size 0 to 5.
Price, Each 35c.

No. 9228.
Composition gold, warranted 15 yrs. Misses ring, very fancy, size 0 to 5.
Price, Each 45c.

No. 9229.
Composition gold, warranted 15 yrs. Any size.
Price, Each 55c.

No. 9230.
Composition gold, warranted 15 yrs. Any size.
.Price, Each 55c.

No. 9231.
Composition gold, warranted 15 yrs. Any size.
Price, Each 80c.

No. 9232.
Composition gold, warranted 15 yrs. Any size.
Price, Each $1.25.

No. 9233.
Composition gold, warranted 15 yrs. Any size.
Price, Each $1.25.'

SOMETHING ABOUT RINGS . . .

Don't Buy a Cheap Ring! A poor gold filled, a gold plated, fire gilt or electro plated ring is not only *worthless* but *dangerous*.

Plain, Solid Gold, Oval and Flat Band Rings.

WE FURNISH THESE RINGS IN EITHER 10 OR 14 KARET.   WARRANTED SOLID GOLD U. S. MINT ASSAY.

Always say size wanted using our scale for size, as described on another page.

No. 9234.
10 kt., **95c.** each.
14 kt., **$1.15** each.
Size 0 to 7.

No. 9235.
10 kt., **$1.10** each.
14 kt., **1.30** each.
Size 0 to 7.

No. 9236.
10 kt., **$1.25** each.
14 kt., **1.50** each.
Size 0 to 10.

No. 9237.
10 kt., **$1.65** each.
14 kt., **1.95** each.
Any size.

No. 9238.
10 kt., **$2.15** each.
14 kt., **2.50** each.
Any size.

No. 9239.
10 kt., **$2.90** each.
14 kt., **3.25** each.
Any size.

No. 9240.
10 kt., **$3.75** each.
14 kt., **4.25** each.
Any size.

No. 9241.
10 kt., **$4.25** each.
14 kt., **4.75** each.
Any size.

No. 9242.
10 kt., **$4.75** each.
14 kt., **5.35** each.
Any size.

No.9243.
10 kt., **$5.90** each.
14 kt., **6.70** each.
Any size.

No. 9244.
10 kt., **$1.25** each.
14 kt., **1.50** each.
Size 0 to 10.

No. 9245.
10 kt., **$1.75** each.
14 kt., **2.05** each.
Any size.

No. 9246.
10 kt., **$2.90** each.
14 kt., **3.25** each.
Any size.

No. 9247.
10 kt., **$4.25** each.
14 kt., **4.75** each.
Any size.

No. 9248.
10 kt., **$5.90** each.
14 kt., **6.70** each.
Any size.

ALL ORDERS FOR RINGS amounting to $2.00 or more, will be sent to anyone, anywhere, C. O. D., subject to examination; less than $2.00 cash must accompany your order. No money in advance. Express collect.

BEST QUALITY SOLID GOLD RINGS.

All hand engraved and warranted solid gold U. S. Mint assay.

Always say size wanted, using our scale for size as described on another page.

No. 9249.
Childs' solid gold, engraved band ring. Size 0 to 5.
Price each, 50c.

No. 9250.
Childs' solid gold, engraved band ring. Size 0 to 5.
Price each, 55c.

No. 9251.
Childs' solid gold, engraved band ring. Size 0 to 5.
Price each, 58c.

No. 9252.
Childs' solid gold, engraved band ring. Size 0 to 5.
Price each, 72c.

No. 9253.
Solid gold, engraved band ring. Any size.
Price each, $1.22.

No. 9254.
Solid gold, engraved band ring. Any size.
Price each, $1.25.

No. 9255.
Childs' solid gold, engraved band ring.
Price each, $1.45.

No. 9256.
Solid gold, engraved band ring. Any size.
Price each, $1.50.

No. 9257.
Solid gold, engraved band ring. Any size.
Price each, $1.60.

No. 9258.
Solid gold, engraved band ring. Any size.
Price each, $1.70.

No. 9259.
Solid gold, engraved band ring. Any size.
Price each, $1.75.

No. 9260.
Solid gold, engraved band ring. Any size.
Price each, $1.80.

No. 9261.
Solid gold, engraved band ring. Any size.
Price each, $1.80.

No. 9262.
Solid gold, engraved band ring. Any size.
Price each, $1.85.

No. 9263.
Solid gold, engraved band ring. Any size.
Price each, $1.85.

No. 9264.
Solid gold, engraved band ring. Any size.
Price each, $1.90.

No. 9265.
Solid gold, engraved band ring. Any size.
Price each, $2.00.

No. 9266.
Solid gold, engraved band ring. Any size.
Price each, $2.10.

No. 9267.
Solid gold, engraved band ring. Any size.
Price each, $2.15.

No. 9268.
Solid gold, engraved band ring. Any size.
Price each, $2.10.

No. 9269.
Solid gold, engraved band ring. Any size.
Price each, $1.90.

No. 9270.
Solid gold, engraved band ring. Any size.
Price each, $1.80.

No. 9271.
Solid gold, engraved band ring. Any size.
Price each, $1.65.

No. 9272.
Solid gold, engraved band ring. Any size.
Price each, $1.90.

No. 9273.
Solid gold, engraved band ring. Any size.
Price each, $1.95.

No. 9274.
Solid gold, engraved band ring. Any size.
Price each, $2.20.

No. 9275.
Solid gold, engraved band ring. Any size.
Price each, $2.35.

No. 9276.
Solid gold, engraved band ring. Any size.
Price each, $2.35.

No. 9277.
Solid gold, engraved band ring. Any size.
Price each, $2.45.

No. 9278.
Solid gold, engraved band ring. Any size.
Price each, $2.40.

No. 9279.
Solid gold, engraved band ring. Extra heavy. Any size.
Price each, $2.90.

No. 9280.
Solid gold, engraved band ring. Extra heavy. Any size.
Price each, $3.00.

No. 9281.
Solid gold, engraved band ring. Extra heavy. Any size.
Price each, $3.50.

No. 9282.
Solid gold, engraved band ring. Extra heavy. Any size.
Price each, $3.50.

No. 9283.
Solid gold, engraved band ring. Extra heavy. Any size.
Price each, $3.75.

☞ All orders for rings amounting to $2 or more will be sent to anyone anywhere C. O. D., subject to examination. No money in advance, express collect. Less than $2 cash must accompany your order.

SOLID GOLD RINGS.

We handle only the finest quality solid gold rings, **14 Karet** fine, with finest grade hand made mountings and best of settings. **Always say size wanted** using our scale for size as described on another page.

No. 9292.
Boys' or ladies' solid gold
Cameo ring.
Raised white cameo figure.
Size 0 to 10.
PRICE EACH, 90c.

No. 9293.
Boys' or ladies' solid gold.
Sardonyx stone.
Engraved mounting, fancy
cut stone. Size 0 to 10.
PRICE EACH, $1.65.

No. 9294.
Gents' solid gold.
Tiger-eye stone beauti-
fully cut. Ring nicely en-
graved. Any size.
PRICE EACH, $1.95.

No. 9295.
Gents' solid gold.
Sardonyx stone, beautiful-
ly cut, ring handsomely
engraved. Any size.
PRICE EACH, $2.55.

No. 9296.
Gents' solid gold, onyx.
Fancy engraved ring.
Very fine, plain polished
onyx setting. Any size.
PRICE EACH, $2.75.

No. 9297.
Gents' solid gold.
Sardonyx, fancy engraved.
Fancy cut stone.
Any size.
PRICE EACH, $2.95.

No. 9298.
Gents' solid gold.
Tiger-eye, very fancy cut
stone, hand made, polished
mounting. Any size.
PRICE EACH, $3.95.

No. 9299.
Gents' solid gold.
Genuine carnelian stone.
Very fine. Any size.
Retails at $10.
OUR PRICE, $4.95.

No. 9300.
Gents' solid gold.
Genuine intaglio, very fine.
Any size.
Retails at $10.
OUR PRICE, $5.25.

No. 9301.
Gents' solid gold.
Very large cut.
Polished garnet.
Any size.
PRICE EACH, $5.95.

No. 9302.
Gents' solid gold.
Genuine onyx, very fine.
Any size.
Retails at $12.
OUR PRICE, $5.95.

No. 9303.
Gents' solid gold.
Genuine intaglio stone.
Large raised and fancy cut.
Any size. Retails at $15.
OUR PRICE, $6.10.

No. 9304.
Gents' solid gold.
Genuine Sardonyx stone.
Very fine. Any size.
Retails at $15.
OUR PRICE, $6.70.

No. 9305.
Gents' solid gold.
Genuine sardonyx stone.
Very fine. Any size.
Retails at $15.
OUR PRICE, $6.95.

No. 9306.
Gents' solid gold.
Genuine intaglio stone.
Very fine. Any size.
Retails at $15.
OUR PRICE, $7.10.

No. 9607.
Gents' solid gold.
Genuine intaglio stone.
Very heavy and fancy.
Any size. Retails at $15.
OUR PRICE, $7.45.

No. 9308.
Gents' solid gold.
Genuine intaglio stone.
Extra fine stone. Any size.
Retails at $15.
OUR PRICE, $8.35.

No. 9309.
Gents' solid gold.
Genuine carnelian stone.
The finest ring we handle.
Any size. Retails at $20.
OUR PRICE, $9.95.

No. 9310.
Gents' solid gold emblem
ring. Oddfellows. We can
furnish this ring with emblem of any society at
same price. Any size.
PRICE EACH, $3.95.

No. 9311.
Gents' solid gold emblem
ring. Masonic. We can
furnish this ring with emblem of any society at
same price. Any size.
PRICE EACH, $3.95.

THERE ARE CHEAPER RINGS, but we don't handle them. **You don't want them.** Buy the best, they are the cheapest. **We handle only the best.** Don't buy cheap imitation stone, lower karet gold mounting.
OURS ARE all hand made 14 karet solid gold mountings, all hand engraved, all extra heavy, **genuine stones;** we use nothing else and we are willing to give you **our personal guarantee** as to price, **personal guarantee** as to quality. We will send the rings to you to examine—let you—let any one be the judge.
RETAIL DEALERS ask double our price. **WHOLESALE DEALERS** ask 50 per cent. more than we.
☞ All orders for rings amounting to $2 or more will be sent to anyone, anywhere C. O. D. subject to ex-amination. **No money in advance,** express collect. Less than $2 cash must accompany your order.

✢ ✢ Solid Gold Initial and Society Rings ✢ ✢

Warranted 14 Karet Solid Gold. Warranted the Best Made.

ALWAYS SAY SIZE WANTED, USING OUR SCALE FOR SIZE, AS DESCRIBED ON ANOTHER PAGE.

No. 9284.
Solid Gold Initial Ring.
Any Initial. Any Size.
Price, Each $3.95.

No. 9285.
Solid Gold Initial Ring.
6 Diamonds.
Any Initial. Any Size.
Price, Each $9.50.

No. 9286.
Solid Gold Initial Ring.
Any Initial. Any Size.
Price, Each $5.90.

No. 9287.
Solid Gold Initial Ring.
6 Diamonds.
Any Initial. Any Size.
Price, Each $13.50.

WE WILL SHIP C. O. D. TO ANYONE, ANYWHERE, SUBJECT TO EXAMINATION. NO MONEY IN ADVANCE. EXPRESS COLLECT.

No. 9496.

Gents' Solid Gold Masonic Ring.
We can furnish this ring for any rank.
Cut is made flat and spread out to show decorations.
PRICE, EACH $4.50.
ANY SIZE.

No. 9497.

Gents' Solid Gold K. of P. Ring.
We can furnish this ring for any rank.
PRICE, EACH $4.50.
ANY SIZE.

No. 9498.

Gents' Solid Gold Odd Fellows Ring.
We can furnish this ring for any rank.
PRICE, EACH $4.50.
ANY SIZE.

We can furnish these rings to order for any society at $4.50 each, but all special orders must be accompanied by cash in full.

No. 9288.
Solid Gold Initial Ring.
Any Initial.
Price, Each $5.55.

WHITE ONYX.
No. 9289.
Solid Gold Initial Ring.
6 Diamonds.
Any Initial. Any Size.
Price, Each $9.95.

No. 9290.
Solid Gold Initial Ring.
6 Diamonds.
Any Initial. Any Size.
Price, Each $12.95.

14 K.FINE.
No. 9291.
Solid Gold Initial Ring.
13 Diamonds.
Any Initial. Any Size.
Price, Each $23.75.

Ladies' Solid Gold Set Rings.

WARRANTED BEST MADE, 14 karet solid gold mounting. Genuine stone settings.
Always say size wanted, using our scale for size as described on another page.

No. 9312.
Childs' solid gold ring.
Emerald doublet setting.
Size 0 to 6.
PRICE EACH, 75c.

No. 9313.
Misses' solid gold ring.
Emerald doublet setting.
Size 0 to 8.
PRICE EACH, $1.10.

No. 9314.
Boys' or ladies' solid gold.
Sardonyx stone, engraved
stone and mounting.
PRICE EACH, 90c.
Size 0 to 10.

No. 9315.
Ladies' solid gold ring.
Amethyst.
Any size.
PRICE EACH, $1.35.

No. 9316.
Ladies' solid gold ring.
Ruby and emerald,
doublet. Any size.
PRICE EACH, $1.75.

No. 9317.
Ladies' solid gold ring.
Garnet.
Any size.
PRICE EACH, $1.95.

No. 9318.
Ladies' solid gold ring.
2 moonstones and ruby.
Any size.
PRICE EACH, $1.95.

No. 9319.
Ladies' solid gold ring.
Amethyst and whole
pearls. Any size.
PRICE EACH, $1.95.

No. 9320.
Gents' or ladies' solid gold.
Tiger eye cameo.
Any size.
PRICE EACH, $1.95.

No. 9321.
Ladies' solid gold ring.
Carbuncle.
Any size.
PRICE EACH, $2.15.

No. 9322.
Ladies' solid gold ring.
Amethyst, 3 stones, very
fancy engraved. Any size.
PRICE EACH, $2.90.

No. 9323.
Ladies' solid gold ring.
Star cluster, 8 real pearls, 1
emerald, doublet. Any size.
PRICE EACH, $3.10.

No. 9324.
Ladies' solid gold ring.
Buckle ring, 6 pearls, 4
turquois. Any size.
PRICE EACH, $3.15.

No. 9325.
Ladies' solid gold ring.
Small marquis, 8 pearls, 3
garnets. Any size.
PRICE EACH, $3.60.

No. 9326.
Ladies' solid gold ring.
4 ruby doublets, 4 genuine
pearls. Any size.
PRICE EACH, $3.75.

No. 9327.
Ladies' solid gold ring.
12 cut turquois, 7 genuine
pearls, fancy engraved.
PRICE EACH, $3.95.
Very fancy. Any size.

No. 9328.
Ladies' solid gold ring.
1........, 6 pearls.
Any size.
PRICE EACH, $4.90.

No. 9329.
Ladies' solid gold ring.
12 turquois, 10 genuine
pearls, doublet marquis.
PRICE EACH, $4.20.
Any size.

No. 9330.
Ladies' solid gold ring.
Cluster, 6 pearls, 1 ruby
doublet. Any size.
PRICE EACH, $4.75.

No. 9331.
Ladies' solid gold ring.
Fancy engraved, 6 whole
pearls, 1 emerald doublet.
PRICE EACH, $5.70.
Any size.

No. 9332.
Ladies' solid gold ring.
6 real pearls, 1 ruby
doublet. Any size.
PRICE EACH, $5.90.

No. 9333.
Ladies' solid gold ring.
6 genuine pearls, 4 emerald
doublets, fancy engraved.
PRICE EACH, $5.90.
Any size.

No. 9334.
Ladies' solid gold ring.
1..........., 10 real pearls.
Very fancy. Any size.
PRICE EACH, $6.95.

No. 9335.
Ladies' solid gold ring.
Marquis, 12 real pearls, 4
real garnets. Very fancy.
PRICE EACH, $6.95.
Any size.

All orders for rings amounting to $2 or more will be sent C. O. D. subject to examination. No money
in advance, express collect. Less than $2 cash in full must accompany your order.

Ladies' Solid Gold Set Rings.

WARRANTED BEST MADE 14 karet solid gold mounting. Genuine stone settings. Always say size wanted using our scale for size as described on rnothther page.

No. 9336.
Ladies' solid gold ring. A beauty. 12 real stones, pearls, garnets, etc. Very fancy. Any size.
PRICE EACH, $8.60.

No. 9337.
Ladies' solid gold ring, Clover leaf, 1 sapphire, 2 ruby doublets. Any size.
PRICE EACH, $1.95.

No. 9338.
Ladies' solid gold ring. 2 moonstones, 1 ruby doublet. Any size.
PRICE EACH, $2.75.

No. 9339.
Ladies' solid gold ring. 2 emerald doublets, 1 ruby doublet. Any size.
PRICE EACH, $3.95.

No. 9340.
Ladies' solid gold ring. Clover leaf, fancy engraved, 1 moonstone, 1 ruby doublet, 1 sapphire doub't.
PRICE EACH, $3.95.
Any size.

No. 9341.
Ladies' solid gold ring. Regular diamond setting, 3 genuine garnets. Any size.
PRICE EACH, $5.95.

No. 9342.
Ladies' solid gold ring. Heart, 13 pearls, 1 carbuncle. Any size.
PRICE EACH, $3.95.

No. 9343.
Ladies' solid gold ing. 3 turquois, 6 pearls. Any size.
PRICE EACH, $3.95.

No. 9344.
Ladies' solid gold ring. 8 pearls, 3 sapphires, fancy engraved. Any size.
PRICE EACH, $3.95.

No. 9345.
Ladies' solid gold ring. 1 emerald doublet, 6 pearls, very fancy.
PRICE EACH, $5.25.
Any size.

No. 9346.
Ladies' solid gold ring. 5 ruby doublets, 20 real pearls, very fancy.
PRICE EACH, $6.95.
Any size.

No. 9346½.
Ladies' solid gold ring. Amethyst.
PRICE EACH, $1.90.
Any size.

TESTIMONIALS.

◄———— **WATCHES.** ————►

GREENSBORO, N. C., November 28th, 1893.

MESSRS. SEARS, ROEBUCK & CO.
  DEAR SIRS:—I take pleasure in writing you these few lines. I would have written to you before now, but I wanted to compliment you and your watch; it is giving satisfaction and I hope to be able to send for another one some time, in short, one that is solid gold. I received all the mail that you sent me, but I was not able to comply with your offers. When you send out another prize offering send to me, that I may be among the first, that I may be in time for the prize. When I send for the next watch I want it to be solid gold through and through.   I remain yours as ever,
                                        B. G. HIGHTOWER,
North Guilmer Street.   Greensboro, N. C.

SEARS, ROEBUCK & CO.   ROCK BRIDGE, Ohio, December 2d, 1893.
       Minneapolis, Minn.
  DEAR SIRS:—The $9.85 watch sent me a few days ago, arrived in good condition. I am well pleased with my bargain. I can readily recommend your house to all wishing to buy a first-class watch. Wishing you success for your fair dealing.   Yours respectfully,
                                        G. W. LATER.

MESSRS. SEARS, ROEBUCK & CO.   GREENVILLE, N. H., December 6th, 1893.
       Minneapolis, Minn.
  GENTLEMEN:—I received the watch, No. 10532, which you sent me. I have delayed to test its merits and find it far ahead of what I expected. Will order more in the near future.
           I beg to remain, yours very truly,
                                        J. F. RILEY.

                              EAST ST. LOUIS, Ill., December 20th, 1893.
  GENTLEMEN:—I received the package of plated ware on the 19th, and am glad to state that the goods were not only satisfactory, but were far superior to anything I have ever seen at such a price. Thanking you I will promise to do all I can for you in the way of orders.   Respectfully,
                                        C. R. TALBOTT.

                                 CLEVELAND, Miss., March 11, 1894.
SEARS, ROEBUCK & CO.,
       Minneapolis, Minn.,
  GENTLEMEN:—I received my watch on the 8th inst., and in reply will say that words are inadequate to express my delight and surprise. It is a "perfect little beauty," and I would not take twice the money I gave for it. You may look for another order real soon. You may use this as a "testimonial" if you feel disposed to do so. I remain,   Yours with best wishes,
                                        J. P. COUCH,
Lock Box 3.   Cleveland, Miss.

BEST QUALITY 14 Karet GOLD FILLED
^^CHARMS AND LOCKETS^^

Made of two plates of SOLID GOLD over composition metal and warranted to wear 20 YEARS.

☞ ALL ORDERS AMOUNTING TO $2.00 OR MORE WILL BE SENT C. O. D. SUBJECT TO EXAMINATION. NO MONEY IN ADVANCE; EXPRESS COLLECT. LESS THAN $2.00 CASH IN FULL MUST ACCOMPANY YOUR ORDER.

Tiger Eye and Agate Setting, Gold Filled Locket No. 9120. Price, each, 40c.

Gold Stone Charm. No. 9121. Price, each, 30c.

Tiger Eye and Agate Locket. No. 9122. Price, each, 55c.

Gold Filled Locket. Hand Engraved. No. 9123. Price, each, 65c.

Horse Shoe. Good Luck. Gold Fil'd Locket. Borneo Diamond. No. 9124. Price, each, 75c.

Borneo Di'mond Charm. No 9125. Price, each. 32c.

Solid Gold Front Locket. Chas'd. No. 9126 Price, e'ch, 90c.

Solid G'ld Fr'nt Locket, set with Borneo Diamond. No. 9127. Price, each, $1.10.

Solid G'ld Fr'nt Locket, Hand Engraved. No. 9128. Price, each, $1.15.

Gold Filled Heart for necklace pendant or charm. Plain polished, set with B'rn'o Dimo'd. No. 9129. Price, each, 55c.

Gold Filled Heart for necklace pendant or charm. Engraved, set with 4 stones. No. 9130. Price, each, 75c.

Fancy Ch'rm, English style, revolves, fancy engraved, set with stones both sides. No. 9131. Price, each, 45c.

Fancy Engraved Charm. No. 9132. Price, each, 50c.

Fancy Engraved Locket. No. 9133. Price, each, 45c.

Fancy Engraved Charm. Set with 3 stones No. 9134. Price, each, 55c.

Gold Filled Mail Pouch Charm. No. 9135. Price, each, 40c.

Fancy Keystone, Masonic. No. 9136. Price, each, 45c.

Odd Fellows Charm, very fancy. Gold filled border and emblem. Pearl one side; Tiger Eye one side. Same with Masonic at same price. No. 9137. Price, each, 50c.

Gold Filled Horse Charm, very fancy. No. 9138. Price, each, 55c.

Best Quality 14 Karet Gold Filled Charms and Lockets.

Made of two plates of Solid Gold over composition metal and warranted to wear 20 years. All orders amounting to $2.00 or more will be sent C. O. D. subject to examination. No money in advance. Express collect. Less than $2.00, cash in full must accompany order.

No. 9144.
Gold filled Bird Dog, solid cast, ruby eyes. Price each, 95c.

No. 9145.
Gold filled Locket fancy engraved. 3 stones. Price each, 85c.

No. 9146.
Gold filled Locket fancy engraved, 3 stones. Price each, 90c.

No. 9147.
Fancy Charm, English style, fancy engraved, stone on each side, charm revolves. Price each, $1.05.

No. 9148.
Gold fil'd Locket, solid gold front, satin finished and engraved, rounded edges. Price each, $1.15.

No. 9149.
Gold filled Locket, solid gold front, polished and engraved, rounded edges. Price each, $1.20.

No. 9150.
Gold filled Locket, solid gold front, raised, satin finish and engraved, rounded edges. Price each, $1.30.

No. 9151.
Gold filled Locket, solid gold front, fancy embossed and engraved. Price each, $1.35.

No. 9152.
Gold filled Locket, solid gold front, fancy engraved, satin finish. Price each, $1.40

No. 9153.
Gold filled Intaglio Charm, swinging charm, very fancy. Price each, $1.45.

No. 9154.
Gold filled Intaglio Charm, swinging charm, hand engraved, very fancy. Price each, $1.55.

No. 9155.
Gold filled Intaglio Charm, very fine stone, ornamental gold filled border. Price each, $1.60.

No. 9156.
Gold filled Locket, beautif'ly finished, 1 Borneo diamond. Price each, $1.65.

No. 9157.
Gold filled Locket, beautif'ly finished, five stones. Price each, $1.80.

No. 9158.
Gold filled Locket, beautif'ly finished, 1 Borneo diamond, gold fronts. Price each, $1.90.

No. 9159.
Gold filled Locket, beautif'ly finished, three stones, gold fronts. Price each, $1.95.

No. 9160.
Gold filled Locket, beautif'ly finished, 1 Borneo diamond, gold fronts. Price each, $1.95.

No. 9161.
Gold filled Locket, beautif'ly finished, three stones, gold fronts. Price each, $2.00.

No. 9162.
Gold filled Locket, gold fronts, raised and colored gold ornamented. Price each, $2.00.

No. 9163.
Gold filled Locket, solid gold fronts, raised and colored gold ornamented. Price each, $2.05.

Best Quality 14 Karet Gold Filled Charms and Lockets.

Made of two plates of solid gold over composition metal and warranted to wear 20 years. All orders amounting to $2.00 or more will be sent C. O.D subject to examination. No money in advance; express collect. Less than $2.00 cash in full must accompany order.

No. 9164.
Gold Filled Locket, solid gold fronts, raised and colored gold ornamentations. Price each, **$2.15.**

No. 9165.
Gold Filled Locket, very fancy, solid gold fronts, 1 Borneo diamond. Price each, **$2.25.**

No. 9166.
Large Gold Filled Locket, very fancy, one Borneo diamond. Price each, **$2.40.**

No. 9167.
Reading or Sun Glass Charm, genuine magnifying glass gold trimmed tiger eye handle. Price each, **$2.40.**

No. 9168.
Ice Tongs Charm, gold filled tongs, genuine crystal. Price each, **$1.95.**

No. 9169.
Crystal Charm, engraved crystal, very fancy, gold filled bale fancy finished. Price each, **$2.10.**

No. 9170.
Gold Filled Locket, fancy horse shoe, 7 stones all very fancy. Price each, **$2.20.**

No. 9171.
Gold Filled Locket, solid gold fronts, fancy raised gold ornamented, 3 fine stones. Price each, **$2.95.**

No. 9172.
Compass Charm, transparent. Price each, **$1.95.**

No. 9173.
Fancy Compass Charm. Price each, **$2.45.**

No. 9174.
Crystal Charm, genuine crystal barrel, gold filled trimmings. Price each, **$1.85.**

No. 9175.
Gold Filled Locket, fancy engraved and raised ornamentations, 1 Borneo diamond. Price each, **$1.65.**

No. 9176.
Fancy Seal Charm, very fine engraved seal, beautifully finished. Price each, **$1.95.**

No. 9177.
Bunch of Shingles, lumberman's charm, gold filled trimmings, tiger eye shingles. Price each, **$1.95.**

No. 9178.
Compass charm, transparent, very accurately poised needle, can be depended on for actual service. Price each. **$2.65.**

No. 9179.
Pearl Logs, gold trimmings. Price each, **95c.**

No. 9180.
Thermometer, very accurate, can be depended on to record the temperature. Price each, **$1.65.**

Best Quality Gold Filled Emblem Charms and Lockets. Warranted to wear 20 years.

All orders for $2.00 or more will be sent C. O. D. subject to examination. No money in advance. When cash in full accompanies the order we prepay all charges.

No. 9181. Christian Endeavor, enameled center, colored enameled letters. Price each, 95c.

No. 9182. Order Railroad Conductors, letters enameled in 3 different colors. Price, each, $1.25.

No. 9183. Order R.R. Conductors, punch closed gold letters enameled in 4 differ't col's. Price each $1.45.

No. 9184. Masonic charm enameled letter. Price, each, $1.05.

No. 9185. Brotherhood R. R. Conductors, letters in 3 different colors, handsom'ly engraved on back. Price, each, $1.45.

No. 9186. Order R. R. Telegraphers, colored enameled letters. Price each, $1.45.

No. 9187. Masonic enameled and engra'd. Price each $1.45.

No. 9188. Odd Fellows, enameled letters, 3 colors. Price, each, $1.45.

No. 9189. Masonic, 2 colors of enamel ruby eyes, morable visor. Price each, $2.25.

No. 9190. Odd Fellows, enameled in 3 col's. Price each, $2.25.

No. 9191. Masonic morable visor. richly enamel'd 3 colors. Price each, $4.25

No. 9192. K. of P. morable visor enameled in 4 colors, ruby eyes. Price ea'h $3.95

No. 9193. Masonic fancy keystone. Price each, $1.35.

No. 9194. Masonic and Oddfellows. Price each, $1.20.

No. 9195. Sons of Veterans fancy enameled. Price each, $1.45.

No. 9196. G. A. R. fancy enameled. Price each, $1.95.

Best 14-Karat Solid Gold Emblem Charms.

Warranted 14-Karat Solid Gold U. S. Mint assay. There is none better made.

TERMS C. O. D. to anyone. No money in advance, express collect. When cash in full accompanies order we prepay all charges.

No. 9197. Masonic. Price each $6.90.

No. 9198. Odd Fellows. Enameled in Colors and Engraved. Price each, $9.95.

No. 9199. Knights of Pythias. Enameled and Engraved. Helmet attached with joint, movable visor. Price ea., $14.50.

No. 9200.

Odd Fellows. Price ea., $11.90.

No. 9201.

Scottish Rite. 32d Degree. Price ea., $16.75.

No. 9203. Knights of Pythias. Enameled and Engraved Helmet attached with joint, movable visor. Price each, $22.90.

No. 9204. Knights Templar. Enameled and Engraved. Helmet attached with joint, movable visor. Set with Diamonds and Rubies. Price each $36.95.

No. 9205. Knights Templar. Enameled and Engraved. Helmet attached with joint, movable visor. Price each, $19.50.

No. 9206. Knights Templar. Heavy wide band around the cross. Center enameled in colors engrv'd Helmet attached with joint, movable visor. Price each, $24.95.

No 9207.

Mystic Shrine. Genuine Tiger Claws. Different pendants can be attached as ordered. Price each, $21.50.

BEST 14 KARET <u>GOLD FILLED</u> EMBLEM PINS MADE

☞ All orders amounting to $2.00 or more will be sent C. O. D. subject to examination. **NO MONEY IN ADVANCE.** When cash in full accompanies order **WE PREPAY CHARGES.**

No. 9347.
Order Railway
Telegraphers.
Price, each, 75c.

No. 9348.
Order Railway
Conductors.
Price, each, 75c.

No. 9349.
Order Railway
Conductors.
Price, each, 85c.

No. 9350.
B. L. E. Price,
each, 85c.

No. 9351.
B. L. F. Price,
each, 85c.

No. 9352.
B. L. F. Price,
each, 95c.

No. 9353.
B. L. E. Price,
each, 95c.

No. 9354.
B. L. E. Price,
each, 95c.

No. 9355.
B. L. F. Price,
each, 95c.

No. 9356.
Switchmen.
Price, each, 85c.

No. 9357.
Order Railroad
Trainmen. Price,
each, 85c.

No. 9358.
Order Railway
Trainmen. Price,
each, 85c.

No. 9359.
Masonic. Price,
each, 65c.

No. 9360.
Masonic. Price,
each, 45c.

No. 9361.
Masonic. Price,
each, 70c.

No. 9362.
Masonic. Price,
each, 55c.

No. 9363.
Masonic. Price,
each, 65c.

No. 9364.
Odd Fellows.
Price, each, 35c.

No. 9365.
Odd Fellows.
Price, each, 65c.

No. 9366.
Odd Fellows
Price, each, 75c.

No. 9367.
Odd Fellows.
Price, each, 75c.

No. 9368.
Forresters.
Price, each, 65c.

No. 9369.
A. O. U. W.
Price, each, 65c.

No. 9370.
Christian En-
deavor. Price,
each, 50c.

No. 9371.
G. A. R. Price,
each, 65c.

No. 9372.
G. A. R. Price,
each, 70c.

No. 9373.
Sons of Veter-
ans. Price, each,
65c.

No. 9374.
K. of P. Price,
each, 85c.

No. 9375.
K. of P. Price,
each, 75c.

No. 9376.
Royal Arcan-
ium. Price, each,
95c.

No. 9377.
Druggist. Price,
each, 65c.

No. 9378.
K. of L. Price,
each, 65c.

No. 9379.
Forresters.
Price, each, 65c.

No. 9380.
Masonic. Price,
each, 50c.

No. 9381.
Masonic. Price,
each, 60c.

No. 9382,
Odd Fellows.
Price, each, 45c.

BEST 14 KARET SOLID GOLD EMBLEM PINS.

☞ Guaranteed the Best ....
.... Emblem Goods Made

All orders amounting to $2.00 or more will be sent C. O. D. subject to examination. NO MONEY IN ADVANCE. When cash in full accompanies order, WE PREPAY ALL CHARGES.

No. 6375. Telegraphers. Price, each, $1.75.

No. 6376. Firemen. Price, each, $1.45.

No. 6377. Engineers. Price, each, $1.45.

No. 6378. Odd Fellows. Price, each, $1.35.

No. 6379. Odd Fellows. Price, each, $1.75.

No. 6380. Encampment. Price, each, $1.85.

No. 6381. Ma. & I.O.O.F. Price, each, $1.00.

No. 6382. Masonic. Price, each, 90c.

No. 6383. Masonic. Price, each, $1.10.

No. 6384. Masonic. Price, each, $1.15.

No. 6385. Masonic. Price, each, $1.60.

No. 6386. Price, each, $1.60.

No. 6387. K. of L. Price, each, $1.35.

No. 6388. Workmen. Price, each, $1.35.

No. 6389. G.A.R. Price, each, $1.05.

No. 6390. S. of V. Price, each, $1.35.

No. 6391. K. of P. Price, each, $1.90.

No. 6392. Foresters. Price, each, $1.90.

No. 6393. Conductor. Price, each, $1.45.

No. 6394. Telegraphers. Price, each, $1.75.

No. 6395. Brakemen. Price, each, $1.55.

No. 9383. B. L. E. Price, each, $1.90.

No. 9384. B. L. E. Price, each, $1.90.

No. 9385. B. L. F. Price, each, $1.90.

No. 9386. B. L. F. Price, each, $1.90.

No. 9387. R'y Trainmen. Price, each, $1.40.

No. 9388. Swhmen. Price, each, $1.35.

No. 9389. Odd Fellows. Price, each, $1.05.

No. 9390. Odd Fellows. Price, each, $1.15.

No. 9391. Odd Fellows. Price, $1.65.

No. 9392. Masonic. Price, $1.15.

No. 9393. Masonic. Price, $1.20.

No. 9394. Masonic. Price, $1.20.

No. 9395. C. E. Price, $1.15.

No. 9396. G. A.R. Price, each, $1.55.

No. 9397. Dr'g'st. Price, each, $1.65.

Best Quality 14 Karet Solid Gold and Gold Filled Scarf Pins.

OUR SOLID GOLD PINS
Are all the best quality made. warranted 14 Karet fine, U. S. mint assay.

OUR GOLD FILLED PINS
Are also the best quality made and are warranted for 20 years.

TERMS. All orders amounting to $2.00 or more will be sent C. O. D., subject to examination. **No Money in Advance**, express collect. When cash in full accompanies order we prepay all charges.

All Full Length, 2 3-4 inches long.

No. 7327. Horse Shoe and Whip, 14K. Gold filled, warranted to wear 20 years. Price each, **45c.**

No. 7328. Horse Shoe and Clover Leaf, Borneo Diamond setting, 14 Karet gold filled, warranted to wear 20 years. Price each, **55c.**

No. 7329. 14 Karet gold filled, Borneo Diamond Setting, warranted to wear 20 years. Price each, **65c.**

No. 7330. 14 Karet gold filled Sword, warranted to wear 20 years. Price each, **85c.**

No. 7331. Horse Shoe, 7 Borneo diamonds, beautifully cut, 14 Karet gold filled, warranted to wear 20 years. Price each, **95c.**

No. 9500. Fish, hand engraved and ornamented warranted to wear 20 years. Price each **35c.**

No. 9501. Mandolin, very fancy warranted to wear 20 years. Price each, **55c**

No. 9502. Crescent and Sword, very fancy, hand engraved and ornamented, warranted 20 years. Each, **60c.**

No. 9503. Crescent and Dagger very fancy hand engraved, warranted 20 years. Price each, **60c**

No. 9504. Fancy Knot, warranted 20 years. Price each, **75c.**

14 KARET SOLID GOLD SCARF PINS.

No. 7332. 14K. Solid Gold, Borneo diamond. Price each, **$1.65.**

No. 7333. 14K. Solid Gold Bow. Price each, **$1.95.**

No. 7334. 14K. Solid Gold Crescent. Crescent and sapphire. Each, **$2.20.**

No. 7335. 14K. Solid Gold, Borneo diamond. Price each, **$2.20**

No. 7336. 14K. Solid Gold Sword. Price each, **$2.75.**

No. 7337. 14K Solid Gold, Horse Shoe, Clover leaf and sapphire. Price each, **$2.95.**

BEST QUALITY 14 KARET GOLD FILLED CUFF BUTTONS

Our Gold Filled Cuff Buttons are made from two plates of Solid Gold over composition metal and are WARRANTED TO WEAR 20 YEARS.

TERMS: All orders amounting to $2.00 or over will be sent C. O. D. subject to examination. No money in advance; express collect. When cash in full accompanies order we prepay all charges.

No. 7315.
Polished and engraved. Price, per pair, 35c.

No. 7316.
Stone set; fancy incrusted. Price, per pair, 40c.

No. 7317.
Hand engraved; Price, per pair, 45c.

No. 7318.
Plain polished Im. diamond. Price, per pair, 65c.

N 7319.
Hand engraved; warranted 20 years. Price, per pair, 75c.

No. 7320.
Hand engraved; warranted 20 years. Price, per pair, 85c.

No. 7321.
Hand engraved; raised and colored gold incrusted; Price, per pair, 95c.

No. 7322.
Hand engraved; warranted 20 years. Price, per pair, 75c.

No. 9398.
Hand engraved; warranted 20 years. Price, per pair, 40c.

No. 9399.
Hand engraved; warranted 20 years. Price, per pair, 50c.

No. 6315.
Gold filled, plain polished; warranted 20 years. Price, per pair, 55c.

No. 6316.
Gold filled; fancy engrav'd; war'ant'd 20 years. Price, per pair, 70c.

No. 940.
Raised gold ornamented. Price, per pair, 55c.

No. 9401.
Raised and hand engraved; very fancy. Price, per pair, 65c.

No. 9402.
Colored enameled and stone set sword hilt. Price, per pair, 85c.

No. 9403.
Intaglio stone setting; hand engraved figure. Price, per pair, 95c.

No. 9404.
Raised gold hand engraved Odd Fellows Button; very fancy. Price, 95c.

No. 9405.
Raised gold hand engraved Masonic Button; very fancy. Price, 95c.

No. 9406.
Tiger Eye; hand engraved; very fancy; gold trimmed. Price, per pair, $1.15.

No. 407.
Very fine raised gold hand engraved. Our price, $1.75.

OUR TERMS

Are
Far
More
Liberal
Than
Any
Other
Concern

No. 9409.
Very fine raised solid gold hand engraved. Price, per pair, $1.75.

No. 9410.
Very fine solid gold hand engraved. Price, per pair, $1.75.

No. 9411.
Very fine solid gold hand engraved. Price, per pair, $1.75.

GENTS' GOLD FILLED SLEEVE LINKS.

Made from two plaies of Solid Gold over composition metal and guaranteed to wear 20 years.

TERMS. All orders amounting to $2.00 or more will be sent C. O. D. subject to examination. No money in advance. Express collect. When cash in full accompanies orders we prepay all charges.

Gold filled link, engraved. Roman gold. **No. 9412.** Price per pair, 45c.

Gold filled link, bright cut engraved. **No. 9413.** Price per pair, 55c.

Gold filled link, fancy raised gold engraved. **No. 9414.** Price per pair, 60c.

Very fancy plain Roman gold. **No. 9415.** Price per pair, 65c.

Very fine, raised solid gold hand ornamented. **No. 9416.** Price per p'r, $1.20

Very fine raised solid gold, hand ornamented, decorated and finished. **No. 9417.** Price per p'r, $1.25

Very fine raised solid gold, hand engraved and ornamented. **No. 9418.** Price per pair, $1.35.

Very fine raised solid gold, ornamented knot. **No. 9419.** Price per p'r, $1.45

SOLID COIN SILVER LINKS

Handsome, hand polished, highly finished Roman gold bright edges. **No. 9420.** Price per p'r, $1.60

Very handsome raised and colored gold, hand engraved and ornamented, can not be told from a $10 solid gold link. **No. 9421.** Price per pair, $1.95.

Coin Silver, satin finished. **No. 9422.** Price, per pair, $1.25.

Coin Silver, raised ornamentations, hand engraved. **No. 9423.** Price per pair, $1.55.

LADIES' GOLD FILLED CUFF BUTTONS

Roman gold. **No. 9424.** Price, pair, 45c.

Hand engraved. **No. 9425.** Price, pair, 50c.

Hand engraved. **No. 9426.** Price, pair, 55c.

Hand engraved. **No. 9427.** Price, pair, 60c.

Hand engraved, raised gold ornamentations. **No. 9428.** Pair, 70c.

Hand engraved, raised gold ornamentat's. **No. 9429.** Pair, 75c.

GENTS' GOLD FILLED COLLAR BUTTONS.

9430
Gold filled collar button, long shank, one piece button. Price each, 10c. Price per doz., $1.00.

9431
Gold filled Collar Button, short shank, one piece button. Price each, 10c. Price per doz., $1.00.

9432
Gold filled Collar Button, patent lever action, extension post. Price each, 8c., per doz., 85c.; for pearl back, 10c, per doz., $1.00.

9433
Gold filled Collar Button, patent lever action for back of collar to hold tie. Price each, 8c.; per doz., 85c.; for pearl back, 10c, per doz., $1.00.

Gents' 14 Karet SOLID GOLD CUFF BUTTONS

Warranted 14 Karet Solid Gold U. S. Mint Assay.

Terms : C. O. D. to any one.   NO MONEY IN ADVANCE; express collect. When cash in full accompanies order WE PREPAY ALL CHARGES.

No. 9434.
Solid Gold, plain polished. Price, per pair, $3.90.

No. 9435.
Roman Gold. Price, per pair, $4.10.

No. 9436.
Roman Gold, bright polished. edges. Price, per pair, $4.25.

No. 9437.
Raised ornamented and bright polished. Price, per pair, $4.45.

No. 9438.
Roman or plain polished. Price, per pair, $3.95.

No. 9439.
Satin engraved. Price, per pair, $5.25.

No. 9440.
Onyx and Intaglio. Price, per pair, $6.95.

No. 9441.
Fancy corrugated Roman gold. Price, per pair, $4.75.

No. 9442.
Fancy finish, hand engraved. Price, per pair, $4.80.

No. 9443.
Raised ornamentation and plain polish. Price. per pair, $4.75.

No. 9444.
Raised ornamentation and plain polish. Price, per pair, $4.75.

No. 9445.
Raised ornamentation and plain polish. Price, per pair, $4.80.

No. 9446.
Raised ornamentation and plain polish. Price, per pair, $4.60.

No. 9447.
Raised ornamentation and plain polish. Price, per pair, $4.95.

No. 9448.
Escolloped and raised ornamentation and plain polish. Price, per pair, $5.25.

Gents' 14 Karet SOLID GOLD Sleeve Links

No. 6324.
Solid 14 karet gold sleeve links. Price, per pair, $4.50.

No. 6325.
Solid 14 karet gold sleeve links. Price, per pair, $5.10.

No. 6326.
Solid 14 karet gold sleeve links. Price, per pair, $6.95.

GOLD HEADED CANES.

Guaranteed best quality Solid Gold Headed Canes made, mounted on finely polished Ebony Sticks.

TERMS. C. O. D. to any one, any where, subject to examination. **No Money in Advance;** express collect. Where cash in full accompanies order we prepay all charges

Round head, hand engraved
No. 9467. ½ inch, 10 Karet
Gold. Price each, $2.75.

POLO CROOK.

Beautifully engraved by hand, polished plate to engrave name.

No. 9470. ⅝ inch, 10 Karet, $9.95 each.
⅝ inch, 14 Karet, 14.95 each.

Round head, hand engraved
No. 9468. ⅝ inch, 10 Karet
Gold. Price each, $3.50.

Round head hand engraved.
No. 9470. ⅝ inch, 10 Karet Gold.
Price each, $4.45.

Round head, hand engraved.
No. 9469. ¾ inch, 10 Karet Gold.
Price each, $3.95.

Round head, hand engraved
No. 9472. ⅝ inch, 14 Karet
Gold. Price each, $5.95.

Round head, hand engraved.
No. 9475. ⅝ inch, 14 Karet Gold.
Price each, $8.95.

Round head, hand engraved.
No. 9474. ¾ inch, 14 Karet Gold.
Price each, $7.95.

Round head, hand engraved
No. 9473. ⅝ inch, 14 Karet
Gold. Price each, $6.95.

Gold, Gold Filled, Gold Plated, and Silver Tooth Picks, Pocket and Charm Pencils

WARRANTED BEST QUALITY GOLD FILLED GOODS MADE. ALL ORDERS of $2.00 or more will be sent C. O. D. subject to examination. **No money in advance**, express collect. When cash in full accompanies order **we prepay charges.**

No. 9452. Price, each, $1.25.
Gold Filled Holder, solid Gold Pick and Ear Spoon.

No. 9453. Price, each, $1.35.
Coin Silver Pencil, beautifully engraved, screw extension.

No. 9454. Price, each, $1.45. Illustration shows pencil closed. Length closed, 3¼ inches; open, 6 inches.

Gold Filled Patent Slide Extension Pencil.

No. 9457. Price, each, $1.40.
Solid Coin Silver, Patent Slide Pencil Watch Charm. Closed, 1¼ inch; open, 3 inches.

No. 9458. Price, each, $1.65.
Gold Filled, Smoked Ivory, Magic Pencil Charm. Closed, 1¼ inches; open, 3¼ inches.

No. 9449. Price, each, 15 cents.
Rolled Plate and Ebony, patent slide Tooth Pick.

No. 9450. Price, each, 20 cents.
Rolled Plate Engraved Screw Tooth Pick.

No. 9451. Price, each, 20 cents.
Rolled Plate Engraved Screw Pencil.

No. 9455. Price, each, 65 cents.
Gold Filled Slide Extension Tooth Pick Holder, with genuine quill pick.

No. 9456. Price, each, 40 cents. Closed, 2 inches; open, 3 inches.
Gold Filled Engraved Screw Extension Pencil.

COMPARE OUR PRICES WITH THOSE OF OTHER HOUSES.

FINE GOLD PENS AND HOLDERS.

ALL ORDERS of $2.00 or more will be sent C. O. D. subject to examination. **NO MONEY IN ADVANCE;** express collect. When cash in full accompanys order **WE PREPAY CHARGES.**

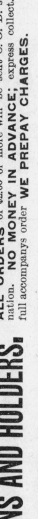

No. 9461. Price, with No. 2 Pen, $1.85; with No. 3 Pen, $2.10; with No. 6 Pen, $2.50. Gold Filled, Ebony Telescope Holder, with 14-karet solid gold pen. In satin lined morrocco case.

No. 9462. Price, $2.65. Gold Filled, Smoked Pearl Fancy Holder, with No. 3 14-karet solid gold pen. In satinlined morrocco case.

No. 9463. Price, $2.35. Gold Filled, White Pearl Fancy Holder, with No. 2 14-karet solid gold pen. In satin lined morrocco case.

No. 9464. Price, $1.95. Gold Filled Ivory Holder, with No. 3 14-karet solid gold pen. In satin lined morrocco case.

No. 9465. Price, $1.85. Gold Filled Ebony Holder, with No. 5 14-karet solid gold pen. In satin lined morrocco case.

No. 9466. Price, $2.75. Gold Filled Pearl Holder, with No. 4 14-karet solid gold pen. In satin lined morrocco case.

No. 9460. Price, $2.75. Gold Filled Engraved. Very beautiful, with No. 2 14-karet solid gold pen. In satin lined morrocco case.

CROWN FOUNTAIN PENS.

Guaranteed the best Fountain pen made. Highest award of merit at **The World's Fair.** Cut shows actual size of complete pen and holder.

No. 9459. Best Hard Rubber Fountain Holder and No. 2 Long Nib 14-karet solid gold pen. Top feed. Our Price, each, $1.25, including filler and case.

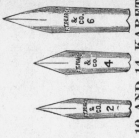

10 AND 14 KARET SOLID GOLD PENS.

Without Holders.

PRICE EACH.

No.	10K	14K
1	$0 45	$0 55
2	50	75
3	55	85
4	75	1 00
5	85	1 25
6	1 00	1 50

DON'T COMPARE our prices with cheap trash advertised by many concerns.

We handle only the best goods. All warranted.

WE GUARANTEE our prices from 30 per cent. to 50 per cent. below all others for the same class of goods.

FINEST QUALITY GOLD PLATED CUFF PINS.

TERMS All orders amounting to $2.00 or more will be sent C. O. D., subject to examination. **No money** in advance. express collect. When cash in full accompanies orders, we prepay all charges.

Gold Plated Cuff Pins, raised gold ornamented. **No. 9566.** Price per pair, 35c.

Gold Plated Cuff Pins, fancy raised gold finish enameled. **No. 9567.** Price per pair, 40c.

Gold Plated Cuff or Baby Pins, fancy raised gold finish enameled letters. **No. 9568.** Price per pair, 40c.

Gold Plated Cuff or Baby Pins, fancy raised gold finish enameled letters. **No. 9570.** Price per pair, 45c.

Gold Plated Cuff or Baby Pins, fancy raised gold finish enameled letters. **No. 9569.** Price per pair, 40c.

Gold Plated Cuff or Baby Pins, fancy raised gold finish enameled letters. **No. 9571.** Price per pair, 45c.

Solid Gold Front Cuff Pins, hand engraved. **No. 9572.** Price per pair, 85c.

Solid Gold Front Cuff or Baby Pins, hand engraved. **No. 9573.** Price per pair, 85c.

Solid Gold Front Cuff or Baby Pins, hand engraved. **No. 9574.** Price per pair, 85c.

Solid Gold Front Cuff or Baby Pins, hand engraved. **No. 9575.** Price per pair, 85c.

FINEST QUALITY GOLD PLATED BAR PINS.

Gold Plated. Engraved, padlock bangle. **No. 9576.** Price each, 50c.

Gold Plated. Engraved; set with 1 stone. **No. 9577.** Price each, 55c.

Gold Plated. Engraved, raised gold ornamentations. Set with one stone. **No. 9578.** Price each, 60c.

Gold Plated. Engraved, raised gold, ornamentations. Set with one stone. **No. 9579.** Price each, 60c.

Gold Plated. Engraved, Raised gold ornamentations. Set with one stone. **No. 9580.** Price each, 65c.

Gold Plated. Engraved, raised gold ornamentations. Set with one stone. **No. 9581.** Price each, 95c.

Gold Plated. Fancy Sword Pin, Roman gold finish. Set with 4 Turquois, 5 Pearls, 1 Imitation Diamonds. **No. 9582.** Price each, $1.45.

Gold Plated. Fancy Sword Pin, Roman gold finish. Set with Pearl, Turquois and Imitation Diamonds. **No. 9583.** Price each, $1.55.

Finest Quality Gold Plated Brooch Pins.

TERMS. All orders amounting to $2.00 or more will be sent C. O. D. subject to examination. No money in advance, express collect. When cash in full accompanies order we prepay all charges.

No. 9556.
Gold plated, raised gold ornamented. Roman gold finish. Price each, **70c.**

No. 9557.
Gold plated, raised gold ornamented. Roman gold finish. Price each, **95c.**

No. 9558.
Gold plated, raised gold ornamented, Roman gold finish. Price each, **95c.**

No. 9559
Gold plated, fancy Roman gold leaves, set with imitation diamond. Price, each, **$1.15.**

No. 9560.
Gold plated, fancy Roman gold leaves, set with pearl. Price each. **95c.**

No. 9561.
Gold plated, fancy Roman gold leaves set with imitation diamond. Price each. **$1.20.**

No. 9562.
Gold plated, fancy Roman gold leaves set with imitation diamond. Price each, **$1.20.**

No. 9750.
Gold plated, fancy Roman gold leaves set with imitation diamond or pearl. Price each, **$1.25**

No. 9751.
Gold plated, raised gold ornamented, Roman gold finish, set with imitation diamond. Price each, **95c.**

No. 9752.
Gold plated, raised gold ornamented. Roman gold finish. Price each, **85c.**

No 9563.
Gold plated, fancy raised gold ornamented Roman gold finish set with imitation diamond. Price each, **$1.05.**

No. 9564.
Gold plated. Roman gold finish, very fancy engraved and raised gold finish set with pearl. Price each. **$1.10.**

No. 9565.
Gold plated, very fancy Roman gold finished wreath and arrows, 9 whole pearls in wreath. This is a beautiful brooch and must be seen to be appreciated. Price each, **$1.85.**

Ladies' Gold Filled Brooch Pins.

BEST HAND ENAMELED GOODS MADE.

TERMS. All orders amounting to $2.00 or more will be sent C. O. D. subject to examination. No money in advance; express collect. When cash in full accompanies order we **prepay** all charges.

No. 9584.
Gold filled brooch, 4 leaf clover, colored enameled leaves, Roman gold stem, imitation diamond center. **Price each, 85c.**

No. 9585.
Gold filled brooch, 3 forget-me-nots colored enameled leaves, imitation diamond center, Roman gold stem. **Price each, $1.15.**

No. 9586.
Gold filled brooch, pansy, colored, enameled leaves, Roman gold stem. **Price each, $1.20.**

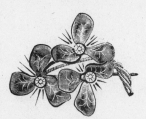

No. 9587.
Gold filled brooch, 3 wood lillies, colored enameled leaves, 3 imitation diamonds. **Price each, $1.50.**

No. 9588.
Gold filled brooch, pansy, colored enameled leaves, Roman gold stem, imitation diamond. **Price each, $1.05.**

No. 9589.
Gold filled brooch, wild lily, colored enameled leaves, Roman gold stem, imitation diamond. **Price each, $1.45.**

No. 9590.
Gold filled brooch, blossom, colored enameled leaves, diamond cluster center, 7 imitation diamonds, plain polished coil stem. **Price each, $1.40.**

No. 9591.
Gold filled crescent brooch, white hard enameled crescent, hand painted ornament with 15 imitation diamonds. **Price each, $2.45.**

No. 9592.
Gold filled brooch, Roman gold finish lilly, ornamented Roman gold stem set with 10 imitation diamonds. **Price each, 75c.**

No. 9593.
Gold filled brooch, Roman gold finish, fancy ornamented, 4 Roman gold blossoms set with rubys,, 11 imitation diamonds. **Price each, 85c.**

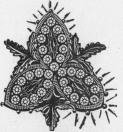

No. 9594.
Gold filled brooch, very fancy colored gold and ornamented leaves, 30 imitation diamonds, 3 imitation emeralds, Roman gold back ground. **Price each, $1.95.**

BEST QUALITY GOLD FILLED BROOCHES, PINS, ETC.

Warranted Best Quality Gold Filled Made! Made of two plates of SOLID GOLD over composition Metal and Warranted to wear 20 YEARS!

All Orders for Jewelry of over $2.00 sent C. O. D. subject to examination. No Money in Advance. Express Collect. Where Cash accompanies order we Prepay Charges.

No. 6360.

Gold Filled Brooch, warranted 20 years. White stone. Price each, 95c.

No. 6363.

Gold Filled Brooch, warranted 20 years. Ruby set. Price each, $1.10.

No. 7380.

Ladies' Gold Filled Sword Brooch. Latest thing out. Gold filled scabbard, chain, pearl handle, Borneo diamond setting, 1-5th solid gold. Warranted 20 years. Price each, 95c.

No. 7381.

Ladies' Crescent Brooch. Gold filled setting, genuine pearl mounting. Set with 3 Borneo diamonds and ornamented in raised and colored gold. 1-5th solid gold. Warranted 20 years. Price each, $1.25.

No. 7382.

Ladies' Gold Filled Brooch. 1-5th solid gold pin, genuine solid pearl Bird, beautifully ornamented, gold pendent, set with a Borneo diamond. Price each, $1.50.

No. 7383.

Ladies' Gold Filled Brooch. 1-5th solid gold, colored gold leaves, beautifully ornamented, genuine pearl Pansy, ornamented Bud, genuine stone, one Borneo diamond. Price each, $1.25.

No. 7385.

Ladies' Gold Filled Brooch. 1-5th solid gold, 2 Borneo diamonds, genuine pearl Anchor, Price each, $1.15.

No. 7386.

Pearl Cross. 1-5th solid gold ornamentation, 2 Borneo diamonds. Price each, $1.15.

No. 9596.

Genuine Pearl Cross. Pendent for neck or watch chain. Solid gold image and gold trimmings. Price each, $1.90.

No. 7384.

Ladies' Gold Filled Brooch. 1-5th solid gold. Maple Leaf, genuine pearl, beautifully finished, colored and ornamented in raised and colored gold and set with one Borneo diamond. Price each, $1.10.

No. 9597.

Gents' 14 Karet Solid Gold Stud. Best hand made mounting, fine imitation diamond, the Saharah Gem. Price each, $1.15.

Ladies' Solid Gold Front

— AND —

GOLD FILLED BAR PINS.

Terms: All orders amounting to $2.00 or more will be sent C. O. D. subject to examination. NO MONEY IN ADVANCE; express collect. When cash in full accompanies order WE PREPAY ALL CHARGES.

No. 9598.
Solid Gold Front Bar Pin. Raised gold ornamented and hand polished and engraved; set with 3 Turquois. Price, each, $1.35.

No. 9599.
Solid Gold Front Bar Pin. Raised gold ornamented and hand polished and engraved; set with 1 whole Pearl and 4 Turquoise. Price, each, $1.50.

No. 9600.
Solid Gold Front Bar Pin. Raised gold ornamented and hand polished and engraved; set with 5 Turquois. Price, each, $1.55.

No. 9601.
Solid Gold Front Bar Pin. Raised gold ornamented and hand polished and engraved; set with 5 Garnets. Price, each, $1.65.

No. 9602.
Solid Gold Front Bar Pin. Raised gold ornamented and hand polished and engraved; set with 2 Garnets. Price, each, $1.85.

No. 9603.
Gold Filled Bar Pin. Fancy raised gold ornamented. Set with imitation Diamond. Price, each, 65c.

No. 9604.
Gold Filled Bar Pin. Colored enameled Clover Leaf; best hard enamel. Price, each, 90c.

No. 9605.
Gold Filled Bar Pin. Roman gold finish; beautifully ornamented; colored enameled Clover Leaf, set with imitation Diamond. Price, each, 95c.

No. 9606.
Gold Filled Bar Pin. Colored enameled Clover Leaves, set with imitation Diamonds. Price, each, $1.00.

No. 9607.
Gold Filled Bar Pin. Colored enameled Clover Leaves, set with imitation Diamonds. Price, each, $1.20.

No. 9608.
Gold Filled Bar Pin. Very fancy raised and colored Gold Leaves; set with 20 imitation Diamonds and 2 large imitation Emeralds. Price, each, $1.35.

No. 9609.
Gold Filled Bar Pin. Very fancy raised and colored Gold Leaves; colored enameled Lillies; 5 imitation Diamonds. Price, each, $1.50.

FINEST QUALITY GOLD FILLED BROOCH PINS.

We guarantee these the highest grade gold filled goods made, equal in appearance, finish and every way, except in intrinsic value, to solid gold. Cannot be told from solid gold, and every pin is warranted for 20 years. **TERMS:** All orders amounting to $2.00 or more will be sent C. O. D., subject to examination. **No money in advance,** express collect. When cash in **full** accompanies order we prepay all charges.

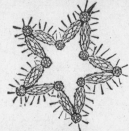

Gold Filled Brooch. Warranted 20 years. Very fancy wreath, enameled in different colors. Fancy hilt to sword enameled in assorted colors and set with imitation Ruby. No. 9543. Price each, **$1.35.**

Gold Filled Brooch. Warranted 20 years. Roman gold, raised gold ornamentations, 3 imitation Ruby Eyes No. 9544. Price each, **$1.55.**

Gold Filled Brooch. Warranted 20 years. Nothing finer made. 10 large imitation Topaz settings, 10 imitation Diamond settings. No. 9554. Price each, **$2.35.**

Gold Filled Brooch. Warranted 20 years. Pansy leaf, raised Roman gold ornamentations. Set with two fine imitation diamonds. No. 9546. Price each, **$1.75.**

Gold Filled Brooch. Warranted 20 years. Fancy Roman gold wreath, 6 fine imitation diamonds. No. 9547. Price each, **$1.75.**

Gold Filled Brooch. Warranted 20 years. Fancy colored gold leaves, beautifully finished and engraved. Set with large imitation Diamond. No. 9548. Price each, **$1.85.**

Gold Filled Brooch. Warranted 20 years. Very fancy Roman gold wreath. Set with 4 imitation Rubys, 4 imitation diamonds. No. 9549. Price each, **$1.90.**

Gold Filled Brooch. Warranted 20 years. Very fancy raised Roman gold finish, fancy engraved. Set with 1 large imitation Ruby, 4 whole Pearls. No. 9550. Price each, **$1.80.**

Gold Filled Brooch. Warranted 20 years. Very fancy raised Roman gold finish. Set with 3 large imitation Rubys. No. 9551. Price each, **$1.90.**

Gold Filled Brooch. Warranted 20 years. Raised fancy Roman gold finish. Set with large imitation Diamond. No. 9552. Price each, **$1.85.**

Gold Filled Brooch. Warranted 20 years. 3 fancy four-leaf clover leaves, each leaf beautifully enameled with hard white enamel, fancy gold border. Set with large imitation Diamonds. No. 9553. Price each, **$1.65.**

Gold Filled Brooch. Warranted 20 years. Fancy Roman gold leaf, raised gold finish. 6 Pearls. No. 9545. Price each, **$1.65.**

Ladies' Solid Gold Bar Pins!

TERMS.—All orders amounting to $2.00 or more will be sent C. O. D. subject to examination. No money in advance, express collect. When cash in full accompanies order we prepay all charges.

No. 9610.

14 Karet solid gold bar pin, plain polished bar set with fine imitation diamond, patent safety catch. Price each, $1.95.

No. 9611.

14 Karet solid gold bar pin, plain polished bar, bird set with turquois, garnets and imitation diamonds, patent safety catch. Price each, $2.35.

No. 9612.

14 Karet solid gold bar pin, very fancy hand engraved, set with 3 large imitation diamonds, patent safety catch. Price each, $2.85.

No. 9613.

14 Karet solid gold bar pin, plain polished bar, very fancy ornamented Roman gold knot, patent safety catch. Price each, $2.65.

No. 9614.

14 Karet solid gold bar pin, plain polished bar, very fancy center set with five stones, (pearls, turquois and garnets), patent safety catch, Price each, $2.55.

No. 9615.

14 Karet solid gold bar pin, very fancy raised ornamented with 2 crescents and 2 stars, set with four turquois and four pearls, patent safety catch. Price each, $2.95.

No. 9616.

14 Karet solid gold bar pin, very fancy engraved bow knot set with two pearls, fancy pin set with large imitation diamond. Price each, $3.15.

No. 9617.

14 Karet solid gold bar pin, very fancy raised gold ornamented, set with 1 large pearl and 6 garnets, beautiful Roman gold heart pendant set with whole pearl, patent safety catch. Price each, $3.95.

No. 9618.

14 Karet solid gold bar pin, very fancy pin set with 10 fine imitation diamonds with saphire, ruby or emerald center; you can't tell this from a genuine diamond cluster pin; patent safety catch. Price each, $4.95.

SOLID SILVER THIMBLES.

No. 6919.

Coin Silver.

Price each,

20c

No. 9620.

Coin Silver, very heavy, hand engraved.

Price each,

45c.

No. 9621.

Coin Silver, very heavy 14 Karet solid gold band, raised gold ornamented and engraved by hand. Price each, 95c.

Solid Gold and Gold Filled Studs, Ear Drops and Ear Hoops.

TERMS. All orders amounting to **$2.00** or more will be sent C. O. D., subject to examination. **No Money in Advance**, express collect. When cash in full accompanies order, we prepay all charges.

No. 6337. Solid Gold Stud. Diamond Cut, **Price ea. $1.50.**

No. 6338. Solid Gold. Per set of 3 studs **$3.75**

No. 6339. 14 karet solid gold Price per pair, 65c.

No. 6340. Gold filled. Warranted 20 years, pearl set, Per pair, 95c.

No. 6341. 14 karet solid gold Plain polished. Per pair, $1.95.

No. 6342. 14 karet solid gold Pearl. Per pair, **$1.95.**

No. 6343. 14 karet gold. Price per pair, **$2.95.**

No. 6344. Solid gold stud. Diamond cut. Price ea., $1.75.

No. 6345. 14 karet solid gold Real Pearl. Per pair, $2.30.

No. 4346. 14 karet solid gold Ruby and Pearls. Per pair, $3.20.

No. 6347. 14 karet solid gold Ruby Set. Per pair, $2.00.

No. 6348. 14 karet solid gold Coil. Per pair, $3.00.

No. 6349. 14 karet solid gold Price per pair $1.05.

No. 6350. Gold filled. Warranted 20 years, per pair 75c

No. 6351. 14 karet solid gold Ruby Sets Per pair, $2.80.

No. 9512. 14 karet, gold filled. Per pair, $1.15.

No. 6353. Gold Filled. Warranted 20 yrs. Ruby Sets. Per pair, 95c.

No. 6354. Gold filled. Warranted 20 yrs. Per pair, 90c

No. 6355. Gold filled. Warranted 20 yrs. Per pair, 70c.

No. 6356. Gold filled. Warranted 20 years. Very Fancy. Per pair, $1.05.

No. 9505. 14 karet solid gold Set with fine Imita'n diamond Per pair, $1.65.

No. 9506. 14 karet solid gold Set with fine Imit'n Diamond. Per pair, $1.95.

No. 9507. 14 karet solid gold Set with fine Imit'n Diamond. Per pair, $2.25.

No. 9508. 14 karet solid gold Set with fine Imit'n Diamond. Per pair, $1.95.

No. 9509. 14 karet solid gold Set with fine Imit'n Diamand. Per pair, $1.85.

No. 9510. 14 karet solid gold Set with Imit'n Diamond. Per pair, $1.60.

No. 9513. Gold Filled. Solid gold wire. Fancy ornamen'd balls. Pair, $1.45

No. 9514. Gold filled, solid gold wire and front. Fancy turquois set. Per Pair, $1.65.

No. 9515. Gold filled. solid gold wire and front. Garnet Sets. Raised ornaments. Pair, $1.70.

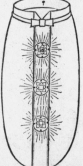
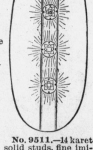
No. 9511.—14 karet solid studs, fine imitation Diamond, 14 karet, solid gold setting. Price per set, of 3, $2.25. (Sold only in sets), C. O. D. No money in advance

No. 9516. Gold filled, solid gold wire, large Ruby Setting. Per pair, $1.75.

No. 9517. Gold filled, solid gold wire, large Moonstone setti'g Per pair, $1.90.

No. 9518. Gold filled, solid gold wire, large Imit'n Diamond, incrusted in blue stone, Pair, $1.95

No. 9519. Solid gold, screw backs, fancy gold coil, set with Whole Pearl. Per pair, $1.90.

Ladies' Gold Filled and Coin Silver Glove Buttoners and Hat and Hair Pins.

TERMS. All orders amounting to $2.00 or over will be sent C. O. D. subject to examination. No money in advance. Express collect. When cash in full accompanies the order we prepay all charges.

Ladies' Gold Filled Glove Buttoner, Roman finish, bright ornamentation. Cut is exact size of buttoner. Silk cord and tassel 5 in. long, "fancy colored." **No. 9487.** Price each, 40c.

Ladies' Gold Filled Glove Buttoner, Roman gold, with silk cord and tassel 5 in. long, **No. 9488.** Price each, 40c.

Ladies' Gold Filled Glove Buttoner, Roman gold, very fancy with silk cord and tassel 5 in. long. **No. 9489.** Price each, 45c.

Ladies' Gold Filled Glove Buttoner, Roman gold, very fancy with silk cord and tassel 5 in. long. **No. 9490.** Price each, 50c.

Ladies' Gold Filled Glove Buttoner, Roman gold, very fancy with silk cord and tassel 5 in. long. **No. 9491.** Price each, 60c.

Ladies' Gold Filled Glove Buttoner, Roman gold, very fancy, hand engraved, with silk cord and tassel 5 in. long. **No. 9492.** Price each, 75c

Ladies' Coin Silver Hat or Hair Pins, very fancy bright cut engraved ball, length 6 inches. **No. 9493.** Price each, 75c.

Ladies' Coin Silver Hat or Hair Pin, very fancy, bright cut engraved ball, length, 6 inches. **No. 9494.** Price each, 75c.

Ladies' Coin Silver Hat or Hair Pin, very fancy, bright cut and engraved sword handle, length 6 inches. **No. 9495.** Price each, 85c.

GOLD FILLED BRACELETS,

Made of two plates of gold over composition metal and guaranteed to wear for 20 years. All orders amounting to $2.00 or more will be sent C. O. D., subject to examination. No Money in Advance, express collect. When cash in full accompanies order we prepay all charges.

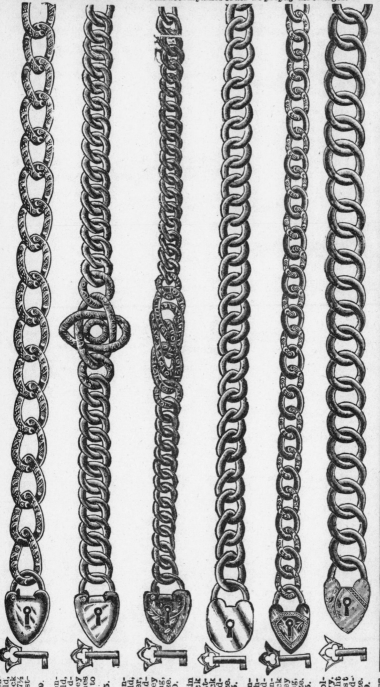

No. 9476. Hand engraved, Roman Gold, with Chain, Padlock and Key attached, 7½ inches long, adjustable to any size. Price, each, $1.80.

No. 9477. Hand engraved Roman Gold, knot Center. Padlock, Chain and Key attached, 7½ inches long, adjustable to any size. Price, each, $2.25.

No. 9478. Hand engraved, Roman Gold, fancy knot center, hand engraved, padlock, chain and key attached, 7⅜ in. long, adjustable to any size. Price, each, $2.40.

No. 9479. Plain polished padlock chain and key attached. Best padlock made. 7½ in. long, adjustable to any size. Price, each, $2.55.

No. 9480. Hand engraved, plain polished. Very fancy padlock. Bright cut engraved, best lock made, chain and key attached, 7½ in. long, adjustable to any size. Price, each, $2.95.

No. 9481. Plain polished, extra heavy. Very fancy bright cut padlock, best made, 7½ in. long, adjustable to any size. Price, each, $3.50.

No. 9482. Latest Thing out. Solid Coin Silver. The most stylish bracelet on the market. Very fancy engraved and ornamented, with six plain polish'd shields for name or initials, patent safe catch or lock. 7½ in. long. Price, each, $3.95.

Ladies' 14 Karet Solid Gold Bracelets.

Waranted 14 Karet Solid Gold, U. S. Mint Assay. Diamond Set, Hand Engraved and Ornamented, All Full Length, 8 inches long, Adjustable to any Size.

TERMS: We send C. O. D. to anyone anywhere subject to examination. No money in Advance, Express collect. When cash in full accompanies order we prepay all charges.

YOU TAKE NO RISK WHEN YOU ORDER FROM US. We guarantee every article to be found exactly as represented. NO ONE MEETS OUR PRICES for same quality of goods. NO CONCERN ON EARTH offers same terms.

NOTHING BUT THE BEST is found illustrated in our Catalogue. We aim to give you only such goods as are found in the best and largest retail stores, goods made on honor, and in this class of goods we guarantee to save you from 20 to 100 per cent.

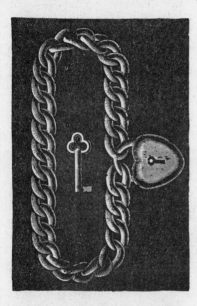

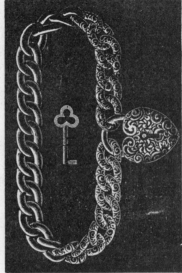

LADIES' CHAIN BRACELET, Roman Finish. Warranted 14 Karet Solid Gold, U. S. Mint assay. Solid Gold Heart Padlock with Solid Gold Key. Price, each, $16.00 No. 9483.

LADIES' CHAIN BRACELET, Roman Finish. Warranted 14 Karet Solid Gold, U. S. Mint assay. Hand engraved, chased and ornamented. Solid Gold Heart Padlock with Solid Gold Key. Price, each, $17.50 No 9484.

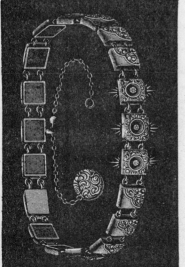

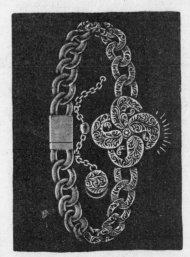

LADIES' FANCY SQUARE BOX LINK CHAIN BRACELET, Roman Finish. Warranted 14 Karet Solid Gold, U. S. Mint assay. Engraved, ornamented and decorated by hand. Solid Gold Safety Chain with Bangle. Three Genuine Diamonds. Price, each, $18.50 No. 9485.

LADIES' CHAIN BRACELET, Roman Finish. Warranted 14 Karet Solid Gold, U. S. Mint assay. Hand engraved, ornamented and decorated. Solid Gold Safety Chain with Bangle. Large Chased Gold Knot set with large genuine Diamond. Very, Heavy Bracelet. No. 9486. Price, each, $29.75

Sterling Silver and Gold Filled Hair and Hat Pins.

Guaranteed Highest Grade Made.

TERMS: All orders amounting to $2.00 or more will be sent C. O. D. subject to examination. No money in advance, express collect. When cash in full accompanies order we prepay all charges.

No. 9520.
Gold filled hat pin, elegantly engraved set with emerald, 5½ inches long. Price each, $1.25

No. 9521.
Solid silver hair pin, fancy engraved sword handle, cut is about ½ size, pin is 6 inches long. Price each, $1.45

No. 9522.
Gold filled hat or hair pin, warranted 20 years, very fancy Roman gold sword handle set with 8 pearls, 1 amethyst. Bright polished silver blade, 6½ in. long, cut is ⅝ size. Price each, $2.15.

No. 9523.
Gold filled hat pin, warranted 20 years, very fancy engraved Roman gold sword handle, set with 6 imitation diamonds, 1 imitation ruby, 6½ in. long, cut is two-thirds size. Price each, $2.25.

No. 9524.
Gold filled hair pin, very fancy engraved and ornamented, imitation tortoise shell prongs, cut is ½ size, 5½ in long. Price each, 95c.

No. 9525.
Gold filled hair pin, very fancy engraved and ornamented, imitation tortoise shell prongs, cut is ½ size, 5½ in. long Price each, $1.15.

No. 9526.
Solid silver hair pin, very fancy engraved, decorated and ornamented, imitation tortoise shell prongs, cut is ½ size, 5½ in. long. Price each, $1.65

No. 9527.
Solid silver hair pin, very fancy engraved, decorated and ornamented, imitation tortoise shell prongs. This pin is very large and showy, 3½ in. wide, 6 in. long. Price each, $2.45.

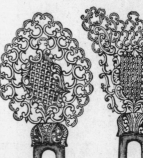

No. 9528.
Solid silver, Roman gold finished and bright cut. This is a very handsome, large and showy pin, cut is about one-half size, pin is 3½ in. wide, 6 in. long, imitation tortoise shell prongs. Price each, $3.95.

No. 9529.
Solid silver Roman gold finished, bright cut, very fancy engraved, decorated and finished, cut is about ½ size, 6 in. long, imitation tortoise shell prongs. Price e'h, $3.35.

No. 9530.
Solid silver, Roman gold finish, bright cut, very fancy engraved, decorated and finished, cut is about ½ size, 6 in long, imitation tortoise shell prongs. Price e'h, $3.15.

No. 9531.
Solid silver, very fancy center, engraved decorated and ornamented, cut is about ½ size, 6 in long, imitation tortoise shell prongs. Price each, $2.85.

STERLING SILVER AND GOLD FILLED HAIR AND HAT PINS

Guaranteed Highest Grade Made.

TERMS: All orders amounting to $2.00 or more will be sent C. O. D. subject to examination. No money in advance; express collect. When cash in full accompanies order we prepay all charges.

No. 9532.
Gold Filled Hair Pin; warranted 20 years. Very fancy hand engraved and ornamented. Cut is two thirds size; 6 inches long. Imitation Tortoise Shell prongs. Price, each, **$3.95.**

No. 9533.
Gold Filled Hair Pin; warranted 20 years. Very fancy hand engraved and ornamented. Cut is exact size; 6 inches long. Imitation Tortoise Shell prongs. Price, each, **$2.95.**

No. 9534.
Gold Filled Hair Pin; warranted 20 years. Very fancy hand engraved and ornamented. **Set with 13 Emeralds.** Cut is two thirds size; 6 inches long. Imitation Tortoise Shell prongs. Price, each, **$4.95.**

Solid Silver Handle Knife.

—TWO FINE STEEL BLADES.   WARRANTED.—

Very fancy raised ornamented Solid Silver Handle. Two blades; warranted best quality steel.
No. 9536. Price, each, **$2.15**, C. O. D., to any one.
No. 9537. Four blades. Price, each, **$2.85.** No money in advance; express collect.

No. 9535.
Gold Filled Hair Pin; **warranted 20 years.** Very fancy engraved, decorated and ornamented; fancy raised gold center piece. Cut is two thirds size; 6 inches long. Imitation Tortoise Shell prongs. Price, each, **$2.65.**

No. 9538.
Solid Silver. Patent Heart Key Ring; very fine. Price, each, 95c.

No. 9539.
Solid Silver. Patent Key Ring; very fancy engraved, raised and ornamented. Price, each, **$1.25.**

DRESS SETS IN GOLD FILLED AND SOLID GOLD.

No. 9540. Plain polished Gold Filled	Price, per set,	**$1.15**
No. 9541. 14 karet Solid Gold. Roman or plain polished.	" "	1.95
No. 9542. 14 karet Solid Gold. Roman or plain polished. Set with Pearls	" "	2.45

SILVERWARE
DEPARTMEMT.

WE FEEL SAFE in claiming, without fear of contradiction, that our Silverware Department is not only more complete, but our prices far lower than any other house.

WE HANDLE EVERYTHING in the Silverware line, in **Single, Triple, Quadruple and Solid Sterling Silver.** If you don't find what you want illustrated, **write for prices;** we can supply you.

OUR TERMS
Are far more liberal than other houses offer. Some goods are so bulky it is not practicable to ship C. O. D. others so heavy we do not feel like taking all the risk, and some cost you so little we must expect cash in full with your order, but so far as possible we either ship C. O. D., no money in advance, or on receipt of a very small deposit.

Terms of Sale will be found on each page.

SOLID SILVER GOODS.
WARRANTED STERLING SILVER.

No. S 1.
Solid Sterling Silver Bon Bon Tongs.
Price, each, $1.75.

No. S 2.
Solid Sterling Silver Napkin Ring.
Price, each, $2.95.

No. S 3.
Solid Sterling Silver Napkin Ring.
Price, each, $2.20.

SOLID STERLING SILVER.

Orders of $2.00 or more will be sent C. O. D., subject to examination, no money in advance, express collect. Under $2.00, cash in full must accompany your order.

No. S 4.

```
Sterling Silver Coffee Spoon, exact size of cut.........................................Price, each, $ .55
    "      "      "      "      "      "      "   gold lined bowl .........................   "      "    .65
    "      "   Tea   "   one-half larger, same pattern as cut.......................   "      "    .58
    "      "      "      "      "      "      "   plain tipped pattern......................   "      "    .55
    "      "   Table Spoons or Forks, fancy handle or plain tipped.....................   "      "   1.75
    "      "   Dessert   "      "      "      "      "      "   ......................   "      "   1.50
```

No. S 5.

```
Sterling Silver Coffee Spoon, exact size of cut.........................................Price, each, $ .55
    "      "      "      "      "      "      "   gold lined bowl.............................   "      "    .65
    "      "   Tea   "   one-half larger than illustration, same pattern as cut......   "      "    .58
    "      "      "      "      "      "      "   plain tipped.............   "      "    .55
    "      "   Table Spoons or Forks, fancy handle or plain tipped.....................   "      "   1.75
    "      "   Dessert   "      "      "      "      "      "   ......................   "      "   1.50
```

No. S 6.

```
Sterling Silver Coffee Spoon, exact size of cut.........................................Price, each, $ .55
    "      "      "      "      "      "      "   gold lined bowl............................   "      "    .65
    "      "   Tea Spoons, one-half larger than illustration, same pattern as cut........   "      "    .58
    "      "      "      "      "      "      "   plain tipped .............   "      "    .55
    "      "   Table Spoons or Forks, fancy handle or plain tipped.......................   "      "   1.75
    "      "   Dessert   "      "      "      "      "      "   ......................   "      "   1.50
```

No. S 7.
Solid Sterling Silver Napkin Ring.
Price, each, $1.70.

No. S 8.
Solid Sterling Silver Napkin Ring.
Price, each, $1.00.

All orders for Solid Silverware amounting to $2.00 or over will be sent C. O. D., subject to examination. **No money in advance, express collect.** Under $2.00, cash in full must accompany your order.

OUR SILVERWARE DEPARTMENT.

Orders of $2.00 or more will be sent C. O. D., subject to examination, no money in advance, express collect. Under $2.00, cash in full must accompany your order.

No. S 25.
Silver Plated Fancy Tray.
Can be used for
Individual Butter Dish.
3 in. square.
Price, each, 10c.

No. S 26.
Silver Plated
Fancy Liberty Bell Tray.
Can be used for
Individual Butter Dish.
3 in. square.
Price, each, 10c.

No. S 27.
Silver Plated
Niagara Falls Tray.
Can be used for
Individual Butter Dish.
3 in. square.
Price, each, 10c.

No. S 28.
Silver Plated Tray.
Can be used for Individual Butter Dish.
Size, 3 in. diameter.
Price, each, 17c.

No. S. 29.
Silver Plated Trinket Tray,
Brooklyn Bridge,
6 in. long.
Price, each, 15c.

No. S. 30.
Fancy Whisk Broom and Holder,
Silver Plated Holder,
Silver Plated Handle.
Price, for Broom and Holder,
$1.10.

No. S. 31.
Silver Plated Trinket Tray,
Niagara Falls,
6 in. long.
Price, each, 15c.

No. S 32.
Silver Plated Lace Tray,
very beautiful ornament, richly decorated,
12 in. long.
Price, each, 25c

No. S 33.
Silver Plated Fan Tray,
very beautiful design,
7 in. long,
Price, each, 28c.

No. S. 34.
Silver Plated Picture Frame,
for cabinet photograph,
beautifully ornamented and
decorated. Size, 11 in. high,
8½ in. wide and very heavy.
Our special price, 90c. each.

No. S. 35.
Key Chains.
20 inches long, with patent fast-
eners at each end. Patent
lock link chain; very
nobby.
Polished Steel, price each, 10c.
" Brass, " " 15c.
" Nickel, " " 17c.
" Nickel Silver, " 25c.
Solid Aluminum, (all
the style) . . " 30c.

No. S. 36.
Silver Plated Salt and Pepper Set,
in satin lined box.
1 Silver Plated Jug Pepper,
1 Salt Dish Basket,
1 Shovel.
Price per set, 37c.

OUR SILVERWARE DEPARTMENT.

Orders of $2.00 or more will be sent C. O. D., subject to examination, no money in advance, express collect.   Under $2.00, cash in full must accompany your order.

No. S 9.
Slipper Cushion.
Silver Plated Slipper,
Plush Cushion,
6 in. long.
Price, each, 35c.

No. S 10.
Shoe Cushion.
Fancy Silver Plated Shoe,
Plush Cushion,
4 in. high.
Price, each, 18c.

No. S 11.
Hat Cushion.
Fancy Silver Plated
Hat, Plush Cushion,
4 in. high.
Price, each, 22c.

No. S 12.
Fancy Silver Plated Boot
Match Holder,
4 in. high.
Price, each, 16c.

No. S 13.
Barrel Cushion.
Fancy Silver Plated Barrel,
Plush Cushion,
4 in. high.
Price, each, 18c.

No. S 14.
Dolphin Cushion.
Fancy Silver Plated
Dpolhin, Plush Cushion,
4 in. high.
Price, each, 18c.

No. S. 15.
Basket Cushion.
Fancy Silver Plated
Basket, Plush Csh'n,
4 in. high.
Price, each, 18c.

No. S 16.
Child's Brownie Napkin
Ring.
Full sized napkin ring,
beautifully engraved, good
quality silver plate.
Price, each, 8c.

No. S 17.
Silver Plated Button Hook.
Engraved handle.   8 in. long.   In satin lined box.   Price, each, 16c.

No. S 18.
Fancy Silver Plated
Hat Match Holder.
4 in. high.
Price, each, 18c.

No. S 19.
Fancy Silver Plated
Bag Match Holder.
4 in. high.
Price, each, 18c.

No. S 20.
Baby Paper Weight.
Silver Plated, 3½ in.
long and heavy.
Price, each, 28c.

No. S 21.
Fancy Silver Plated Shoe
Match Holder.
4 in. high.
Price, each, 16c.

No. S 22.
Silver Plated Fan Tray.
Very beautiful design, 7 in. long.
Price, each, 25c.

No. S 23.
Hand Mirror.
Silver Plated, 9 in. long.
Price, each, 27c.

No. S 24.
Moon Mirror.
Silver Plated, 6 in. high.
Price, each. 27c.

OUR SILVERWARE DEPARTMENT.

Orders of $2.00 or more will be sent C.O.D., subject to examination, no money in advance, express collect.   Under $2.00, cash in full must accompany your order.

No. S 54.
National Souvenir Tea Spoons.
Good quality,
Price, per set of 6, in satin lined box, 60c.

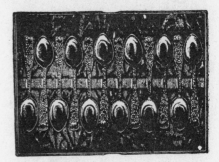

No. S 55.
Fine Quality Silver Plated Tea Spoons.
In fancy box.

Price, for 12 in box	$2.55
" " 6 "	1.55
" " 6 Table Spoons in box	2.55
" " 6 Forks in box	2.55
" " 6 Knives "	2.55

No. S 56.
Very Fine Quality Silver Plated Knives and Forks.
Beautifully finished, highly ornamented and fully warranted.
6 knives and 6 forks in beautiful case.
Price, per case, $2.95.
With plain handles, 30c. less.

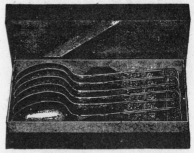

No. S 57.
Good Quality Silver Plated Spoons, in fancy box.

Price, for 6 Tea Spoons in box	29c.
" " 6 Table "	58c.
Better quality Tea's	49c.
" " Table's	98c.

No. S 58.
Extra Fine Quality Silver Plated Knives and Forks.
Beautifully finished and ornamented handles, warranted in every respect.
6 knives and 6 forks in a beautiful case.
Price, per case, $2.38.
With plain handles, 25c. less.

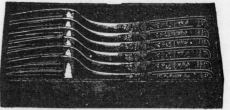

No. S 59.
Good Quality Silver Plated Forks.
In fancy box.

Price, for 6 Forks in box	$ .58
" " 6 " " better quality	.98
" " 6 Knives "	.65
" " 6 " " better quality	1.20

OUR SILVERWARE DEPARTMENT.

Orders of $2.00 or more will be sent C. O. D., subject to examination, no money in advance, express collect.   Under $2.00, cash in full must accompany your order.

No. S 46.
Child's 4-piece Set, in Plush Box.
1 Knife, 1 Fork, 1 Spoon and 1 Napkin Ring, all in beautiful plush case, made of plush, satinette lined, nickel clasps. Size, 4x8 in. Price, per set, 90c.

No. S 47.
Child's 4-piece Set, in Plush Case.
1 Knife, 1 Fork, 1 Spoon and 1 Napkin Ring, extra quality Triple Silver Plate, all in a beautiful plush case, made of plush, satinette lined, nickel clasps. Size, 4x8 in. Price, per set, $1.20.

No. S 48.
Child's 3-piece Set, in Satin Lined Box.
Extra quality triple silver plate, beautifully finished handles. 1 Knife, 1 Fork, 1 Spoon. Size of case, 4x8 in. Price, per set, 60c.

No. S 49.
Child's 3-piece Set, in Satin Lined Box.
Extra quality triple silver plate, beautifully finished handles. 1 Knife, 1 Fork, 1 Spoon. Size of case, 4x8 in. Price, per set, 85c.

No. S 50.
Fine Silver Plated Coffee Spoons. "Columbias."
Price, each, 1 in a fine box............ 10c.
      "   per set of 6, in one box.......... 42c.

No. S 51.
Child's 3-piece Set, in Satin Lined Box.
Extra good silver plate, fancy handles. Size of case, 3½x7 in. Price, per set, 30c.

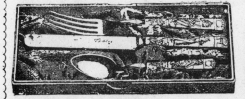

No. S 52.
Child's 3-piece Set in Satin Lined Box.
Extra quality triple silver plate, very fancy handles. Size of case, 4x8 in. Price, per set, 75c.

No. S 53.
Fine Quality Silver Plated Butter Knife and Sugar Shell, in Satin Lined Box.
Price, per box, 40c. Better quality, 75c.
Best quality made, $1.20.

OUR SILVERWARE DEPARTMENT.

Orders of $2.00 or more will be sent C. O. D., subject to examination, no money in advance, express collect.   Under $2.00, cash in full must accompany your order.

No. S 60.
Child's 3-piece Set.
Finest quality made. Best quadruple plated Knife, Fork and Spoon in an elegant heavy plush case.
Price, per set, $1.75.

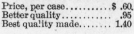

No. S 61.
Fine quality Silver Plated Butter Knife and Sugar Shell.
In plush case, satin lined.
Price, per case...........$ .60.
Better quality............ .95
Best quality made........ 1.40

No. S 62.
Silver Plated Fruit Knives.
In fine plush and satin lined case.
12 knives in case.
Price, per case.............. $2.50
Better quality................ 2.95
Finest quality............... 3.95

No. S 63.
Fine Quality Silver Plated Orange Spoon. "Columbus."
Price, each, 1 in a fine box, 12c.   Price, per set of 6 in one box, 55c.

No. S 64.
Fine Quality Silver Plated Sugar Shell. "Columbus."
Price, each, 1 in a fine box, 12c.

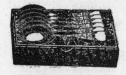

No. S 65.
Fine Quality Silver Plated Tea Spoons, in fancy box.
Price, per set of 6 Spoons....$ .60
Better quality................ .90
Set of 6 Table Spoons........ 1.20
Better quality............... 1.80

No. S 66.
Fine Quality Silver Plated Tea Spoons. "Columbus."
Price, each, 1 in a fine box, 12c. Per set of 6 in one box, 55c.
Per set of 6 Table Spoons. $1.10.

No. S 67.
Fine Quality Silver Plated Tea Spoons.
Very fancy pattern, as shown in cut.
Price, per set of 6, 62c.   Per set of 6 Table Spoons, $1.20.

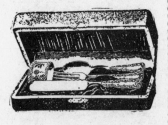

No. S 68.
Child's 4-piece Set.
Finest quality made. Best quadruple plated Knife, Fork, Spoon and Napkin Ring, in an elegant heavy plush case. This set would retail at $4.00.
Our price, per set, $1.95.

No. S 69.
Very Fancy Coffee Spoons.
Price, per set of 6 in very fancy silk plush and satin lined case, $1.45.

OUR SILVERWARE DEPARTMENT.

Orders of $2.00 or more will be sent C. O. D., subject to examination, no money in advance, express collect. Under $2.00, cash in full must accompany your order.

No. S 72.
27-piece Combination Silverware Set.
Consisting of

6 Silver Plated Knives.
6 " " Forks.
6 " " Table Spoons.
6 " " Tea Spoons.
1 " " Sugar Shell.
1 " " Butter Knife.
1 " " Napkin Ring.

Our price, common grade, per set..... $3.95
" better grade, " 4.80
" very fine grade, " 5.90

C. O. D. to anyone. No money in advance.

No. S 70.
Fine Quality Silver Plated Set.
Consisting of 6 Tea Spoons, 1 Sugar Shell, 1 Butter Knife.
In beautiful silk plush, satin lined case.
Price, per case, fair quality.....$ .85
" " better quality.... 1.40
" " extra fine quality. 1.85
" " best sect'n'l plate,
Wm. Rogers' 1846 ware....... 2.35

No. S 71.
Silver Plated Pickle Caster.
Warranted best quality triple plate.
Height, 12 inches.
Price, each, $1.25.

Knives, Forks, Table and Dessert Spoons.

We quote price per set of six, nicely wrapped in tissue paper:

TEA SPOONS.

	Plain Tipped Handles.	Fancy Pattern Handles.		Plain Tipped Handles.	Fancy Pattern Handles.
Common quality	$ .25	$ .25	Still finer quality	$ .70	$ .85
Better "	.40	.40	Best Wm. Rogers' 1846	1.50	1.75
Extra "	.60	.70			

TABLE SPOONS.

	Plain Tipped Handles.	Fancy Pattern Handles.		Plain Tipped Handles.	Fancy Pattern Handles.
Common quality	$ .50	$ .50	Still finer quality	$1.40	$1.70
Better "	.80	.80	Best Wm. Rogers' 1846	2.70	2.95
Extra "	1.20	1.40			

FORKS.

	Plain Tipped Handles.	Fancy Pattern Handles.		Plain Tipped Handles.	Fancy Pattern Handles.
Common quality	$ .55	$ ...	Still finer quality	$1.20	$1.35
Better "	.75	.85	Best Wm. Rogers' 1846	1.60	1.75
Extra "	.95	1.05			

KNIVES.

	Plain Tipped Handles.	Fancy Pattern Handles.		Plain Tipped Handles.	Fancy Pattern Handles.
Common quality	$ .75	$ ...	Still finer quality	$1.40	$1.60
Better "	.95	1.05	Best Wm. Rogers' 1846	1.70	1.95
Extra "	1.20	1.35			

OUR SILVERWARE DEPARTMENT.

Orders of $2.00 or more will be sent C.O.D., subject to examination, no money in advance, express collect. Under $2.00, cash in full must accompany your order.

No. S 37.
Silver Plated Nut Pick and
Cracker Set.
6 nut picks, 1 cracker, in paper box.
Price, per set, $1.05. Size, 4x6.

No. S 38.
Silver Plated Nut Pick Set.
6 nut picks in fancy paper box.
Price, per set, 38c.
Size, 3x5 in.

No. S 39.
Silver Plated Nut Pick Set.
6 nut picks in very fancy hardwood
case. Size, 3½x5½.
Price, per set, 95c.

No. S 40.
Four Piece Tea Set.
1 Tea Pot........9 in. high. | 1 Sugar Bowl....7 in. high.
1 Spoon Holder, 5 in. high. | 1 Cream Pitcher, 5 in. high.
Warranted best quality Triple Plate.
Retail price, $20.00. Our price, per set, $5.25.
C.O.D. to anyone. No money in advance.
A beautiful set, gold lined, hand engraved.

No. S 41.
Silver Plated Nut Pick and
Cracker Set.
6 nut picks, 1 cracker, in very fancy
hardwood case.
Price, per set, $1.75. Size, 4x6.

No. S 42.
Silver Plated Nut Pick and
Cracker Set.
6 nut picks, 1 cracker, in paper box.
Price, per set, 95c.
Size, 4x6.

No. S 43.
Four Piece Tea Set.

1 Tea Pot ....8 in. high.
1 Spoon Holder.........5 "   "
1 Sugar Bowl...........7 "   "
1 Cream Pitcher........5 "   "

Warranted best quality triple
plated, beautifully finished, hand
engraved and ornamented. This
set would retail at $20.00.
Our price, $5.75, C.O.D. to any-
one. No money in advance. You
pay express charges.

No. S 44.
Silver Plated Fruit Knives. Beautifully finished
and warranted. Per set of 6 knives, in
box, $1.20. Size of box, 5x7 in.

No. S 45.
Silver Plated Child's Set. Knife, Fork and Spoon,
in beautiful satin lined box. Size, 4x8 in.
Price, per set, 28c.

Finest Quality Quadruple Plated Ware.

These goods are the very finest quality made, warranted in every respect, and will wear a lifetime. There is nothing better made. They can only be found in the finest jewelry stores, and always at nearly, if not fully, double our price. **Every Article** listed under this head is guaranteed quadruple silver plated on best quality **Nickel Silver,** and in this class of goods we handle only goods of highest reputation, made by the largest and most reliable manufacturers.

OUR TERMS

On Silverware are alike on everything. **All Orders** amounting to $2.00 or over will be sent C. O. D., subject to examination, to anyone. No money in advance. You can examine the goods at express office, and if found perfectly satisfactory, pay the express agent our price and **express charges,** otherwise **refuse it,** and the express agent will return it at our expense.

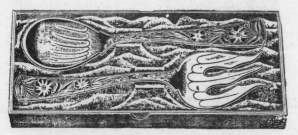

No. S 73.

			Plain Handle.	Fancy Handle.
Cream Ladle, in plush box		Price, each	$ .55	$ .65
Gravy " " "		" "	.70	.80
Oyster " " "		" "	1.40	1.70
Medium " " "		" "	1.90	2.10
Soup " " "		" "	1.95	2.15

No. S 74.
Napkin Ring. Fancy Chased.
Price, each, 38c.
Cut is ¼ size.

No. S 75.
Magnolia Salad Set, Silver or Old Silver, Gold Bowls.
Spoon and Fork in plush lined case, per set, $3.90.

No. S 76.
Napkin Ring. Fancy Chased.
Price, each, 46c.
Cut is ¼ size.

No. S 77.
Pie Knife, Silver or Old Silver.
In plush lined case, engraved blade. Price, $1.95.

No. S 78.
Napkin Ring. Fancy Chased.
Price, each, 51c.
Cut is ¼ size.

OUR SILVERWARE DEPARTMENT.

Orders of $2.00 or more will be sent C. O. D., subject to examination, no money in advance, express collect.   Under $2.00, cash in full must accompany your order.

No. S 92.
Lunch Caster.
Decorated China bottles,
gold lined napkin ring.
Price, each, $3.22.
Height, 7½ in.

No. S 93.
Lunch Caster.
Decorated China bottles,
very fancy.
Price, each, $3.25.
Height, 8 in.

No. S 94.
Lunch Caster.
Decorated.
Price, each, $1.48.
Height, 7 in.

No. S 95.
Puff Box, with French puff,
raised ornamented corru-
gated cover, all very fancy.
Price, per set, $1 45.
Cut is ¼ size.

No. S 96.
Silver Cup, Hand Made,
very fine, gold lined.
Price, each, $1.15.
Cut, ¼ size.

No. S 97.
Fancy Ink Stand, Cut Glass
bottle, very fancy ornamented
silver tray. Price, each, $1.15.
Cut, ⅛ size.

No. S 98.
Fancy Ink Stand, Cut
glass, beveled edge bottle
silver tray.
Price, each, 68c.
Cut, ⅛ size.

No. S 99.
Puff Box with French
puff, fancy celluloid.
fancy silver covered.
Price, per set, $1.75.
Cut, ¼ size.

No. S 100.
Card Receiver, Very Fancy Hand
Engraved and Ornamented.
Retail price, $4.50; our special price,
$2.45. Length, 8 in.

No. S 101.
Finest Ink Stand Handled.
Two very fancy cut glass ornamented bottles. Large ornamented
and decorated tray. Very
handsome design.
Price, each, $2.75. Cut, ⅛ size.

No. S 102.
Fancy Ink Stand.
Very fancy cut glass and
ornamented bottle. Beautiful
engraved and ornamented tray.
Price, each, $1.38. Cut, ⅛ size.

No. S 103.
Silver Plated Work Basket.
Very fancy design.
Retail price, $6.00.
Our special price, $3.75.
9 in. diameter.

No. S 104.
Baking Dish, Finest Quality Silver Plated.
Polished or Satin, as desired.
Removable porcelain lining.
Our special price, $5.95. Height, 5½ in.
Capacity, 7 half-pts; diameter lining, 9 in.

No. S 105.
Smoking Set, 3 pieces.
Bright cut, fancy engraved.
Gold lined, beautifully ornamented.
Price, per set, $4.65.
Size, 8 in. long, 5 in. high.

OUR SILVERWARE DEPARTMENT.

Orders of $2.00 or more will be sent C. O. D., subject to examination, no money in advance, express collect.   Under $2.00, cash in full must accompany your order.

No. S 79.

Cream Ladle in Plush lined box ....$ .60
Gravy   "   "   " 80
Oyster   "   "   " 1.70
Soup   "   "   " 2.25

Plain handles 15c. less.

No. S 80.
Napkin Ring.
Very Fancy.
Price, each, $1.05.
Cut is ¼ size.

No. S 81.
Napkin Ring.   Very Fancy.
Price, each. $1.05.
Cut is ¼ size.

No. S 82.
Napkin Ring.
Very Fancy.
Price, each, $1.28.
Cut is ¼ size.

No. S 83.
Napkin Ring.
Very Fancy.
Price, each, 98c.
Cut is ¼ size.

No. S 84.
Napkin Ring.
Beautifully Finished
and Engraved.
Price, each, 75c.
Cut is ¼ size.

No. S 85.
Napkin Ring.
Very Fancy.
Price, each, 95c.
Cut is ¼ size.

No. S 86.
Napkin Ring.   Very Fancy.
Price, each, 88c.
Cut is ¼ size.

No. S 87.
Napkin Ring.   Fancy Chased.
Price, each, 58c.
Cut is ¼ size.

No. S 88.
Napkin Ring.   Very Fancy.
Price, each, $1.35.
Cut is ¼ size.

No. S 89.
Napkin Ring.   Very Fancy.
Price, each, $1.45.
Cut is ½ size.

No. S 90.
Napkin Ring,
Very Fancy.
Price, each, $1.40.
Cut is ¼ size.

No. S 91.
Napkin Ring.   Very Fancy.
Price, each, $1.75.
Cut is ¼ size.

OUR SILVERWARE DEPARTMENT.

Orders of $2.00 or more will be sent C. O. D., subject to examination, no money in advance, express collect.   Under $2.00, cash in full must accompany your order.

No. S 117.
Pickle Caster.
Fancy bottle, nicely
finished.
Price, $1.45.   Height, 11 in.

No. S 119.
Berry or Fruit Dish.
Very fancy, hand engraved and ornamented.
Fancy ground, cut and ornamented glass.
Our special price, $7.20.   Height, 11 in.

No. S 118.
Pickle Caster.
Very fancy, engraved and ornamented, crystal bottles.
Price, each, $3.75.
Height, 12½ in.

No. S 120.
Pickle Caster.
Very fancy, engraved and
ornamented.
crystal bottle.
Price, each, $1.95.
Height, 12½ in.

No. S 122.
Berry or Fruit Dish.
Fancy, hand engraved and
ornamented.
Our special price, $5.60.
Height, 9 in.

No. S 121.
Pickle Caster.
Very fancy, engraved and ornamented.   Hand painted,
colored and ornamented glass.
Price, each, $3.40. Height, 11 in.

No. S 123.
Silver Plated Salver.
Very fancy, fancy border.
Our special price, $4.95.
Size, 12 in.

No. S 124.
Cake Basket.   Very beautiful.
Hand engraved and ornamented.
Hammered border and finish.
Our special price, $4.95.   Size, 9 in.

No. S 125.
Berry or Fruit Dish.
Very fancy, hand engraved and
ornamented.   Ornamented, ground
and colored glass.   Height, 9½ in.
Our special price, $3.65.

OUR SILVERWARE DEPARTMENT.

Orders of $2.00 or more will be sent C. O. D., subject to examination, no money in advance, express collect.   Under $2.00, cash in full must accompany your order.

No. S 106.
Bon Bon Dish.
Very fancy hand engraved and
ornamented.
Our special price, $1.95.
Height, 4½ in.

No. S 107.
Silver Cup.
Fancy engraved, gold lined.
Price, each, 90c.
Height, 4½ inches.

No. S 108.
Silver Cup.
Fancy engraved, bright cut.
Price, each, $1.85.
Height, 3½ inches.

No. S 109.
5 Bottle Caster.
Very fancy caster, beautifully ornamented and engraved by hand. Very fancy ornamented bottles.
Our special price, $4.50.
Height, 18 inches.
C. O. D. No money in advance.

No. S 110.
5 Bottle Caster.
Fancy Silver Plated, hand engraved. Fancy bottles.
Our Special price, $3.95.
Remember, all these goods are best quality, quadruple plate. None better made.
Height, 16 inches.
C. O. D. No money in advance.

No. S 111.
6 Bottle Caster.
Very fancy, engraved and embossed, highly finished and ornamented. The nicest caster handled. Very heavy base and all closed in; 6 large square cut and ground fancy bottles.
This caster would retail at $12.00 to $15.00.
Our special price is $6.45.
Height, 17 inches.
C. O. D. No money in advance.

No. S 112.
Pickle Caster.
Very fancy, engraved and ornamented; hand painted, colored and ornamented glass.
Price, each, $4.95.
Height, 13¾ inches.

No. S 113.
Silver Plated Bread Tray.
Beautiful design.
Retail price, $10.00.   Our special price, $4.95.
Length, 15 inches.

No. S 114.
Card Receiver.
Very fancy, hand engraved and ornamented.
Length, 8 inches. Retail price, $5.00.
Our special price, $2.95.

No. S 115.
Cake Basket.
Fancy engraved.
Our special price, $2.95.
Height, 11½ inches.

No. S 116.
Card Receiver.
Very fancy, hand engraved and ornamented.
Length, 7⅞ in. Retail price, $4.00.
Our special price, $1.91.

OUR SILVERWARE DEPARTMENT.

Orders of $2.00 or more will be sent C. O. D., subject to examination, no money in advance, express collect.   Under $2.00, cash in full must accompany your order.

No. S 126.
Berry or Fruit Dish
Very fancy hand engraved and
ornamented, figures on either
side, very fine glass, white on
inside and colored on outside
One of the most beautiful
dishes made.
Our special price, $8.35
Height, 12 in.

No. S 127.
Berry or Fruit Dish.
Very fancy hand engraved and
ornamented, fancy hand paint-
ed and ornamented glass, red
outside, white inside.
This dish would retail at
$12.00.
Our price, $6.95.
Height, 10 inches.

No. S 128.
Berry or Fruit Dish.
A work of art.
Finest imported French glass,
beautifully cut.
Our special price, $9.85.
Height, 10 inches.

No. S 129.
Berry or Fruit Dish.
Finest made.   It must be seen to be appreciated.
The frame is a work of art, beautifully finished,
and the bowl is imported, fancy colored and orna-
mented glass.   This piece would retail at $20.00.
Our special price, $12.85.
Height, 8 inches.

No. S 130.
Soup Tureen.
Very fancy, silver plated and ornamented.
Our special price, $7.95.
Height, 8 inches.   Capacity, 8 half-pints.

No. S 131.
Baking Dish.
Very fancy, engraved and ornamented.
With removable porcelain lining.
Our special price, $9.95.
Height, 7¾ inches.   Capacity, 9 half-pints.
Diameter of lining, 11½ inches.

No. S 132.
Baking Dish.
Fancy engraved Silver Plated, with removable
porcelain lining.
Our special price, $8.90.
Height, 7 inches.   Capacity, 9 half-pints
Diameter of lining, 11 inches.

OUR SILVERWARE DEPARTMENT.

Orders of $2.00 or more will be sent C. O. D., subject to examination, no money in advance, express collect. Under $2.00, cash in full must accompany your order.

No. S 138.
6-piece Tea Set.

Finest thing made. Nothing spared. You can't buy better. Every piece a work of art. Beautifully engraved, decorated and finished by hand. Gold lined throughout.

SIZE.

Coffee Pot	8½ inches high.	
Tea Pot	7 " "	
Hot Water Pot	6½ " "	
Sugar Bowl	7 " "	
Spoon Holder	6 " "	
Cream Pitcher	4½ " "	

OUR SPECIAL PRICE.

For Coffee Pot	$7.80
" Tea Pot	6.90
" Hot Water Pot	7.50
" Sugar Bowl	4.35
" Spoon Holder	4.50
" Cream Pitcher	4.95

We furnish the complete set of six pieces for $34.95. C. O. D. to anyone. No money in advance.

No. S 139.
Baking Dishes.

Fancy engraved, silver plated, satin finish, with removable porcelain lining.
Our special price, $6.95.
Height, 6 in.   Capacity, 9 half pints.
Diameter of lining, 10 in.

No. S 140.
4-piece Water Set.

Nothing better made. Latest style and fanciest design in market.

12-in. hand engraved Tray | 9-in. hand engraved Pitcher
7-in. " " Goblet | 4-in. " " Slop Bowl
Gold lined.
Our special price, $19.85.

No. S 141.
4-piece Tea Set.

Best quality quadruple plate made. Latest style border and finish. Hand engraved throughout. Very fancy. Gold lined throughout.

SIZE.

Tea Pot	8 inches high.	
Cream Pitcher	6 " "	
Spoon Holder	6 " "	
Sugar Bowl	6 " "	

OUR SPECIAL PRICE.

For Tea Pot	$3.90
" Sugar Bowl	2.45
" Cream Pitcher	1.95
" Spoon Holder	1.90

We furnish the complete set of four pieces for $9.25. C. O. D. to anyone. No money in advance.

No. S 142.
Butter Dish.

Finest we handle. One of the finest made. Square corners, very handsomely engraved, finished and decorated by hand. Silver plated drainer.
Our special price, $4.95.

SIZE.

6 inches long.
5 " high.

OUR SILVERWARE DEPARTMENT.

Orders of $2.00 or more will be sent C.O.D., subject to examination, no money in advance, express collect. Under $2.00, cash in full must accompany your order.

No. S 143,

5-Piece Tea Set.

Best quality quadruple plate made. Money can't buy better. All hand engraved on both sides. Gold lined.

SIZES:

Tea Pot.........7 inches high.   Cream Pitcher....6 inches high.
Sugar Bowl.......6 "   "   Spoon Holder.....6 "   "
Butter Dish............................6 "   "

OUR SPECIAL PRICES:

For Tea Pot...............$3.00 ' For Cream Pitcher $1.50
" Sugar Bowl .... 2.00   " Spoon Holder 1.50
" Butter Dish.. 2.25

We furnish the complete set of 5 pieces for $9.45.

Remember, all orders for Silverware amounting to $2.00 or over will be sent C. O. D., subject to examination. No money in advance.

No. S 144.

Butter Dish.

Very fancy, hand engraved and ornamented.
With silver plated Drainer.
Our special price, $3.45.
Height, 7 inches.

No. S 145.

Butter Dish.

Very fancy, hand engraved and ornamented.
With silver plated Drainer.
Our special price, $2.95.
Height, 6½ inches.

No. S 146.

4-Piece Water Set.

Nothing better made.

12 inch hand engraved Tray.   7 inch hand engraved Goblet.
9 "   "   "   Pitcher.   4 "   "   "   Slop Bowl.
Gold lined.
Regular retail price, $30.00.
Our special price, $14.95.

OUR SILVERWARE DEPARTMENT.

Orders of $2.00 or more will be sent C. O. D., subject to examination, no money in advance, express collect.   Under $2.00, cash in full must accompany your order.

No. S 133.
4-Piece Tea Set.

Best quality quadruple plate made. Hand engraved, throughout. Gold lined.
Sizes—Teapot, 8 inches high ; Cream Pitcher, 6 in. high ; Spoon Holder, 6 in. high ; Sugar Bowl, 6 in. high.
Our Special Prices:
For Tea Pot, $4.40 ; Sugar Bowl......... $2.75 ; Cream Pitcher...... $2.25 ; Spoon Holder, $2.25.
We furnish the complete set of 4 pieces for $10.95.
C. O. D. to anyone.   No money in advance.

No. S 134.
Water (Ice) Pitcher.
Beautifully finished, porcelain lined,
hand engraved and ornamented.
Our special price, $6.95
Height, 11 inches.

No. S 135.
Water (Ice) Pitcher.
Beautifully finished, hand engraved
and ornamented, porcelain lined.
Our special price, $9.45.
Height, 13 inches.

No. S 136.
4-Piece Water Piece.
Nothing better made.
12 inch hand engraved Tray ; 9 inch hand
engraved Pitcher ; 7 inch hand engraved
Goblet ; 4 inch hand engraved
Slop Bowl. Gold lined.
Regular retail price, $30.00.
Our special price, 17.35.

No. S 137.
4-Piece Water Set.
Nothing better made.
12 inch hand engraved Tray ; 9 inch hand
engraved Pitcher ; 7 inch hand engraved
Goblet ; 4 inch hand engraved
Slop Bowl. Gold lined.
Our special price, $18.90.

OUR
CLOCK DEPARTMENT.

We offer in this Department a complete variety of high grade Clocks, made by manufacturers of the highest reputation; goods we can guarantee in every respect, and **at prices heretofore unheard of.**

OUR TERMS.

We will send Clocks by express C. O. D., subject to examination, to anyone anywhere. On some we require a small deposit as a guarantee of good faith, the balance to be paid at express office after you have examined the Clock and found it satisfactory.

ON OUR LEADERS Clocks, we are pushing the sale of, and handling in immense quantities, **we require no money** in advance, but send C. O. D. to anyone. **No money in advance.** You can examine it at express office, and, if found perfectly satisfactory, pay the express agent **our price and express charges,** and the Clock is yours; **otherwise, PAY NOTHING,** and the agent will return it at our expense.

YOU CAN TELL under the description of each Clock whether a deposit is required or not, and how much, as we state plainly in each case. We can save you 100 per cent. on Clocks.

No. T 1.

No. T 2.   No. T 3.   No. T 4.

AN $8.00 CLOCK FOR $2.75.

(ONE DAY.)

This clock cannot be duplicated in any retail store for less than $8.00.

Silver plated, highly ornamented, fancy dial, 13 inches high, 9 inches wide, easel rest. This clock is a work of art.

A LEADER AT $2.75.

C. O. D. to anyone. No money in advance.
The greatest bargain we have.

YOUR CHOICE FOR $3.25.

THEY ARE ALL LEADERS.

We will send you any one C. O. D., subject to examination. No money in advance. If found perfectly satisfactory, pay the express agent $3.25, and **express charges;** otherwise, **pay nothing,** and the agent will return it **at our expense.**

DESCRIPTION.

Fancy silver plated, best quality, first-class lever movement. They are works of art.

Height, 10 inches.

Special Clock Bargains.

NICKEL ALARM CLOCK FOR 75 CTS.

Retails at $1.50 to $2.00.

Cash in full must accompany all orders for this clock. **GUARANTEED** a first-class nickel alarm clock. Good time keeper and a rare bargain. **DIAL IS 4 INCHES.** Our special price 75 cents. **POSTAGE 25 CENTS EXTRA,** if to be sent by mail.

No. T 22.

$2.15 Buys a $5.00 Clock

DESCRIPTION.—Nickel or gold plated as desired. Visible movement, can be seen through the plate glass, very fine, white enameled dial, with second hand. Stands on a frame with 4 legs. One day lever movements; 2 inch dial; height 2¼ inches; smallest lever clock made. **MOVEMENT** is beautifully finished, and warranted an accurate time keeper. Cut to left shows clock out of case; cut to right shows clock in case.

CASE for traveling is made of fine morrocco, beautifully finished, with handle as shown in cut.

No. T 23.
This Cut shows Clock in case.

No. T 23.
This Picture shows Clock out of case.

OUR SPECIAL PRICE, without Case, - - - **$ 2.15**
"   "   "   with   " complete, - - **2.65**

TERMS C. O. D. to any one. No money in advance. Examine the clock at express office, and if found Satisfactory, **PAY THE AGENT** our price and express charges. Otherwise, **PAY NOTHING.**

Genuine Onyx Clock for $2.35.

RETAILS EVERYWHERE FOR $6.00. IS A THING OF BEAUTY.

Beautiful ornament, perfect time keeper, and a wonderful bargain. Three inches high, 2 inch dial, dial white enameled, beveled edge, French crystal. **FRAME IS WARRANTED GENUINE ONYX,** white or colored, beautifully finished or polished. **IT WILL COST YOU NOTHING** to see and examine this clock. We will send it to anyone anywhere C. O. D., subject to examination. **NO MONEY IN ADVANCE.** **$2.35** and express charges to be paid at express office.

No. T 24.

$3.95 BUYS A $10.00 CLOCK.

CLOCK AND TRAVELING CASE COMPLETE.

Smallest Striking Clock Made.   Bargain of Bargains.

DESCRIPTION.—Gold or silver plated as desired, visible movement, beveled edge French plate glass on both sides. **WHITE ENAMELED DIAL. PATENT STRIKING.** Strikes hour and half hours, impossible to strike wrong. Beautifully finished movement. **CLOCK STANDS ON FOUR LEGS.** Is 4½ inches high, 3 inches wide, 2 inch dial. **TRAVELING CASE** is made of fine imitation morrocco, **CANNOT BE TOLD FROM MORROCCO.** Made with telescope, slide, handles and all complete. **OUR SPECIAL PRICE** for Clock and case complete, $3.95. C. O. D. to any one. No money in advance.

T 25. This picture shows Clock out of Case.

T 25.
This picture shows Clock in Case.

No. T 5.
FANCY SILVER PLATED CLOCK.

Our silver plated clocks are all of the very best quality quadruple silver plate, and warranted. **THIS CLOCK** is a most beautiful pattern, full engraved and ornamented by hand. Fancy easel. Height, 10 inches. Retail price, $7.50.

OUR SPECIAL PRICE, $3.75.

A LEADER. C. O. D. No money in advance.

No. T 6.
FANCY SILVER PLATED CLOCK.

Height, 10 inches. Retail Price, $8.00.

OUR SPECIAL PRICE, $4.95.

A LEADER. C. O. D. No money in advance. **Understand.** These are not nickel clocks, but the highest grade quadruple silver plate, warranted, and will wear a lifetime.

No. T 7.
A $6.00 CLOCK FOR $2.45.
(ONE DAY.)

This clock cannot be duplicated in any retail store for less than $6.00. Silver plated, highly ornamented. 7 inches high.

A LEADER AT $2.45.
C. O. D. No money in advance.

No. T 8.
FANCY SILVER PLATED CLOCK.

Fancy easel. Hand engraved and ornamented, Height, 10 inches. Retail price, $6.00.

Our Special Price, $2.95.

A LEADER.
No money in advance.

No. T 9.
QUADRUPLE SILVER PLATE.
A thing of beauty. Stylish pattern, full hand engraved, on easel. Height, 10 in. Retail price, $8.00.

Our Special Price, $4.95.

A LEADER. C. O. D. to anyone. No money in advance.

LOOK AT OUR PRICES.
70c. for a $2.00 CLOCK.

READ! READ!

Wood frame clock, imitation mahogany. One day. Good time keeper.

Our Special Cut Price, 70c.

No. T 10.

Extra for alarm, 25 cents. Dial, 5 inches. Height, 11 inches.

AT 70 CENTS.

Cash in full must accompany all orders for this clock. This clock retails at $1.50 to $2.00. **We cut price to 70c.**

No. T 11.

Best Silver Plated.

A work of art.

Hand engraved and ornamented.

Height, 9 inches.

Retail price, $9.00.

OUR SPECIAL PRICE, **$4.95**

A LEADER.

C. O. D. No money in advance.

BLACK WALNUT OR ANTIQUE OAK.

 $2.75 Buys a $7.00 Clock.

READ. This beautiful clock is furnished with either solid black walnut or antique oak case, nicely carved and ornamented. Size: Dial, 6 inches; height, 22 inches.

OUR PRICE.

One day, strike $2.75
Eight-day, half-hour strike........................... 3.50
Eight-day, half-hour strike, gong 3.80
Alarm, extra, 30c.

TERMS.—C. O. D. on receipt of $1.00, balance to be paid at express office.

No. T 12. **No charge** for boxing or shipping.

BLACK WALNUT OR ANTIQUE OAK.

 $2.95 Buys an $8.00 Clock.

C. O. D. to any one, on receipt of **ONE DOLLAR**, as a guarantee of good faith, balance to be paid at express office if found satisfactory.

DON'T PAY THREE PRICES for a clock. **We will save you one-half** on every clock.

DESCRIPTION.

Solid black walnut or antique oak case, as desired, beautifully engraved and ornamented. Very fine grade movement, **Warranted as a timekeeper.** Size: Dial, 6 inches; height, 24 inches (a very large clock).

OUR PRICES.

One-day, strike...................................... $2.95
Eight-day, half-hour strike........................... 3.75
Eight-day, half-hour, gong strike..................... 4.15
Extra for alarm, 30c.

No. T 13.

WONDER · OF · THE · AGE.

RETAILS AT $12.00.

OUR PRICE TO ALL, $4.95.

GRANDEST BARGAIN EVER OFFERED.

JUST READ. An eight-day, half hour strike, calendar, thermometer and barometer—**all combined** in a 24-inch high clock—for $4.95. **Nothing like it ever heard of before.** Read

DESCRIPTION.

This Clock is furnished with solid black walnut or antique oak case as desired, beautifully carved, ornamented and decorated; in fact, it is a work of art. Very large, 24 inches high; dial, 6 inches. One of the best clock movements made, warranted an accurate timekeeper. Will last a lifetime. **A most perfect calendar**, showing day of month, working automatically and always correct **A perfect thermometer** on one side, beautifully finished. **A perfect barometer** on one side, giving condition of atmosphere, correctly indicating the weather probabilities.

No. T 14. **THIS CLOCK RETAILS EVERYWHERE FOR $12.00.**

OUR OFFER IS: Send us **ONE DOLLAR** as a guarantee of good faith and we will send it to you C. O. D., subject to examination. If found satisfactory, pay the express agent the balance of $3.95 and express charges. We furnish this clock with eight-day, half-hour strike. (Cannot be fitted with alarm.)

BLACK WALNUT OR ANTIQUE OAK.

RETAILS AT $6.00 TO $8.00.

Our Special Cut Price, $3.95.

C. O. D. to anyone on receipt of **ONE DOLLAR** as a guarantee of good faith, balance, $2.95, and express charges, to be paid at express office.

═══ DESCRIPTION. ═══

Eight-day, half-hour strike, gong. Size: Height, 16 inches; dial, 5½ inches. American white dial, Roman or Arabic figures, or American gilt dial, Arabic figures, as desired. Case is very massive, beautifully finished, carved and ornamented. Movement is a perfect timekeeper and so warranted. No alarm furnished to this clock.

No. T 15.

SOLID CHERRY OR ANTIQUE OAK.

A WORK OF ART.

ONE OF THE MOST BEAUTIFUL CLOCKS MADE.

RETAIL PRICE, $8.00 to $10.00.

OUR SPECIAL PRICE, $4.95.

C. O. D. to anyone. **ONE DOLLAR** in advance, balance, $3.95, and express charges, payable at express office.

═══ DESCRIPTION. ═══

Eight-day, half-hour strike, gong. Size: Height, 16 inches; dial, 5½ inches; fine hand carved and decorated cherry or antique oak case. Very fancy dial, ornamented. Fancy pendulum, visible.

All clocks are shipped from Chicago carefully packed and boxed, for which **we make no charge.**

No. T 16.

IMITATION MARBLE CLOCK.

Cannot be Told in Appearance from the Finest French Marble,

GOLD PLATED TRIMMINGS AND ORNAMENTATIONS.

This Clock Retails at $10.00 Everywhere.

OUR • SPECIAL • PRICE, • $4.95.

C. O. D. to anyone. **No Money in Advance.**

No. T 17.

THIS IS A LEADER. Costs you nothing to see it. Costs you nothing to examine it.

We will send it to you by express, C. O. D., subject to examination. **Don't send us a cent in advance.** You can examine it at the express office, and if found perfectly satisfactory, pay the express agent **$4.95** and express charges and it is yours; **otherwise pay nothing,** and the agent will return it at our expense.

DESCRIPTION.
Imitation French marble, made from polished wood to so closely resemble marble that it can only be detected in the weight, **beautiful brocatel, gold plated ornamentations.** Eight-day, half-hour strike, beautiful gong, Star movement (guaranteed as a timekeeper). Size: Height, 11¾ inches; length, 10 inches; dial, 5½ inches. Roman or Arabic figures, as desired.

NO MONEY IN ADVANCE. COSTS NOTHING TO SEE IT.

IMITATION BLACK MARBLE.

OUR SPECIAL PRICE, $4.75.

C. O. D. to anyone anywhere on receipt of $1.00, balance, $3.75, and express charges to be paid at express office after you examine the clock.

DESCRIPTION.

Polished wood, imitation black marble, cannot be told from marble, gilt engraved, eight-day, half-hour strike, gong, Star movement. **Size.**—Height, 9⅜ inches; length, 10⅛ inches; dial, 5⅛ inches. Very fancy dial; Roman or Arabic figures, as desired.

No. T 18.

IMITATION BLACK MARBLE.

Our Special Price, $6.75.

C. O. D. to anyone on receipt of $1.00, balance, $5.75, and express charges payable at express office.

RETAILS AT $15.00 TO $20.00.

DESCRIPTION. Black marble frame, fancy white marble pillars, gold plated trimmings, eight-day, half-hour strike, gong, Star movement. **Size.**—Height, 10⅜ inches; length, 16 inches; dial, 5⅛ inches. Fancy Roman or Arabic dial, as desired.

No. T 19.

IMITATION BLACK MARBLE.

Retails Everywhere at $15. OUR SPECIAL PRICE, $7.25.

C. O. D. to anyone on receipt of $1.00, balance, $6.25, and express charges to be paid to the express agent after you have examined the clock.

DESCRIPTION.

Black marble frame, white marble trimmings and pillars, gold plated legs and trimmings, 8-day, half-hour strike, gong, Star movement. Warranted as a time keeper. **Size.**—Length, 17 inches; height, 11¼ inches; dial, 5⅛ inches. Roman or Arabic figures on dial, as desired.

No. T 20.

IMITATION BLACK MARBLE.

Retails Everywhere at $15.00.

Our Special Price, $7.95.

THE FINEST CLOCK WE HANDLE.

Sent C. O. D. to anyone on receipt of $1.00, balance, $6.95, and express charges payable at express office.

DESCRIPTION.

Black marble frame, white marble trimmings, gold plated legs and ornamentations, eight-day, half-hour strike, gong, Star movement. Warranted as a time keeper. **Size.**—Length, 18 inches; height, 12 inches; dial, 5½ inches. Roman or Arabic figures, as desired.

No. T 21.

SEWING MACHINE HEADQUARTERS!

WE SAY HEADQUARTERS because we honestly believe we are prepared to furnish sewing machines direct to familes, *for less money*, than any other concern in existance.

We added sewing machines to our business believing the large masses were opposed to paying the enormously high prices charged by country dealers, and that they would place their orders direct if a thoroughly reliable house, with an established reputation, would offer a line of machines equal to the very best made and at a LOW PRICE.

It has been a Grand Success.
Our old customers began patronizing us from the start. Many so-called manufactures, agents, etc., (some of them unreliable) have been advertising sewing machines at various prices, but in nearly every case the question of RELIABILITY came up; people knew nothing about them. When we started **ALL THIS WAS CHANGED,** our reputation had been long established in the watch business, we were well known in nearly every city, town and hamlet in the United States, being incorporated under the laws of the State of Minnesota with a cash capital paid in full of $75,000.00, any bank or financial institution could tell of our responsibility. We refer to any commercial agency, any bank in the United States, or you can ask any express agent anywhere about us. Nearly every agent knows and can tell you of our reliability, or any stranger not feeling absolutely safe can, if he chooses, send his order and money to the Union National Bank, Minneapolis, Minn., with instructions not to turn it over to us unless they know us to be thoroughly reliable, or they can send for our big book of testimonials, thus convince the most skeptic that we are not only reliable but will in all cases carry out our every promise to the word and letter.

THAT'S WHAT PEOPLE WANT FIRST CONFIDENCE!

We believe we establish that in every case. Next, **Do You Need a Machine?** If so, we are now prepared to supply you at a great saving. We not only claim our prices lower than any other house but with our 10 year binding guarantee for the workmanship and quality of our machine, we also include a guarantee the machine shall be in every respect exactly as represented, and the price less than the same grade is sold by any other house.

WE HAVE MANY ADVANTAGES
over other houses. We do not depend on machines alone for our support, on the contrary, our sales of over 300 watches daily comprises the bulk of business; and by utilizing the one clerical force to attend to the office work of both sewing machines and watches we save the salaries of many clerks. **WE SELL FOR CASH,** no bad debts, no traveling men's salaries or big hotel bills to pay, no poor notes, no collections, no interest. Our customers pay the actual cost to manufacture with the smallest profit added consistant with a thoroughly safe, honest and reliable business.

PLAIN TALK.

How much ough I to pay for a first-class serviceable Sewing Machine, complete with all the latest attachments? Put this question to your friends, individually, and you will be surprised to learn how little they know about the actual value of Sewing Machines. The majority of them will tell you they secured theirs from an agent, hence at *exorbitant* prices.

The sale of sewing machines is conducted so expensively under the agency system that it is impossible for the purchaser to secure a good machine without paying double what he ought.

Consider the expense of maintaining an army of Officers, General Managers and Managers of lesser degree, together with a legion of Agents, Sub-Agents, Offices and Branch Offices, Canvassers, Wagons, Horses, etc., and the few sales each agent makes. This extravagant system of selling machines, canvassing from house to house, *costs more than it does to manufacture the machine itself*. All these wasteful expenses compel a price that is in most cases more than double what we ask for a Sewing Machine equally as handsome and really superior in mechanism and durability. In no other kind of business is such a false system maintained. It is a shame to those manufacturers whose Sewing Machines cannot be sold without resorting to such wasteful methods. It is to be expected that those who profit by these devices will join in defaming us because we strike at the system which makes such plundering of purchasers possible. Agents for high-priced machines will try to make you believe all sorts of stories concerning our Machines. **Beware of them!** Do not allow their falsehoods to influence you. By taking advantage of our economical system you pay **one profit only,** viz: The manufacturers, and therefore you get them at strictly guaranteed factory cost. This is a progressive age, and you will find it a wise policy to investigate, as far as possible, every new departure. In this case you may satisfy yourself as to the truth of our statements at the cost of very little time and trouble. We invite a comparison of our Sewing Machines with others, and to make comparison before purchasing possible we will ship by freight any style of our Minnesota Sewing Machine to anyone, anywhere in the United States, *at wholesale price*, and allow all purchasers the privilege of **10 Days FREE Trial in Their Own Homes.** This is an unparalleled offer, and one which clearly demonstrates our fearless method of conducting business. Consider this privilege carefully, and avail yourself of it before paying exorbitant Agents' prices.

DEALERS AND AGENTS.

In their efforts to prevent our making sales, unprincipled dealers and agents often advise purchasers not to test our Machines. This is mistaken advice, because you take no responsibility until you examine the Machine in your own home, and if it is not as represented, you return it to us at our expense. Dealers buy from the manufacturers, and must take such machines as are sent, and they must sell them without regard to quality, and to those who are not well informed they must give the poorest and keep the best ones for more critical customers. We cannot favor one above the other, but must send *PERFECT MACHINES TO ALL*. Our Machines must speak for themselves — the agent can hide the defects of his — we must send you one so good that its superiority is apparent. It will pay you to consider carefully which system will produce the most perfect Machine and give the greatest assurance of satisfaction.

OUR TERMS, CONDITIONS, ETC.

WE WILL SHIP ANY MACHINE ON 10 DAYS TRIAL FREE! No Money in Advance. You needn't send one cent.

Select the machine you want, write your order plainly and then get some banker, merchant or express agent to endorse your order saying you will do exactly as you agree, or if you prefer, give us the names of three reliable parties who know you, we will write to them and if they answer favorable we will send you the machine by freight. You can **use it 10 days** and then if entirely satisfactory send us the money, otherwise return it **at our expense.**

THE BEST WAY

Is to send cash with your order, it is just as safe, you take no risk for we will return your money if you are not perfectly satisfied. **BESIDES,** where cash in full accompanies your order, **WE WILL SEND AN EXTRA DOUBLE SET OF ATTACHMENTS FREE. FURTHER,** where cash in full accompanies the order we always send free as a gift some nice and useful present.

BEAR IN MIND, You take no risk as our binding 10 years guarantee covers everything and protects you always.

SEARS, ROEBUCK & CO.

IMPROVED LOW-ARM SINGER!

These machines are made after the latest models of the Singer Mfg. Co.'s machines, and are perfect fac-similes of their machines in shape, ornamentation and appearance, with the exception of the lettering on the arm of machine, and the trade mark. All the parts are make to gauge exactly the same as the Singer Co.'s parts, and are constructed respectively of precisely the same materials. The utmost care is exercised in the selection of the metals used, and only the very best quality is purchased. Each machine is thoroughly well made and is fitted with the utmost nicety and exactness, and no machine is permitted by the inspector to go out of the shops until it has been fully tested and proved to do perfect work, and run light and without noise.

NOTE.—Self-Threading Shuttle. Only used in the Improved Singer Sewing Machine. A perfect STEEL SHUTTLE with delicate and perfect tension opened to allow the bobbin to be inserted without displacing any part of the shuttle; holds more thread than any other Singer machine shuttle; runs loose in shuttle with spring center and point bearings, thus insuring an even tension and all annoyance resulting from shuttle thread breaking while the machine is in motion, which is common to many machines, is entirely obviated.

The Stand is among the handsomest in design. Finely japanned. Has large drive wheel. It rests on four castors and can be easily moved. The treadle is set on anti-friction bearings that run light and never need oil, thus saving the carpet from grease and spots. The dress-guard over band wheel is large and protects the operator's dress from oil.

With Every Machine is Furnished Registered Warranty for Ten Years. Any Machine not Satisfactory can be Returned and Money will be Refunded. Where can you buy a Machine on more Favorable Terms?

COMPLETE SET OF BEST ATTACHMENTS WITH EACH MACHINE WITHOUT EXTRA CHARGE, AS MENTIONED HEREON.

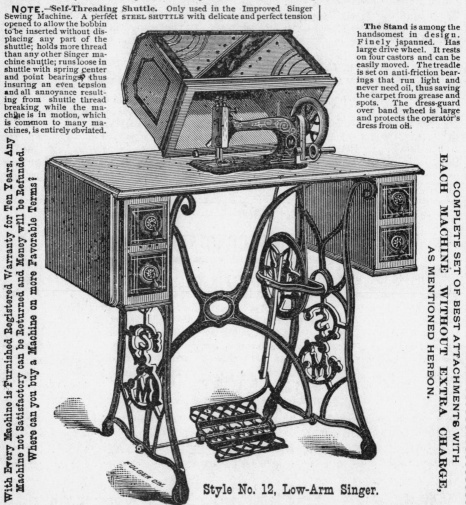

Style No. 12, Low-Arm Singer.

								Price,	
No. 10, Low-Arm Singer, with one Drawer, no Cover,								Price, $	8.50
No. 11,	"	"	"	"	"	and Cover,		"	10.00
No. 12,	"	"	"	3 Drawers and Cover,				"	11.90
No. 13,	"	"	"	5	"	"	"	"	12.90
No. 14,	"	"	"	7	"	"	"	"	13.90

READ AND REFLECT.

Ornamented Head, Nickel-Plated Balance Wheel, Handsome Oil-Polished Best Walnut or Oak Woodwork of latest design; Gothic Cover, with Beautiful Veneered Panels, Convenient

Drawers, with Nickel Plated Drop-Ring Handels and Good Locks; Iron Stand and Castors as Illustrated above, with all the attachments.

The Singer is a perfect working Sewing Machine in every particular. It is finely finished, the wood being of the best seasoned walnut or oak, and the greatest care is exercised in the manufacture of each part. Money will be refunded if not just as represented.

Remember, The Singer is not a cheap machine in quality, but in price.. Our great reduction in prices is to increase the demand for our goods.

QUICK SALES AND SMALL PROFITS

are the proper principles on which to do business, and we are determined to see how much the people will appreciate it.

Each machine is nicely packed in a wooden crate, free of charge, also the following attachments free accompany.

Each machine, of whatever style, is furnished with the following equipment of tools and accessories:

One Foot Hemmer, One Screw Driver, One Wrench, One Oil Can and Oil, One Gauge, One Extra Throat Plate, One Extra Check Spring, One Package of Needles, Six Bobbins and One Instruction Book. *In addition to the above we furnish with each machine an EXTRA SET OF ATTACHMENTS, FREE OF CHARGE, consisting of the following:* **One Tucker, One Foot Ruffler, One Set of Plain Hemmers, 5 different widths up to 7-8 of an inch, One Binder and One Thread Cutter.**

When ordering give plain shipping directions, giving the Town, County and State, the number and of price of the machine, and where to ship machine. You can send money by P. O. Money Order, Registered Letter or Bank Draft, either of which is perfectly safe.

REMEMBER where Cash in Full Accompanies your Order
WE WILL SEND YOU FREE AN EXTRA

double set of attachments; we will also send free some nice present.

BEAR IN MIND by the conditions of our binding 10 years' guarantee you are absolutely safe as you can return the machine at any time and have your money refunded.

REMEMBER we also send machines freight collect, and allow **ten days trial** free, no money in advance.

Read What the People Say!

"I CANNOT FIND ANY FAULT WITH IT."

MACON, MISSISSIPPI.

Gents.— This is to say, your machine does just as you recommended it. I cannot find any fault with it by any means. If the second one does as well as the first one I will be perfectly satisfied. Every one who has seen the machine likes it very much. There is nothing short about it that I can see. It does all you claim for it. Everybody in our town is "stuck" on your machine.

Yours truly, G. L. CONNER.

"AMPLY WORTH THE MONEY."

CANTON, KANSAS.

Gents.— The machine has now been in use for two years and has given perfect satisfaction in every respect, and is amply worth the money paid for it. If all your goods are as straight as your sewing machines, you deserve every success in your business, and have my best wishes for same.

Yours truly, F. H. McCLELLAN,

Agt. C. R. I. & P. Ry. and U. S. Express.

"WIFE THINKS IT SPLENDID. LIGHT RUNNING."

BLANKET, TEXAS.

Gents.— I purchased a machine of you about eighteen months ago. My wife thinks it splendid. In fact, it does as nice work as machines of a higher price, is light to work and does not take as much power to run it as those of a higher price. It is as good now as on the day of purchase. Respectfully yours, DR. D. P. COBB, M. D.

"WILL DO ALL I CAN TO HELP YOU."

BEACH CHESTERFIELD, VIRGINIA.

Gents.— I received the sewing machine I ordered of your house Sept. 20, 1890, and am well pleased with it. It has given perfect satisfaction. I am also well pleased with your way of doing business, and will do all I can to help you. Yours truly, J. R. ELDER.

"FULL SATISFACTION IN EVERY SHAPE AND FORM."

WAHL, WASHINGTON.

Gents.— I was pleased with the sewing machine I bought from you about eighteen months ago. I take pleasure in saying that the machine reached me in good order, and gives full satisfaction in every shape and form. I will recommend your house to all who are in need of a machine or any article you may carry in your business. Respectfully, AUGUST KUEHNVEL.

IMPROVED HIGH-ARM SINGER!

NOTE.—Self-Threading Shuttle. Only used in our Improved Singer Sewing Machine. A perfect **steel shuttle** with delicate and perfect tension, opened to allow the bobbin to be inserted without displacing any parts of the shuttle; holds more thread than any other Singer machine shuttle; runs loose in shuttle with spring center and point bearings, thus insuring an even tension and all annoyance resulting from shuttle thread breaking while the machine is in motion, which is common to many machines, is entirely obviated.

NOTE.—The Stand is among the handsomest in design. Finely japanned. Has large drive wheel. It rests on four castors and can be easily moved. The treadle is set on anti-friction bearings that run light and never need oil, thus saving the carpet from grease and spots. The dress-guard over band wheel is large and protects the operator's dress from oil.

With every Machine is Furnished Registered Warranty for Ten Years. Any Machine not Satisfactory can be Returned, and Money will be Refunded.

WHERE CAN YOU BUY A MACHINE ON MORE FAVORABLE TERMS?

Automatic Bobbin Winder and Complete Set of Best Attachments with Each Machine Free of Charge as Mentioned Hereon.

STYLE No. 14, HIGH-ARM SINGER.

Ornamented Head, Nickel Plated Balance Wheel, Handsome Oil-Polished BEST Walnut or Oak Woodwork of Latest Design; Gothic Cover, with Beautiful Veneered Panels; Convenient Drawers, with Nickel-Plated Drop Ring Handles, Good Locks, Iron Stand and Castors, with all the attachments.

Style No. 12, High-Arm Singer, with 3 Drawers and Cover, Price, $13.25
Style No. 13,   "   "   " 5 "   "   "   " 14.25
Style No. 14,   "   "   " 7 "   "   "   " 15.25

THE CABINET WORK OF ALL OUR MACHINES IS OF ELEGANT OIL POLISH, BEST WALNUT OR OAK OF THE LATEST DESIGN, WITH GOTHIC COVER.

The above cut represents our No. 14, High-Arm Improved Singer Sewing Machine, which is known the world over. Our machines are made after the latest models of the Singer Mfg. Co.'s machines, and are perfect fac-similes of their machines in shape, ornamentation and appearance, with the exception of the lettering on the arm of the machine, and the trade mark. All the parts are made to gauge exactly the same as the Singer Co.'s parts, and are constructed respectively of precisely the same materials.

The utmost care is exercised in the selection of the materials used, and only the very best quality is purchased. Each machine is thoroughly well made and is fitted with the utmost nicety and exactness, and no machine is permitted by the inspector to go out of the shops until it has been fully tested and proved to do perfect work, and run light and without noise.

During the life of the patents under which this machine was formerly made prices were kept up, and as the sewing machine is such a necessity people were compelled to buy, notwithstanding the prices were extortionate. All sewing machine manufacturers who have operated under the protection of U. S. patents have become immensely wealthy, and the bulk of their fortunes have come from the poor sewing woman, who, in order to get easy terms, has paid seven or eight times what her machine is worth.

We are now prepared to sell our machines at prices within reach of all, being positively the **Lowest Cash Prices** made by any concern in this line.

The loose balance wheel is a very **important improvement,** and constructed so that the Bobbins can be wound without running the machine or removing the work therefrom.

Another marked improvement is the Self-threading Eyelet, Check Lever and Needle Clamp. Each machine, of whatever style, is furnished with the following equipment of tools and accessories Free of Charge:

One Foot Hemmer, One Screw Driver, One Wrench, One Oil Can and Oil, One Gauge, One Extra Throat Plate, One Extra Check Spring, One Package of Needles, Six Bobbins and One Instruction Book. *In addition to the above we furnish with each machine an EXTRA SET OF ATTACHMENTS, FREE OF CHARGE, consisting of the following:* **One Tucker, One Foot Ruffler, One Set of Plain Hemmers, 5 different widths up to 7-8 of an inch, One Binder and One Thread Cutter.**

Each machine is nicely packed in a wooden crate, FREE OF CHARGE, and we guarantee the safe delivery of each machine.

Remember, WHERE cash in full accompanies your order WE WILL SEND FREE a double set of extra attachments and also send some nice and valuable present.

IF YOU WANT 10 DAYS TRIAL FREE

Get 3 Reliable Men to Endorse Your Order.

Read What the People Say!

"DOES GOOD WORK."

WATERTOWN, SOUTH DAKOTA.

Gents.—I wrote to you when I got my sewing machine. It runs well, and I like it all right. It does good work.   Respectfully,   JEREMIAH MINTZ.

"HAVE USED IT TWO YEARS. ITS ALL RIGHT."

WINDFIELD, TENNESSEE.

Gents.—I will inform you that I am well pleased with my machine. It gives perfect satisfaction. It is nearly two years since I ordered my machine, and it is all right.
                    Yours truly,   H. C. DOUGHERTY.

"JUST WHAT YOU REPRESENTED."

ELMVILLE, ALABAMA.

Gents.—The sewing machine you sold me gives perfect satisfaction and am well pleased with it. I have had it twelve months and it has proved to be just what you represented. I am well pleased with your way of doing business and will recommend your Company.
                    Yours respectfully,   A. A. POWELL.

"LIKE YOUR MANNER OF DOING BUSINESS."

LEWISTON, UTAH.

Gents.—I bought a sewing machine from you about eighteen months ago, and it gives good satisfaction in work. I like your manner of doing business and you were prompt in sending the machine.   Yours truly,   EDWARD KEMP.

"MY LADY FRIENDS ARE PLEASED WITH IT."

TUNIS, TEXAS.

Gents.—I am well pleased with the machine I received from you. I have had the machine eight months and have not had an hours trouble with it. Machine is all that you said it was. I like it very much indeed and I showed it to a great many of my lady friends and they seem to be well pleased with it. I think I can sell a great many next fall. There is no money among the farmers at this season of the year.   Very respectfully yours,   GEORGIANA LOCKHART.

"O. K. ON HEAVY WORK."

TABLE ROCK, NEBRASKA.

Gents.—I received a sewing machine of you over a year ago, and it has given perfect satisfaction. I use it a great deal in sewing rubber-duck for carriage trimming and it never refused to sew.   Respectfully,   A. F. HANSON.

The Minnesota Sewing Machine

Is the only machine that can be called modern ; it is up to the times. Runs so quietly and steady that a lamp may be set on the stand with safety. It is not an old style machine improved, but built on new mechanical principles. Sews fast and makes perfect stitch with all kinds of thread on all classes of material ; it is always ready. As time rolls on, will drive all other Sewing Machines from first-class homes and dressmaking establishments. It is unrivaled for speed, durability and quality of work. Sell that ancient machine of thine and buy the MINNESOTA.

A Complete Set of Attachments with each Machine, FREE.

The Late Improved Automatic Bobbin Winder Fitted to Each one of these Machines.

A Written Guarantee for 10 years accompanies each Machine.

The Late Improved Automatic Bobbin Winder Fitted to Each one of these Machines.

•• STYLE No. 13 •• **MINNESOTA** SEWING MACHINE.

No. 12, New Minnesota, with 3 Drawers and Cover............Price, $16.55
No. 13, " " " 5 " " " (Same as Cut). " 17.55
No. 14, " " " 7 " " " .... " 18.55

Handsome Oil Polished Walnut or Oak Cabinet Work, Nickle Plate Balance Wheel. Stands on Castors.

READ THE DESCRIPTION.

The Minnesota has been manufactured in order to meet a growing demand for a machine of this kind. The Minnesota is made with great care, and has no superior in the world. The special points claimed for it are as follows : *Double Eccentric* on main shaft for operating the shuttle and feed levers, made of one piece, and so perfectly balanced that vibration is reduced to the minimum, requiring but one adjustment, no slipping of eccentrics, and therefore throwing machine out of time. Feed mechanism much lighter ; less material to be vibrated by spring ; mechanical in construction ; no knocking or "side lash" ; hence no *raw hide* to deaden sound required. Double feed, so operated that whether long or short stitch is used, the middle section of teeth always start immediately behind the needle, insuring thereby a perfect and uniform stitch. Also so arranged that the feed does not fall until point of needle enters the goods, the benefit of which is obvious. The guard for thread controller on inside of face plate prevents injury or displacement, a frequent source of annoyance in some machines. Loose pully device, easily and quickly adjusted, relieving the shaft from friction and allowing shaft end to be neatly finished off, avoiding the unsightly "wabbling" of balance wheel which in time wears out of true. Cylinder shuttle, *self-threading*, large loose bobbin, a delicate and perfect tension; oil holes large and free. The stand is beautiful in design, light and graceful in appearance, and at the same time strong and substantial. The *belt replacer* is simple and effective, the utility of which the ladies will thoroughly appreciate. Treadle hung on ball bearings requiring no oil, hence no soiled carpets. The New Minnesota is a perfect working sewing machine in every particular, and is equal to any $65.00 machine in the market. It is finely finished, the wood being of seasoned walnut or oak, and the greatest care is exercised in the manufacture of each part. Each machine is furnished with the following equipment of tools and accessories:

One Foot Hemmer, one Screw Driver, one Wrench, one Oil Can and Oil, one Gauge, one Package of Needles, six Bobbins, and one Instruction Book. In addition to the above we furnish an extra set of attachments, consisting of the following: One Tucker, one Foot Ruffler, one Set of Plain Hemmers, five different widths up to 7-8 of an inch, one Binder, one Thread Cutter and Quilter, packed in plush-lined case.

Each Machine is Neatly Packed in a Wooden Crate Free of Charge, and we Guarantee Safe Delivery.

SEND CASH IN FULL WITH YOUR ORDER, and we will MAKE YOU A NICE PRESENT,

Send you a **Double Set of Extra Attachments,** and also send you some nice present.

Our Binding 10 Year Guarantee covers everything and makes you **absolutely safe**. We guarantee to refund money in any case a machine does not prove entirely satisfactory and exactly as represented.

Read What the People Say!

"COULDN'T ASK ANYTHING BETTER."

GLENDIVE, MONTANA.

Gents.—We have had the sewing machine you sold us since Dec. 29, 1890, and are well pleased with the work it does. Couldn't ask for anything better. Yours truly, JOHN HARBSTER.

"I CAN RECOMMEND YOU."

WAKEFIELD, VIRGINIA.

Gents.—This is to say, your machine does just as you recommended it. I have had it about ten months, and have found no fault with it. I feel that I can recommend you to the public, and would do you any favor that I can in selling a machine. Yours truly, MRS. A. W. HOLLOWAY.

"TRUTHFUL REPRESENTATIONS."

RINGWOOD, NORTH CAROLINA.

Gents.—The machine I purchased from you gives and has been giving satisfaction. I found you truthful in your representations of the same. Very truly, WM. C. FINCH, Attorney at Law.

"PERFECTLY SQUARE AND HONEST."

ALLENTOWN, RHODE ISLAND.

Gents.—I had a sewing machine from your place nearly two years ago, and I like the machine very much. It is just what it was said to be. Your manner of doing business with me was perfectly square and honest. Yours truly, MRS. JENNIE L. ARNOLD.

"WELL PLEASED WITH IT."

WESTMINSTER, SOUTH CAROLINA.

Gents.—We received our sewing machine December 15, 1890, and are well pleased with it. We have found no fault with it so far. Respectfully, W. N. WILSON.

"A SPLENDID MACHINE FOR THE PRICE."

MERIDIAN, TEXAS.

Gents.—In stating how I am pleased with the machine I received I can say it is a splendid machine for the price and is giving perfect satisfaction. It has now been in use about seventeen months. I think your manner of doing business is splendid. Yours truly, A. J. McCURRY.

OUR BICYCLE DEPARTMENT.

We sell the highest grade wheels, make the lowest prices and give the most liberal terms.

No concern will compete with us on bicycles. We have been very careful to select for our line only the finest wheels, and we are not only prepared to offer you the best bicycles made, but we are also prepared to furnish them to you at far less money than they were ever offered before. At our prices everyone can own a bicycle, and on our most liberal terms, everyone can see and examine the bicycle thoroughly before paying.

Terms, conditions of shipments &c.——

We will send any bicycle to any address, by express C.O.D. subject to examination on receipt of $1.00 as guarantee of good faith, you can examine it at the express office, and if you do not find it exactly as represented, by far the best bicycle ever offered at anything like the price, in fact if you do not find it in every way satisfactory and fully equal to bicyles which sell at retail everywhere at double our price, refuse it—Don't pay a cent and the agent will return it at our expense.

No other concern——

Makes any such terms. No other concern can afford to. Why we make our terms so easy! We know our bicycles are the highest grade made, we know our prices are below all others, we know when you have seen and examined one of our bicycles you will be convinced you are saving one-half by buying direct from us, we know everyone who orders a bicycle, will upon examination, pay the express agent our price less the one dollar sent with order, and take the bicycle, if a bicycle is ordered in good faith they are always taken, never come back, we are never put to loss of express charges.

Our guarantee——

We issue a binding written guarantee for one year which goes with each bicyle we sell, they will, with care, last a life time.

Express charges——

You pay the express charges, but express charges are very low, we ship all bicycles from Chicago, and we have arranged with the different express companies for the lowest express rate, our bicycles weigh less than 50 pounds, and the express charges for 100 miles or less is about 35c; 200 miles, 60c; 300 miles, 80c; 400 miles, $1.00; 600 miles, $1.50; 1,000 miles, $2.00.

We make no charge——

For crating or packing. We deliver all bicycles securely crated on board the cars in Chicago, free of charge.

We take all the risk——

Ourselves, and as you take no risk and our terms are made so very easy, we earnestly request a trial order.

No. 10. THE PET.

Order by Number.

Our Drive Price $11.90

SELLS EVERYWHERE AT $20.00

WE DEFY COMPETITION.

No Concern on earth can meet our Prices.

No Concern on earth will meet our Terms.

This is the strongest and best finished bicycle made at anything like the price.

Heretofore this bicycle has retailed at anywhere from $20.00 to $25.00 and never sold at wholesale for less than $15.00.

WE MADE A CONTRACT with a large manufacturer for their entire product, and by so doing we have got the prices so far below all others that there is actually **no room for comparison. This wheel is designed** for children of either sex from **6 to 10 years** of age, it is **easy running**, made after the **very latest model**, as follows: **FRAME** improved 1894 drop pattern; **WHEELS** 22 inches, Crescent rims and 1-inch rubber tire, direct spokes; **STEERING FORK**, semi hollow, light and strong, fitted with rubber coasters; **HANDLE BAR**, adjustable, properly curved; **CRANKS**, detachable and adjustable; **PEDALS**, steel axle fitted with rubbers; **CHAIN**, detachable link, rear adjustment; **SADDLE**, Garford, and supplied with tool bag, wrench and oiler; **FINISH**, all bright parts tinned, frame finely enameled.

WE FURNISH THIS BICYCLE with all bright parts **nicely nickeled**, wheels nickel plated, with the very best quality patent cushion tyres, $14.90.

YOU CAN EXAMINE THIS BICYCLE at your own express office **All at Our Risk.** Send us your order with $1.00 as a guarantee of good faith, and we will send the bicycle by express C. O. D., subject to examination; you can examine it at express office and if found perfectly satisfactory you can pay the express agent our price, less $1.00, and **the bicycle is yours**, otherwise **refuse it** and the agent will return it **at our expense.**

Our Drive Price $17.45.

RETAILS EVEYWHERE AT FROM $30.00 to $35.00.

YOU CAN SAVE $13.00 to $20.00 on this wheel by sending your order to us. We were the **first concern** to offer bicycles to the consumer at wholesale prices, and the **first concern** to offer them at anything like our terms. **At our heretofore unheard of prices** every one can own a bicycle, and at our **incomparable terms** any one can see and examine them.

IT TAKES BUT A VERY FEW DAYS to deliver a bicycle to any point in the United States, your order is received one day and we ship the bicycle the next **This bicycle** is designed for boys from **12 to 18 years** of age.

DESCRIPTION OF WHEEL. FRAME, improved 1894, cross frame strongly braced; **WHEELS** 25 inches, Crescent rims, fitted with finest quality 1-inch cushion tires, direct spokes; **STEERING FORKS**, semi hollow, light and strong, fitted with adjustable coasters; **HANDLE BAR**, adjustable, nicely curved; **CRANKS**, detachable and adjustable; **PEDALS**, steel axle, properly fitted with fluted rubbers; **CHAIN**, detachable link and noiseless, rear adjustment; **SADDLE**, Garford, and supplied with tool bag, wrench and oiler; **FINISH**, all bright parts nickeled, frame finely enameled.

No. 11. THE TRUSTY.

Order by Number.

C. O. D. TO ANY ONE ONLY $1.00 IN AD-VANCE.

$34.90 Our Drive Price $34.90.

RETAILS EVERYWHERE AT FROM
$50.00 TO $75.00.

Never before offered even at wholesale, at anything like our price. **This Wheel** is designed for boys from **12 to 15 years** of age and we **guarantee** it the best 24-inch **Pnuematic tyre** bicycle made.

WE ARE EXTREMELY ANXIOUS to get your order, and to get you to give us a trial we will make you **the grandest offer ever made.** Send us $1.00 as a guarantee of good faith and we will send the bicycle to you by express C. O. D., subject to examination. After you have examined it if you are not thoroughly satisfied **refuse it** and the agent will return it **at our expense** and we will refund your $1.00.

ORDER BY NUMBER.

No. 12.

THE WONDER.

DESCRIPTION OF WHEEL. FRAME, improved pattern "diamond" made of steel tubing, with vital part of drop forgings; **WHEELS,** 24 inches, corrugated rims with tangent spokes and brass nipples, fitted with 1½-inch **Morgan & Wright** pneumatic tyres; **STEERING FORK,** made of steel tubing, adjustable nickeled coasters; **HANDLE BAR,** made of steel tubing, curved downward and backward, and brought well into position for rider; **BEARINGS,** made of high grade steel, carefully hardened, dust proof, full balls to wheels, crank axle, streering head and pedals; **CRANKS,** detachable and adjustable, from 4 to 5 inches throw; **PEDALS,** made of steel, fitted with moulded rubbers; **CHAIN,** Humber pattern block chain ⅜-inch, 1-inch pitch, true to guage, **rear adjustment; BRAKE,** improved plunger pattern; **GEAR,** Sprocket wheels, 17x9, geared to 45 inches; **SADDLE,** improved Garford, style as shown in cut, tool bag, inflater, oiler and necessary tools; **WEIGHT,** all on 33 lbs.; **FINISH,** All bright parts finely nickeled, japaned with our special enamel, which puts the best finish on the wheel that can be obtained. Our illustration shows the wheel stripped, but our price includes, and we furnish it complete with mud guards, brake and all **attachments.**

We furnish the same Wheel with best quality cushion tyres at $31.60.

OUR GUARANTEE is the best, strongest and most binding guarantee issued by any bicycle house in existence. It warrants the wheel in every respect for 1 year. "With fair usage it will last a lifetime."

No. 13. THE ONWARD.

Order by Number.

Our Drive Price $42.25

Retails everywhere at $75.00 and upwards.

Sent C. O. D. to any one on receipt of $1.00 as a guarantee of good faith.

We furnish the same Wheel with best quality 1-inch Cushion Tyre at $39.20.

DESCRIPTION. FRAME, improved 1894 pattern diamond frame, made of steel tubing, with important parts of steel drop forgings; **WHEELS,** 26 inches, corrugated rims with tangent spokes and brass nipples, fitted with 1½-inch Morgan & Wright pneumatic tyres; **STEERING FORK,** made of steel tubing with adjustable nickeled coasters; **HANDLE BAR,** made of steel tubing, fitted with cork grips with nickeled ferrules, properly curved downward and backward, and brought well into position for rider; **BEARINGS,** all high grade steel, carefully hardened, dust proof, full balls to wheels, crank axle, steering head and pedals; **CRANKS,** detachable, 5½-inch throw; **PEDALS,** made of steel, hardened and fitted with moulded rubbers; **CHAIN,** Humber pattern, ⅜-inch block chain, 1-inch pitch, true to gauge, **rear adjustment; BRAKE,** improved Plunger pattern; **GEAR,** Sprocket wheels, 17x9 geared to 49 inches; **SADDLE,** improved 1894 Garford style, as shown in cut, with tool bag, inflater, oiler and necessary tools; **WEIGHT,** all on, 36 lbs.; **FINISH,** all bright parts finely finished, japanned with our special enamel which produces the best finish on the wheel which can be obtained.

ILLUSTRATION shows the bare wheel, but our price includes and we furnish it complete with mud guard, brake, and all attachments. **This Wheel is designed** for boys from 12 to 18 years of age.

Our Drive Price $42.95.

C. O. D. TO ANY ONE ON RECEIPT OF $1.00 AS A GUARANTEE OF GOOD FAITH.

DESCRIPTION. FRAME, Improved 1894 pattern **for girls,** with detachable bar for boys use, made of steel tubing, with principal parts of steel drop forgings; **WHEELS,** 26 inches, corrugated rims with tangent spokes and brass nipples, fitted with 1½-inch Morgan & Wright pneumatic tyres; **STEERING FORK,** made of steel tubing, fitted with adjustable nickeled coasters; **HANDLE BAR,** made of steel tubing, fitted with cork grips with nickeled ferrules, properly curved downward and backward, and brought well into position for rider; **BEARINGS,** made of high grade steel, carefully hardened and dust proof, full balls to wheels, crank axle, steering head and pedals; **CRANKS,** detachable, 5½ inch throw; **PEDALS,** made of steel, fitted with moulded rubbers; **CHAIN,** Humber pattern, ⅜-inch block chain, 1-inch pitch, true to guage, **rear adjustment; BRAKE,** improved Plunger pattern; **GEAR,** Sprocket wheels; 17x9, geared to 49 inches; **SADDLE,** improved 1894 Garford style, as shown in cut, with tool bag, inflater, oiler and necessary tools; **WEIGHT,** All on, 37 lbs.; **FINISH,** All bright parts finely nickeled, japanned with our special enamel, which produces the best finish on the wheel which can be obtained.

No. 14.

THE FORWARD.

We furnish same Wheel with 1-inch Cushion Tyre at $39.20.

Order by Number.

GUARANTEED BEST ON EARTH. OUR SPECIAL PRICE, $55.95

We Stand Ready to Match this Machine Against any Bicycle Made.
Retails Everywhere at $135.

WE HONESTLY BELIEVE we are furnishing, as we advertise, the very best wheel in the market—a wheel without an equal in strength, general finish, and all the essential parts, and at the same time, at a price $79.00 below the usual retail price, and even far below the regular wholesale price.

YOU MAY BE THE JUDGE. We will send the bicycle to you C. O. D., subject to examination, on receipt of $1.00 as a guarantee. **Examine it yourself, let your friends examine it, call in an expert. The wheel stands on its merits, and the price is something heretofore unheard of.** If you are thinking of buying a bicycle, if you are tired of your old wheel, **now is your chance.**

DON'T BE PERSUADED to buy any certain make, or to pay a fancy price. **The Electric** is the **latest, handsomest** and most complete wheel out. It combines the advantages of all, with the defects of none, and what's more **we save you money.** Our reputation, our binding guarantee, our representations, our most liberal offer **all is at stake.** We can't afford to disappoint you. It is of the most vital importance that we please you in every respect, and thus make every bicycle **a moving advertisement.**

YOU CAN MAKE MONEY selling these wheels and with **very little effort,** if you own one yourself, **your friends will want the same wheel,** and you can sell them easily at a **big profit,** if you do not care to sell bicycles, but will be kind enough to tell your friends where you got it and what you paid we **will be sure to get more orders** from your neighborhood. **That's how we are able to make the price so low.**

WE DEPEND on one bicycle causing the sale of more and they always do it.

CONSIDER THE PRICE, $55.95, for a $135 wheel.

No. 15.
THE ELECTRIC.
Order by Number.

Consider the terms, C. O. D. to any one on receipt of $1.

DESCRIPTION OF THE ELECTRIC. FRAME, most improved pattern of 1894, with long head and wheel base, made entirely from cold drawn seamless tubing and steel drop forgings; **STEERING FORK,** made of cold drawn seamless tubing, with steel drop forged crown head; **WHEELS,** 30-inch front 28-inch rear, corrugated steel rims, with swaged tangent spokes and brass nipples, fitted with **Morgan & Wright** pneumatic tyres, 1⅞-inch to rear, and 1¾-inch to front wheel. **We also furnish** the above with 28-inch front and rear wheels, when so desired. **HANDLE BAR,** made from 13-16 cold drawn seamless tubing, dropped pattern, brought well into place for comfortable and perfect steering, fitted with cork grips with nickeled ferrules; **BEARINGS,** all tool steel, hardened and drawn in the most perfect manner, balls to every part, dust proof; **CRANKS,** round pattern, made from steel drop forgings, 6½ inches throw; **CHAIN,** Brampton's patent beveled roller chain, true to guage, **rear adjustment; GEAR,** drop forged steel sprocket wheel, hardened, 18x8 teeth, geared to 63 inches; **PEDALS,** dust proof, fitted with large rubbers; **SADDLE,** Garford, as shown in cut, tool bag, inflater, patent oiler and all necessary tools; **FINISH,** enameled with our special enamel, with the usual bright parts heavily nickeled on copper; **WEIGHT,** all on 39 lbs., stripped 33 lbs. **ILLUSTRATION** shows bicycle stripped, but the price includes, and we furnish it with mud guards, brake and all attachments complete.

We furnish the Electric with best quality 1¼-inch Cushion Tyre at $52.95.

OUR LADIES ELECTRIC or Combination Wheel. We furnish the same wheel, designed for either lady or gentleman. It has a perfect ladies' drop frame, with detachable bar for gentleman's use, and weighs all on, 41 lbs. **OUR PRICE** is the same for either ladies' or gent's **Electric Pneumatic Tyre, $55.95; Cushion Tyre, $52.95.**

Baby Carriage

DEPARTMENT.

BABY CARRIAGES AT YOUR OWN PRICE.

We say your own price for the reason we are in a position to supply you at one-half the price charged by retail dealers.

WE HANDLE THE BEST grades of goods only, and always strive to send our customers such goods that when they are received they will not only give satisfaction, but prove even better than represented.

WE WANT every carriage to advertise our house. If we sell you a carriage and you find you have saved one-half by buying from us, you will tell your neighbors, and speak a kind word for us, and thus in many cases cause the sale of at least one more carriage, and **THAT'S OUR MOTTO**—make a carriage sell a carriage.

✤ WE WANT YOUR TRADE. ✤

All we ask is a trial order to convince you we are in a position to furnish you more for your money than you can possibly get elsewhere.

○ ○ ○ ○ ○ ○ ○

OUR TERMS, CONDITIONS, ETC.

NOTHING COULD BE MORE LIBERAL.

WE SHIP C. O. D. To anyone anywhere, subject to THOROUGH examination. Read, select any carriage you want, and send us your order with $2.00 as a guarantee you are ordering in good faith, and we will send the carriage to you by express C.O.D., subject to examination. You can examine it at the express office, and if found perfectly satisfactory, pay the express agent our **special advertised price,** less the $2.00 you sent us, and the carriage is yours.

THE BEST WAY Is to send cash in full with your order. Then we will always ship by freight, which is **far cheaper** than by express. The freight on one carriage, to points within 1,000 miles of Chicago is from 50 cents to $1.00; to Pacific Coast and far distant points, from $1.00 to $2.00.

YOU TAKE NO RISK, For if the carriage is not found perfectly satisfactory, you can return it at our expense, and we will refund your money.

OUR GUARANTEE. We warrant all our carriages for three years, and a binding guarantee accompanies each carriage.

COLORS. We use the leading colors to match the upholstering and parasols, and if any special color is desired please state in ordering. **WE CAN SUPPLY** Gold, Brown, Peacock, Old Gold, Mahogany, Cardinal, Red, Olive, and Old Rose.

FREE. All our carriages are nicely packed in wooden crates, and delivered at our freight or express depot. We make no charges for crating or cartage.

CHEAPEST ON EARTH.

No house can compete with us in this line. **We are acknowledged** headquarters.

Investigate, Look where you may, compare our prices with those of any other concern and decide for yourself.

This Carriage for $2.68.

Retails everywhere at from $6.00 to $9.00. Never before sold at wholesale by the dozen for less than $4.00. **We want your trade.** We want you to advertise our house. We want you to become a steady customer. To do this, we have got to please you, and the way to do it, is by giving you more value for your money than you can possibly get elsewhere.

B 20.
ORDER BY NUMBER.

READ OUR DESCRIPTION.

This Carriage is made of white reed and maple, medium size, bottom 12½ by 26 inches, oil cloth in bottom, seat only upholstered, solid bent handles, iron reach, iron brace, iron axle, four steel springs, trimmings all nicely finished.

Our Special Price, Without Top,   -   -   -   - $2.68.
Our Special Price, with Parasol, Silesia, unlined, with scalloped edges, **$3.42.**

$4.95 FOR A $10.00 CARRIAGE.

YOU CAN SAVE from $5.00 to $20.00 by buying a carriage from us.

VERY LITTLE TROUBLE to send us your order.

YOU CAN'T MAKE MONEY EASIER.

Don't let your retail dealer discourage you. He wants to make $5.00 or $10.00 on a carriage, **WE DON'T.**

REASON FOR YOURSELF. The retail dealer's sales are small. **He only buys a few carriages a year,** consequently pays a big price. His sales are comparatively small, consequently his entire income for the year must be made on his few sales. **What's the result?** If you only purchase a baby carriage in a season, you contribute at least several dollars towards his year's profits.

WITH US IT'S DIFFERENT. We handle thousands of carriages annually, figuring the cost down as low as they can possibly be made. We don't ask several dollars profit on a carriage. We can't think of getting even $1.00 profit on a carriage. **On the contrary,** our margin of profit is figured as low as possible, consistent with **thoroughly reliable business methods.**

WHAT'S THE RESULT? When you order a carriage from us you are paying the lowest net cash cost to manufacture, with our profit added, and are buying a carriage for less money than your local dealer can possibly buy.

DO YOU BELIEVE US? If you will **stop to consider,** we sell only for cash, make no bad debts, no traveling men's expenses to pay; **stop to think** all it costs us to sell the thousands of carriages per year is but the simple cost of a few pages in this catalogue, you will readily see we stand in a position against which **NO ONE CAN COMPETE.**

B 21.
ORDER BY NUMBER.

DESCRIPTION OF B 21.

Warranted strong and substantial, and will give the best of satisfaction. Each part well fitted and glued, oil cloth in bottom, upholstered in cretonne, with crushed plush roll. Parasol, silesia, unlined, with scalloped edges. Solid bent handles, iron reach, iron brace, iron axle, four strong steel springs, best steel wheels, trimmings all nicely finished and plated.

WE FURNISH the above carriage in Satin Russe with Crushed Plush Roll at   -   - **$5.65.**
Best Steel Wheels with Rubber Tire on the above, $2.00 extra.

BARGAIN OF BARGAINS

The above applies to this carriage, but not more so than to any other. **Every Carriage we handle is a bargain.** We can't call any one a leader, or in fact we might say, **they** are all leaders. Our sales on these goods are enormous.

NO WONDER!

Our prices are so far below all competitors that there is absolutely no room for comparison, no chance for doubt.

PICTURES DON'T DO JUSTICE.

We have tried to give you some idea of the general style and appearance of our carriages by small illustrations. These pictures are all engraved by hand from photographs of the carriages, but want of space compels us to make them so small that you can get but a faint idea of the artistic manner in which our carriages are constructed and finished, and the handsome appearance they make.

NOTHING COMPARES with THEM

at anything like the same price. If you buy a carriage from us, say this our number B 22, at $5.65, it will be so far superior in every way to your neighbor's, which they paid $12.00 or $15.00 for that you will have difficulty in convincing them that it is possible to make such a carriage for $5.65.

B 22.
ORDER BY NUMBER.

DESCRIPTION. This carriage is made of reed and maple, strong, substantial and durable, upholstered in cretonne, with crushed plush roll, oil cloth in bottom. Parasol, silesia, unlined, with scalloped edge. Solid bent handles, iron reach, iron brace, iron axle, four strong steel springs, best steel wheels, plated, trimmings all nicely finished and plated.

SAME STYLE AS ABOVE, upholstered in satin russe, with crushed plush roll, Brussels carpet in bottom, parasol sateen, with lace edge, $6.25.

BEST STEEL WHEELS with Rubber Tires on the above, $2.00 extra.

YOURS * FOR * $5.95.

WE WANT YOUR TRADE,

And if you are in need of a Baby Carriage we want your order, and are willing to do everything in our power to secure it. We can't sell you a baby carriage for less than cost,

BUT WE CAN sell you one for one-half the price your retailer will ask you, and at from 15 to 30 per cent. less than the same carriage was ever offered by any house in America (wholesale or retail). You will find everything exactly as we have represented. Our goods will even excel our representations.

YOU WILL FIND US PROMPT.

We will acknowledge receipt of your order and money the day it is received. The carriage will be shipped the following day. You will find we use extreme care in crating, boxing and shipping our goods. Your letters will be answered promptly, courteously and in detail.

OUR INSTRUCTION to every employe intrusted with orders is to treat every customer at a distance exactly as he or she would like to be treated, were they in his or her place.

DON'T HESITATE TO WRITE

about anything pertaining to these goods. You may want something special, made to order, or you may wish to make inquiry regarding some carriage, or other information. If so, we will consider it a favor if you will write us. No matter whether you buy or not, we will feel equally grateful for you kind consideration.

B 23.
ORDER BY NUMBER.

DESCRIPTION. Reed and maple frame, strong and well made, as shown in cut, upholstered in cretonne, with crushed plush roll, oil cloth in bottom. Parasol, silesia, unlined, scalloped edge. Solid bent handles, iron reach, iron brace, iron axle, four strong steel springs, best steel wheels, plated. Trimmings all nicely finished and plated.

SAME AS ABOVE, Upholstered in satin russe, with silk plush roll, Brussels carpet in bottom, parasol of sateen, with lace edge, $6.55.

BEST STEEL WHEELS with Rubber Tires on the above, $2.00 extra.

Our Price, $7.20; Retail Price, $18.00.

B 24.
ORDER BY NUMBER.

YOU MAY HESITATE to order, not from lack of confidence, not because you don't consider our prices extremely low, or that you question our reliability—

YOU CAN'T DO THAT.

The bona fide testimonials we have spared space in this book for, will convince you of the manner in which we do business. The fact that we refer by permission to the Union National Bank of Minneapolis, any express company doing business in Minneapolis, any express company doing business in Chicago, any commercial agency, or any financial institution in the United States; the fact that we are duly authorized and incorporated under the laws of the State of Minnesota, with a cash capital of $75,000.00, and a cash surplus of nearly $100,000.00, places our responsibility, in the eyes of every one,

Beyond the Least Possible Shadow of a Doubt.

WE MAKE IT EASY. Send us your order and the carriage will be shipped to you accompanied by our three-years' binding guarantee, and if you don't find it satisfactory and exactly as represented you can return it at our expense and we will cheerfully refund your money.

DESCRIPTION OF B 24.

THIS FANCY CARRIAGE is very strong and substantial, made of the best material and warranted to give entire satisfaction. Best reed body, Brussels carpet on bottom; upholstered in damask, with silk plush roll; parasol, sateen, with lace edge, solid bent handles; iron reach, iron brace, iron axle, four strong steel springs, best steel wheels, plated. Trimmings all nicely finished and plated.
  SAME STYLE AS ABOVE, upholstered in best silk plush, with best silk plush roll; parasol best silk satin, lined, with lace edge, $8.75.
  BEST STEEL WHEELS, with Rubber Tires, on above, $2.00.

Our Price, $7.65; Retail Price, $20.00.

DON'T ASK for any concession in price.
DON'T ASK us to deviate from our fixed terms.

WE WILL ACCOMMODATE, but we believe the greatest accommodation we can offer is in dollars and cents, and we feel confident when you have made a purchase from us, and found you have saved nearly one-half, you will agree we are accommodating indeed, but in order to maintain our heretofore unheard of prices, we are compelled to adhere rigidly to certain iron-clad rules, but after all you must admit **our terms are easy.** We will send any carriage to any address by express, C. O. D., subject to examination, on receipt of $2.00 as a guarantee of good faith. You can examine the carriage at the express office, and if found perfectly satisfactory pay the express agent our price and express charges, less the $2.00.

But we recommend you to **have your carriage shipped by freight,** although where carriages are to be shipped by freight, **cash in full must accompany all orders,** as railroad companies will not accept goods to be sent C. O. D., subject to examination.

FREIGHT IS LOW on a carriage, as they only weigh fifty lbs. crated ready for shipment, and they can be shipped to the most distant points at a small expense to the purchaser.

B 25.
ORDER BY NUMBER.

DESCRIPTION OF B 25.

WARRANTED to be made of the best material. Brussels carpet bottom, reed body; upholstered in damask, with silk plush roll; parasol sateen, with lace edge; patent wheel lock; solid bent handles; iron reach, iron brace, iron axle, four strong steel springs; best steel wheels, plated. Trimmings all nicely finished and plat d.
  SAME STYLE AS ABOVE, upholstered in silk plush, with silk plush roll; parasol special quality silk satin, lined, with lace edge, $8.95.
  BEST STEEL WHEELS, with Rubber Tires, on the above, $2.00 extra.

Our Price, $8.95; Retail Price, $20.00

WE HAVE A GREAT VARIETY OF STYLES

Want of space prevents our showing the great variety we handle. In this catalogue we illustrate a few of the most desirable and best selling styles, carriages we have carefully selected from our entire line. We can furnish you anything in baby carriages and you will find our prices uniformly low on everything. In connection with the price, let us again say one word in regard to **Freight Charges.** We can't make this matter too plain. Some customers think the freight charges will add too much to the cost.

DON'T DECEIVE YOURSELF!

If you buy from your local retail dealer—no matter where you buy—you must pay the freight, as your local dealer pays the highest local freight rate on all the carriages he buys, and when he sells them he adds the freight and his enormous profit to the generally high price he has paid for the carriage at the factory, and **THAT IS WHAT YOU PAY.**

WE WANT as much trade in your town as we can possibly get. If we are to secure and hold your trade and the trade of your friends, we fully realize we must make strong inducements—we must save you money—save you money on everything you buy from us. We can't make a low price on a few things and a high price on others; everything must be a money saver. **Our price must be squeezed down to the lowest possible notch.**

B 26.
ORDER BY NUMBER.

TRUST US FOR THAT when you see our goods, when your neighbors see them, your retail dealers see them, they will think our prices have been squeezed, **even by Hydraulic Pressure.**

DESCRIPTION OF B 26.

A fine, large and roomy carriage, with reed-wood body, Brussels carpet in bottom. Made of the best material, shellaced, varnished, and handsomely finished. Warranted to wear and give the best of satisfaction. Upholstered in fine damask, with silk plush roll, parasol silk satin, lined, and lace edge. Solid bent handles, iron reach, iron brace, iron axle, four strong steel springs, plated wheels, trimmings all nicely finished and plated.

SAME STYLE AS ABOVE upholstered in silk plush, parasol silk satin, lined, with lace edge..............**$9.85**
BEST STEEL WHEELS, with Rubber Tires, on the above...extra, **2.00**

OUR SPECIAL PRICE, $8.35

IT WILL PAY YOU TO ORDER ONE OF THE BEST; YOU WILL BE FAR BETTER SATISFIED.

While our low grade carriages are very fine and will give the best of satisfaction, you will be far better satisfied if you buy one of our better grades. Every additional dollar you pay will add wonderfully to the appearance and general finish of the carriage. It would surprise you to see what we could do for even one dollar, and if you could but see, we know you would order one of our better grade carriages. Don't misunderstand us. Our cheapest carriages are very strong and thoroughly well made, but we wish to urge you to buy a nice job. **WHY?** Because it will please you—advertise us—attract the attention of everyone who sees it, and bring us orders from your neighbors and friends.

Don't Pay Less Than $8.35,

the price of this, our No. B 27, if you can possibly afford it. If necessary make a special effort to get this grade or higher.

IT WILL PAY YOU!

B 27.
ORDER BY NUMBER.

DESCRIPTION! This extra fine special price carriage is made of the best material, reed body, Brussels carpet on bottom, finely finished and varnished. Upholstered in damask, with silk plush roll. Parasol, best sateen, with lace edge. Solid bent handles, iron reach, iron brace, iron axle, four strong steel springs, best steel wheels, patent wheel lock. Trimmings all nicely finished and plated.

SAME AS ABOVE, upholstered in silk plush, parasol silk satin, lined, with lace edge..........................**$9.95**
BEST STEEL WHEELS, with Rubber Tires, on the above...extra, **2.00**

YOUR CHOICE <u>FOR</u> $9.95.

B 28.
ORDER BY NUMBER.

It's very hard to give you an idea of the appearance of our carriages, ranging in price from $9.00 and upwards.

They are Things of Beauty. Nothing you have ever seen at anything like the price will give you the slightest idea.

Don't stick to the ancient stereotyped theory that you must protect home trade. This is a progressive age; every man, no matter what his calling, whether farmer, laborer, mechanic or otherwise, must be a business man if he would succeed, and in business the key to success is buying at the right price.

DO YOU BUY AT THE RIGHT PRICE? If not, it's your own fault. The opportunity is laid plainly before you.

If you have not begun, it is high time you had, and the proper time is NOW. You may believe in reciprocity; SO DO WE; but you may misconstrue the meaning of the word. We believe when ▀▀▀ ▀▀ money for an article you are entitled in return for same the greatest value it is possible to give.

DO YOU GET THAT AT HOME? NO. Did you ever study the matter? The

retail dealer buys his goods on time from the jobber, the jobber figures on a certain percentage for loss each year, interest on money due him from retailers, and adds all this to the price when he sells to the retail dealer. The retail dealer in making his price must figure a certain percentage for bad debts, clerk hire, rent, general expenses. On top of this comes his profit, which must necessarily be large, for his living expenses are generally big while his sales are comparatively small. Now when you patronize him with your money you pay for all this! WHERE DOES THE RECIPROCITY COME IN? Does this class of retailers assist you in any way? No. On the contrary, you are contributing every year to maintain this unreasonable loss, and to sustain an unreasonable expense.

We don't say there should not be retail stores, but there are altogether too many. You are supporting too many people. Within every radius of a few miles you will find a country village; in this village is a large number of people living, often in comparative luxury, off of the hard earnings of the farmer and laboring man. IT'S ALL WRONG! There is only one way to remedy it—

Don't Pay Too Much for Your Goods.

We are forcing the price of goods down everywhere. Cut off their excessive profits and you cut off their support.

Our Motto is: "LIVE AND LET LIVE," and at our live and let live prices we are saving the consumers throughout the United States thousands of dollars annually. We are making customers everywhere, and of customers fast friends. THESE CARRIAGES, like everything we handle, are based upon Live and Let Live Prices. They are the wedges that will break the strongest combinations, gotten together to maintain high prices. They are the sledge-hammers that are driving prices down from ocean to ocean.

WE DEFY combinations, trusts, associations and competition of all kinds, that would endeavor to hold up fictitious values. WE APPEAL to the 60,000,000 consumers of the United States and ask:

Do You Want the Bottom Price?

B 29.
ORDER BY NUMBER.

DESCRIPTION OF OUR NOS. B 28 AND B 29.

Beautiful patterns, as shown in cuts, body of best reed, Brussels carpet in bottom. Warranted throughout. A Special Certificate of Guarantee for three years accompanies each carriage. Upholstered in fine satin russe with piped silk plush roll. Parasol, fine silk satin, lined and lace edge. Solid bent handles, iron reach, iron brace, iron axle, four strong steel springs, patent wheel lock, plated wheels, trimmings all nicely finished and plated.

SAME STYLE AS ABOVE, upholstered, piped with extra quality silk plush; parasol extra silk satin, lined and lace edge, $11.95.

BEST STEEL WHEELS, with Rubber Tires, on the above, $2.00 extra.

BARGAIN AFTER BARGAIN

Is offered you in this line.

STYLES to suit any taste.
PRICES to suit any purse.

THIS CARRIAGE FOR $10.65

While we only get one half the price usually charged by others

WE ARE SATISFIED.

Our profit is small, but our sales are large.

WE WILL SEND this Carriage to any address C. O. D., subject to examination, on receipt of $2.00 as a guarantee of good faith, the balance, $8.65, and express charges to be paid after you have examined the carriage at the express office and found same satisfactory.

IF NOT SATISFACTORY refuse it, and the agent will return it at our expense, and we will refund your money cheerfully.

THIS CARRIAGE is a thing of beauty, very strong and well made, maple and reed, wrapped, and protected by a hand finish of shellac and varnish, Brussels carpet in bottom, special design, upholstered in fine imported damask, piped, with silk plush pillow at back, tied with silk cords and tassels. Parasol, silk satin, lined and lace edge. Solid bent handles, iron reach, iron brace, iron axle, plated wheels. Trimmings all nicely finished and plated.

B 30.
ORDER BY NUMBER.

OUR SPECIAL PRICE IS $10.65.

 | **SAME STYLE AS ABOVE,** |

Upholstered in silk plush, special quality silk satin parasol, lined, - - - - - - $11.65.
BEST PLATED STEEL WHEELS with Rubber Tires on above for $2.00 extra.

OUR $11.90 CARRIAGE

THIS IS ONE OF THE VERY BEST CARRIAGES MADE.

Everything is strictly first-class. Reed body, upholstered in fine English broad-cloth, with piped roll of same. Parasol, special quality of silk, satin lined, with silk lace edge. Best quality solid handles, iron reach, iron brace, iron axle, plated wheels. Trimmings all nicely finished and plated.

This carriage retails everywhere at $25.00.

Our former price was $13.00, but it has been a great seller with us and handling them in such large quantities we are able to cut the price to

$11.90.

B 31.
ORDER BY NUMBER.

SAME STYLE AS ABOVE,

Upholstered in fine Silk Plush. with piped roll of same, parasol special quality of same. lined, and fine silk lace edge, $12.90.

BEST PLATED STEEL WHEELS, with Rubber Tires, on the above, $2.00 extra.

PRICE CUT TO $14.10.

Our old price was $16.00. This Carriage sells everywhere at $30.00 and upwards.

FEW PEOPLE EVER SEE SUCH A FINE PIECE OF WORK.

Heretofore this class of goods could only be found in the homes of the wealthy, but at our prices we bring it

WITHIN THE REACH OF ALL.

THIS CARRIAGE has reed body, finest quality Wilton carpet bottom, wound with best webbing, finished in best manner. Nothing but best of material used; design new and very fancy; upholstered in fine English broadcloth, with fancy rolls of same; parasol special quality silk satin, lined with fancy silk lace edge; best solid handles; iron reach, iron brace, iron axles, plated wheels; trimmings all nicely finished and plated.

B 32.

ORDER BY NUMBER.

Same Style as Above, upholstered in best quality silk plush,   .   .   .   **$15.35**

Best Plated Steel Wheels, with rubber tires, on the above, $2.00 extra.

$19.95 FOR A $45.00 CARRIAGE.

NOTHING LIKE IT

EVER BEFORE OFFERED AT ANYTHING LIKE OUR PRICE.

THIS CARRIAGE is one of our special designs, very fancy, well made and strong. Best rattan reed, shellaced and extra finished, with cane bottom, each part being close and well wrapped. No danger of end becoming loose, as is common with many,

- - UPHOLSTERED - -

B 33.

ORDER BY NUMBER.

In the best extra quality, imported Brocatelle plush; soft pillows, with tassels; back lined with fine silk satin; parasol extra quality silk satin lined, and fine silk lace edge; solid bent handles; iron reach, iron brace, iron axles.

Best Steel Wheels, Plated, and Rubber Tires.

Trimmings all nicely finished and plated.

WE HANDLE THE BEST

B 34.

ORDER BY NUMBER.

BUGGIES

AT HALF PRICE.

WE SAY HALF PRICE for the reason we sell direct to the consumer all grades of **BUGGIES, CARRIAGES, ROAD WAGONS, ROAD CARTS, WAGONS, SLEIGHS and CUTTERS** at about **one-half** the price usually charged by retail dealers.

A comparison of our prices with those of any other concern will convince you that you can buy far cheaper from us than from any other house.

IF YOU DON'T find what you want in this catalogue write for it. We can supply you with any kind or grade of vehicle. Want of space only prevents us from showing a far greater variety. We illustrate the most saleable goods in the line, and what we consider the best bargains.

OUR TERMS. Cash in full must accompany all orders. We sell for cash only which alone enables us to make such extremely low prices. **You take no risk,** for if you do not find the vehicle exactly as represented **you can return it** at our expense and we will refund your money.

HOW WE SHIP. We ship direct from the factory in Indiana or from our store rooms in Chicago, Ill., or Minneapolis, Minn., depending on where our customer is located and from which point we can secure the lowest freight rate. **WE MAKE NO CHARGE** for boxing, crating or delivering on board the cars at factory or in Chicago. **ALL THIS IS FREE.**

ABOUT THE FREIGHT. You pay the freight, but don't think it is too high, don't think you live too far away. We will secure the **LOWEST FREIGHT RATE POSSIBLE.** It will not be as much as you think.

The freight to points in Illinois, Indiana, Michigan, Wisconsin and Ohio will be on a road cart from 30 cents to $1.25, on a top buggy from 75 cents to $3.00, on a two-seated top carriage $1.25 to $4.00 To points 500 to 1,000 miles from Chicago, the freight on a road cart, $1.25 to $2.75; on a top buggy, $3.50 to $6.00; on a two-seated top carriage, $5.00 to $10.00. To greater distant points the freight will be about in proportion, **so you can well afford** to pay the freight, for you will still have your vehicle at about one-half the retail price.

OUR GUARANTEE. We issue a two years' binding guarantee with every vehicle we sell, agreeing to replace free of charge at the factory any part that may prove defective, either in material or workmanship within two years.

HOW TO ORDER. Write your orders plainly and always say to what freight depot you wish goods shipped. Order by name and number. Be sure to sign your name plainly and in full. Be sure to send the full amount of cash with your order, either by bank draft, check, money order or express.

GENERAL DESCRIPTION OF OUR VEHICLES.

We not only aim to furnish first-class work at our extremely low price, but we try to make every job so good that when you receive it you will find it even better than described and superior in every way to the goods so generally advertised. **IF WE SELL YOU ONE BUGGY** we shall expect in time to sell you more and also your neighbors. To do this we must give you goods of such quality that you will be in every way satisfied. The description will give you a general idea of the way our work is finished, but you must see it to fully appreciate it.

Wood Work.

WHEELS—We begin with wheels because we think they are the most important feature in the durability of a vehicle; our wheels are manufactured of carefully selected and thoroughly seasoned hickory, either Sarven's Patent with 16 spokes, or Banded Wood Hub, or Shell Band with 14 spokes, and every wheel guaranteed. Buggy and phaeton wheels, ¾ inch, ⅞ inch, and 1 inch tread; carriage and surrey wheels, 1 inch and 1⅛ inch tread, all with screwed rims. The regular height for buggy wheels is 42 inch front and 46 inch back; for phaeton, 36 inch front and 44 inch back; for carriages, 38 inch front and 46 inch back. Tires bolted between every spoke. (We can furnish different sizes of wheels if desired).

GEARS—Made of best hickory, thoroughly seasoned, with fine, handsome scrolls.

BODIES—Made of thoroughly seasoned lumber, ash frame, poplar panels, joints put together with glue, and panels carefully screwed and plugged; corners all mitered and strengthened by corner irons.

POLES AND SHAFTS—Very best second growth hickory, carefully and neatly finished and trimmed. All poles are furnished complete and single tree, double tree and neck yoke ready for use.

Iron Work.

TIRES—Best refined steel with round edges, and FULL BOLTED BETWEEN SPOKES.

AXLES—Double collar, steel fantail, Anchor Brand, best quality on all work.

BRACES—Clips, king bolts, fifth wheels, etc., all carefully finished of best Norway iron.

SPRINGS—First quality of English steel, oil tempered and fully warranted.

Painting.

The very best colors and varnishes are used on every job, well filled and rubbed out with pumice stone; bodies all black, gears black, brewster green or wine color, with fine-line striping. (Special styles of painting if desired).

Trimming.

TOPS—Four-bowed or three-bowed, (as desired). No. 1 leather used in quarters and back stays; roof, best heavy rubber drill; back curtains, rubber drill lined with cloth, side curtains, rubber flock; steel bow sockets and wrought iron joints and top props; cloth head lining. **WE USE THE CELEBRATE BREWSTER PATENT SILVER FASTENINGS on all our tops INSTEAD of THE OLD-FASHIONED BUCKLES.** We can furnish full leather tops with leather back curtain when desired, on buggies at $5 extra, and on two-seated vehicles at $9 extra. We, however, never advise our customers to go to this extra expense which is unnecessary, as the superior quality of our regular style tops look as well and are fully as durable.

CUSHIONS—Best No. 1 trimming leather, either black or fancy is used, unless cloth is especially ordered, in which case we use green English wood-dyed broadcloth. All top vehicles are furnished with side and back curtains.

CARPETS—TOE CARPETS in all vehicles. Full leather dash.

BOOTS—Each buggy furnished with Patent Boot for buggy body bock of seat.

☞We also furnish a special grade imitation leather top at a special price.

Compare our prices with those of any house in America. Compare our work with any and you be the judge.

SEARS, ROEBUCK & CO.,

Minneapolis, Minn.   **Chicago, Ills.**

OUR $8.95 ROAD CART $8.95

Retails every where at $15.00

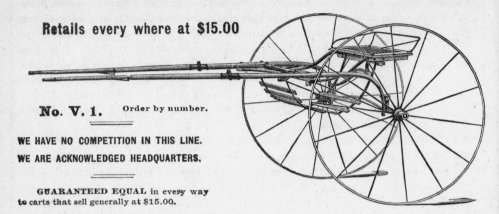

No. V. 1.   Order by number.

WE HAVE NO COMPETITION IN THIS LINE.

WE ARE ACKNOWLEDGED HEADQUARTERS.

GUARANTEED EQUAL in every way to carts that sell generally at $15.00.

NO SUCH BARGAINS EVER OFFERED BEFORE, we are determined to lead all others in this line by lower prices, better goods and larger sales.

THIS CART is very strong, thoroughly well made, nicely finished in the natural wood, carries two passengers, all second growth hickory, 1 inch double collar steel axle, square at shoulders, octogon and round in center, steel tire bolted on, low bent seat arms, perfectly balanced, long easy riding oil tempered springs, best patent wheel, width of tire 1 inch, width of seat from rail to rail 30 inches, weight 125 pounds shipping weight 140 pounds.

AT OUR PRICE $8.95, no one need be without one of these road carts, many of our customers but them to sell again, you can make money on this cart, you can sell them to all your neighbors at $12.00 each the weight is only 140 pounds crated so the freight will be very little.

THIS CART FOR $10.95

Regular wholesale price is $15.00.
Retails every where at $20.00.

No. V. 2.   Order by number.

WE MAKE THE PRICE $10.95
And ship to any one any where,

OUR BINDING GUARANTEE
Goes with every cart.

NO SUCH BARGAINS EVER OFFERED BEFORE, we are determined to lead all others.

This cart is very much the same as V 1, except it is better finished in every way, has the best oil tempered springs hung on a patent link, while our V 1 cart at $8.95 is in every way a good job and the best cart ever sold for the money, for a really first class job we recommend this cart at $10.95.

☞ **YOU WON'T BREAK IT.   RIDES VERY EASY.   HAS NO HORSE MOTION.** ☜

Weight 140 pounds crated, so freight will be very little.   **YOU TAKE NO RISK** when you order from us, if everything is not satisfactory we **will refund your money** and pay all the freight both ways.

LIKE A THUNDERBOLT

Our unheard of prices are being sounded from ocean to ocean. **We are waging war against high prices. Down with the credit system. Down with monopoly, trusts and combinations.**

GOOD GOODS, LOW PRICES, CASH. We are armed to the teeth, nothing can defeat us. **Our fortification is Cash.** No bad debts, no extra expense. The great price destroyer is **Cash.**

GIVE US CASH and we will furnish you more goods for a dollar than you ever dreamed was possible.

THIS BUGGY $36.90 CASH.

Don't say you can buy it as cheap elsewhere. Don't say you ever see it advertised before for **$36.90.** **Don't say you ever heard of such a bargain before.**

TELL THE TRUTH, acknowledge it's the most wonderful bargain you ever heard of.

If you are a dealer, if you are a manufacturer, **be honest, don't shrink from the truth ; say what you think, say what you know. The first time on record a top buggy was ever offered for $36.90.**

RETAILS FOR $75.00 everywhere. No retail dealer can possibly sell it for less than $75.00.

IT IS GUARANTEED.— A binding two years' written guarantee goes with every buggy. We will ship to any one anywhere on receipt of said special price, $36.90. We pack carefully and deliver F. O. B. at factory or Chicago. Our freight rates are low, our prices bottom. Can't we have your trade?

YOU CAN SELL IT for $50.00 any day. You can make big money selling these buggies.

No. V. 3.

☞ Order by Number.

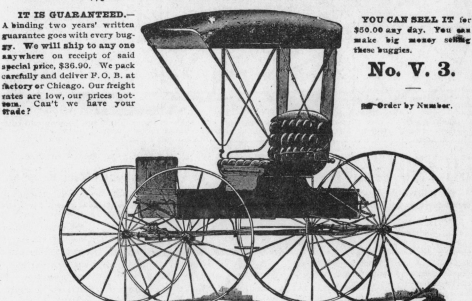

DESCRIPTION. This buggy is built to supply the demand of those who want a substantial rig at a **low price,** yet do not feel like buying a high grade job. This buggy has 1 inch double collar steel axle, ⅞ inch round edge steel tire, Sarven Patent Wheels, full rubber top, cloth cushions and back, carpet full length of body. **Your choice,** either end spring, Brewster spring or Timpkin side spring. **The price includes the buggy complete as described, with shafts.** If you wish pole in place of shafts, we require **$4.00 additional. Extra poles** will be furnished with neck yoke and singletrees complete, at **$6.00.**

WITHOUT TOP. We furnish this buggy with full cushioned back at $31.90. Understand, this is a very strong job; has a capacity of 480 pounds and is thoroughly adapted to general use.

THE FREIGHT IS VERY LOW. The buggy weighs 400 pounds, including crate, and to all points within 1,000 miles of Chicago, or the factory, the freight on this buggy will be from 75c to $6.00. Send your order direct to us, either Chicago or Minneapolis. Be sure to send the full amount of cash with your order, and the buggy will be promptly shipped to you. Understand, you take no risk, for, if you do not find it in every way as represented, and entirely satisfactory, you can return it by freight at our expense and we will cheerfully refund your money.

WE FURNISH ON ALL BUGGIES WHEN DESIRED

American Queen Springs	$3.00 extra.
National Springs	2.00 "
Thomas' Patent Coil Springs	1.50 "

OUR GREATEST DRIVE.

Positively the grandest bargain we have to offer. Grandest for the reason that it is a thoroughly first-class job in every respect and yet offered at one-half the price charged by retailers.

We furnish on all buggies when desired American Queen Springs $3 extra, National Springs $2 extra, Thomas' Patent Coil Spr'gs $1.50 extra. For pole in place of shafts add $5.

OUR SPECIAL DRIVE
PRICE IS $49.50

DESCRIPTION: The general description of our best work fully describes this job, which we furnish in either end spring, Timpkin, or Brewster side spring as desired. Everything about it is thoroughly first-class as described in our general description.

Trimming is No. 1 leather in quarters, and back stays, roof best heavy rubber drill, back curtains rubber drill lined with cloth, side curtains, rubber flock steel bow sockets, and wrought iron joints and top props, cloth head lining.

Don't Forget our binding 2 years guarantee goes with every buggy, and we always refund money if you are not perfectly satisfied.

V. 4. $49.50

While our V. 3 is the best buggy ever offered for anything like the price, we by all means, **recommend this job** for it is much better finished, and will be a standing recommendation for us wherever it is owned.

DO YOU WANT THE BEST?

DON'T PAY $150 FOR A BUGGY.
OUR FINEST BUGGY $58.00 to $68.00

We Guarantee our $68.00 job fully equal to any buggy you can buy at retail for $150. **No other concern** advertises this class of work. This buggy is built for our finest trade. **Has wonderful sale in the cities.**

YOUR CHOICE either end spring, Timpkin, or Brewster side spring. The material, workmanship, and finish is thoroughly first-class in every respect. A general description of this buggy can be summed up in three words, **Everything the Best.**

Our price complete with shafts, three-fourths leather top, **$58.00;** our price for our **special extra finished** job, with full leather top, **$68.00.**

We furnish pole in place of shafts at $5.50. Extra poles will be furnished with neck yoke and single tree complete, $7.00.

V. 5.

$58.00 to $68.00

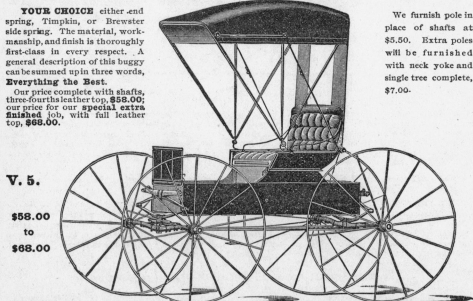

YOU CAN OWN THE BEST for we have put the price within the reach of all. **Don't compare this job** with that advertised by many catalogue houses, **they have nothing to compare** with this in quality, finish and general appearance.

OUR ROAD WAGON $22.95.

V. 6.   PRICE $22.95.

This job is thoroughly well made wagon, *warranted* for two years; with proper care will last a life time. **WE MAKE IT A LEADER** and ship to any one, complete with shafts, on receipt of $22.95.   Pole in place of shaft $3.00 extra.   Painted, or natural wood, as desired.

OUR $58.00 PHAETON.

We furnish pole with neck yoke and whiffletrees complete in place of shafts at $5.00 extra.   Wing Dash $4.00 extra.

V. 7.

PRICE
$58.00,
$68.00
and $88.00.

THE BEST MATERIAL is used in the construction of all our Phaetons. The difference in price is governed by the amount of work and the general finish; also in top and cushions. Our $58.00 Phaeton is a good job and a most wonderful bargain. It comes complete with *Lamps, Fenders* and shafts, best quality immitation leather top. Our $68.00 grade is better finished throughout, fine quality broadcloth cushioned seat and back, full three-fourths leather top. Our $88.00 grade is our very finest work, best of finish throughout, including full leather top, finest quality broadcloth spring cushion seat and back, finished in fourteen coats of paint and guaranteed equal to Phaetons which retail everywhere at $200. Lamps in front in place of back. $2.00 extra.

FINEST PHAETON MADE. Our Price $105.00 and $117.00.

BUILT FOR THE FINEST CITY TRADE. GUARANTEED EQUAL TO PHAETONS THAT RETAIL EVERYWHERE AT FROM $250.00 TO $300.00.

Any description we could give this job, would hardly do it justice. Every piece and part is of the very finest material, and the workmanship is unexcelled.

There is Nothing Better Made.

V 9.

PRICE

$105.00 and $117.00.

We Recommend Our $105.00 Grade as it will compare favorably with the finest work carried by the best dealers. It is finely finished, has ¾ leather top, fine broadcloth spring cushion seat and back, complete with lamps, fenders and shafts.

Our $117.00 Grade is a special finished job. Where something extra fine is required. Full leather top and in every respect the finest grade we handle. We furnish pole with neckyoke and whiffletrees complete, in place of shafts, at $6.00 extra.

FINEST PHAETON CART $13.90.

We Are Selling This Cart at ONE-HALF the Regular Price.

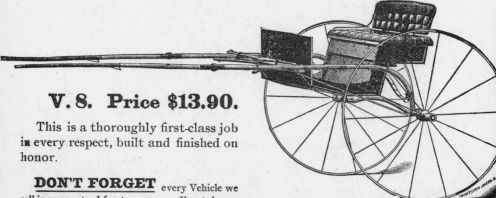

V. 8. Price $13.90.

This is a thoroughly first-class job in every respect, built and finished on honor.

DON'T FORGET every Vehicle we sell is guaranteed for two years. You take no risk. If not found satisfactory you can return it by freight, at our expense, and we will cheerfully refund your money. Painted or Natural wood as desired.

OUR $27.00 ROAD WAGON.

NOTHING LIKE IT EVER OFFERED BEFORE FOR LESS THAN $40.00.

V. 10. Price $27.00.

WE GUARANTEE every vehicle for two years, and guarantee this wagon equal to any wagon sold elsewhere for $40.00. We furnish this in the natural wood or painted as desired. Trimmed in corduroy or Evans leather. Price, complete with shafts, $27.00. For pole, neck yoke and whiffletrees complete in place of shafts, $3.00 extra.

HALF PLATFORM SPRING WAGON

WE BREAK ALL RECORDS AND MAKE THE PRICE $37.50. RETAILS EVERYWHERE AT $60.00 to $75.00.

V. 11. Price $37.50.

THIS IS OUR LEADER in spring wagons and the best value ever offered for the money, guaranteed for two years, with fair usage will last a lifetime. Trimmed in corduroy or Evans leather, weighs, crated, 550 lbs. The freight within 1,000 miles of Chicago, or factory, will be from $1.50 to $9.00. Our price is for wagon complete with shafts. For pole complete with neckyoke and whiffletrees in place of shafts add $4.00.

OUR $31.00 ROAD WAGON. LIGHT, STYLISH, DURABLE.

Retails Everywhere at $45.00 to $50.00.

V. 12. Price $31.00.

THE GREATEST thing of the season; better than any other of the kind. A very fancy and thoroughly first-class job. We furnish it in natural wood or painted, as desired. Trimmed in either corduroy or Evans leather, as desired. Our price, complete with shafts, $31.00. For pole with neck-yoke and whiffletrees complete in place of shafts, add $3.00. **With Canopy Top $10.00 extra.**

ONE OF THE HANDSOMEST VEHICLES BUILT

Price quoted is for job complete with shafts. For pole with neck-yoke and whiffletrees complete, add $5.00.

V. 13.

Price $55.00 to $61.00.

Our Special Price $55.00 to $61.00

Retails Every-where at $80.00 to $100.00.

The most convenient, best made *Jump Seat* carriage in the market. We furnish this carriage with either end or side springs. Our $55.00 grade is thoroughly well built with best quality imitation leather top. Our $61.00 grade has ¾ leather top.

WE DEFY COMPETITION! OUR PRICE IS $29.85.

WE CHALLENGE ANY CONCERN ON EARTH TO MEET THIS PRICE.

V. 14. Price $29.85.

THE GREATEST BARGAIN EVER OFFERED in a two-seated wagon. This wagon is well built—nothing but the best material is used in its construction; finished in the natural wood or painted as desired. Trimmed in corduroy or Evans' leather. We furnish this job complete with shafts, at $29.85. With pole, neck yoke and whiffletrees complete, in place of shafts, add $3.00.

OUR EXTENSION TOP SURREY.

$79.00.

Retails Everywhere at $125.00 to $150.00.

PRICE, $79.00.

V. 15.

WE GUARANTEE THIS SURREY in every respect. All thoroughly well made of the best material, and warranted for two years. Our price complete, with shafts, ¾ leather top, $79.00; with full leather top, $88.00. Extra for pole in place of shafts, $5.00. **DON'T THINK** the freight too high. **This Surrey** weighs **700** pounds crated and ready for shipment, and the freight will be but a few dollars to any point.

$69 BUYS A $150 CARRIAGE

V 16

THIS BEAUTIFUL WAGON is a well made, guaranteed job, constructed of the best material **on honor. Trimmings,** corduroy or Evans' leather as desired, finest quality **Leatherine top,** fully warranted. **$69.00** includes wagon complete with shafts. For pole in place of shafts add $5.00.

OUR FREIGHT RATE is the lowest. A few dollars at the most will deliver it at your door.

WE REFUND YOUR MONEY if you are not perfectly satisfied.

OUR PRICE, $89.50. RETAIL PRICE, $150.

V 17

ONE OF THE FINEST jobs made. Everything strictly first-class. Full spring seat, and back made of extra heavy, fine broadcloth, ¾ leather top. Our price includes everything complete, with shafts; for pole in place of shafts, add $5.

$105 OUR PRICE $105

RETAIL PRICE $200.

One of the Finest Cut-Under Surreys Made.

V. 18. Price $105.00.

EVERYTHING FIRST-CLASS. Best quality broadcloth upholstered spring seats and cushions. Our price, complete in canopy top, with shafts $150. We furnish this job with extension top, three-fourths leather, at $112. For pole in place of shafts add $5.00; for wing dash add $4.00.

WRITE TO US about anything you don't understand. We are always ready to answer all inquiries promptly, pleasantly and in detail, no matter whether you buy or not.

ABOUT THE FREIGHT. Understand you pay the freight, but we have figured to make that as low as possible. We will ship either from the factory, Chicago, or Minneapolis, depending on which point we can get the lowest rate to your place.

WE CAN TELL YOU to a cent what the freight will cost you on any vehicle, in case you wish to know before purchasing. Write us what you contemplate buying, tell us to what railroad station you wish it shipped, and we will inform you just what the freight will be. We will also be pleased to give you a full description, or any special information you may desire concerning any vehicle.

WE FINISH TO ORDER any vehicle to suit our customers, with very little, and often no additional expense. Tell us how you want a job finished, give us a few days time to do the work and we will endeavor to fill your order to the letter, and in nearly every case we can do so without putting you to any extra expense.

FINEST JOB WE MAKE

WE ARE NOT AFRAID to match it against any extension top, four-passenger phaeton in the market. We have spared nothing in its construction.

THIS CARRIAGE WAS BUILT for our best trade. We have had a call from our customers in cities and large towns for an extra fine two-seated top phaeton, and to supply this demand we offer this

Elegant New Style Carriage.

IT WAS BUILT WITH A VIEW TO SUPPLY A HIGH CLASS TRADE,

**OUR PRICE,
$129.75.**

**RETAIL PRICE,
$250.00.**

V. 19.

PRICE, $129.75.

IN OUR WAR AGAINST MONOPOLY PRICES IT COMES WITHIN THE REACH OF ALL.

NOTHING SPARED—Nothing Left Undone in This Job.

HUNG VERY LOW, exceedingly roomy and comfortable, furnished with beautiful lamps, wide double fenders and storm aprons all around. Finest quality extra heavy broadcloth spring cushioned seats and backs, ¾ leather top with shafts. Complete $129.75. This job complete with full leather top, $139.75. This job complete with canopy top, $123.75. Forpole in place of shafts, add $5.00.

COSTS YOU NOTHING to see and examine our goods.

WE MAKE NO CHARGE FOR BOXING, CRATING or CARTAGE.

We ship to any one anywhere, and in any quantity. Always send our binding two years' guarantee.

WE TAKE ALL THE RISK, as we always refund all money where goods are not found perfectly satisfactory.

Harness and Saddles...

On the following pages we illustrate and describe a full line of Harness and Saddles at prices as low as any wholesale house in existence. - - - - - -

We Are Prepared to save you money on everything in this line. We can furnish you a harness or saddle at one-half the price charged by retail dealers.

We Handle Nothing but the best grade goods, all our harness are made from carefully selected oak tan stock. Our machine made harness are made on the most improved machines, and we guarantee it equal to the average hand made goods; while our hand made work is of a specially fine quality, and far superior than it is possible for the average harness-maker to produce.

Our Terms and Conditions of Shipments. We will ship any single harness or saddle to any address C. O. D., subject to examination, on receipt of $1.00 as a guarantee of good faith. You can examine it at the express office and if found perfectly satisfactory you can pay the express agent our price, less the $1.00 you have paid us; if not satisfactory refuse it and the agent will return it at our expense.

We Send Double Harness by express C. O. D., subject to examination on receipt of $2.00 as a guarantee of good faith.

Where Cash in Full accompanies the order, we send free, with each single harness, a *Fine Saddle Pad* worth $1.00, and with each set of double harness we send free a full set of *Sweat Pads* worth $2.00.

It is Far Better to Send Cash in Full with your order, for you not only get a present, but it enables us to ship the harness by fast freight, a thing which we cannot do when we send C. O. D.

By Fast Freight we get a very low rate. To points within 1,000 miles of Chicago, we can ship from one to six harness, for from 25c. to 50c., according to the line of railroad.

How to Order Harness. Always give the weight and height of the horse they are to fit. If the harness is ordered with collar and hames, be sure to give the size of collar. All styles of harness in this catalogue are made in full size and will fit any average size horse. Always state the style of mountings or trimmings wanted; also whether side rein or over-check is wanted with bridle, and whether you want the lines fair or black. *If nothing is mentioned* concerning the lines, or reins, it is understood we have the privilege of using our own judgment, in which case we will do our best to please you.

We Make No Charge for boxing, crating, packing or cartage, but deliver all harness and saddles to any express office, or freight depot in Chicago, or Minneapolis, *free of charge*.

We Make to Order anything in the harness line. If you want anything special, anything different from that illustrated in our catalogue, write for it; we are prepared to furnish anything in that line.

C. O. D. ANYWHERE FOR $4.95.

RETAILS
EVERYWHERE
AT $10.00.

YOU KNOW OUR TERMS

No. H. 11.
ORDER BY NUMBER.

Where cash in full accompanies the order we send free a fine Saddle Pad worth $1.00, or send C. O. D., subject to examination, to any one on receipt of $1.00 as a guarantee of good faith.

DESCRIPTION

Our Number H. 11 Single Buggy Harness comes in full X. C. Plate. **BRIDLES**—⅝-inch cheeks, box loops, patent leather blinds, flat winker braces, ring bits, fancy fronts and rosettes, flat over or side reins. **LINES**—¾-inch flat, all black. **BREAST COLLAR**—Folded with full length straight lay and narrow loops, folded neck strap with ⅝-inch lay. **HAMES**—3½ lb., full X. C. with 1-inch box loop hame tugs. **TRACES**—1-inch, doubled and stitched "buckle to breast collar." **GIG SADDLE**—2½-inch japanned seat and jockey, enameled cloth bottom, doubled and stiched bearers. **SHAFT TUGS**—⅞-inch, doubled and stitched, with ⅞-inch belly-band billets. **BELLY-BANDS**—⅞-inch flat. **BREECHING**—Folded, with full length lay, ⅝-inch flat hip straps, ¾-inch turn backs lapped and stitched to crupper pieces, folded crupper docks sewed on, breeching straps ¾-inch.

OUR PRICE for this harness as described $4.95.

WITH COLLAR AND HAMES in place of breast collar, $1.50 extra.

$3.87 BUYS THIS HARNESS. < < < < <

NO HARNESS CONCERN ON EARTH CAN BEAT THIS PRICE.

Cash in Full must accompany all orders for this harness. **We send all other grades C. O. D.**, subject to examination, but on this our cheapest harness there is but a very few cents profit, and we believe you will agree, we are not at all unreasonable when we ask you to send cash in full with your order.

No. H. 10.
ORDER BY NUMBER.

DESCRIPTION

Our Number H. 10 single buggy harness comes in full X. C. Plate only; imitation hand sewed. **Bridles**—⅝-inch cheeks, patent leather blinds, flat winker braces, ring bits, fancy fronts and rosettes, flat over-checks or side reins as desired. **Lines**—¾-inch flat, all black, to loop into bit. **Breast Collar**—Single strap, with 1-inch full length lay, and 1-inch doubled and stitched traces attached, single strap neck piece. **Gig Saddle**—2½-inch enameled cloth bottom, doubled and stitched bearers. **Shaft Tugs**—1¼-inch, with ⅞-inch buckles and ¾-inch belly-band billets. **Belly-Bands**—⅞-inch flat. **Breeching**—Single strap with full length lay, ⅝-inch flat hip straps, ⅝-inch turn-backs lapped and stitched to crupper pieces, folded crupper docks sewed on, breeching straps ¾-inch.

OUR SPECIAL PRICE $6.45

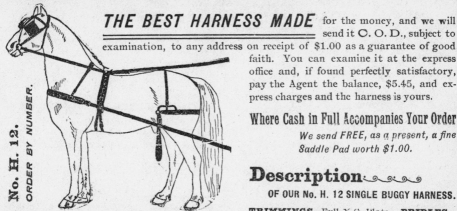

No. H. 12. ORDER BY NUMBER.

THE BEST HARNESS MADE

for the money, and we will send it C. O. D., subject to examination, to any address on receipt of $1.00 as a guarantee of good faith. You can examine it at the express office and, if found perfectly satisfactory, pay the Agent the balance, $5.45, and express charges and the harness is yours.

Where Cash in Full Accompanies Your Order

We send FREE, as a present, a fine Saddle Pad worth $1.00.

Description

OF OUR No. H. 12 SINGLE BUGGY HARNESS.

TRIMMINGS—Full X C Plate. **BRIDLES**—⅝-inch cheeks, full box loops, nicely finished, creased and polished patent leather blinds, flat winker braces, half cheek bits, fancy fronts and rosettes, flat over-checks or side reins as desired. **LINES**—All black flat, ⅞-inch, to loop or buckle into bit. **BREAST COLLAR**—Folded, with full straight lay and full length fancy box loops, folded neck strap, with ⅝-inch lay. **HAMES**—3½ lb. steel with 1-inch patent leather swell end hame tugs, box loops and safes. **TRACES**—1-inch, fancy raised, beveled and stitched. **SADDLE**—2½-inch japanned seat and jockey, enameled drilled bottom, padded full length leather loops, doubled and stitched bearers. **SHAFT TUGS**—⅞-inch, doubled and stitched, with ⅞-inch belly-band billets. **BELLY-BANDS**—⅞-inch flat. **BREECHING**—Folded, with full length lay, ⅝-inch flat hip straps, ¾-inch turn-backs lapped and stitched to crupper pieces, round crupper-docks sewed on.

OUR PRICE for this harness as described $6.45. With full leather collar and hames in place of breast collar $7.95.

For Full Nickel or Davis Rubber Trimming in Place of X. C., 75c. extra.

SPECIAL SINGLE BUGGY HARNESS. A GREAT LEADER A GREAT BARGAIN

$7.95 BUYES A $15.00 HARNESS.

No. H. 13. ORDER BY NUMBER.

Let us Send You One to Examine. *You examine it carefully at the express office, and if you don't say it is fully equal to any harness you ever see offered for $15.00,* **DON'T TAKE IT** *but let the agent return it at our expense.*

YOU KNOW OUR TERMS *C. O. D., subject to examination, on receipt of $1.00.*

A $1.00 SADDLE PAD FREE where cash in full accompanies your order.

DESCRIPTION of our No. H 13 Single Buggy Harness

Finest quality full nickel or Davis rubber trimming, as desired. **BRIDLES**—⅝-inch cheeks, full box loops, very fancy, creased, finished and polished patent leather blinds, with two rows of carving, round winker braces, layers on crown pieces, half cheek bits, band fronts and fancy rosettes, flat over-check or side reins as desired. **LINES**—⅞-inch flat, all black, to buckle or loop into bit. **BREAST COLLAR**—Folded, with straight raised lay and box loops throughout, folded neck strap, with ⅝-inch raised lay, doubled and stitched points. **HAMES**—3½ lbs. steel, with 1-inch leather swell end hame tugs, box loops and safes. **TRACES**—1-inch solid raised, doubled and stitched. **SADDLE**—2½-inch japanned seat and jockey, leather loops, enameled leather pad and welt, raised, doubled and stitched bearers. **SHAFT TUGS**—⅞-inch, doubled and stitched, ⅞-inch belly-band billets. **BELLY-BANDS**—Short folded belly-band, with one row of straight stitching and ⅞-inch buckles. **BREECHING**—Folded, with straight raised lay, ⅝-inch flat hip straps, ¾-inch turn backs lapped and stitched to crupper pieces, round crupper docks sewed on, breeching strap ⅞-inch.

OUR PRICE FOR HARNESS AS DESCRIBED $7.95.

WE FURNISH this harness with hames and leather collar, in place of breast collar, at $8.45.

WE USE NOTHING but the best selected oak tanned leather and the best grade trimmings in all our goods. **WE GUARANTEE** our harness in every respect, and will make good any breakage, or damage, resulting from defect in material or workmanship.

OUR $9.75 SINGLE HARNESS

No. H. 14. ORDER BY NUMBER.

GUARANTEED equal to harness which retail at $20.00 and upwards.

Remember all our goods are of the best oak tanned stock, and trimmings the best.

OUR TERMS ARE VERY EASY

We make no charge for boxing or drayage, **you pay our price** and the freight or express charges, **nothing more.**

DESCRIPTION OF OUR No. H. 14 SINGLE BUGGY HARNESS.

TRIMMINGS—Full Nickel or Davis Rubber, blackened on the flesh throughout. **BRIDLES**—⅝-inch cheeks, full box loops, patent leather blinds, with two rows of carving, round winker braces, layers on crown pieces, half cheek bits, band fronts and fancy rosettes, flat over-checks or round side reins, as desired. **LINES**—⅞-inch flat, with 1-inch hand parts, all black. **BREAST COLLAR**—Folded, with full length straight raised lay and full box loops throughout, folded neck strap with ⅝-inch raised lay, doubled and stitched points. **HAMES**—3½ lb. iron, with 1-inch leather swell end hame tugs, with box loops and safes. **TRACES**—Extra heavy 1⅛-inch solid raised, doubled and stitched. **SADDLE**—3-inch japanned seat, patent leather skirts and jockey, plain leather welt and loops, enameled leather pad, ⅞-inch raised, doubled and stitched bearers. **SHAFT TUGS**—1-inch, doubled and stitched with box loops, and ⅞-inch belly-band billets. **BELLY-BANDS**—Folded, with one row of straight stitching, ⅞-inch buckles. **BREECHING**—Folded, with straight raised lay and round breeching stays, ⅝-inch flat hip straps with round crupper-docks sewed on, breeching straps ⅞-inch.

OUR PRICE for this harness as described $9.75.

We Furnish the same harness with hames and leather collar in place of breast collar at $11.25

OUR $12.00 HARNESS.

SELLS EVERYWHERE AT $25.00.

BEST LEATHER. TRIMMINGS. OF EVERYTHING.

No. H. 15. ORDER BY NUMBER.

FULLY WARRANTED.

SENT C. O. D. TO ANYONE.

Fine Saddle Pad FREE on all Cash Orders.

Description

Of Our No. H. 15 Single Buggy Harness.

Trimmings—Full Nickel or Davis rubber, as desired. **Bridles**—⅝-inch cheeks, box loops, patent leather blinds, with three rows of stitching, round winker braces, waved layers on crown pieces, half cheek bits, leather fronts and fancy rosettes, flat over-checks or round side reins as desired. **Lines**—⅞-inch flat, 1-inch hand parts, all black with buckles and billets. **Breast Collar**—Folded, with scalloped and wave stitched raised lay, box loops throughout, folded neck strap, with ¾-inch doubled and stitched raised lay. **Hames**—3½ lbs. iron, with patent leather swell end hame tugs, with two rows of stitching, box loops and safes. **Traces**—1⅛-inch solid raised, doubled and stitched. **Saddle**—3-inch japanned seat, patent leather jockey, leather loops, enameled leather pad, doubled, raised and straight stitched bearers. **Shaft Tugs**—Doubled and stitched with box loops, and ⅞-inch belly-band billets. **Belly-Bands**—1½-inch short flat belly-band, with ⅞-inch buckles, ⅞-inch long flat belly-band. **Breeching**—Folded, with straight raised lay, and three ring round breeching stays, with box loops, ⅝-inch flat hip straps, fancy stitched turn backs, round crupper docks sewed on, breeching straps ⅞ inch.

OUR PRICE, for this harness as described, $12.00.

WE FURNISH THE SAME HARNESS WITH HAMES AND LEATHER COLLAR FOR $13.75.

DO YOU WANT OUR BEST? OUR BEST IS $18.95

A REGULAR $35.00 HARNESS.

CANNOT BE DUPLICATED IN ANY HARNESS SHOP FOR LESS THAN $35.00.

YOU CAN EXAMINE it at the Express Office.

No. H. 17. ORDER BY NUMBER.

SENT C. O. D. to any one anywhere on receipt of **$1.00** as a guarantee of good faith; balance to be paid at the express office if satisfactory.

FREE Our Special Made Fine Saddle Pad with all Cash Orders.

DESCRIPTION

Of our No. H. 17 Best Grade Single Buggy Harness. READ this Carefully, it's our Bargain of Bargains.

Trimmings—Genuine rubber throughout, or full nickel, as desired; blackened on the flesh throughout, sewed 8 and 10 to the inch, is all hand creased and has round edges. **Bridles**—⅝-inch checks, extended laps, box loops, patent leather fancy stitched blinds, round winker braces, fancy stitched layers on crown pieces, half cheek bits, fancy fronts and rosettes, flat over-check or round side reins. **Lines**—1-inch flat, all black, hand finished. **Breast Collar**—Boarded fold, with very fancy stitched raised lay and box loops through-out, folded neck strap, boarded with ¾-inch solid raised lay. **Hames**—3½ lbs. steel, with patent leather swell end hame tugs and box loops. **Traces**—1⅛-inch solid raised, doubled and stitched. **Saddle**—3-inch japanned seat, patent leather jockey and loops, enameled leather pad doubled, raised and fancy stitched bearers. **Shaftings**—⅞-inch, doubled and stitched box loops, and ⅞-inch belly band billets. **Belly Bands**—Boarded fold, with one row of stitching and ⅞-inch buckles. **Breeching**—Boarded fold, with fancy stitched raised lay and three ring round breeching stays, with box loops, ⅝-inch flat hip straps, fancy stitched turn-backs, round crupper docks sewed on, breeching straps ⅞-inch.

OUR PRICE, for this harness as described, $18.95.

WE FURNISH the same harness with hames and leather collar in place of breast collar at $21.75. The above prices include martingales.

OUR $14.75 HARNESS. Best Stock. Best Everything.

Retails Everywhere at $25.00 to $30.00.

C. O. D. TO ANY ONE SUBJECT TO EXAMINATION.

Nice Saddle Pad **FREE** on all cash in advance orders.

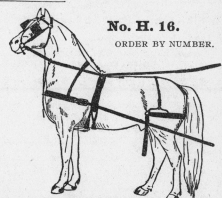

No. H. 16.

ORDER BY NUMBER.

Description

Of Our No. H. 16 Single Buggy Harness.

Trimmings—Full Nickel or Davis rubber, as de-sired; blacked on the flesh throughout. **Bridles**—⅝-inch checks, box loops, patent leather blinds, with three rows of stitching, round winker braces, layers on crown pieces, half cheek bits, fancy fronts and rosettes, flat over checks or round side reins. **Lines**—⅞-inch flat, 1-inch hand parts, all black with buckles and billets. **Breast Collar**—Folded, with full length straight raised lay, and box loop throughout, folded neck strap, with ¾-inch raised lay. **Hames**—3½ lbs. iron, with swell end hame tugs, with box loops and safes. **Traces**—1⅛-inch raised, doubled and stitched. **Gig Saddle**—3-inch japanned seat, patent leather jockey, leather loops, enameled leather pad, doubled, raised and straight stitched bearers. **Shaft Tugs**—⅞-inch doubled and stitched with box loops, and ⅞-inch belly band billets. **Belly Bands**—1½-inch short flat belly band, with ⅞-inch buckles, ⅞-inch long flat belly band, **Breeching**—Folded, with straight raised lay, and three ring round breeching stays, with box loops, ⅝-inch flat hip straps, fancy stitched turn backs, round crupper docks sewed on, breeching straps ⅞-inch.

OUR PRICE FOR THIS HARNESS AS ABOVE DESCRIBED, $14.75.

WE FURNISH the same harness with hames and leather collar in place of breast collar for $16.75.

SINGLE TRACK HARNESS
OUR PRICE $7.85

RETAILS AT $12.00.

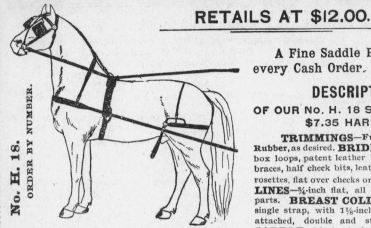

No. H. 18. ORDER BY NUMBER.

A Fine Saddle Pad FREE with every Cash Order.

DESCRIPTION

OF OUR No. H. 18 SINGLE TRACK, $7.35 HARNESS.

TRIMMINGS—Full Nickel or Davis Rubber, as desired. **BRIDLES**—5/8 inch cheeks, box loops, patent leather blinds, round winker braces, half check bits, leather fronts and fancy rosettes, flat over checks or side reins as desired. **LINES**—3/4-inch flat, all black, 7/8-inch hand parts. **BREAST COLLAR**—1 3/4-inch, solid single strap, with 1 1/8-inch single strap traces attached, double and stitched trace ends. **SADDLE**—3-inch, single strap, japanned seat, enameled leather pad, metal loops, 7/8-inch solid raised and stitched bearers. **SHAFT TUGS**—Doubled and stitched with box loops. **BELLY BANDS**—1 1/2-inch solid single strap with Griffith girth buckles and 3/4-inch billets to buckle around shafts. **BREECHING**—1 1/2-inch solid single strap, doubled and stitched breeching stays, 5/8-inch flat hip straps, 3/4-inch turn backs lapped and stitched to crupper pieces, round crupper docks sewed on, breeching straps 3/4-inch.

C. O. D. TO ANY ONE ON RECEIPT OF $1.00 AS A GUARANTEE OF GOOD FAITH.

OUR $11.40 HARNESS.
Retails at from $20.00 to $25.00.

OUR BARGAIN OF BARGAINS.

GUARANTEED the Greatest Value ever offered in a Single Strap Track Harness.

It Will Pay to buy a good Harness and this is a **Good One** and sure to please you.

SENT ANYWHERE C. O. C. SUBJECT TO EXAMINATION.

WE SEND FREE a Fine Saddle Pad with every cash order.

DESCRIPTION of our No. H. 19 Fancy Single Track Harness.

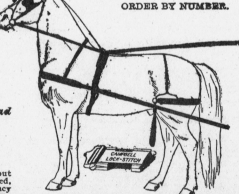

No. H. 19. ORDER BY NUMBER.

Trimmings—Full Genuine Rubber throughout Finest Quality Nickel or Davis rubber, as desired, blackened on the flesh throughout, plain or fancy creased as desired, sewed 8 and 9 to the inch. **Bridle**—5/8-inch cheeks, box loops, patent leather blinds, round winker braces, layers on crown pieces, half check bits, leather fronts and fancy rosettes, flat over checks or round side reins, as desired. **Lines**—7/8-inch flat, all black, with buckles and billets, scalloped and waved stitched laps, 1-inch hand parts. **Breast Collar**—1 3/4-inch, solid single strap, fancy creased, scalloped and waved stitched raised lay and box loops, with 1 1/8-inch single strap traces attached. **Saddle**—3-inch, single strap track covered seat, with patent leather jockey, enameled leather pad, and metal tips, 1-inch fancy creased single strap bearers. **Shaft Tugs**—1-inch, doubled and stitched with box loops. **Belly Bands**—1 1/2-inch solid single strap, with Griffith girth buckles and 7/8-inch billets to buckle around shafts. **Breeching**—1 1/2-inch solid single strap, fancy creased, scalloped and waved stitched raised lay, and three ring doubled and stitched breeching stay, with box loops, 5/8-inch flat hip straps, scalloped and waved stitched turn backs, round crupper docks sewed on breeching straps 7/8-inch.

OUR PRICE, for the above harness with Full Nickel or Davis Rubber Trimmings, **$11.40.**

WE FURNISH the same harness with genuine rubber trimmings throughout at **$14.40.**

OUR $18.75 HARNESS.

C. O. D. to any one on receipt of $1.00 as a guarantee of good faith.

OUR VERY BEST Single Strap Track Harness.

No. H. 20. ORDER BY NUMBER.

WE SAVE YOU $12.00 to $25.00 on this harness. *Warranted* in every way, and strictly first-class throughout.

Free a fine Saddle Pad with every order accompanied by cash in full.

WE REFUND YOUR MONEY and all express or freight charges if you are not perfectly satisfied.

DESCRIPTION
OF OUR No. H. 40 BEST GRADE SINGLE TRACK HARNESS.

Trimmings—Genuine rubber, full nickel or Davis rubber, as desired, blackened on the flesh, throughout fancy waved, creased and sewed, 10 and 12 to the inch. **Bridles**—⅝-inch cheeks, extended laps, box loops, patent leather blinds with three rows of stitching, round winker braces, waved layer on crown pieces, half cheek bits, leather fronts, fancy rosettes, flat over checks, with folded nose bands. **Lines**—1-inch flat, all black with spring billets scalloped and waved, stitched laps, 1⅛-inch boarded hand parts. **Breast Collar**—1¾-inch solid single strap with 1⅛-inch single strap traces attached, scalloped and wave stitched raised lay, with box loop. **Saddle**—2¾-inch patent leather track, with enameled leather pad, laced in ⅞-inch doubled and stitched bearers. **Shaft Tugs**—⅞-inch doubled, raised and stitched with box loops. **Belly Bands**—2¼-inch, solid single strap, with Griffith girth buckles, and ⅝-inch billets to buckle around shafts. **Breeching**—1¾-inch solid single strap, scalloped and wave stitched breeching stays with box loops, ⅝-inch flat hip straps, scalloped, waved and fancy stitched turn-backs, round crupper-docks sewed on, breeching straps ⅞-inch.

Our Price, For the above Harness with Full Nickel or Davis Rubber Trimmings, **$18.75.**

WE FURNISH the same harness with genuine rubber trimmings at $21.75.

RUSSET LEATHER HARNESS.

No. H. 21.
ORDER BY NUMBER.

DON'T BUY A POOR Russet Leather Harness. A poor one is a poor investment.

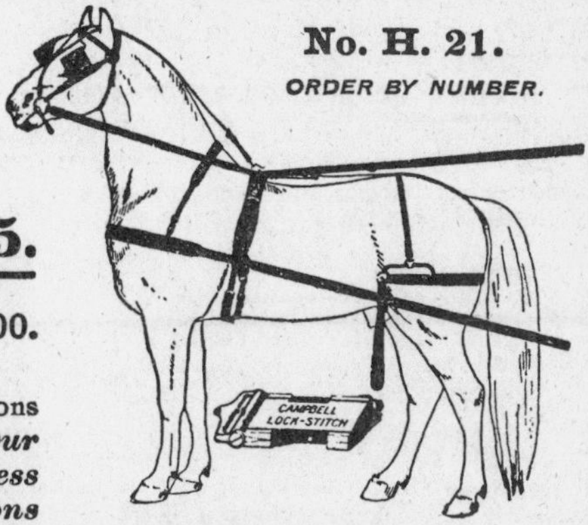

This Harness for $12.75.

Sold at Retail from $20.00 to $25.00.

MADE ESPECIALLY to match our road wagons and road carts, finished in the natural wood. *Our No. H. 21, Russet Leather Track Harness* and one of our *Natural Wood Road Wagons* makes a *handsome, nobby* turn out. *You should see it to appreciate it.*

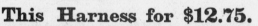

DESCRIPTION OF OUR No. H. 21, RUSSET LEATHER, SINGLE TRACK, FANCY HARNESS.

TRIMMINGS—Full nickle, highly polished, sewed, 8 and 10 to the inch. **BRIDLES**—⅝-inch cheeks, box loops, russet leather blinds with three rows of stitching, round winker braces, layers on crown pieces, half cheek bits, leather fronts and fancy rosettes, flat over checks or round side reins as desired. **LINES**—⅞-inch flat, with box loops to loop into bit, scalloped and wave stitched laps, 1-inch hand parts. **BREAST COLLAR**—1¾-inch solid, single strap with 1⅛-inch single strap traces attached, scalloped and wave stitched, raised lay and box loops. **SADDLE**—2½-inch russet single strap leather, covered seat with metal tips, ⅞-inch raised and straight stitched bearers. **SHAFT TUGS**—⅞-inch doubled and stitched with box loops. **BELLY BANDS**—1¾-inch solid, single strap, with Griffith girth buckles and ⅞-inch billets to buckle around shafts. **BREECHING**—1½-inch solid single strap, with scalloped and wave stitched raised lay, and three ring doubled and stitched breeching stays with box loops, ⅝-inch flat hip straps, scalloped and wave stitched turn backs, crupper docks sewed on. Breeching Strap, ⅞-inch.

OUR $23.95 SUREY HARNESS

THE BEST MADE.

No. H. 23.
ORDER BY NUMBER.

Description

TRIMMINGS—Full Nickel or Davis Rubber, as desired. **BRIDLES**—⅝-inch cheeks, extended laps, box loops, patent leather swell blinds, with three rows of stitching, round winker braces, layers on crown, pieces, half cheek bits, chain fronts, fancy rosettes, round side reins. **LINES**—⅞-inch flat, with buckles and billets, 1-inch hand-parts. **HAMES**—3½ pound iron, with box loops, safes and patent leather swell end hame tugs, with three rows of stitching, ⅝-inch hame-straps. **TRACES**—1⅛-inch solid raised, doubled and stitched. **SADDLE**—3½-inch coupe, patent leather jockey, enameled leather pad, tufted and laced in, 1-inch raised doubled and stitched bearers. **SHAFT TUGS**—1-inch, doubled and stitched, with dees, box loops and 1-inch belly-band billets. **BELLY BANDS**—Folded, with one row of straight stitching. **BREECHING**—Folded, with scalloped and waved stitched raised lay, with box loop breeching tugs, ⅝-inch hip straps scalloped, and waved stitched turn-backs, with round crupper-docks to buckle on. **BREECHING STRAPS**—⅞-inch. **MARTINGALES**—1-inch single strap, to buckle around collars.

Complete with Patent Leather Collar.

$13.45 EXPRESS HARNESS.

RETAILS at from $20.00 to $25.00.

<u>NO ONE</u> pretends to meet our price.

No. H. 22.
ORDER BY NUMBER.

WE SEND this harness to any one C. O. D., subject to examination, on receipt of $1.00 as a guarantee of good faith.

FREE————

With all Cash Orders a fine Saddle Pad worth $1.00.

DESCRIPTION OF OUR $13.45 EXPRESS HARNESS.

Trimmings—Brass, full nickel or X C as desired. **Bridles**—Blackened on the flesh throughout, ¾-inch cheeks, box loops, harness leather blinds, round winker braces, half check bits, fancy fronts and rosettes, round side reins. **Lines**—1-inch flat, all black, with buckles and billets. **Hames**—Wood, with bent ball top. **Traces**—1¼-inch, doubled and stitched with cock-eyes. We furnish 1½-inch extra heavy traces, when desired, for $1.00 extra. **Saddle**—4-inch iron jockey skirts, with 1-inch stitched bearers. *We furnish* an extra quality 5-inch express, kersey lined saddle, with best harness leather skirts and 1½-inch doubled and stitched bearers, when desired, at $1.00 extra. **Shaft Tugs**—1-inch, doubled and stitched, plain loops. **Belly Bands**—Folded. **Breeching**—Folded, with layer, with double hip straps ⅞-inch wide, side strap 1-inch. **Collar**—All leather, Tan or Black.

OUR PRICE for the above harness in X C Plate Trimmings, $13.45.

WE FURNISH this harness in Brass or Full Nickle Trimmings at $14.45.

DOUBLE BUGGY HARNESS.

Our Bed Rock Price $16.90.

RETAILS Everywhere at from $25.00 to $30.00.

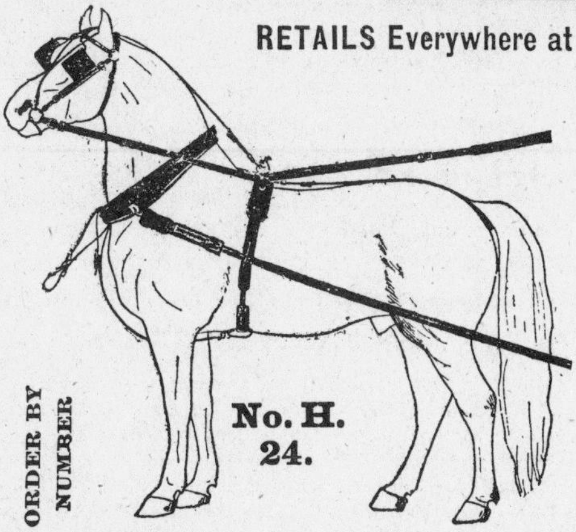

ORDER BY NUMBER

No. H. 24.

You Can't meet our prices anywhere.

We Are Far Below all others on Single Buggy Harness.

OUR TERMS on all Double Harness are **Express C. O. D.,** subject to examination to any one, anywhere, on receipt of **Two Dollars ($2.00)** as a guarantee of good faith. The two dollars you pay in advance is a guarantee of gook faith, and will be deducted from the price of the harness you buy. **WE SEND FREE as a present** with every **double harness** a fine set of sweat pads **when cash in full accompanies** your order and we **always refund your money** if you are not satisfied.

DESCRIPTION of our No. H. 24 Double Buggy Harness.

Trimmings—Davis rubber, full nickel or X C as desired. **Bridles**—⅝-inch cheeks, full box loops, patent leather blinds, round winker braces, half cheek bits, fancy fronts and rosettes, flat over-checks, round side reins. **Lines**—¾-inch flat, all black, with buckles and billets, ⅞-inch hand parts. **Hames**—7 lbs. steel, box loop, hame tugs, ⅝-inch hame straps. **Traces**—1-inch, machine raised, doubled and stitched. **Pads**—**Special coach,** with doubled and stitched skirts and trace bearers, 1¼-inch flat belly bands, ⅞-inch buckles, ¾-inch turn backs lapped and stitched to crupper-pieces, round crupper-docks sewed on, no hip straps. **Martingales**—⅞-inch to buckle around collar. **Pole Straps**—1⅛-inch. **Collars**—Plain leather. **Hitch Straps**—⅝-inch. **Breast Collar**—(When so desired) Folded with full length lays, box loops, folded neckstraps with straight lays, ⅝ and ¾-inch billets, breast collar irons.

OUR PRICE *WITH FULL X C PLATE AND BREAST COLLAR,* **$15.90**
WITH COLLAR AND HAMES, - - - - - - - **16.90**
DAVIS RUBBER OR FULL NICKEL TRIMMINGS AND BREAST OOLLAR, **16.90**
SAME WITH COLLAR HAMES, - - - - - - - - - - - - - **17.60**

DOUBLE BUGGY HARNESS. Our Bed Rock Price $22.75

Retails Everywhere at from $35.00 to $40.00.

DO YOU EVER LOOK FOR

BARGAINS

Then Read This Catalogue.

There's nothing else in it. **ALL BARGAINS, ALL MONEY SAVERS.** We want you to feel when ordering from us you are at **HEADQUARTERS.**

No. H. 25.

ORDER BY NUMBER.

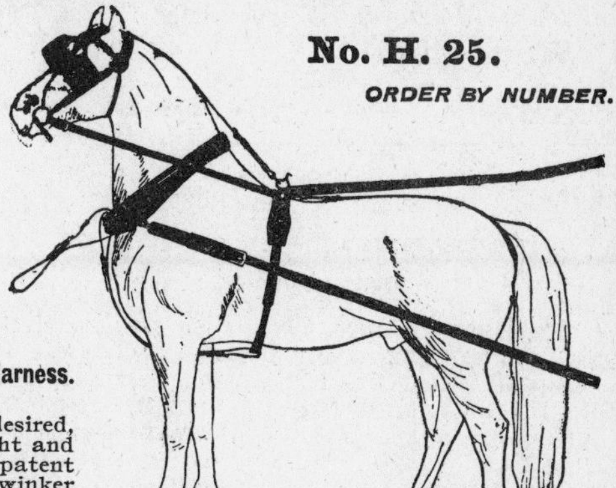

DESCRIPTION of Our No. H 25 Double Buggy Harness.

Trimmings—Full nickel or Davis rubber, as desired, blackened on the flesh, throughout and sewed, eight and nine tothe inch. **Bridles**—⅝-inch cheeks, box loops, patent leather blinds with three rows of stitching, round winker braces, scalloped layers on crown pieces, half cheek bits, band fronts and fancy rosettes, flat over checks, or round side reins as desired. **Lines**—⅞-inch flat, all black with buckles and billets, 1-inch hand parts. **Hames**—7 lb. steel, with patent leather swell end hame tugs, box loops and safes, ⅝-inch hame straps. **Traces**—1⅛-inch, solid raised, doubled and stitched. **Pads**—Immitation *Park Coach*, with fancy housing scalloped and fancy stitched trace bearers, folded belly bands with fancy stitching and 1-inch buckles, scalloped and fancy stitched turn backs, with round crupper docks sewed on. **Martingales**—1-inch to buckle around collar. **Pole Straps**—1¼-inch. **Collars**—Extra quality patent leather. **Breast Collar**—Folded, with full length solid raised straight stitched lays with box loops, folded neck straps with raised lays, ⅝ and ¾-inch billets, breast collar irons.

OUR PRICE furnished in full nickel or Davis rubber with beast collars $22.75

FULL NICKEL or DAVIS RUBBER with Collar and Hames $24.75.

OUR $12.05 FARM HARNESS

WE ARE BELOW ALL OTHERS.

ORDER BY NUMBER.

No. H. 26.

SENT C. O. D. to any one on receipt of $2.00 as a guarantee of good faith.

WE GIVE FREE a fine set of sweat pads with all orders for double harness accompanied by cash in full.

DESCRIPTION OF OUR No. H 24 FARM HARNESS.

This is a well made team or farm harness and can be used for all purposes on the farm. As the traces can be lengthened by the trace chains. **TRIMMINGS**—Japanned or X C Plate, as desired. **BRIDLES**—¾-inch stock, well made. **LINES**—¾-inch, 18 feet long with snaps. **TRACES**—1½-inch, 4 feet long with 3½ feet stage chains. **PADS**—Folded, with loop for back strap. **HAMES**—Varnished, iron over top. **BREAST STRAPS**—1¼-inch, with snaps and breast strap slides. **NECKYOKE STRAPS**—1¼-inch, back straps ⅞-inch, with folded crupper, hip straps ⅞-inch, belly bands flat.

OUR PRICE, FOR HARNESS COMPLETE WITHOUT COLLARS, $12.05.

COLLARS.—All Leather Immitation Cloth, $2.00 extra net.

BREECHING AND SIDE STRAPS, $3.00 extra net.

OUR $16.45 FARM HARNESS

UNDERSTAND we use nothing but best selected oak tanned stock. **Everything Warranted.**

C. O. D. to any one on receipt of $2.00 as a guarantee, the balance to be paid after you examine the harness.

DESCRIPTION OF OUR NO. H. 25 FARM HARNESS.

ORDER BY NUMBER.

No. H. 27.

TRIMMINGS—Full Japanned or X C Plate, as desired. **BRIDLES**—¾-inch, checks flat, rein square or concord style blinds. **LINES**—⅞-inch, flat, 18 feet long with snaps. **HAMES**—High top, X C trimmed. We will furnish low hames if so desired. **TRACES**—1½-inch doubled and stitched with cockeyes, champion trace buckles. **PADS**—Flat, 2½-inch, folded, with loops for back straps, 1¼-inch billets, back straps 1-inch with folded crupper dock, patent trace carriers. **HIP STRAPS**—⅞-inch, with wear leathers for traces to work in. **BREAST STRAPS**—1½-inch, with snaps and breast slides. **NECKYOKE, MARTINGALES**—1½-inch, with collar straps.

OUR PRICE, FOR THE ABOVE HARNESS AS DESCRIBED, WITHOUT COLLARS, $16.45.

For all KIP COLLARS $2.00 extra. BREECHING AND SIDE STRAPS $2.00 extra.

1¾-INCH TRACE in place of 1½-inch $1.00 extra.

OUR $26.75 TEAM HARNESS

The Best Concord Team Harness Made.

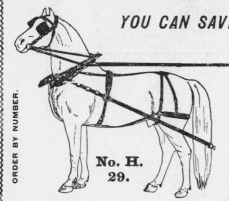

ORDER BY NUMBER.

No. H. 29.

YOU CAN SAVE $15.00 to $20.00 on this harness by sending your order to us.

DESCRIPTION OF OUR No. H. 27, $26.75 TEAM HARNESS.

Trimmings—Full X C Plate or Japanned, as desired; hand sewed, five to the inch. **Bridles**—¾-inch cheeks, box loops, square harness leather blinds, round winker braces, round side reins, ring bits, fancy fronts and rosettes. **Lines**—⅞-inch by 18 feet, with buckles, billets and snaps. **Hames**—X C over-top, with spread straps and rings, 1½-inch long, folded hame tugs with X C champion three loop buckles. **Traces**—1½-inch, doubled and stitched with cock-eyes. **Pads**—Folded, with 1¼-inch full length lay, hooks and terrets, soft pads and patent leather team housings, folded belly-bands with one row of straight stitching, 1¼-inch buckles, 1-inch turn-backs, ⅞-inch flat hip-straps with safes, sewed into trace carriers, ¾-inch folded crupper-docks buckled on. **Martingales**—1½-inch. **Breast Straps**—1½-inch, with snaps and slides. **Breeching Bodies**—Folded, with full length lay, ⅞-inch side straps, ⅞-inch hip-strap buckles, Campbell Lock-Stitched.

OUR PRICE, FOR ABOVE HARNESS COMPLETE WITHOUT COLLARS OR BREECHING, **$26.75.**

BREECHING AND SIDE STRAPS, $3.25 extra net.   COLLARS, $3.00 extra.

1¾-INCH TRACES, $1.00 EXTRA.

OUR $19.90 FARM HARNESS

Nothing Like it Ever Offered For Less than $30.00.

DESCRIPTION.

TRIMMINGS—Full X C Plate or Japanned, as desired. **BRIDLES**—¾-inch cheeks, narrow loops, square harness leather blinds, flat winker braces, round side reins, X C ring bits, fancy fronts and rosettes. **LINES**—⅞-inch by 18 feet, with buckles, billets and snaps. **HAMES**—X C over-top, with 1½-inch long hame-tugs, and X C champion three loop buckles. **TRACES**—1½-inch, doubled and stitched, with cock-eyes. **PADS**—Folded, with 1-inch full length lay, hooks and terrets, soft pads and patent leather housings, 1-inch turn backs, ⅞-inch flat hip-straps, with trace carriers, folded crupper-docks buckled on. **BELLY BANDS**—Folded, with one row of straight stitching. **MARTINGALES**—1-inch. **BREAST STRAPS**—1-inch, with snaps and sides. **BREECHING-BODIES**—Folded, with full length lays, ⅞-inch side straps, ⅞-inch hip-strap buckles.

No. H. 28.

ORDER BY NUMBER.

OUR PRICE, FOR ABOVE HARNESS COMPLETE WITHOUT COLLARS OR BREECHING, **$19.90.**

BREECHING AND SIDE STRAPS, $3.25 extra net.   COLLARS, $2.25 extra.

1¾-INCH TRACES, $1.00 EXTRA.

Morgan Saddle. Morgan Saddle.

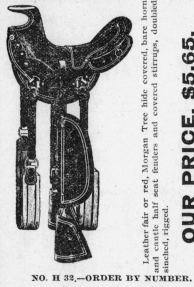

Plain, fair leather, hide covered tree and horn.

Without fenders..............$1.75

With fenders.................2.50

OUR PRICE—

C. O. D. On Receipt of $1.00.

No. H 30.—ORDER BY NUMBER.

Fine leather, Morgan Tree, bare and cantle, fenders and wood stirrups, girth stamped.

OUR PRICE, $3.95.

C. O. D. to any one on receipt of $1, balance to be paid at express office.

NO. H 31.—ORDER BY NUMBER.

MORGAN DOUBLE.----SINCHES.

MULEY MORGAN,

Leather fair or red, Morgan Tree hide covered, bare horn and cantle half seat fenders and covered stirrups, doubled sinched, rigged.

OUR PRICE, $5.65.

C. O. D. on receipt of $1.00, balance at express office.

NO. H 32.—ORDER BY NUMBER.

Russet leather, Morgan Tree. Stamped, with hand hold, covered bars.

OUR PRICE, $7.75.

C. O. D. to any one on receipt of $1, balance to be paid after saddle is examined at express office

NO. H 33.—ORDER BY NUMBER.

WE SEND FREE with every saddle a very fine saddle blanket, where cash in full accompanies your order.

IT IS BETTER to send cash in full with your order for saddles, as you not only get a **NICE SADDLE BLANKET FREE,** but you also save charges on return of C. O. D. money; besides, where we can get a low rate we can ship by fast freight and save you money.

Somerset Saddle

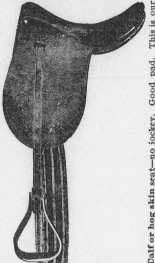

No. H 34—ORDER BY NUMBER.

Calf or hog skin seat—no jockey. Good pad. This is our gentleman's easy riding saddle and we offer it at half the usual retail price.

OUR PRICE, $4.10.

C. O. D. to any one on receipt of $1, balance to be paid at express office.

Best Somerset Saddle

No. H 35—ORDER BY NUMBER.

Quilted, enameled leather, **Calf or Hog Skin**, hood seat, fair leather stamped, full pad, ground seat. This is ONE of the Best Saddles Made and you will find it in every way equal to saddles that retail at $12 and upwards.

OUR PRICE, $7.75.

C. O. D. to any one on receipt of $1.00, balance to be paid at express office.

Fine Pad Saddle

No. H 36—ORDER BY NUMBER.

Full quilted enameled drill—**OUR PRICE, $3.95.**
Full quilted Hog skin—**OUR PRICE, $5.20.**
☞**TERMS ALIKE ON ALL SADDLES.**
C. O. D. to any one on receipt of $1.00 as a guarantee of good faith. Balance to be paid at express office.

Race Saddle.

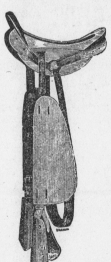

No. H 37—ORDER BY NUMBER.

St. Louis Race Tree, felt lined bars, good girth and light wood stirrups. This Saddle retails everywhere at double our price.

OUR PRICE, $3.95.

C. O. D. to any one on receipt of $1.00, balance to be paid at express office.

We Send Free

with every saddle a very fine **Saddle Blanket,** where cash in full accompanies your order.

IT IS FAR BETTER TO SEND CASH IN FULL with your order for Saddles, as you not only get a nice **Saddle Blanket FREE,** but you also save charges on return of C. O. D. money. Besides, where we can get a low rate we can ship by fast freight and save you money.

McClellan Saddle...

No. H. 38. ORDER BY NUMBER.

McClellan tree, plain half seat, short skirts, fenders and covered skirts, carved border, all black leather.

ON THIS class of goods you will find our prices about one half the usual retail price, and much lower than the same goods were ever advertised.

OUR PRICE $6.95.

C. O. D. to any one on receipt of $1.00; balance $5.95 to be paid at express office.

$1.75 Boys' Morgan.

Plain fair leather, hide covered tree and horn.

OUR PRICE without fenders $1.75.

OUR PRICE with fenders $2.50.

IT IS CHEAPER and better to send cash in full for saddles as you save C. O. D. express charges. All saddles sent C. O. D. on receipt of $1.00; balance payable at express office.

No. H. 39. ORDER BY NUMBER.

Boys' Hannible.

No. H. 40. ORDER BY NUMBER.

C. O. D. to any one on receipt of $1.00; balance, $5.95, to be paid at express office.

Light or black leather, Morgan tree, covered horn and cantle, fenders and covered stirrups, single sinch rigged, hair sinch.

OUR SPECIAL CUT PRICE ON THIS SADDLE $6.95.

Texas Saddle.

All black leather, Morgan tree, hide covered bare horn and cantle open seat, fenders and covered stirrups, single sinch rigged, hair sinch, finely carved. Don't pay two prices for a saddle.

OUR PRICE FOR THIS SADDLE $9.45.

C. O. D. to any one on receipt of $1.00; balance, $8.45 payable at express office.

No. H. 41. ORDER BY NUMBER.

WE SEND FREE with every saddle a very fine SADDLE BLANKET where cash in full accompanies your order.

IT IS BETTER to send cash in full with your order for saddles as you not only get a **nice Saddle Blanket free**, but you also save charges on return of C. O. D. money, besides where we can get a low rate we can ship by fast freight and save you money.

Texas Saddle.

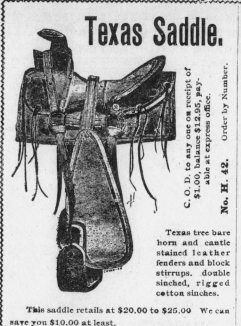

C. O. D. to any one on receipt of $1.00, balance $12.95, payable at express office.

No. H. 42. Order by Number.

Texas tree bare horn and cantle stained leather fenders and block stirrups. double sinched, rigged cotton sinches.

This saddle retails at $20.00 to $25.00 We can save you $10.00 at least.

OUR PRICE $13.95.

Stock Saddle. Our Special PRICE $16.90

Retails for $30.00.

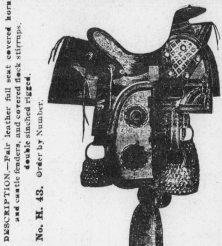

DESCRIPTION.—Fair leather full seat covered horn and cantle fenders, and covered flock stirrups. double sinched rigged.

No. H. 43. Order by Number.

OUR TERMS Alike on all saddles. We send any saddle C. O. D. on receipt of $1.00, balance payable at express office.

Stock Saddle. ——————

Our Best Regular California StockSaddle.

DESCRIPTION Freseka. Tree, oiled, skirting, solid seat with iron strainers. California stirrup strap with fenders, tapideroes, double sinch rigged, hair sinches, creased border.

No. H. 44.

Order by Number.

OUR PRICE $19.95.

C. O. D. to any one on receipt of $1.00, balance payable at express office.

Ladies' Side Saddle.

OUR PRICE $4.95.

DESCRIPTION.—Fancy creton or red plush seat, good pad, stamped skirt.

No. H. 45. Order by Number.

OUR TERMS.—C. O. D. to any one on receipt of $1.00, balance $3.95 to be paid at express office.

WE SEND FREE with every saddle a very fine saddle blanket where cash in full accompanies your order.

IT IS FAR BETTER to send cash in full with your order for saddles as you not only get a **nice saddle blanket free,** but you also save charges on return of C. O. D. money, besides where we can get a low rate we can ship by fast freight and save you money.

CLOTHING DEPARTMENT!

Showing Different Styles.

For Rules for Self Measurement see following pages.

Style No. 1

Style No. 2

Style No. 3

Style No. 4

Style No. 5

Style No. 6

Style No. 7

Style No. 10

Style No. 12

Style No. 13

Style No. 14

Style No. 16

Style No. 17

OUR
CLOTHING
DEPARTMENT.

Rules for Measurement, Terms, Conditions of Shipments, Etc.

RULE
For Measurement:

FOR COAT.

Measurement to be taken over vest. Chest measure, adjust tape measure at figure 1, in cut, giving number of inches *around body*. Length of sleeve to elbow, 7 to 8, per cut; from elbow to hand, 8 to 9 per cut.

FOR VEST.

Measurement to be taken over vest and should be same as for coat.

FOR PANTS.

Measure around the body *under* vest for waist measure, at figure 2, per cut; at figure 3 for hip measure, per cut; and for measure of inside seam, from 4 to 5, per cut.

FOR OVERCOAT.

Same as for coat.

REMARKS. — Give your height, weight and age. State whether you have stooping or square shoulders.

WE ARE MAKING this one of our most important Departments, and at our prices you can save money and dress better than ever before. *We are prepared* not only to furnish you Clothing as cheap as your local dealer can buy, but also prepared to give you an infinitely better selection *and a far better fit.*

If a Tailor has been making your clothing, DISCHARGE HIM. If you have been buying your clothing ready-made, STOP IT! We will furnish you clothing at from ONE-HALF to TWO-THIRDS the price asked by retailers and give you cloths that will compare in *quality, finish* and *fit* with any clothes a tailor will make to order.

Follow our Rules for Measurement and we Guarantee a Perfect Fit, and Guarantee every garment in every respect.

YOU CAN SAVE more money on the clothing you buy than on any other necessity of life. *Manufacturers, Jobbers* and *Retailers* profit is *Larger* on clothing than on any other commodity of necessity handled. Sold on the longest time, consequently *greatest Risks* and *greatest Losses* as well as greatest profit.

Why pay all this year after year?

FOR CASH WE WILL SAVE YOU this enormous profit of three or four who handle your clothing, the amount you pay for losses, interest, etc.

COMPARE OUR PRICES AND SEE.

TERMS

We will fill any order for clothing, "no matter" how *large or small,* and ship to anyone anywhere in the United Stated, C. O. D., subject to examination, **on receipt of One Dollar** as a guarantee of good faith, the one dollar you pay in advance will always be deducted from amount of the bill, you can examine the goods, and if not found satisfactory, you can return them and we will refund you **ONE DOLLAR,** less Express charges.

We Do More. We always send instructions to the Express Agent to collect the amount of C. O. D. and Express charges, and hold the same three days, and allow you to take the clothing home and examine and try it on in your own home, and if not found a perfect fit and in every way satisfactory, give you the privilege of returning same to the Express Agent who will return you ALL YOUR MONEY.

THE BEST WAY is to send Cash in full with your order, in which case WE PREPAY ALL EXPRESS CHARGES on amounts of $10.00 OR OVER, and send FREE AS A PRESENT a beautiful Silk Handkerchief.

You Take No Risk for we will always refund your money cheerfully if you are not perfectly satisfied.

NOTICE : The illustrations on preceding page show cuts and shape of clothing, as follows:

STYLE No. 1 represents Single-Breasted Sack Suit.

STYLE No. 2 represents Single-Breasted Square-Cut Suit.

STYLE No. 3 represents Double-Breasted Sack Suit.

STYLE No. 4 represent One-Button Cutaway, or Frock Suit.

STYLE No. 5 represents Three-Button Cutaway, walking or Dress suit.

STYLE No. 6 represents Single-Breasted Prince Albert Dress Coat.

STYLE No. 7 represents Double-Breasted Prince Albert Dress Coat.

STYLE No. 10 represents Single-Breasted Fly Front Sack Overcoat.

STYLE No. 12 represents Double-Breasted Storm Ulster, extra heavy.

STYLE No. 13 represents Single-Breasted Prince Charles or Storm Coat, extra long.

STYLE No. 14 represents Double-Breasted Loop Overcoat.

STYLE No. 16 represents Double-Breasted Sack Overcoat.

STYLE No. 17 represents Double-Breasted Pea Jacket.

OVERALLS & JUMPERS.

BLUE OVERALLS.

No.   **PRICE PER PAIR**

1. Blue drilled denim, 2 top pockets, double stitched seams and crotch, does not lose color through washing, double belt and fly, japanned buttons, hand made button holes 35c

2. Heavy blue twilled denim, 2 top pockets, double stitched seams throughout, seat and crotch, hand made button holes, japanned bar buttons, 2-ply belt and fly, extra good value at 39c

3. CROWN, extra heavy blue drilled denim, well made, double stitched throughout, 2 top and 1 hip pockets, wide 2-ply band and fly, hand made button holes, never-pull-out large brass buttons, patent riveted 47c

4. REPUBLIC, extra heavy quality, changeable blue drill denim, full pantaloon cut, double stitched overlapped seam, long reinforced button flap, patent brass riveted buttons, 2 top and 1 hip pockets, hand worked button holes, reinforced crotch, 2-ply belt and fly 55c

5. Extra heavy weight blue denim, 2 top and hip pockets, overlapped and double stitched seams, reinforced crotch, wide 2-ply band and fly, patent riveted buttons, hand worked button holes; this line is manufactured for durability and comfort 68c

6. Changeable, extra heavy quality blue denim, reinforced seat, never-rip crotch, hand sewed button holes, non-pull-out buttons, wide full shaped pantaloon cut, patent 2-ply band and fly, 2 top and 1 hip pockets. The reputation this overall has for durability and honest make is sufficient guarantee for its satisfaction 64c

7. CROWN, superior quality, extra heavy, blue drilled denim, 2-ply wide fly and band, 2 top and 1 hip pocket, overlapped and double stitched seams throughout, reinforced crotch, will not rip; a very popular make 68c

8. Heavy drilled blue denim, overlapped seams, double stitched throughout, reinforced crotch, will not rip, 2 top, 1 hip and watch pocket, patent japanned riveted buttons, hand worked button holes, western style high cut back 65c

9. The Anchor Overall, extra heavy weight blue denim, patent long reinforced button flaps, extra wide 2 top and one hip pockets, double stitched and overlapped seams, hand sewed button holes, non-pull-out brass rivet buttons, reinforced seat and never rip crotch. We claim that this overall is a rare bargain at 72c

10. Superior quality, extra heavy drill denim, western style high cut back, double stitched seams throughout, strong reinforced crotch, extra wide 2 ply band and fly, japanned riveted buttons, hand worked button holes, 2 top, 1 hip and 1 watch pocket; for finish and durability we have nothing better to offer at 72c

11. THE REPELLANT, heavy quality blue denim with high cut back, full pantaloon shape, 2 top, 1 watch and 1 hip pockets, enameled non pull out rivet buttons, reinforced seat, never rip crotch, welted seams, extra wide 2 ply band and fly 78c

12. Extra heavy weight, blue denim, two top and hip pockets, overlapped, double stitched seams with patent reinforced crotch which can never rip, regular pantaloon cut, has a double front and is two for one. After the knees and front of these overalls has worn out, the top layer can easily be removed and you can have an overall almost as good as new for the price of one pair. 90c

13. Same make as above in changeable blue drilled denim 85c

14. The Challenge pantaloon overall, changeable dark blue denim, piped seams, 2 ply band and fly, 2 top, 1 watch and 2 hip pockets, double front and seat. The advantages of this overall over others are, that when the top is worn off it can be taken off, and in this way you can obtain two pairs for one. Seams are all felled and double stitched, non pull out brass buttons, hand sewed button holes. This overall is extra heavy quality denim .... $ 1 07

STRIPED OVERALLS.

15. Heavy twilled denim, dark and gray mixed, medium width stripes, double stitched seams, crotch and seat, 2 top pockets, japanned bar buttons, hand worked button holes, extra wide 2 ply band and fly 58c

16. Brown duck, extra well made, pantaloon cut, double stitched, 2 top pockets, wide 2 ply band and fly, japanned button holes, reinforced crotch, overlapped seams, assorted in fancy wide and narrow checks in browns, blues and gray mixed, a popular assortment 59c

17. CROWN, heavy quality drilled denim, full pantaloon cut, overlapped and double stitched throughout, reinforced crotch, wide 2 ply band and fly, patent riveted buttons, hand made button holes, 2 top and 1 hip pocket, assorted in fancy light mixed and dark ground stripes; these overalls in appearance are an accurate imitation of cottonade pants 65c

18. Light brown checked duck, welted seams, 2 ply band and fly, reinforced seat, never rip crotch, western style, high cut reinforced extension back, non pull out Japan buttons, hand sewed button holes, 2 top, 1 watch and 1 hip pockets. For extra fine finish and durability we have nothing better to offer at 85c

19. Pepper and salt, mixed, western style, high backed pantaloon cut, non pull out Japanned buttons, hand sewed button holes, 2 top, 1 watch and 1 hip pockets, extra wide 2 ply band and fly reinforced seat and crotch. This pantaloon is made up in the latest shades of woolen goods; when worn has the appearance of genuine wool. 92c

GRAY AND BROWN YORK.

20. High back pantaloon cut, gray, heavy quality denim, pipe seams, extra wide 2 ply band and fly, with extension welted side seam, reinforced seat with never rip crotch, wide pantaloon cut, enameled bar buttons, 2 top and 1 hip pockets. This overall is very popular with the best class of indoor workmen, as it is an accurate imitation of the latest shades in woolen goods; will not show dirt as quickly as other overalls 59c

21. CROWN, medium brown, heavy drilled denim, pantaloon cut, 2 top and 1 hip pocket, overlapped, double stitched seams throughout, reinforced seams throughout, reinforced crotch, wide 2 ply band, patent riveted buttons; these overalls are very popular with the best class of workmen as they are neat and do not show dirt as easily as others 76c

22. CROWN, same as above in steel gray 76c

23. 9 oz. YORK, heavy twilled dark brown denim, overlapped, double stitched seams throughout, reinforced crotch and seat, wide 2 ply belt and fly, 2 top and 1 hip pocket, patent brass riveted buttons, hand worked button holes 75c

24. Same as above in gray 75c

25. Extra heavy weight gray denim, 2 top and hip pockets, overlapped double stitched seams, patent reinforced crotch, guaranteed against ripping; regular pantaloon style cut, has a double front, and is two pairs for one; after the knees and front of these overalls has worn off, the top layer can be easily removed and you have an overall almost as good as new for the price of one pair. 93c

26. Same as above in medium and light shades of brown. 93c

BROWN DUCK.

27. Good quality brown duck, 2 top and 1 hip pockets, strengthened crotch, double stitched throughout, wide 2 ply band and fly; impossible to get anything better for 37c

28. REPUBLIC brown duck, extra heavy weight, well made throughout, overlapped double stitched seams, full pantaloon cut, reinforced button flaps and crotch, wide 2 ply band and fly, patent riveted buttons, hand made button holes, 2 top and 1 hip pocket 55c

29. Extra heavy brown duck well made throughout overlapped, double stitched seams, 2 top and 1 hip pocket, wide 2 ply band and fly, hand worked button holes; these overalls are worn largely by commission house employes as they always present a tidy appearance 58c

BROWN DUCK—Continued.

No.   Per Pair.

C30. Made of extra weight brown ducking, regular full pantaloon cut, patent never rip crotch, double front, is virtually two pairs of overalls for the price of one; when top layer is worn off it can be easily removed, and your overall is better than ever. Overlapped double stitched seams throughout and manufactured so as to wear as long as two pairs........................ 85c

APRON OVERALLS.

C31. Heavy blue denim, extra well made, double stitched seams all through, double stitched large apron front with strap suspenders, buckle in front on side, open on side with top pockets.. 42c

C32. Super quality drilled denim, patent apron front, double seams all through, extra well finished, best value in the market.................. 68c

C33. The Royal, heavy twilled blue denim, patent apron front with patent buckle, suspender straps, top, hip and tool pocket, reinforced crotch and sides, double seams all through, well made and finished............................. 72c

C34. Blue twilled denim overlapped double-stitched seams all through, reinforced crotch which can never rip, top, hip and large tool pocket, apron front with patent suspenders, straps and buckles reinforced sides................................. 78c

C35. Super changeable blue twilled denim, apron front and back, double suspender straps with patent buckle catch, extra well made, double stitched welt seams all through, open reinforced sides and fly, outside top, hip and tool pockets, extra strengthened crotch, pat. snap buttons.... 80c

PAINTERS' OVERALLS.

C36. White medium weight, twilled denim, extra well made, double stitched all through, with apron front, strap suspenders, metal buttons, 1 top pocket and rule pocket on side, double stitched crotch, assorted sizes in a dozen, open on side................................... 35c

C37. Heavy white denim, extra well made, double stitched all through, reinforced front and extra strengthened crotch, apron front, strap suspenders, outside pocket in front and hip rule pocket on side; this overall is put up in good large sizes, open on side.............................. 40c

BOYS' OVERALLS.

C38. Blue denim, medium weight, 2 top pockets, well made, extra strengthened crotch, double stitched seams, two ply belt and fly, extra finish 35c

C39. Heavy twilled denim, dark and gray mixed, medium width stripes, double stitched seams, crotch and seat, 2 top pockets, Japanned bar buttons, hand worked button holes, extra wide 2 ply band and fly........................ 42c

CHECKED COATS.

Price Each.

C40. Medium weight checked cheviot jumper, with rolling collar, metal bar buttons, full size band cuffs................................... 30c

C41. Good quality, small checked cheviot jumper, with large rolling collar, wide pocket, white metal bar buttons, 2 ply band cuffs, assorted in three shades..................... 35c

C42. Extra quality medium checked cheviot, with wide rolling collar, overlapped double stitched seams, 2 ply cuffs and front fly, shaped sleeves, reinforced laps 50c

C43. Heavy weight extra wide checked cheviot jumper, large rolling collar, non pull out rivet metal buttons, overlapped seams. The reputation that this jumper has for its excellence of material and finish is a sufficient guarantee for its ready sale and satisfaction.................. 60c

BLUE JUMPERS.

C44. Heavy weight dark blue denim, 2 ply band collar and wide cuffs, japanned bar buttons, one wide pocket, double stitched seams throughout, full sack coat shape............................. 35c

C45. Changeable, extra quality denim, piped seams throughout, 2 ply band collar and extra wide cuffs, japanned bar buttons, one large pocket. We guarantee this jacket to be made of the best material and workmanship for the money......

No.   Price Each.

C46. Well made, extra good quality twilled denim, with 2 ply band collar, welted seams throughout, one large pocket, full size sack coat cut extra wide, 2 ply band cuffs, japanned bar buttons, trimmed. This jumper is made of extra heavy quality goods, and can be worn the same as any coat.... .... 45c

C47. Denim shirt, full length, made of good quality heavy weight denim, overlapped, double stitched and welted seams, 2 ply rolling collar and band cuffs, japanned bar buttons. We guarantee this to be extra good value at....................... 60c

C48. Superior quality heavy brown duck, with low cut wide rolling collar, full sack coat shaped, large pocket, 2 ply band cuffs, overlapped double stitched seams, non pull out brass buttons, hand sewed button holes. This jumper is very popular with commission house employees, as it always presents a neat appearance............. 70c

C49. Western style high cut 2 ply rolling collar, good quality denim, overlapped and double stitched welted seams, japanned non pull out buttons, hand sewed button holes, two large pockets, sack coat cut, full shaped sleeves, 2 ply band cuffs, assorted in dark and light shades... 75c

C50. Superior quality, medium blue denim, with low cut 2 ply rolling collar, overlapped, double stitched and welted seams, with side 2 ply cuffs, one pocket. This jumper is extra heavy weight goods, and is very popular with outside workmen all the year around........................ 75c

GRAY MIXED AND LIGHT BROWN.

C51. Double breasted sack coat with large rolling collar, overlapped, double stitched and welted seams, two large front pockets, metal non pull out buttons, hand sewed button holes, full shaped sleeves, 2 ply band cuffs made of extra quality denim. We guarantee this to be extra good value................................. 80c

C52. Strong Hold Changeable, superior quality heavy denim, with two lower and one top front pocket, overlapped, double stitched seams throughout, 2 ply rolling collar and extra wide band cuffs, non pull out metal buttons, hand sewed button holes. We guarantee this jumper to be heavy quality denim, and to possess all the qualifications that makes it a genuine bargain 85c

COMBINATION COAT AND VEST.

C53. THE MACHINIST'S PRIDE, changeable, extra quality denim, two pockets, small 2 ply rolling collar and band cuffs, overlapped, double stitched seams throughout. Vest with two pockets, japanned bar buttons, shaped arms and sleeves, 2 ply band cuffs, well finished throughout, hand sewed button holes................... 90c

PANTALOONS.

Quotations under this heading are for pants only. All men's sizes. Smallest waist 30 inches, largest waist 40 inches. Read rules for measurement before ordering.

KENTUCKY JEAN PANTALOONS.

No.   Price.

C54. Kentucky Jean Pants, dark gray mixed....... $ .75

C55. Kentucky Jean Pants, Oxford mixed, spring bottom.................................. 1.05

C56. Kentucky Jean Pants, Oxford mixed......... 1.30

C57. Kentucky Jean Pants, dark Oxford mixed.... 1.75

OUR $2.90 ALL WOOL PANTS.

C58. All wool, black and gray hair line cassimere pants 2.90

C59. All wool, brown mixed hair line cassimere... 2.90

C60. All wool, black ground, with narrow gray stripe.................................. 2.90

C61. All wool, black ground with neat stripe of gray and fine red mixture...................... 2.90

C62. All wool, brown ground with medium stripe of gray................................. 2.90

C63. All wool, navy blue cassimere, guaranteed indigo blue, medium weight.................. 2.90

PANTALOONS, COTTONADE, CASSIMERE, UNION, WORSTED, AND DOESKIN.

No.		Price.
C64.	Cottonade pants, fancy stripe	$ .75
C65.	Black diagonal cotton worsted pants	.98
C66.	Black and gold mixed diagonal cotton worsted pants	1.25
C67.	Dark mixed striped satinet cassimere	1.75
C68.	Dark mixed fancy striped satinet	2.40
C69.	Black and gray striped Union cassimere	2.50
C70.	Brown Corduroy	2.50
C71.	Drab Corduroy	2.50
C72.	Black and gray pin head cassimere	2.75
C73.	Dark mixed, fancy striped worsted pants	3.20
C74.	Steel mixed striped worsted	3.35
C75.	Brown corduroy, fine cord	3.50
C76.	Drab corduroy, fine cord	3.50
C77.	Black and blue striped worsted with fine red silk thread	3.50
C78.	Gray cassimere with black stripe worsted finish	3.95
C79.	All wool, black and gray hair line striped cassimere pants	4.15
C80.	Black and blue striped worsted pants	4.45
C81.	Steel gray ground worsted with brown and blue stripes	4.65
C82.	Brown and gray mixed striped cassimere, velvet finish	4.95
C83.	Medium light gray and black broken plaid cassimere, velvet finish	4.95
C84.	Black and gray pin striped English cassimere	4.95
C85.	Black imported worsted with neat gray mixed stripes	5.30
C86.	Blue and steel gray, neat stripes of English cassimere	6.35
C87.	Black and blue gray, neat stripes of imported worsted	6.95
C88.	Black imported English worsted with neat gray stripes	7.35

BLACK PANTALOONS.

No.		Price.
C89.	Black diagonal cotton pants	1.15
C90.	Black diagonal worsted corkscrew weave	1.80
C91.	Black diagonal worsted corkscrew weave	2.50
C92.	Black diagonal worsted corkscrew weave	3.95
C93.	Black diagonal, imported, worsted corkscrew weave	4.15
C94.	Black diagonal, imported, worsted corkscrew weave	4.90
C95.	Black diagonal, imported, worsted corkscrew weave	5.65
C96.	Black Doeskin pants, all wool	5.35
C97.	Black worsted corded pants	4.35
C98.	Black diagonal Clay worsted pants	4.15
C99.	Black diagonal, imported, Clay worsted pants	5.15

COATS AND VESTS.

The quotations under this heading are for coats and vests together. All men's sizes, 34 to 42. Before ordering read instructions for measuring.

No.		Price for Coat and Vest.
C100.	Black diagonal cotton worsted, style 1	2.35
C101.	Black diagonal cotton worsted, old gold mixed style 1	2.85
C102.	Black diagonal cotton worsted, old gold mixed style 4	2.95
C103.	Dark mixed satinet cassimere, style 1	3.60
C104.	Black diagonal worsted, corkscrew weave style 1	4.75
C105.	Black diagonal worsted, corkscrew weave, style 5	5.25
C106.	Black and gray pin head check union cassimere, style 1	6.25
C107.	All wool navy blue cloth, medium weight style 1	6.00
C108.	All wool navy blue cloth, medium weight style 2	6.00
C109.	All wool navy blue cloth, medium weight, style 4	6.40
C110.	All wool navy blue cloth, medium weight, style 3	6.75
C111.	All wool navy blue cloth, medium weight, extra sizes, 43 to 48, style 1	7.25
C112.	Drab corduroy, cassimere lining, two very large pockets on inside of coat, style 1	8.25
C113.	Brown corduroy, cassimere lining, two large pockets on inside of coat style 1	8.25
C114.	Black corduroy, colored flannel lining, fine cord, style 1	10.00
C115.	Drab corduroy, colored flannel lining, fine cord style 1	10.00
C116.	Black corduroy, colored flannel lining, two very large pockets on inside of coat, style 3	10.25
C117.	Drab corduroy, colored flannel lining, two very large pockets on inside, style 3	11.25

No.		Price for Coat and Vest.
C118.	Black diagonal worsted, corkscrew weave, style 1	7.25
C119.	Black diagonal worsted, corkscrew weave, style 5	8.00
C120.	Black diagonal worsted, style 1	8.25
C121.	Black diagonal worsted, corkscrew weave, style 1	9.00
C122.	Black diagonal worsted, corkscrew weave, style 5	9.25
C123.	Black diagonal worsted, corkscrew weave, style 1	10.25
C124.	Black diagonal worsted, corkscrew weave, style 5	10.50
C125.	Black diagonal imported clay worsted, unbound, style 1	10.00
C126.	Black diagonal imported clay worsted, unbound, style 5	10.25
C127.	Black diagonal imported clay worsted, bound, style 1	11.75
C128.	Black diagonal imported clay worsted, bound, style 5	12.00
C129.	Black diagonal imported clay worsted, bound, style 1	12.50
C130.	Black diagonal imported clay worsted, bound, style 5	13.50
C131.	Black diagonal imported clay worsted, bound, style 5	15.00
C132.	Black diagonal imported worsted., style 6	15.00
C133.	Black diagonal worsted, corkscrew weave, style 7	12.25
C134.	Black diagonal worsted, corkscrew weave, bound, style 7	13.50
C135.	Black diagonal worsted, corkscrew weave, silk faced and bound, style 7	15.75
C136.	Black diagonal imported clay worsted, bound, style 7	15.75
C137.	Black diagonal imported clay worsted, bound, style 7	17.00
C138.	Black diagonal imported clay worsted, silk faced and bound, style 7	19.00
C139.	Black imported broadcloth, style 6	15.25
C140.	Black imported broadcloth, style 7	16.00

Note.—Prices regulate quality on all Black Worsteds and Corkscrews.

VESTS.

Before ordering vests, read instructions for measurement and remarks under same. Be sure to make your figures plain and correct. Sizes, chest measure, 34 to 42.

SINGLE VESTS ONLY.

Single vests, 10 to 15 ounces, according to size and quality.

No.		Price for Vest.
C140½	Black diagonal cotton worsted, old gold mixed	$ .80
C141	Black and brown check satinet cassimere	.90
C142	Black and blue check satinet cassimere	1.25
C143	Black and gray check union cassimere	1.60
C144	Black and fancy mixed striped cassimere	1.60
C145	All wool, navy blue cloth, medium weight	1.60
C146	All wool, black and gray hair line cassimere	1.80
C147	Black diagonal worsted corkscrew weave	1.35
C148	Black diagonal imported worsted	2.10
C149	Black diagonal worsted, corkscrew weave	2.25
C150	Black diagonal imported worsted	2.50
C151	Black broadcloth, all wool, single breasted	2.75
C152	Black diagonal imported worsted	3.25

PANTALOONS & VESTS.

The quotations under this heading are for **Pants** and **Vests** together. All men's sizes, chest measure from 35 to 42.

No.		Price for Pants and Vest.
C153	Black diagonal worsted, corkscrew weave	$ 3.25
C154	Black and gray pin head check cassimere	3.60
C155	Black and gray hair line cassimere	4.00
C156	All wool black and gray hair line cassimere	5.00
C157	All wool navy blue cloth, medium weight	4.50
C158	All wool black and gray hair line cassimere	6.00
C159	Black diagonal worsted	6.25
C160	Black diagonal imported worsted	7.25
C161	Black diagonal worsted, corkscrew weave	7.25
C162	Black diagonal, imported worsted	9.00
C163	Black doeskin pants and black broadcloth vests	8.10

COATS.

The quotations under this heading are for coats only. Sizes 35 to 42.

Before ordering coats read instructions for measurements and remarks under same. Be sure to make your figures plain and correct.

Coats weigh from 1¾ to 2¼ pounds, according to size, style and quality.

COATS—Continued.

No.   PRICE FOR COAT.

C164 Black diagonal cotton worsted, old gold mixed. Style 1...........................$ 2.00
C165 All wool indigo blue flannel coats. Style 1... 4.50
C166 Black diagonal worsted coats. Style 6...... 11.70
C167 Black diagonal imported worsted coats. Style 7 13.50
C168 Black broadcloath coats. Style 6............ 12.75
C169 Black broadcloth coats. Style 7............ 13.25

MEN'S BLACK and BLUE WORSTED SUITS.

A black suit of clothes is never out of fashion.

Our line is complete. A trial order will convince you how cheap we sell them.

We charge you less for a suit of black clothes made first-class than is usually charged for inferior makes by your merchants. Sizes 34 to 42 chest measure. Pant size 30 to 40 inch waist measure and 30 to 35 inside seam measure. Half-sizes are not made in ready-made clothing.

No.   PRICE FOR SUIT.

C170 Black diagonal cotton worsted. Style 1.....$ 3.50
C171 Black diagonal worsted corkscrew weave. The best black suit made for the money. Send for sample. Style 1.......................... 5.40
C172 Black diagonal worsted, corkscrew weave. Style 5............................... 6.90
C173 Black worsted, heavy, diagonal pattern. Style 2................................ 9.00
C174 Blue worsted, heavy, diagonal pattern. Style 2................................ 9.00
C175 Black diagonal worsted, corkscrew weave. Style 1............................... 10.45
C176 Black worsted, heavy diagonal pattern. Style 5................................ 10.45
C177 Black diagonal worsted, corkscrew weave. Style 5............................... 10.80

Corkscrews are very serviceable.

C178 Black diagonal worsted. Style 1............ 11.75
C179 Black diagonal corkscrew worsted, fancy weave, solid black. Style 2............... 12.00
C180 Black diagonal imported clay worsted, guaranteed all fine worsted. Fine stitched edge. Style 1, our price for suit................. 12.00
C181 Black diagonal worsted, corkscrew weave. Guaranteed pure worsted. Send for sample. We recommend it. Style 1................. 12.60
C182 Black diagonal worsted, corkscrew weave. Guaranteed pure worsted. An excellent suit for wear; will not turn gray with wear. Suitable for business or dress. Style 5............ 12.75
C183 Black diagonal imported clay worsted. Guaranteed all fine worsted. Fine stitched edge. The effect of this suit is simply elegant for the price. A soft, rich black, well made and neatly trimmed. Style 5, 3-button cutaway. Send for sample................................. 12.75
C184 Black diagonal worsted. Style 4............ 13.00
C185 Black corkscrew worsted, with raised effects, fancy weave. Style 5................... 13.00
C186 Blue corkscrew worsted, with raised effects, fancy weave. Style 5................... 13.00
C187 Black diagonal imported clay worsted, stitched edges. Style 1.................... 14.00

Clay worsteds are worn by all the leaders of fashion.

C188 Black corkscrew worsted, fancy weave and effect. Style 2...................... 14.50
C189 Black diagonal imported clay worsted, stitched edges. Style 5.................. 14.50
C190 Black diagonal imported worsted. Style 1... 15.25
C191 Black diagonal, worsted corkscrew weave. Style 1............................... 15.50
C192 Black worsted, small seed pattern. Style 2... 15.50
C193 Blue worsted, small seed pattern. Style 2... 15.50
C194 Black diagonal imported clay worsted. Style 1 16.25
C195 Black diagonal imported clay worsted, bound. Style 5............................... 16.25

If you want a neat, dressy suit buy a clay worsted.

C196 Black diagonal imported clay worsted, bound. Style 2............................... 16.35
C197 Black diagonal imported clay worsted, stitched edge. Style 3.................... 16.35
C198 Black worsted, small seed pattern. Style 5.. 16.35
C199 Blue worsted, small seed pattern. Style 5... 16.35
C200 Black diagonal worsted, wide wale pattern. Style 5............................... 16.35
C201 Blue diagonal worsted, wide wale pattern. Style 5............................... 16.35
C202 Black diagonal imported clay worsted, bound. Style 1............................... 18.00
C203 Black diagonal imported worsted. Style 1... 18.00
C204 Black diagonal imported clay worsted. Style 5 19.00
C205 Black diagonal imported clay worsted, bound. Style 3............................... 19.75
C206 Black diagonal imported clay worsted, bound. Style 5............................... 20.75

SINGLE AND DOUBLE BREASTED PRINCE ALBERT SUITS.

Sizes 34 to 42 Chest Measure.

No.   PRICE FOR SUIT.

C207 Black diagonal worsted, corkscrew weave. Style 1..............................$14.50
C208 Black diagonal worsted, corkscrew weave, coat and vest bound. Style 7.............. 18.00
C209 Black diagonal imported worsted. Style 7... 19.00
C210 Black diagonal imported worsted. Style 6... 21.00
C211 Black diagonal imported clay worsted, coat and vest bound. Style 7.................. 21.00
C212 Black diagonal worsted, corkscrew weave, silk faced and bound. Style 7............ 21.25
C213 Black diagonal, imported worsted. Style 7... 21.75
C214 Black diagonal imported clay worsted, coat and vest bound. Style 7.................. 23.10
C215 Black diagonal imported clay worsted, silk faced and bound. Style 7................ 24.50

BROADCLOTH SUITS.

BROADCLOTH SUITS, STYLES 6, 7 AND 8.

Sizes 34 to 42.

No.   PRICE FOR SUIT.

C216 Black broadcloth. Style 6...............$21.50
C217 Black broadcloth. Style 7................ 24.00

BLUE FLANNEL SUITS.

Sizes 34 to 42.

No.   PRICE FOR SUIT.

C218 Blue flannel suits, light weight, all wool. Style 1..............................$ 8.00
C219 Blue flannel suits, light weight, all wool. Style 2................................ 8.00
C220 Blue flannel suits, light weight, all wool. Style 4................................ 8.50
C221 Blue flannel suits, light weight, all wool. Style 3................................ 9.00
C222 Indigo blue regulation pilot cloth, heavy weight. Style 2........................ 11.50
C223 Indigo blue regulation pilot cloth, heavy weight. Style 3........................ 11.50
C224 All wool, heavy weight, navy blue uniform cloth. Style 2......................... 14.00
C225 All wool, heavy weight, navy blue uniform cloth. Style 3......................... 15.00
C226 All wool, navy blue Middlesex cloth, heavy weight. Style 2........................ 15.75
C227 All wool, navy blue Middlesex cloth, heavy weight. Style 3........................ 16.50

GRAND ARMY SUITS.

Sizes 35 to 42.

No.   PRICE FOR SUIT.

C228 Regulation G. A. R. blue flannel, fast colors; G. A. R. brass buttons. Style 2.............. 8.50

EXTRA SIZE SUITS.

43 to 48 inches chest measure.

No.   PRICE FOR SUIT.

C229 Black and grey mixed, pin check, Union Cassimere. Style 1.......................$10.00
C230 All wool black and gray hair line cassimere.. 13.00
C231 Blue black cassimere, with invisible gray check. Style 1......................... 15.00
C232 All wool black and gray mixed tricot cassimere. Style 1........................ 16.00
C233 Black cassimere, interwoven with white silk threads. Style 1...................... 17.50
C234 Indigo blue, regulation pilot cloth, heavy weight. Style 2........................ 13.50
C235 All wool black and gray hair line, cassimere. Style 4................................ 14.00
C236 Black diagonal worsted, corkscrew weave. Style 5................................ 18.00
C237 Black diagonal imported worsted. Style 4... 18.00

MEN'S SUITS.

The quotations under this heading are for coat, vest and pants together. All men's sizes.

Before ordering suits, read instructions for measurement and remarks under same. Be sure and make your figures plain and correct. We cannot exchange single coats for another if size is wrong. Return full suit. Half sizes are not made in ready made clothing.

Sizes, 34 to 42 only. Larger than 42 chest measure comes under the head of extra sizes. Waist measure for pants under this heading—smallest, 30 inches; largest, 40 inches.

NOTE.—We take pleasure in announcing to our customers that we will offer the most complete line of suits, from the lowest (well made) to the best grade in ready made clothing. All made from the best standard materials, and are absolutely correct in style, shape and finish. A great many people who are not thoroughly posted on clothing imagine that if a suit is not all wool it will not

MEN'S SUITS—Continued.

wear well. Such was the case years ago, but owing to the improved machinery and skilled workmen of the present time, we are able to manufacture some of the finest grades which have a fine cotton warp in the back, which adds weight, strength and durability and cheapens the cost of production, while the face of the fabric is strictly all wool or sometimes silk mixed; will wear equally as well as any all wool suit. We never misrepresent our clothing, but late in the season we are sometimes obliged to substitute, using our best judgment, always to your advantage.

No.		PRICE FOR SUIT.
C238	Black cotton worsted diagonal suits. Style 1.	$ 3.50
C239	Black and gold mixed diagonal emerald worsted suits. Style 1	4.25
C240	Black and gold mixed diagonal emerald worsted suits. Style 4	4.25
C241	Dark mixed fancy plaid satinet cassimere. Style 1	5.40
C242	Brown mixed wool cassimere, diagonal cheviot pattern. Style 1	7.00
C243	Blue and gray mixed cassimere, fancy weave. Style 1	7.20
C244	Black and gray pin head check union cassimere; an old standard, never out of style. Style 1	8.90
C245	Dark gray cassimere, with invisible plaid of blue and red, solid weave. Style 1	9.00
C246	Black and dark blue cassimere, with broken plaid of red and blue threads. Style 1	9.00
C247	Brown mixed kersey cheviot, check and plaid combined, made from long heavy wool. Style 1	9.00
C248	Dark brown mixed melton, heavy and close woven. Style 1	9.00
C249	Black diagonal cheviot, has a fine cotton warp in back. Style 1	9.00
C250	Blue whipcord cheviot, something new and nobby. Style 1	9.00

OUR CELEBRATED $9.00 SUITS.

The following numbers of our **All Wool $9.00 Suits** we are willing to place before any competitor, made from so confident of their superiority over all others sold at the price. You can buy them from us for the same price that your merchant pays for them, saving you his profit (which is usually 50 per cent) and a larger assortment of styles to select from. We guarantee them to be strictly all wool and free from all shoddy and other impurities which are often worked in to cheapen the cost of production. We will furnish samples of cloth for inspection on application. Sizes run from 34 to 42 inch chest measure. We do not break suits.

No.		PRICE FOR SUIT.
C251	Black and dark blue with a neat mixture of dark olive diagonal cheviot pattern, made from long staple, strictly all wool. Style 1 only...	$ 9.00
C252	Black and gray medium dark color, strictly all wool, fine basket pattern weave. Style 1 only	9.00
C253	Black and gray medium dark color. strictly all wool, fine basket pattern weave. Style 2 only..	9.00
C254	Dark blue cassimere, well covered with a golden brown mixture. Cheviot pattern, strictly all wool. Style 1 only	9.00
C255	Dark blue cassimere, well covered with a golden brown mixture. Cheviot pattern, strictly all wool. Style 3 only	9.00
C256	Black and blue mixed cassimere, interwoven with a neat red mixture. Very neat pattern, strictly all wool. Style 1 only	9.00
C257	Black and blue mixed cassimere, interwoven with a neat red mixture. Very neat pattern, strictly all wool, three button cutaway. Style 5 only	9.00
C258	Brown and gray mixed cassimere, diagonal cheviot pattern. Very nobby and dressy, strictly all wool. Style 1 only	9.00
C259	Brown and gray mixed cassimere, diagonal cheviot pattern. Very nobby and dressy, strictly all wool, three button cutaway. Style 5 only	9.00

N. B.—Numbers C251 to C259 inclusive, we consider are the best value ever offered for the money.

C260	Black worsted, with very fine neat check of brown and blue. Style 1	9.00
C261	Black and blue mixed cassimere, worsted finish, interwoven with fine white threads. Style 1	9.00
C262	All wool gray and black mixed diagonal cheviot. Style 1	9.00
C263	Drab corduroy, fancy plaid cassimere lining, with large pockets on inside of coat. Style 1..	9.00
C264	Brown corduroy, fancy plaid cassimere lining, with large pockets on inside of coat. Style 1...	9.00

MELTON SUITS.

These suits we recommend very highly; they are the most serviceable goods made for actual wear. The cloth is very heavy and solid and closely woven, has an all wool face and back with a fine hard twist cotton warp, which adds weight, strength and durability. The price is moderate; make is first-class; color a dark brown mixture.

N. B.—We do not break suits, or send samples of any ready made clothing.

No.		PRICE FOR SUIT.
C265	Dark brown mixed melton suits. Style 1...	$11.50
C266	Dark brown mixed melton suits. Style 2....	11.50
C267	Dark brown mixed melton suits, plaid cassimere lining. Style 3	11.50
C268	Dark brown mixed melton suits. Style 5...	11.50
C269	All wool black and gray hair line cassimere. Style 1	11.50
C270	Blue diagonal wool cassimere. Style 1	11.50
C271	Blue, gray and black, small check all wool cheviot. Style 1	12.75
C272	Brown mixed pin head pattern all wool cassimere. Style 1	12.75
C273	Black cassimere, with neat gray check. Style 1	12.75
C274	Black and gray mixed diagonal cassimere, English pattern. Style 1	13.50
C275	Black corduroy, flannel lining. Style 1	13.50
C276	Drab corduroy, flannel lining. Style 1	13.50
C277	Brown and blue gray, very fine check cassimere. Style 1	14.50
C278	Blue and black mixed cheviot, well covered with a mixture of brown and red. Style 1	14.50
C279	Dark brown mixed melton, extra heavy. Style 1	15.10
C280	Oxford or dark gray mixed melton, extra heavy. Style 1	15.10
C281	Black diagonal worsted, interwoven with red and blue silk threads. Style 1	15.50
C282	Black and black mixed fancy pattern worsted, with fine red silk threads. Style 1	15.75
C283	Blue and black fine hair line cassimere. Style 1	15.75
C284	Black diagonal imported worsted, interwoven with fine white silk threads. Style 1	15.75
C285	Black and steel blue fine check worsted. Style 1	16.50
C286	Blue cassimere, black mixed, soft finish, with fine silk threads. Style 1	16.75
C287	Black and gray diagonal pattern imported English worsted. Style 1	19.90
C288	Black and blue mixed worsted, neat pattern, fancy weave. Style 1	22.10

N. B.—We do not sample any ready made clothing.

SACK SUITS.

SINGLE AND DOUBLE BREASTED, SQUARE CUT.

Sizes 34 to 42 in. chest measure; waist measure 30 to 40 in.

No.		PRICE FOR SUIT.
C289	Black and gray check satinet cassimere. Style 2	$ 5.40
C290	Brown mixed melton, extra heavy. Style 3..	6.50
C291	Black, gray and brown mixed check satinet cassimere. Style 2	6.75
C292	Black and blue fancy satinet cassimere. Style 3	7.10
C293	Dark mixed cassimere, fancy patterns. Style 2	9.00
C294	Brown mixed kersey cheviot, plaid cassimere lining. Style 3	9.90
C295	Black cheviot, fancy plaid cassimere lining, double breasted vest and coat. Style 3	9.90
C296	Blue whipcord cheviot, plaid lining, double breasted vest and coat. Style 3	9.90
C297	Navy and steel blue fancy pattern and weave worsted. Style 2	10.80
C298	Black and gray mixed wool cheviot. Style 3.	11.70
C299	Black, blue, green and invisible red small check cassimere. Style 2	12.00
C300	Black and gray check cheviot, double breasted vest and coat. Style 3	12.00
C301	Blue and black mixed worsted with broken plaid of red. Style 2	12.00
C302	Blue diagonal cassimere, double breasted vest and coat. Style 3	13.00
C303	Brown mixed wool cheviot, fancy pattern, double breasted vest and coat. Style 3	13.00
C304	Black diagonal cheviot, heavy, wide pattern, double breasted vest and coat. Style 3	13.50
C305	Black corduroy, colored flannel lined, two large pockets on inside of coat. Style 3	13.50
C306	Drab corduroy, colored flannel lined, two large pockets on inside of coat. Style 3	13.50
C307	All wool black and gray check cassimere, double breasted vest and coat. Style 3	13.75
C308	Black and blue mixed cheviot, very rough. Style 2	13.75
C309	Black and blue all wool cassimere with gray check. Style 2	14.50
C310	Black cheviot, extra heavy, plaid lining. Style 2	14.50
C311	Black cheviot, silk facing, double breasted vest and coat. Style 3	15.00
C312	Brown mixed melton, extra heavy. Style 2..	15.25
C313	Oxford or dark gray mixed melton, extra heavy. Style 2	15.25

SACK SUITS—Continued.

No. PRICE FOR SUIT.

C314 Black worsted, fancy weave, mixed with red silk threads. Style 2 .... 16.20

C315 Brown mixed melton, extra heavy, double breasted vest. Style 3 .... 16.20

C316 Oxford or dark gray mixed melton, extra heavy, double breasted vest. Style 3 .... 16.20

C317 Blue diagonal cassimere, interwoven with gold silk threads, double breasted vest. Style 3 .... 16.40

C318 All wool black cheviot, slightly mixed with gray, double breasted vest and coat. Style 3 .... 17.90

C319 Blue and black fancy plaid, imported worsted. Style 2 .... 17.90

THREE BUTTON CUTAWAY SUITS.

Sizes 34 to 42 inch chest measure; waist measure 30 to 40 inch.

N. B.—We do not sample any suits.

No. PRICE FOR SUIT.

C320 Gray mixed cassimere suits. Style 5 .... $ 8.00

C321 Black and gray pin head check, union cassimere. Style 5 .... 9.00

C322 Black and blue mixed worsted interwoven with silk threads. Style 5 .... 10.20

C323 All wool gray and black mixed diagonal cheviot. Style 5 .... 10.20

C324 Black and brown mixed worsted, interwoven with white threads. Style 5 .... 10.20

C325 Blue diagonal wool cassimere. Style 5 .... 12.20

C326 Black diagonal wool cheviot. Style 5 .... 12.20

C327 Black, brown and blue small check worsted. Style 5 .... 12.70

C328 Black diagonal cassimere, slightly mixed with gray. Style 5 .... 13.50

C329 Black cassimere, with small broken check of gray. Style 5 .... 14.50

C330 Black and steel gray mixed diagonal cassimere. Style 5 .... 15.50

C331 Black and blue small check worsted. Style 5 16.20

C332 Brown mixed melton, extra heavy. Style 5.. 16.20

C333 Oxford mixed melton, extra heavy. Style 5.. 16.20

C334 Black diagonal cassimere, interwoven with fine white silk threads. Style 5 .... 17.10

C335 Black and gray diagonal English clay worsted pattern. Style 5 .... 17.95

C336 Black diagonal imported worsted, interwoven with white and gold silk threads. Style 5 .... 18.90

C337 Blue and black imported diagonal worsted. Style 5 .... 21.65

CHILDREN'S SUITS.

For ages 4 to 14 years. Coat and knee pants suits two pieces.

N. B.—We do not sample and ready made clothing.

Children's suits weight from 1¼ to 2 lbs., according to age and quality.

No. PRICE FOR SUIT.

C338 Black and gray mixed jean suits, 4 to 12 years. $ .75

C339 Fancy mixed satinet cassimere. Made plain. .75

C340 Fancy mixed gray and brown, broken plaid satinet cassimere. Made plain 1.05

C341 Black diagonal cotton worsted, old gold mixed, corded front and back 1.25

C342 Brown mixed fancy plaid satinet cassimere, corded front and back 1.30

C343 Gray and blue striped satinet cassimere, pleated front and back 1.55

C344 Black and dark mixed satinet cassimere, pleated front and back 1.75

C345 Black and gray mixed pinhead check satinet cassimere, corded front and back 1.75

C346 Black ground union cassimere, with neat stripes of brown and red, pleated front and back 2.05

C347 Black and gray mixed hair-line satinet cassimere, single breasted square cut coat 2.30

C348 Fancy mixed plaid satinet cassimere, double breasted square cut coat 2.30

C349 Black, brown and white mixed, hard twist union cassimere, small neat check 2.40

C350 Dark mixed small pattern satinet cassimere, double breasted square cut coat 2.40

C351 Brown and gray mixed, small check, medium light colored satinet cassimere, double breasted square cut coat 2.40

C352 Black diagonal worsted corkscrew weave, pleated front and back 2.40

C353 Blue diagonal worsted corkscrew weave, pleated front and back 2.40

C354 Brown corduroy, pleated front and back 2.60

C355 Drab corduroy, pleated front and back 2.60

C356 Brown gray and black mixed check, made from Kersey wool, corded front and back, with sliding band storm cap of same material 2.60

C357 Blue gray and red mixed striped wool cheviot, pleated front and back 2.60

No. PRICE FOR SUIT.

C358 Monitor suits, made for boys who are rough on clothes. All wool brown mixed diagonal pattern double and twist cassimere, extra well sewed, heavy weight; double knees and seat in pants. This is a big bargain 2.60

C359 Black and blue gray striped union cassimere. Style 1 coat 3.05

C360 Brown mixed fancy plaid wool cheviot, double breasted square cut coat 3.10

C361 Brown and gray mixed wool kersey, basket pattern weave, double breasted square cut coat. 3.15

C362 Brown gray and white mixed hard twist cassimere, small neat pattern. Double breasted coat, double knees and seat in pants, sliding band winter storm cap of same material with each suit free. Sizes 6½ to 7⅛ 3.15

C363 Fancy mixed plaid union cassimere, velour finish; double breasted square cut coat 3.60

C364 Black and dark brown mixed diagonal wool cheviot. Style 1 coat 3.95

C365 All wool navy blue tricot cassimere, corded front and back 3.95

C366 Monitor suits, made for boys who are rough on clothes. All wool, blue and gray, neat check; double knees and seat in pants, extra well sewed. Cast iron cheviots 3.95

C367 Monitor suits for boys who are rough on clothes. All wool brown and gray kersey double knees and seat in pants, extra well sewed 3.95

C368 Monitor suits for boys who are rough on clothes. Fancy mixed cast iron wool cheviot, double knees and seat in pants; double breasted square cut coat. Sliding band winter storm cap of same material with each suit free 4.45

C369 Dark brown mixed extra heavy union melton cassimere; double breasted, square cut coat. Sliding band winter storm cap of same material with each suit and one extra pair pants. We will not sell separate or give two different size of pants 4.45

C370 Black diagonal wool cheviot, pleated front and back 4.45

C371 Navy blue corduroy, double breasted, square cut coat 4.90

C372 Myrtle green corduroy, double breasted, square cut coat 4.90

C373 All wool blue and red mixed cheviot, double breasted, square cut coat 4.90

C374 All navy blue tricot cassimere pleated and corded front and back 5.40

C375 Black wool cheviot, fancy plaid cassimere lining, double breasted, square cut 5.40

C376 Black and blue small check cassimere, velour finish 5.80

C377 Black and blue small check cassimere, velour finish, double breasted, square cut coat 6.55

C378 Fancy weave black worsted with neat fine threads of wine. Style 1 coat 6.65

CHILDREN'S ZOUAVE SUITS.

Zouave coat and knee pants. Ages 4 to 7.

No. PRICE FOR SUIT.

C379 Brown mixed diagonal wool cheviot; buckle and braid on bottom of pants $2.60

C380 Brown and gray mixed diagonal kersey with invisible red plaid, braided front and sleeves; buckle and braid on bottom of pants 3.50

C381 Blue corduroy, with buckle and braid on bottom of pants 3.60

C382 Myrtle green corduroy, with buckle and braid on bottom of pants 4.00

C383 Blue black fancy weave worsted, revere front trimmed with silk braid, buckle and braid on bottom of pants 4.25

C384 Navy blue tricot cassimere coat trimmed with silk cord, buckle and braid on bottom of pants.. 5.40

C385 Boucle cloth or fine nigger head, gray and black mixed with silk threads of peacock and red, trimmed with pearl buttons, buckle and braid on bottom of pants 6.65

C386 Boys' double breasted reefer coat and pants 4 to 7 years; navy blue corduroy 4.95

C387 Boys' double breasted reefer coat and pants, 4 to 7 years; myrtle green corduroy 4.95

BOYS' THREE PIECE SUITS.

No. PRICE FOR SUIT.

C388 Black and brown small check satinet cassimer, double breasted coat; ages 10 to 15 .... $ 3.30

C389 Black and gray mixed diagonal wool cheviot double breasted coat; ages 6 to 15 .... 5.40

C390 All wool brown and blue mixed diagonal cheviot, double breasted coat; ages 6 to 15 .... 6.30

C391 Navy blue serge, cheviot, fancy plaid cassimere lining, double breasted coat; ages 6 to 15.. 6.75

C392 Black diagonal Imported clay worsted, double breasted coat; ages 6 to 15. .... 8.75

CHILDREN'S BLOUSE SUITS.

No.   PRICE FOR SUIT.

C393 All wool navy blue jersey cloth blouse suits with silk ribbon bow at neck; ages 3 to 7........$ 2.25

C394 All wool navy blue jersey cloth blouse suits with silk ribbon bow at neck and silk cord trimming on collar........................... 2.70

C395 All wool navy blue jersey cloth blouse suits with silk ribbon bow at neck and silk cord trimming on collar........................... 3.10

C396 All wool navy blue jersey cloth blouse suits, fancy silk embroidered collar and front, bow at neck..................................... 3.60

C397 All wool navy blue jersey cloth blouse suits, large shawl collar embroidered with silk cord, vest front.............................. 4.45

SCHOOL SUITS.

Chest measure 25 to 29 inches, or ages 9 to 13. Coat, vest and long pants.

No.   PRICE FOR SUIT.

C398 Fancy mixed broken check satinet cassimere. 2.65

C399 Black diagonal cotton worsted............... 2.65

C400 Black diagonal cotton worsted, yellow mixed. 2.90

C401 Black and gray hair line satinet cassimere.... 3.60

C402 Black and gray mixed, small check satinet cassimere............................... 3.60

C403 All wool black, with gray plaid, double and twist cassimere; for boys who are rough on clothes this has no equal for the price.......... 4.20

C404 Black diagonal worsted, corkscrew weave..... 4.45

C405 Blue diagonal worsted, corkscrew weave..... 4.45

C406 Black and gray mixed diagonal wool cheviot. 5.35

C407 Black and gray striped union cassimere...... 5.35

C408 All wool blue and gray, small check, cast iron cheviot; one of the best suits made for actual wear............................... 6.75

BOYS' SUITS.

Ages 14 to 18; sizes 30 to 34 inch chest measure.

N. B. Where sizes are quoted up to 19 years, the chest measure is 35 inches, pants size run from 26 to 32 inch waist and 26 to 32 inside seam measure; larger sizes than these will have to be selected from men's sizes.

No.   PRICE FOR SUIT.

C409 Fancy mixed broken check satinet cassimere, 14 to 18 years......................... 2.60

C410 Black diagonal cotton worsted, 14 to 18 years. 2.90

C411 Black and old gold mixed diagonal cotton worsted, 14 to 18 years................. 3.10

C412 Black and gray mixed satinet cassimere, diagonal pattern, 14 to 18 years........... 3.60

C413 Black and gray mixed satinet cassimere, small check, 14 to 18 years................... 4.10

C414 Black and gray hair line satinet cassimere, 14 to 18 years......................... 4.30

C415 Black and gray small check satinet cassimere, double breasted..................... 4.30

C416 Black and invisible blue plain satinet cassimere............................... 4.45

C417 All wool black with gray, plaid double and twist cassimere. For boys who are rough on clothes this has no equal for the price; 14 to 19 years. Send for sample............... 4.60

C418 Black diagonal worsted, corkscrew weave, 14 to 18 years......................... 4.80

C419 Black ground with brown stripes, union cassimere, 14 to 18 years...................... 4.95

C420 Black and brown mixed satinet cassimere, disgonal pattern, double breasted, 14 to 18 years. 4.95

C421 Black cassimere interwoven with white and red threads, 14 to 18 years............... 5.40

C422 Black and gray mixed diagonal wool cheviot, 14 to 18 years......................... 5.70

C423 Blue, brown and black heavy weight wool kersey, double breasted, 14 to 19 years..... 6.25

C424 Black and gray mixed striped union cassimere, 14 to 18 years.................... 6.50

C425 Blue diagonal worsted, corkscrew weave, 14 fo 19 years............................. 6.60

C426 Black diagonal worsted, corkscrew weave, 14 to 18 years............................ 6.75

C427 Fancy pattern and weave black worsted, 14 to 19 years............................. 6.85

C428 All wool blue and gray small check cast iron cheviot. One of the best suits made for actual wear. Send for sample. 14 to 19 years....... 7.25

C429 Black diagonal wool cheviot, double breasted, square cut coat, 14 to 19 years............. 7.25

C430 Brown mixed extra heavy melton cassimere, double breasted, 14 to 19 years........... 7.25

C431 Black and blue mixed fancy cassimere, worsted finish, interwoven with white threads, single breasted square cut coat, 14 to 19 years... 8.00

C432 Black and dark brown mixed diagonal wool cheviot, single breasted square cut coat, 14 to 19 years................................. 8.00

No.   PRICE FOR SUIT.

C433 Brown mixed fancy plaid wool cheviot, plaid cassimere lining, double breasted, 14 to 19 years. 8.00

C434 All wool navy blue tricot cassimere, 14 to 19 years................................. 8.50

C435 All wool blue and brown mixed diagonal kersey cheviot, double breasted, 14 to 19 years.. 9.00

C436 Black diagonal cassimere, worsted finish, interwoven with white and gold silk threads, double breasted, 14 to 19 years........... 9.00

C437 Black diagonal wool cheviot, 14 to 19 years.. 9.00

C438 All wool navy blue tricot cassimere, 14 to 19 years................................. 10.00

C439 Brown mixed melton extra heavy, double breasted, 14 to 19 years.................. 10.00

C440 Black diagonal clay worsted pattern, 14 to 19 years................................. 10.80

C441 Blue cassimere, with neat gray check, 14 to 19 years................................. 10.80

C442 Blue and brown striped wool cassimere, fancy plaid lining, double breasted, 14 to 19 years.... 10.80

C443 Black and wine mixed kersey, fancy plaid satin lining, double breasted, 14 to 19 years....... 11.00

C444 Black diagonal imported clay worsted, 14 to 19 years............................. 11.75

C445 Black and blue mixed diagonal worsted, interwoven with fine red silk threads, 14 to 19 years................................. 11.75

C446 Black diagonal imported clay worsted, double breasted, 14 to 19 years.................. 12.50

C447 Black diagonal imported clay worsted, coat and vest bound, 14 to 19 years............. 13.25

CHILDREN'S KNEE PANTS.

Sizes 4 to 14 years.

No.   PRICE FOR PAIR.

C448 Kentucky Jeans, Oxford mixed.............$ .20

C449 Fancy mixed satinet cassimere............. .25

C450 Black diagonal cotton worsted............. .25

C451 Fancy striped cotton worsted.............. .30

C452 Fancy striped cottonade................... .30

C453 Dark mixed plaid satinet cassimere......... .35

C454 Black and brown mixed check satinet cassimere............................... .40

C455 Fancy mixed striped satinet cassimere....... .45

C456 Drab corduroy pants..................... .65

C457 Brown corduroy pants.................... .65

C458 All wool black and gray hard twist cassimere. .65

C459 Black, gray and red mixed striped wool cassimere................................. .75

C460 Brown and gray small checked wool kersey.. .75

C461 All wool navy blue jersey cloth............ .90

C462 Brown corduroy pants.................... .90

C463 Drab corduroy pants..................... .90

C464 Brown and gray mixed striped union cassimere................................. .90

C465 Black and gray striped union cassimere...... .90

C466 All wool navy blue jersey cloth............ 1.25

C467 All wool blue tricot cassimere............. 1.30

C468 All wool blue and red mixed cheviot......... 1.30

BOYS' LONG PANTS.

Scale of sizes in boys' pants.

Waist	27	27	28	28	29	29	29	29	30	31	31
Inside seam	26	27	27	28	29	29	28	29	30	30	31

Weight of pants under this heading 1¼ to 1½ lbs. according to size and quality.

No.   PRICE FOR PAIR.

C469 Striped cottonade pants.................. .90

C470 Fancy striped satinet cassimere............ 1.15

C471 Black and gray striped satinet cassimere..... 1.25

C472 Drab corduroy pants..................... 1.60

C473 Brown corduroy pants.................... 1.60

C474 Black, gray and red striped wool cassimere... 1.80

C475 Black and brown striped union cassimere.... 2.25

C476 Black diagonal worsted with neat silk stripes. 2.75

C477 Blue, black and gray mixed striped kersey cheviot................................. 2.75

C478 Black and purple mixed herring bone pattern worsted............................... 3.25

C479 Black with neat stripes of dark wine fancy weave worsted.......................... 4.25

CHILDREN'S OVERCOATS.

Children's overcoats, weight from 2½ to 4 lbs. according to age and quality.

No.   PRICE FOR COAT.

C480 Gray and brown mixed satinet overcoat, 4 to 12 years............................... 1.25

C481 Fancy mixed plaid satinet ulster, with cape, 4 to 12 years............................ 1.55

C482 Brown, black and red mixed plaid ulster, with cape, 4 to 12 years...................... 1.75

C483 Black and gray plaid overcoat, with cape, 4 to 12 years............................. 1.80

C484 Black and gray broken plaid ulster, with cape, 4 to 12 years...................... 2.25

CHILDREN'S OVERCOATS.—Continued.

No.	PRICE FOR COAT
C485 Black and gray broken plaid ulster, with cape, 4 to 12 years	2.50
C486 Black and brown plaid satinet ulster, double breasted, with cape	2.50
C487 Brown and gray fancy plaid ulster, double breasted, 4 to 13 years	3.15
C488 Brown, black and red mixed kersey cheviot ulster, with cape, 4 to 12 years	3.60
C489 Fancy mixed nickerbocker wool cheviot ulster, with cape, 4 to 12 years	4.00
C490 Brown mixed melton overcoat, extra heavy, with cape, 4 to 12 years	4.25
C491 Gray mixed melton ulster, double breasted, with large collar, plaid cassimere lining, 6 to 12 years	5.40
C492 Black, brown and red mixed cheviot overcoat, with cape, 4 to 14 years	5.40
C493 Plain black melton overcoat, with cape, 4 to 12 years	5.40
C494 Oxford mixed melton overcoat, with cape, 4 to 14 years	6.25
C495 Brown mixed Shetland chinchilla ulster, fly front, shawl collar, plaid cassimere lining, 6 to 12 years	6.25
C496 Brown mixed invisible plaid Irish frieze plaid cassimere lining, double breasted, large collar, 6 to 12 years	7.25

CHILDREN'S KILT OVERCOATS.

2½ to 7 years.

Kilt overcoats are all made with pleated skirt in back, half belt and buckle and large cape.

No.	PRICE FOR COAT
C497 Fancy mixed satinet kilt overcoat with cape, 2½ to 7 years	2.75
C498 Gray and blue mixed broken check kilt ulster, with cape, 2½ t o 7 years	3.25
C499 Brown, black and red mixed plaid kersey kilt ulster, with cape, 2½ to 7 years	3.60
C500 Brown and mixed kersey medium light colored invisible plaid, kilt ulster, with cape, 2½ to 7 years	4.10
C501 Brown and gray large broken plaid cassimere, with cape, kilt ulster, 2½ to 7 years	4.50
C502 Blue wool cheviot with mixtures of brown and black, kilt ulster with cape, 2½ to 7 years	5.50
C503 Brown and gray mixed rough wool cheviot mixed with red and blue silk floss; very nobby kilt ulster with cape, 2½ to 7 years	7.00

BOYS' OVERCOATS AND ULSTERS.

Ages	13	14	15	16	17	18	19
Chest measures	29	30	31	32	33	34	50

No.	PRICE FOR COAT
C504 Black and gray mixed satinet ulster, single breasted, 13 to 18 years	2.25
C505 Brown and mixed plaid satinet ulster, single breasted, 13 to 18 years	2.50
C506 Black, brown and gray broken plaid satinet ulster, single breasted, 13 to 18 years	3.50
C507 Black and gray mixed check satinet ulster, single breasted, 13 to 18 years	3.60
C508 Black and brown mixed diagonal satinet cassimere ulster, single breasted	4.25
C509 Black and brown mixed satinet overcoat fly front, 13 to 18 years	4.50
C510 Black, brown and gray mixed satinet long overcoat, 13 to 18 years	5.00
C511 Blue chinchilla overcoat, velvet collar, fly front, 13 to 18 years	5.00
C512 Brown mixed melton overcoat, extra heavy velvet collar, fly front, 13 to 19 years, plaid cassimere lining, style 10	5.50
C513 Gray mixed melton ulster, plaid cassimere ltning, double breasted, 13 to 18 years	6.25
C514 Plain black melton ulster, plaid cassimere lining, double breasted, 13 to 19 years	6.25
C515 Brown mixed Shetland chinchilla ulster, plaid cassimere lining, 13 to 19 years	6.75
C516 Gray and snowflake Shetland chinchilla ulster, extra heavy, plaid cassimere lining, double breasted, 13 to 19 years	7.25
C517 Blue gray mixed melton overcoat, velvet collar, plaid cassimere lining, double breasted, 13 to 19 years	8.10
C518 Brown mixed frieze, fly front ulster, shawl collar, medium light color, plaid cassimere lining, 13 to 19 years	8.90
C519 Navy blue chinchilla ulster, large fur collar and cuffs, loop fastners, style 14; 13 to 19 years	8.90
C520 Navy blue beaver overcoat, smooth finish, velvet collar, fly front, style 10; 13 to 19 years	9.00

No.	PRICE EOR COAT
C521 Brown mixed invisible plaid Irish frieze ulster, plaid cassimere lining, double breasted, 13 to 19 years	10.00
C522 Navy blue chinchilla fly front ulster, shawl collar, 13 to 19 years	10.00
C523 Navy blue chinchilla ulster, large fur collar and cuffs, loop fastners, style 14; 13 to 19 years	11.00
C524 Navy blue beaver fly front ulster, shawl collar, plaid cassimere lining, 13 to 19 years	12.75

MEN'S OVERCOATS AND ULSTERS.

All men's sizes; 35 to 42.

Take measure for overcoats; over vests same as for undercoat.

Heavy overcoats weigh from 5 to 7 pounds, according to style size and quality.

No.	PRICE FOR COAT
C525 Black and gray mixed satinet, single breasted ulster, style 13	3.60
C526 Black and gray check satinet cassimere, velvet collar	4.25
C527 Brown and gray satinet cassimere, single breasted ulster, style 13	5.00
C528 Blue chinchilla overcoat, velvet collar, fly front, style 10	5.25
C529 Gray mixed melton, plaid lining, velvet collar, fly front, style 10	5.42
C530 Black beaver overcoats, double breasted, style 16	5.40
C531 Fancy brown plaid satinet ulster, fancy back, double breasted, style 12	5.40
C532 Black, Brown and gray satinet ulster, plush collar and cuffs, single breasted	5.40
C533 Brown and gray diagonal satinet cassimere, single breasted, Prince Charles ulster, fancy back, style 13	6.00
C534 Black and gray mixed melton ulster, double breasted, style 12	6.50
C535 Black chinchilla, velvet collar, fly front, style 10	6.35
C536 Black diagonal worsted, corkscrew weave, medium weight, style 10	6.35
C537 Black and blue satinet cassimere overcoat, plaid lining, velvet collar, double breasted, style 16	6.35
C538 Dark Oxford gray mixed melton, heavy weight storm ulster, plain cassimere lining, double breasted, style 12	6.35
C539 Blue chinchilla, double breasted ulster, storm coat, plaid lining, shawl collar, style 12.	6.75
C540 Dark Oxford gray mixed melton, heavy weight storm ulster, large astrakhan collar and cuffs, plaid cassimere lining, made from same material as 538	7.25
C541 Black and brown plaid satinet, large astrakhan collar and cuffs, double breasted storm ulster, fancy back	7.25
C542 Black beaver, smooth finish velvet collar, fly front, style 10	8.10
C543 Black diagonal cheviot, fly front, style 10	8.10
C544 Brown and red mixed kersey, fancy back, single breasted storm ulster, style 13	8.10
C545 Black chinchilla, velvet collar, fly front, style 10	8.10
C546 Blue chinchilla, velvet collar, fly front, style 10	8.10
C547 Brown mixed melton, velvet collar, fly front, style 10	8.10
C548 Blue diagonal wool cassimere, velvet collar, fly front, style 10	8.10
C549 Black and brown hard twist diagonal cassimere, fancy back, single breasted storm ulster, style 13	8.90
C550 Blue chinchilla, velvet collar, fly front, style 10	9.00
C551 Brown mixed kersey, plaid lining, shawl collar, double breasted storm ulster, style 12	9.00
C552 Black beaver, smooth finish, velvet collar, fly front, style 10	9.00
C553 Blue beaver, smooth finish, velvet collar, fly front, style 10	9.00
C554 Brown beaver, smooth finish, velvet collar, fly front, style 10	9.00
C555 Blue chinchilla, large nutria fur collar, storm ulster, frog and loop fastners, style 14	9.00
C556 Brown mixed melton, double breasted storm ulster, plaid cassimere lining, shawl collar, style 12	9.00
C557 Brown mixed melton, velvet collar, fly front, plaid cassimere lining, style 10	10.00
C558 Black melton, velvet collar, fly front, plaid cassimere lining, style 10	10.00
C559 Black kersey beaver, plaid cassimere lining, velvet collar, fly front, style 10	10.00
C560 Blue kersey beaver, plaid cassimere lining, velvet collar, fly front, style 10	10.00

MEN'S OVERCOATS AND ULSTERS.—
Continued.

No.   Price for Coat.

C561   Brown kersey beaver, plaid cassimere lining, velvet collar, fly front, style 10.................. 10.00

C562   Fawn colored kersey beaver, plaid cassimere lining, velvet collar, fly front, style 10.......... 10.00

C563   Blue chinchilla, double breasted storm ulster, plaid cassimere lining, shawl collar, style 12.... 10.00

C564   Gray mixed Shetland chinchilla, double breasted storm ulster, cassimere lined, style 12. 11.00

C565   Brown mixed Shetland chinchilla, double breasted storm ulster, cassimere lined, style 12.. 11.00

C566   Black kersey beaver, plaid cassimere lining, velvet collar, fly front, style 16............... 11.00

C567   Blue kersey beaver, plaid cassimere lining, velvet collar, fly front style 16.............. 11.00

C568   Brown kersey beaver, plaid cassimere lining, velvet collar, fly front, style 16..... 11.00

C569   Medium colored Fawn, kersey beaver, plaid cassimere lining, velvet collar, fly front, style 16. 11.00

C570   Oxford or gray mixed Irish frieze, double breasted storm ulster, shawl collar, plaid cassimere lining, style 12............................ 11.25

C571   Black Irish frieze, extra heavy, double breasted storm ulster, shawl collar plaid cassimere lining, style 12.......................... 11.75

C572   Black beaver, smooth finish, velvet collar, fly front, style 10.............................. 12.60

C573   Blue beaver, smooth finish, velvet collar, fly front, style 10............................... 12.60

C574   Fawn colored beaver, smooth finish, velvet collar, fly front, style 10..................... 12.60

C575   Gray mixed rough chinchilla beaver, double breasted storm ulster, plaid cassimere lining, style 12................................. 12.60

C576   Black kersey beaver, plaid cassimere lining, velvet collar, fly front, style 10............. 12.60

C577   Blue chinchilla storm ulster, large nutria fur collar and cuffs, frog and loop fastners, style 14. 12.60

C578   Brown mixed Irish frieze, double breasted storm ulster, striped cassimere lining, shawl collar, style 12............................... 13.50

C579   Oxford or dark gray mixed Irish frieze, double breasted storm ulster, colored cassimere lining, shawl collar, style 12...................... 13.50

C580   Black diagonal worsted corkscrew weave, medium weight, fly front, style 10.............. 13.50

C581   Brown mixed diagonal wool cheviot, shawl collar, plaid cassimere lining, double breasted storm ulster, style 12........................ 13.50

C582   Black beaver, smooth finish, velvet collar, fly front, style 10............................... 14.00

C583   Brown mixed Irish frieze, double breasted storm ulster, plaid cassimere lining, style 12.... 14.50

C584   Blue kersey beaver, plaid cassimere lining, velvet collar, fly front, style 10............... 14.50

C585   Kersey overcoats, satin yoke, and plaid cassimere lining, velvet collar, double breasted, colors black or brown, style 16................. 16.25

C586   Blue chinchilla storm ulster, large nutria fur collar and cuffs, frog and loop fastners, style 14. 16.25

C587   Oxford or dark gray mixed double breasted storm ulster, plaid cassimere lining, shawl collar, style 12............................... 16.25

C588   Fawn colored Iceland beaver, plaid cassimere lining, double breasted, style 16............... 17.10

C589   Blue beaver, smooth finish, large nutia fur collar and cuffs, frog and loop fastners, style 14. 17.10

C590   Iceland beaver, very heavy, velvet collar, fly front, style 10, colors black, navy blue, or seal brown................................. 17.10

C591   Blue chinchilla, silk cord edged, velvet collar, fly front, style 10, colors black or blue 17.10

C592   Kersey beaver, with inside satin yoke on shoulders, plaid cassimere lining, velvet collar, double breasted, style 16, colors black seal brown or fawn.............................. 19.00

C593   Black Irish frieze, double breasted, storm ulster, plaid cassimere lining, shawl collar, style 12.................................... 22.25

C594   Imported kersey, with inside satin yoke on shoulders, plaid cassimere lining, velvet collar, double breasted, style 16, colors black, blue or fawn.................................... 23.50

C595   Imported kersey, with inside satin yoke on shoulders, plaid cassimere lining, velvet collar, double breasted, style 16, colors black or blue... 27.00

PEA JACKETS AND VESTS.

Weights 4½ to 5½ lbs., according to size and quality.

No.   Price per Pair.

C596   Gray mixed satinet, pea jacket and vest, double breasted, style 17................... 4.00

C597   Blue chinchilla, pea jacket and vest, double breasted, plaid lining, style 17............... 5.40

No.   Price per Pair.

C598   Blue chinchilla pea jacket and vest, double breasted, serge lining, style 17.................. 8.10

C599   Blue chinchilla pea jacket and vest, double breasted, plaid lining, style 17.................. 9.00

C600   Gray mixed Irish frieze, pea jacket and vest, double breasted, plaid lining, style 17.......... 9.00

C601   Black plush, pea jacket and vest, double breasted, serge lining, style 17.................. 10.00

C602   Seal brown plush, pea jacket and vest, double breasted, serge lining, style 17.................. 10.00

C603   Blue chinchilla, pea jacket and vest, plaid cassimere lining, double breasted, style 17...... 13.50

C604   Black curly astrakhan plush, black Italian lining, double breasted, style 17.................. 16.25

OVERCOATS.
EXTRA SIZES.
Sizes 43 to 44.

No.   Price for Coat.

C605   Blue chinchilla, velvet collar, fly front, style 10. 9.00

C606   Black beaver, velvet collar, fly front, style 10. 11.00

C607   Blue beaver, velvet collar, fly front, style 10.. 11.00

C608   Gray mixed cassimere, smooth finish, fly front, style 10. .... 12.00

C609   Black beaver, velvet collar, fly front, style 10. 19.00

FUR OVERCOATS.

Weight, 7¼ to 9 lbs., according to size and quality.

Sizes run from 38 to 48 tailor measure.

There are cheaper grades of goat and dog coats manufactured, but we do not handle them as they give very poor satisfaction to the consumer.

No.   Price for Coat.

C610   Graygoat overcoats, cotton lined, 50 in. long. 10.00

C611   Black goat overcoats, cotton lined, 50 inches long................................... 11.00

C612   Yellow dog overcoats, cotton lined, 52 inches long................................... 11.00

C613   Yellow dog overcoats, medium dark color, cotton lined, 52 inches long............... 12.25

C614   Natural black dog overcoats, cotton lined, 52 inches long............................... 13.50

C615   Natural black goat overcoats, quilted lining, 50 inches long........................... 14.00

C616   Natural black goat overcoats, large nutria fur collar and cuffs, quilted lining, 50 inches long.. 15.50

C617   Natural black dog overcoats, large nutria collar, cotton lined, 52 inches long........... 17.00

C618   Wombat or Australian bear overcoats, medium light color, quilted Italian lining, 52 inches long................................... 18.00

C619   Natural brown calf overcoats, quilted Italian lining, 52 inches long...................... 18.00

C620   Natural black calf overcoats, quilted Italian lining, 52 inches long...................... 20.00

C621   Wild cat overcoats, quilted Italian lining, 52 inches long............................... 20.25

C622   Natural black calf overcoats, quilted Italian lining, large nutria fur collar................. 22.50

C623   Black Bulgarian lamb overcoats, quilted Italian lining, 52 inches long................. 22.50

C624   Black hair seal overcoats, large nutria fur collar, quilted Italian lining, 52 inches long... 31.50

C625   Raccoon overcoats, quilted lining, 52 inches long................................... 33.50

C626   Raccoon overcoats, quilted lining, large nutria fur collar, 52 inches long................... 37.50

C627   Raccoon overcoats, quilted lining, large nutria fur collar and cuffs, 52 inches long...... 39.50

LEATHER CLOTHING.

Leather clothing, commonly called Dongola goat, is made of oil-tanned and dressed Rocky Mountain sheepskin. It is very soft and pliable, and is strictly waterproof. Sizes in leather clothing are 36, 38, 40, 42 and 44. No odd sizes. Weight of leather coats, 3¼ to 4 pounds. Vest, 1 to 2 pounds.

No.   Price Each.

C628   Black leather coats, double breasted, patent snap buttons, plaid cassimere lining........... 3.50

C629   Brown 10 ounce waterproof duck, lined with russet leather, double breasted, patent snap buttons.................................. 3.60

C630   Black leather coats, double breasted, patent snap buttons, plaid lining.................... 4.00

C631   Black leather coats, double breasted, patent snap buttons, gray blanket lining............. 4.00

C632   Black leather coats, No. 1 stock, red flannel lined, double breasted, patent snap buttons..... 4.50

C633   Black leather coats, drab corduroy lining, double breasted, patent snap buttons.......... 4.50

C634   Black leather coats, Kentucky jeans lining, double breasted, patent snap buttons.......... 4.50

LEATHER CLOTHING.—Continued.

No.   PRICE EACH.
C635 Black leather coats, double breasted, plaid
Mackinaw lining, sheep pelt roll collar, patent
snap buttons................................... 5.40
C636 Russet leather coat, red flannel lining, double
breasted, patent snap buttons................ 5.40
C637 Black leather coats, plaid Mackinaw lining
double breasted, patent snap buttons.......... 5.25
C638 Black leather coats, reversible, ½ z. brown
duck, double breasted, patent snap buttons.... 5.40
C639 Black leather coats, reversible, black twilled
flannel, double breasted, patent snap buttons... 5.40
C640 Black leather coats, reversible, drab corduroy,
double breasted, patent snap buttons.......... 5.75
C641 Black leather coats, chamois lining, double
breasted, patent buttons...................... 6.00
C642 Brown duck, lined with sheep pelt, corduroy
collar, storm fly front, patent snap buttons..... 6.00
C643 Black leather coats, reversible, extra heavy
mottled blanket lining, double breasted, patent
snap buttons.................................. 7.25
C644 Russet leather coats, reversible, drab corduroy
lining, double breasted, patent snap buttons... 7.50
C645 Black leather coats, reversible, green cordu-
roy, double breasted, patent snap buttons..... 7.75
C646 Tan brown genuine ooze calfskin coat, revers-
ible, soft and as pliable as cloth............... 10.00
C647 Black leather vests, red flannel lined, each... 2.25
C648 Black leather vests, drab corduroy lined, each. 2.75
C649 Russet leather vests, red flannel lined, double
breasted..................................... 2.00
C650 Black leather vests, chamois lined........... 3.25
C651 Black leather vests, with sleeves, red flannel
lined... 3.50
C652 Tan brown genuine ooze calfskin vests, re-
versible...................................... 5.00
C653 Black leather pants, per pair................. 4.00
C654 Black leather apron pants, lined, per pair.... 4.75
C655 Tan brown genuine ooze calfskin pants....... 10.00

Leather pants are made in the following sizes only: 32,

34, 36, 38, 40 and 42 waist, and 30, 31, 32, 33 and 34 inside
seam measure.
C656 Black leather overcoat, red and black plaid
Mackinaw blanket lining each................. 8.75

LINED DUCK SUITS and COATS.

Mens sizes in duck goods are 34, 36, 38, 40, 42 and 44.
No odd sizes. Duck clothing weighs as follows: Suit, 6½
and 7½ pounds; ulsters 5 to 6½ pounds; single coats, 2 to
9 pounds.
C657 Brown duck coats, drab cotton flannel lined
each.. 1.35
C658 Brown duck coats, dark gray mixed blanket
lined, each................................... 1.60
C659 Brown duck coats, red cotton flannel lined,
corduroy collar, each......................... 1.60
C660 Brown duck coats, lined with red Mackinaw
blanketing, corduroy collar, each.............. 2.10
C661 Black duck coats, waterproof gray blanket
lined, corduroy collar, each................... 2.70
C662 Men's brown duck ulsters, 10 oz. goods, gray
blanket lining................................ 4.25
C663 Men's brown duck ulsters, 10 oz. goods, red or
blue Mackinaw lining......................... 6.00
C664 Brown duck pants, gray blanket lined. Size
32 to 42 waist, 30 to 34 leg measure. Per pair.. 1.65
C665 Brown duck pants, gray blanked lined, 32 to
42 waist, 30 to 34 leg measure. Per pair..... 1.80
C666 Brown duck vests, gray blanket lined. Each .90
C667 Brown duck vests, gray blanket lined. Each 1.15
C667 Men's gray duck suit, 10 oz. goods, gray
blanket lined; full suit....................... 4.75
C668 Men's duck suits, 10 oz. goods, red blanket
lined... 6.30
C669 Men's duck suits, 10 oz. goods, better lining,
red blanket lined............................. 7.00
C670 Men's brown duck suits, 10 oz. goods, lined
with heavy plaid Mackinaw flannel............. 8.10

PIANOS AND ORGANS.

MONEY SAVING prices on **Pianos and Organs** is what we are able to offer you. **Want of space** prevents our showing the complete line. **If you don't find what you want, write us,** and we will furnish prices on the work you want. **We illustrate** the most desirable instruments only, and such as we are able to offer at extremely low prices.

WE DON'T HANDLE CHEAPER GRADES. They will not give satisfaction. We could sell you an **organ for $20.00,** and a **piano for $75.00,** but it would be a loosing purchase for you and a discredit to us. If you want an instrument, **buy a good one,** and you will always be satisfied.

· · OUR TERMS · ·

WE GIVE 10 DAYS TRIAL FREE on the following conditions: Deposit the price of the instrument with any bank and send the banker's receipt to us, which should always read as follows:

We have this day received from..........................$..........for one Organ or Piano, this amount to be held by us until instrument has been received and tried for ten days, the amount then to be forwarded to SEARS, ROEBUCK & CO., Chicago, unless the instrument is found unsatisfactory and the same returned to SEARS, ROEBUCK & CO., Chicago, within the ten days, when the money shall be returned to .... Banker should sign here.

OR YOU CAN have any banker or reliable business house of good financial standing endorse your order, guaranteeing the instrument will be paid for or returned in good order within 10 days, and we will ship on **10 days trial.**

WE WILL SHIP C. O. D. subject to examination, by freight, on receipt of $5.00 as a guarantee of good faith, the balance to be paid after you have received the instrument.

THE BEST WAY is to send cash in full with your order, when we will ship direct to you and send **free as a present** a nice **Piano Stool** with every Piano, and a nice **Organ Stool** with every Organ.

YOU TAKE NO RISK as we always refund all your money and pay freight charges both ways, if you are not perfectly satisfied.

OUR PEERLESS CHAPEL.

ENTIRELY NEW CASE, MADE OF SOLID BLACK WALNUT.

DESCRIPTION.

This is a new Chapel Organ of modest and chaste design. Its beauty and simplicity will recommend themselves to those who do not feel disposed to pay for a more elaborate case. This is just what they want. We fit these up with same actions we put into our higher priced cases. It is provided with handles, lamp stands and music folios. It has also our patent pedal frames, is finely finished, polished front and back, all the accessories which make up a beautiful and durable organ are here combined. Solid black walnut case, carved and turned ornamentations, panel ends, paneled front and back, handles, castors and lamp stands, pedals covered with best brussels carpet, with nickel plated pedal frames, patent stop knobs with solid bronze rims, best three ply bellows stock with best dull color rubber cloth on bellows, finest material and workmanship throughout, a plain and durable organ for churches, Sunday schools or lodge rooms.

FIVE OCTAVE ACTION.

Case Illustrated on Opposite Page.

Contains 4 sets of reeds. Two of three Octave, two of two octave each. Eleven (11) stops, as follows: Diapason, Cremona, Echohorn, Dulcet, Melodia, Principal Forte, Celeste, Bass Coupler, Principal, Vox Angelica, Treble Coupler. Grand Organ and Knee Swell, 122 Reeds.

DIMENSIONS.

Height, 52 inches.   Length, 51 inches.   Depth, 24 inches.   Weight, boxed, 300 pounds.

REASONS WHY THE PEERLESS ORGAN IS THE BEST.

1. Our tone is mathematically and theoretically correct; is based on principles and proved.
2. Our cases are the latest and most unique in architectural beauty, and always popular.
3. Cases are heavy and of solid walnut. Never misrepresented.
4. Cases all framed and paneled. No wide boards. No warping or splitting.
5. Large bellows and wind-chest. Full capacity; gauged accurately.
6. Our pedals are boxed up close, leaving no open space that would be unpleasant to the sight.
7. **Our Action** is trim and practical and cannot get out of order. Wires are copper bronze, and the simplest mechanism used with direct results, giving largest variety of tone effects from stop combinations.
8. **Our Foundation-Boards** are of three-ply stock; cannot warp nor split, consequently, bellows never leak.
9. **Our Keys** never fail, pitmans and valves being so arranged that they cannot possibly be displaced.
10. Our keys do not stick; the pitman rods are thoroughly relieved and holes to receive them large enough to allow of swelling and shrinking.
11. **Action** bushed with fine felt at every bearing, to prevent jarring or rattling.
12. **Key Board Frame** is screwed down solidly **on each end**, and iron brace in back-center and **front.**

Handsome in Design. Moderate in Price.

Solid in Construction. Warranted 5 Years.

13. Our organs have the Wilcox octave cuppler, the best in use; is simple in mechanism, never gets out of order, and for endurance is without an equal.
14. We use the dull rubber cloth; lasts longer and is in keeping with good work and material.
15. Our closing music pocket protects and keeps sheet music free from dust.
16. Many of our cases have elegant French plate mirrors, the most costly and perfect, with the indestructable patent back.
17. The stop-knob is the latest made; is of high grade celuloid face, with bronze rim; will never become in the least affected by time, wind or weather. Old defects cease. Cannot crack. Letters or faces never wear off.
18. The swinging fall-board never sticks at side; always runs perfect and smooth.
19. Highest grades of felt are used.
20. Highest grades of specially tanned leather are used.
21. Highest grades of all stock material are used.
22. Our pedals are absolutely non-squeaking.
23. We use but one grade of actions—that the best.

Factory Price . . . $100.00
OUR PRICE 44.60

OUR CELEBRATED PEERLESS ORGANS.

THE FINEST MONEY AND SKILL CAN PRODUCE. WE USE ONLY THE SILVER TONGUED.

We only show two styles of cases—one for the Parlors and one for Halls, Churches, etc. The Parlor style is our choice of all the various designs produced. It is of a high order of architecture and something entirely new in design and still moderate in price. We furnish it in either **Solid Black Walnut or Antique Oak Case.**

The Tuning and Voicing of our Organs is not Surpassed by Any.

The Material used in Constructing our Organs is the finest. Our Peerless Organ Pleases Everyone.

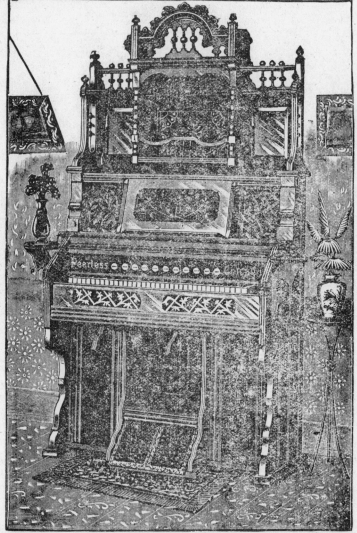

Height, 81 inches.   Length, 48 inches.   Depth, 23 inches.   Weight, boxed, 375 pounds.

DESCRIPTION.

The free-hand carving and turning is costly, but modern taste demands the latest and best, and we consider this one of our handsomest cases. It has large bevel plate mirror in each outside panel, adding to the beauty of the case. The Safety Lamp Stand, Scroll Fretwork, Music Rest and Pocket with fretted Bric-a-Brac shelves and corners, all call for their value and price.

This case is made of Black Walnut or Oak, finished in oil, hand rubbed, with Handles, Castors, Lamp Stands, Nickel Plated Pedal Frames, best brussels carpet on pedals, best rubber cloth used on all bellows and three ply stock used on bellows frame. Best material of all kinds used in constructing our Organs.

CONTAINS 5 Octave Action of 4 sets of reeds. Two of three octave, two of two octave each. Eleven (11) stops as follows: Diapason, Dulcet, Principal, Ecremona, Vox Angelica, Base Coupler, Melodia, Echohorn, Celeste, Treble Coupler. Grand Organ and Knee Swell, 122 Reeds.

Factory Price $110.00
OUR PRICE 47.90

OUR PEERLESS PIANOS.

THE FINEST ON EARTH FOR THE MONEY ASKED.
HANDSOME NEW DESIGN OF CASES.

So great has been the demand for our goods, that it has been necessary to secure double our floor space, and we have now a capacity of about twenty pianos per week.

The action of our pianos is the finest attainable, and is carefully and thoroughly gone over in detail and improved in many ways. Great care is exercised in bringing out the splendid results as shown in our matchless pianos. Extreme care is used in the development of the touch, and the delicate and quick response is but one of our many points of superiority. Our workmen are experienced and skillful and the best the country affords.

STYLE S.   UPRIGHT.

Height, 4 feet 6 inches.   Width, 4 feet 11½ inches.   Depth, 2 feet 1½ inches.
Weight, boxed, about 800 pounds.   All our cases are double veneered.

In the powerful, grand and mellow tone, sustained throughout the entire register, lies the secret of success. Its depth and quality is a source of wonder and satisfaction to the musician, and the many testimonials which we have received are extremely gratifying, and we are justly proud of the success attained.

Our scales are original and the marvelous tone which is the result, proves our claim.

Our cases are all double veneered both sides and highly finished, and our styles modern, unique and highly satisfactory to the trade and public.

Unequalled in volumn of tone and quality. 7¼ octaves, strong iron plate, original and perfect scale, Overstrung bass, three unisons, international pitch, repeating action, nickel plated continuous hinge, closed engraved panels, carved trusses, high art finish.

FACTORY PRICE $325 00
OUR PRICE 155 00

OUR PEERLESS PIANOS.

THE FINEST ON EARTH FOR THE MONEY ASKED.
HANDSOME NEW DESIGN OF CASES.

The aim of our company is to produce a piano which shall have no equal, and a reputation which shall be lasting, and to lay a sure foundation which becomes necessary for all true and lasting success. We shall endeavor at all times to carry a large and full stock of pianos and to fill all orders promptly. Our aim is to please, and our methods, enterprise and energy warrant a fair share of patronage.

STYLE R. UPRIGHT GRAND.

Height, 4 feet 9½ inches.   Width, 5 feet 3½ inches.   Depth, 2 feet 4½ inches.
Weight, boxed, 850 pounds.   All our cases are double veneered.

Unequalled in volume of tone and quality. 7⅓ octaves, full iron plate, original and perfect scale, overstrung bass, Three unisons, international pitch, repeating action, **Three Pedals, Sostenuto Pedal,** ivory keys, nickel plated continuous hinge, closed engraved panels, carved trusses, high art finish. All our pianos contain the Exposed Pin Block and Wood End Bridge.

FACTORY PRICE	**$400 00**
OUR PRICE	**174 00**

MUSICAL GOODS DEPARTMENT.

WE FEEL CONFIDENT we offer the most complete line of Musical Goods at prices far below all competitors, and **our terms we know are far more liberal** than any other concern in the business. **You can save from 25% to 100%** by placing your order with us, besides know you are getting goods of the highest grade, as we buy nothing but the better grades from manufacturers of established reputation.

OUR TERMS.
All Musical Goods will be sent to any one, anywhere, C. O. D. subject to examination, on receipt of One Dollar as a guarantee of good faith. You can examine them at the express office and if found perfectly satisfactory pay the express agent our price and express charges; but if not found satisfactory and in every way exactly as represented, **refuse the goods,** and the agent will return them at our expense and we will refund your one dollar. **THE BEST WAY** is to send cash in full with your order, as you save return express charges on money and, **What's Better, we send you a nice present.** Every order for Musical Instruments amounting to $2.00 or more, if accompanied by cash in full, will be promptly filled, and in addition to the goods ordered, a **nice, useful and valuable present** will be sent you.

··· ACCORDIONS. ···

We buy all our Accordions direct from European manufacturers, select the styles with a view to durability, quality of material, tone and workmanship, and our instruments will invariably be found far better than those sold by others at greatly advanced prices.

No. 11006.

No. 11006. Our price **$1.95.** Retails at $5. Description; Ebonized cases, size 10x5¼ x5¾ inches, two sets reeds, two stops, ten nickel keys, double bellows, open action. Weight boxed, seven pounds.

WE LEAD ALL OTHERS
for fine goods at low prices, and ship to any one **C. O. D. Subject to Examination.**

No. 11007.

No. 11007. Our price, **$3.35.** Retails at $6.00. Description: Highly polished ebonized case, hand painted decorations, double bellows, open action, sunken keybo'rd, two sets reeds, two stops, ten patent nickel keys, nickel trimmings. Weight boxed, seven lbs. This accordion is made by one of the most noted Berlin makers, and is without doubt the best instrument in the world for the money. Sent C. O. D. to any one.

No. 11008.

No. 11008. Our price, **$3.95.** Retails at $7.00. **Imperial Patent 12-Keyed Accordion.**

Description: Polished black case, double leather bound bellows, patent nickel clasp, two sets broad reeds, two stops, two basses, 12 nickel keys, cases 10½x 5¼ inches. The extra keys are so arranged as to obviate the necessity of two rows of keys, and being adapted for the execution of the most difficult music, are suitable for professional players; besides are easily mastered by beginners. Weight boxed, 8 pounds. C. O. D. to any one on receipt of $1.00.

11009.
Our price **$4.45.** Retails at $9.00.
IMPERIAL PICCOLO ACCORDION. Description: Very fancy finished case; size, height 9 inches, width 6¾ and depth 4½ inches; 10 nickel keys, 2 bases, open action, double bellows, 2 sets broad reeds, one stop, leather bound bellows frame, nickel trimmings. In neat case with handle and hooks manufactured expressly for us.

C. O. D. to anyone on receipt of $1.00 balance, $3.45, to be paid after you have seen and examined it.

No. 11010.
Our price **$4 90.** Retails at $10 00.

Imperial Accordian, with vox humana or tremola attachment.

Description: Handsome mahogany case, highly polished; size 10½x5½ in., 2 sets extra broad, steel bronze reeds 10 patent nickel keys, 2 stops, open action, double bellows, nickel trimmings. Weight, boxed, 10 pounds.

C. O. D. to anyone on receipt of $1.00.

MUSICAL GOODS DEPARTMENT.

No. 11011. Our price, **$4.95.** Retails at $10.00. Description: Ebonized case, beaded mouldings, bellows, has nine folds, each fold bound with nickel, 10 patent keys, 2 sets reeds, 2 stops, tremolo attachment. Miniature size; wt., boxed, 10 pounds. Sent C. O. D. to any one on receipt of $1.00.

No. 11011.

No. 11003. Our price, **$5.95.** Retails at $10.00. Description: Ebonized case, nickel trimmings, 19 nickel valves, ivory key buttons, 4 sets reeds, 4 basses, double bellows; weight, boxed, 12 pounds, length, 9 inches; width, 5½ inches; depth, 6 inches. C. O. D. to any one on receipt of $1.00; balance to be paid at express office.

No. 11003.

No. 11005. Our price, **$5.35.** Retails at $10.00. **Professional Accordion.** Description: Mahogany case, size, 10¾x5½x7½ in., 3 sets reeds, 10 long nickel keys, 6 stops, 2 basses, 3 double bellows, nickel corners, 2 rows mirror trumpets, excellent tone; weight, boxed, 10 pounds. C. O. D. to any one on receipt of $1.00, balance, $4.35, to be paid at express office.

No. 11005.

No. 11004. Our price, **$5.75.** Retails at $10.00. **Cornettina Accordion.**

Latest thing out and very popular. It consists of an ordinary accordion, full size and well made. Description: Very fancy case, has 2 sets reeds, 2 stops, 10 keys, 2 basses, double bellows, directly under the regular row of keys are 5 extra keys, the reeds of which are tuned in imitation of the cornet, bugle, and military signals. The bugle call, etc., can be perfectly executed. This instrument also has 3 other attachments by which you can imitate either coo-coo, nightingale, or cock crowing. The Cornettina with the different combinations is capable of producing the most pleasing musical effects. Set C. O. D. to any one.

No. 11004.

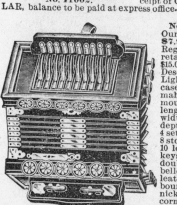

No. 11002. Our price, **$7.85.** Retails at $15.00. Description: Ebonized case, with nickel mouldings, size 11¾x6½x6½ inches, weight, boxed, 18 pounds; has 21 long nickel keys, 4 sets reeds, 2 stops, 4 basses, double leather bound bellows. We guarantee our prices far below all others and to convince you we are willing to send any accordion to any one C. O. D., subject to examination, on receipt of ONE DOLLAR, balance to be paid at express office.

No. 11002.

No. 11001. Our price, **$7.95.** Regular retail price, $15.00. Description: Light wood case with mahogany mouldings; length 14 in., width, 7½ in., depth, 9 in.; 4 sets reeds, 8 stops, 10 long nickel keys, 2 basses, double bellows, leather bound, with nickel corners, 2 rows of fancy trumpets; weight, boxed, 20 pounds. C. O. D. to any one on receipt of $1.00.

No. 11001.

No. 11012.

No. 11012. Our price, **$5.90.** Retails at $12. **Professional Imperial Accordion.**

Description: Ebonized case; size, 12½x6¾ in., fine hand painted mouldings, gilt ornaments, 5 double bellows, 2 sets broad steel bronz' reeds, 2 stops, 10 nickel keys, nickel trimmings; weight, boxed, 10 pounds. C. O. D. to any one on receipt of $1.00.

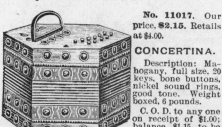

No. 11017.

No. 11017. Our price, **$2.15.** Retails at $4.00.

CONCERTINA.

Description: Mahogany, full size, 20 keys, bone buttons, nickel sound rings, good tone. Weight boxed, 6 pounds.

C. O. D. to any one on receipt of $1.00; balance, $1.15, to be paid at express office.

READ OUR GRAND OFFER FOR CASH IN ADVANCE.

MUSICAL GOODS DEPARTMENT.

No. 11021.

No. 11021. Our price, **$8.25.** Retails at $15. Description: "Imperial," ebonized mouldings and panels, open key board, nickel keys, corners and clasps, double bellows, 10 keys, 3 stops, 3 sets reeds, very fancy leatherette bellows, nickel bordered panels, "very fancy. Weight, boxed, 15 pounds. C. O. D. to anyone on receipt of $1 00, balance $7.25, to be paid at express office.

No. 11014.

No. 11014. Our price, **$11.75.** Retails at $20. **Very Fancy Accordion.** Description: Ebonized mouldings and panels. Size 12x7x6 inches, leatherette covered bellows, open action, 21 nickel keys, 2 stops, double bellows, 4 sets reeds, 6 basses. Weight, boxed, 15 pounds.

Nothing we could say would do this instrument justice, you can only form an idea by seeing it and you can see it. We will send it C. O. D., subject to examination, on receipt of one dollar, balance to be paid after examination if found satisfactory.

NO. 11000.

No. 11000. Our price, **$8.95.** Regular retail price, $15.00. Description: Mahogany case, size 12 in. long by 6x6½ in., ebonized keys, gilt and nickel ornaments, 10 keys, double bellows, 2 sets of reeds, 2 basses, 3 stops. This new araphone accordion combines the real tones of an accordion, with the tones or chime of bells, the bell attachment is fastened directly over the keys and they may be played together or by drawing the proper stop either the accordion or bells may be used separately. Sent C. O. D. to anyone on receipt of one dollar; balance, $7.95, to be paid at express office.

No. 11020. Our price, **$3.95.** Retails at $7.00.

CONCERTINA.

Description: Mahogany case, beautifully finished and ornamented, 20 keys, broad reeds. Weight boxed, 7 pounds.

C. O. D. to any one on receipt of $1.00.

No. 11020.

No. 11019. Our price, **$5.90.** Retails at $10.00.

CONCERTINA.

Description: Mahogany case, German silver inlayings, leather bound bellows, 20 keys, broad reeds, heavy tone, finely finished. Wt. boxed, 8 pounds.

C. O. D. on receipt of $1.00.

No. 11019.

No. 11013.

No. 11013. Our price **$9.25.** Retails at $18. Description: Ebonized case, size 12½x7 inches. 19 long nickel keys, 4 sets broad reeds, 2 stops, open action, double bellows, leather straps, nickel trimmings. Weight, boxed, 12 pounds. Everything about it is the best. We imported them direct from one of the most noted European makers and for the first time we offer them at a price fully one-half cheaper than they were ever before sold. C O D to anyone to examine. One of the finest instruments made.

No. 11018.

No. 11018. Our price, **$9.90.** Retails at $20.00.

ENGLISH CONCERTINA.

Description: Anglo-German pattern, made of mahogany, 20 keys, leather bound bellows, 5 folds in wood case. Weight boxed 6 pounds.

This is one of the finest instruments made and our price is about one-half the regular retail price.

READ OUR GRAND OFFER FOR CASH IN ADVANCE.

MUSICAL GOODS DEPARTMENT.

THE LATEST NOVELTIES.

No. 11015.
Our price, 85c. Retails at $2.00.
Flute Accordion. 10 keys, 2 basses, metal mouth pieces. Weight, 21 ounces.

No. 11016.
Our price, $1.15.   Retails at $2.50.
New Flute Accordion Or Clariophon. Length 15 inches, diameter 2 inches. Made of fine imitation mahogany wood, 10 keys, 2 basses, well made. Weight, 20 ounces.

HARMONICAS.
OUR "WINDSOR."

No. 11030.
Our improved Windsor Harmonicas are made expressly for us by one of the first makers of Europe, under our own name and brand, and after giving them a thorough trial, we feel justified in pronouncing them the BEST Richters ever put on the market. They have ten single holes, 20 German silver reeds, extra heavy nickel plated reed plates, extension ends, nickel covers. Especial attention has been given to tuning, and we guarantee every one to be absolutely perfect.   Each is stamped with firm name.   Price each, **20c.** Per dozen, **$2.15.** Weight, each, 3 oz.

No. 11031.

The "GOLDEN LARK" RICHTER Harmonicas, ten single holes, 20 reeds, nickel plated reed plates gild gilt, covers, satin finished, perfectly tuned. Each in satin lined plush case. Weight, 4 ounces.   Price each, **40c.** Per dozen, **$4.30.**

No. 11032.
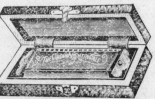

The "GOLDEN LARK" CONCERT Harmonicas, ten double holes, 40 reeds, nickel plated reed plates, extension ends gold gilt covers, satin finish, tuned in octaves and absolutely perfect. Each in satin lined plush case.   Price each, **75c.** Per dozen, **$8.10.** Weight, five ounces.

No. 11021.
Harmonicas with celluloid covers. Have proven very acceptable to our trade, and we have added the very latest production (see cut). They are the Richter pattern with nickel plated reed plates, 10 single holes, 20 reeds. The mouth piece and backs are covered with heavy white celluloid and sides with fancy colored celluloid, giving them a handsome appearance. The covers can also be removed by sliding, thus giving access to the reeds. Can furnish the following colors: White, green, amber, transparent and imitation tortoise shell. The quality of the instrument is first-class. Price each, **35c.** Per dozen, **$7.35.** Weight, each, 3 oz.

No. 11022.
Consists of a set of four harmonicas, No. 11021, one each, green, amber, transparent and imitation tortoise shell. Assorted keys in neat cloth bound case.   Price, per set, **$1.50.** Weight, per set, 10 oz.

No. 11023.
Richter Harmonicas, fine quality, 10 single holes, 20 reeds, brass reed plates, celluloid covers, correctly tuned.   Each, **35c.** Per dozen, **$3.75.**
No. 11024. Concert Harmonica, 10 double holes, 40 reeds, brass reed plates, celluloid covers, absolutely perfect in tone.   Each, **55c.** Per doz., **$6.00.**
The seamless celluloid shell into which the harmonica, slides, acts as a resonator as well as cover for the instrument, and avoids putting the lips in contact with the brass plates.

HOHNERS.

No. 11025.
Hohner, 10 single holes on one edge. Brass reed plates, nickel covers.   Each, **20c.** Weight, 3 oz.

No. 11026.
Ten double holes on one edge, double reeds, nickel plated covers.   Each, **45c.** Weight, 5 oz.

READ OUR GRAND OFFER FOR CASH IN ADVANCE.

MUSICAL GOODS DEPARTMENT.

No. 11027.

Ten double holes on each edge, double reeds, nickel covers. Each, 90c. Weight, 7 oz.

CARL ESSBACH'S

No. 11028.

Carl Essbach's Richter Harmonica, good quality, 10 single holes, 20 reeds, brass reed plates, nickel cover. Each, 10c. Per dozen, $1.00. Weight, 3 oz.

No. 11029.

Carl Essbach's New French Harp extra fine quality, pure tone, perfectly tuned; ten single holes, 20 German silver reeds, brass reed plates nickeled, nickel covers, extension ends. Each, 15c. Per dozen, $1.60. Weight, 3 ounces.

No. 11033.

Essbach's Miniature concert harmonica. 10 double holes, 40 reeds, brass reed plate, nickel covers. This harmonica "fills a long felt want," it being a full "concert," but of small size, therefore the tones are easily produced, besides, it can be covered with the hands, same as the Richters. Each, 35c. Per doz. $3.75. Weight, 4 oz.

KOCH.

We now carry in stock the celebrated Andreas Koch Harmonicas, and can recommend them for either professionals or amateurs. They are perfectly tuned and easy to blow.

No. 11034.

Koch Richter 10 single holes, 20 reeds, brass plates, extension ends, nickel covers all keys. Each, 15c. Per doz., $1.60. Weight, 3 ounces.

No. 11035.

Koch Double Richter. 10 single holes on each edge, 40 reeds, brass plates. nickel covers, extension ends. assorted keys. Price each, 29c. Per doz., $3.00. Weight, 6 ounces.

No. 11036.

Koch Professional Richter, Organ tone. 16 double holes. 32 reeds tuned in octaves, brass plates, nickel covers, excellent tone; every player should have one. Price each, 35c. Per doz., $3.75. Weight, 5 ounces.

No. 11037.

Koch Concert Harmonicas, ten double holes, 40 reeds, brass plates, nickel covers, extension ends, every one a gem. Price each, 40c. Per doz., $4.35. Weight, 6 ounces.

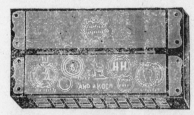

No. 11038.

Koch Double Concert Harmonica, ten double holes on each edge, 80 reeds, brass plates, nickel covers. Price each, 80c.

LUDWIG'S.

No. 11039.

The Genuine Gebr. Ludwig Harmonica, Richter pattern, 10 single holes, brass, reed plates, nickeled single holes, nickel covers, extension ends, assorted keys. Weight, 3 ounces. Each, 12c. Per doz., $1.30.

No. 11040.

Ludwig's Royal Steel Reed Harmonica, 10 single holes, brass reed, plates, German silver covers, excellent tone, assorted keys. Each, 30c. Per doz., $3.20. Weight, 3 ounces.

MISCELLANEOUS MAKES

No. 11041.

Price each, 5c. Per dozen 50c.

No. 11041.

Common Richter Harmonica.

10 single holes, double reeds, brass reed plates, nickel covers, extension ends, weight (2 ounces)

READ OUR GRAND OFFER FOR CASH IN ADVANCE.

Musical Goods Department.

No. 11043.

No. 11043. Price each, 95c.
EMPEROR DOUBLE.
10 double holes on each side, German silver reeds, brass plates, nickeled covers, each in two keys. Weight 8 ounces. You know our terms; all goods sent C. O. D. subject to examination.

No. 11043½. Price per set, 75c.

Set of 4 Thie Harmonicas in Pocket Case.

Each has 10 single holes on one edge, brass reed plates, German silver covers. Each in different key. Weight 12 ounces.

No. 11043½.

No. 11045.
No. 11044. Price each, 35c.
BELL HARMONICA.
Richter German silver, 10 holes, 1 bell. Weight 4 ounces.
No. 11045. Price, 58c.
Bell Harmonica, Richter German silver, 10 holes, 2 bells. Weight 5 ounces.
No. 11046. Price each, 65c.
Bell Harmonica, Concert German silver, 10 holes, double, 1 bell. Weight 6 ounces.
No. 11046½. Price each, 85c.
Bell Harmonica, Concert German silver, 10 holes, double, 2 bells. Weight 7 ounces.

Harmonica Pocket Cases.

No. 11047. Price each, 10c.
Pocket case for Richter harmonicas made of kid, nickel plated frame at top with clasp.

No. 11048. Pocket case for Concert Harmonica, same style as No. 11047. Price, 15c.

No. 11047.

No. 11042. Price each. 90c.
EMPEROR SET.
Contains two harmonicas—one an Emperor tuned in octaves, the other a Conqueror, tuned for duet. Both 10 holes and double reeds. They can be used for duet playing to good effect. Weight 9 ounces.

No. 11042.

Harmonica Holders.
No. 11049. Price each, 50c.
Excelsior harmonica holders, (see cut) are constructed on an entirely new principle and are giving excellent satisfaction. They consist of a wood breast plate to which is attached heavy spring wire shoulder pieces. Harmonicas of any size are held firmly in proper position for playing by two springs, thus leaving the hands free to play accom-

No. 11049.

paniment on any other instrument. They are quickly and easily adjusted. Weight 8 ounces.
No. 11050. Price each, 10c.; per dozen, $1.00.
Harmonica Holder, consists of heavy metal tube painted and varnished with opening at top for either Richter or Concert harmonica. Also opening at one end and is used to regulate the tone and produce tremolo vibrations. Weight 6 ounces.

FLUTES.

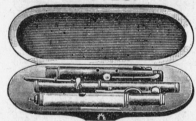

No. 11061.
Instruction Book free with each flute. No music dealer will warrant flutes, clarionets, piccolos or fifes, not to check or crack. This often happens by change of temperature. Great care should be exercised in the use of such instruments, not to suddenly expose to heat when they have been in cold air. They are always examined and leave in perfect shape. We will not be responsible for them after they arrive at destination.
No. 11056. Price each, $1.75.
Description. D, one key with tuning slide. German silver trimmed, in paper case. Weight 12 ounces.
No. 11057. Price each, $2.95.
Description. D, 4 keyed, Grenadillo. German silver rings and slide. in paper case. Weight 13 ounces.
No. 11058. Price each $3.95.
Description. D, 6 keyed, Grenadillo, German silver rings and slide, cork joints, paper case. Weight 14 ounces.
No. 11059. Price each, $6.95.
Description. D, 8 keyed, Grenadillo, German silver rings and slide, cork joints, in leather case. Weight 26 ounces.
No. 11060. Price each, $9.95.
Description. D, made of Grenadillo, with 10 German silver keys and trimmings, slide, cork joints, each in fine morrocco case. Weight 26 ounces.
No. 11061. Price each, $17.45.
Description. D, 10 keyed Grenadillo, ivory head with slide, in fine case like illustration. Weight 26 ounces.

READ OUR GRAND OFFER FOR CASH IN ADVANCE.

MUSICAL GOODS DEPARTMENT.

VIOLIN CASES.

No. 11051. Price each, $1.
Description. Wood American, black varnished, half lined with flannel, handle and hooks, without locks.

No. 11053.

No. 11052. Price each, $1.40.
Wood, American, black varnished, half lined with flannel, handle and hooks with lock.

No. 11053. Price each, $2.00
Wood, black with lock and clasps, lined throughout with felt or flannel.

No. 11054. Price each, $2 95.
Papiermache, French violin shape, lined with baize, lock, handle and clasps.

No. 11055. Price each, $4.45.
Genuine Leather, black, finely finished, lined throughout with velvet, leather handles, nickel clasps.

PICCOLOS.

No. 11064.

Each in a paper case, weight 6 ounces, (instruction book 45c.)

No. 11062. Price each, 60c.
E flat or D, 1 key, cocoa, German silver tipped.

No. 11063. Price each, 95c.
E flat or D, 1 key, cocoa, German silver tipped, tuning slide.

No. 11064. Price each, $1.95.
E flat or D, 4 keys, German silver tipped, and tuning slide.

No. 11065. Price each, $2.45.
E flat or D, 6 keys, cocoa, German silver tipped, and tuning slide.

No. 11066.

No. 11063. Price each, $4.90.
E flat or D, 6 keys, Grenadillo, ivory head, tuning slide, cork joints, German silver tipped.

FLAGEOLETS.

No. 11070.

Each in pasteboard box.

No. 11067. Price each, $1.65.
Flageolet, key of D, made of Grenadillo wood, German silver trimmed, 1 key.

No. 11068. Price each, $1.05.
Flageolet, key of B flat, Grenadillo wood, German silver trimmed, 1 key.

No. 11069. Price each, $2.45.
Flageolet, key of D, Grenadillo wood, 4 keys, German silver trimmings.

No. 11070. Price each, $2.65.
Flageolet, key of D, Grenadillo wood, German silver trimmings, 6 keys.

No. 11071.

No. 11071. Price each, 25c.
Nightingale Flageolets, (see cut) made of brass, nickel plated, finely finished, correctly tuned, made in following keys, Bb, C, D, Eb, F and G. Weight 6 ounces.

PICCOLO FLAGEOLETS.

This combination consists of a piccolo, with an extra flageolet head and can be used as either instrument.

No. 11072. Price each, $2.00.
Description. Piccolo Flageolets, key of D, made of boxwood, German silver trimmed, 1 key.

No. 11073. Price each, $2.95.
Piccolo Flageolet, key of D, made of Grenadillo wood, German silver trimmed, 6 keys.

FLUTE AND PICCOLO CASES.

No. 11074. Price each, $1.95.
Flute Case, morocco covered, velvet lined, for 4 or 6 keyed flute.

No. 11074.

No. 11075. Price each, $2.45.
Flute Case, morocco covered, velvet lined, for 8 to 10 keyed flute.

No. 11076. Price each, $1 35.
Piccolo Case, morocco covered, velvet lined, for Eb, or D piccolo.

FIFES.

No. 11077.
(Instruction book 12c.)
Fifes are made in the key of Bb and C only.

No. 11077. Price each, 20c.
Description. Fifes made of maple, brass tipped.

No. 11078. Price each, 40c.
Fifes made of cocoa, German silver tipped.

No. 11079. Price each, 55c.
Fifes made of ebony, German silver ferrules.

No. 11080. Price each, 80c.
Fifes, (Crosby) made of ebony or cocoa, long model. U. S. regulation pattern, long German silver ferrules.

No. 11081.

No. 11081. Price each, $1.20.
Fifes made of German silver, raised holes.

CLARIONETS.

Clarionets are made in the following keys only; A, Bb, C, D, and Eb. We give an instruction book free with instrument. Always mention what key is desired.

No. 11082. Price each, $12.75.
Description. Clarionet, made of Grenadillo wood, black, with 13 German silver keys, German silver trimmings, any key. Weight 20 ounces.

No. 11083. Price each, $17.35.
Description. Clarionet, Grenadillo wood, black, Albert system, with 13 German silver keys, 2 patent rings, German silver trimmings, in any key. Weight 22 ounces.

No. 11084. Price each, $19.65.
Description. Clarionet, Grenadillo, black, Albert system, with 15 German silver keys, (extra Bb and C sharp) 2 rings, German silver trimmings, any key. Weight 23 ounces.

No. 11085. Price each, $34.50.
Description. Clarionet, Albert system, made by Buffet, Crampon & Co., Paris, Grenadillo wood, 15 German silver keys, 2 rings, with trill keys, each has 2 mouth pieces.

No.   No.   No.
11082   11083   11084.

CLARIONET REEDS.

(Weight each 1 ounce.)
Give key of Clarionet for which reed is wanted.

No. 11086. Price each 5c. Per dozen, 50c.
Martin brand, good quality, any key.

No. 11087. Price each, 10c. Per dozen, $1.00.
Lefin brand, superfine quality, any key.

No. 11088. Price each, 15c. Per dozen $1.60.
Artists' brand, the best brand in the market made expressly for soloists.

READ OUR GRAND OFFER FOR CASH IN ADVANCE.

MUSICAL GOODS DEPARTMENT.

Clarionet Reed Cases.

No. 11089.

Clarionet Pocket Reed Case, leather covered, holds six reeds. Each, $1.25. Weight, 5 ounces.

Clarionet Cases.

No. 11090.

Leather case, lined, with handle strap. Give key of clarionet. Each, $2. Weight, 9 ounces.

No. 11091.

No. 11091.

Clarionet Case (see cut), leather covered, lined with flannel, handle, hooks and lock; for set of three clarionets. Each,

$3.50. Weight, 4 lbs.

Clarionet Music Racks.

Always state key of instrument for which rack is wanted.

$11092.

German silver, with adjustable ring. Each, $1.00. Weight, 4 oz.

No. 11092

Clarionet Mouthpieces.

Weight, 4 ounces. Give key of Clarionet.
No. 11093. Cocoa or Ebony, without reed holder, any key. Each, 45c.
No. 11094. Cocoa or Ebony, with German Silver reed holder, any key. Each, 70c.

Clarionet Mouthpiece Caps.

Weight each, 3 ounces.

No. 11095. Clarionet Mouthpiece Cap or Protector, made of cocoa. Each, 35c.
No. 11096. Clarionet Mouthpiece Cap, nickel plated. Each, 45c. Give key of clarionet.

Music Boxes.

We now import our entire line of music boxes, buying of the leading manufacturers of Switzerland, and a careful inspection of description and prices given below will convince the most skeptical that we are headquarters for this line of goods.

No. 11097.

11097. Round Nickel Case, 2¾ inches in diameter, decorated top and bottom, 18 notes, one air, operated by turning small crank on top. Weight, 10 ounces. Price, each, 50c.

No. 11098.

No. 11098. Square wood case, size 4x3½ inches, decorated top, 18 teeth, operated with crank, plays two airs. Weight, 16 ounces. Price, each, 80c.

No. 11099.

No. 11099.

Highly polished Mahogany Case. Size, 4¾x3½x 2⅜, interior glass cover to protect works, covers decorated with pretty chromos, self-acting cylinder, 2½ inches long with mainspring, winds like a watch, with attached key, has 36 notes, plays 2 airs. Weight 16 ounces. Each, $3.00.

No. 11100.

Imitation Rosewood, highly polished. Size 12 x6½x4½. Swiss carved and decorated, spring lever movement, self-starting. Plays 6 airs. Price each, $9.00.

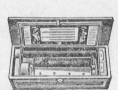

No. 11100.

No. 11100½.

Imitation Rosewood Case, size 18x8½x5½ inches 7½ in. cylinder, cylinder tune indicator, zither attachment. Plays 10 airs. Weight, boxed, 25 lbs. Each, $16.80.

No. 11100½.

No. 11101. Imitation Rosewood, same style as 11100½, size 20½x9x5¾, with 9¾ in. cylinder tune indicator, zither attachment; plays 12 airs. Weight, boxed, 30 lbs. Each, $27.
No. 11102. Imitation Rosewood, same style as 11101, 23½x9½x9, 13 inch cylinder, plays 10 airs, has zither attachment, speed regulator, tune indicator; a very fine instrument. Each, $31.50.

Mandolins.

Weight, boxed, 8 pounds.

This instrument is becoming very popular, our sales having more than doubled during the last year. We would state for the benefit of those desirous of learning to play the mandolin, that they are "tuned" same as the violin, and fingering is the same, so that one who can play a violin may easily learn to manage the mandolin. Instruction book free with each instrument.

No. 11103. Mandolin, American, full size, maple and sycamore ribs. Highly polished plain front, rosewood finger board, brass patent head, correct scale, finely finished, warranted for one year not to split or warp. The best mandolin ever put on the market for the money. Price, each, $6.50.
No. 11104. Our Conservatory Mandolin, full size, American made, rosewood and maple ribs, rosewood band, all French polished orange front, ebony finger

READ OUR GRAND OFFER FOR CASH IN ADVANCE.

MUSICAL GOODS DEPARTMENT.

Mandolins—Continued.

board, position dots, inlaid striking piece, rosewood tipped, fully warranted. German silver patent head. Price, **$9.50.**

No. 11105. Our professional Concert Mandolin, American manufacture, rosewood and mahogany ribs, white inlaid edges, rosewood bound lined soundhole, ebony finger board, position dots, full French polished, Italian patent head, warranted not to split or warp. Price, each, **$13.00.**

No. 11106. The Joseph Bohman American Mandolin, full concert size, 19 maple ribs, highly polished, rosewood finger board, pearl position dots, patent tail piece, inlaying around soundhole, patent head, scale guaranteed absolutely perfect. Warranted one year. Each, **$15.00.**

Mandolin Cases.

No. 11106½.

Mandolin Case, made of brown canvass, leather bound, flannel lined strap fastenings. Each, **$1.50.**

No. 11107. Mandolin case, leather covered, russet or black color, hand sewed, flannel lined, fine quality. Each, **$5.50.**

No. 11107½. Mandolin case, wood, black, lined with flannel, lock, handle and spring clasps. Each, **$2.25.**

No. 11108. Mandolin Bags, made of green cloth. Each, **75c.**

No. 11109. Mandolin Bags, canvass, fleeced lined, patent fasteners. Each, **90c.**

No. 11110. Mandolin Bags, made of silk plush, extra fine quality. Each, **$4.50.**

Violoncellos.

Instruction book and bow free with each Violoncello. Each one in case ready for shipping. Weight, boxed, 43 pounds.

No. 11111. Violoncello, German make, common peg head. Each, **$7.75.**

No. 11112. Violoncello, of better quality, reddish brown color, peg head. Each, **$9.00.**

No. 11113. Violoncello, light red color, patent head, polished, good tone. Each, **$11.50.**

No. 11114. Stradivarius model, dark brown color, inlaid edges, patent head, fine quality, excellent tone. Each, **$18.00.**

Violoncello Patent Heads.

Weight, per set, 11 ounces.
No. 11115. Iron plates and screws, maple pegs with pearl dot inlaid in head. Each, **$1.75.**

No. 11116. Brass plates, iron screws, maple pegs with pearl dot inlaid in head. Each, **$2.00.**

Double Bass Viols - Patent Heads.

Instruction book and bow free with each. Weight, boxed, about 125 pounds.

No. 11117. Double Bass, half size, dark red, shaded and polished, 3 strings, good quality. Each, **$19.50.**

No. 11118. Double Bass, same size and style as No. 11117, with 4 strings. Each, **$21.00.**

No. 11119. Double Bass, three-quarter size, 3 strings, dark red shaded and polished, good quality. Each, **$22.00.**

No. 11120. Double Bass, same size and style as No. 11119, with 4 strings. Each, **$24.00.**

No. 11121. Double Bass, half size, 3 strings, dark red, polished, inlaid edges, fine quality. Each, **$30.**

No. 11122. Double Bass, three-quarter size, 4 strings, dark red, polished, inlaid edges, fine quality. Each, **$35.**

No. 11123. Double Bass, three-quarter size, 4 strings, dark red, polished, inlaid edges, swelled back, extra fine quality. Each, **$45.**

Double Bass Bows.

No. 11124. Maple, red painted, light wood frog. Each, **$1.30.** Weight, 10 ounces.

No. 11125. Red wood, natural color, ebony frog, good quality. Each, **$2.50.** Weight, 12 ounces.

No. 11126. Pernambuco wood, natural color, ebony frog, German silver lined, inlaid eye (professional model). Each, **$4.75.** Weight, 12 ounces.

Double Bass Bridges.

No. 11127. Maple, plain scroll, good quality, for half size bass. Weight, 3 ounces. Each, **45c.**

No. 11128. Maple, plain scroll, good quality, for three-quarter size bass. Weight, 4 oz. Each, **55c.**

Guitars.

Instruction book free with each guitar.

We have discontinued quotations on all imported guitars, and hereafter will handle only American made instruments. This is due to the fact that on account of the difference in the climate imported guitars will, with hardly an exception, crack and warp out of shape. On the other hand, the American instruments are made in a more scientific manner, possesses a superior tone, besides we warrant each regardless of price, for ONE YEAR not to split or warp, provided no *steel* strings are used. Our guitars are made in the largest and best factory in this country. Every instrument is thoroughly inspected before being shipped and are all guaranteed to be perfect in scale, tone and construction.

No. 11129. Our leader. American made Guitar, standard size, back and sides made of maple and handsomely finished in imitation of either Rosewood, Mahogany, or Oak, all highly polished, yellow top, imitation ebony finger board, position dots; patent head, raised frets, warranted for one year. Price, **$4.50.**

No. 11130. Our Kenwood. American made, standard size, back and sides made of "quarter-sawed" oak, highly polished, finely finished cedar sounding board, walnut neck, raised frets, patent head, excellent tone and warranted not to split or warp. Weight, boxed, 25 lbs. Price each, **$6.**

No. 11131. Our Columbian. American made guitar, standard size, solid mahogany back and sides, edges inlaid with celluloid, highly polished Rosewood finger board, correctly fretted, cedar neck, patent heads, manufactured expressly for us and warranted not to split or warp. Weight, boxed, 25 lbs. Price, **$9.00.**

No. 11132. Our "Windsor." American made, Conservatory Guitar, solid rosewood back and sides, yellow cedar top, cedar neck, ebony finger board, inlaid stripe in back, standard size, finely polished and fully warranted in every respect. Weight, boxed, 25 lbs. Each, **$12.00.**

11133. Our Windsor Concert Guitar, American made, same as 11132, only they are the large or concert size, each is absolutely perfect in every respect, and warranted not to split or warp. Weight, boxed, 25 lbs. Price each, **$14.00.**

NOTE.—The "Windsor" Guitars are manufactured expressly for us in one of the very best factories in the country, and we can safely say they are *the best* instrument ever offered for the money.

11134 Washburn American Guitar, solid Rosewood body, mahogany or cedar neck, patent head, ebony finger board, warranted not to split or warp, standard size. Weight, boxed, 25 lbs. Each, **$22.00.**

11135 Washburn American Guitar, of solid rosewood body, mahogany or cedar neck, ebony finger board, inlaid, warranted not to warp or split, concert size. Weight, boxed, 25 lbs. Each, **$26.00.**

NOTE.—On our American Guitars gut and silk wound strings are recommended under all circumstances. The efforts of the manufacturers are directed toward the production of a rich mellow tone,

READ OUR GRAND OFFER FOR CASH IN ADVANCE.

MUSICAL GOODS DEPARTMENT.

GUITARS--Continued.

and in order to accomplish this result they use a sensitively constructed sounding board, which is not made to withstand the strain of wire strings. By using great care some of them will stand this heavy strain without serious detriment, but we wish it understood that we will not be responsible for the failure of a guitar where steel strings are used.

Capo D'Astros.

11136 Capo D'stros, brass with cork lined string cap and adjusting screw, like cut. Weight 3 oz. Each, **40c.**
11137 Capo D'Astros, same as above, nickel plated. Weight 3 oz. Each, **50c.**
NOTE.—The Capo D'Astro is used to clamp on guitar finger board at first fret to facilitate playing in flat keys.

11136.

Guitar Tail Pieces.

11138 Guitar tail pieces, made of *Celluloid*. Each, **50c.**
11139 Guitar Tail pieces, made of brass, nickel plated, (see cut). Weight 5 oz. Each, **75c.**

11138. NOTE.—If steel strings are to be used on a guitar it is essential to the tone and durability of the instrument that they should be attached to a tail piece.

GUITAR CASES.

11140 Brown canvas, leather bound, with opening in the end for standard size guitar. Weight 5½ lbs. Each, **$1.75.**
11141, Brown canvas, same as above, for concert size Washburn guitar. Weight 5½ lbs. Each, **$2.**
11142, Wood, half lined, with handle and hooks, for standard size guitar Weight, boxed, 18 lbs. Each, **$1.90.**
11143, Wood, half lined, with lock, handle and hooks, for standard size guitar. Weight, boxed, 18 lbs. Each, **$2.00.**
11144, Wood, full lined, with lock, handle and spring clasp, for concert size Washburn guitar. Weight, boxed. 20 lbs. Each, **$2.85.**

GUITAR BAGS.

11145, Green felt, for either standard or concert size guitars. Weight 9 ounces. Each, **$1.**
11146, Gossamar rubber, for standard or concert size guitars. Weight 12 ounces. Each, **$1.50.**
State size of guitar.

GUITAR AND BANJO FRETS.

11147, Guitar or Banjo frets, brass, per set of 18, **20c.**
No 11147. **11148,** Guitar or Banjo frets, German silver, per set of 18, **30c.** Weight, per set, 3 ounces.
NOTE.—We do not break sets.

BANJOS.

(Weight of banjos boxed, 18 lbs.)
Instruction book free with banjo.
11149, Maple Shell, 10 inch, imitation cherry, sheepskin head, four brass brackets, marked frets. each, **$1.75.**
11150, Nickel shell, 10 inches in diameter, wood lined, imitation cherry neck, marked frets, calfskin head, 7 brass brackets. Each, **$2.75.**
11151, Nickel shell, 11 inches in diameter, wood lined, highly polished birch neck, imitation ebony finger board, raised frets, inlaid position dots, celluloid pegs, 21 nickel brackets, calfskin head. Each, **$4.50.**
11152, Nickel shell, 11 inches in diameter, wood lined grooved hoop, 24 nickel brackets, French polished birch neck, imitation ebony finger board, inlaid position dots, wired edge, celluloid pegs, patent tail piece, calfskin head. Each, **$5.50.**

11153, German silver shell, 11 inches in diameter, wood lined, both edges wired, grooved hoop, 24 nickel brackets, French polished birch neck, ebony veneered finger board, fancy inlaid position dots, handsome scroll, elaborately inlaid with pearl, patent pegs, an extra fine instrument. Each, **$9.00.**
11154, German silvered shell, 11 inches in Diameter, wood lined, both edges wired, corrugated hoop, 28 nickel brackets, French polished neck, full ebony finger board, highly polished, fancy pearl inlaid position dots, excellent tone, fine calfskin head, a perfect banjo every way. Each, **$12 00.**
11155, Professional banjo, Steward model, 12 inches in diameter, nickel plated German silver shell, both edges wired, wood lined finely polished birch neck, extra heavy strainer hoop, ebony finger board, raised frets, 29 nickel brackets, neck ornamented with pearl, calfskin head. Each, **$13.00.**

11156, Our Windsor Professional banjo, 11 inches in diameter, polished German silver shell, 30 nickel brackets, wood lined, both edges wired, grooved corrugated hoop, patent tail piece, raised frets, French polished walnut neck, full ebony finger piece extending over head piece, elaborately inlaid with pearl, back of head piece covered with ebony, German silver name plate, patent pegs, calfskin head; this banjo is a new model made expressly for us, and is one of the most beautiful as well as perfect instruments ever put on the market. Banjos of no better quality are sold daily at double our price. Each, **$17.00.**

BANJO THIMBLES.

11156. **11157,** Banjo thimbles of German silver. Price each, **5c.;** per dozen, **50c.** Weight, each, 1 ounce.

BANJO CASES.

11158, Pasteboard, marbled, weight, boxed, 12 lbs. Each, **45c.**
11159, Wood, black, varnished, flannel lined, with lock, handle and hooks, for 11 inch banjo. Weight, boxed, 17 lbs , **$2.00.**
11160, Brown canvas, leather bound, with opening in end for 9, 11 or 12-inch banjo. Weight 6 lbs. **$1.75.**
11161, Banjo case, made of sol'd leather, flannel lined, hand sewed, fine quality, with opening at end for 11 inch banjo. Weight 7 lbs. Each, **$4.50.**

BANJO BAGS.

11162, Green felt, for 9, 10 or 11 inch banjo. Weight 7 ounces. **90c.**
11163, Gossamer rubber, for 9, 10 or 11 inch banjo. Weight 9 ounces. **$1.35.**

ZITHER, PLAIN HEAD.

(Weight, boxed, 12 lbs.)

11163½, Imitation rosewood, full strung, neatly inlaid, good quality and finish, in paper box, **$5.00.**
11163½, Rosewood, full strung, neatly inlaid, finely finished, in paper box. **$8.00.**
11165, Rosewood, polished, inlaid sound holes and edges with patent head, in pasteboard case. Each, **$11.00.**

ZITHER RINGS.

11166, German silver, plain. Each, **3c.**
11167, Horn, plain. Each, **5c.**

ZITHER STRINGS.

11168, Steel and brass for finger board. Each, **5c.**
11169, Accompaniment and bass wound on steel wire. Each **7c.**
11170, Full set wound on steel wire. Weight per set, 6 ounces. **$1.75.**
NOTE.—When ordering strings for zither be sure and give number and letter of string wanted.

READ OUR GRAND OFFER FOR CASH IN ADVANCE.

MUSICAL GOODS DEPARTMENT.

ZITHER CASES.

(Weight, boxed, 10 lbs.)

11171, Wood, black varnished, flannel lined, with lock, handle and hooks. Each, $2.00.

11172, Wood, black varnished, velvet lined, with lock, handle and spring clasp. $6.50.

ZITHER TUNING PINS.

11173, Steel, blued. Per dozen, 20c.

11174, Nickel plated. Per dozen, 30c.

Weight, per dozen, 4 ounces.

DULCIMERS.

11175.

11175. Dulcimers, American made, imitation Rosewood, neatly decorated, body finely finished, chromatic can be perfectly tuned in all keys; in short, it is the most complete and carefully made instrument of the kind produced. Price each, $16.00.

DULCIMER OR ZITHER WIRE.

11176, English steel, best quality, in ¼ pound coils. Per lb., $1.20.

11177, Brass, best quality, on 1 pound spool. Per lb., $1.00.

11178, English steel on spools, 2 yards each. Per dozen spools, 45c.

11179, Brass on spools, 2 yards, each per doz. spools, 40c.

Weight, per dozen spools, 5 ounces.

DULCIMER TUNING PINS.

11180, Steel, blued, with square or oblong heads. Per dozen, 12c.

Weight, per dozen, 6 ounces.

AMATEUR VIOLIN OUTFIT.

Each one with instructor free.

11180½.

11180½, Violin outfit consisting of violin of good quality bow, box of resin, set of strings, instruction book, all in marbled pasteboard case. Weight, boxed, 10 lbs. Price each, complete, $2.00.

11181, Violin outfit, consisting of full sized violin, good model, bow, box of resin, set of strings, instruction book, in pasteboard case. Price complete, $3.00.

11182, Violin outfit, with better violin, bow and wood case, with handle and hooks, also strings, etc. Weight, boxed, 20 lbs. Price each, $4.50.

11183, Violin outfit with finely polished violin, good model and tone, bow, strings, etc., in wood case, with lock, handle and hooks. Price complete, $5.75.

11184, Violin outfit, with violin of extra fine quality, handsome model, ebony trimmings, well made, polished, smooth tone, each in full lined wood case, with patent spring clasps and lock, bow, extra set strings, etc. Weight, boxed, 20 lbs. Price each, complete, $10.00.

VIOLINS ALONE.

(Weight, boxed, 10 pounds.)

We import our entire line of violins, comprising a large collection, and instead of putting on fabulous prices, which is the case with music dealers generally, we sell all grades on reasonable margins. We guarantee satisfaction in every case, and any violin purchased from us may, if unsatisfactory, be returned after a trial of five days and money will be refunded, providing the transportation charges are paid by the purchaser. Instruction book, bow and paper case free with each violin.

11185, Italian, dark red color, good model and finish. Each, $4.00.

11186, Dark brown color, handsomely inlaid with pearl, fine model, highly polished. Each, $5.00

11187, Stainer model, swelled back and top, red shaded, highly polished ebony trimmings, good tone. Each, $6.00.

11188, Stradavarius model, red shaded and polished, well made ebony trimmings, loud tone. Each, $7.00.

11189, Stradivarius model, fine imitation of old amber varnish, loud, heavy tone, full ebony trimmed. Each, $8.00.

11190, Magini model, fine quality, red shaded, double purfling around edges, dull finish, ebony trimmings. Each, $9.00.

11191, Bergonzi model (narrow) swelled body, imitation old amber varnish, ebony trimmings, extra fine quality. Each, $10.50.

11192, Stradivarius model, light red color, highly polished, loud, clear tone, ebony trimmings. Each, $12.50

11193, Stradivarius model, American style, light red color, amber varnish, ebony trimmings. This is a new instrument and possesses a fine tone. Each, $15.00.

11194, "Sarasate" Amatus model, imitation old amber varnish, ebony trimmings, loud, clear tone, especially adapted for orchestra playing. $22.00

11195, Our Artist's violin made by Henry Eichheimer, Berlin. This is a new line of violins and on account of their exceptionally fine qualities are bound to become famous. They are of the popular rich red color, oil varnish, and polished, beautiful model (rather favoring Stradivarius), small neck, fine scroll, polished ebony trimmings and possesses a tone which in *volume* and *purity* is seldom equaled in a new instrument. They are the *best* violin we have ever quoted, regardless of price. We guarantee *perfect* satisfaction and will refund money in any case if not perfectly satisfactory. Each, $25.00.

11194.

N. B. When testing a violin be sure and tune it to "concert pitch." This can be done by using a tuning pipe or fork. You will then get full strength and volume of the tone. Violins are often condemned simply because they are tuned too low.

BOYS' VIOLINS.

(Weight, boxed, 8 pounds.)

Instruction book and bow free. No case.

We can furnish Boys' violins in either half or three-quarter sizes at same price.

11196, Good model, light red shaded, imitation ebony finger board. Each, $2.00.

11197, Dark brown color, perfect model, well made, imitation ebony trimmings. Each, $4.00.

11198, Conservatory, fine model, amber color flamed back, ebony trimmings, good tone. Each, $6.00.

VIOLAS OR TENOR VIOLINS.

Prices quoted include bow and instruction book.

11199, Viola, light reddish color, inlaid edges, good model and finish. Each, $5.00.

11200, Viola, medium brown color, good model, well finished, fancy tail piece. Each, $7.00.

11201, Viola, Guarnerius or Stradivarius model, reddish brown color, polished, finely finished, full ebony trimmings. Each, $14.00.

VIOLIN BOWS.

(Weight, packed, 10 ounces.)

11202, Maple, red painted ebony frog, bone slide and button. Each, 40c.

11203, Maple, imitation Snakewood, ebony frog, pearl slide, German silver button. Each, 60c.

11204, Redwood ebony frog, pearl inlaid dot, pearl slide, German silver button. Each, 90c.

11205, Brazil wood, ebony frog, pearl slide and eye, full German silver lined, German silver button. Each, $1.20.

MUSICAL GOODS DEPARTMENT.

11206, "Remenyi," Brazil wood, dark color, ebony frog, double, pearl eye, pearl slide, German silver lining and button. Each, **$1.75.**

11207, Pernambuco wood, ebony frog, pearl inlaid eye, pearl slide, German silver lining and button. Each, **$2.00.**

11208, Genuine snakewood, carved ivory frog, German silver lined, fine hair. Each, **$2.50.**

11209, "Imperial" genuine pernambuco wood, fine ebony frog, silver heart in side, full lined, extra quality hair. Each, **$3.50.**

11210, "Tourte" model for artist genuine Pernambuco wood, octagon, ebony frog, full German silver lined, finely finished, heavy hair. Ea., **$4.50.**

VIOLIN BOW FROGS WITH SCREWS.

11211, Ebony with German silver button and slide. Each, **25c.**

11212, Ebony, pearl eye inlaid in slides, full German silver lined, German silver button, pearl slide. Each, **40c.**

OCARINAS.

11213.	Each.
11213, Key of C, Sop	$ .20
11214, Key of Bb, Sop	.23
11215, Key of G, Sop	.25
11216, Key of F, Sop	.30
11217, Key of E, Sop	.35
11218, Key of E.b, Alto	.35
11219, Key of D, Alto	.35
11220, Key of C. Alto	.40
11221, Key of Bb, Alto	.45
11222, Key of A, Alto	.50
11223, Key of Ab, Alto	.55
11224, Key of G, Alto	.60
11225, Key of F, Alto	.70
11226, Key of E, Alto	.85
11227, Key of Eb, Alto	.95
11228, Key of D, Bass	1.40
11229, Key of C, Bass	1.60
11230, Key of B, Bass	1.75
11231, Key of A, Bass	2.00
11232, Key of G, Bass	2.40
11233, Key of F, C, Bass	2.50
11234, Key of Eb, C, Bass	3.00
11235, Key of D, C, Bass	3.25

NOTE.—When ordering quartet or sextet sets, be sure and have all the same key.

Weight of Ocarinas: Sopranos, 4 oz.; altos, 14 oz.; bass, 26 oz.; contra-bass, 40 oz.

METALLOPHONES.

After some experience with metallaphones we have found that only the best grade of these instruments are really of any use. We therefore recommend the following to be of excellent quality in manner of finish and tone. Put up one in box with mallets.

11236.

11236, Metallophones, 3 octaves, 22 bronzed steel bars on fancy wood frame, tuned for use, each one with instruction book. Weight 8 pounds. Each, **80c.**

PARLOR BELLS.

11237.

11237, Twelve lettered blue steel bars fastened on finely gilded wood frame, key of C, perfectly tuned to concert pitch. Produces a fine effect when played with piano, organ or guitar, or as solo instrument. Weight, 51 ounces. Price in pasteboard box, including two beaters, **$1.50.**

THE AUTOHARP.

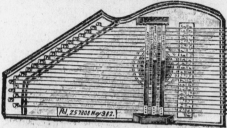

11238.

(A practical and ingenous musical novelty.)

11238, Consists of a zither with an attachment for producing the chords used in accompanying music for singing or solo playing. The attachment consists of three or more bars, which are placed across the strings in the center of the instrument, and are made with dampers, which deaden all the strings not used in the chord. It will therefore be seen that it is only necessary to draw the ring over every string on the instrument in order to produce a perfect chord when either of the bars are lowered. It has 18 treble strings and three bass strings, making 21 in all. Six pieces of music, a ring and full instructions are furnished with each instrument. Weight 53 ounces. Price each, **$2.75.**

11239, Autoharp No. 2, with 4 bars, 23 strings, producing four chords, furnished with extras, the same as No. 11238. Weight 60 ounces. Each, **$3.25.**

11240, Autoharp No. 2¾, has 23 strings, 5 bars, producing 5 chords. Weight 62 ounces. Each, **$3.60.**

11241, Autoharp No. 3, has 28 strings, 4 bars with shifters, producing 9 chords. Weight 6 lbs. Each, **$8.60.**

11242, Autoharp No. 5, "Concert," top and sides rosewood veneered, edges inlaid, highly polished, has 28 strings, 5 bars with shifters, producing 13 chords. Weight 6¼ pounds. Each, **$13.50.**

11243, No. 6, same style as No. 5, has 32 strings, 6 bars with shifters, producing 16 chords. Weight 8½ lbs. Each, **$18.50.**

Autoharp Strings.

We do not sell less than full set.

11244, Full set for No. 11238	$ .40
11245, Full set for No. 11239	.45
11246, Full set for No. 11240	.50
11247, Full set for No. 11241-42	.60
11248, Full set for No. 11243	.65

Autoharp Picks.

11249, Horn, good quality. Each, **6c.**

11250, Celluloid, good quality. Each, **10c.**

Autoharp Cases.

11251, Autoharp cases, wood, black varnished, half lined with flannel, handle, hooks and lock for Nos. 11238 to 11242 inclusive. Weight, boxed, 8 lbs. Each, **$1.40.**

11252, Autoharp cases, wood, black varnished, full lined with flannel, nickel lock and hook harps for Autoharp No. 11243. Weight, boxed, 10 lbs. Each, **$2.00.**

Tambourines.

11253, 10-inch, plain maple rim, tacked sheepskin head. Weight 7 ounces. Each, **40c.**

11254, 10-inch fancy painted, tacked sheepskin head. Weight 8 ounces. **50c.**

11255, 10-inch fancy painted, tacked, calfskin head. Weight 9 ounces. **70c.**

11256, 10-inch, nickel rim, lined with redwood, calfskin head, tacked, 3 pr. jingles. Weight 13 ounces. **90c.**

READ OUR GRAND OFFER FOR CASH IN ADVANCE.

Musical Goods Department.

Tambourines—Continued.

11257, 10-inch, narrow metal hoop, nickel plate, wood-lined, professional, tacked calfskin head, 6 set jingles. Weight 12 ounces. Each, **$1.75.**

11258, Tambourine, Salvation Army, 11-inch maple hoop, calfskin head, 19 sets brass jingles, band fastenings. Weight 17 ounces. Each, **$1.50.**

11259, Tambourine, Salvation Army, 11-inch, nickel hoop, wood lined, 19 sets of brass jingles, metal band fastenings. Weight 20 ounces. Each, **$2.00.**

BONES.

11260, Bones, rosewood, large, set of four. Weight 6 ounces. Per set, **20c.**

11261, Bones, rosewood, small, set of four. Weight 5 ounces. Per set, **15c.**

11262, Bones, ebony, large, set of four. Weight 7 ounces. Per set, **35c.**

11263, Bones, ebony, small, set of four. Weight 6 ounces. Per set, **25c.**

11264, Bones, walnut, patent clappers. Weight 3 ounces. set of two, **10c.**

11265.

11265, Cymbalet, a new musical novelty made of hard bent wood, with two brass jingles at each end loosely attached to a steel rod, gives the same effect as the tambourine and is much easier to handle. Weight 4 ounces. Each, **5c.** Per dozen, **50c.**

TRIANGLES.

11266, 6-inch, polished steel, with hammer. Weight 9 ounces. Each, **35c.**

11267, 7-inch, polished steel, with hammer. Weight 12 ounces. Each, **50c.**

11268, 8-inch, polished steel, with hammer. Weight 15 ounces. Each, **75c.**

11266.

PIANO STOOLS.

11269, Imitation rosewood, hardwood pedestal, iron feet, hair cloth, red or green reps. Retail price, $2.50 to $3.00. Our price, **$1.25.** Weight boxed, 25 lbs.

11270, Same, with plush seat, maroon or crimson. Weight, boxed 25 lbs. Retail price, $6.00. Our price, **$3.00.**

11271, Imitation rosewood, framed, oblong seat, 13x16½ inches, handsome wood pedestal, maroon or crimson silk plush, plain or embossed. Weight, boxed, 30 lbs. Retail price, $7.20. Our price, **$3.50.**

11269.

Violin Tail Pieces. Musical Stands.

11272, Tail pieces, imitation ebony, plain, **5c.**

11273, Tail pieces, ebony plain, **10c.**

11274, Tail pieces, inlaid, similar to cut. Each, **30c.**

11275, Violin tail pieces made of celluloid, finely carved, imitation ivory, or tortoise shell; very popular. Each **50c.**

11276, Tail pieces, very fine ebony, inlaid, similar to cut. **75c.**

11276.   **11277-78.**

Weight of tail pieces, 2 ounces.

11277, The "Ideal" folding music stands, made of steel, japanned, light and convenient for carrying. Each, **75c.** Per dozen, **$8.10.**

11278, "Ideal" music stands, same as above, nickel plated. Each, **$1.25.** Per dozen, **$13.50.**

Violin Finger Boards.

11278½, Violin Finger Boards; ebony polished; weight, 6 ounces. Each **25c.**

Banjo Pegs.

Weight per set, 3 ounces.

11279, Imitation ebony, hollow shape, polished, with pearl dot in head. Each **3c.**

11280, Side peg to match No. 11279. Each **3c.**

11281, Ebony, hollow shaped, polished, with pearl dot in head. Each **6c.**

11282, Side peg to match 11281. Each **6c.**

11283, Celluloid, white or imitation amber, hollow shape, polished. Each **8c.**

11284, Side peg to match 11283. Each **8c.**

11285, Greek Cross, polished, (see cut.) Each **12c.**

11285.   **11286,** Side peg to match 11285. Each **12c.**

Peerless Patent Banjo Pegs.

11287, Nickel-plated with ebony thumb piece. Turns easily but can be adjusted so it will not slip. Each **30c.**

Per set of five, **$1.35.**

Weight, per set, 3 ounces.

11287.

Banjo Brackets.

Weight per dozen, 9 ounces.

11288, Spread Eagle pattern, brass, with bolt and nut. Per dozen **60c.**

11289, "Leaf" pattern, brass, with bolt and nut. Per dozen **70c.**

11290, "Leaf" pattern, nickel-plated with bolt and nut. Per dozen **$1.00.**

11291, Gold pattern, brass turned and polished, with bolt and new pattern safety nut (see cut). Per dozen **90c.**

11292, Globe pattern, nickel-plated, turned and polished, with bolt and new pattern safety nut. Per dozen **$1.25.**

11291.

READ OUR GRAND OFFER FOR CASH IN ADVANCE.

MUSICAL GOODS DEPARTMENT

Banjo Tail Pieces.

11293, Ebony, common, good model and finish, wt. 1 oz. each **8c.**
11294, Imitation ivory, carved, weight 1 ounce, each **35c.**
11295, Wood's Patent Adjustable Banjo Tail Piece, made of a peculiar metal, highly polished, strings are easily and quickly attached, besides it will not break them, weight 2 ounces. Price each, including bolt, **40c.**

11295.

Banjo Bridges.

11296, Banjo bridges, common. Each **3c.**
11297, Banjo bridges, better, made of ebony, weight 1 ounce. Each **6c.**

Violincello Bridges.

11298, Maple, good quality, with two scrolls, weight 3 ounces. Each **20c.**
11299, Maple, fine quality, with 3 scrolls, weight 3 ounces. Each **30c.**

Violincello Tail Pieces.

11300, Maple, imitation ebony finish, pearl dot inlaid on top, weight 4 ounces. Each **30c.**
11301, Ebony, plain, best model and finish, weight 4 ounces. Each **75c.**

Violincello Bows.

11302, Redwood, plain ebony frog, bone button, good quality, weight 8 ounces. Each **75c.**
11303, Redwood, ebony frog, pearl eye, German silver button, weight 10 ounces. Each **$1.10.**
11304, Brazil wood, ebony frog, double pearl eye, full German silver lined, pearl slide, German silver button, weight 10 ounces. Each **$1.75.**
11305, Pernambuco wood, ebony frog, double pearl eye, full German silver lined, German silver button, weight 10 ounces. Each **$2.50.**

Violincello Bow Frogs with Screws.

11306, Ebony, pearl dot inlaid in side, pearl slide, bone button. Each **30c.**
11307, Ebony, pearl dot inlaid in sides, German silver lined, pearl slide, German silver buttons, weight 2 ounces. Each **50c.**

Violin Nuts and Saddles.

11308, Violin nut, ebony, for upper end of finger board. Each **4c.**
11309, Violin saddles, ebony, for supporting tail piece string. Each **4c.**

Violin Bridges.

11310, Violin bridges, good. Each **4c.**
11311, Violin bridges, better, weight 1 ounce. Each **10c.**

Bow Hair.

11312, Violin bow hair, white, good quality. Per bunch **15c.**
11313, Violin bow hair, white, finest quality, for artists' use. Per bunch **20c.**
11314, Violincello bow hair, best quality, white. Per bunch **20c.**
11315, Double Bass bow hair, best quality, black. Per bunch **25c.**
11316, Double Bass bow hair, best quality, white, weight per bunch 1 ounce. Per bunch **30c.**

Resin.

11317, Resin in pasteboard box, weight 2 ounces. Per box **3c.**

11318, Resin, better quality, on metal spools, weight 3 ounces. Per box **7c.**
11319, Double Bass resin, good quality, in oblong pasteboard boxes. Per box **10c.**
11320, Double Bass resin, Koehler's improved, in round boxes. Per box **30c.**

Mouthpieces.

11321, Mouthpieces for flute, composition, with adjustable screws. **20c.**
11322, Mouthpieces for fife. **12c.**
11323, Mouthpieces for piccolo, weight 2 ounces. **12c.**

11321-22.

Violin Mutes.

11324.   **11326.**

11324. Violin mute made of ebony (see cut). Each **10c.**
11325, Violin mute made of German silver. Each **20c.**
11326, German silver with tuning pipe. A and string gauge, weight each 1 ounce, **35c.**

Piano Tunning Hammers.

11327, Piano tuning hammers, steel with extension rosewood handle, three heads, square, oblong and star; weight 20 ounces. Price each, complete, **$1.75.**

Strings.

We wish to caution our trade in buying strings against being misled by "fancy names and high prices quoted by other dealers. We buy all our gut strings (steel and wound strings are made in this country) direct from the best European manufacturers, select only *first quality*, and are selling them at "rock bottom" prices. A trial order will convince you that this statement is correct.
Violin and banjo strings, weight 2 ounces per set; guitar and violincello strings, 4 ounces per set.

Violin Strings.

		Each	Per doz.
11328, E, best Italian, 4 lengths polished		**$0 12**	**$1 25**
11329, E, best quality, rough finish		12	1 25
11330, A, best Italian, 2½ lengths		12	1 25
11331, D, best Italian, 2½ lengths		15	1 60
11332, G, best Italian, 1 length		08	85
11333, Per set of 4, **40c.**			

Steel Violin Strings.

	Each	Per doz.
Silver-plated		
11334, E, 1 length, best quality	2c	**$0 20**
11335, A, 1 length, best quality	2c	20
11336, D, 1 length, best quality covered, silver-plated	6c	65
11337, G, 1 length, best quality covered, silver-plated	6c	65
11338, Full set, **10c.**		
11339, Silk violin strings, E, 4 lengths, very fine quality, French	12c	1 25

Banjo Strings.

	Each	Per doz.
11340, B or 1st, and E or 5th	8c	**$0 85**
11341, G or 2nd	10c	1 00
11342, E or 3d	10c	1 00
11343, A or 4th bass	8c	85
11344, Full set of 5, best quality, **35c.**		

READ OUR GRAND OFFER FOR CASH IN ADVANCE.

MUSICAL GOODS DEPARTMENT.

Steel Banjo Strings.

	Each	Per doz.
11345, B or 1st, E or 5th	2c	20c
11346, G or 2nd	2c	20c
11347, E or 3d	2c	20c
11348, A or 4th	7c	65c
11349, Full set of 5, per set, 12c.		

Guitar Strings.

	Each	Per doz.
11350, E or 1st, best quality gut	12c	$1 25
11351, B or 2nd best quality gut	12c	1 25
11352, G or 3d, best quality gut	15c	1 60
11353, D or 4th, silvered wire on silk	10c	1 00
11354, A or 5th, silvered wire on silk	10c	1 00
11355, E or 6th, silvered wire on silk	10c	1 00
11356, Full set of 6, 60c.		

Steel Guitar Strings.

	Each	Per doz.
11357, E or 1st, silvered steel, best quality	02c	$0 20
11358, B or 2nd, silvered steel, best quality	02c	0 20
11359, G or 3d, compound silvered wire wound on steel and silk	10c	1 00
11360, D or 4th, compound	10c	1 00
11361, A or 5th, compound	10c	1 00
11362, E or 6th, compound	10c	1 00
11363, Full set of 6, steel, 38c.		

Mandolin Strings.

11364, First string, steel wire, silver-plated. Each 4c.
11365, Second string, steel wire, silver-plated. Each 4c.
11366, Third string, steel, wound with silver wire, Each 8c.
11367, Fourth string, steel wound with silver wire. Each 8c.
11368, Full set of 8, 40c.

Violincello Strings.

	Each
11369, A, best Italian	15c
11370, D, best Italian	20c
11371, G, best wired gut	15c
11372, C, best wired gut	20c
11373, Full set of 4 strings, per set 65c.	

Double Bass Strings.

	Each
11374, G or 1st, genuine Italian, fine quality.	$0 60
11375, D or 2d, genuine Italian, fine quality.	75
11376, A or 3d, genuine Italian, fine quality.	90
11377, A or 3d, wound silvered wire on gut...	1 00
11378, E or 4th, wound silvered wire on gut.	1 10
11379, Per set of 3	2 00
11380, Per set of 4	3 00

NOTE.—When ordering sets of double bass strings state whether you want "A" string plain or wound.

Guitar Finger Boards.

11381 Each

11381, Guitar finger boards, ebony, plain, without fret | $0 60
11382, Guitar finger boards, ebony, with frets, weight 16 ounces | 1 00

Guitar Bridges.

	Each
11383, Ebony, plain, good model and finish.	25c
11384, Ebony, polished, with pearl inlaid ends	60c
11385, Celluloid, imitation amber, weight 4 ounces	90c

Guitar Patent Heads.

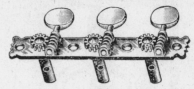

11386-7.

Weight 6 ounces.

11386, Brass, per set | $0 75
11387, Nickel-plated, per set | 1 00

Guitar Bridge Pins.

Weight per set of 5, 1 ounce.   Each

	Each
11388, Ebony, polished, with pearl dot in end Per set of 6, 10c.	2c
11389, Celluloid, imitation ivory, amber or tortoise shell Per set of 6, 15c.	3c
11390, Ivory, polished, pearl dot in head Per set of 6, 30c.	6c

Violin End Pins.

Each

11391, End pins, maple, No. 1 | 3c

11392, End pins, ebony, No. 3, weight 1 ounce... | 5c

11392.

Violin Pegs.

11393, Violin pegs, imitation ebony polished. Each 4c.
Per set of 4, 12c.
11394, Violin pegs, ebony, polished, Each 6c.
Per set of 4, 20c.
11395, Violin pegs, ebony, finely inlaid (similar to cut). Each 20c.
Per set of 4, 75c.
11396, Violin pegs, celluloid, polished with white, black or amber. Each 8c.
Per set of 4, 25c.

11395.

11397.

11397, Peerless patent violin pegs, made of the new metal, aluminum, white thumb pieces; will not slip. Price per set of 4, **$1.00.**

READ OUR GRAND OFFER FOR CASH IN ADVANCE.

MUSICAL GOODS DEPARTMENT.

Jew's Harp.

11398, English harp, club pattern, weight 2 oz., each **10c.**
11399, English harp, fancy pattern, wt. 2 oz., each **10c.**
11400, Jew's harp, common style, good quality, wt. 2 oz., each **5c.**
11401, Jew's harp, white metal frame, best quality, medium size,

11398.   11399 to 11404.
weight 2 ounces, each **12c.**
11402, Jew's harp, large size, weight 3 ounces, each **20c.**
11403, Jew's harp, extra large size, weight 3 oz., each **25c.**
11404, Jew's harp, Jumbo, lacquered, weight 4 ounces, each **40c.**

Drums.

We quote below two of the latest improved styles of snare drums. The "Prussian" pattern has square headed metal rods for holding the hoops in place. The "Regulation" pattern has cords and hooks.

Prussian Pattern Snare Drum.

11405, Brass shell 16 inches in diameter, 6 inches high. 8 rods, white metal plated hooks and trimmings, 8 rawhide snares, 2 calfskin heads weight 16 pounds, each, **$5.00.**
11406, Nickel-plated shell, 16 inches in

11405.

diameter, 6 inches high. 8 rods, white metal plated hooks and trimmings, 8 rawhide snares, 2 calfskin heads, weight 16 pounds, each **$6.00.**

Regulation Pattern.

11407, Rosewood shell, (army pattern) 16 inches in diameter, 12 inches high, best Italian hemp cord, improved snare strainer, 2 calfskin heads, tinnec cord hooks, wt. 16 lbs., boxed; each **$4.40.**
11408, Birds-eye Maple shell, 16 inches in diameter, 9½ inches high, fine varnish finish, best Italian hemp cord,

11409.

tinned cord hooks. 8 braces, 3 snares, new pattern snare strainers, 2 calskin heads weight 14 lbs.; each **$5.50.**
11409, Bird's-eye Maple shell, 16 inches in diameter, 6 inches high, fine varnish finish, best quality Italian hemp cord, tinned cord hooks, 12 braces, 8 snares, new pattern snare strainers, 2 calfskin heads (CH), weight 13 lbs.; each **$5.75.**

Youth's Snare Drums.

11410, Brass shell, Regulation pattern. 14 inches in diameter, 7 inches high, red hoops. 6 snares with strainer. 1 calf skin and 1 sheepskin head, 2 sticks, weight 10 lbs.; each **$3.00.**
11411, Brass shell, Prussian pattern. 14 inches in diameter, 4½ inches high, 6 rods. red hoops. 6 snares with snare strainers, 1 calfskin and 1 sheepskin head, 2 sticks, weight 11 lbs.; each **$3.50.**

Bass Drums.

11412. Regulation pattern. bird's-eye Maple shell, 24 inches in diameter, 12 inches high, 13 braces, best quality Italian hemp cord, improved cord hooks. 1 calfskin and 1 sheepskin head. 1 stick, weight 50 lbs.; each **$10.50.**
11413, Regulation pattern, bird's eye Maple

shell, 30 inches in diameter, 12 inches high. 14 braces' best quality Italian hemp cord, improved cord hooks, 2 calfskin heads, 1 stick, weight 55 pounds; each **$13.50.**

Cymbals.

(TURKISH.)

11414, Composition metal, 8 inch, with leather handles, weight 35 ounces; **$4.50.**
11415, Composition metal, 9 inch, with leather handles, weight 45 ounces; **$5.25.**
11416, Composition metal, 10 inch, with leather handles, weight 50 ounces; **$6.25.**

(GERMAN.)

11417, Brass, 12 inch, leather handles, weight 45 ounces; **$2.50.**
11418, Brass, 13 inch, leather handles, weight 50 ounces; **$3.25.**

Calfskin Heads for Drums, Banjos and Tambourines.

	Each
11419, 12 inch head for 10 inch shell	**$0 22**
11420, 13 inch head for 11 inch shell	30
11421, 14 inch head for 11½ inch shell	35
11422, 15 inch head for 12 inch shell	40
11423, 16 inch head for 13 inch shell	50
11424, 17 inch head for 14 inch shell	60
11425, 18 inch head for 15 inch shell	70
11426, 19 inch head for 16 inch shell	80
11427, 20 inch head for 17 inch shell	90
11428, 22 inch head for 19 inch shell	1 00
11429, 28 inch head for 24 inch bass drum	1 50
11430, 30 inch head for 26 inch bass drum	1 80
11431, 32 inch head for 28 inch bass drum	2 00
11432, 34 inch head for 30 inch bass drum	2 25
11433, 36 inch head for 32 inch bass drum	2 75
11434, 38 inch head for 34 inch bass drum	3 00
11435, 40 inch head for 36 inch bass drum	3 50
11436, 42 inch head for 38 inch bass drum	4 00

Weight of calfskin drum heads: 10 to 15 inches, 4 ounces; 15 to 20 inches, 5 ounces; 20 to 28 inches. 9 oz. 30 to 36 inches, 12 ounces; 38 to 40 inches, 16 ounces.

Snare Drum Sticks.

	Per pair
11437, Rosewood. polished, weight 6 ounces.	**$0 25**
11438, Ebony, polished, weight 8 ounces	50
11439, Ebony, with nickel-plated ferrules, highly polished. weight 9 ounces	1 00
11440, Snakewood, highly polished. weight 9 ounces	1 20
11141, Snakewood, with nickel-plated ferrules, highly polished, weight 9 oz.	2 00

Bass Drum Sticks.

11442, Hickory handles with chamois skin head, weight 10 ounces; **40c.**

Snare Drum Slings.

11443, Red webbing, small, for boy's drum, with snap, weight 3 ounces; each **25c.**
11444, White or stripped webbing, improved pattern, best quality, with snap, weight 3 oz.; each **40c.**

Bass Drum Slings.

11445, White or stripped webbing. improved pattern, best quality, with snap, weight 4 oz.. each **60c.**
11446, Leather, fine quality, weight 6 ounces; each **80c.**
Any musical instrument made furnished at lowest rates. Also parts of all kinds of musical instruments furnished if desired.

Music Wrappers.

11447. Imitation morocco sides, plain, with gilt letters, assorted, weight 26 oz.; each **75c.**

11448. Imitation morocco side, fine, similar to illustration, weight 6 oz.; **$1.25.**

11447-8.

MUSICAL GOODS DEPARTMENT

11450.

11449. Solid leather music rolls, similar in style to No. 11450; finely finished, hand stitched, in either russet, lemon or orange color, weight 9 ounces; each 75c

11450, Music roll, made of the finest embossed leather; colors, black, russet or orange; weight 8 ounces; each $1.00.

11451.

11451, Music wrapper, made of silk plush, extra fine quality, with flat handle, weight 9 ounces; each $1.50.

Tuning Forks.

Weight 2 ounces.

11452, Philharmonic A................................ $0 10
11453, Philharmonic C................................ 10
11454, Tuning forks, heavy blued steel, finely finished, warranted the new American pitch; each in case, Key of A; price each.................... 35
11455, Tuning fork, same quality as 11454; Key of C; each...................... 35

Tuning Pipes.

11457.

11456. Set of two, A and C; combined weight 2 oz., per set 15c.
11457, E, A, D and G, combined, for tuning violin or mandolin (like cut), weight 3 oz.; per set 35c.
11458, Set of 5, B, G, E, A and E, combined, for tuning banjo, weight 3 oz.; per set 45c.
11459, Set of 6, E, G, B, D, A and E, combined, for tuning guitar, weight 3 ounces; per set 55c.

NOTE—New beginners on violin, mandolin, banjo or guitar will find apove sets very convenient for tuning instruments. They are made of German silver and tuned to a standard concert pitch.

Batons.

For the use of singing teacher, band masters, etc.

11460, Baton made of rosewood, polished, tapering, length 16 inches; 25c.
11461, Baton made of ebony, tapering, nickel-plated tip at each end, French polished, length 16 inches; 75c.
11462, Baton made of ebony, highly polished with richly carved and inlaid ivory handle and point (see cut), length 16 inches; each $4.00.

Metronomes.

This instrument consists of a short pendulum with a sliding weight; is operated by clock work, and is fixed to measure or to beat "time" in music. They are very useful for beginners in learning to read music.

11463, Metronome, made of mahogany, Mælzel system, best French make, without bell; each $2.85.

11464, Metronome, same as No. 11463, with bell; each $4.

11463.

Ruling Pens.

11465.

11465, Ruling pens, with five liness for drawing staff, weight 1 ounce; 10c.
11466. Steel pens, with three points, for writing music, weight per dozen 1 ounce; 20c.

Violin Chin Rests.

11467, Violin chin rests, ebony, double action, screw fastenings, Richard's patent, weight 3 ounces; each 50c.
11468, Violin chin rests, gutta-percha, ratchet fastenings, C. F. Albert's patent; weight 6 ounces; each $1.00.
11469, Violin chin rest and shoulder rest combined (Becker's patent), made of celluloid and nickel. This is a new and useful invention, as it holds the violin in proper position for playing; weight 6 ounces; each $1.15.

11468.

Violin Patent Heads.

11470, Violin Patent Head, brass, engraved on sides, bone buttons. Per set, 40c.

11471, Violin Patent Head, nickel plated, engraved on sides, good quality. Per set. 60c.

Weight each, 4 ounces.

11470.

Violin Necks.

11472.

11472, Violin Necks, maple, unfinished, carved scroll. Weight 8 ounces. Each, 20c.
11473, Violin Necks, maple, unfinished, fine quality, finely carved scroll. Weight 8 oz. Each, 75c.
11474, Violin Necks, curly maple, unfinished, best quality, finely carved scroll. Weight 8 ounces. Each, $1.25.

Music Paper.

	Per Quire.
11475, 10 Staves, superfine royal, 10x15......	$0.35
11476, 12 Staves, superfine royal, 10x15......	.35
11477, 14 Staves, superfine royal, 10x15......	.35
11478, 16 Staves, superfine royal, 10x15......	.35

Weight per quire, 21 oz.

Blank Music Books.

11479, 6 staves, 40 pages, cloth back, marbled paper covers, oblong; size 7½x9½ inches. Weight. 7 oz. Each, 15c.
11480, 8 staves, 64 pages, same size and style as No. 11479. Weight 10 ounces. Each, 20c.
11481, 12 staves, 84 pages, same size and style as No. 11479. Weight 14 ounces. Each, 30c.
11482, 10 staves, 52 pages, cloth back and sides, full gilt; size 7½x9½ inches. Weight 12 oz. Each, 40c.
11483, 12 staves, 80 pages, leather back and corners, cloth sides; size 9x11½ inches. Weight 22 oz. Each, 60c.
11484, 14 staves, 80 pages, leather back and corners, cloth sides; size 10½x13¾ inches. Weight 31 oz, Each, 75c.

READ OUR GRAND OFFER FOR CASH IN ADVANCE.

MUSICAL GOODS DEPARTMENT.

Roller Organs.

The roller organs are new and very popular mechanical musical instruments, and our prices are so low that our sales are already very large. The music is produced from reeds (regular organ size) 20 in number, which are perfectly tuned and covered with steel valves. The latter are operated by the music roller which is supplied with pins similar to those on an ordinary music box. The roller is made to revolve with gearing, which also drives the bellows. All the working parts are made of solid metal, easily accessible, and on the whole are well made and durable. They have a tone of good volume. Any child can play them, and we can furnish all styles of music.

11485, The Gem roller organ as described above, imitation black walnut case, length 16 inches, width, 14 inches, height, 9 inches. Price complete, including three rollers, $4.50. Weight, boxed, 15 pounds.

11485.

11486, The Concert roller organ, larger in size, hence greater volume of tone, hand some black walnut case, glass top, finely finished, length, 19 inches, width 16 inches, height, 14 inches. Price complete, including five

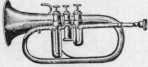

11486.

rollers, $9.00. Weight, boxed, 30 lbs.

We can furnish extra rollers for above at 23c. each; extra by mail, 7c. Each roller plays one tune. Music lists furnished on application.

BAND INSTRUMENTS.

The German Piston Valve Instruments are made expressly for us by a reliable manufacturer in Germany, and we can recommend them as being equal to any German Piston line on the market. We have also taken the exclusive agency for the celebrated French Piston Valve Instruments manufactured by Jules DeVere & Co., of Paris, which are now being largely used by French military bands. While we do not claim these instruments to be "the best in the world," we can safely say they are equal to the better grades that other dealers are selling at from 20 to 50 per cent. higher than our prices. The fact that we buy direct from manufacturers, and that we are always willing to give our customers all benefits possible, enables us to make prices lower than ever offered before.

On orders of 5 or more band instruments we will be pleased to quote special prices on applicatson.

German Piston Valves.

Water key, music rack and German silver mouthpiece with each instrument.

11487, Eb cornet, brass. Each $6.25.
11488, Eb cornet, nickel plated. Each $7.75. Weight, boxed, 6 pounds.
11489, Bb cornet, brass, same

11487-88.

style as No. 11487. Weight 7 pounds. $7.10.
11490, Bb cornet, nickel plated. Weight 7 pounds. $8.50.

11491-92.

11491, Eb Alto Valve Trombone, brass. $8.50.
11492, Eb Alto Valve Trombone, nickel plated. Each, $11.30. Weight, boxed, 8 lbs.

11493, Bb Tenor Valve Trombone, same style as 11491. brass. Weight, boxed, 9 pounds. $11.15.
11494, Bb Tenor Valve Trombone, same style as 11411, nickel plated. Weight, boxed, 9 lbs. $13.90.

11495-96.

11495, Eb Alto, bell up, brass. Weight, boxed, 8 pounds. $8.50.
11496, Eb Alto, bell up, nickel plated. Weight, boxed, 8 pounds. $11.30.
11497, Bb Tenor, bell up, same style as 11495, brass. $11.15.
11498, Bb Tenor, bell up, same style as 11495, nickel plated. Weight, boxed, 9 pounds. $13.90.
11499, Bb Baritone, bell up, same style as 11495, brass. $12.90.
11500, Bb Baritone, bell up, same style as 11495, nickel plated. Weight, boxed, 10 pounds. $16.50.
11501, Bb Bass, bell up, same style as 11495, brass. $14.60.
11502, Bb Bass, bell up, same style as 11495, nickel plated. Weight, boxed, 15 pounds. $19.25.

Eb Basses.

11503, Eb Bass, bell up, brass..............$20.25
11504, Eb Bass. bell up, nickel plated........ 25.75
Weight, boxed, 18 pounds.

Improved French Piston Instruments.

With genuine light action valves, manufactured by Jules DeVere & Co., Paris. Water key, music rack and German silver mouthpiece with each instrument.

11505, Eb Cornet, brass. $8.00.
11506, Eb Cornet, nickel plated. $9.40. Weight, boxed, 6 pounds.

11505. Eb Cornet.

11507, Bb Cornet, brass. $8.75.
11508, Eb Cornet, nickel plated. Each, $10.55.

Weight, boxed, 7 pounds.

11507-8.

11509, Eb Solo Alto, bell front, brass. Each, $11.80.
11510, Eb Solo Alto, bell front, nickel plated. Each, $14.60. Weight, boxed. 8 lbs.

11509-10.

11511, Eb Alto, Valve Trombone, bell front. Each, $11.80.
11512, Eb Alto Trombone, bell front, nickel plated. Each, $14.60. Weight, boxed, 9 lbs.

11511-12.

11513 Bb Tenor Valve Trombone, same style as No. 11511. Brass, $14.00.
11514, Bb Tenor Valve Trombone, same style as No. 11511 Nickel plated. $16.80. Weight, boxed, 10 pounds.
11515, Bb Baritone Valve Trombone, same style as No. 11511, brass. $16.00.
11516, Bb Baritone Valve Trombone, same style as 11511, Nickel plated. $19.80. Weight, boxed, 11 pounds.

READ OUR GRAND OFFER FOR CASH IN ADVANCE.

MUSICAL GOODS DEPARTMENT.

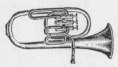

11517 and 11518.
boxed, 8 pounds. Nickel plated. **$12.00.**

11517, Bb Ten-or slide Trom-bone, brass. $9.25.
11518, Bb Ten-or slide Trom-bone. Weight,

11521 and 11522.

11519, Eb Alto, bell up, brass. $11.80.
11520, Eb Alto, bell up, nickel plated. $14.60.
Weight, boxed, 8 lbs.
11521, Bb Tenor, bell up, same style as No. 11519, brass. $14.00.
11523, Bb Tenor, bell up, same style as No. 11519,
nickel plated. **$16.80.** Weight, boxed, 10 pounds.
11525, Bb Baritone, bell up, same style as No.
11519, brass. Each, **$16.00.**
11527, Bb Baritone, bell up, same style as No.
11519, nickel plated. Each, **$19.80.**
Weight, boxed, 11 pounds.
11529, Bb Bass, bell up, same style as No. 11519,
brass. Each, **$18.10.**
11530, Bb Bass, bell up, same style as No. 11519,
nickel plated. Each, **$22.90.**
Weight, boxed. 16 pounds.

Eb Basses.

11531, Eb Bass, bell up, brass..............$26.40
11532, Eb Bass, bell up, nickel plated...... 32.00
Weight, boxed, 25 pounds.

Solo Bb Cornets.

11533, Bb Cornet, brass, long model, German silv-er, light ac-tion, French piston valves, water key German silve mouthpiece, "A" set piece, a superb in-strument.
11533.   Price, $9.75.
Weight, boxed. 7 pounds.
11534, Bb Cornet, same as above, nickel plated. $11.50.
11535, Bb Cornet, light action, improved short model French manufacture, extra quality, richly mounted with figured metal, German silver pistons and mouthpiece, with double water keys and "A" set piece, Brass, $20.50. Weight, boxed, 8 pounds.
11536, Nickel plated, same as above. $22.50.
11537, Silver plated, satin finish, same as above. 28.50.
11538, C Cornet, "Besson" model, German silver piston valves with water key, brass. $9.75.
Weight, boxed, 7 pounds.
11539, C Cornet, nickel plated, same as above. $11.50.
NOTE.—We guarantee our band instruments to be in perfect condition, as each one is thoroughly ex-amined by an experienced workman before being shipped.

Band Instrument Mouthpieces.

11540, German silver for Eb or Bb Cornets. Each, 40c. Weight 2 ounces.
11541, German silver for altos and tenors. Each, 65c. Weight 2 ounces.
11542, German silver for Bb baritones, or Eb basses. Each, **$1.00.** Weight 3 ounces.
11543, "Professional" silver plated and burnish-ed. "Higham" or "Austin" models, for Eb or Bb cor-nets. Each, 70c. Weight 2 ounces.
11544, "Professional," same as No. 11543, for altos or tenors. Weight 3 ounces. Each, **$1.00.**
11545, "Professional," same as No. 11543, for bari-tone. Weight 3 ounces. Each, **$1.40.**
11546, "Professional," same as No. 11543, for Bb or Eb bass. Each, **$1.65.**

Band Instrument Music Racks.

11547, Music Rack, improv-ed pattern, 3 prongs for band instrument, brass. Each, **50c.**
11548, Music Rack same as No. 11547, nickel plated. Each, 75c.
11549, Music Racks for slide trombone. brass 75c. each, nickel plated **$1.00** each.

11547.

Bugles.

Weight, boxed, 6 pounds.

11550, Cavalry Bugles, key of F, brass. Each, **$2.25.** Nickel plated. Each, **$3.00.**

11550.

11551, In-fantry Bugles, key of C, with Bb crook, brass. Each, **$3.00.** Nickel plated Each, **$4.00.**

11551.

11552, Artil-lery Bugles, key of G, brass, Each, **$3.25.** Nickel plated. Each, **$4.25.**

11552.

11553, Hunting horns, brass, one turn. Each, **$1.00.**
11554, Hunting horns, brass, three turns. Each, **$1.50.**

11553.

Cornet Cases.

11555, Wood, black varnished, lined, lock, handle and hooks. Each, **$1.25.**
11556, Brown can-vas satchel form leather bound, flan-nel lined. with shoul-der strap. Each, **$1.70.** Weight 22 oz.
11557, Pebbled leather, black satch-el form, flannel lined, nickel plated trim-mings, with shoulder **11557.** strap, (see cut.) **$1.90.** Weight 25 ounces.
11558. Leather, russet color, satchel form. flannel lined, nickel plated trimmings, with shoulder strap. Weight 25 ounces. **$2.00.**

Vocal and Instrumental Musical Collections.

We wish to call special attention to our new music books quoted below. We have selected only the latest and most popular music, and the price is low-er than ever offered before. The music contained in each book if purchased in sheet music form sep-arately, would cost at least $20. Postage on music books will average about 15 cents.

MUSICAL GOODS DEPARTMENT.

Vocal Music.

SUPERB SONGS.

11559, Superb Songs, a new book which contains over 200 pages of choice music and words, arranged for piano or organ accompaniment. This is a companion to the celebrated "Song Folio," the most popular book of the class ever issued. It has illuminated paper covers and contains 15 elegant lithograph portraits of the celebrated singers of the day, both male and female. The publisher's price is 50 cents for this book. Extra by mail, 11c. Our price, 40c.

11560, The Trumpet of Reform, by Geo. F. Root. A song book for all industrial and reform organizations. Contains a well arranged collection of stirring music, designed for general use in the Grange Club and school room. Price each, 45c. Postage, 8c.

11561, The Standard Song Album. A collection of old and new popular songs, just published, containing 224 pages and 62 pieces, among which are some selections from the "The Mikado," "Nanon" and "Beggar Student;" also "The Bridge," "Ave Maria," "Free as a Bird" and "Old Sexton." Price each, 40c.

11562, Selected Songs, by eminent composers. A new collection of the latest and best vocal music. Full sheet music size, paper covers. Price each, 40c. Extra, by mail, 8c.

11563, Whitney's Song Casket, a fine collection of vocal gems, including ballads, duets, songs with choruses, quartettes, etc. 150 pages, full sheet music size; paper covers. Price each, 40c. Postage, 10c.

11564, Whitney's Song Offering; a companion to the Song Casket, and contains a selection of melodies throughout. Price each, 40c. Postage, extra, 10c.

11565, Whitney's Golden Folio for the cabinet organ, containing a choice variety of music, both vocal and instrumental, by well known authors. Price each, 40c. Postage, extra, 10c.

11566, Whitney's Silver Folio, a companion to the Golden Folio, arranged on the same order. Every piece a gem. Price each, 40c. Postage 10c.

11566½. Grand Army Songs. A valuable collection of war and camp songs, to which is added a selection of memorial songs and hymns for Decoration Day, etc.; choruses all arranged for male voices, organ or piano accompaniment; 100 pages, heavy paper covers. Price, 45c. Extra, by mail, 5c.

11567, *The Treasury of Song.* A mammoth collection of the very best vocal gems, both sacred and secular, selected from the works of the best composers. Every piece a favorite. A book of 550 pages; size, 10x7, handsomely bound in cloth. The largest collection ever put on the market. Regular price, $2.50. Our price, $1.25. Extra, by mail, 24c.

11568, Songs of Scotland, full sheet music size, containing 100 of the most popular Scotch Songs, with piano or organ accompaniment. Paper covers, 40c. Extra, by mail, 7c.

11569, Song Folio No. 4. This is the latest publication of this popular series of song collections. Contains over 100 popular songs with accompaniment for organ or piano. Price each, 40c. Extra by mail, 10c.

11570, Famous Comic Songs, the best collection of comic songs ever published. Contains 35 of the very latest, including "A Job Lot," "What a Difference in the morning," "Irish Spree," "I've Worked Eight hours To-day," "Mary and John," "Near It," "Sweet Katie Connor," "When You Wink the Other Eye," etc., etc. Words and music complete with piano and organ accompaniment. Price each, 45c. Extra, by mail, 8c.

11571, Choice Baritone and Bass songs. A collection of twenty-six of the latest and best songs for male voices with piano or organ accompaniment published by T. B. Harms, full sheet music size. Price each, 40c. Extra, by mail, 8c.

11572, Minstrel Songs, old and new, book of 214 pages, board covers, containing a collection of over 100 of the famous minstrel and plantation songs, including the most popular of the celebrated Foster melodies; arranged with piano or organ accompaniment, $1.25.

11573, Vocal Duet Folio. A rare collection of late and popular vocal duets for similar and mixed voices; 96 pages; full sheet music size. Price, 40c. Postage extra, 10c.

11574, College Songs. A collection of eighty new and popular songs (with music) sung in American colleges. This new and already widely used collection contains not only the college songs proper, but the light, comic songs one hears everywhere. It is brimful of fun, and can hardly be spared from any social party, where they are all musical. Price, paper covers, 45c. Extra, by mail, 8c.

11575, Male Quartette and Chorus Book by J. Herbert. A new collection of music for male voices designed for use in glee club, concert, college or home; contains 108 pieces. Board covers. Price, 55c. Extra, by mail, 8c.

11576, Musical Chatterbox No. 2 contains both vocal and instrumental music, every piece a popular favorite, choice, easy and medium piano pieces; beautiful songs for the young folks; just the collection for home; it contains, besides the music, eight beautiful illustrations. Weight 24 oz. Price, 40c. Extra, by mail, 8c.

11577, The Song Bouquet. A companion to the parlor bouquet, a beautiful collection of the latest popular songs, everything new, complete and unabridged. Size, 10x12½ in., 224 pages. Nothing like it ever before published. Price, 40c. Extra by mail, 8c.

11578, The "Maywood" Folio, a new collection of popular songs and instrumental music by George Schleifforth, 111 pages, every piece new and good. Price, 40c. Postage, 16c.

11579, "Recent Gems of Song," containing some of the most popular songs of the day. Price, 10c.

11580, The celebrated Dockstader Songster, containing 50 minstrel and variety songs, with words and music. Price, 8c. Postage, 2c.

11581, The Gem Songster. A fine collection of 200 pieces, including comic and patriotic songs, popular ballads and favorite Negro melodies. Price, paper covers, 15c. Postage, 5c.

Gospel Hymns.

11582, Consolidated, Nos. 1, 2, 3, 4. Large type words and music. 400 pages. Each, 75c. Per dozen, $7.72. Postage, 10c.

11583, Same as 11582, bound in ½ leather, red edges, words and music. Each, $1.50. Per dozen, $15.40. Postage each, 10c.

11584, Words only, Nos. 1, 2, 3, 4. Each, 20c. Per dozen, $2.15. Postage, 4c.

11582.

11585. Gospel Hymns, No. 5, with words and music. Board covers. Each, 30c.; per doz., $3.10; postage, each, 6c.

11586. Same as No. 11585, bound in limp cloth, very handsome. Each, 50c.; per doz. $5.40; postage, each, 6c.

11587. Gospel Hymns, No. 6, bound in boards. Each, 30c.; per doz. $3.10; postage, each, 6c.

11588. Same as No. 11587, bound in limp cloth, very handsome. Each, 50c.; per doz., $5.40.

11589. Just out. Nos. 5 and 6, combined. Words and music. Each, 70c.; per doz.; $7.00; postage, each, 8c.

11590. Same as 11589. Words only. Each, 22c; per doz., $2.30; postage, each, 4c.

11591. Gospel Choir, by Ira D. Sankey and James McGranahan; 128 pages, board covers. Each 40c.; per doz., $4.00; postage, each, 10c.

Instrumental Music.

11592. The Parlor Bouquet, companion to the "Song Bouquet," a fine collection of instrumental music, comprising new and sparkling gems and standard favorites. Every piece complete. Sheet music size, 224 pages. The Parlor Bouquet should adorn every piano in the land, and the low price brings it within the reach of all. Each, 40c; extra by mail, 10c.

11593. Whitney's Folio of Pearls, containing brilliant pieces for the piano, also pieces especially arranged for cabinet organ. 150 pages full sheet music size. Each, 40c.; extra by mail, 10c.

11594. Kinkel's Folio, Vol. 1, a rare collection of bright instrumental gems for young players, arranged for piano and organ. No better books for pupils can be obtained, and we especially recommend them to teachers. Price, 40c.; extra by mail, 10c.

11595. Kinkel's Folio, Vol. 2, containing pieces of an advanced order. Price, 40c., extra by mail, 10c.

MUSICAL GOODS DEPARTMENT.

11596. Gems of Strauss, containing 100 of this great composer's popular pieces, including waltzes, polkas, marches, etc., arranged for piano or organ, full sheet music size, paper covers. Price, **40c.**; extra by mail, **7c.**

11597. Whitney's "Folio Gems," a choice collection of recent composition, including marches, waltzes, polkas, schottisches, etc., by popular composers, 150 pages. sheet music size. Price each, **40c.**; extra by mail, **10c.**

11598. Whitney's "Folio Leaves," a companion to Folio Gems, containing same style of music (no duplicates), 150 pages. Price each, **40c.**; extra by mail, **10c.**

11599. Reed Organ Companion, composed of easy pieces for the reed organ, suitable for beginners, contains many useful hints on organ playing, fills a long-felt want for just such a volume as the "Companion," containing a collection of bright, pretty and pleasing pieces for the parlor or cabinet organ, 36 p'eces, bound in boards. Our price, **40c.**

11600. Famous Dance Music, a new collection of the very latest and most popular waltzes, polkas, marches, etc., by Waldteufel, Roeder, and others. arranged for piano or organ, full sheet size. Price **40c.**; extra by mail, **10c.**

11601. Parlor Dance Folio, contains choice collection of the latest dances; also the German, with quadrille calls, etc., arranged for piano or organ, full sheet music size, paper covers, just the book for parlor dancing. Price, **40c.**; extra by mail, **10c.**

SUPERB SOLOS.

11602. An instrumental book of 200 pages, containing the popular music of the day, arranged for piano or organ, with handsomely illuminated cover. Companion book to Superb Songs. Price, **40c.**; extra by mail, **11c.**

11603. Queen of Waltzes, a splendid collection of beautiful waltzes, every one a gem, nearly 100 pages, sheet music size. (Brainard's Dollar Library.) Price, **40c.**; extra by mail, **11c.**

11604. The "Monarch" Waltz Collection, 16 of the very latest and best waltzes, arranged for organ or piano. Published by T. B. Harms. Every one a favorite. Price each, **40c.**; extra by mail, **8c.**

11605. The Organ at Home, a fine collection of standard pieces, including polkas, marches, schottisches, and contra dances, especially arranged for the reed organ. Price, **40c.**; extra by mail, **10c.**

11566. Reed Organ Folio, a new collection of the best and most popular music of the day, arranged especially for the 5 octave organ. Over 60 pieces, full sheet music, paper covers. Each, **40c.**; extra by mail, **10c.**

11567. Melodies of the Gospel Hymns, Nos. 1, 2, 3, 4 consolidated. Arranged for the cornet by Hayslip, for use in Sabbath schools, gospel meetings, etc. A piano or organ played from the regular edition will agree perfectly with the cornet played from this. Price, paper covers, **$1.00**; extra by mail, **8c.**

11608. Gospel Hymns No. 5, arranged for the cornet, containing the melodies and altos of all the members. Price, paper covers, **80c.**; postage, **5c.** extra.

Orchestra Music.

11609. Favorite Dance Album, first series, arranged for orchestra of nine instruments, viz.: 1st and 2nd violin, cornet, clarionet, flute, viola, trombone, bass and piano; contains 11 pieces of assorted dance music, each piece new and good. Price, each book (except piano) **25c.**; Piano book, **35c.**; extra by mail, **3c.**

11610. Favorite Dance Album, second series, arranged for same instruments as No. 11609, contains 11 pieces choice dance music. Price. each book (except piano) **25c.**; Piano book, **35c.**; Extra by mail, **3c.**

11611. Beginners' Orchestra Journal, No. 1, by A. S. Bowman. Contains 25 easy and popular pieces of dance music arranged for orchestra of 8 instruments, viz: 1st and 2nd violin, cornet, clarionet, flute, trombone (either clef) bass and piano, each part separate. Price, each book (except piano), **25c.**; Piano book, **50c.**; Extra by mail, **3c.**

11612. Beginners' Orchestra Journal, No. 2, by A. S Bowman; 25 pieces dance music arranged for orchestra, same as No. 1, but contains a more diffi-

cult grade of music. Price, each book (except piano) **25c.**; Piano book, **50c.**; Extra by mail, **3c.**

11613. Popular Duets for violin and piano, No. 1. This is a new collection of the very latest music, including "Loves' Dreamland" Waltzes, Mendelsshon's "Wedding March," "Hornpipe Polka," etc., 84 pieces, 122 pages. Full sheet, music size, paper covers. Every piece a gem. Price each, **40c.**; postage **10c.** extra.

11614. Popular Duets for violin and piano, No. 2, contains a collection of still later music. Full sheet music size, 120 pages. These are the best collections ever put on the market in book form. Price each, **40c.**; postage **10c.** extra.

11615. Gems of the ball room, No. 1, by McCosh and others. A collection of 33 pieces of choice dance music, all kinds, arranged for orchestra of eight instruments, viz: 1st and 2nd violin, cornet, clarionet, flute, trombone, (double clefs), bass and piano, each part separate. Price, each book, (excepting piano), **50c.**; price, each book, in lots of 5 or more (excepting piano), **45c.**; prices piano book each, each, **$1.00.**

11616. Gems of the Ball Room, No. 2. A collection of the latest dance music, arranged for orchestra of eight instruments, same as Gems No. 1. contains 33 pieces, including the new military schottische "Berlin," "York," etc. Price, each book, (excepting piano), **50c.**; price, each book in lots of five or more (excepting piano), **45c**; price, piano books each, **$1.00.**

11617. Gems of the Ball Room, No. 3, arranged for same instruments as Nos. 1 and 2, and contains 33 pieces of new dance music, also some of the old "Contra" dances. Price, each book, (excepting piano), **50c.**; price, each book, in lots of five, **45c.**; price piano books, each **$1.00.**

11618. Gems of the Ball Room, No. 4, arranged for same instruments as the other numbers, contains 32 pieces of the latest and best dance music. Price, each book (excepting piano) **50c.**; price, each book (excepting piano), in lots of five, **45c.**; price piano book, **$1.00.**

11619. Gems of the Ball Room, No. 5; this is the latest edition of these very popular orchestral collections, and contains 32 piecss of the best new dance music. Arranged for same instruments as Nos. 1 and 2. Price, each book (excepting piano), **50c.**; price, each book (excepting piano), in lots of five, **45c.**; price piano books, **$1.00**; extra by mail, each **2c.**

There are no duplicates in Gems of the Ball Room and every orchestra leader should have the complete set.

11620. Echoes from the Ball Room. This collection contains everything in music essential to dancing. It includes the latest dances, also the old standards, 31 pieces, arranged for 1st and 2nd violin, cornet, clarionet, bass, flute, viola, trombone and piano. Price, each book (excepting piano), **50c.**; price, each book, in lots of five, **45c.**; price piano **$1.00.**

11621. Musician's Omnibus. A book containing 1,500 pieces, arranged for violin, consisting of waltzes, polkas, schottisches, galops, quadrilles, jig and clog dances, etc. Publisher's price, **$2.00**; our price, **$1.50.**

11622. Ryans 1050 Reels and Jigs, a very popular collection of lively music arranged for violin. Price each, **$1.50**; extra by mail, **12c.**

Brass Band Music.

11623. The Combination Band Book, arranged by McCosh, just published, and is already becoming very popular, as it contains 16 pieces of choice music for every occasion. "Marches," "Quicksteps," "Waltzes," "Polkas," "Overtures," etc., etc, Just the book for young bands. Arranged for full band of twenty pieces. Price, single book, each, **25c.**; set of six or more, each, **20c.**

11624. National Band Journal No. 1. Contains 8 pieces of music, including our national airs, together with the best of our grand old war songs, arranged for full band. Price, all parts, complete, **90c.**; postage, **4c.**

11625. The Ever Ready Band Books. A new collection of choice "Quicksteps," "Marches," "Waltzes," etc., by McCosh, Fox, Ruby and other composers, arranged for full brass band. Price single books, each, **25c**; set of 6 or more, each **20c.** Postage 4 cents.

11626. Sacred Band Journal, contains 10 familiar hymns arranged for full band. This journal is invaluable for Sunday playing, Sunday school picnics, concerts, etc. Price, all parts complete, **90c.**

READ OUR GRAND OFFER FOR CASH IN ADVANCE.

MUSICAL GOODS DEPARTMENT

Guitar and Banjo Music

11627, Hamilton's Banjo Folio. A splendid collection of beautiful banjo music, suitable for amateur or artist. Contains collections for solos and duet. Full sheets music size 40c. Postage 10 cents.

11628, "Banjoists' Budget," a grand collection of 50 jigs, hornpipes, reels, clog dances, walk-arounds, etc., etc., arranged and correctly fingered for the banjo, by A. Bauer. Best collection of banjo music published. Paper covers. Price 45c. Extra by mail 5 cents.

11629, Benjamin's Amateur Mandolin and Guitar Collections. No. 1 contains 13 easy and popular pieces, arranged for mandolin or violin with guitar accompaniment, also the piano accompaniment. Price 30c. Extra by mail 4 cents.

11630, The Royal Guitar Folio, one superior collection of the latest and best guitar music, both vocal and instrumental. Arranged in good style by the best professionals. Paper covers; each 40c. Extra by mail 10 cents.

11631, The Guitarist (vocal.) We confidently claim for this collection of guitar music a place at the head of all similar productions. It is not an instruction book, but a collection of the latest and best music with accompaniment for the guitar. Full sheet music size, bound in cloth. Price $1.10. Extra by mail 11 cents.

11632, The Guitarist (instrumental.) A collection of new and standard walzes, polkas, marches, etc., arranged for the guitar in the most artistic manner. Bound in cloth. Price $1.10. Extra by mail 11 cents.

Miscellaneous.

11633, The true Musical Directory, an invaluable book containing all the musical terms, their definitions, etc., now in use. Weight 3 ounces; 20c.

11634, The True Piano Tuner, containing concise instruction for tuning and regulating pianos. This useful little book will be welcomed by all amateurs who wish to know more about the structure and care of instruments. Price 25c. Postage 3 cents.

11635. Organ Voicing and Tuning, a thoroughly practical work on organ tuning, voicing and repairing. This book is illustrated and a careful study of it will obviate the necessity of send ng for a tuner every time your organ gets out of order. Each 25c. Postage 3 cents.

11636, Rudiments of Music, a concise and thoroughly practical course of instruction on the art of singing by note, prepared by J. R. Murray. Teachers' classes and individuals will find in the above inexpensive work every thing that is necessary to a complete understanding of the art of reading and singing by note. Each 10c. Postage 12 cents.

Instruction Books.

11637, Lebert & Stark Piano School, Parts 1.2 and 3; board covers, retail price per volume $2.00; our price per volume, $1.25. Postage 14 cents.

We have elegant plate editions of this celebrated school carefully edited and corrected. This work is endorsed by the greatest musicians, and is fast coming into popular favor.

11638, Karl Merz' Piano Method, complete. Publisher's price, $3.00; our price, $2.00. Postage 24 cents.

11639, Palmer's Theory of Music, a practical guide to the study of thorough bass, harmony and composition, and for acquiring a knowledge of the science of music in a short time with or without the aid of a teacher. Each 90c. Postage 5 cents.

11640, Richardson's New Method for Piano. Publisher's price, $3.00; our price, $2.10. Postage 28 cents.

11641, Root's New Musical Curriculum, complete and revised. Publisher's price, $3.00; our price, $2.10. Postage 28 cents.

11642, The Normal Music Hand Book, by Geo. F. Root. This work contains statements of elementary principles, short lecture, full method of teaching singing classes, elementary harmony and composition. Also a defining and pronouncing index of musical terms. Price, complete (five books in one), each $2.60. Postage 10 cents.

11643, Whitney's Improved Easy Method for the parlor organ. New and enlarged edition. This is a a new and attractive system by which the pupil may rapidly learn to play the organ. Besides a thorough course in music, this book contains a choice collection of vocal and instrumental pieces, progressively arranged, so that a careful study of each in their order will enable the student to correctly perform all the different styles of music. Publisher's price, $1.50. Extra by mail, 13 cents. Our price, 60c.

11644, Root's New Course in Voice Culture and Singing, by Frederick W. Root. This is a graded course, adapted to guide the young voice, correct the faults of mature singers, and develope the voice systematically. State whether it is wanted for male or female voice. Price, $1.40. Extra by mail, 10 cents.

11645, White's Method of Reed Organ. Publisher's price, $2.50. Extra by mail, 15 cents. Our price, 80c.

11646, Karl Merz's Modern Method for Reed Organ. Publisher's price, $2.50. Extra by mail, 18 cents. Our price, $1.25.

11647, Getze's Method for Reed Organ. Publisher's price, $2.50. Extra by mail, 16 cents. Our price, $1.00.

11648, Fifty Organ Voluntaries, composed and selected by F. W. Sudds, including service preludes, offertories, marches, etc., arranged for the pipe or reed organ: board covers. Extra by mail, 12 cents. Price each, $1.30.

11649, Maza's Complete Violin School. Publisher's price, $2.00. Extra by mail, 7 cents. Our price, 75c.

11650, Benjamin's Illustrated Violin Method. This is the latest publication in the way of a violin instructor, and is the best work for the beginner ever put on the market. It contains the complete elementary course, is profusely illustrated; also contains a collection of popular music; 79 pages sheet music size. Extra by mail, 5 cts. Each 50c.

11651, Wichtl's Young Violinist. Publisher's price, $2.25. Extra by mail, 10 cts. Our price, 80c.

11652, Henning's Practical School for Violin, complete with English and German text. Publisher's price, $1.50. Extra by mail, 14 cents. Our price, $1.00.

11653, Howe's Original Violin School. new and enlarged edition. Contains complete rules and exercises, together with a collection of over 450 pieces of every variety. Hundreds of old familiar airs never before published for violin. Extra large type and fine paper. Extra by mail, 4 cents. Each 40c.

11654, Howe's "Diamond" School for the Violin, contains complete instruction, full directions for bowing, and 558 pieces of dance music. Extra by mail, 4 cents. Each 45c.

11655, Student's Recreation. A magnificent collection of violin solos, with or without piano accompaniment. This work contains 12 well known popular airs, with variations arranged progressively from the 1st to the 7th positions. When necessary, the fingering as well as the bowing is marked, Price, violin part alone, paper covers, 45c. Extra by mail, 5 cents.

11656, Student's Recreation. Violin and piano, in one volume, paper covers. Extra by mail 12 cts. Price, 90c.

11657, Benjamin's Illustrated Method for the Mandolin, containing complete course in the rudiments of music, is fully illustrated and contains a choice collection of music, Extra by mail, 5 cents. Price, 50c.

11658, Howe's Army and Navy Fife Instructor, containing complete course of instructions. also calls, signals, and the complete camp and garrison duties as practiced in the United States army and navy, besides the National Airs and a large collection of marches, quicksteps, waltzes, etc., etc. Price each, paper cover, 40c. Extra by mail, 4 cts.

11659, Pepper's Universal Dancing Master. Prompter's Call Book and Violinists' Guide, This work is intended as a complete instructor in the art of dancing and prompting. It contains an elaborate description of the steps and figures used in the round, square and fancy dances, including the very latest, such as the "York," "Berlin," "Leemo," "German," etc., etc.; also an appropriate collection of music easily arranged for the violin and plainly marked for prompter's calls. Over 200 pages. board covers. Every violinist should have one of these books. Extra by mail, 14 cents. Price each, 80c.

11660, Wessenberg's Thorough Banjo. A new and standard method for banjo, containing a complete elementary course, besides a fine collection of solo and duet music; board covers. Price each, 90c. Extra by mail, 10 cents.

READ OUR GRAND OFFER FOR CASH IN ADVANCE.

MUSICAL GOODS DEPARTMENT.

11661. Carcassi's Guitar Method, complete $1.00. Extra by mail, 12 cents.

11662, Diagram School for the Guitar, by J. T. Rutledge. This is the latest, and without doubt the most complete, method for the guitar that has ever been offered to the public. It contains a thorough course of instruction, is profusely illustrated with diagrams of the finger board, showing all the positions, etc., besides a fine collection of music, bound in boards Publisher's price, $2.50, Extra by mail, 16 cents. Our price, **$2.10.**

11663, Ryan's True Mandolin Instructor. Publisher's price, 75c. Our price, **25c.**

11664, Ryan's True Zither Instructor. Publisher's price, 70c. Our price, **25c.** Extra by mail, 3 cts.

11665, Ryan's True Double Bass Instructor; publisher's price, 72c. Our price, **25c.** Extra by mail, 3c.

11666, Ryan's True Occarina Instructor; publisher's price, 75c. Our price, **25c.** Extra by mail, 3c.

11667, Ryan's True Harmonica Instructor; publisher's price, 75c. Our price, **25c.** Extra by mail, 3c.

11668, Arban's World Renowned Method for the Cornet, four books in one. This edition contains a complete method of instruction. Arban's 14 solos with variations. 60 beautiful duets for 2 cornets, and the art of phrasing, consisting of 100 operatic, classic and popular melodies. Every cornetist should have one. Extra by mail, 16 cents. Price, in paper binding, **$1.35.**

11669. Arban's World Renowned Cornet Method. in cloth binding, gilt letters. Extra by mail, 16c. Each, **$1.60.**

The following works by Sep. Winner are all 1893 edition, condensed and revised. Extra by mail, 2 cents:

11670, Winner's Instruction Book for Accordion; retail price, 25c. Our price, **12c.**

11671, Winner's Instruction Books for Organ; retail price, 25c. Our price, **12c.**

11672, Winner's Instruction Book for Violin; retail price, 25c. Our price, **12c.**

11673, Winner's Instruction Book for Guitar; retail price, 25c. Our price, **12c.**

11674, Winner's Instruction Books for Banjo; retail price, 25c. Our price, **12c.**

11675, Winner's Instruction Book for flute; retail price, 25c. Our price, **12c.**

11676, Winner's Instruction Books for Fife; retail price, 25c. Our price, **12c.**

11677, Winner's Instruction Book for Cornet; retail price, 25c. Our price, **12c.**

11678, Winner's Primary School for Accordion, Organ, Violin, Guitar, Banjo, Flute, Fife, Violoncello, Clarionet and Cornet. Not condensed; unabridged. (Specify for which instrument book is wanted.) Price per volume, **18c.** Extra by mail, 3c.

11679, Pepper's New Self Instructor for the Piccolo. Contains complete instructions for this popular instrument. Each, **45c.** Extra by mail, 4c.

11680, Instruction Book of Chords for the guitar. A new system of learning to play the chords of the guitar without notes or teacher. Each, **25c.** Extra by mail, 1c.

11681, Instruction Book of Chords for Banjo; publisher's price, 50c. Our price, **25c.** Extra by mail, 1c.

Gun and Sporting Goods

DEPARTMENT.

Limited space prevents our illustrating all the various Guns, Rifles, Revolvers, etc., that are made. We have endeavored to select the most desirable goods—those which offer the best value for the money, and such goods as we can furnish you for *less money* than you can possibly buy elsewhere.

☞ **WE HANDLE EVERYTHING** in the Sporting Goods line, including all the standard makes of American and imported hammer and hammerless shot guns, rifles, revolvers, gun implements, ammunition, leather and canvass goods, sportsmen's clothing, rubber goods, coats, decoys, tents and awnings, indian clubs, boxing gloves, etc., etc. **If you don't find what you want illustrated, WRITE FOR IT,** we can supply you with anything and everything in this line at the **lowest wholesale** prices.

☞ **ABOUT PRICES.** By a close comparison of our prices with those of other houses, you will find you can save money, yes, from 20 % to 70 % on any article in this line. Our goods are purchased in large quantities **for cash,** direct from American and European manufacturers, and we have based our selling price on the closest basis of profit consistent with first class goods. In calculating our profit, we have not had to figure any expense for **traveling salesmen, bad debts,** extensive newspaper advertising, etc., but have simply added to the actual net cost of the goods a close conservative profit for handling.

TERMS. We honestly believe our terms are far more liberal than any other concern, in fact there is no concern that will ship goods to anyone anywhere **on our terms,** but we know **our goods are the best, our prices lower** than others and that they are sure to please, consequently we are not afraid to ship to anyone anywhere on the most liberal terms.

WE SHIP C. O. D. BY EXPRESS, subject to examination, to anyone anywhere on the following conditions: **All Orders for Revolvers** amounting to **$2.00** or more will be sent to anyone anywhere **C. O. D.** subject to examination. **No Money in Advance.** You can examine the goods at express office and if found perfectly satisfactory pay the agent our price and express charges, **otherwise pay nothing.** All orders for **Revolvers** amounting to less than $2.00 must be accompanied by 50 cents (postage stamps taken). You can examine the goods at express office and if found satisfactory pay the express agent our price and express charges **less the 50 cents** paid in advance.

☞**WE SHIP GUNS** to anyone anywhere **C. O. D.** subject to examination, on receipt of **$3.00** as a guarantee of good faith, examine them at the express office and if found perfectly satisfactory pay the express agent our price and express charges less the $3.00 sent in advance. If not satisfactory, refuse it and we will refund your $3.00 less express charges. **All other goods in this line,** including ammunition, sportsmen's clothing, implements, etc., etc., will be sent to anyone by express C. O. D. subject to examination on receipt of one-fourth the amount of bill, the balance and express charges to be paid after you receive the goods.

HEAVY GOODS, such as shot, loaded shells, tents, decoys, boats, canvass goods, etc., should be sent by freight as the express charges are so very much higher. **Where goods are to be sent by freight Cash in full must accompany all orders.**

Special Offer for Cash Orders.

When you send cash in full **for a revolver** we will always **send you free** some nice, useful and valuable present.

When you send **cash in full for a gun** we will send you free a very fine complete set of reloading tools, consisting of one loader, one re-caper, one powder and shot measure and one shell extractor. Besides when you send cash in advance **you have no return express charges** to pay on money.

YOU TAKE NO RISK by sending cash in full with your order, as we **guarantee** everything to be found exactly as represented and entirely satisfactory, and if not found so you can return the goods and we will cheerfully refund your money.

Revolvers at Your Own Price.

WE SAY REVOLVERS AT YOUR OWN PRICE for the reason we have made our prices so low that all who receive this Catalogue will be **WONDERFULLY SURPRISED** how cheap revolvers can be sold. **FROM US YOU DONT PAY RETAIL PRICES, NOT EVEN WHOLESALE PRICES,** but merely a small percentage above the lowest price made by the different manufacturers.

DON'T FORGET OUR TERMS on Revolvers.

ALL ORDERS for Revolvers amounting to **$2.00** or more will be sent to any one any where by express C. O. D., subject to examination. **NO MONEY REQUIRED IN ADVANCE,** you can examine the revolvers at the express office, and if found perfectly satisfactory and exactly as represented, **PAY THE EXPRESS AGENT** our price, and **EXPRESS CHARGES,** and keep it; otherwise **PAY NOTHING** and the agent will return it at our expense. **ORDERS AMOUNTING TO LESS THAN $2.00,** must be accompanied by **AT LEAST FIFTY CENTS** (postage stamps taken,) as a guarantee of good faith, when we will ship the revolvers by express C. O. D., subject to examination. Examine it at express office, and if found satisfactory, **PAY THE EXPRESS AGENT** our price and express charges **LESS THE FIFTY CENTS** sent with order

A NICE PRESENT will be sent with every revolver when **CASH IN FULL** accompanies your order. **IT WILL PAY YOU** to send cash in full with your order, and get one of our nice presents. If you are not perfectly satisfied, **WE WILL CHEERFULLY REFUND YOUR MONEY.** All revolvers can be sent by mail when so ordered. Postage one cent per ounce. **IF YOU WISH REVOLVER SENT BY MAIL SEND CASH WITH YOUR ORDER,** and always send enough extra to pay postage. **REMEMBER,** you get a nice present with every revolver when cash in full accompanies your order.

NO. 29.
PRICE 52 CTS.
By mail extra 7 cts.

NO. 30.
PRICE 68 CTS.
Postage extra 10 cents.

DESCRIPTION. (No. 29.)—Vest pocket single shot pistol, nickel plated, wood stock, 2¼ in. barrel, weight 5 ounces, for BB and conical caps, and 22 caliber cartridges.

DESCRIPTION. (No. 30.) — Defender, wood stock, full nickel plated, plain cylinder, 7-shot, 22 caliber, rim fire long or short, 2¼ in. barrel, weight 7 ounces, safe and reliable.

$3.75 Buys a $7.00 Revolver

NEVER SOLD AT RETAIL FOR LESS THAN $7.00. AT OUR SPECIAL PRICE OF $3.75 they should be wonderful sellers. Besides our terms are so easy. It costs you nothing to see and examine the revolver. We will send it to any one, any where, C. O. D. subject to examination. **No money in advance.** Express collect. You can examine it at the express office and if found perfectly satisfactory and exactly as represented, pay the express agent **$3.75** and express charges. Otherwise pay nothing. If you wish the revolver sent by mail, postage paid by us, send 23 cents extra to pay postage. **WE SEND YOU A PRESENT** free if cash in full accompanies your order, and we always refund all money if goods do not prove satisfactory.

Description: HARRINGTON & RICHARDSON, Police Automatic, Safety Hammer, Double Action, Self-Cocking, Automatic Shell Extractor, Rebounding Locks, Fancy Rubber Stock, Full Nickel Plate.

5 Shot. 32 or 38 Caliber.

Center Fire.

Guaranteed as good a shooting revolver as there is on the market.

NO. 42.
PRICE, $3.75.

We Make a Special Price of $3.75.

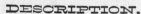

FRONTIER REVOLVER.

THE BEST REVOLVER FOR THE MONEY for frontier use.
LARGE, STRONG SHOOTING, and well finished.

OUR SPECIAL PRICE, $3.95.   *RETAILS EVERYWHERE AT $10..00*

No. 35.
PRICE, $3.95.

DON'T FORGET OUR TERMS. We ship to anyone anywhere C. O. D., subject to examination. No money in advance. You can examine the revolver at the express office, and if found satisfactory, pay the express agent our price and express charges, otherwise **PAY NOTHING.**

DESCRIPTION. Frontier Revolver, large 5½ inch barrel, 6-shooter, weighs 35 ounces, fine engraved rubber stock, 44 calibre, central fire, full nickel plated. This revolver is adapted to 44 calibre Winchester cartridges, so that a person having a rifle need not change ammunition, but can use same cartridges in both.

REMEMBER, when cash in full accompanies your order, you always get a nice present, and we always refund all money if goods are not perfectly satisfactory.

GRANDEST BARGAIN YET.

FREE TO EXAMINE DOUBLE ACTION AUTOMATIC POLICE REVOLVER $1.68 FOR HOME AND POCKET

$1.35 BUYS A $5.00 REVOLVER.

NO. 39. PRICE $1.35.

If you send cash with your order you get a nice present.

DESCRIPTION.—FOREHAND & WADSWORTH'S NEW DOUBLE-ACTION, SELF-COCKING REVOLVER, full nickel plated, fancy engraved rubber stocks, rifled barrels, safe, reliable and accurate. **REBOUNDING LOCKS** and all parts interchangeable. **WE GUARANTEE** this the best revolver in the market for the money, and the **GRANDEST BARGAIN EVER OFFERED. AT OUR PRICE** you can make money selling these revolvers. **NO RETAIL DEALER** can buy them at anything like the price we offer. **THEY ARE NEVER SOLD** for less than **$3.00** and often for **$5.00. OUR SPECIAL PRICE** for this revolver, 32 or 38 caliber, 5 shot, 12 ounces, is **$1.35. WE WILL SEND IT** C. O. D. to anyone on receipt of **50 CENTS** (postage stamps taken), balance 85 cents to be paid at express office. **THE BEST WAY** is to send cash in full, when we will send you a **NICE PRESENT.** We will ship by mail POSTPAID for 17 cents extra.

$3.45 Buys a $6.00 Revolver.

NEVER SOLD AT RETAIL FOR LESS THAN $6.00.

TERMS: C. O. D. TO ANY ONE, ANY WHERE. No money in advance. If found satisfactory pay the express agent $3.45 and express charges, **OTHERWISE PAY NOTHING. FREE.** A nice present if cash in full accompanies your order.

WE WILL SHIP by mail, post paid, on receipt of 23 cents extra to pay postage, **provided** cash in full accompanies your order.

Description. HARRINGTON & RICHARDSON IMPROVED AUTOMATIC, SHELL EXTRACTING, DOUBLE ACTION, SELF-COCKING REVOLVER (modeled on the Smith & Wesson pattern.) Guaranteed fully equal to the Smith & Wesson. Beautifully nickel plated, Rubber Stock. As accurate and durable as any revolver in the market. No better shooter made.

NO. 41.

Weight, 18 to 20 ounces. Five Shooter. 3¼ inch Barrel. 32 or 38 Caliber. Compare Our Prices with those of other houses. We can save you money on everything in this line. **We are reasonable and our terms are easy.**

PRICE, $3.45.

GREATEST BARGAIN EVER OFFERED

No such bargain ever offered before.

$3.38 BUYS A $7.00 REVOLVER.

GUARANTEED equal to any $7.00 revolver in the market.
GUARANTEED as good a shooter as any revolver in the market.
✳ ✳ ✳ ✳ **NO BETTER** material is put in any revolver.
NO BETTER workmanship in any revolver.
AS A LEADER to get new customers and to advertise our house,
WE MAKE THE PRICE $3.38.

OUR TERMS

are more liberal than any other house. **WE WILL SHIP** to anyone anywhere C. O. D., subject to examination. **NO MONEY** in advance. Examine the revolver at the express office, and if found satisfactory, pay the express agent **$3.38 and express charges,** and it is yours. **If you want it sent by mail, POST-PAID,** send cash in full, $3.38, and 23 cents extra to pay postage, and **you will get a present.**
We send a nice present with every revolver when cash in full accompanies order.

No. 43. PRICE,

$3.38

DESCRIPTION. FOREHAND & WADSWORTH REVOLVER, manufactured by the **Forehand Arms Co.**, Worcester, Mass. **The most wonderful bargain in a revolver in the market. Warranted by the manufacturers. Guaranteed by us.** Latest model, new improved, automatic shell extracting, self-cocking, rebounding locks, double action, simple and accurate, interchangeable parts (made from steel drop forgings). The frame is cast steel, no malleable iron about it. Fine polished nickel plated. Fancy ornamented rubber stocks. Length of barrel, 3¼ inches; weight, 17 ounces; entire length, 7¾ in.; **32 or 38 calibre; 5 shots.** Uses Smith & Wesson central fire cart'gs.

Our Special Price, **$3.38.**
Special Price with 5-in. Barrel, **$4.48.**

BUY THIS REVOLVER. It is the biggest bargain in the market; the greatest seller we have. **There is no better revolver made.**

COLT'S REVOLVERS.

THE SAME TERMS on Colt's Revolvers, C. O. D. to anyone anywhere, subject to examination. **No money** in advance. Examine them at the express office, and if found satisfactory, pay our price and express charges, **otherwise pay nothing,**
IF CASH IN FULL accompanies your order, **we send free** a nice present. Besides, we will ship any Colt's revolver by mail, postage paid, on receipt of 25c. extra to pay postage.

DESCRIPTION. Colt's New Pocket Revolver, 32 calibre, central fire, adapted to long and short Colt's C. F. cartridges, double action, self cocking, blued or nickel plated as desired, jointless solid frame, with simultaneous extractor. Weight about 14 ounces.

OUR SPECIAL PRICE.
32 calibre, 2½ or 3½ inch barrel........... $10.00
32 calibre, 6 inch barrel 11.00

COLT'S NEW POCKET 32 CALIBRE.

NO. 47. PRICE, $10.00

COLT'S ARMY MODEL 1892.

C. O. D. to anyone. No money in advance.

COLT'S ARMY MODEL 1892. 38 & 41 CALIBRES.

DESCRIPTION.

Colt's New Army Model 1892. Double action, self-cocking, jointless solid frame with simultaneous ejector. Blued or nickel plated, as desired. Weight 2 lbs., 6 shooter, 38 or 41 caliber, length of barrel 3, 4½ or 6 in. as desired. Our special price, **$12.00.**

No. 51. Price, $12.00.

SMITH & WESSON REVOLVER.

Terms: C. O. D. to anyone. No money in advance. If cash in full accompanies your order we will send free a nice present. If to be sent by mail send cash in full and 20 cents extra to pay postage.

NO. 45.

PRICE, $9.95.

DESCRIPTION Warranted genuine Smith & Wesson, manufactured by Smith & Wesson, Springfield, Mass. Self cocking, double action, automatic shell extractor, fine rubber stocks, full nickel plated or blued as desired.

OUR SPECIAL PRICES AS FOLLOWS:

32 Calibre, 5 Shot, 3 and 3½ inch Barrel, Best Double Action								$9 95
32 " " 6 inch " " " " "								11 00
38 " " " 3¼ " " " " " "								11 00
38 " " " 4 " " " " " "								11 25
38 " " " 5 " " " " " "								11 50
38 " " " 6 " " " " " "								12 00
44 Calibre, Winchester, 5 Shot, Cartridge, 4 inch Barrel, Best Double Action								13 00
44 " " " 6 or 6½ " " " " "								13 75
Extra for Ivory Stock, 32 or 38 Calibre								1 25
" " " 44 "								2 00
Extra for Pearl Stock, 32 or 38 Calibre								1 75
" " " 44 "								2 00

COMPARE THESE PRICES WITH ANY OTHER HOUSE.

Smith & Wesson Hammerless Revolver

Terms: C. O. D. to any one. No money in advance. If cash in full accompanies your order, we will send free a nice present. If to be sent by mail send cash in full and 20 cents extra to pay postage.

NO. 46.

PRICE, $10.95.

DESCRIPTION.

Genuine Smith & Wesson.

Made by Smith & Wesson, at Springfield, Mass.
Latest Style, New Model, Hammerless, Automatic Shell Ejector, Patent Safety Catch, Self Cocking, Rebounding Locks, Double Action, full Nickel Plated, or Blued, as desired.

——— OUR SPECIAL PRICES. ———

32 Calibre, 3 or 3½ inch Barrel.........$10 95	38 Calibre, 5 inch Barrel..............$12 50
38 " 3¼ " " 12 00	38 " 6 " 13 00
38 " 4 " " 12 25	

OUR RANGER FOR $1.25.

TERMS. Less than $2.00 at least 50 cents must accompany order, balance to be paid at express office. $2.00 or over, no money in advance. **If cash in full** accompanies your order you get a nice present.

DESCRIPTION.—Full nickel plated, fine engraved rubber stock, octagon barrel, rim fire. A good shooter and a fine arm.

NO. 46½.

PRICE, $1.25.

Our price, 22 caliber, $1.35; Our price, 32 caliber, $1.85

Colt's Army Double Action Revolver.

SENT TO ANY ONE C. O. D. subject to examination. No mondy in advance. **IF CASH IN FULL** accompanies your order **WE SEND FREE** a nice present.

DESCRIPTION.

COLT'S
ARMY DOUBLE ACTION
44 & 45 CALIBRES.
No. 49. Price $13.75.

Colt's Double Action, 44 and 45 caliber. **EVERY ONE WARRANTED.** Made by the Colt's Patent Fire Arms Co., Hartford, Conn. Colt's revevolver army size, double action, self-cocking, 44, 45 or 38 caliber. Winchester center fire, case hardened, nickel plated or blued as desired. Rubber stock with sliding spring ejector barrels, 4½, 5½ or 7½ in. long, as desired; 6 shooter. **Price $13.75.**

Colt's Double Action Revolver

C. O. D. to any one. No money in advance.

DESCRIPTION.

Colt's Double Action, Sliding Ejector. Every one warranted. **38 or 41 caliber, 6 shooter, center fire,** nickel plated or blued, as desired, 4½, 5 or 6 in. barrel as desired. Our special price, **$12.00.**

REMEMBER! You get a nice present, if cash in full accompanies your order.

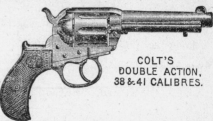

COLT'S
DOUBLE ACTION,
38 & 41 CALIBRES.

No. 50. Price $12.00.

COLT'S SINGLE ACTION ARMY, FRONTIER AND TARGET REVOLVERS.

Barrels 7½ inches, weight 2 pounds and 5 ounces. **C. O. D.** to any one; No Money in advance..

Description: Single action, six Shooter, rubber stock solid frame, the best quality and finish, warranted perfect and accurate in every detail. Nickel plated or blued, as desired. Barrel 7½ inches; length 12½ inches; 32, 38, 44, 41 or 45 caliber as desired.

No. 52, Our Special Price $12.95.

COLT'S NEW NAVY.

Made by the Colt's Patent Fire Arms Co., New Haven, Conn.

This revolver has been adopted by the U. S. Navy, and every one has to pass a rigid inspection.

COLT'S
NEW NAVY,
38 & 41 CALIBRES.

NO. 48. PRICE, $12.00.
Shows how ejector works.

DESCRIPTION.

Col''s New Navy, double action, self cocking, automatic shell ejecting revolver, nickel plated or blued as desired, rubber stock, beautifully finished, finest material, **length** about 12½ inches, 6-shooter, weight 2 pounds, 3, 4½ or 6 inch barrels as desired, 38 or 41 calibre as desired. **OUR SPECIAL PRICE, $12.00. C. O. D.** to anyone. **No money in advance. A nice present sent you,** if cash in full accompanies your order.

COLT'S NEW NAVY,
38 & 41 CALIBRES.

NO. 48. PRICE, $12.00.
Shows same revolver closed.

Single Barrel Breech Loading Shot Gun for $5.95

TERMS. C. O. D. subject to examination to anyone anywhere on receipt of $3.00, balance, $2.95, and express charges to be paid after you see and examine it. **If you send cash in full with order we will send you free a fine set of reloading tools.**

DESCRIPTION.

Walnut stock, pistol grip, Scott top lever break, blued, rolledsteel barrel, choke bored, rebounding lock, center fire, checkered patent fore end, fancy butt plate, 30 or 32 inch barrel, 6½ to 7½ pounds. 12 guage, each, $5.95; 16 guage, each, $5.95.

NO. 1. PRICE, $5.95. ORDER BY NUMBER.

Forehand & Wadsworth Single Barrel Breech Loading Shot Gun for $6.90.

Made by the Forehand Arms Co. at Worcester, Mass., and guaranteed one of the best single guns made. **Retails for $12; we sell it at $6.90.**

C. O. D. to anyone on receipt of $3.00; balance, $3.90, and express to be paid after you examine it. **If cash in full accompanies your order** you get FREE a fine set of reloading tools.

DESCRIPTION.

F. & W. top snap break, fine walnut stock, pistol grip, rebounding locks, snap fore end, nicely checkered, solid block strikers, choke bored, finest blued steel barrels, 12 guage, 30 or 32 inch barrel; 7 pounds. Price, $6.90.

NO. 2. PRICE, $6.90. Order by number.

CAN YOU MATCH IT FOR $6.95

Our Special Price is $6.95.   It Retails for $12.

You can examine it at your near t express office by sending $3.00 as a guarantee of good faith; the balance, $3.95, and expres charges to be paid after you get the gun. **You will get free a complete set of re-loading tools if you send cash in full with your order** and we will refund your money if you are not perfectly satisfied.

Remington Semi Hammerless Single Barrel Breech Loading Shot Gun.

HANDSOME AND WELL MADE.

DESCRIPTION

The Remington Semi-Hammerless Single Barrel Breech Loading Shot Gun, top lever break, the best break made, blued steel barrels choke bored, side cocking lever, case hardened frame and butt plate, pistol grip stock, re-

NO. 3. PRICE, $6.95.
Order by number.

bounding lock. The material finish and shooting qualities are the same high standard as the Remington double barrel guns. Every gun is warranted perfect and a strong shooter. They are all put to a test before leaving the factory and none are allowed to go out until a perfect patern has been shown.

You take no risk in buying the old and reliable **Remington.** 12 guage only; 30, 32 and 34 inch barrel, 6 to 6½ pounds. **Our special price $6.95.**

The Best Hammer Single Barrel Gun Made.

Made by the Crescent Fire Arms Co.

Retails at $15.

Our Special Price, $7.65.

Compare our prices with those of other houses. You will find our prices below all others. **Consider our terms:** C. O. D. to any one on receipt of $3, balance to be paid at express office. **FREE—** a full and complete set of reloading tools if cash in full accompanies your order.

NO. 4. PRICE $6.75.
Order by Number.

DESCRIPTION.—This single barrel breech loading Shot Gun we guarantee the best in the world for the money. Fine walnut stock, pistol grip, improved fore-end nicely checkered, rebounding lock, plated frame, fine twisted steel barrel, choke-bored, self acting shell extractor, center fire, Scott's best top lever break. Guaranteed as good a shooter as any 12-guage double barrel gun made. Central fire using Paper or Brass shells; 30 or 32 inch barrel, 6¼ to 7½ pounds; 12 guage only.

Hammerless Single Barrel Breech Loader,

Made by the FOREHAND ARMS CO.

The Finest, the Best single barrel breech loading shot gun made. **Retails everywhere at $20 and upwards. OUR SPECIAL DRIVE PRICE, $12.35.**

NO. 5. PRICE, $12,35.
Order by Number.

TERMS.—C. O. D. to anyone on receipt of $3.00, balance $9.35, and express charges to be paid after you have received and examined the gun. WE SEND FREE a fine complete set of reloading tools if cash in full accompanies your order, and always refund money if you are not thoroughly satisfied.

DESCRIPTION.—Best, Safest, Most Durable, single barrel shot gun made.. Top snap break, pistol grip nicely checkered and finished, patent snap fore-end, automatic action, with an absolute safety-catch to lock the trigger to prevent accidental discharge, simple in construction, perfectly safe and made of the very best material, choke bored, finest twist steel barrel, using brass or paper shells, center fire, 12 gauge, 30 inch barrel, weight 7 pounds.

We **Guarantee** the shooting qualities of this gun fully equal to any 12 guage gun made.

Winchester Repeating Shot Guns

Six Shooter. Retails at $25. Our Price, $16.88.

OUR TERMS.—The same on all shot guns, C. O. D. to any one on receipt of $3.00, balance payable at express office.

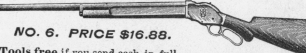

NO. 6. PRICE $16.88.

A nice set of Reloading Tools free if you send cash in full with your order. **Money refunded if you are not satisfied.**   Order by number.

DESCRIPTION.—No better shooting gun made. The barrel can be examined and cleaned from the breech. The magazine and carriers hold five cartridges, which with the one in the chamber, makes six at the command of the shooter. The forward and backward motion of the finger lever, which can be executed while gun is at shoulder, throws out empty shells, raises a new cartridge from magazine, and puts into the barrel. The gun is then ready to be fired. Finest quality rolled steel barrels, case hardened frame and pistol grip, walnut stock. All guns are full choked, and no gun will be sent out that will not make a perfect target. The standard gun will have a stock 12¼ inches in length and 2⅜ inches drop, any variation from standard length or drop will be charged for extra.

    12 guage, 30 or 32 in. barrel, weight 7 3-4 lbs.   Our special price, $16.88.
    10 guage, 30 or 32 in. barrel, weight 9 lbs.   Our special price, $16.88.

The BEST GUN MADE for ducks, chickens, partridges, etc., as you can fire much more rapidly than with any double barreled gun, besides the penetration of these guns is simply wonderful.

Latest Repeating Shot Gun Made.

JUST PUT ON THE MARKET. MODEL OF 1893.

Retails at $25.00. Winchester Repeating Shot Gun. Shoots 6 Times. **Our Special Price $16.88.**

NO. 7. PRICE, $16.88.
Order by number.

We will ship C. O. D. to anyone anywhere on receipt of $3.00 as a guarantee of good fiaith, examine the gun at express office and if found satisfactory pay the express agent the balance, $13.88, and express charges, otherwise pay nothing and the agent will return it to us and we will refund your $3.00 less express charges.

You get a present of a fine and complete set of reloading tools if you send cash in full with your order.

DESCRIPTION.—Best gun made for ducks, chickens or partridges, no stronger shooting gun made, has wonderful penetration and makes a perfect patern. Operated by sliding fore arm below the barrel. When the hammer is down the backward and forward motion of this slide unlocks and opens the breech lock, ejects the cartridge or fired shell and replaces it with a fresh cartridge. The construction of the arm is such that the hammer cannot fall, or the firing pin strike the cartridge until the breech lock is in place and locked fast, while the hammer stands at the full cock notch, the gun is locked against opening. In this position the firing pin must be pushed forward to open the gun; when the hammer stands at half-cock, the gun is locked both against opening and pulling the trigger.

To load the magazine turn the gun with the guard upwards, lay the cartridge on the underside of the carrier and push it into the magazine.

Finest quality, patent rolled steel barrels, fine selected walnut stock, pistol grip; length of stock 13 inches, drop of stock 2¾ inches, weight 7¾lbs, shoots six times, 12 guage only, 30 or 32 inch barrel. **Our Special Price $16.88.**

This gun is simple in construction, very few parts and not liable to get out of order, most rapid action made, choke bored to do the best shooting possible.

New Model Spencer Repeating Shot Gun.

OUR SPECIAL PRICE $27.65. RETAILS AT $40.00.

Six Shooter, Single Barrel, Latest Model. Can be taken apart to pack.

We will send this gun to anyone C. O. D. subject to examination on receipt of $3.00, balance, $24.65, and express charges, to be paid at express office. **A present** of a fine complete set of reloading tools will be sent with every gun where cash in full accompanies order. **NO.8.** Order by number

PRICE, $27.65.

DESCRIPTION.—The magazine is located under the barrel and will hold five cartridges. Fine Genuine Damascus barrels, fine selected Italian walnut stock, pistol grip, handsomely checkered, beautifully finished throughout and is far superior to any double barrel shot gun in precesion and penetration. Has few parts and is solid and substantial, can be used as a single loader and cartridges in magazine held in reserve. 30 and 32 inch barrels, 7¾ to 8¼ pounds, 12 guage.

Compare our prices with those of other houses. **Consider our terms. We can save you money.** Can we have your trade?

DOUBLE BARREL BREECH LOADING SHOT GUN FOR $6.68.

Retails for $15. Never sold at

WE SEND FREE a fine complete set of reloading tools if cash in full accompanies your order.

wholesale for less than $20. Our price is and it will be sent to anyone C. O. D. subject to examination on receipt of $3.00 as a guarantee of good faith, the balance, $3.68, and express charges to be paid after you have received the gun. **$6.68**

NO. 9.
PRICE, $6.68.
Order by number.

DESCRIPTION
The celebrated Lefaucheux action, no stronger action made, guaranteed the best gun of this make in the market, double barrel, blued decarbonized steel barrels, back action lock, checkered grip, bottom lever, automatic shell ejector, 30 or 32 inch barrel. 12 guage, weight 7¼ to 8¼ lbs, our special price, **$6.68**; 10 guage, weight 8¼ to 9¼ lbs., our special price, **$6.68**; 16 guage, 30 and 32 inch barrel, **$7.45.**

The World is Ours on Guns.

WE LEAD ALL OTHERS. NONE CAN MEET OUR PRICES.

Our Special Slaughter Price, $8.69

NO ONE ON EARTH CAN MEET IT.

How we make the price:
We import these guns direct, every gun is a direct blow at monopoly. The cost in Belgium, the import duty and an extremely low profit FOR US and US ONLY, is all you pay.
THE RESULT is you buy a gun for less than one-half the retail price, 40 per cent. cheaper than other houses advertise, and FAR BELOW the price your retail dealer pays.
WE MAKE IT EASY for you to buy from us for we send any gun C. O. D. subject to examination on receipt of $3.00, the balance to be paid after you get the gun.
WE DO MORE, we send you free with every gun a fine complete set of reloading tools *if cash in full accompanies your order.*
WE DO MORE, *we guarantee every gun*, and if you are not perfectly satisfied we refund all your money on the return of the gun to us.

DESCRIPTION.—Special Complete Double Barrel Breech Loader, top lever, snap action, rebounding back-action locks, walnut stock, checkered grip and foreend, case hardened lock plates and mountings, automatic shell ejector, blued steel barrels.

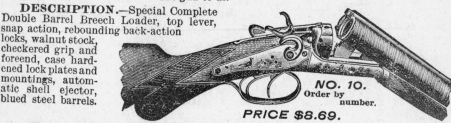

NO. 10.
Order by number.

PRICE $8.69.

12 guage, 30 or 32 inch barrel, 7¼ or 8¾ lbs. - - - - Our special price, $8.69.
10 guage, 30 or 32 inch barrel, 8½ or 9¼ lbs. - - - - Our special price, 8.69.

$10.75 Buys a $20.00 Gun.

We will send the gun C. O. D., subject to examination, to anyone anywhere, on receipt of $3.00, as a guarantee of good faith, the balance $7.75. and express charges to be paid after you receive the gun. **If you are not satisfied,** return the gun and we will refund your $3.00 less express charges.
A PRESENT of a complete set of reloading tools will be sent you, if cash in full accompanies your order

You take no risk. We guarantee every gun to be exactly as represented, and if not found so, we will cheerfully refund your money.

NO. 11.
Order by number.

PRICE $10.75.

DESCRIPTION.
Fine laminated steel twist finish barrels, back action, rebounding locks, pistol grip stock, fancy butt plate, patent fore end beautifully checkered and finished, large firing pins, top snap break.

12 guage, 30 or 32 inch barrels, 7¼ to 8¼ lbs.   Our Special Price, - - $10.75
10 guage, 30 or 22 inch barrels, 8½ to 9¼ lbs.   Our Special Price, - - 10.75

We aim to save you money on everything in this line. Compare our prices with those of other houses, and judge for yourself.

Look Well Before You Buy.

We can save you 25 to 100 per cent. on everything in the Gun and Sporting Goods line. Everything at greatly reduced prices, and at terms and conditions never before offered. **This Gun at $12.95** is 25 per cent be- low wholesale price and far below any retail dealers price. DON'T BUY guns, shells, ammunition and sporting goods at retail. YOU THROW AWAY your money. Study our prices, consider our terms, and *GIVE US A TRIAL ORDER.*

DESCRIPTION.
Complete bar lock, top snap break (the best made,) fine twist finish steel barrels, rebounding hammer, strong extension rib, pistol grip, selected walnut stock finely checkered, patent fore end, large strong firing pins, fancy rubber butt plate. 12 guage, 30 or 32 inch barrel, 7¼ to 8½ lbs. Our special price, **$12.95.** 10 guage, 30 or 32 inch barrel, 8½ to 9½ lbs. Our special price, **$12.95.** **Remember,** if you send cash in full with your order, WE SEND YOU FREE a complete set of reloading tools.

NO. 12. PRICE $12.95.
Order by number.

A GREAT DRIVE at $13.65.

Many imitate us, but none furnish the same gun at the same money. **They can't do it.** This gun, like all foreign made guns, *WE IMPORT DIRECT FROM EUROPE.* We buy them in BELGIUM from the very best makers at the lowest price for cash, pay the import duty, and add the smallest profit possible, consistent with a safe business, and **That's what you pay.** We make the terms easy. C. O. D. to any one on receipt of $3.00, balance to be paid after you examine the gun.

CLEANING OUTFIT—
a complete set, sent free if you send cash in full with your order.

DESCRIPTION.—
SPECIAL COMPLETE BACK ACTION, double-barrel, breech loader, Scott patent top lever brake, fine rebounding bar locks, polished insides, pistol grip, oiled walnut stock, fine checkered grip and fore end, case hardened locks, plates and mountings, laminated steel barrels, large head firing pins, extension rib, low circular hammers out of sight, patent snap fore end, will balanced, well made, finely finished locks and action. The best gun for the money ever put on the market. 12 guage, 30 or 32 inch barrel, 7¼ to 8¾ lbs. Our special price, **$13.65.** 10 guage, 30 or 32 inch barrel, 8½ to 9¾ lbs. Our special price, **$13.65.**

NO. 13. PRICE $13.65.
Order by number.

Consider our Special Offer for cash in advance.

$12.95 and $16.35 for a T. Parker Gun

Your Choice, Damascus or Steel Barrels:
Lamanated Steel Barrels, $12.95.
Royal Damascus Steel Barrels, 16.35.

FREE, a complete set of reloading tools if cash in advance accompanies your order.

C. O. D. to anyone on receipt of $3.00 as a guarantee of good faith, balance to be paid at express office.

DESCRIPTION.—T. PARKER.
This is a genuine Belgium T. Parker double barrel breech loading shot gun and the finest gun in the market for the money. Scott top brake, bar rebounding hammers, extension rib, pistol grip, patent fore end, matted rib, circular hammers, engraved lock plate and action. 12 guage, 30 or 32 inch barrels, 7¼ to 8½ lbs; 10 guage, 30 or 32 inch barrels, 8½ to 9¾ lbs.

NO. 14.
PRICE $12.95 & 16.35.
Order by number.

Our special price with Lamanated Steel Barrels, - - - - **$12.95**
Our special price with fine Royal Damascus Steel Barrels and beautifully engraved and ornamented trimmings throughout - - - **16.35**

PRIZE MACHINE GUN.

NO BETTER SHOOTING GUN MADE.

Everything about it is first-class. Top Lever Brake, Extension Rib, Bar action Matted Rib, Etc.

NO. 18.

PRICE

$19.75.

ORDER BY NUMBER.

DESCRIPTION.—Although we make our price far lower than other houses, this gun combines all the latest improvements, and all the advantages in shooting qualities of the highest priced guns made. The parts are interchangeable and are finished in the best manner. The gun is closely fitted, working smooth and easy. In elegance and durability it is equal to the most celebrated guns of English and American make. The barrels are soldered by a special contrivance and patented machine, and soldering is done entirely with copper. By this process, strength, rigidity and perfect boring are secured. The uniform shooting qualities of these guns are their greatest recommendation, and their style and finish are unsurpassed.

Top lever, fine Twist Barrels, Bar Locks, Rebounding **New Style Circular Hammers** (below line of sight) Double Bolt, Elevated Extension Rib, Pistol Grip, Patent Fore End, Solid Plungers, **Matted Rib,** fancy ornamented Rubber Butts.

12 gauge 30 or 32 inch barrel, weight 7¾ to 8½ lbs.
10 gauge 30 or 32 inch barrel, weight 8¾ to 10 lbs.

OUR TERMS always the same, C. O. D. to anyone on receipt of $3.00 balance, $16.75 to be paid at express office if satisfactory.

A PRESENT of a complete set of reloading tools will be sent you if you send cash in full with your order.

The Improved Baker Gun for $19.95

Retails everywhere at $30.00 to $40.00.

JUST SEE HOW MUCH WE CAN SAVE YOU!!

Manufactured by the Baker Forging and Gun Company, Batavia, N. Y. **Not fancy, but a good one.** The makers claim for this gun, Even challenge any equal it for plicity.

pattern, powerful shooter, and gun in the market to durability and sim-
DESCRIPTION.—
Best English twist barrels, extension rib, checkered pistol grip, English walnut stock, rubber butt plate, low circular hammer, solid striker, r e b o u n d i n g

NO. 20, PRICE $19.95.
Order by Number.

locks, top snap break, interchangeable parts, choke bored (unless otherwise ordered). No better shooting guns at any price. A plain, well balanced, neatly finished gun, made of best materials. Compensating fore-end cannot get loose and shaky in hinge joint. In fact just the gun for business, at a moderate price. EVERY GUN WARRANTED.

The manufacturers guarantee the New Baker to shoot equal to any gun made, and should any part fail through defect in material or workmanship, they agree to replace the same **free of charge.** 12 guage, 30 and 32 inch barrels, weight 7¼ to 9 lbs. Our price, **$19.95.** 10 guage, 30 and 32 inch barrels, weight 8¼ to 11 pounds. Our price, **$19.95.**

We have the Baker gun in Damascus barrels beautifully finished and engraved, and handsome in design at **$28.75. Terms alike on all guns,** C. O. D. to anyone on receipt of $3.00, balance to be paid after the gun is received. **Complete set of reloading tools free** if cash in full accompanies your order.

A GREAT BARGAIN AT $18.60

C. O. D. subject to examination to anyone on receipt of $3.00, balance to be paid after you receive the gun.

This Gun Retails at $30.00.

Our Drive Price, $18.60.

FREE.—A complete set of reloading tools if cash in full accompanies your order.

DESCRIPTION.
Fine Lamanated Steel Barrels, top snap brake, rebounding bar locks, solid plungers, low circular hammers, tapered extended matted rib, snap fore end, English walnut pistol grip stock, checkered and engraved, fancy rubber butt plate. left barrel full choked, right barrel modified choke. 10 guage, 30 and 32 inch barrel, weight 8¾ to 10¼ lbs.; 12 guage, 30 and 32 inch barrels, weight 7½ to 9 lbs.

NO. 15.
PRICE, $18.60. Order by number.

We want your trade on everything in this line and we will save you money on everything you buy.

A WONDERFUL BARGAIN.

Genuine C. G. BONEHILL GUN for $19.90.

Never before offered at anything like our price. And our terms are fair, alike on all guns. C. O. D. to any-one on receipt of $3.00, balance to be paid at ex-press office.

Re-loading Tools.—A complete set if cash in full accompanies your order.

PRICE, $19.90.
NO. 16. Order by number.

We Guarantee everything exactly as represented and if you find it different at any time return the goods and we will refund your money.

DESCRIPTION—Fine lamanated steel barrels, top snap break, rebounding bar locks, solid plungers, low circular hammers, tapered extended matted rib, double bolt, snap fore end, English walnut pistol grip stock, checkered and engraved, rubber butt plate, left barrel full choked, right barrel modified choke. 12 guage, 30 and 32 inch barrel, weight 8 to 9lbs; 10 guage, 30 and 32 inch barrel, weight 9 to 10 lbs.

We carry everything in stock. We can supply you with anything in this line at great-ly reduced prices.

GENUINE C. G. BONEHILL. New Model 1891.

This Gun retails at $40.00.   **WE SELL IT AT $23.95.**

JUDGE our prices, by comparison, compare our prices with those of any other concern, wholesale or retail, then you will know the difference, then you will know how much you are saving by sending your orders to us.

OUR TERMS are reasonable. You couldn't expect us to do more. We will send the gun on receipt of $3.00, the balance to be paid after you get the gun.

THE COMPLETE set of reloading tools will be sent free only to those who send cash in full with their order.

DESCRIPTION.
Very Finest Laman-ated Steel Barrels, nicely finished and per-fectly bored, **full choke.**

No. 17.

PRICE, $23.95. Order by number.

"Doll's Head" extension rib, rebounding bar locks, latest pattern low circular hammer (out of line of sight), solid block striker, double bolt, both lumps through frame, elevated (mat-ted) rib, fancy rubber butt plate, finely checkered extra quality oil-finished walnut stock, pistol grip, checked hand, and Deeley & Edge patent fore end, choke bored, 12 guage, 30 and 32 inch barrel, weight 7½ to 9 lbs.; 10 guage, 30 and 32 inch barrel, weight 9 to 10 lbs. **For Long Range Shooting** this gun cannot be excelled. We have received many unsolicited testimonials from prominent sportsmen who have used this gun and would have no other kind.

$19⁸⁵ Buys a Genuine Remington Gun

New Model Remington Double Barrel Breech Loading Shot Gun.

This Gun Retails at $30.00 to $40.00.

NO. 21.

PRICE, $19.85. ORDER BY NUMBER.

At Our Price, $19.85,

YOU SAVE FROM $10 TO $20.

SEND US $3.00, and we will send the gun to you by express C. O. D. subject to examination; balance to be paid after you receive the gun. **SEND US $19.85** and we will send you free with the gun a complete set of reloading tools.

DESCRIPTION.—Manufactured by the Remington Arms Co., Ilion, N. Y. The very latest improved model, top lever brake, extension rib, rebounding bar locks, large head strikers, patent fore end. All have pistol grip and all are choke bored. Every gun is carefully and rigidly tested before leaving the factory and satisfaction is guaranteed. Length.—12 guage, 30 and 32 inches, weighs 7¼ to 9 lbs.; 10 guage, 8½ to 10 lbs. The barrels of the **Remington** guns are choke bored on the best principle, and the parts are all interchangeable, only the best material and wormanship are used in the construction of these guns and there are no better shooters at any price, or more desirable guns.

We furnish the Remington in several grades as follows: **Grade 1,**—Fine decarbonized steel barrels, walnut stocks, 10 or 12 guage, pistol grip; just as good a shooter as Damascus, at **$19.85. Grade 2,**—Twist barrels and a little more fancy than Grade 1, **$22.85. Grade 3,**—Damascus steel barrels and finely finished throughout, **$24.35.** ☞The decarbonized steel barrels used in Grade 1 are made by the Remington Co. and are a very high grade of soft steel and will stand as much wear and hard shooting as the other grades, and not more liable to rust and as easily kept bright inside. **We Recommend Grade 1**, at $19.85, and further, we honestly believe our prices are below all competition.

The New Ithaca Gun for $23.45

No one pretends to meet our prices on guns. THEY CAN'T DO IT. We have many advantages and give our customers the benefit.

WE SAVE YOU MONEY

on anything in this line and always ship to any one **C. O. D.** subject to examination, on receipt of $3, balance to be paid at express office.

NO. 22.

PRICE, $23.45.

FREE.—The complete set of reloading tools, if cash in full accompanies your order.

DESCRIPTION.

Manufactured by the **ITHACA GUN CO.**, Ithaca, N. Y., a **GREAT DUCK GUN,** and wonderful gun for long range shooting. Made of the best materials, simplest and best locks, low hammers, top lever swinging over them when cocked, self compensating, taking up wear at every point. Never get loose and shaky. Matted rib, and all have walnut pistol grip finely checkered stock, case hardened lock plates and blued mountings. All guns are choke bored to shoot the closest pattern. Only the best English twist and Damascus steel barrels are used. All have fancy rubber butt plate, all have top lever, all have extension rib, all are choke bored. **EVERY GUN WARRANTED.**

We furnish these guns in either 10, 12 or 16 guage, best English twist or Damascus barrels as follows:

10 guage, 30 or 32 inch barrels, weight 8½ to 11 lbs.
12 " 30 or 32 " " " 7½ to 10½ "
16 " 28, 30, 32 " " " 6¼ to 7½ "

OUR SPECIAL PRICE for BEST ENGLISH TWIST Barrels, any guage or weight.................................. **$23.45**

OUR SPECIAL PRICE for FINE DAMASCUS STEEL Barrels, any guage or weight.................................. **$35.65**

For long range shooting and big game, a 10 guage Ithaca has no superior.

CHEAPEST GUN ON EARTH. ≡≡≡ BEST GUN ON EARTH.

Nothing like it ever offered for the money.

GUARANTEED equal to any gun made, **English** or American, in shooting qualities, workmanship and mechanical finish. **Pattern and Penetration** guaranteed equal to any gun made. In fact it is the **greatest value for the money ever offered.**

OUR SPECIAL PRIZE MACHINE GUN.

OUR SPECIAL PRICE, $22.75, WORTH $35.00.

For ducks, geese, chickens, partridge and such game it can't be beat. **It's the greatest bargain we have to offer,** and if you are intending to purchase we want you to see and examine this gun before buying.

WE WILL SEND YOU ONE, C. O. D. subject to examination, on receipt of $3.00. You can examine it at the express office, and if found satisfactory and **the most wonderful** bargain you ever saw, pay the express agent the balance, **$19.75,** and express charges, and it is yours. **If not satisfactory,** return it, and we will return your $3.00.

A COMPLETE set of reloading tools will be sent you free if you send cash in full, and your money refunded if you are not satisfied.

DESCRIPTION.

Choke bored to make closest pattern possible (unless otherwise ordered), Scott's patent top lever break (the best break made), elevated extension rib, bar action, matted rib, very finest twist

No. 19. *PRICE, $22 75.*
Order by Number.

barrels (warranted), bar locks, rebounding, **new style circular hammer** (below line of sight), double bolt, pistol grip, patent fore-end, solid plungers, fancy ornamented rubber butt plate.

We furnish this gun in either 10 or 12 guage at same price, $22.75. Barrels either 30 or 32 inches. 12 guage weighs from 7¾ to 8½ lbs; 10 guage weighs from 8¾ to 10 lbs.

Nothing has been spared to make this gun equal to the very best in shooting qualities and durability, and we honestly believe it is **the grandest bargain** in the market.

IMPROVED ITHACA HAMMERLESS GUN FOR $33.65.

BOTTOM. Thats where we put our prices, and at bottom prices we hope to merit your trade. **OUR TERMS ARE EASY.** We send any gun to any one anywhere, C. O. D., subject to examination, on receipt of $3.00, balance to be paid at express office.

WE SEND FREE, a full set of reloading tools if cash in full accompanies your order.

WE GUARANTEE every gun to be exactly as represented, and if not found so, we

NO. 23.

PRICE, $23.65.

cheerfully refund your money. **IT IS NOT NECESSARY** for us to say much about **THE ITHACA GUN,** as they are too well known to need any comment from us. There is no better shooting gun made. For long range, hard shooting; they can't be beat.

DESCRIPTION. — Latest Improved **Ithaca Hammerless Double Barrel Shot Gun,** bored for nitro and black powder. Barrels can be put on and taken off, same as a hammer gun, whether gun is cocked or not. Locks are rebounding, automatic safety, can be changed to independent by the touch of the thumb, for rapid firing. All have pistol grip, all have extension rib, all choke bored, all finely finished and greatly improved for this year. All have matted ribs. **THE STUB TWIST** barrels used on these guns are better than lamanated or cheap Damascus barrels. We furnish these guns in either 10, 12 or 16 guage as desired.

We furnish any guage or weight at the same price

	guage						weight	
12	guage,	30 or 32 inch barrels,	weight	7½	to	9¼	lbs.
10	"	30 or 32 "	"	"	8¼	to	11	"
16	"	30 or 32 "	"	"	6½	to	7¼	"

OUR PRICE for Gun with FINE ENGLISH STUB and TWIST BARRELS, $33.65.
OUR PRICE for Gun with DAMASCUS STEEL BARRELS, and extra fine finish throughout, $39.75.

The Improved Lefever Hammerless Gun.

LATEST PATTERN.   MODEL OF 1893.

RETAILS EVERYWHERE AT $75.00 AND UPWARDS.

We make the Price $43.10. and send to any one C.O.D. subject to examination on receipt of $3.00, balance to be paid after you receive the gun. **FURTHER WE SEND YOU FREE,** a fine and complete set of **RELOADING TOOLS,** if cash in full accompanies your order.

NO. 25.

PRICE, $43.10.

DESCRIPTION. The Lefever is a well balanced, symetrical and finely made gun, of highest grade, and has an unexcelled record for pattern and penetration. Compensated action to take up wear at all points. Trigger pull regulated by a screw

without removing locks, Engine turned rib, all guns bored on the taper system, all warranted good shooters, and latest models. All have Damascus barrels and matted ribs. **WE FURNISH** these guns in 8, 10 or 12 guage. 8 guage is a special gun, and is only made to special order. 10 guage, 30 or 32 inch barrels, weight 9 to 10 lbs. 12 guage, 30 or 32 inch barrels, weight 7¼ to 9 lbs. **WE FURNISH** these guns in five grades, as follows:—

Grade G—Damascus Barrels.			Fine Engraved, 10 or 12 guage,				$ 41.25
" F—	"	"	Better	"	"	"	57.40
" E—	"	"	Fine	"	"	"	75.00
" D—	"	"	Finer	"	"	"	93.75
" C—	"	"	Very Finely	"	"	"	112.50

Still finer grades to order at $200.00, $250.00, $300.00, $350.00 and $400.00. 8 guage guns, any quality, $10.00 extra.

Colt's New Hammerless Breech-Loading Gun

MADE BY THE COLT'S PATENT FIRE ARMS CO., HARTFORD, CONN.

LATEST IMPROVED MODEL.

$59.75 BUYS AN $80.00 GUN.

SAME TERMS. C. O. D. to any one on receipt of $3.00, balance $56.75 and express charges payable at express office, if found satisfactory. **If not satisfactory,** the gun will be returned at our expense, and your $3.00, less express charges, refunded you.

DESCRIPTION.

No better shooting gun made. This gun ranks among the very highest priced guns made in America. Simple, few parts to get out of order. All have pistol grip, all are choke bored, all have extension rib. In fact, in the manufacture of

RELOADING TOOLS. A complete set sent free as a present if cash in full accompanies your order.

No. 27.

PRICE, $59.75. **ORDER BY NUMBER.**

these guns nothing but the best of material is used, and nothing has been left undone.

Our $59.75 Gun has fine Damascus steel barrels, neatly engraved, fancy imported walnut stock, pistol grip, fancy rubber butt plate, fancy checkered grip and fore-end, case hardened lock plates and actions, and finely finished.

12 Guage, 30 and 32 inch Barrels, 7½ to 9 lbs.,	-	OUR PRICE, $59.75.
10 Guage, 30 and 32 inch Barrels, 8½ to 10 lbs.,	-	OUR PRICE, $59.75.

OUR $94.75 GRADE. Has very finest Damascus steel barrels, very elaborate engraving, decorating and finish throughout. **10 or 12 Guage. Our Special Price, $94.75.**

All have the best improved automatic safety, and every gun is a beauty.

The Famous L. C. Smith Hammerless Gun.

(Made by the Hunter Arms Co., Fulton, N. Y.)

Every Gun warranted by the Manufacturers

For long distance shooting they can't be beat. Every gun guaranted to make a perfect pattern, and the penetration is something wonderful.

There is no better gun made. Our Special Price,

$41.95

DESCRIPTION
All have top levers, all are choke bored, all have pistol grip, every gun warranted.

NO. 26.

PRICE, $41.95. Order by number.

WE FURNISH them in all grades, as follows:

NO. I QUALITY. Fine stub twist steel barrels, imported walnut stock, pistol grip, checkered grip and fore end, rubber butt plate, case hardened lock-plates and actions. No fancy engravings, but well made and desirable, and just as good a shooter as a higher price gun. 10 or 12 guage, 30 and 32 inch barrel, 7¼ to 10¾ lbs. **OUR PRICE $41.95.**

NO. 2 QUALITY. Good Damascus steel barrels, imported walnut stock, pistol grip, checkered and engraved, finely finished. (The regular $80.00 grade.) 10 or 12 guage, 30 or 32 inch barrel, weight 7¼ to 10¾ lbs. **OUR PRICE $57.20.**

NO. 3 QUALITY. Finer finished throughout, elaborately engraved and decorated. Very finest Damascus steel barrels. **OUR PRICE $69.75.**

The L. C. Smith Ejector Gun.

QUALITY AI. Very finest Damascus steel barrels, very fine imported English walnut stock, elaborate checkering and engraving, choke bored on the multiplied system, warranted close, hard shooter. 10 or 12 guage. **$116.75.**

The Smith Hammerless

has won more prizes than any other gun in the market, and for durability, finish and shooting qualities, it has no superior.

OUR TERMS are the same on all guns, C. O. D. to any one on receipt of $3.00, balance to be paid at express office. **IF CASH IN FULL** accompanies your order, you get an elegant **SET OF RELOADING TOOLS AS A PRESENT.**

REMEMBER, everything we sell is guaranteed, and if not found satisfactory **RETURN THE GOODS AT OUR EXPENSE,** and we will refund your money.

Double-Barrel Muzzle-Loaders $5.35 TO $9.60

OUR TERMS. C. O. D. subject to examination to anyone anywhere on receipt of $3.00, balance to be paid at express office. **If not satisfactory,** return the gun at our expense, and we will refund your $3.00, less express charges.

This is a Picture of our $8.95 Muzzle Loader.

NO. 54.

DESCRIPTION.

PRICE, $5.35 TO $9.60.

A. Imitation twist barrels, back action locks, plain breech, guage 11, 12, 13, 14.
OUR PRICE, $5.35

B. Genuine twist barrels, oiled walnut stock, patent breech, back action locks, checkered grip, 12 to 14 bore, 7 to 8¼ lbs., 30 to 34 inch barrel. A good, safe and reliable gun.
OUR PRICE, $7.95

C. Lamanated steel barrels, back action lock, oiled walnut stock, patent breech and break-off, checkered pistol grip. **OUR PRICE, $8.95**

D. Genuine twist barrels, bar lock, walnut stock, checkered pistol grip, guage 11, 12, 13 and 14, length of barrels 30 to 34 inches, weight 7½ to 8¼ lbs. **OUR PRICE, $9.60**

The Well-Known Parker Gun

LATEST IMPROVED. See that your Parker Guns are stamped "Parker Bros," All others are **ONLY IMMITATION** and only cheap grade of common guns.

OUR PRICES: $39.75 TO $73.75 ACCORDING TO GRADE, FINISH, ETC. . . . .

The PARKER Gun is too well known to need much description from us. Their reputation the past years is enough. **ANY SPORTSMAN** can tell you what the **Parker Gun** is.

OUR TERMS: C.O.D. to anyone on receipt of $3.00, balance to be paid after you receive the gun. **IF YOU SEND CASH IN FULL** you get a handsome **SET OF RELOADING TOOLS FREE.**

NO. 28.

PRICE, $39.75 TO $73.75.

DESCRIPTION.—All Parker Guns are hard shooters and so warranted, there are none better, all choke bored and all have all modern improvements. Accompaning each gun is a target made by the gun at the factory. Parker guns are 30 or 32 inch barrels, 12 guage, weight 7¼ to 9 lbs; 10 guage, weight 8¼ to 10 lbs.

OUR PRICES FOR PARKER HAMMER GUNS.

Parker Gun, very fine twist barrels, 12 guage, - - **$39.75**; 10 guage, **$43.75**
Parker Gun, very fine Damascus barrels, 12 guage, - **57.50**; 10 guage, **62.50**

OUR PRICES FOR PARKER HAMMERLESS GUNS.

All Parker Hammerless Guns; will have fine Damascus steel barrels, all very fine imported walnut stocks, handsomely engraved and finished.

Grade E. H., 10 guage, regular wholesale price $85.00; our price, - - **$62.75**
Grade G. H., 12 or 16 guage, regular wholesale price $80.00; our price, - **57.50**
Grade D. H., 10, 12 or 16 guage, regular wholesale price $100; our price, - **73.95**

We can furnish these guns to order with any finish, any length or drop of stock wanted. Prices quoted on application.

BOYS' MUZZLE LOADER, SINGLE BARREL.

OUR SPECIAL PRICE, $3.35. RETAILS AT $7.00.

A GREAT BARGAIN.

CASH IN FULL must accompany your order for this gun. If you don't find it satisfactory, return it at our expense, and we will immediately refund your money.

No. 53. PRICE, $3.35. Order by Number.

DESCRIPTION. Boys' muzze loader, single barrel, wood ramrod, blued barrel, a good, safe gun. small nipple for GD or EB caps, 31 inch barrel, 4¼ pounds, 16 guage.

Our Leader of Leader of Leaders

IT BEATS THEM ALL.

$29.75 BUYS A REGULAR $50.00 GUN
$34.75 BUYS A REGULAR $80.00 GUN

THE GRANDEST BARGAIN EVER OFFERED.

ON THIS GUN — **WE MAKE SPECIAL TERMS, WE MAKE SPECIAL CONDITIONS.**

It will Cost you Nothing

to see and examine this gun. **DON'T SEND US ONE CENT,** until after you see and examine it, and after you have seen and examined it, **DON'T PAY A CENT** unless you find the gun exactly as represented, and entirely satisfactory. But **REFUSE IT,** and let the agent return it **AT OUR EXPENSE.** If you find it satisfactory, and the **GRANDEST BARGAIN** you ever saw, **EQUAL TO ANY GUN MADE,** yes, in many respects superior to any other gun, pay our price and the express charges, and the gun is yours.

Five Years' Guarantee. WE GUARANTEE EVERY ONE OF THESE GUNS FOR 5 YEARS.

The New Forehand Arms Co.

HIGH GRADE HAMMERLESS.

KING OF THE FIELD. MONARCH OF THE SWAMP.

12 GUAGE ONLY. — **12 GUAGE ONLY.**

SOMETHING ABOUT THIS WONDERFUL GUN.

NO. 24.
Price $29.75 & $34.75

PERFECT PATTERN guaranteed. Penetration simply wonderful. **IN THIS GUN** you have a long distance, hard shooter, a fine duck and goose gun, and get a 12 guage gun, weighing

7 to 8 pounds, adapted to all kinds of shooting. **IT MUST BE SEEN** to be appreciated. **IT HAS MANY ADVANTAGES** over other hammerless guns, far safer, more convenient. The barrels can be taken off and put on again without cocking the gun, and when cocked the hammer can be let down gradually and without the full force of the blow. These are improvements found on no other gun. **IT IS VERY SIMPLE IN CONSTRUCTION, HAS MANY LESS PIECES** than any other hammerless gun, and the tipping of the barrels and cocking of the gun is very easy indeed. **NO BETTER MATERIAL, NO BETTER WORKMANSHIP,** in a $200.00 gun. **ALL FULL PISTOL GRIP,** fine imported Italian walnut stock, finely checkered and engraved. We furnish the Forehand Hammerless Shot Gun in two grades. The $29.75 grade has fine imported twist barrels. The $34.75 grade has finest quality Damascus barrels; 12 guage only, barrels 28, 30 and 32 inches long.

YOU GET MORE for your money in this than any other gun made, and in our anxiety to give our customers the greatest value possible, **WE URGE** you to select this gun, and as an inducement, **WE MAKE SPECIAL TERMS. NO MONEY IN ADVANCE,** but ship C. O. D. to any one subject to examination. If satisfactory, after examination, pay the express agent our price and express charges.

YOUR PRESENT will be a fine **COMPLETE SET OF RELOADING TOOLS,** if you send cash in full with your order. **WE WILL REFUND** your money, every cent, promptly and cheerfully if you are not perfectly satisfied with the gun.

AIR RIFLES and BELONGINGS

OUR PRICES on all **Air Rifles** are far below all others, and our assortment is complete. **CASH IN FULL** must accompany all orders for these guns. If not found perfectly satisfactory, you can return them at our expense, and we will refund your money.

THE CHICAGO AIR RIFLE. NO. 56.

DESCRIPTION. PRICE, 89c.

The Chicago Air Rifle shoots regular air gun darts and bullets. Entire length over all, 33 inches. Price each, 89 cents. It will shoot a common BB shot 40 rods, and kill small game at 50 feet. No powder or caps, no noise, not dangerous to handle. By its use a person can become a perfect shot. It costs but one cent to shoot 100 times. The barrel, air chamber and all working parts are made of brass and steel. The stock is maple, nicely stained and varnished, representing rosewood. The air chamber and barrel are of mandrel drawn brass, accurately bored and polished. The barrel has a perfect device for holding the ball tight to place. The plunger or piston is of the very best of steel, and made specially for this purpose. All parts are made to stand continued usage and not get out of order.

Price, 98 Cents.

THE KING AIR RIFLE. NO. 57.

All metal, nickel plated, shoots BB shot. Length of barrel, 19 inches; length over all 34 inches; weight 2 lbs. The King Air Rifle shoots common BB shot accurately and with sufficient force to go through ¼ inch soft pine. The barrel and all working parts can be easily removed by simply unscrewing the metal cap on front part of gun, a feature when seen that must be appreciated, as it makes the removal of shot that are sure to become lodged in all muzzle-loading air guns, a very simple and easy matter. Each gun is sighted with movable sights, and packed in a paper box, with sample package of shot and directions.

The DAISY AIR RIFLE.

Price, $1.00.

Made entirely of metal, latest improved pattern; length of barrel, 19 inches; total length, 33 inches; weight, 2½ lbs.

NO. 58.

THE DANDY REPEATING AIR RIFLE. NO. 59.

Shoots 45 times without reloading. Full **PRICE, $1.75.** length 29 inches. Nickel plated barrel, 16 inches long. One movement in loading. Nice light colored hardwood stock, shoots BB shot, cocking lever works similar to those on the Winchester repeating rifle.

MATCHLESS REPEATING AIR RIFLE. NO. 59½.

PRICE, $1.75.

Shoots 65 times without reloading. Length of gun, 36 in.; weight, 3 lbs. 4 oz.; weight packed ready for shipment, 5 lbs. The Matchless for BB shot. The accompanying cut gives a good idea of the shape of the "Matchless" rifle. The stock is made of black walnut, nicely finished. The barrel is made of heavy brass tubing, nickel plated with block nickel.

PRICE, $6.95

QUACKENBUSH IMPROVED NICKEL PLATED AIR GUN.

No. 1.—$\frac{21}{100}$ caliber: full length, 36 inches; weight, 4½ **NO. 60.** lbs. Shoots darts and slugs. Each gun is neatly boxed, with six patent darts, six paper targets, 100 slugs, together with a combined claw and wrench. The gun can be instantly taken apart for the convenience of carrying in trunk or valise.

DARTS, SLUGS, ETC.

$\frac{17}{100}$ Darts for Quackenbush Rifle, per doz. . . . . . 50c.		$\frac{17}{100}$ Felted Slugs for Quackenbush Rifle, per 100, . . . 15c.
$\frac{21}{100}$ " " " " " . . . . . 50c.		$\frac{21}{100}$ " " " " " . . . . 15c.
BB Shot, 5-lb. bag 50c.;	25-lb. bag . . . . . $2.00.	

FLOBERT RIFLES.

$1.65 BUYS A $3.00 RIFLE.

NO. 53. PRICE $1.65.

DESCRIPTION.—This rifle is made for BB caps, has side extractor, bright mountings, varnished stock, 22 inch barrel, weighs about 4½ lbs.

OUR SPECIAL PRICE $1.65

NO. 54.

Remington System

PRICE, $2.85. **Flobert Rifle.**

Our Special Price $2.85

DESCRIPTION—Remington system, for 22 caliber (rim fire) five cartridges, polished barrel, Remington action, scroll guard, light barrel, rifled, oiled stock, dark mountings, fine checkered pistol grip, 22 inch barrel, weighs about 4½ pounds.

Warnant System Flobert Rifle.

NO. 55. **PRICE $3.35.**

DESCRIPTION.—Warnant, or Springfield action, polished heavy barrel, rifled, pistol grip, fancy butt, scroll guard, carved stock, dark mountings, 24 inch barrel, weight about 6 lbs. Uses 22 caliber rim fire cartridges. **OUR SPECIAL PRICE, $3.35**

The Quackenbush Junior Safety Rifle.

$4.25 Buys an $8.00 Rifle.

DESCRIPTION.

The **Quackenbush Junior Safety Rifle** has a fine steel nickel-plated

NO. 115. PRICE $4.25.

skeleton stock which can be easily detached for carrying in small space. Nickel plated barrels, finely rifled. Whole length 33 inches. Weight 4 pounds, 22 inch caliber, rim fire only. **SAFE**, accurate and reliable, and **Fully Warranted** by the manufacturers. Our special price, $4.25.

Quackenbush's Safety Cartridge Rifle.

$5.00

BUYS A $10.00 RIFLE.

C. O. D. to anyone on receipt of $3.00, balance payable at express office.

NO. 116. PRICE $5.00.

DESCRIPTION.—Fine steel barrel, automatic cartridge extractor, and adjustable rear sight. Stock is black walnut, handsomely finished, and so fastened to the barrel that the two may be easily and quickly separated, making the arm handy to carry in a trunk, valise or package. The barrel and parts are well and durably nickeled, except the breech block, which is case hardened in color. Whole length 33 inches, 18 inch barrel, weight about 4½ lbs., 22 caliber, for regular rim fire, "BB" or long and short cartridges. Plain open sights, as shown in cut.

Our price with 18 inch barrel, $5.00.   Our price with 22 inch barrel, $5.85.

Winchester Rifles.

ON RIFLES our terms are exactly the same as on all other guns: C. O. D. to anyone **ON RECEIPT OF $3.00** as a guarantee of good faith, the balance and express charges to be paid after you receive the rifle. **IF NOT SATISFACTORY** return the rifle to us and we will refund your money, less express charges.

A NICE PRESENT will be sent you if cash in full accompanies your order. **YOU TAKE NO RISK.** If the rifle is not in every way satisfactory **RETURN IT AT OUR EXPENSE** and we will refund your money.

DESCRIPTION.

Although this rifle is a recent production it has become almost as famous as the "Winchester Repeat-

NO. 61.

PRICE, EACH, $10.13.

er" and stands in the "front rank" with the very best target rifles of this and other countries. **THIS GUN** has the old Sharp's breech block and lever and is as safe and solid as a Sharps. The firing pin is automatically withdrawn at the first opening movement of the gun and held back until the gun is closed. The hammer is centrally hung, but drops down with the breech block when the gun is opened and is cocked by the closing movement. It can also be cocked by hand. This arrangement allows the barrel to be wiped and examined from the breech. In our line everything has been done to make the gun pleasing to the eye. All of these guns have case hardened lock plates and dark walnut stock, other styles and caliber made to order.

EVERY RIFLE WARRANTED perfect and accurate. These rifles are not made with double trigger. The set locks are adjustable by a little screw in rear of trigger and can be set to pull as desired or not used at all. Pushing the trigger forward places it in the "hair pull" notch, same as working a double trigger. All rifles have sporting rear sights.

Our Special Prices:

	EACH.
No. 61. 22 caliber (rim fire), BB caps, short or long cartridge, 24 inch octagon barrel, weight 7 lbs., (plain trigger)	$10 13
No. 62. 22 caliber (rim fire) BB caps, short or long cartridge, 26 inch octagon barrel, weight 7 lbs, (plain trigger)	11 00
No. 63. 32 caliber, (rim fire) extra short, short or long cartridges, 26 inch, octagon barrel, weight 7 lbs , (plain trigger)	10 13
No. 64. 22 caliber (center fire), 26 inch octagon barrel, weight 7 lbs, (plain trigger)	10 75
No. 65. 25 caliber, (center fire) 28 inch octagon barrel, weight 7 lbs, (plain trigger)	10 13
No. 66. 32 caliber (center fire), 28 inch octagon barrel, weight 8¼ lbs, (plain trigger)	10 40
No. 67. 32-40 caliber (center fire) 30 inch octagon barrel, weight 9 lbs, (plain trigger)	10 13
No. 68. 32-40 caliber, (center fire) 30 inch octagon barrel, weight 9 to 9½ lbs, (set trigger)	12 13
No. 69. 38 caliber (center fire) 28 inch octagon barrel, weight 8½ lbs, (plain trigger)	11 00
No. 70. 38-55 caliber (center fire) 30 inch octagon barrel, weight 9 lbs, (plain trigger)	10 13
No. 71. 38-55 caliber (center fire) 30 inch octagon barrel, weight 9 lbs, (set trigger)	12 75
No. 72. 40-60 caliber (center fire) 30 inch octagon barrel, weight 9½ lbs, (set trigger)	12 75
No. 73. 40-82 caliber (center fire) 30 inch octagon barrel, weight 9½ lbs, (plain trigger) long range	10 13
No. 74. 40-90 caliber (center fire) 32 inch octagon barrels, weight 9½ to 11 lbs, (set trigger)	14 75
No. 75. 45-70 caliber, (center fire), 30 inch octagon barrel, weight 9½ lbs, (plain trigger), long range	11 00
No. 76. 40-65 caliber (center fire) 30 inch octagon barrel, weight 9¼ lbs, a good target rifle	11 00
No. 77. 45-90 caliber (center fire) 30 inch octagon barrel, weight 9½ lbs, long range	11 00

Special guns made to order. Prices quoted on application.

Winchester Rifles. MODEL OF 1873

No. 78—Winchester Sporting Rifle (Model 1873) Repeating, round barrels, and length of barrel 24 in., center fire, 44 caliber, 15 shots, weight 8¼ lbs. **$10.94**

No. 79—Octagon Barrel, length of barrel 24 inches, center fire, 44 caliber, 15 shots, weight 9 lbs..................................... **11.86**

No. **80—Octagon Barrel,** 24 inches, center fire, 15 shots, weight 9 lbs., 38 cal. **11.86**

No. **81—Round Barrel,** 24 inches, 15 shot, weight. 8¼ lbs., 38 caliber.......... **10.94**

No. **82—Octagon Barrel,** 24 inches, 15 shots, weight 9 lbs., 32 caliber......... **11.86**

No. **83—Round Barrel,** 24 inch, 15 shots, weight 8¼ lbs., 32 caliber,.......... **10.94**

No. **84—Octagon Barrel,** 24 inch, 25 shot, weight 9 lbs., 22 caliber, (Rim fire,) short only.. **11.86**

Sent C. O. D. to any one on receipt of $3.00, balance payable at express office.

WINCHESTER RIFLES, MODEL 1886.

No. 85—Octagon Barrel, 26 inches or under, 9¼ lbs., 40-82 caliber, 260 grain bullet, 8 shot................ **$14.18**

No. 86—Round Barrel, 40-82 caliber................................ **13.16**

No. **87—Octagon Barrel,** 26 inches or under, 9¼ lbs., 45-70 caliber, 405 grain bullet, using a regular (government cartridge) 9 shot........................ **14.18**

No. **88—Round Barrel.** 26 inches or under, 9 lbs., 45-70 caliber................ **13.16**

No. **89—Octagon Barrel,** 26 inches or under, 9¼ lbs., 45-90 caliber, 300 grain bullet, 8 shot.. **14.18**

No. **90—Round Barrel,** 26 inches or under, 9 lbs., 45-90 caliber................ **13.16**

No. **91—Octagon Barrel,** 26 inches, 9¼ lbs., 38-56 caliber, 8 shot............. **14.18**

No. **92—Round Barrel.** 26 inches, 9¼ lbs., 38-56 caliber....................... **13.16**

No. **93—Octagon Barrel,** 26 inches, 9¼ lbs., 40-65 caliber..................... **14.18**

No. **94—Round Barrel,** 26 inches, 40-65 aliber............................... **13.16**

No. **95—Octagon Barrel,** 26 inches, 50-110 caliber, Express................... **14.18**

The standard length of barrel will be 26 inches. Guns taking the 45-70 cartridge will have the Sporting Leaf Sight, and all other the Sporting Rear Sight. Each gun will be accompanied by a cleaning rod FREE. Set Triggers, $2.25 extra.

Winchester 22 Caliber Repeating Rifle.

MODEL '90.   "TAKE DOWN."

DESCRIPTION.

Winchester Model, 1890, Repeating Rifle. Loads and ejects the shell by the sliding motion of the forearm. All 24 inch Octagon barrels, and 5½ pounds weight. **New Model** stock and barre., can be separated by removing a screw.

No. **96—For** 22 caliber, Rim fire short, only 15 shot. Our special price........... **$9.72**

No. **97—For** 22 caliber; Rim fire long, 12 shot. Our special price............... **9.72**

SENT C. O. D. to anyone, anywhere, on receipt of $3.00, balance to be paid at express office after the gun is received and examined.

Stevens' Open Sight Rifle.

C. O. D. to anyone on receipt of $3.00, balance payable at express office.

DESCRIPTION. Stevens' Open Sight Rifle, 22 caliber, rim fire, short cartridges; or 25-20 caliber center fire, as desired Weight, 6½ to 7½ lbs for 24 inch barrel; 7½ to 8 lbs. for 28 inch barrel.

No. **102.** Our special price for 24 inch barrel....................... **$12.00**

No. **103.** Our special price for 28 inch barrel....................... **13.25**

Remington Rifle.

NEW MODEL NO. 4.   SINGLE SHOT

DESCRIPTION.—Remington Rifle No. 4, oiled walnut stock, case hardened frames and mountings, open front and rear sights. As finely rifled as any rifle in the market, and made of the very best rifle material. Perfectly accurate, and every one warranted. **No better or longer range rifles made** of these calibers. Warranted as represented.

No. **123**—Our special price, 22 caliber, rim fire, 22½ inch octagon barrel, weight 4¼ lbs., rifle butt. A fine little rifle and an accurate shooter................ **$5.25**

No. **124**—Our special price, 32 caliber, rim fire, 24 inch octagon barrel, weight 4½ lbs., rifle butt.. **5.25**

REMINGTON FINE TARGET RIFLE.

No. **125**—Rim fire, 22 caliber, using "B. B." cap, or 22 long or short cartridge, 24 inch octagon barrel, weight 5¼ to 6 pounds. Our special price............ **8.72**

No. **126**—Rim fire. 32 caliber, using long or short rim fire cartridges, 28 inch octagon barrel, weight 5¾ to 6 lbs. Price..................................... **8.75**

Remington No. 3, Long Range Target Rifle.

THEIR BEST RIFLE.   *OVER 1,000,000 SOLD.*

No other Single Shot Rifle has had such wonderful sale. **LATEST MODEL GUARANTEED.** Every rifle warranted by the manufacturers. **THIS RIFLE** is especially designed for long range hunting, and target purposes. It has a solid breech block, with direct rear support, rebounding hammer, so that it always stands with the trigger in the safety notch, rendering premature discharge impossible. This rifle makes a flatter tragectory than other rifles, and is unequaled for **TARGET** and sporting use. **NO BETTER** or more accurate rifle in the market. All have side lever, oiled walnut stock, pistol grip checkered, rebounding hammer, case hardened frame and mountings, open front and rear sights, full octagon barrels. Set trigger $2.75 extra.

No. **127**—32-30 caliber, 30 inch, 8½ to 9 lbs. Price.................................. **$14.75**

No. **128**—32-40 caliber, 30 inch octagon barrel, 8¼ to 9 lbs. Sure at 200 yards.... **14.75**

No. **129**—38-55 caliber, 30 inch octagon barrel, 8¾ to 9½ lbs. Sure at 100 to 500 yds. **14.75**

No. **130**—40-65 caliber, 30 inch octagon barrel, 4¾ to 10 lbs. weight. sure at 150 to 600 yards.. **14.75**

No. **131**—40-90 caliber, 32 inch octagon barrel, 10 to 11 lbs. weight. Long range. **16.65**

No. **132**—45-70 caliber, 30 inch octagon barrel, 10 lbs. Sure at 20 to 1000 yards... **14.75**

OUR REMINGTON RIFLES are the best and every rifle is fully warranted. **YOU KNOW OUR TERMS:**—C. O. D. to any one on receipt of $3.00, balance to be paid at express office. **IF YOU SEND CASH IN FULL** with your order, a nice present will be sent you. **YOU TAKE NO RISK** for we will cheerfully refund your money if you are not perfectly satisfied.

Merwin, Hulburt & Co.'s Rifle and Shot Gun Combined.

NO. 135.

PRICE, $13.50.

The above illustration shows rifle, also shot gun barrel. **OUR PRICE** includes full combination, making a rifle and shot gun complete in one arm. **THE BARRELS** are interchangeable, and can be easily taken apart by withdrawing a thumb screw, which, being tapered, takes up all wear that any gun is subject to, and makes it the most solid single barrel breech loader. **THIS COMBINATION SHOT GUN AND RIFLE** is provided with rebounding locks and automatic shell ejector. **OUR SPECIAL PRICE,** for 22 or 32 caliber (as desired), rim fire, 26 inch rifle barrel, and 16 guage, 30 inch shot gun barrel, **$13.50.** **OUR TERMS.** Always the same, C. O. D. to anyone on receipt of $3.00, balance to be paid at express office. **A NICE PRESENT** sent you if you send cash in full with order.

MERWIN, HULBERT & CO.'S RIFLES

No. 133. Price, $5.20.

This picture shows the rifle together.

DESCRIPTION. Merwin, Hulburt & Co.'s Junior Rifle, single shot, barrel easily removed from stock for packing or cleaning, blued barrel, case hardened lock plates, 22 inch round barrel, weighs 4½ lbs., perfectly reliable and accurate, barrel as well rifled as the best rifles, 22 caliber, rim fire, using BB caps and 22 long and short cartridges, ejects the empty shell from the gun when lever is **thrown down.**

OUR SPECIAL PRICE, $5.20.

For 32 caliber, 22 inch round barrel, rim fire, long and short cartridge, ivory bead and sporting rear sights......................................**$6.75.**

NO. 133.
PRICE, $5.20.

This picture shows rifle taken apart.

Merwin, Hulbert & Co.'s Rifle.

NO. 134.   PRICE, $8.90.

DESCRIPTION. Rebounding locks, set trigger, ivory front and sporting rear sight, pistol grip, nicely checkered, rubber butt plate. The barrel can be detached from the frame **without the aid of any tool,** and then can be made into compact shape for trunk, valise or canvas cover. Owing to its fine shooting qualities this rifle is fast becoming very popular.

OUR SPECIAL PRICE, for 22 caliber, rim fire, 28 inch barrel, weight 7 lbs., **$8.90.**
OUR SPECIAL PRICE, for 32 caliber, rim or central fire as desired, weight 7 lbs., length of barrel 28 inches..................... **$8.90.**

Colt's New Lightning Magazine Rifles.

Manufactured by **COLT'S PATENT FIRE ARMS MANUFACTURING CO.,** Hartford, Conn. Constructed upon entirely new principles. The workmanship is of the same high standard as that of other arms manufactured by this company. Old shell ejected and new cartridge inserted by sliding motion of the forearm, and as it can be done with the left hand, it is at once convenient and rapid. **EVERY RIFLE WARRANTED.** All center fire, using same cartridges as Winchester rifles of same caliber, or U. M. C. special make.

No. 98—32	Caliber,		15 shot,	weight	6¾ lbs.,		26 inch round barrel	....	$11.00
No. 99—32	"		15 "	"	7¼ "		26 inch octagon "	....	12.00
No. 100—38	"		15 "	"	6¼ "		26 inch round "	....	11.00
No. 101—38	"		15 "	"	7¼ "		26 inch octagon "	....	12.00
No. 102—44	"		15 "	"	6¾ "		26 inch round "	....	11.00
No. 103—44	"		15 "	"	7¼ "		26 inch octagon "	....	12.00
No. 104—38-56	"		10 "	"	9¼ "		28 " " "	....	15.00
No. 105—45-85	"		10 "	"	10 "		28 " " "	....	15.25

TERMS the same on all rifles, C. O. D., subject to examination on receipt of $3.00, balance payable at express office.

MARLIN MAGAZINE RIFLES.

Like all other guns, we send them C. O. D. to anyone on receipt of $3.00, balance to be paid at express office. If cash in full accompanies your order, we send free a nice present.

DESCRIPTION. Model of 1893 Marlin Safety Rifle. Side Ejector. This model is similar in principle to the 1889 model, and is made in response to the many demands for a rifle in 32-40 and 38-55 calibers. It is the only repeater on the market using these cartridges. The Marlin Fire Arms Co. were the originators of these cartridges, and for years made their finest Ballard target rifles to use them. These rifles are to have exactly the same barrels as were used in the famous Ballards. For deer or similar game, we recommend this model above any in the market. The standard length of barrel will be 26 inches, and a rifle with octagon barrel of this length will weigh about 7¾ pounds. This weight we believe will b found about right for hunting purposes. All rifles of this model will have case hardened frames. Ejects the shell at the side of receiver.

No. 117. 26 inch octagon barrel, 10 shot, 32-40 caliber, weight 7½ lbs.... **$14.18**
No. 118. 26 inch round barrel, 10 shot, 32-40 caliber, weight 7½ lbs....... 13.16
No. 119. 26 inch octagon barrel, 10 shot, 38-55 caliber, weight 7¾ lbs.... 14.18
No. 120. 26 inch round barrel, 10 shot, 38-55 caliber, weight 7½ lbs....... 13.16

We can furnish either the 32-40 caliber or 38-55 caliber with 28 in. barrels at $15.66 each. With 30 inch octagon barrels, $17.25.

Marlin Repeating Rifle. Model of 1891.

TERMS. The same: C. O. D. to anyone anywhere subject to examination on receipt of $3.00, balance to be paid at express office.

DESCRIPTION.— No better Rifle made, very simple in construction, can not get out of order. A novel feature of this rifle is the ease with which the lock mechanism can be cleaned. The unscrewing of the thumb screw on the right hand side of the action allows the entire side of the receiver to be removed, and also in turn the carrier block, finger lever and breech bolt. From the breech bolt may be taken the firing pin and extractor; all this can be done without any tools whatever, and with the lever in any position. This allows the action to be **THOROUGH-LY CLEANED WITHOUT TROUBLE OR TOOLS,** and allows the barrel to be wiped out from the breech, which is very desirable in a small bored gun, and, if the action becomes clogged, one minute is time sufficient to open the gun and remove the obstruction.

IMPORTANT. IN THE 22 CALIBER RIFLE, without adjustment, may be used the following rim fire cartridges, 22 caliber short, 22 caliber long, 22 long rifle, 22 long shot: ☞**READ.** The **32 caliber** takes rim or central fire cartridges in the same rifle by changing the firing pin:

No. 121. **OUR SPECIAL PRICE FOR 32 CALIBER,** 24 inch barrel: Number shots, short rim or central fire, 18; number shots, long rim or central fire, 15; weight, 6¼ to 6½ pounds. Round barrel................................. **$12 15**
Octagon barrel 13 17
No. 122. **OUR SPECIAL PRICE FOR 22 CALIBER,** 24 inch barrel, number of shots, short cartridges (all rim fire), 19; number shots, long or 22-50 shot cartridges, 16; number shots, long rifle cartridges, 14; weight, 6¼ lbs;
Round barrel, ... 12 15
Octagon barrel 13 17

EXTRA for 26 inch barrel, $1.50. **EXTRA** for 28 inch barrel, $3.00.
REMEMBER If you send cash in full with your order **YOU GET A NICE PRESENT. YOU TAKE NO RISK** as we always refund your money if you are not perfectly satisfied.

Stevens' New Model Pocket Rifle

DESCRIPTION.
A fine target or squirrel rifle. **Good for 100 yards.** Latest model, 22 caliber, rim fire, shoots short cartridge or BB caps.

No. 107. 12 inch barrel, weight 2½ lbs. **Our Special Price, $8.95**
No. 108. 15 inch barrel, weight 2½ lbs. **Our Special Price, 10.13**

C. O. D. to anyone on receipt of $3.00, balance payable at express office.

Stevens' Hunter's Pet Rifle.

NO. 114. PRICE $12.15.

22 or 32 caliber, rim fire cartridge.

OUR PRICE $12.15. Extra for 20 inch barrel, 85 cents.

C. O. D. to anyone on receipt of $3.00. Balance and express charges to be paid at express office.

Hunter's Pet Rifle, 18 inch barrel, weight 5¼ lbs., and good 40 rods.

Stevens' Rifles.

SENT C. O. D. to anyone on receipt of $3.00, balance payable at express office. **You get a nice present free,** if you send cash in full with your order, and we refund all your money if you are not perfectly satisfied.

NO. 106.
PRICE $6.75.

DESCRIPTION.

New Model Stevens Rifle, "Sure Shot." The Sure Shot is an entirely new model. The barrel swings to extract the shell instead of "tipping-up," as in the old models. Barrels are rifled same as in the higher grades, and is a wonderful shooter. Frame nickel plated, walnut stock, rebounding lock, German silver front sight, finely finished throughout. Stock and barrels easily separated to clean or pack. Barrel 20 inches long. Entire length 34 inches, weight 3½ pounds, 22 caliber, rim fire short, long or long rifle cartridge. Every rifle warranted as long range and as accurate as any 22 caliber rifle in the market. Our special price, $6.75.

Stevens' Favorite Rifle.

DETACHABLE BARREL.

DESCRIPTION. Guaranteed as well finished and rifled a barrel as found in the most costly rifles. Entirely new model. **The** barrel is held to stock by a set screw, and easily separated or put together. Rifling and quality of barrel same as the higher cost rifle. Case hardened frame, walnut stock, finely finished, warranted accurate, rim fire, 22 caliber, using long or short cartridges, 22 inch barrel, weight 4½ lbs.

OUR SPECIAL PRICE, $6.95. C. O. D. to anyone on receipt of $3.00, balance, $3.95, and express charges, payable at express office after you receive rifle.

This picture shows barrel and stock detached.

PRICE,

$6.95

NO. 136.

This picture shows gun complete.

STEVENS' LATEST IDEAL RIFLE.

DESCRIPTION.

Lever action, like Sharp's, same as Stevens' Favorite.
THE IDEAL RIFLE is perfection for all gallery work, or for use of any of the sporting sizes of rim or central fire cartridges. It is also especially adapted for long range practice with the following central fire cartridges: 25-20 Stevens, 32-30 Stevens, 30-40, 38-55, and others.

No. 109. Our special price, 22 or 25 caliber, 24 inch barrel..............$17.40
No. 110. With extra fancy walnut stock, 22 or 25 caliber, 24 inch barrel. 19.20
No. 111. With extra fancy walnut stock, wind guage and front sight, 22, 25, 32 or 44 caliber, 24 inch barrel......................... 20.70

Extra for mid-range Vernier sight, 60 cents.
Extra for each 2 inches in length of barrel over 24 inches, $1.20.

SPORTING AND MILITARY RIFLE SIGHTS.

All orders for sights must be accompanied by cash in full. **IF NOT FOUND SATISFACTORY** we will cheerfully refund your money.

Lyman's Patent Combination Sight.

Any one can attach these sights to a rifle in a few minutes. Lyman sights of all kinds can be furnished for almost every kind of rifle on the market. These sights more than double the value of a rifle, either for hunting or target shooting, for instantaneous aim can be taken with great accuracy. The sights are made in all sizes. When ordering give the make and gauge of rifle.

The sight stem is illustrated separately to show the point blank stop pin. Price of sight, **$2.45.**

No. 830. Price, $2.45.

Lyman's Patent Ivory Shotgun Sight, with Reamer.

No. 837. Price 55c.

Lyman's Patent Combination Ivory Front Sight.

One cut shows the sight with the ivory open part in use and the other with the globe turned up. **No. 838.** Price 85c.

Beach Combination Sight.

No. 839. Price, 90c.

As open.   As globe.

An excellent spirit level, which can be used in place of blank piece. **No. 840. Price, 85c.**

Lyman's Patent Wind Gauge Sight.

When used without the large disk, the principle of this sight is the same as the combination sight. For target shooting it is unequaled, and it is an improvement on the combination sight for hunting. **No. 830. $4.00.**

Lyman's Patent Ivory Bead Front Sight.

This sight gives the sportsman a clear, white bead which can be seen distinctly against any object in the woods or in bright sunlight.

No. 831.   **No. 832. Price, 85c.**

Rocky Mountain Front Sight.

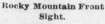

No. 841. Price each 48c.

No. 842. Price, 23c.

Black piece to replace the crotch sight, which is usually on the barrel when the rifle is purchased, this should always be removed when peep sights are used.

Lyman's Patent Improved Ivory Front Sight.

This sight is better than the bead sight for a hunting rifle. **The Ivory is** so well protected by the surrounding metal that there is no danger of its being injured. **No. 833.   Price 42c.**

Midrange Vernier Peep sight, complete with screws to fasten to stock of rifle. **No. 843. Price, $3.90.**

Sporting Rear Sight.

Graduated from 50 to 300 yards. **No. 834. Price, 78c.**

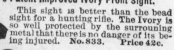

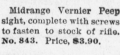

Wind Gauge Sight, With Spirit Level.

with 3 discs, always mention name and caliber of rifle when ordering sight. **No. 844. Price, $3.85.**

No. 835. Price, $3.85.

No. 845. Price, $3.90.

Graduated peep sight, complete, with screws to fasten to stock of rifle. **No. 836. Price, $2.25.**

LOADED METALLIC CARTRIDGES.

ALL ORDERS FOR CARTRIDGES, LOADED AND EMPTY SHOT SHELLS AND AMMUNITION must be accompanied by cash in full.

ALL ORDERS FOR GUN IMPLEMENTS, TOOLS, SPORTING GOODS, Etc., must be accompanied by at least ONE-FOURTH of catalogue price; if to be sent by express, C. O. D.; if to be sent by freight cash in full must accompany order.

WE ALWAYS REFUND ALL MONEY if goods are not perfectly satisfactory.

We do not send Cartridges C. O. D. Cartridges cannot go by mail. We can furnish all kinds of cartridges not on this list at lowest market price.

Cartridges can be shipped with other goods by express or freight.

Prices subject to change without notice. U. M. C., U. S., Lowell and Winchester makes, all the same price and kept in stock.

RIM FIRE CARTRIDGES.

140 Cartridge, 22 caliber, BB cap, 100 in box; per box, 14c; per 1000, $1.41; weight, ¾ lb. per box.

141 Conical Ball Cap Cartridge, 22 caliber, rim fire, box of 100, 22c; per 1000, $2.00; weight ¼ lb. per box.

142 Cartridges, 22 caliber, short, rim fire, U. M. C. make "U," 100 in box, 24c; per 1000, $2.30.

143 Cartridges, 22 caliber, short, rim fire, Winchester make "H," 100 in box, 24c; per 1000, $2.30.

144 Cartridges, 22 caliber, short, rim fire U. S. make, 100 in box, 24c; per 1000, $2.30.

145 Cartridges, 22 caliber, short, rim fire, 100 in box 25c; per 1000, $2.25.

146 Cartridges, 22 caliber, long, rim fire, 100 in box, 30c; per 1000, $2.85; weight 1¼ lbs. per box.

147 Cartridges, 22 caliber, long rifle, rim fire, 100 in box, 30c; per 1000 $2.85.

148 Cartridges, 22, extra long, rim fire, 100 in box, 47c; per 1000, $4.30; weight 1¼ lbs. per box.

149 Cartridges, special 22 caliber, for Winchester model '90, repeating rifle, 7 grains powder, 45 grains lead; per 100 48c; per 1000 $4.57.

149

150 Cartridges, 25 caliber, for Stevens, Maynard and Winchester single shot rifles, 11 grains powder, 65 grain ball, rim fire, 50 in box 40c; per 100 70c

151 Cartridges, 30, short. rim fire 50 in box 23c; per 100 44c; Weight ¾ lb.

151

152 Cartridges, 30, long. rim fire, 50 in box 28c; per 100 51c; weight ¾ lbs.

152

153 Cartridges, 32 caliber, extra short, rim fire, 50 in box 25c; per 100 46c; weight ⅓ lb. per box.

153 Cartridges, 32 caliber, short, rim fire, 50 in box, 26c; per 100 48c; weight ¾ lbs.

154

155 Cartridges, 32 caliber, long, rim fire, 50 in ox 30c; per 100 56c; weight 1 lb.

155

156 Cartridges, 32 caliber, extra long rim fire, 50 in box 48c; per 100 80c; weight 1¼ lbs per box.

156

157 Cartridges, 38 caliber, short, rim fire, 50 in box 42c; per 100 79c; weight 1¼ lbs.

158 Cartridges, 38 caliber, long, rim fire, 50 in a box 47c; per 100, 87c; weight 1½ lbs.

158

159

159 Cartridges, 38 caliber, extra long, rim fire, 50 in box, 65c; per 100 $1.20; weight 1¾ lbs.

160 Cartridges, 41 caliber-rim fire, for Remington Der; ringer pistol, per box of 50 40c, per 100 72c; weight 1¼ lbs.

160

161 Cartridges. 41 caliber, long, rim fire, 50 in box 45c; per 100 85c.

162

162 Winchester, model '66, rim fire, 28 grains powder, 200 grain ball. 50 in box 62c; per 100 $1.17; weight 1¼ lbs. per box.

163 Cartridges, 56 - 46, Spencer carbine, rim fire, 25 in box 52c; per 100 $1.94; weight 2 lbs.

164 Cartridges, 56 - 50 Spencer carbine,, rim fire, 25 in box 52c; per 100 $1.94; weight 2½ lbs, per box.

164

165 Cartridges, 56-52, Spencer rifle, rim fire, 25 in box, 52c; per 100 94c.

165

166 Cartridges, 56-56, Spencer carbine, rim fire, 25 in box 52c; per 100 $1.94.

166

LOADED METALLIC CARTRIDGES.

ALL ORDERS FOR CARTRIDGES, LOADED and EMPTY SHOT SHELLS and AMMUNITION must be accompanied by cash in full.

ALL ORDERS for GUN IMPLEMENTS, TOOLS, SPORTING GOODS, Etc., must be accompanied by at least ONE-FOURTH of catalogue price; if to be sent by express, C. O. D.; if to be sent by freight cash in full must accompany order.

WE ALWAYS REFUND ALL MONEY if goods are not perfectly satisfactory.

CENTER FIRE PISTOL AND RIFLE CARTRIDGES.

167 Cartridges, 22 caliber, center fire, 15 grs. powder, 45 gr. bullet for Winchester *single shot* rifle, box of 50 **60c**; per 100 **$1.10**; weight 1 lb. per box.

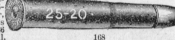

168 Cartridges, 25-20 caliber, 19 grains powder, 86 grain ball, for Stevens', Maynard and Winchester single shot rifles, box of 50 **75c**; per 100 **$1.35**; weight 1¼ lbs.

169 Cartridges, 32 cal., Smith & Wesson, center fire, 50 in box **44c**; per 100 **80c**; weight 1¼ lbs. Using No. 1 primers if made by W. R. A. Co.; using No. 0 primer if made by U. M. C. Co.

170 Center fire, 32 caliber, short, for Colt's revolver, 50 in box **44c**; per 100 **80c**; weight 1¼ lbs.

171 Center fire, 32 caliber, long, Colt's or Ballard, 50 in box **48c**; per 100 **88c**; weight 1½ lbs.

172 Cartridges, 32 caliber, extra long, center fire, 50 in box **72c**; per 100 **$1.32**; weight 1¼ lbs.

173 Cartridges, center fire, 32 caliber, for Colt's lightning repeating rifle, 20 grs. powder, 100 grs. lead; box of 50 **64c**; per 100 **$1.16**; weight 1¾ lbs.

174 Cartridges, for Winchester rifle, 32 caliber, center fire, 20 grs. powder, 115 grs. lead, weight 1¾ lbs., per box of 50 using No. primer **64c**; per 100 **$1.16**.

175 Cartridges, 38 caliber, center fire, Smith & Wesson, 60 in box **54c**; per 100 **98c**; weight 2 lbs. per box

176 32 Ideal Cartridge, 1¾ inch straight shell, 25 grains powder, 150 grains lead; per box of 50, **75c**; per 100 **$1.70**.

177 Center fire, 38 caliber, short, for Ballard rifles, Colt's and Remington revolvers, 50 in box **54c**; per 100 **98c**; weight 2 lbs.

178 Center fire, 38 caliber, long, for Ballard rifle and Colt's revolvers, 50 in box **58c**; per 100 **$1.06**; weight 2¼ lbs. per box.

179 Center fire, 38 calibar, extra long, 38 grains powder, 148 grains lead, for Ballard rifle, No. 2, 50 in box **92c**; per 100 **$1.67**; weight 2½ lbs.

181. Winchester (model '73), center fire, 38 caliber, 40 grains powder, 180 grains lead, 50 in box, using No. 1 primer. Per box, **72c**; per 100, **$1.40**; weight, 2¾ lbs. per box.

182 Cartridges, center fire, 38 caliber for Colt's Lightning Repeating Rifle, 40 grains powder, 180 grains lead. Per box of 50, **72c**; per 100, **$1.40**; weight, 2¾ lbs. per box.

183 Colt's revolver, caliber 41, center fire, (long DA), 50 in a box. Per box, **70c**; per 100, **$1.28**; weight 1½ lbs. per box.

184 Cartridges, Colt's revolver, 41 caliber, center fire (short DA), 50 in a box. Per box, **60c**; per 100, **$1.15**; weight, 1½ lbs. per box.

185 Cartridges, 44 caliber Smith & Wesson, center fire, No. 3 Russian, 50 in a box. Per box, **80c**; per 100, **$1.45**; w'ght 2½ lbs

186 Smith & Wesson, American model, caliber 44, center fire, 50 in a box. Per box, **76c**; per 100, **$1.38**; weight, 2½ lbs.

187 Cartridges for Colt's pistol, 44 caliber, center fire, 50 in a box. Per box, **80c**; per 100, **$1.45**; weight 2½ lbs. per box.

188 Cartridges for Winchester rifle, model '73, 44 caliber, centre fire, 40 grs. powder, 200 grs. lead, 50 in box, using No. 1 primer. Per box **72c**; per 100 **$1.38**; weight 1¾ lbs.

189 Cartridges, 44 caliber, long, center fire, for old Ballard rifles, 50 in a box. Per box **88c**; per 100 **$1.60**; weight 2½ lbs.

191 Cartridges, Evans' old model repeating rifle (34 shot), shell 1 inch long, 33 grs. powder, 220 grs. bullet, 50 in a box. Per box **88c**; per 100 **$1.60**; weight 2½ lbs. per box.

192 Cartridges, caliber 44, Webley center fire, for bull dog revolver, 50 in a box. Per box **68c**; per 100 **$1.20**; weight 2½ lbs. per box.

LOADED METALLIC CARTRIDGES.

ALL ORDERS for CARTRIDGES, LOADED and EMPTY SHOT SHELLS and AMMUNITION must be accompanied by CASH IN FULL.

ALL ORDERS for GUN IMPLEMENTS, TOOLS, SPORTING GOODS, ETC., must be accompanied by at least ONE-FOURTH of Catalogue price; if to be sent by express C. O. D.; if to be sent by freight, cash in full must accompany order.

WE ALWAYS REFUND ALL MONEY if goods are not perfectly satisfactory.

193 Cartridges, center fire, caliber 44, for Colt's Lightning repeating rifle. 40 grains powder, 217 grains lead. Per box of 50 **76c**; per 100 **$1.40**; weight 2¾ lbs.

194 Colt's Army and DA revolvers, 45 caliber, center fire. Per box of 50 **88c**; per 100 **$1.60**; weight 3¼ lbs. per box.

Central Fire Cartridges for Target and Sporting Rifles.

195 Cartridges, for Ballard, Marlin and Winchester single shot rifles, center fire, 32 caliber, 40 grains of powder, 165 grains lead, weight 1¼ lbs. Per box of 20 **48c**; per 100 **$2.33**.

196 Cartridges, for Ballard, Marlin and Winchester single shot, short range, 32-40 caliber, 13 grains of

powder. 98 grains lead, weight 1¼ lbs. Per box of 20 **48**; per 100 **$2.33**.

197 Center fire, 38-55 caliber, 55 grains powder. 255 grains lead, for Ballard, Marlin and Winchester single shot rifles of this caliber, 20 in a box, weight 1¼ lbs., **60c**; per 100 **$2.72**.

198 Cartridges, for Ballard, Marlin and Winchester single shot, 38 55 caliber, short range, 20 grains of

powder, 155 grains lead, same length shell as No. 197. Per box of 20 **60c**; per 100 **$2.72**.

199 Cartridges, for Winchester rifles, models 1886, 38-56 caliber, 255 grains, weight 1⅜ lbs. Per box of 20 **60c**; trade price per 100 **$2.72**.

200 Cartridges, center fire, for Colt's lightning rifle, 40 caliber, 60 grains powder, 260 grains lead, weight 1¾ lbs. Per box of 20 **60c**; trade price per 100 **$2.64**.

201 Cartridges, for Winchester rifle, 40-60 caliber, 60 grains powder, 210 grains lead, weight 1 5-16 lbs. Per box of 20 **60c**; trade price of 100 **$2.64**.

202 Cartridges for Winchester repeating rifle, model 1886, 40-65 caliber, center fire, weight 1½ lbs. Per box of 20 **60c**; trade price per 100 **$2.72**.

203 Cartridges, for Marlin rifle, 40-60 caliber, center fire, 60 grains powder, 260 grains lead, weight 1½ lbs. Per box of 20 **60c**; trade price per 100 **$2.72**.

204 Cartridges, 40-70-330 straight shell, grooved ball, weight 1¾ lbs. Per box of 20 **70c**; trade price per 100 **$3.30**.

209 Cartridges, for Winchester rifle, model 1876, 45 caliber, center fire, straight shell, 60 grains powder, 300 grains lead. Per box of 20 **60c**; per 100 **$2.72**; weight per box 1⅜ lbs.

210 Cartridges, for Winchester rifle, model 1876, 45 caliber, center fire, 75 grains powder, 350 grains lead. Per box of 20 **63c**; per 100 **$3.00**; weight 1⅛ lbs.

205 Cartridges, 40 caliber, 82 grains powder. 260 grain bullet, center fire, for Winchester rifle, model 1886. Per box of 20 **64c**; per 100 **$2.97**.

206 Cartridges, 40-85 caliber, center fire, straight shell, for Ballard rifle this caliber, 85 grains powder, 370 grains lead. Per box of 10 **45c**; per 100 **$4.12**.

207 Cartridges, for Sharp's rifle, 40-90, Sharp's, Remington and Winchester single shot rifles, center fire, 3¼ inches, straight shell, 90 grains powder, 370 grains lead. For shape of shell see 40-85 Ballard. Per box of 10 **45c**; per 100 **$4.12**.

208 Cartridges, 40-110 Express, 3¼ inch shell, 110 grs. powder, 260 grs. lead. Per box of 10 **72c**; per 100 **$6.80**.

LOADED METALLIC CARTRIDGES.

ALL ORDERS FOR CARTRIDGES, LOADED and EMPTY SHOT SHELLS and AMMUNITION must be accompanied by cash in full.

ALL ORDERS for GUN IMPLEMENTS, TOOLS, SPORTING GOODS, Etc., must be accompanied by at least ONE-FOURTH of catalogue price; if to be sent by express, C. O. D.; if to be sent by freight cash in full must accompany order.

WE ALWAYS REFUND ALL MONEY **if goods are not perfectly satisfactory.**

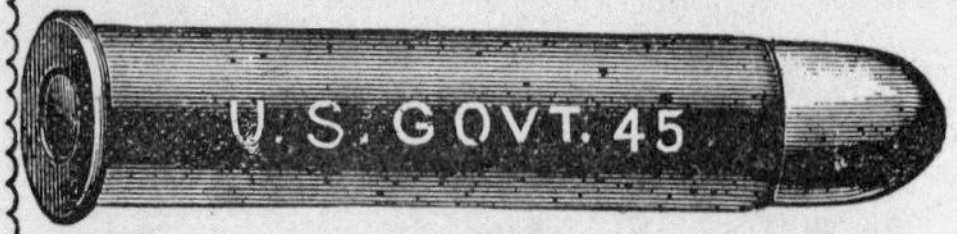

211 Cartridges, 45 caliber, center fire, for Winchester rifle, model 1886, 70 grains powder, 405 grains lead, weight 36 oz. Per box of 20 **68c**; per 100 **$2.98.**

212 Cartridges, for Marlin rifle and Winchester model '86 rifle, 45 caliber, center fire, 70 grs. powder, 405 grains lead. Per box of 20 **67c**; per 100 **$2.98**; weight 36 oz.

213 Cartridges, for single shot rifles, 45-70 caliber, for armory practice, 5 grains powder, 140 grains lead, round ball Per box of 20 **67c**; per 100 **$2.98**; weight 20 oz.

214 Cartridges, for Marlin rifle or any other 45-70 caliber rifle, 45 caliber, 45-85 grains powder, 285 grain bullet. Per box of 20 **67**; per 100 **$2.98**; weight per box 30 oz.

215 Cartridges, for Winchester repeating rifle, model 1886, 45 caliber, 90 grains powder, 300 grains bullet. Box of 20 **70c**; 100 **$3.17**; wt. per box 28 oz.

216 Sharp's, only 2¼ inch necked shell, 44-77-405. Box of 20, **80c**; 100 **$3.62**; weight per box, 30 oz.

217 Cartridges, U. S. government, 45 caliber, 70 grs. powder, 2 1-10 inch shell, 500 grain ball, special long range target, for Winchester and other 45-70 caliber rifles. Box of 20 **72c**; 100 **$3.23**; wt. per box 36 oz.

218 Cartridges, 50 caliber, U. S. Government, center fire, 70 grains powder, 1¾ inch shell, weight 44 oz. Per box of 20 **80c**; per 100 **$3.62.**

219 Cartridges, regular and Remington, 44-77-470, necked 2¼ inch shell, weight 44 oz. Per box of 20 **80c**; per 100 **$3.62.**

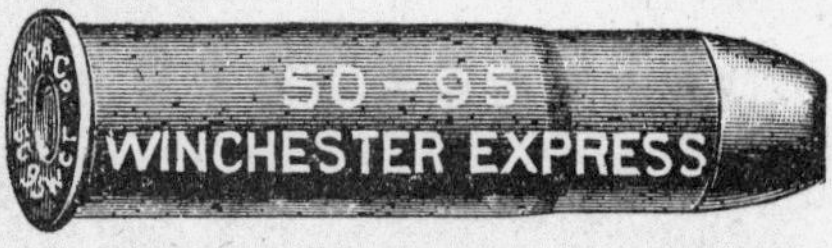

219½ Sharp's straight 2 7-8 inch shell, 45-105-550. Box of 20, **$1.08**; wt., 55 oz.

220 Cartridges, 50-95 Winchester Express rifle, 95 grains powder, 300 grains bullet, Per box of 20 **76c**; per 100 **$3.35.**

221 Cartridges, 50-110-300, Winchester Express. Per box of 20 **87c**; per 100 **$3.92.**

Cartridges for Remington Rifle.

222 32 caliber, center fire, 30 grains powder, 125 grs. lead, weight 36 oz. Per box of 50 **90c**; per 100 **$1.70.**

223 38 caliber, center fire, 1¾ inch, 40 grains powder, 245 grs. lead, straight shell. Box of 20 **60c**; 100 **$2.65.**

224 38 caliber, center fire, 2¼ inch straight shell, 50 grains powder, 245 grs. lead. Box of 20 **63c**; 100, **$2.88**

225 40 caliber, center fire, 45 grains powder, 265 grs. lead, 1⅞ inch straight shell, weight 24 oz. Per box of 20 **62c**; per 100 **$2.88.**

226 40 caliber, center fire, 65 grains powder, 330 grs. lead, 2¾ inch straight shell, weight 38 oz. Per box of 20 **71c**; per 100 **$3.30.**

227 32-44 caliber, center fire, S. & W. target cartridge, grooved ball, 19 grains powder, 83 grain ball Per box of 50 **71c.**

228 32-44 S. & W. gallery cartridges, center fire, round ball, 6 grs. powder, 50 grain bullet. Per box of 50 **68c.**

229 38-44 caliber, center fire, S. & W. target cartridge, grooved ball, 23 grins powder, 140 grain ball. Per box of 50 **87c.**

230 38-44 caliber, center fire, S. & W. gallery, round ball, 6 grains powder, 70 grain ball. Per box of 50 **70c.**

Patent Metal Patch Bullet Cartridges.

These cartridges are made up with the regular shell, and vary only in charge of powder and weight and kind of bullet. The patent metal patched bullet gives increased accuracy, penetration and cleanliness. The bullet has a covering of copper instead of paper patch, and is smooth instead of being grooved.

231 Metal patch cartridge, 38-56-255, for Winchester model 1886 rifle, per box of 20 **65c**; per 100 **$3.00.**

232 Metal patch cartridge, 40-65-245, for Winchester rifle, model 1886, per box of 20 **65c**; per 100 **$3.00.**

233 Metal patch cartridge, 40-82-245, for Winchester rifle, model 1886, per box of 20 **68c**; per 100 **$3.20.**

234 Metal patch cartridge, 45-90-295, for Winchester rifles, per box of 20 **75c**; per 100 **$3.30.**

Blank Cartridges.

Order No. 235.

Primed and regular powder charge, but without ball. Weight per box of 50, ¾ to 1¼ lbs.

22 caliber, rim fire, per box of 100	$0.18
32 caliber, rim fire, per bxo of 50	.22
45-70 caliber, per box of 25	.57
50-70 caliber, per box of 25	.72

Empty Rifle and Pistol Shells.

Order No. 236.

Sold in any quantity from one shell to a thousand. All center fire. Shells can be sent by mail.

	Weight		Per 100
22 caliber, Winchester	1	lb.	$0.77
25-20 caliber	1	"	1.02
38 caliber, for Smith & Wesson	1⅛	"	.55
32 caliber, for Winchester, 1873 model	1⅜	"	.75
32-44 S. & W., gallery	¾	"	.90
32-44 S. W., target	¾	"	.91
32 caliber, for Colt's rifle	1⅝	"	.78
32 caliber, for Smith & Wesson	1⅛	"	.64
38 caliber, for Colt's pistol		"	.63
38 caliber, for Winchester, model 1873	1¾	"	.85
38-44 S. & W., gallery	1⅛	"	1.08
38-44 S. & W., target	1⅛		1.08
41 caliber, for Colt's long DA pistol	2	"	.63
44 caliber, for Smith & Wesson, Russian	2	"	.85
44 caliber, for Winchester, model 1873	1¾	"	.85
44 caliber, for Colt's Lightning rifle	1¾	"	.86
44 caliber, for Evan's rifle, new model	1 5-16	"	1.00
44 caliber, Webley	⅞	"	.68
45 caliber, for Colt's revolvers	1 5-16	"	.90
32-40 caliber, Ballard & Marlin	2	"	1.30
38-55 caliber, Ballard & Marlin	2½	"	1.50
40-60 caliber, Winchester, mod. '76, 210 gr.	2¾	"	1.68
40-85 caliber, Ballard	2¾	"	2.20
40 65 caliber, Winchester, model 1886	2¾	"	1.55
45-60 caliber, Winchester, model 1876	2½	"	1.68
40-82 caliber, Winchester, model 1886	2¾	"	2.00
45-70 caliber, U. S. government	2¾	"	1.90
45-75 caliber, Winchester, model 1876	2¼	"	1.75
44-77 caliber, Sharp's only, necked	2¼	"	2.00
40-90 Ballard	2¾	"	2.20
45-90 Winchester	2⅞	"	2.00
50-70 Government	2¾	"	1.80
40-70 Remington, straight	2½	"	1.85
40-90 Sharp's, straight	3¼	"	2.26
38-56 Winchester	2⅞	"	1.60
40-90 Sharp's, necked	2⅝	"	2.20

Prices of cartridges, shot and ammunition in general are subject to market changes without notice.

LOADED METALLIC CARTRIDGES.

ALL ORDERS for CARTRIDGES, LOADED and EMPTY SHOT SHELLS and AMMUNITION must be accompanied by CASH IN FULL.
ALL ORDERS for GUN IMPLEMENTS, TOOLS, SPORTING GOODS, ETC., must be accompanied by at least ONE-FOURTH of Catalogue price; if to be sent by express C. O. D.; if to be sent by freight, cash in full must accompany order.

***WE ALWAYS REFUND ALL MONEY* if goods are not perfectly satisfactory.**

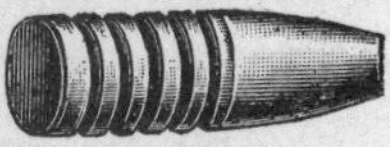

Grooved Bullets.

Order No. 237.

Weight, per 100, 1¾ lbs to 4 lbs., according to size.

32-165

Sizes.	Description.	Weight Grains.	Price per 100.	Weight per 100.
22	Winchester	45	$0.21	1 lb.
32-40	Short range	98	.45	2 "
38-55	Short range	155	.63	2¼ "
25-20	Stevens'	86	.35	1¾ "
32	Smith & Wesson	85	.25	1¾ "
32-73	Winchester	115	.35	2 "
32-40	Ballard & Marlin	165	.60	2½ "
32-40	Ballard & Marlin	185	.81	4 "
32-44	S. & W.	85	.47	1 "
32-44	S. & W., round ball	146	.36	1½ "
38-44	S. & W.	140	1.08	1¼ "
38-44	S. & W., round	70	.37	1 "
38	Smith & Wesson	145	.38	3 "
38-73	Winchester	180	.42	4 "
38-55	Ballard & Marlin	255	.78	4 "
40-60	Winchester	210	.66	3½ "
40-60	Marlin	260	.75	4½ "
45		285	.95	4½ "
44-73	Winchester	200	$0.50	3¼ lbs.
44	Smith & Wesson, Russian	256	.54	4 "
45	Colt D. A.	260	.58	4¼ "
45-60	Winchester	300	.75	4½ "
45-75	Winchester	350	.79	5¼ "
45-70	Government	405	1.00	6 "
45-70	Government	500	1.25	7¼ "
50-70	Government	450	1.35	6¾ "
50-95	Hollow Ball Express	300	.90	5¼ "
50-95	Solid Ball Express	312	.76	

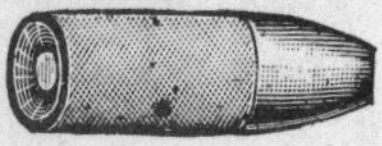

Patched Bullets,

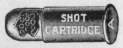

Order No. 238.

Sizes.	Description.	Weight Grains.	Weight Per 100.	Price Per 100.
32-40	Ballard	135	3¼ lbs.	$0.82
32-40	Ballard	135	3¼ "	.82
38-55	Ballard	255	4¼ "	.85
40-85	Ballard	370	5¾ "	1.05
40-90	Sharp & Winchester, straight	370	4¾ "	1.05
44-77	Remington	470	7 "	1.35
44-90	Remington	550	8 "	1.40
45-70	Sharp's	420	6¼ "	1.25
45-105	Sharp's	550	10¼ "	1.89
45		500	7½ "	1.48
40		330	5 "	.76

Everlasting Shells.

No.	Size.	Description.	Each
239	45-70	Ballard Everlasting shells	$0.08
240	45-100	Ballard Everlasting shells	.07

By mail, 1 cent extra.

Shot Cartridges.

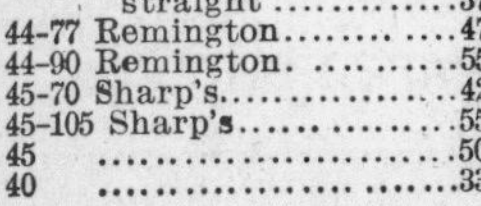

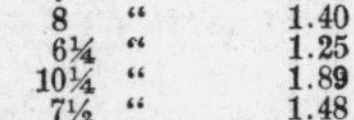

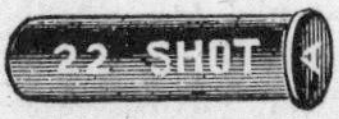

Loaded with shot instead of ball. For use in rifles and revolvers

No.	Description	Weight.	Per box.
241	22 caliber, rim fire, 50 in box, per 100	¾ lbs.	$0.50
242	32 caliber, long rim fire, 25 in box, per 100	2 "	1.10
243	32 caliber S & W., center fire, 50 in box, per 100	2 "	1.17
244	38 caliber, S & W., center fire, 50 in box, per 100	4 lbs.	1.30
245	44 caliber, Winchester, model 1873, center fire, 50 in box, per 100	5 "	1.64
246	32 caliber, center fire, Winchester, model 1873, 50 in box, per 100	2½ "	1.36
247	38 caliber, center fire, Winchester, model 1873, 50 in box, per 100	4½ "	1.65
248	56-52 caliber, Spencer, rim fire, per 100		2.50
249	56-56 caliber, Spencer rim fire, per 100, 25 in box		2.50

Pin Fire Pistol Cartridges.

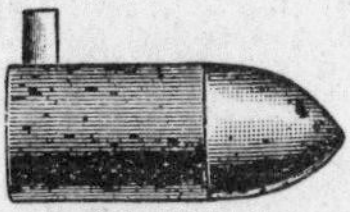

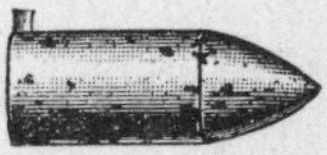

250 7 M-M per box of 50, weight 18 oz.............. $0.32
251 9 M-M per box of 50, weight 24 oz.............. .45

In sizes 7 M-M is 32 caliber, 9 M-M is 38 caliber. 12 M-M is 44 caliber.

252 12 M-M per box of 50, weight, 24 oz........ $0.53

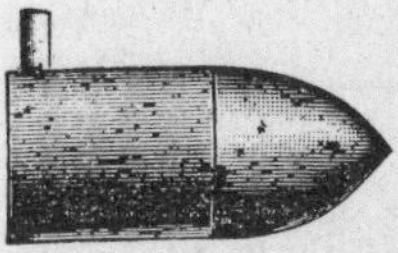

Machine Loaded Paper Shot Shells.

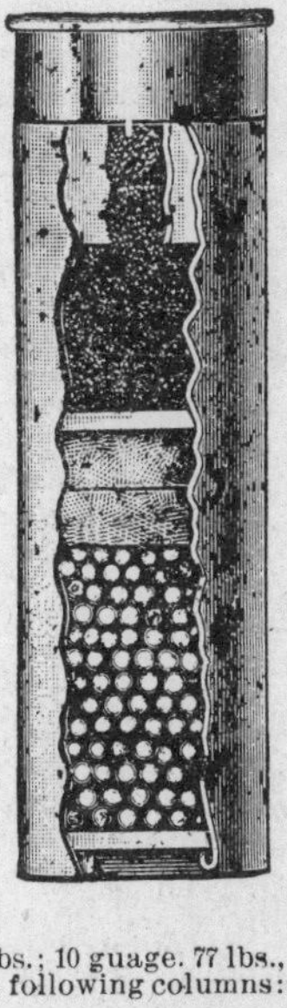

Every Shell warranted.
Loaded Shells can go by freight, or express, alone or with other goods.

The shells used are the celebrated WATERPROOF RIVAL and Club, U. M. C. and Winchester make, (Waterproof paper shells.) Put up in boxes of 25 shells, 20 boxes or 500 shells to the case. These shells are loaded with two thick black edge wads, and one CARDBOARD wad over the powder, and one thin cardboard wad over the shot.

NO BETTER MADE.

The uniformity of the material used and the regularity of the machine work, insure level seating of wads and even pressure of powder, the compression being such as to secure the *highest explosive force*, thereby giving absolute perfection of loading, and becoming at once the most salable form of fixed amunition. We can usually furnish these goods, loaded with Dupont, Laflin & Zand, or Hazard dead shot powders.

PRICES SUBJECT TO CHANGE WITHOUT NOTICE.

Weight per case, 12 guage, 65 lbs.; 10 guage, 77 lbs., 500 shells in a case. See prices in following columns:

Loaded Metallic Cartridges.

ALL ORDERS for CARTRIDGES, LOADED and EMPTY SHOT SHELLS and AMMUNITION must be accompanied by cash in full.

ALL ORDERS for GUN IMPLEMENTS, TOOLS, SPORTING GOODS, ETC., must be accompanied by at least ONE-FOURTH of Catalogue price; if to be sent by express C. O. D.; if to be sent by freight cash in full must accompany order.

WE ALWAYS REFUND ALL MONEY if goods are not perfectly satisfactory.

Order No. 253. 12 Guage.

BLACK POWDER.

Load No.	Am't of powder	Am't of shot	Size shot.	Adapted to shooting	Price per 25	Price p'r100
701	3 dr.	1 oz.	10	Woodcock...........	$0.34	$1.29
703	3¼ dr.	3⅛ oz.	9	Snipe................	35	1.36
705	3¼ dr.	1 oz.	8	Quail................	34	1.31
707	3¼ dr.	1¼ oz.	8	Quail &PrairieCh'ks	36	1.36
709	3½ dr.	1⅛ oz.	8	Prairie chicken.....	37	1.39
711	3 dr.	1¼ oz.	8	Inanimate targets.	37	1.39
713	3¼ dr.	1¼ oz.	8	Inanimate targets .	38	1.41
715	3½ dr.	1¼ oz.	8	Live pigeons.	38	1.44
717	3¼ dr.	1¼ oz.	7	Clay pigeons........	38	1.41
719	3¼ dr.	1⅛ oz.	7	Ruffed Grouse......	36	1.36
721	3½ dr.	1⅛ oz.	7	Teal.................	37	1.39
723	3½ dr.	1¼ oz.	7	Live Pigeons........	39	1.44
725	3¼ dr.	1⅛ oz.	6	Bluebill	36	1.36
727	3½ dr.	1⅛ oz.	6	Pintail	37	1.39
729	3½ dr.	1⅛ oz.	5	Mallard..............	37	1.39
731	3¾ dr.	1⅛ oz.	4	Red-head............	38	1.41
733	3¾ dr.	1⅛ oz.	3	Canvas back........	38	1.41
735	4 dr.	1⅛ oz.	2	Turkey..............	38	1.44
737	4 dr.	1⅛ oz.	1	Brant................	38	1.44
739	4 dr.	1⅛ oz.	BB	Goose	45	1.54
741	3 dr.	1 oz.	9	....	34	1.28
743	3 dr.	1 oz.	8	....	34	1.28
745	3 dr.	1⅛ oz.	8	....	36	1.34
747	3 dr.	1 oz.	7	....	34	1.28
749	3 dr.	1 oz.	6	....	34	1.28
751	3¼ dr.	1⅛ oz.	5	....	36	1.36
752	3 dr.	1⅛ oz.	7	....	35	1.25
753	3 dr.	1¼ oz.	7	....	35	1.30

Order No. 254. 10 Guage.

MACHINE LOADS. BLACK POWDER.

Load No.	Am't of powder	Am't of shot	Size shot.	Adapted to shooting.	Price per 25	Price p'r100
700	4 dr.	1⅛ oz.	10	Woodcock	$0.40	$1.49
702	4 dr.	1⅛ oz.	9	Snipe...............	40	1.49
704	4 dr.	1⅛ oz.	8	Quail ....[en	38	1.49
706	4¼ dr.	1⅛ oz.	8	Quail&Prai'eChick-	40	1.51
708	3¾ dr.	1¼ oz.	8	Inaminate Targets.	40	1.51
710	4 dr.	1¼ oz.	8	Inaminate Targets.	41	1.54
712	4¼ dr.	1¼ oz.	8	Inaminate Targets.	42	1.57
714	4½ dr.	1¼ oz.	8	Live Pigeons........	42	1.59
716	4¼ dr.	1¼ oz.	7	Clay Pigeons........	42	1.51
718	4¼ dr.	1⅛ oz.	7	Ruffed Grouse......	40	1.51
720	4½ dr.	1⅛ oz.	7	Teal	41	1.54
722	4½ dr.	1¼ oz.	7	Live Pigeons	42	1.59
724	4¼ dr.	1⅛ oz.	6	Bluebill	42	1.57
726	4½ dr.	1⅛ oz.	6	Pintail	41	1.54
728	4½ dr.	1⅛ oz.	5	Mallard	41	1.54
730	4½ dr.	1⅛ oz.	4	Red Head...........	41	1.54
732	4¾ dr.	1⅛ oz.	3	Canvass Back......	42	1.57
734	5 dr.	1⅛ oz.	2	Turkey..............	42	1.59
736	5 dr.	1⅛ oz.	1	Brant	42	1.59
738	5 dr.	1⅛ oz.	BB	Goose...............	55	1.70
740	3½ dr.	1¼ oz.	8	....	40	1.49
742	3½ dr.	1⅛ oz.	7	....	39	1.44
744	3¾ dr.	1⅛ oz.	6	....	39	1.47
746	4 dr.	1⅛ oz.	6	....	40	1.49
748	4 dr.	1⅛ oz.	7	....	40	1.49
750	4¼ dr.	1⅛ oz.	5	....	40	1.51

Order No. 255. 16 Guage.

MACHINE BLACK POWDER.

Load No.	Am't of powder	Am't of shot.	Size shot.	Adapted to shooting.	Price per 25	Price p'r100
800	2½ dr.	⅞ oz.	10	....	33	1.26
802	2¾ dr.	1 oz.	10	....	37	1.34
804	2½ dr.	⅞ oz.	9	....	35	1.26
806	2¾ dr.	1 oz.	8	....	37	1.34
808	2¾ dr.	1 oz.	8	....	37	1.34
810	2¾ dr.	1 oz.	7	....	37	1.34
812	2¾ dr.	1 oz.	6	....	37	1.34
814	3 dr.	1 oz.	6	....	38	1.36
815	2½ dr.	1 oz.	8	....	37	1.35
816	2½ dr.	1 oz.	7	....	37	1.35

SHOT SPREADERS—PATENTED.

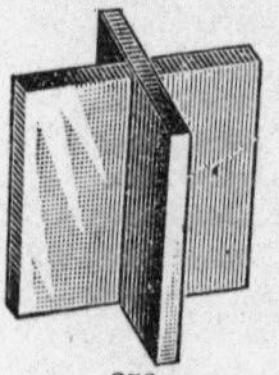

256.

256 Full chokes made to spread MORE than cylinders. SHOT SPREADERS do it. A FULL CHOKE makes a circle of about 12 inches at 15 yards. Shot spreaders make the same gun scatter from 24 to 30 inches. No use of carrying two sets of barrels on a hunting trip. They are made of pasteboard, and pass loosely through the choke. Very successful in the bushes where shooting is done at short range. Just right for quail, woodcock, partridge and rabbits. Do not mangle the game at close quarters. No trouble to load them.

12 gauge and 10 gauge. To load: In a 2⅝ inch shell use 2¾ drs. powder; 1 B. edge and 1 card wad on powder. Drop the spreader down onto the powder wads and then pour in 1⅛ ounces shot. 1⅛ ounce fills the spreader and a little over. Lay on an ordinary card wad and turn over the shell. If your shell is more than 2⅝ inches long use any load of powder and wads you have room for. Price, per hundred **50c.** Box of fifty **25c.**

EMPTY PAPER SHOT GUN SHELLS.

Pin-Fire.

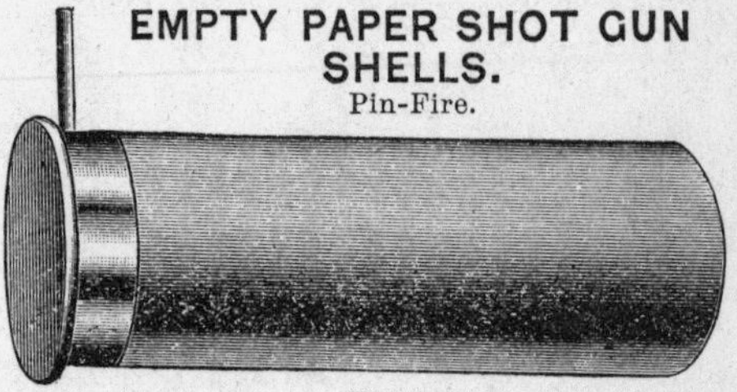

257.

257 Pin-fire paper shells, 20 gauge; per box of 100; weight 2 pounds, **75c.**

258 Pin-fire paper shells, 14 gauge; per box of 100, weight 2 pounds, **75c**

259 Pin-fire paper shells, 16 gauge; per box of 100, weight 2 pounds, **75c.**

260 12 gauge; per box of 100, pin-fire, weight 4¼ pounds, **90c.**

261 10 gauge, pin-fire, paper shells, per box of 100, **$1.45.**

SMOKELESS PAPER SHELLS.

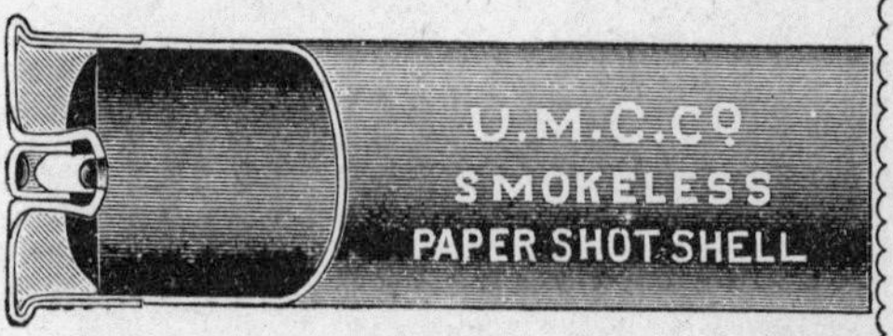

262.

The Smokeless Shell is the boss paper shell.

262 The New U. M. C. Smokeless Red or Salmon color paper shell, made expressly for (SS) smokeless powder and the best low-priced shell for E. C. Schultze and Wood powders, using the long, strong No. 3 primer made by the U. M. C. Company only. With "Nitro" powder of any kind this is much the *quickest* and strongest shell now upon the market for the price. See that your shells take the LONG No. 3 PRIMER, for they are *much* the *best.* (The long No. 3 primer is twice as long as other primers.)

12 gauge, 2⅝ inches, per box of 100; Weight 2¼ lbs., **85c.** Per 1,000, **$8.10.**

12 gauge, 2¾ inch, per box of 100; weight 2½ lbs., **92c.** Per 1,000, **$8.69.**

10 gauge, 2⅞ inch, per box of 100; weight 2¾ lbs., **92c.** Per 1,000, **$8.69.**

LOADED METALLIC CARTRIDGES.

ALL ORDERS for CARTRIDGES, LOADED and EMPTY SHOT SHELLS and AMMUNITION must be accompanied by cash in full.

ALL ORDERS for GUN IMPLEMENTS, TOOLS, SPORTING GOODS, ETC., must be accompanied by at least ONE-FOURTH of catalogue price; if to be sent by express C. O. D.; if to be sent by freight cash in full must accompany order.

WE ALWAYS REFUND ALL MONEY if goods are not perfectly satisfa ctory.

TRAP U. M. C.

263.

Prices subject to change without notice. (Empty shells, not loaded.) All center fire.

Weight, per box, 12 gauge, 2½ lbs.: 10 gauge, 3¼ lbs.; 8 gauge, 4¼ lbs.

The Trap Shell is the best and strongest paper shell made, and is used by all experts in live bird "matches," and where heavy charges are required, and are warranted gas-tight.

263 Paper U. M. C. Trap shell, metallic lined, green colored paper, gas tight especially adapted to E. C. Schultze, Wood and all nitro powders, crimp same as any paper shell; reloadable, using No. 3 long, quick, strong primer.

10 gauge, 2⅞ inch; per 100 **$1.32.** Per 1,000 **$12.57.**
12 gauge, 2⅝ inch; per 100 **$1.25.** Per 1,000 **$12.00.**
12 gauge, 2¾ inch; per 100 **$1.32.** Per 1,000 **$12.55,**
12 gauge, 2⅞ or 3 in.; per 100 **$1.32.** Per 1,000 **$12.57.**

"CONICAL."

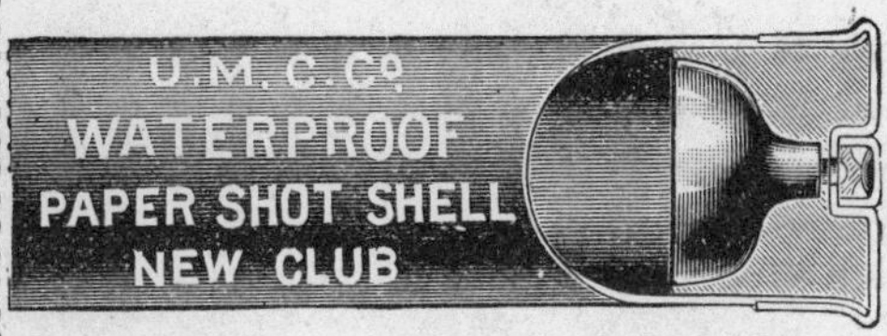

264.

264 The New Club U. M. C., "Conical · base paper shot shells, reinforced base, gas tight, *extra strong* primers for S. S., E. C. Schultze, Wood or black powders, all waterproofed, extra quality, high grade paper (almost transparent). Reloabadle many times, using No. 2 primers.

12 gauge, per box of 100 2⅝ inch 2¼ lbs., **50c.** Per 1,000 **$4.75.**

10 gauge, per box of 100 2⅞ inch, 2½ lbs., **60c.** Per 1,000 **$5.40.**

12 gauge, 2¾ inch, 2 5-16 lbs., **59c.** Per 1,000 **$5.39.**

New Nitro Club Paper Shell.

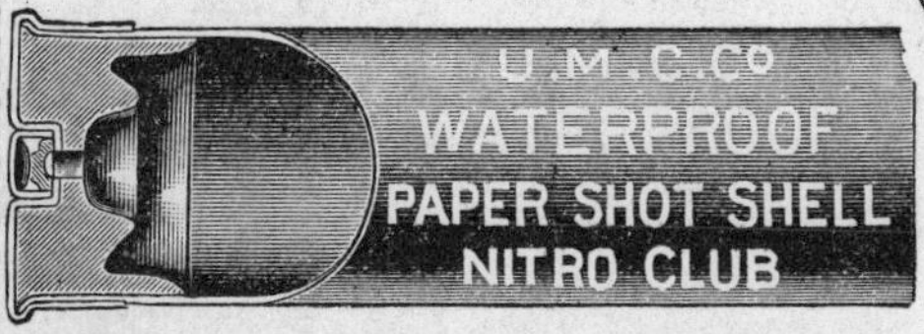

266 The new club Nitro or Black Powder shell, with special strong primer. Strong and quick. **No. 2.**
12 gauge, 2⅝ inch, per 100, **50c.** Per m, **$4.79,**
12 gauge, 2¾ inch, per 100, **60c.** Per m, **5.39.**
10 gauge, 2⅞ inch, per 100, **60c.** Per m, **5.39.**

CLIMAX "CONICAL."

267 The New U. S. Lowell "Climax" paper shell, black water proof, conical base, re-enforced base, gas tight, extra strong, quick primer, for E. C. Wood, Schultze or black powders, can be reloaded using No. 2 primer

12 gauge, per box of 100, 2⅝ inch; weight 2¼, per box **50c** Per 1,000 **$4.75.**

12 gauge, per box of 100, 2¾ inch; weight 2 5-16, per box **63c.** Per 1,000 **$5.40.**

12 gauge, per box of 100, 2⅞ inch; weight 2⅜, per box **60c.** Per 1,000 **$5.39.**

10 gauge, per box of 100, 2⅞ inch; weight 1⅞, per box **60c.** Per 1,000 **$5.38.**

16 gauge, per box of 100, **56c.** Per 1000, **$5.39.**

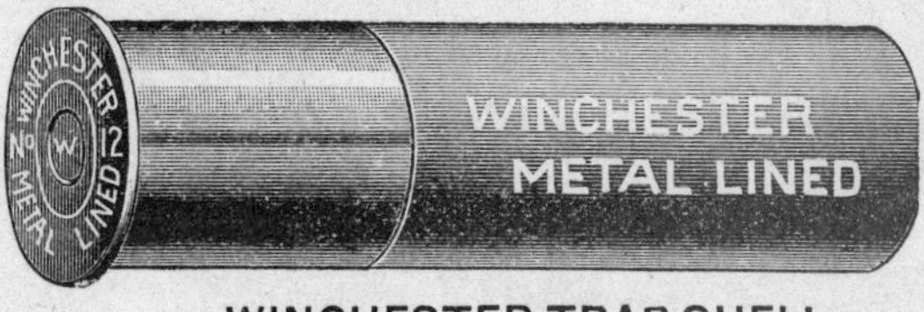

WINCHESTER TRAP SHELL.

268.

268 The New Trap Paper Shell made by the W. R. A. Co. Re-inforced inside and outside with brass, as shown in cut, for nitro or black powder, new, strong No. 3 W. primer

12 gauge, 2⅝ in., per box of 100 **$1.25.** Per m, **$12.00.**
12 gauge, 2¾ in., per box of 100 **1.33.** Per m, **12.60.**
10 gauge, 2⅞ in., per box of 100 **1.33.** Per m, **12.60.**

Nitro=Rival Paper Shells.

269 Winchester "Rival" Paper Shells, warranted perfect, a good shell, waterproof, U. M. C. or Winchester, No. 3 W. or No. 2 primer, can be reloaded.
12 gauge, weight 2¼ lbs., per box **50c.** Per m, **$4.75.**
10 gauge, weight 2½ lbs., per box **60c.** Per m, **5.35.**

270 Paper shells, Winchester club or climax, center fire, using No. 2 primer, first quality, 14 gauge, per box of 100; weight 2 1-16 lbs., per box **60c.** Per m, **$5.75.**

271 Same as No. 270, 16 gauge, per box of 100; weight 1⅞ lbs., **58c.** Per m, **$5.75.**

272. Same as No. 270, 20 gauge, per box of 100; weight 1⅝ lbs., **59c.** Per m, **$5.75.** (Using No. 2 any make of primers).

273 Paper Shells, Winchester; center fire, first quality, 8 gauge, in boxes of 100; weight 3⅞ lbs., per box **$1.90.** Per m, **$18.75.**

Empty Brass Shells.

Give gauge and length when ordering shells.

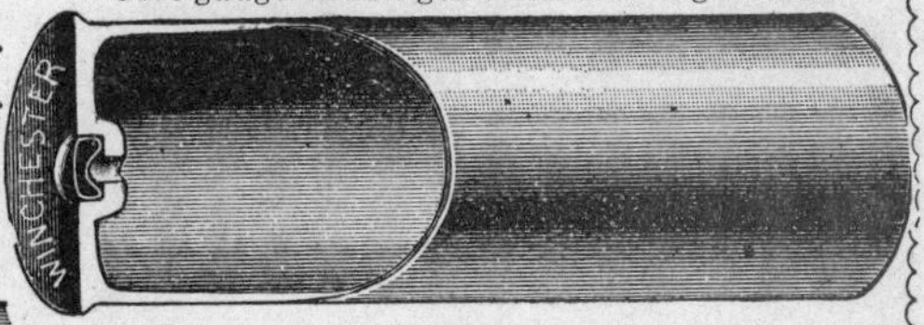

274

Weight, per box of 25 shells, about 1¾ lbs.

Don't forget to give gauge wanted when ordering shells.

We always send 2½ inch in 12 gauge and 2⅞ inch in 10 gauge unless length is given, as this is the size most used.

Winchester "Rival" Brass Shell.

274 Brass shells, "Rival," using any No. 2 primer. A good, strong shell, but lighter than the first quality, 12 gauge, 2½ and 2⅝ inches long, each, **4½c.** Per box of 25 **80c.**

275 Brass shells, "Rival," 10 gauge, 2⅝ inches long, each, **4½c.** Per box of 25 **80c.**

N. B.—The Rival Shells are sold by many dealers as "The very best quality." Don't be fooled. Send to us for samples at box rates.

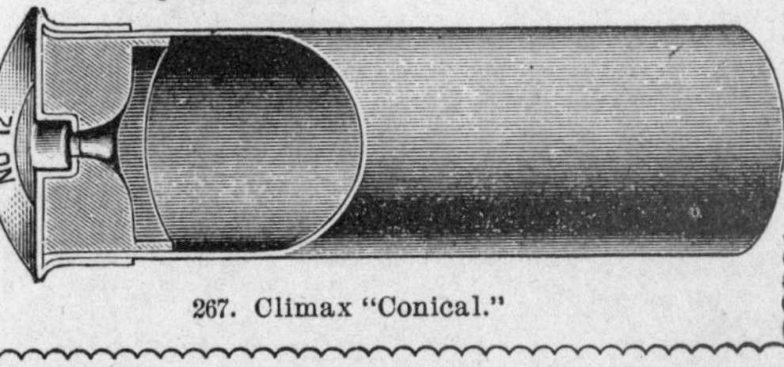

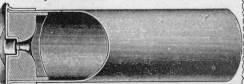

267. Climax "Conical."

Sporting Goods Department

ALL ORDERS for CARTRIDGES, LOADED and EMPTY SHOT SHELLS and AMMUNITION must be accompanied by cash in full.

ALL ORDERS for GUN IMPLEMENTS, TOOLS, SPORTING GOODS, ETC., must be accompanied by at least ONE-FOURTH of Catalogue price; if to be sent by express, C. O. D.; if to be sent by freight cash in full must accompany order.

WE ALWAYS REFUND ALL MONEY if goods are not perfectly satisfactory.

Winchester "Best" Brass Shells.

ORDER No. 276.

Winchester brass shells, first quality, using Winchester No. 2 primer.

20 gauge, 2½ inches long, per box of 25 **$1.15**.

16 gauge, 2½ inches long, each **5c**. Per box of 25 **$1.16**.

14 gauge, 2⅝ inches long, each **5c**. Per box of 25 **$1.17**.

12 gauge, 2½ and 2⅝ inches long, each **5c**. Per box of 25 **$1.18**.

12 gauge, 2¾ and 2⅞ inches long, each **5c**. Per box of 25 **$1.19**.

10 gauge, 2⅝ inches long, each **5c**. Per box of 25 **$1.20**.

10 gauge, 2⅞ and 3 inches long, each **5½c**. Per box of 25, weight 1¾ lbs., **$1.21**.

8 gauge, 3 inches long, each **9c**. Per box of 25, weight 2¼ lbs., **$2.10**.

In ordering shells, be careful to give gauge of gun for which you wish the shells.

U. M. C. Brass Shells.

ORDER No. 277.

Give gauge and length when ordering shells.

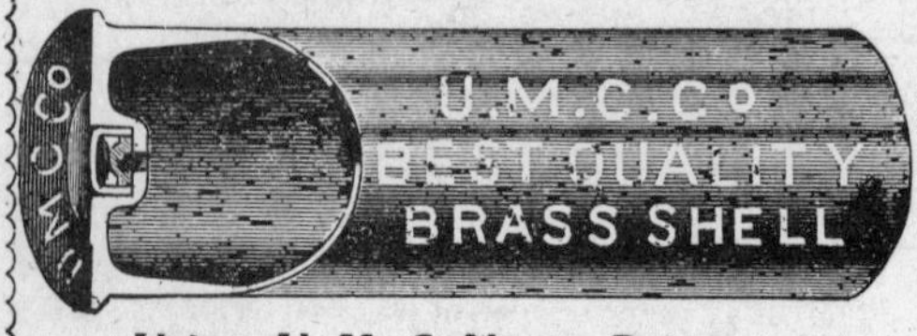

Using U. M. C. No. 2. Primer.

Brass shells, 20 gauge, 2⅝ inches, each, **5c**. Per box of 25, **$1.15**.

Brass shells, 16 gauge, 2½ inches, each **5c**. Per box of 25 **$1.16**.

Brass shells, 14 gauge, 2⅝ inches, each **5c** Per box of 25 **$1·17**.

Brass shells, 12 gauge, 2½ or 2⅝ inches long. Per box of 25 **$1.18**.

Brass shells, 10 gauge 2⅜ or 2⅞ inches long. Per box of 25 **$1.18**.

Brass shells, 10 gange, 2⅝ or 2¾ inches long. Per box of 25 **$1.20**.

Brass shells, 10 gauge, 2⅞ inches long. Per box of 25 **$1.25**.

Brass shells, 10 gauge, 3 inches long. Per box of 25; weight, 1¾ lbs. **$1.25**.

Brass shells, 8 gauge, 3 inches long. Per box of 25; weight, 2¼ lbs., **$2.10**.

Gun Caps and Primers.

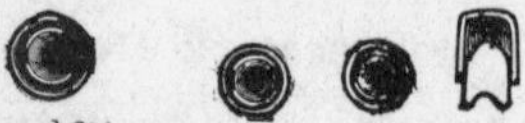

Showing size of No. 2 and 2½.

Showing size of primer No 1, 1½ and 3.

Cannot go by mail.

276 Primer for pin-fire paper shell, per box of 250, **60c**. Per m, **2.00**.

277 Primer for pin-fire pistol cartridges. Per box of 250, **50c**. Per m, **$1.80**.

278 The W. R. A. Waterproof gun caps for mnzzle loaders, per box, **06c**. Per m, **45c**.

279 U. S. musket caps, 10 boxes (1,000 caps). Per box **5c**. Per m, **65c**.

280 Gun caps, G. D. percussion, per box, **4c**. Per m, **40c**.

281 Gun caps (Ely E. B.), single waterproof, 10 boxes (1,000), per box, **7c**. Per m, **65c**.

282 Primers, center fire, for shot gun shells and cartridges, U. M. C. No. 2½. 2, 1, 1½, 0, per box of 250, **35c**. Per m, **$1.20**.

283 Primers for Winchester cartridges and shot gun shells, Nos. 1, 1½, 2 and 2½, per box of 250, **35c**. Per m., **$1.20**.

284 Primers No. 3 for U. M. C. Trap and "Smokeless" grade paper shells. These primers are twice as long as the regular primers and are the only No. 3 primer known to the trade. They are much stronger and quicker than any other primer. per box of 250, **35c**. Per m, **$1.20**.

285 Winchester No. 3 W primer for Rival paper shells, when nitro powder is used, per box **35c**. Per m, **$1.20**.

When ordering *Primers* be sure to give *manufacturer's name* of shell or *our* catalogue number. *Primers connot go by mail.*

GUN WADS.

A New Top Shot Wad.

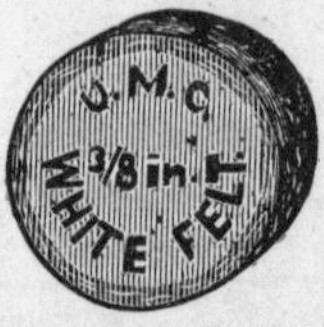

286 The new thin top shot wad. For trap shooting, made of specially prepared paper, less than ¼ as thick as regular card wads. Advantages of this wad: Evener distribution of shot; closer pattern; more space for powder, wads and shot; blows to pieces when "fired," and offers less resistance to the shot, and yet stiff enough to hold shot in place when crimped and does not "bulge" in crimping.

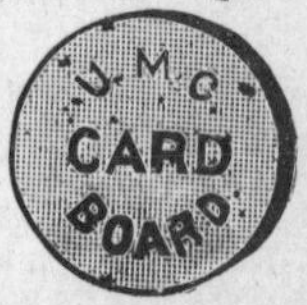

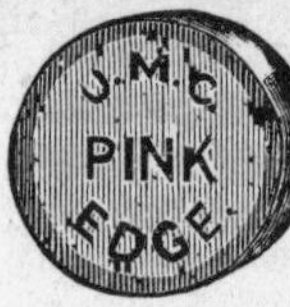

10 gauge, per box of 500; weight, 7 ounces, per 1,000. Per box **20c**. Per 1,000 **35c**.

12 gauge, per box of 500; weight, 6 ounces per 1,000. Per box **18c**. Per 1,000 **30c**.

Top Shot Wads.

287 Engraved "THIN" Top Shot Wad. THE BEST YET. Try them once and be convinced. Size of shot engraved on both sides. Sizes of shot: Nos. 5, 6, 7, 8 and 9.

12 gauge, per box of 500; weight, 6 ounces per 1,000. Per box **15c**. Per 1,000 **25c**.

10 gauge, per box of 500; weight, 7 oz. per 1,000. Per Box **18c**. Per 1,000 **30c**.

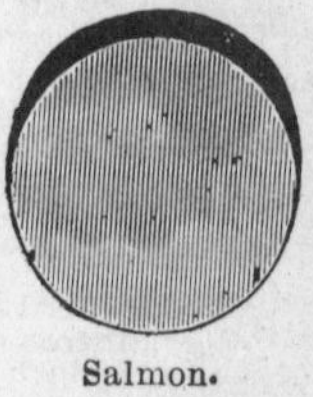

Salmon.

288 Salmon Felt Wads, "soft," for use over nitro powder. Gives the best satisfaction of any wad in the market for "top powder" use. Has soft hair on one side, thin salmon colored paper glued on the other side.

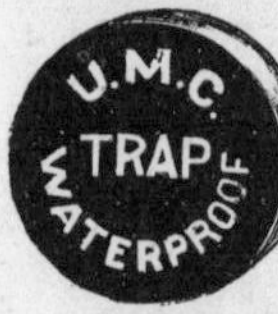

293.

12 gauge, package of 259; weight, per 1,000, 1 lb. Per box **20c**. Per 1,000 **68c**.

10 gauge, package of 250; weight, 1¼ lbs per 1,000, Per box **25c**. Per 1.000 **82c**.

Wads—U. M. C. and Winchester Make.

289 Cardboard wads for use over shot. Weight per 1,000, 1¼ lbs.

	Per box.	Per 1,000
7 gauge, per box of 250	$0.12	$0.35
8 gauge, per box of 250	.10	.32
9 or 10 gauge, per box of 250	.09	.28

Sporting Goods Department

Wads--U. M. C. and Winchester Make.

(CONTINUED.)

	Per box.	Per 1000
11 to 20 gauge, per box of 250	.08	.24

290 Black edge wads, for use over powder. Weight per 1,000, 2 to 3½ lbs., according to size.

6 gauge, per box of 250	.28	1.12
7 gauge, per box of 250	.23	.88
8 gauge, per box of 250	.21	.77
9 or 10 gauge, per box of 250	.17	.66
11 to 20 gauge, per box of 250	.14	.55

291 Pink edge wads, for use over powder. Weight per 1000, 2 to 3½ lbs.

6 gauge, pink edge, per box of 250	$0.42	$1.60
7 gauge, pink edge, per box of 250	.37	1.44
8 gauge, pink edge, per box of 250	.35	1.36
9 to 10 gauge, pink edge, per box of 250	.32	1.20
11 to 20 guage, pink edge, per box of 250	.24	.92

292 White felt wads, ⅜ inch thick, for use over powder. Weight per 1,000, 5 to 6 lbs.

7 gauge, per box of 125	.47	3.60
8 gauge, per box of 125	.41	3.20
9 or 10 guage, per box of 125	.37	2.80
11, 12, 14, 20 gauge, per box of 125	.32	2.40

293 The new "trap" wool felt wad one side black waterproof, reverse side salmon-color paper; some times called express or field wads; about the same thickness as a pink edge, for over powder, not as hard "finish" as most wads of this kind, and consequently better than any other wad of this kind on the market; weigh 1½ to 1¾ lbs per 1000.

10 guage, per box of 250	.25	.90
11, 11½ and 12 guage, per box of 250	.24	.85

294 Black edge, ¼ inch wads, U. M. C.; weight per 1000, 2¼ to 3 lbs.

9 or 10 guage, per box of 250	.27	1.00
11 and 12 guage, per box of 250	.23	2.88

295 Black edge wads, ⅜ in. thick, 125 in a box, 9 and 10 gauge | .26 |

11 and 12 gauge; weight, per 1000, 3¼ to 4¼ lbs	.24	1.95

N. B.,--In 12-gauge brass shells, use 10-guage wads; in 10-guage brass shells, use 8-guage wads. In paper shells use wads the same size as shell. Always put the wad down to place flat and evenly, otherwise the shooting quality of your gun will be greatly impaired.

Wad Cutters.

Postage, 5 cents extra. *Be sure and give guage wanted.*

296 Wad cutters,	
7 and 8 guage	35c
297 9 and 10 gauge	20c
298 11 to 20 gauge	15c
299 Any size pistol or rifle and 24 gauge	45c

American Wood Powder for Shot Guns only. It Must Not be used in Rifles.

Wood powder does not weigh as much as black powder, bulk for bulk. A 1-lb. can weighs about 8 ounces. Recoil much lighter than when using black powders, and little or no smoke.

300 10 and 12 guage, trap grade. Very quick and strong. Pound can (bulk) 65c
6¼ pound can (bulk) $3.75

Schultze Powder.

These powders are made for first-class guns.

301 Schultz Powders for shot-guns, very little smoke.
1-pound (bulk) cans 68c
10-pound (bulk) drums $6.50
Follow directions on can for loading.

E. C. Powder.

302 E. C. Shot Gun Powder, little or no smoke. It is becoming more popular every year.

1-pound (bulk) cans 70c
10-pound (bulk) per can $6.50

Great care must be taken in loading these powders to obtain the best results. Directions for use on each can.

Wood, S. S. Schultz, or E. C. Powder can go by express or freight, as it will not explode unless confined. The great advantage of Wood, Schultz, S. S. and E.C. powders over common powder is the fact that there is much less recoil and no smoke to prevent seeing game or target for second shot.

The New Grade. (S. S.) Smokeless Powder.

303 The New Smokeless (S. S.) Shot Gun Powder; does not weigh as much bulk for bulk as black powder.
1-pound can (bulk) price 65c
10-pound cans (bulk) $6.00

The superiority of the (S. S.) powder consists in its high velocity, long range, reduced recoil, reduced smoke, reduced fouling and more regular patterns. (S. S.) is the highest development in "Nitro" compounds. In consequence of the absence of "jar," and the reduced recoil it is the most agreeable of powders to shoot.

S. S. The Best Smokeless or Nitro Powder Yet Produced.

Dupont Rifle and Shot Gun Powder.

The Messrs. Dupont & Co. are the oldest powder makers and have the most extensive works in the country. We consider their powder the best. Every pound warranted good and clean. In air tight metallic kegs; Fg, coarse FFg, medium; FFFg, fine.

304. Kegs, Fg, FFg, FFFg, 25 lbs $3.50.

305. ½ kegs, Fg. FFg, FFFg, 12½ lbs, $2.00.

306. ¼ kegs, Fg, FFg, FFFg, 6¼ lbs. $1.26.

307. 1 lb. cans. Fg, FFg, FFFg, per can 30c.

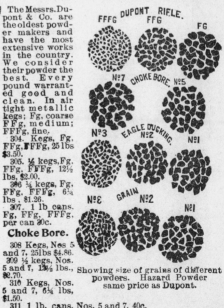

Choke Bore.

308 Kegs, Nos 5 and 7, 25 lbs $4.86.

309 ½ kegs, Nos. 5 and 7, 12½ lbs., $2.70.

310 Kegs, Nos. 5 and 7, 6¼ lbs, $1.50.

311 1 lb. cans, Nos. 5 and 7, 40c.

Showing size of grains of different powders. Hazard Powder same price as Dupont.

SPORTING GOODS DEPARTMENT.

ALL ORDERS for CARTRIDGES, LOADED and EMPTY SHOT SHELLS and AMMUNITION must be accompanied by cash in full.

ALL ORDERS for GUN IMPLEMENTS, TOOLS, SPORTING GOODS, ETC., must be accompanied by at least ONE-FOURTH of Catalogue price; if to be sent by express, C. O. D.; if to be sent by freight cash in full must accompany order.

WE ALWAYS REFUND ALL MONEY if goods are not perfectly satisfactory.

Dupont Eagle Duck.

312 Kegs, Nos. 1, 2, 25 lbs., $11.
313 ½ Kegs, Nos. 1, 2, 12½ lbs., $5.75.
314 ¼ Kegs, Nos. 1, 2, 3, 6¼ lbs., $3.00.
315 1 lb cans, No. 1, 2, 3, 60c.

Powder cannot be shipped by express, but must be sent in separate kegs or cases and marked "gunpowder," and sent by freight. Freight charges are double first-class rates on powder.

"V. G. P." Dupont's. "V. G. P."

316 The new Trap Powder—black, moist, quick, clean and strong (not a nitro); 12½ lb. kegs... $2.00
6¼ pound kegs........................$1.15

Prices Quoted on Any Make of Powder in the Market.

SHOT AND BAR LEAD.

Subject to market changes without notice.
Chilled and dropped shot in sacks of 5 pounds and 25 pounds at lowest market rates. We do not sell less than a sack. The price of shot fluctuates so much that we cannot quote permanent price.

317 Drop shot, all sizes, 1 to 12, per 25-lb sack $1.30
318 Drop shot, all sizes, 1 to 12, per 5-lb sack, 40
319 Chilled shot, all sizes, 2 to 10. Per 25-lb sack, 1.60
320 Chilled shot, all sizes, 2 to 10, per 5-lb sack, 45
Buck shot, B to No. 8, 25-lb sack............ 1.60
Buckshot, B to No. 8, 5-lb sack.............. 45

In case of fluctuation chilled shot is always 25 cts. higher in 25 lb. sacks and ten cents higher in 5 lb. sacks than drop shot. We will always bill shot at the lowest market rates.

321 Bar lead for running bullets at market price, average price about 6¼ cents per pound.

We always bill at lowest market prices.

We guarantee lowest market price on cartridges, shells, primers, powder, shot, etc.
Prices subject to change without notice.
We cannot sell 5 lb. sacks at 25 lb. sack rates.

Gallery Targets.

Bird and Star Target.

The birds and stars fall back out of sight when hit, and are reset by rope from shooting stand. It is one of the most satisfactory targets in the market, and is made to last. Heavy wrought iron face plate.
322 (ex) Target of 6 extra heavy birds and stars; weight, 14 to 18 pounds. Each...................$3.50
323 (o) Target of 8 extra heavy birds and stars, weight, 18 to 22 lbs.........................$3.75

Round Iron Targets.

Bell rings when bull's eye is hit, and self-setting round iron, no figure.
324 (C) 12 inches diameter, for Flobert ball caps; weight, 12½ pounds......................$1.10
325 (A) 12 inches diameter, heavy, for 22 cartridges..$1.35

Round Iron Figure Targets.

Figure springs up and rings bell when bull's eye is hit; reset with rope from shooting stand.
326 (B) 12 inch diameter, for Flobert ball caps; weight, 15 lbs, $1.95.
327 (R) 12 inch diameter, heavy, for 22 cartridges; weight, 15 to 18 lbs 2$.40.
328 12 inch diameter, steel faced, ¼ inch thick. Bird is thrown up and bell rings when bull's eye is hit. For air guns or cartridges not larger than 22 long; weight, 12½lbs. Each, $2.90.

Paper targets for Rifle and Pistol practice furnished. Write for prices.

331 The Standard Keystone Trap Puller, made entirely of iron. Ropes or wire can be used to pull the trap. Price 3 trap pull $3.75
Price 5 trap pull............. 6.00

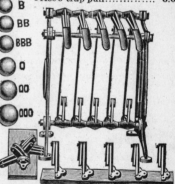

Standard Keystone Trap and Target.

329 The New Standard Keystone Target, improved in every way; best target yet made. **Can use in** ny trap except the Peoria Black Bird trap. **Try** 1000 and you will not use any other target.
Per (barrel) 500 targets.................$3.00
Per 1000 Targets per barrel................ 6.00
Weight, 148 lbs.
330 The Standard Keystone Expert trap, Weight, packed about 35 lbs. Each................$5.50
Other Targets same price as Keystones.

Blue Rock Extension Trap.

332 Blue Rock Extension Trap.
Each........$4.50

Standard Keystone Targets work just as well in Blue Rock Traps as other Targets.

Other Targets same price as Keystones.

We furnish Score Cards Free.

Sporting Goods Department.

ALL ORDERS FOR CARTRIDGES, LOADED and EMPTY SHOT SHELLS and AMMUNITION must be accompanied by cash in full.

ALL ORDERS for GUN IMPLEMENTS, TOOLS, SPORTING GOODS, Etc., must be accompanied by at least ONE-FOURTH of catalogue price; if to be sent by express, C. O. D.; if to be sent by freight cash in full must accompany order.

WE ALWAYS REFUND ALL MONEY if goods are not perfectly satisfactory.

Blue Rock Trap.

333 The New Blue Rock "Expert" Traps. Ea. **$6.50**
334 Paul North's Electric Trap Pulls, complete with wire and battery. Weight, 35 lbs.

For One Trap....	**$10.00**
For Three Trap..	25.00
For Five Traps..	30.00

Shooting Clubs are being formed all over the country, even among the farmers. They find it pays in the increased amount of "work" the boys and "hired" men perform.

Midget Traps.

335 U. S. Midget Traps, The smallest trap made; will throw U. S. Pigeons, Blue Rock or Standard Keystones 40 yards. Weight, 13 lbs.
Each.... ......**$2.50**
Prices on targets are subject to market changes.

335

Rudolph's Ground Pigeon Trap.

336

336 Rudolph's Ground Pigeon Trap, for live Pigeon match shooting. The most satisfactory trap for the purpose and used by many of the State Associations for 8 years. Made of heavy galvanized sheet iron. This trap has filled a long felt want for a good trap at a reasonable price. Every club should have a set.
Each.................... .... **$2.60**
Weight 6½ lbs. each.

Winchester Make Reloading Tools, Including Bullet Molds, Complete Set.

337

A set of implements comprises the reloading tool, a bullet mold and charge cup. The reloading tool removes the exploded primer and fastens ball in the shell, at the same time swaging the entire cartridge to the exact form and with absolute safety. Wood handles on bullet molds. Blued finished and polished. Perfect in every respect.

337 Extra by mail 42 and 45 cts.

					Per set
22 caliber, center fire, Winchester					**$1.70**
25-20	"	"	"	"	1.71
32	"	"	"	model '73...	1.76
38	"	"	"	" " ...	1.77
44	"	"	"	" " ..	1.78
32	"	"	"	S. & W.	1.68
38	"	"	"		1.69
38-90 Winchester Express					2.75
44 caliber, center fire, Webley Cartridge					1.80
40-90 " Sharp's Patched Straight					2.80
40-70 Ballard patch Ball					2.81
40-110 caliber, Winchester Express					2.40
40-60 "					2.15
44 S. & W. Russian					1.80
44 S. & W. American					1.80
45-75 caliber, Winchester					2.26
50-95 " Express					2.70
50-70 " U. S. Government					2.50
45-60 " Winchester					2.22
50-110 Express					2.40
337½ Reloaders. only 22 to 44 caliber					1.45
Reloaders, only from 40.90 to 45-60 caliber.					
Each					1.85
338 Bullet Molds. any caliber. Each					.85
339 Brass charge cups					.10

Mention caliber when ordering tools.

New Model Winchester Tool, Including Bullet Mold, and Complete Set. Reloads and Resizes the Shell.

Polished blued finish. Wood handle on bullet molds. Perfect in every respect.

340—Weight 4¼ lbs.		Per set
38-56 Winchester		**$2.12**
40-65 "		2.13
40-82 "		2.14
45-90 "		2.15
45-70 "		2.16
45-70 Gov't, 405		2.17
45-70 " 500		2.18
50-110 Winchester Express		2.45

WINCHESTER NEW MODEL TOOL, including bullet mold with wood handles. A complete set. Reloads and resizes the shell. Weight 3¼. Bolished blued finish. Perfect in every respect.

341 32-40 cal. **$2.15**
38-55 cal. 2.16

341

Ideal Combined Reloading Tools.

IDEAL RELOADING TOOLS.

These tools will reload shells using patched balls, but to run smooth balls you require an extra bullet mold.

Ideal Combined Reloading Tools.

A set of reloading tools includes: Bullet Mold, Recapper, Decapper, Ball Seater, all in one tool. Powder Measure with each set.

342

IDEAL RELOADING TOOLS.

342 Any caliber. State caliber wanted.

		Per set
22 caliber, center fire, U. M. C		**$1.59**
32 " short		1.59
32 " long		1.59
32 " S. & W.		1.59
32 " extra long		1.59
38 " short		1.59
38 " long, outside lubricator		1.59
38 " extra long		1.59
38 " S. & W.		1.59
41 " Colt's D. A. pistol		1.59
41 " long, Colt's D. A. pistol		1.59

Postage on above tools about 30c extra.

Sporting Goods Department.

ALL ORDERS for CARTRIDGES, LOADED and EMPTY SHOT SHELLS and AMMUNITION must be accompanied by cash in full.

ALL ORDERS for GUN IMPLEMENTS, TOOLS, SPORTING GOODS, ETC., must be accompanied by at least ONE-FOURTH of Catalogue price; if to be sent by express C. O. D.; if to be sent by freight cash in full must accompany order.

WE ALWAYS REFUND ALL MONEY if goods are not perfectly satisfactory.

343 Ideal Tools.
State caliber when ordering.
32-44 S. & W. grooved Ball. Per set, $3.50
32-44 S. & W. gallery, round ball.
38-44 S. & W. target grooved.........$3.50
38-44 S. & W. gallery round.........$3.50

343
38 Long Colt Pistol, inside lubricator, per set 3.00
Postage on above tools, about 40c extra.

344 Ideal Tools.
25-20 caliber, Winchester.
Per set....$1.70
32 caliber, Colt's Lightning Rifle.
Per set....$1.71

32 caliber, Winchester Rifle, Model '92 and '73 $1.72
32-20 "   Marlin................................ 1.73
32-30 "   Remington......................... 1.75
38-40 "   Winchester Model '73 and '92.. 1.74
38-40 "   Colt's Rifle........................ 1.75
38-40 "   Marlin Rifle....................... 1.76
44-40 "   Colt's Rifle........................ 1.77
44-40 "   Winchester Model '73 and '92.. 1.78
44-40 "   Marlin............................. 1.79
44   "   S. & W. Russian Model.......... 1.80
44   "   S. & W. American Model......... 1.80
45   "   Colt's Pistol....................... 1.70

Postage on above tools about 40c extra.

345 Ideal Reloading Tools. State caliber wanted.

32-40   Ballard and Marlin. Per set $2.10
32-40 caliber, Remington. Per set $2.11
38-40 caliber, Remington. Per set, $2.12
38-50 caliber, Remington................ "   2.13
38-55 Marlin.............................. "   3.14
38-56 Winchester and Colt............... "   3.15
40-60 Winchester......................... "   2.16
40-60 Colt and Marlin.................... "   2.17
40-65 Winchester......................... "   2.18
40-70 Sharp's straight groove........... "   2.70
49-82 Winchester......................... "   2.19
44 Evans' new model.................... "   2.30
45-60 Winchester......................... "   2.20
45-70 405 Government.................... "   2.21
45-70 500 Government.................... "   2.24
45-70 Marlin.............................. "   2.23
45-85 285................................. "   2.25
45-90 Winchester......................... "   2.22
50-70 Government......................... "   2.24
40-90 Sharp's straight 3¼ inch shell... "   2.25
Postage on above tools about 45c. extra.
Can furnish any other caliber in the Ideal Tools that are made, including those for Winchester rifles, etc.

346 Shell Reducer and Resizer for any size from 32-40 and larger.
Each....................$1.75
Order size wanted.
Every good rifle shooter needs these tools.
Postage extra, 15c.

347 Ideal Bullet Sizer for making bullets to exact size, and one standard die
Each.......................... $1.75
Extra dies................. .50
You require a die for each style of bullet. Postage, extra, 18c.

348 Ideal Re- and De-capper for pistol cartridges. One tool will only re- and de-cap the one size shell.
Each......... .. $1.00
Postage, extra, 8c.
349 Ideal Loading Flask No. 1 for rifle. 38 to 50 cali., $2.25

No. 2 for Rifles and Pistols, 38 to 22 caliber, $2.20
Extra shell receiver from 22 to shot gun size, .50
Postage, extra, 20c.

Bullet Molds Only.

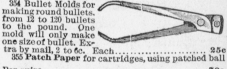

Be sure and give size wanted.
For all sporting and military sizes of cartridges.
Extra by mail...16c

350 To make Grooved Balls.............each $0.85
351 "   Express Balls.......... "   1.25
352 "   Round Balls............ "   1.15
353 "   Smooth Balls for cartridges made only with patched bullet................. 1.00

354 Bullet Molds for making round bullets. from 12 to 120 bullets to the pound. One mold will only make one size of bullet. Extra by mail, 2 to 6c. Each................. 25c

355 **Patch Paper** for cartridges, using patched ball
Per quire................................... 70c
Per sheet.................................... 7c

356 Ideal Dipper for running bullets.
Each............40c
Postage, extra, 10c.

Ideal Melting Pot.

357 Ideal Melting Pot for melting lead 40c; postage, extra, 15c.
357½ Adjustable Cover to fit any stove for Id'l Melting Pot 40c; extra for postage 24c.
Melting pot. Cut ½ size.

Cover.

Melting Ladles.

Weight 1 to 3 lbs.

358 Melting ladles, for melting lead, etc.   Each.
3-inch diameter bowl.........................$0.22
4-inch diameter bowl......................... 25
5-inch diameter bowl......................... 40
6-inch diameter bowl......................... 45

Loaders, 10 and 12 Guage.

Extra by mail, 4c.

359 Cocobolo Loader, complete, 10 & 12 guage. Each 15c.
360 Common Loader, complete, each 10c.

361 Loader without tube, 10 and 12 guage, each, 8c.

Sporting Goods Department

ALL ORDERS for **CARTRIDGES, LOADED** and **EMPTY SHOT SHELLS** and **AMMUNITION** must be accompanied by **CASH IN FULL.**
ALL ORDERS for **GUN IMPLEMENTS, TOOLS, SPORTING GOODS, ETC.,** must be accompanied by at least **ONE-FOURTH** of Catalogue price; if to be sent by express **C. O. D.;** if to be sent by freight, cash in full must accompany order.
WE ALWAYS REFUND ALL MONEY if goods are not perfectly satisfactory.

All with extracting pin. Be sure and give guage wanted.

362 Barclay Loader with inside spring wad starter, 10 and 12 guage, each, **55c**; 8 guage, **75c.**

363 Nitro Powder Loader, cocobolo rammer and base, nickel tube, spring equal to 10 ℔ pressure in rammer, 10 or 12 guage only. Each, **35c.**

Reloading Tools.

For 14, 16 and 20 guage only. These are the only styles and prices we have in these guages.
In ordering state size wanted.
364 Cocobolo Loader with nickel tube and extracting pin, 14, 16 or 20 guage only, **18c**; extra by mail 3c.
365 Recapper, bronzed iron, for 14, 16 or 20 guage only, **15c**; extra by mail 3c.
366 Shell Crimper, best quality, for 14, 16 or 20 guage only, **70c**; extra by mail 10c.
367 Ring Shell Extractor, for 14, 16 or 20 guage only, **10c**; extra by mail 1c. (State guage wanted.)

8-Guage Reloading Tools.

These tools are of the very best quality and are the only style made for this guage.
368 Cocobolo Loader with tube and extracting pin, weight 4 ounces, 8 guage only, **50c.**
369 Shell Crimper, best quality, 8 guage only, weight 24 oz., **$1.50.**
370 Recapper, red japanned, polished joints, 8 guage only, weight 5 oz., **84c.**
371 Ring Shell Extractor, 8 guage only, **20c.**

Re-Capper and De-Capper.

Shell Extractor and Rammer.

372 The Ideal Shell Loader, including funnel & base, bronze finish, compact and handy to carry in the pocket, re- and de-caps and seat wads, weight 4 oz.
Each, 16 guage........**42c** | Each, 12 guage........**40c**
Each, 10 guage........**40c**

373 The Ideal Hand Shell Closer for paper shells; handy to carry

"Ideal" Hand Closer.

in pocket; always ready for use; weight 5 oz.
Each, guage 16........**28c** | Each, guage 12........**29c**
Each, guage 10........**30c**

374 Ideal Powder and Shot Measure combined. Nickel plated cap, wood handle. Each **10c**; postage, extra, 2c.

10 and 12 Guage Reloading Tools.

375 Red Japanned Re-capper, neat and handy, 10 and 12 guage, weig't 2 oz., each **9c**; 16 or 20 guage **12c.**

376 Recapper, with flat automatic spring handle, 10 and 12 guage, weight 3 oz., each **15c.**

377 Remington De- and Re-capper, 10, 12, 14, 16 and 20 guage, each **50c.** Be sure and give guage wanted when ordering de-and-re-cappers or implement sets. Postage, 11c extra.

If you haven't got Mann's De-and-Re-Capper,
don't find fault if your gun missfires.

378 Mann's De-and-Re-capper is first-class in every respect, nickel plated shell post, cocobolo handle. A simple, convenient and effective implement, de-capping and re-capping the cartridge shell without removing from the shell post or reversing the lever, doing its work easily, rapidly and perfectly. Miss-fires will be avoided by its use. Weight 8 oz. 12 guage **90c**; 10 guage **95c.** *When de-cap'g.*

379 Paper Shell Crimper, bronzed iron, 10 & 12 guage. State guage wanted; a crimper will only crimp one guage. Weight 10 oz. Each **35c**; 16 guage **45c.**

380 Paper Shell Crimper, bronzed and brass, with expelling pin, 10 and 12. State guage wanted. Weight 12 ounces. Price, each, 10 or 12 guage **40c**; 16 or 20 guage, **50c.**

381 The B. G. I. Paper Shell Closer, red japanned, brass and ebony trimmings, expelling pin; a good, strong closer. Guage 10 or 12, each, **60c**; guage 16 or 20, each, **72c**; weight 13 ounces.

382 The New Improved Spangler Square Crimper. New straight feed lever, with steel grip. The only tool that will crimp every shell alike, no matter what the variations of load may be. The only tool having an automatic plunger, that prevents the end of the shell from spreading over the wad. All wearing parts are of steel. The best crimper ever made; 10 or 12 guage only. Weight 30 oz. Each, **$1.88c.**

Showing style of crimp.

Sporting Goods Department.

ALL ORDERS for CARTRIDGES, LOADED and EMPTY SHOT SHELLS and AMMUNITION must be accompanied by cash in full.

ALL ORDERS for GUN IMPLEMENTS, TOOLS, SPORTING GOODS, ETC., must be accompanied by at least ONE-FOURTH of catalogue price; if to be sent by express C. O. D.; if to be sent by freight cash in full must accompany order.

WE ALWAYS REFUND ALL MONEY if goods are not perfectly satisfactory.

383 The New No. 3 B. G. I. Crimper, with reversible crimp, making either the oval or the square crimp with the same tool, a good, strong and durable article, 10 or 12 guage, $1.35. Postage extra, 32c. Order by guage or shell you wish to crimp. A 10 guage will not crimp a 12 guage.

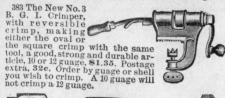

384 Cleaning Rods, hardwood, patent brass joints and three implements, swab, scratch brush and wiper, 10, 12, 16 gauge. Weight 7 oz., per set 33c.

385 Cleaning rod, 3 joints, lancewood, nickel trimmings, four implements, swab, scratch brush, wormer and wiper; 10, 12 and 16 gauge. Weight, 7 ounces; each 66c.

386 Cleaning rod, three joints, ebony wood, nickel trimmings, four implements, swab, scratch brush, wormer and wiper; a fine rod, 10, 12 and 16 gauge; weight 7 ounces. Each $1.09.

387 Snake wood, cleaning rod nickel trimmings and implements, 10 or 12 gauge, $1.25.

388 Brass Wire Brush, for removing lead caking and rust spots; can be attached to any joint rod; 10, 12, 16 and 20 gauge. Order by gauge, as one brush will fit but one gauge. Each 45c. Postage extra, 2 cents.

389 Field cleaner, large bristle brush slotted wiper, string and oil bottle weight, fine leather pouch with clasp; 10 and 12 gauge. Weight, 3 ounces. Each 90c.

389.

390 Expansion Felt swab, to fit jointed rod, 10 or 12 gauge; weight 2 oz. Each 35c.

390. 391.

391 Three Row Wire Brush, to fit jointed rods. 10 and 12 gauge. Each 30c. Weight, 3 oz. 16 and 20 gauge. Each 45c.

392. 393. 394.

392 Wool swab, to fit jointed rods, 10 and 12 gauge; Weight. 2 ounces. Each 12c.

393 Flannel wiper, to fit jointed rods, 10 and 12 gauge; weight, 1 oz. Each 12c.

394 Wire Scratch Brush, to fit jointed rods, 10 and 12 gauge; weight, 1 oz. Each 8c.

BUDD'S PAT. CLEANER
B. G. I. Co. PAT SEPT 19 1876

By mail 3c. extra.

395.

395 Budd's Improved Petmecky Gun cleaner, 10 or 12 gauge; screws onto all jointed rods; the best cleaner in the market, 65c.

396 Ferris gun cleaner, the best gun cleaner in the market, for removing lead spots rust and burnt powder The cleaner has an India rubber cone, and is adjustable to 10 or 12 gauge. Each 70c. Postage extra, 5 cents.

396.

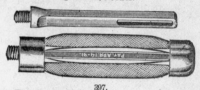

397.

397 The Tomlinson gun cleaner, for shot gun. Wire gauze cleaner. Fits any standard jointed cleaning rod. Each 80c. Postage extra, 4 cents.

Shell Extractor.

398 The Universal shell extractor will extract any shell from 8 to 22 caliber; 20c. By mail, 1c. extra.

MACMILLAN PATENT.

398.

400. 401. 399.

399 Wormers to fit jointed rods, 10 and 12 gauge. Weight, 1 oz. Each, 8c.

400 Ring shell extractor, polished, 10 and 12 gauge, nickel finish; weight 1 oz. Each, 12c.

401 Powder and shot measure combined, ring handle, polished nickel finish; weight 1 oz. Each, 15c.

402 Powder and shot measure, combined, cocobolo handles, polished, nickel finish; weight, 2 oz. Each, 10c.

402.

403 B. G. I. Standard Nitro powder measures, 3¼ drams, 45 grains, or 3½ drams, 49 grains, will only measure one size charge. Each, 35c.

Rifle Cleaning Rods.

404 Twisted wire, bristle brush on end; 22 caliber. Weight, 2 oz., 4c.

405 Plain Brass Wire, slotted, for 22 caliber; weight, 4 oz., 12c.

406 French Iron Wire Rod, with screw off and bristle and wire scratch brushes, 22 caliber, 19c; 32 caliber, weight 4 oz., 18c.

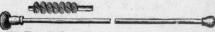

407 Cocobolo Handle, brass wire jagged, slotted and knob for 32 and 22 caliber; weight 4 oz, each, 35c.

Sporting Goods Department.

ALL ORDERS FOR CARTRIDGES, LOADED and EMPTY SHOT SHELLS and AMMUNITION must be accompanied by cash in full.

ALL ORDERS for GUN IMPLEMENTS, TOOLS, SPORTING GOODS, Etc., must be accompanied by at least ONE-FOURTH of catalogue price; if to be sent by express, C. O. D.; if to be sent by freight cash in full must accompany order.

WE ALWAYS REFUND ALL MONEY if goods are not perfectly satisfactory.

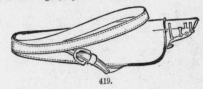

408 Four jointed Brass Cleaning Rods; can be carried in the pocket. Postage extra, 6c.

22 Caliber	$0.39	32 Caliber	$0.39
40 Caliber	.39	45 Caliber	.39
38 Caliber	.39	44 Caliber	.39
50 Caliber	.40		

409 Brass Wire Brush to fit 408. Rods, 12, 32, 38, 40, 44, 45 and 50 calibers.
Postage extra, 2c. Each........$0.23

410 Revolver Cleaners, brass rod, snake wood handle, brass wire brush, Order caliber wanted. Same brush only good for one caliber. Each. **38c.** Postage extra, 3 cents.

Gun Implement Set.
State gauge wanted.

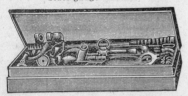

411 The complete gun implement set, embracing loader, paper shell crimper, re and de-capper, shell extractor, powder and shot measure, and cleaning rod with implements. This set comes in a strong pasteboard box, neatly divided into compartments for each article, and each implement is made of *good material*, and recommends itself to every owner of a breech-loading shot gun. The best ever offered for the money. Size of box, 5x13 inches. Price per set, best quality, 10 or 12 gauge, with 20 hole loading block; weight 3 pounds, **$1.89.**

412 Price per set, medium quality, 10, 12, 16 and 20 gauge, with loading block with 20 holes, **$1.25.**

413 Price, good every day quality, 10 or 12 gauge; weight 2 lbs., **95c.**

(State gauge wanted.)

414 Reloading set consisting of rammer and de-capper, with base block, nickel loading tube and re-capper, ring extractor, and patent paper shell crimper, graduated powder and shot measure, all inclosed in a strong paper box, making a neat and convenient set of tools. Per set, 16 or 20 gauge, weight 1 lb., **60c.**

414.

415 Per set, 10 or 12 gauge, **63c.**
416 Per set, for brass shells only, no crimper, 10 or 12 gauge only, weight 12 oz., **25c.** 16 or 20 gauge, **32c.**

Shell-Loading Block.

New model, made of white wood, holes bored with shoulder to fit entire length of shell; top of hole reamed out in place of wadstarter: shell does not come within ⅓ inch of top of block; shells cannot "bulge

417.

or break down." Just the thing to load shells for Smith or Parker guns, or where wads larger than shell are required; weight, 3 lbs.

417 Holding 50 12-gauge shells, **85c.**
Holding 50 10-gauge shells, **85c.**
418 Metal-lined block, same as above. Each, **$5.55.** Weight, 6¾ lbs.

419.

By mail, 3 to 5c extra.

419 Single Belts, with Irish charger, **$6.35.**
420 Single Belts with lever charger, **70c.**
421 Couble Belts, with patent charger, **$1.00**

422 Pouches, 2½ lbs., with common Irish charger, not illustrated. Each, 30c.
423 Pouch, 2½ lbs., with lever charger. Each, 60c. Extra, by mail, 3 to 5c.

Powder Flasks.

424 8 oz., with cord, common top, 29c.
425 12 oz., with cord, common top, 48c.
426 16 oz., with cord, common top, 50c.
Postage, extra, 6c.

Pouch.

Shell Bags.

427 Brown Canvas Bags, leather bound with pocket, weight 12 oz.

50 shells	28c
75 shells	30
100 shells	33

Weight 15 oz.
428 Leather bags, extra finished; weight 10 to 20 oz.

100 shells	$1.18
75 shells	1.06
50 shells	.93

429 Heavy drab colored canvas shell bag, bound with red leather, 2 pockets, extra shoulder piece, handsome and durable. Each.

50 shells	$0.58
75 shells	.65
100 shells	.79

Weight 9 to 14 ounces.

Game Bags.

430 Brown canvas game bags, leather bound, with pockets. No. 100; weight 8 oz. Each, **80c.**

431 Leather game bags, leather flaps and backs, canvas pockets, square corners, No. 3. Each, **$1.12;** weight 12 oz.

432 Leather game bags, leather flaps, and back, large pocket and small canvas pocket, round corners, with fringe; weight 16 oz. Each, **$1.95.**

SPORTING GOODS DEPARTMENT

<u>ALL ORDERS</u> FOR CARTRIDGES, LOADED AND EMPTY SHOT SHELLS AND AMMUNITION must be accompanied by cash in full.

ALL ORDERS FOR GUN IMPLEMENTS, TOOLS, SPORTING GOODS, Etc., must be accompanied by at least ONE-FOURTH of catalogue price; if to be sent by express, C. O. D.; if to be sent by freight cash in full must accompany order.

WE ALWAYS REFUND ALL MONEY if goods are not perfectly satisfactory.

Bedells' Patent Game Skirt.

433 Bedells' patent game and cartridge holder, heavy russet leather belt with game hooks, double leather shoulder straps, heavy brown canvas skirt with pocket to carry 100 shells. The best game and cartridge holder for field shooting in the market. Each, $2.00. Postage, extra, 26 cents.

Gun Covers.

By mail, 15 to 20 cents extra.

Gun Covers, Nos. 434—36.

434 Brown Canvas, leather bound, leather handle and muzzle protector, cotton flannel lining, 30 to 40 inch barrel. Each 50c. Per doz., $5.50.

435 Brown canvas, same style as 434 but lighter material, for single barrel shot guns and small rifles 24 inch to 34 inch. Each, 38c.

436 Best Quality Brown Canvas, leather bound, with leather lock and muzzle protector and handle, cotton flannel lined. Each, 70c. Per doz., $7.50.

Rifle Covers—waterproof.

437 Rifle Cover, best brown canvas, leather bound, leather sling, cotton flannel lined, best quality, 24 to 32 inch barrel. Each, 58c.

438 Rifle Cover, same as 437, with heavy leather lock and muzzle protector. Each, 75c. Per doz., $8.40.

439 Rifle Cover, with sling straps, all heavy bag leather, russet color, made same style as the canvas covers. Waterproof and a good one, $1.50. Extra by mail, 24 cents.

Rifle and Carbine Sheath or "Saddle Holster." $1.15.

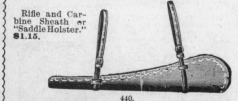

440.

Weight for carbines, 13 oz., model 73, 16 oz., mod. 76 and 86, 26 oz.

440 Rifle and Carbine Sheath, best russet leather, for Winchester carbines and models 1873, 1876 and 1886 rifles. These sheaths are not full length covers, but are for carrying rifle on saddle, leaving the stock of rifles exposed to be easily grasped. Each, $1.15.

441 Victoria Gun Case, best brown canvas, leather bound, with leather handle, lock and muzzle protector, with heavy leather and with tool pocket on outside; weight 32 oz. Each $1.00. Per doz., $11.00.

442 Victoria Gun Case, same as 441, but without lock and muzzle protector; weight 25 oz. Each, 65c. Per doz., $7.20.

443 Victoria Gun Case, brown canvas, leather bound, with leather handle, cotton flannel lined, no tool pocket, a good cover; weight 20 oz. Each, 44c. Per doz., $4.80.

Victoria.

444 Victoria Gun Case, extra heavy russet leather, good, strong and durable, 30 and 32 inch barrels, with tool pocket outside, $2.40.

445 Victoria Gun Case, heavy russet sole leather, cotton flannel lined, tool pocket outside, 30 and 32 inch barrels. Weight 36 oz. Each, $2.63.

446 Victoria Gun Case, extra heavy leather, good, strong and durable, no outside pocket, 30 32 inch barrels. Each, $2.00.

447 Victoria Gun Case, extra heavy russet colored sole leather, highly finished, with tool pocket, flannel lined, 30 and 32 inch barrels; weight 44 oz. Each, $3.75.

448 California style gun case. Heavy brown canvas, leather muzzle protector, tool pocket and sling strap. Well made, strong and durable. Each, $1.00. Postage extra, 25 cents.

449.

449 Victoria Gun Case, heavy waterpr't canvas reenforced on stock and barrel with pocket for cleaning rod, also shell bag to hold 50 shells. The most complete cover offered to sportsmen and trap shooters. Each, $1.27. Postage, extra, 35 cents.

Sporting Goods Department.

ALL ORDERS for CARTRIDGES, LOADED and EMPTY SHOT SHELLS and AMMUNITION must be accompanied by cash in full.

ALL ORDERS for GUN IMPLEMENTS, TOOLS, SPORTING GOODS, ETC., must be accompanied by at least ONE-FOURTH of Catalogue price; if to be sent by express C. O. D.; if to be sent by freight cash in full must accompany order.

WE ALWAYS REFUND ALL MONEY if goods are not perfectly satisfactory.

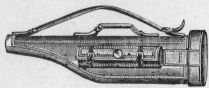

Weight 40 to 60 ounces.

450 English Victoria Gun Case, extra heavy oak tanned russet leather, embossed, nickel plated trimmings, patent fastening, staple for lock. A fine case, well made and very durable, 30 and 32 inch barrels. Each, **$4.00.**

451. English Victoria, oak tanned russet colored leather, brass trimmings, a beauty. 28, 30 or 32 inch barrel. Flannel lined, each **$4.75.**

452 Same as 451 with tool pocket on outside, each **$5.25.**

453

453 English Victoria, imitation alligator, chestnut colored leather, heavy and strong, a fine case; each **$4.75.**

Any of above cases lined with lambskin with the wool left on for $2.00 extra, to order chamois lined $2.50 extra.

454 English Victoria Gun Case, made of the very best orange color finish sole leather, burnished brass trimmings, made up in the very best style; no tool pocket; elegant in design and finish; each, **$5.50.**

455 Victoria Case, same as 454, with tool pocket on the outside; each **$6.00.**

All leather Victoria cases are the best and handsomest covers for guns. The leather being thick and heavy protects the guns from being injured or getting rusty. These cases are called sole leather and are almost as heavy as sole leather. (Mention length of gun barrels.)

Leather Trunk Gun Cases.

For breech loading guns with 30 to 32 inch barrels. Weight, 8 to 10 lbs.

456 Sole leather trunk case, nickel corners, iron frame, shell top, holding 75 shells for 30 or 32 in. barrels, each **$10.00**

457 Sole Leather Trunk Case, same as 456, without metal corners or shell top, for 30 or 32 inch barrel, each **$8.90.**

458 Heavy Leather Trunk Case, same as 456, metal corners, and without shell top, 30 or 32 inch barrel, each **$6.25.**

In ordering trunk cases, give length of barrel.

Shell Boxes.

Weight, 5 lbs.

458½ Sole Leather Shell Boxes, tin lined, with compartments, nickel plated trimmings. Dimensions, 12¾ in. long, 6 in. wide, 7½ in. high; holding 200 shells; each **$2.95.**

459 Sole Leather Shell Boxes, same as 458½. Dimensions: 13¾ in. long, 8½ in. wide, 8 in. high; holding 300 shells; each **$3.50.**

460 Metalic shell box; length 11 in., width 6½ in. depth 5 in.; capacity 100, No. 12; each **$1.75.** Weight 3 lbs.

461 Length 13 in., width 8½ in., depth 7½ in.; capacity, 400 No. 12; each **$2.75.** The material of this box is very heavy, so it could be used for a seat or a stool to sit upon

without damage. All are nicely painted and ornamented; weight about 4 lbs.

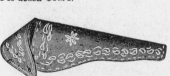

462 Trap Shooter's Leather Ammunition Cases; heavy russet sole leather, tin lined, partitioned for 25 shells in each space; tray for cleaning rod and three partitions for sundries; holds 150 shells. Each.............. **$4.96** Weight 5 lbs.

Pistol Holsters.

463 Russet Leather Pocket Holster as adopted by police officers), heavy russet leather, for 3½ inch barrel, 32 and 5 caliber. Made to wear in the hip pocket; sweat proof; each 30c. Per dozen $3.24.

Army and Navy Holsters, by mail 5c. extra.

424½-25

464 Pistol Holster with loop similar to cut, heavy russett leather. 32 caliber; each 25c.

465 Pistol Holster with loop similar to cut, russet leather, 38, 44 and 45 caliber; each 38c.

466 Rubber Pocket Holster with steel hook.
32 caliber...... ..... 50c
38 " 60c
44 " 80c
Postage, 4 cents extra.

The rubber Holster is rust proof, and being soft and pliable, it is the best and most convenient holster ever made to carry a revolver in the pocket. Will hold revolvers with 3½ inch barrel, or shorter.

467 Pocket Pistol Holster, soft russet leather (no loop for belt) for pocket use only; 22, 32 and 38 calibers. Each, 15c.; Per dozen $1.65. Postage, 3 cents.

Sporting Goods Department.

ALL ORDERS FOR **CARTRIDGES, LOADED** and **EMPTY SHOT SHELLS** and **AMMUNITION** must be accompanied by cash in full.

ALL ORDERS for **GUN IMPLEMENTS, TOOLS, SPORTING GOODS,** Etc., must be accompanied by at least **ONE-FOURTH** of catalogue price; if to be sent by express, C. O. D.; if to be sent by freight cash in full must accompany order.

WE ALWAYS REFUND ALL MONEY if goods are not perfectly satisfactory.

Pistol Holsters
(By mail, 5 cents extra.)

468 Pistol Holster with loop for belt; heavy russet leather, 22 and 32 caliber; each **20c.**

469 Pistol Holster with loop for belt; best russet leather, 38 caliber; each. **25c.**
470 Pistol Holster with loop for belt, best russet leather, 44 caliber; each. **30c.**
471 Pistol Holster with loop for belt, best russet leather. 45 caliber; each. **35c.**

472 Mexican Holster, best russet leother, heavy and durable, 32 and 38 caliber; each, **40c.**
44 " " 47c.
45 " " 50c.
By mail, 6 cents extra.

Leather Belts.

Our Leather Goods are the Best in the Market.

473 Belts only. russet leather, without loops for cartridges. By mail, 5 cents extra. Each. **15c.**

474 Belts only, russet leather, with loops for cartridges; 32 and 38 caliber, 1½ inches. Wide plain roller buckle. By mail, 5 cents extra. Each, **30c.**

475 Belts only, fine russet leather, with loops for cartridges. 32, 38, 44 and 45 caliber, 2½ inches wide, large nickel plated buckle. By mail, 10 cts. extra. Each, **45c.**

Rifle Cartridge Belts.

By mail, 5 cents extra. **Be sure and mention caliber of cartridge you wish to carry.**
476 Webb rifle belt, 32, 38, 44, 45 caliber, heavy and strong, **35c.**
477 Leather rifle belt, 32, 38, 44, 45 caliber, 2½ inches wide, best quality, heavy, **50c.**

Cartridge and Shot Belts.

478 The woven cartridge belt, invented by Coi. Anson Mills, U. S. A. The main body of the belt as well as the loops which hold the cartridge, is woven in one solid piece. The belt is soft and pliable, particularly adapted to rifle cartridges. In ordering be sure to give caliber and name of cartridges you wish to carry. 32 to 50 caliber. By mail 20 cents extra. Each, **$1.20.**

479 The Anson Mills woven shot shell belts, 10 guage and 12 and 16 guage, with shoulder strap and game hooks. By mail 22 cents extra. **$1.20.**

Shell Belts.

480 Anson Mills hunters' belt. The loops are woven, closed at the bottom, protecting the cr.mped end of shell, no sewing on the belt whatever; weight, 5 ounces; 10 or 12 guage. Each **90c.**
481 Light Webb shell belts; no shoulder straps or welt on bottom; weight, 4 oz. **18c.**

482 Canvas shell belts. 10, 12, 16 and 20 guage. with shoulder strap, weight 15 oz. **40c.**
483 Russet leather shell belt, with shoulder strap, 10, 12, 16 and 20 guage, Each, **46c.**

484 Russet leather shell-belt, with shoulder strap, 8 guage only. Each **$1.00.** By mail, extra, **16c.**

485 Mexican combined Cartridge and Money Belt, made of the very best russet leather; belt 3 inches wide, soft and pliable and will not get hard and crack; neatly embossed; 32 and 38 caliber, **95c.** 44 caliber, **96c.** 45 caliber **97c.** By mail, 13 cents extra. Don't forget to state caliber wanted.

486 "The Pop" shoulder holster, with breast and shoulder strap to wear under coat, on the left side, as shown in cut. Made of fine soft russet leather, any caliber or length of barrel. Ea. **63c.** Extra by mail, each, **7c.**
Always forget to state caliber if you are in a hurry for your goods, and then it will be necessary to write you for size.

Money Belts.

By mail 3 cents extra.
487 Money belts, chamois skin, with 3 compartments widths 3 inches; to be worn around waist under clothing. Each, **40c.** Per dozen, **$5.00.**
488 Money belts, soft pliable leather, 3 compartments, sweat proof, never get hard or stiff, the best thing in the world. Each, **75c.** Per dozen, **$7.70.**

489 Heik's Hand Protector, for shot gun barrels; a protection from cold barrels or hot barrels, made of spring steel, leather covered. A necessity to trap shooters. Each, **69c.** By mail 3 cts. extra.

SPORTING GOODS DEPARTMENT.

ALL ORDERS for CARTRIDGES, LOADED and EMPTY SHOT SHELLS and AMMU-NITION must be accompanied by cash in full.
ALL ORDERS for GUN IMPLEMENTS, TOOLS, SPORTING GOODS, ETC., must be accompanied by at least ONE-FOURTH of Catalogue price; if to be sent by express, C. O. D.; if to be sent by freight cash in full must accompany order.
WE ALWAYS REFUND ALL MONEY if goods are not perfectly satisfactory.

Recoil Pads.

By mail, 5 cents extra.

490 Rudolph's Popular Recoil Pad leather, with lacing; will not become loose. Each, **95c.** Postage extra, 10c.

491 The Rubber Recoil Pad, made enterely of rubber, well padded, and will fit any gun, its elasticity keeping it in position, and preventing the shock of the recoil doing injury to the shoulder. Price, each 35c. Per dozen, **$3.95**.

490 491

492 Pure Red Rubber Recoil Pad, the best pad in the market. Two sizes. Nos. 3 and 4. No. 3 smallest. Give length of heel plate on gun for which you want the pad. Each, **75c.** Postage, extra, 7c.

493 The "Cow Boy" Holster, made of heavy red, oiled leather, raised embossed work; made to match in color and style our Cow Boy Saddles. The best holster on the market.

38 caliber, **$1.40.**
44 " **1.50.**
45 " **1.60.**

Postage, extra, 11c.

494 The "Cow Boy" Combined Cartridge and Money Belt. made of heavy red, oiled leather, strong and durable, designed to match our Cow Boy Saddles. 38, 44 and 45 caliber. Each, **$2.25.** Postage, extra, 8 cents.

Hunting Knives.

All these knives are of very best quality steel.

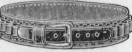

446—Deer Foot.

495 Hunting Knife, deer's foot handle, 7-inch clip blade, best steel, leather sheaths, with loops to attach to belt, nickel bolstered (see cut) **$1.85.**

Spear point

Club blade

496 Hunting Knife, buck horn handle, -inch steel clip blade, leather sheath , with loop to attach to belt; entire length. 11 inches; by mail, 8c extra. **90c.**

497 Hunting Knife, same description as No. 496, 6 inches, spear point; by mail, 8c extra. **95c.**

498 Hunting Knife, same description as No. 496, 9 inches, spear point weight, 13 oz. **$1.65.**

(By mail, 8c extra.)

499 Hunting Knives, scored ebony handle, bolstered with guard, best steel blade, 6-inch blades. Each, **50c.** 6½-inch blades; each, **60c.** 7-inch blades; each, **70c.**

Sheaths and Belts.

(By mail, 8c extra.)

500 Leather Knife Sheaths.
6-in. **10c.** 7-in. **12c.**
8-in. **15c.** 9-in. **18c.**

501 Leather Belts for knife sheaths, 1¼ inches wide, **15c.**

Hunter's Ax.

Hunters' Ax and Sheath.

502 Hunters' Ax, with handles, extra cast steel, steel poll; weight, 1¾ lbs.; with heaviest russet leather sheath, per cut. This is a very convenient tool. It makes a light ax or a heavy hatchet. Price, each, **$1.40.**

Pocket Oilers.

503 The C. & D. Perfection Gun Oiler, the best and handiest gun and revolver oiler in the market. Each, **23c.**

504 The Pocket Oiler, flat, nickel plated, with brass screw on top, entirely preventing the escape of oil; can be carried in the vest pocket; about the size, of a watch. Each, **12c.** Per dozen, **$1.25.** Extra, by mail, 2c.

456

Gun Oil, Etc.

Winchester Gun Grease, put up by the Winchester Repeating Arms Company.

505 The Winchester Gun Grease is the best rust preventer manufactured. It has been in use in this factory for years. For any steel or polished iron surface, and for inside or outside of gun or rifle barrels, it has no equal. Put up in neat metalic tubes. Per tube, **11c.** Per box of 10 tubes. **$1.15.** Postage, 12 cents extra.

506 Parafine Gun Oil, put up exclussvely for guns, gun locks, and fine machinery and furniture; removes rust and will not gum. 2-oz. bottles, Price per dozen, **50c.** 3 bottles for 15 cts. Postage 18 cts. per bottle.

507 Popular Lubricating Oil; best oil in the market for guns, locks, sewing machines, bicycles, and any small machines; will not freeze, gum, rust, or corrode or become rancid. Per bottle, 8c. Per dozen, **80c.** Unmailable.

508 **RUST REMOVER,** coarse, for removing russ from iron, steel, brass or any metal where cutting properties are desired. Per bottle, **20c.**

509 Rust Remover, medium, **18c.**

510 Rust Remover, fine, **19c.** Postage, 5c extra.

511 **WOOD POLISH.** Nothing like it for bright, clean and lustrous polish on furniture, desks, gun stocks and all walnut, oiled or varnished furniture. Per bottle, **20c.** Unmailable.

Sporting Goods Department

ALL ORDERS for CARTRIDGES, LOADED and EMPTY SHOT SHELLS and AMMU-NITION must be accompanied by cash in full.

ALL ORDERS for GUN IMPLEMENTS, TOOLS, SPORTING GOODS, ETC., must be accompanied by at least ONE-FOURTH of Catalogue price; if to be sent by express, C. O. D.; if to be sent by freight, cash in full must accompany order.

WE ALWAYS REFUND ALL MONEY if goods are not perfectly satisfactory.

Bird Calls.

By mail, 2 to 3 cts. each.

512 Grubb's Improved Illinois River Duck Call The most natural toned call made; easy to blow; not easy to get out of repair, having a fine tempered reed; makes it so you can call teal, woodduck and bluebill, as well as mallard. This is the only call you can do this with. Each, 50c.

513 The Perfection Duck Call, made of red cedar, silver mounted, with silver reed which gives it a perfect tone. This is the finest duck call made, perfect, similar in style to the Grubb's call, and are warranted. Each, $1.00.

514 Allen's Improved Wood Duck Caller, the most natural toned, easiest blowing. Used in the field by all the best duck shooters in America. Ea., 45c.

515 Duck Calls, horn, with rosewood mouth piece. Each, 33c.

516 Turkey Calls, horn, with rosewood mouth piece. Each, 32c.

Extra, by mail, 3c.

Allen's Turkey Call. Duck Call.

517 Snipe Calls (no cut). Each, 21c. Postage, 2 cts. extra.

518 Fuller's Metalic Wild Goose Caller. Each, 80c. Extra by mail, 5c,

Barnum's Patent Game Carrier.

By mail, 3 cents extra.

Barnum's. Rudolph's.

519 Worth its weight in gold; a blessing to feathered game shooters; weight 2½ ozs. folded; 8½ in. long; ½ in. thick; can be carried in the pencil pocket, yet holds securely 18 ducks, balanced on the shoulders, on the belt, gun barrel, or in the hand. Price, each 15c. Per dozen, $1.40.

520 Rudolph's Compact Game Carrier, with leather shoulder strap. Each, 30c. Per dozen, $3.00. By mail, 3c. extra.

Decoys

In making these decoys great care has been used to select only sound white cedar for their construction and to secure a perfect balance. They are light, substantial and naturally painted. Assortments: Mallard, canvass back, red head, blue bill, teal, pin or sprig tails. Weight, per dozen, 35 to 40 pounds.

Decoys.

521 No. 1 best decoy ducks, per doz.,......... $3.90
522 No. 2 good decoy ducks, per doz.,....... 3.00
523 Cords and anchors for decoys, per doz. .75

The Brinkop Metal Duck Decoy.

Its the best.

The body is stamped in one piece, and the head and neck in another, from thin sheet metal, and can be connected firmly in an instant, then thrown into the water. They always assume and hold their proper position, can be used with or without the board float; being open underneath. If perforated with holes its buoyancy is not affected. They are neatly painted and on the water closely resemble a live duck, being so light the least wind gives them an easy, graceful motion. A dozen of these ducks do not weigh much more than two wooden ones, and occupy, when nested, about as much space; cheaper and better than wooden decoys.

524 Per dozen, all mallards, with board float and anchors, complete...........................$4.95
Each, weight 17 oz..... 45
Mallard decoys are good for decoying almost any kind of ducks.

Folding Canvas Decoys.

525 Folding Canvass Decoys. The best immitation of the natural duck in the market. Made of best canvass, beautifully painted in natural colors, waterproofed. Weight, 4 oz. each. Packed 1 dozen in a neat wooden box 2¾x9 inches. We do not sell less than a dozen. Mallards, red heads, canvass back and blue bills. Per dozen.............. $7.00
Weight, per dozen, packed, 9 lbs.
526 Folding or collapsible convass geese, packed in boxes of one dozen. Sold in one half dozen lots at dozen prices; not less than one-half dozen sold. Per dozen,................................. $14.40
Weight, per dozen, packed, 11½ lbs.

SPORTING GOODS DEPARTMENT.

ALL ORDERS FOR GUN IMPLEMENTS, TOOLS, SPORTING GOODS, ETC., must be accompanied by at least one-fourth of Catalogue price; if to be sent by express, C. O. D.; if to be sent by freight, cash in full must accompany order.

WE ALWAYS REFUND ALL MONEY if goods are not perfectly satisfactory.

Grass Suits.

527 For wild goose, duck and all kinds of shore bird shooting, made of long, tough marsh grass into cape coat with hood. Weigh less than four pounds, are convenient to wear and shoot from. Make good waterproofs in rainy weather, are easily packed and carried. Hunters appreciate the value of these suits, as no blind or bough house is necessary when shooting on marshes. Single suits, each,......**$3.00**

Hunter's Clothing.

Also good for Farmers, Teamsters and Mechanics. Finest quality and the best made goods in the market. All double stitched and never rip. Extra by mail 40 to 50 cents on canvass coats.

535 The Barnard Hunting Coat, best quality water proof canvas, dead grass color, corduroy collar, leather bound; waist lined with corduroy, and made to button close if desired. Sizes, 36, 38, 40, 42 and 44. Each, **$3.00**.

489

536 The Barnard Hunting Coat, same as No. 535, not leather bound. Each, **$2.75**.

Barnard coats, flannel lined, **$1.50** extra.

537 (No. 1) Vest made of best 8 oz. duck, waterproof, color to match coat, with four pockets, which will carry forty shells or more; sizes 36 to 42. Price each, **75c.** 20 cents extra by mail.

528 Hunting coat, made of heavy 12 oz. duck, dead grass color, otherwise same as 529. Leather bound, made in the best possible manner, heavy and durable. Each,..... **$4.00**

529. (No. 1) Hunting coat, is made of heavy 8 oz. duck, dead grass color and waterproof, bound with leather to prevent wearing out of edges, has six pockets, entrance to game pocket from outside; shoulders reinforced corduroy collar, no better coat in the market; sizes 36 to 46. Price each, **$2.90**

530. Coat, same as No. 1, without leather binding; sizes 36 to 46. Price each, **$2.35**.

531. Coat, lighter duck, 6 pockets outside, full game pocket inside, corduroy collar; sizes 36 to 46, a good coat. Each, **$1.55**.

532 Coat, same as No. 531, except leather bound all around. Each, **$1.80**.

533. Hunting coat, dead grass color, duck, 4 outside pockets, one large game pocket, full size of coat inside, with outside entrance on each side. Each, **90c.** Extra by mail 25cts.

534 Hunting suit, greenish drab color, 8 oz. duck for hunting or fishing, before the foliage is dead, or

in the south, 6 outside pockets, full inside game pocket, entrance on the outside, shoulders reinforced. Made in first class manner; a good suit, coat, pants and vest. **$4.50**.

Coat only, **$2.40**. Vest only, 95c.

Pants only, **$1.27**.

Caps and hats, any hunting style, same prices as the DEAD GRASS colored.

N. B.—We can furnish the above coats heavy flannel lined, **$1.50** extra. No other coat is needed where No. 1 coat is lined.

538 Vest same as 537, but with shell bands instead of pockets; sizes, 36 to 44. Price each, **$1.00**. Extra by mail, 15cts. Give chest measure for coat and vest.

539 Hunting Pants, made of heavy, 8 oz. waterproof duck to match coat and vest, with two long pockets in front, one hip pocket, full length, regular make, double stitched, never rip until worn out. Each, **$1.30**. Extra by mail, 25c.

539

538

540 Canvas Vest, dead grass color, with sleeves; sizes, 36 to 44. Each, **$1.15**. Extra by mail, 16 cts

541 Skeleton coat canvas, dead grass color with game pockets. Sizes breast measure, 36 to 44. Each, **90c.** Extra by mail, 16c.

540   541

Best Imported Corduroy Suits.

Weights—coat, 42 oz; Pants, 33; Vest, 16 to 20 oz.

542 Corduroy coat; size 36 to 44.... ....**$6.15**
543 Corduroy vest; size 36 to 44............... 2.93
544 Corduroy Pants; give waist and inside seam measure; full length, regular make.... 4.45
545 Corduroy Hunting Coat, dark drab color not as heavy as 545, but well made and durable. (Many prefer them to the heavier goods.) Each..................................... 4.13
546 Corduroy pants, same..................... 3.15
547 Corduroy vest, same...................... 1.80

Our Corduroy clothing is made of **Imported** goods, and is free from any "objectionable odor," such as is found in some "so called" imported corduroys. They are well made and nice fitting goods, and all warranted as represen3ed. Coats are all sack style, similar to our hunting coats in design and finish.

Oil Tanned Horsehide Suits.

Weight—Coats, 56 to 60 oz.

Positively the best garment made in this or any other country for those exposed to rough weather They are water and windproof, pliable and soft as kid, and will always remain so. Made with outside pockets.

548 Horsehide coat, reversible with corduroy; sizes, 36 to 44............... **$11.65**

549 Horsehide coat, heavy cassimere lined......**$9.79**

548

Sporting Goods Department.

ALL ORDERS FOR CARTRIDGES, LOADED and EMPTY SHOT SHELLS and AMMUNITION must be accompanied by cash in full.

ALL ORDERS for GUN IMPLEMENTS, TOOLS, SPORTING GOODS, Etc., must be accompanied by at least ONE-FOURTH of catalogue price; if to be sent by express, C. O. D.; if to be sent by freight cash in full must accompany order.

WE ALWAYS REFUND ALL MONEY if goods are not perfectly satisfactory.

Oil Tanned Horsehide Suits.—Continued.

550 Vest, Cassimere lined horsehide..........$3.90
551 Vests, reversible, with corduroy.......... 5.60
552 Pants, horsehide cassimere lined, weight about 3 lbs. Full length regular make........ 6.95
553 Horsehide Pants, reversible, with corduroy.................................... 8.50

Our horsehide clothing is genuine horsehide, and not "goatskin" or "sheepskin" or "dogskin" (which is another name for "sheepskin" in most cases), and will never peel off or get rough, no matter how sharp the thorns or how thick the brush and trees are, and can be oiled like a boot or harness, grows softer and more pliable the longer it is worn.

554 The Hunters' Shirt, made of lamb's wool. They pull down over the head and make a close-fitting wind-proof garment. Being elastic they are also good for trap shooters. Colors: white, tan, black and navy blue. Extra heavy. (Retail price, $6.00. Each.... $3.75 Medium heavy (Retail price. $4.00.) Each.............. $2.75 Weight, 22 to 30 oz.

Shooting Blouse.

555 Thurman's Shooting Blouse. For trap shooters; made of the very best knit jersey. Colors: brown or navy blue.
Each.............$1.80
Postage, 10c. extra.

Chamois Shirt.

556 This shirt is made of fine Swiss Chamois and lined with a light cassine.e—has the extra protector on chest. It is pronounced by our leading trap shooters to be the most comfortable garment on the market. It is proof against the wind. Soft and light. Does not interfere with the proper handling of the gun. For measure, send size of collar worn, breast measure and length of sleeve.

Price, net..................................... $6.25
Weight, 35 to 40 oz.

Hunting Hats and Caps.

557 558

557 Hunting Cap (No. 1) made of heavy dead grass colored duck, with double visor. Give size of hat worn, Weight, 5 oz. Each.......... 42c
558 Hunting Cap, same as above, one visor, has havelock cape to pretect the neck from starm or sun. Taped seams, light flannel lined. Weight, 12 oz. Each............................ 48c

Our Canvas goods are the best in the market.

We do not handle the cheap stuff.

559 560

559 Hunting Hat, dead grass colored duck, all around rim, taped seams, weight 10 oz. Each, 38c
560 Solar Hunting Hat, dead grass crlor, with ventilated sweat band inside.................... 60c
561 Corduroy Hats, round top, light drab color, taped seams............................... 85c
562 Corduroy Hat, square top, light drab color, taped seams.............................. 85c
563 Corduroy Cap, double visor, light drab color, taped seams............................ 60c
546 Corduroy Cap, with short cape, light color, taped seams............................... 75c
Postage extra, 12c.

565 Corduroy Cap.
Each.............. 75c
Postage, extra, 12c.
For lined duck clothing, see "Clothing Department."

Clothes Bags.

566 Made of heavy white duck, with drawing strings fastened on the top, with round bottom; weight, 2 lbs................................. 95c
Postage extra, 35c.

Leggings.

For Hunting Boots and Shoes see Index.

When ordering leggings, be sure and give size of calf of leg outside of pants.

567 Reynold's Army Style, Leggings made of heavy 10 oz. brown water-proof canvas, with eyelets and hooks to lace all the way; 12 inches long. In ordering send size around calf of leg.
Per pair............................... 75c
Per dozen............................. $8.00
568 Men's Knee Legging to buckle; brown canvas. Per pair...........................50c
Per dozen...........................$5.40
Postage extra, 4 cents.

569 (AH) Men's Leggings, brown waterproof canvas, to button on side, 16 inches long.
Postage extra, 12c.
Per pair...............60c
Per dozen.........$6.00

570 (AX) Men's Leggings, brown waterproof canvas, leather facings to button on side,
Per pair................75c
Per dozen.............$8.00
569 Postage extra, 15c. 571

Give measurement around calf of leg for all kinds of leggings.

571 (AM) Men's Leggings, brown canvas, water-proof, leather facings, to buckle. Like cut, 16 inches long. Per pair...................... .. 78c
Per dozen............................$8.20
Postage extra, 21c.
572 Men's Leggings, same as 573, except has steel spring fastenings on side instead of buckles or buttons. Each............................$1.00
Per dozen.............................11.00
Postage extra, 25c,

Sporting Goods Department

ALL ORDERS for CARTRIDGES, LOADED and EMPTY SHOT SHELLS and AMMUNITION must be accompanied by CASH IN FULL.

ALL ORDERS for GUN IMPLEMENTS, TOOLS, SPORTING GOODS, ETC., must be accompanied by at least ONE-FOURTH of Catalogue price; if to be sent by express C. O. D.; if to be sent by freight, cash in full must accompany order.

***WE ALWAYS REFUND ALL MONEY* if goods are not perfectly satisfactory.**

573 (AB) Men's Leggings, brown canvas, water-proof, leather facings to buckle and button. Like cut, extra long, 25 inches long; wt. 28 oz. Per pair....................................$1.10
Per dozen....................................11.40
Postage extra, 30c.

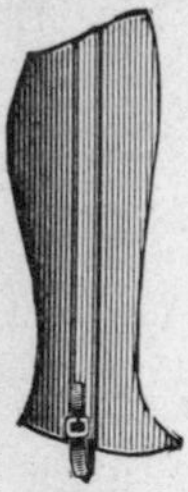

574-5

574 (AO) Men's Leggings black grain leather, with steel spring stiffner on side, the new and convenient fastening like cut; 19 in. long. Weight, 44 oz.
Per pair................$1.85
Per dozen..............19.85

575 Men's Leggings, russet grain leather, with steel spring stiffener on side, the new and convenient fastening, like cut, 18 inches, weight, 40 oz.
Per pair....................................$1.85
Per doz....................................19.85
Postage extra, 45c.

572

576 (OAP) Men's Leggings, black grain leather, to buckle all the way up, 18 inches long, weight, 32 oz. Per pair $1.75
Per doz....................................18.70
Postage extra, 35c.

577 Men's Leggings, russet grain leather, like cut 572, to buckle all the way up; 18 inches long. Weight, 32 oz. Per pair..................$1.75
Per dozen....................................18.70

Thigh

Horsehide Leggings, either "Knee" or "Thigh" lengths. To lace all the way. Same price as to buckle.

578 Men's Knee Leggings, russet tanned horsehide, to lace, weight 28 oz.
Per pair....................................$2.39
Per dozen....................................25.00

579 Men's Thigh Leggings, russet tanned horsehide, to buckle and lace; weight, 36 oz. Per pair..........$3.20
Per dozen pair....................$33.75

Showing shape of thigh legging, all buckle.

N. B.—The horsehide leggings are the handsomest and best in the market; are always soft and pliable.

Horsehide leggings to lace all the way; same price as buckle.

580 Men's Knee Leggings, imported corduroy, to buckle. Each $1.48
Per doz.............................. 15.00
Weight, 23 oz. To lace.
Per pair.............................. 1.50
Per doz..............................16.00

Always send measurement around calf of leg for leggings, or we will be obliged to hold the order and write you for size.

Dog Collars—Big Bargains.

By mail, 5 to 14c extra.

581 Dog Collar, nickel, wide, flat links, nickel name plate, with staple for padlock. The most popular and a big seller; very attractive; 14, 16, 17 and 18 in,; width, 1 inch.
Each....................$.20

582 Dog Collar, fine orange leather, chamois lined, large nickel plated studs, nickel name plate and trimmings, to lock; length, 17, 19 and 21 in.; 1 in. wide. Each..$.69

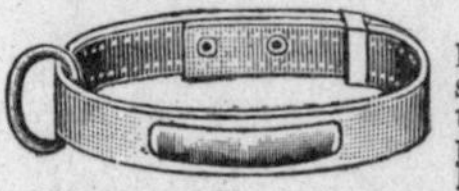

583 Dog Collar, double harness leather, black, stitched edges, nickel trimming, ring name plate and staple to lock; length, 17 to 21 inches; width, 1 in. Each.......................................$0.49

584 Length, 19 to 23 in.; width, 1¼ in., each, .50
585 Length, 21 to 25 in.; width, 1½ in., each, .55
586 Dog Collar, same as 583, except to buckle; length, 17 to 21 in., width, 1 in., each.............. .38
587 Length, 19 to 23 in.; width, 1⅛ in., each... .44
Length, 21 to 25 in.; width, ⅛ in., each.... .47

588 Dog Collar, polished steel name plate, chain and padlock in one; strong and durable; will last a lifetime; single chain, 14 and 16 in.
Each.......................................$0.35

589 Same style, double chain, 14, 15, 17, 18 and 20 in. Each.......................................$0.65

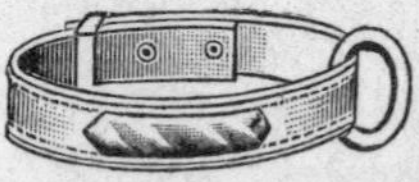

590 Dog Collar, fancy leather, assorted colors, nickel trimmings and name plate; length, 8, 9, 10, 12 and 13 in.; width, ⅝ in. Each..............$0.18
Per doz.............. 1.60

591 Length, 13, 14, 15 or 16 inches; width, ⅞ in.
Each.......................................$0.27
Per doz....... .... 2.75

592 (ABOt) Dog Collar, best English single russet harness leather, studded, nickle name plate and ring to buckle; length, 14, 15, 16, 17, 18 and 20 in.; width, 1 in.; all collars have nickel name plates.
Each.......................................$0.45

593 Dog Collar, same as 592; double row, heavy plated studs, is 1¼ to 1½ inches wide; to buckle, 21 inches; 22 inches long. Each .... .44
594 Dog Collar. same as No. 592; fine nickle plated studs. is 1½ inches wide, to buckle, 15, 16, 17, 18 and 20 inches long. Each .... .59
595 Dog Collar, same as 592, except to lock, 1¼ in. wide, 2 rows, heavy nickle plated studs, fine russet leather, 16, 17, 18, 19, 20, 21 in. long. Each .... .65
595½ Dog Collar, extra quality, single harness leather, studded, to lock (locks not included in price named) 1 in. wide, 17, 19 and 21 in. Each.................................. .55
596 Three rows studs, with staple to attach lock, 1¼ to 1½ inches wide, 14. 15, 17, 19, 21 and 23 in. Each.................................. .60
597 Dog Collar, same as No. 595, with staple to attach lock, 2¼ inches wide, four rows nickel plated studs, 15, 16, 17, 18, 19, 20, 21, 22 and 24 inches long. Each.............................. 1.00
Postage extra, 12c.

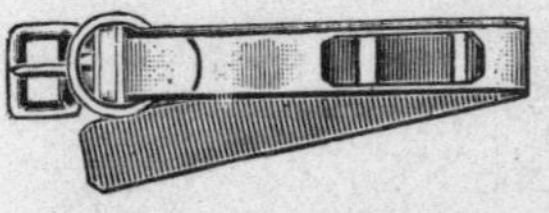

598 (AOCt) Dog Collar, russet leather, nickel name plate and ring to buckle; length, 14 to 18 in.; width 1 in., each..$0.22
Per doz...... 2.15
Length 9 to 12 in., ½ in. wide. Each .... .20

599 (CTP) Scalloped russet leather, to lock, chamois lined, new style ornaments. Width ¾ in.; length, 13, 15 or 17 inches.
Each $0.35
Per doz...... 3.60

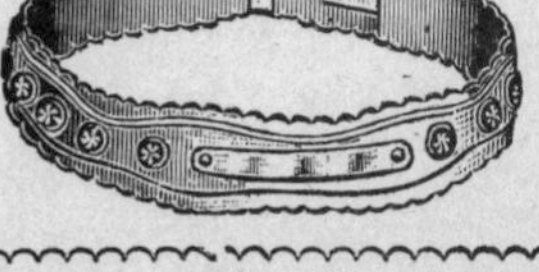

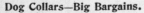

Sporting Goods Department.

ALL ORDERS FOR CARTRIDGES, LOADED and EMPTY SHOT SHELLS and AMMUNITION must be accompanied by cash in full.

ALL ORDERS for GUN IMPLEMENTS, TOOLS, SPORTING GOODS, Etc., must be accompanied by at least ONE-FOURTH of catalogue price; if to be sent by express, C. O. D.; if to be sent by freight cash in full must accompany order.

WE ALWAYS REFUND ALL MONEY if goods are not perfectly satisfactory.

600 (ctHc(Cl) Nickel plated, woven steel wire chain.leather and chamois lined, handsome and stylish, 1 in. wide, staple to lock. Lengths: 17, 19, 21 in. Each ..**$0.60** Per doz.....**$6.48**

601 Round Dog Collar, to buckle. Fine heavy block leather,with name plate, 16, 18, 20 in. Each.......**$0.75** Round Dog Collars, orange leather, very light weight, no name plate, to buckle. 14, 16, 18 in. Each.................**$0.75**

603 D. Watter's Spike Collar, pronounced by all dog trainers the best collar ever made for training purposes. Simple and durable, and cannot twist. Hence the points are always towards the dog's neck. It works freely, and will not mutilate any dog. Punishment can be applied or ended instantly in forcing a dog to retrieve. Every owner of a dog should have one. Made of good black leather. Each **$1.40**

Extra by mail, 10c.

604 (CTARcl) Nickel plated ladder link chain, leather and chamois lined; a big seller (to lock); width, ¾ in. Length, 13, 15 and 17 in. Each .....**$0.30** Per doz...**$3.00**

605 Dog Collar, lined with fancy colored leather, making a handsome and durable collar; width, ½ in.; length, 9, 10, 12 and 14 in. Each...........................**$0.30** Width, ¾ in.; length, 13, 15 and 16 in...........**.40** Width, 1 in.; length, 14, 15, 16, 17, 18 and 20 in. Each ....**.50**

Dog Combs.

606 Rubber Dog Combs, best quality. Ea. **$0.25**

Dog Collar Padlocks.

607 Padlock, 1x¾ in., all nickel plated, with key. Each..... **$0.20** Per dozen .... **2.20** **608** Padlock, 1x¾ in., brass, with key. Each............**$0.20** Per doz.,**$2.20**. Extra by mail, 1c.

607-8

609 Scandinavian Padlock for dog collar.

Small ....**$0.20** Large............ **.25** Postage extra, 2c

610 Dog Collar Padlock, made of aluminum, almost as light as a feather, ¾ in. by 10-16 in. (CTC). Each ....**$0.20** Per doz. **2.25**

Dog Leads.

By mail 5 to 8 cents extra.

611 Dog leads, polished steel. cable link, very light weight, snap on end. Each, **25c.** **612** Dog leads, fancy silver link, light weight, but strong and durable, 4½ feet. Each, **35c.** **613** Dog lead, polished steel, cable link, large size, with swivel and snap, 4½ feet. Each, **30c.**

614 Dog Lead, polished iron, flat safety link, neatly polished, and very strong and durable, also makes the best of halter chains, 4½ feet. Small, each, **15c.** Medium, each, **18c.** Large, each, **25c.** **615** Dog Leads, hand braided leather, round with loop and snap, 40 in. Each, **39c.** **616** Kennel Dog Chains, polished iron, flat link, 5½ feet, with snap and swivels. Weight, 16 oz., **44c.** **617** Kennel Dog Chains, polished steel, round wire, new style safety links, 3 swivels, 2 hooks, well made and durable; no dog can break it; 9 feet. Each, **65c.** Weight, 16 oz.

618 Dog Couplings, polished steel, large ring in center, snap hook on each end, two swivels; weight 5 oz. Each, **40c.**

The Surprise Whistle.

By mail, 1c. extra.

619 TheSurpriseWhistle, the loudest and best dog call in the market. By squeezing in the bulb at the end you can regulate the sound and produce any effect, from purling, or muffled notes up to a great swelling booming, two mile piercing note. A good snipe or plover call also. Each, **20c.** Per doz., **$2.00**. Postage extra, 2c.

Whistles.

620. Celluloid Dog Call or Whistle. A loud one Small, each......**20c.** Large, each .....**25c.**

Postage extra 2 cts.

Sporting Goods Department.

ALL ORDERS for CARTRIDGES, LOADED and EMPTY SHOT SHELLS and AMMUNITION must be accompanied by cash in full.

ALL ORDERS for GUN IMPLEMENTS, TOOLS, SPORTING GOODS, ETC., must be accompanied by at least ONE-FOURTH of catalogue price; if to be sent by express C. O. D.; if to be sent by freight cash in full must accompany order.

WE ALWAYS REFUND ALL MONEY if goods are not perfectly satisfactory.

Dog Whips.

By mail, 8 cents extra.

621 Whips, hand braided russet leather, whistle on handle, heavy and durable. Each 73c.

622 The Never Break Whip, same as 621, with snap on end instead of whistle, making a good lead as well as whip, can be folded into small compass and carried in pocket. Each, 50c.

623 The Never Break Whip, 12 plait braided leather, with leather loop on end, loaded butt, strong tnd durable. Each, 80c.

Dog Muzzles.

By mail, 4 to 6 cents extra.

624 Dog Muzzles, common iron wire, with strap to buckle around the neck. Basket style to cover nose and mouth. Each, 25c.

Safety.

625 "The Safety" Dog Muzzle, made of iron wire with strap to buckle around neck. Each, 25c.

626 Leather strap Dog Muzzle, to buckle around neck and buckle to take up around head if too large. Small size, 15c. Medium size, 30c. Large size, 39c.

Give measurements from tip of nose to top of head.

627 Automatic Dog Muzzle, wire and leather. Permits dog to open mouth to drink or eat. Each, 70c.

628 The Echo Call, the loudest yet, beautifully nickel-plated. Can be carried in the vest pocket. Each, 233.

626

Drinking Cups.

629. Drinking Cups. Britannia collapsing telescope height, full length 3¼ inches, width across top 2⅜ in., flaring bottom, comes in round japanned box; size 2½x1⅜ in. One of the handiest and most convenient articles ever invented for hunters, tourests and teamsters; can be carried in pocket easily. Price only 20 cts; per doz. $2.00; By mail, 4c extra.

630. Soft, White Rubber Drinking Cup, tumbler shape, will hold about as much as a common table tumbler, flexible and can be folded and put in pocket.

Each .... 18c.

By mail, 3 cts. extra.

630½. Patent Collapsing Pocket Cup, in nickeled tin watch case. Cup stands about 2 inches high when open. Case exact size of a watch. One of the best novelties ever invented. Price each .... 25 cts. By mail .... 4c extra.

631. Olry Pocket Flasks, leather covered, with metal drinking cup on bottom, and white metal screw-off top or stopper. Almost a household necessity.

¼ Pint	$0 75
½ Pint	87
¾ Pint	1 10
1 Pint	1 25
1 Quart	2 10

Dog Remidies.

631½ "Spratts Patent" Tonic Condition Pills for debility arising from disease, and of great value in preparing dogs for work requiring endurance. Unequaled in preparing dogs for bench shows.

Price per box	$0 35
Postage	04

632. "Spratts Patent" Mange Cure, which rarely fails to speedily cure mange in every form, and the destruction of fleas, lice, ticks, etc., in the Dog, Horse, Ox, Pig and other animals, is non-poisonous, full directions wrapped around each bottle.

Price	$0 40
Postage	10

633. "Spratts Patent" Worm Cure. A speedy and sure destroyer of these troublesome parasites, which are the source of so many forms of canine diseases.

Price per box	$0 35
Postage	04

634. "Spratts Patent" Distemper Cure, the new antiseptic remedy. an effective cure for the scourge of the kennel; each packet contains very minute directions for the treatment of dogs suffering under distemper.

Price per box	$0 70
Postage	04

GENUINE UNLESS NONE ARE SPRATTS PATENT STAMPED

635. "Spratts Patent" Fibrine Dog Cakes (with Beetroot), these celebrated biscuits are supplied to all the leading kennels and are used at the principal dog shows in America and England, and have been before the public for more than a quarter of a century.

Price per 50 lb. bag	$3.25
25 lb. boxes per box	1.70
5 lb. boxes per box	.40

636. "Spratts Patent" Dog Soap; this is of the greatest value to dog owners as it is entirely free from poison and at the same time most effective in the destruction of lice, fleas and ticks; it is the only soap that should be used in preparing dogs for exhibition, as it leaves the coat smooth and glossy. Printed directions for using the soap on each wrapper

Price per cake	$ 20
Extra by mail	07

Plaited Billy.

637. Plaited Billy black leather each $0.30

638. Braided Leather Billy, 12 plat, loaded with shot, made of the best material and cannot be broken. 9½ inches; weight 6 oz. Each 0.95

Postage extra 06

SPORTING GOODS DEPARTMENT.

ALL ORDERS for CARTRIDGES, LOADED and EMPTY SHOT SHELLS and AMMU-NITION must be accompanied by cash in full.
ALL ORDERS for GUN IMPLEMENTS, TOOLS, SPORTING GOODS, ETC., must be accompanied by at least ONE-FOURTH of Catalogue price; if to be sent by express, C. O. D.; if to be sent by freight cash in full must accompany order.
WE ALWAYS REFUND ALL MONEY if goods are not perfectly satisfactory.

Braided Leather Pocket Billy, made of the best material, cannot be broken.

Each $0.50
Postage, extra .... .05

The Duplex Police Call or Bicycle Whistle.

640 Duplex Call, nickle plated, Each $0.15
641. Duplex Call, with guard chain. Each .... .20
Extra by mail, 3c.

Lawn Tennis Goods, Etc.

642. Best Jointed Poles, polished, with brass ferrules, ornamented. Per pair......... $1.70
643. Ordinary Jointed Poles. Per pair...... .90
644. Lawn Tennis Guy Ropes and Pins; complete, 2 ropes, 4 guys and 4 pins; per set, 25c, 50c, 75c, according to quality.
645. Tennis Marking or Boundary Tapes for marking out the court with pins and staples; per set................................. 3.90
646. Dry Powder Court Marker, cylinders and handle complete................................. 1.70
647. Tennis Fork to hold net up in center, made of smooth iron. Each.............. .75
Weight 2¼ lbs.
648. Tennis Marking Plates for marking angles of court. Made of iron; per set of 10 plates .... .90

Each
649. Tennis nets, 27 x 3 feet, 12 threads, weight 27 oz........................... $0.90
650. Tennis nets, 36 x 3 feet, 15 thread, weight 32 oz 1.40
651. Tennis nets, 42 x 3, 15 thread, weight 32 oz 1.55
652. Back stop nets, 50 x 7 feet, No. 12 thread Each...................................... 3.35

652½. Popular Lawn Tennis set contains 4 strung gut bats, 4 balls, portable poles, net 3 x 27 feet lines and runners, mallet and book complete in box, a good plain set, small bats, per set **$8.45**
653. Popular lawn tennis set, contains 4 regulation bats. 4 balls, good net, 3 x 33 feet, portable poles, lines and runner ,mallet and book of instructions, complete in box **$10.35**.
654. Picnic lawn tennis set, contains 4 regulation racquets, regulation net, 4 regulation balls, painted poles, jointed guys, ropes, pegs, and mallet, with book of instructions, complete in case. **$13.00.** Better sets, complete **$18.00, $20.00, $25.00, $30.00.**

Lawn Tennis Balls.

655. Plain rubber for wet weather use........$0.18
656. Regulation covered......................... .28
657. Tournament, regulation covered......... .35
658. Champion Tennis Balls. Wright and Distons.................................... .40

Lawn Tennis Bats. "Racquets."

Our Tennis Bats this year are the latest improved.

Made by A. G. Spaulding Bros. and best makers, and warranted A 1 quality. If not satisfactory for price, can be returned at our expense after examination, These prices are from 30 to 50 per cent less than regular retail prices.
669. Boys bat. ash frame, gut strung 80c.
670. Boy's and Gil'r's favorite; made of good ash, cedar handle, gut strung, $1.10.
671. No.A bat made of good ash, cedar handle, gut strung. 10 to 14 oz., a good bat for beginners, 10 to 11½ oz., $1.65.
672. No. M bat, made of good ash, cedar handle, domestic gut, length 26½ in., bow 7½ x 10½, $2.00.
673. No. B bat made of good white ash, cedar handle, fair qulity of domestic gut. A well finished bat, 11 to 15 oz. $2.40.
674. No. P bat, made of fine white ash, cedar handle, good quality all redgut, a strong bat, 11 to 15 oz. checkered handles, cherry throat piece, $3.24.
675. Same as 674, with cork handle, $3.40.
676. Bat No. O, made of the finest white ash, cedar handle, strung with finest red and white gut, 12 to 15 oz., Slocum Pattern, fine finish, $4.00.
677. Bat same as 676, cork handle, $4.40.
678. Tournament Racquet, extra fine all Oriental gut, polished mahogany handle. Slocum Pattern $5.75.
679. Tournament Racquet, oval handle, finest white gut, handsomely finished, checkered on side of handle, mahogany throat Piece........$6.00
680. Tennis Bat Covers, made of green felt, ea.   45
681. Tennis Ball Covers, made of canvass, ea.   90
682. Rubber Handle Covers for Tennis Bats.....   45

Croquet Sets.

Weight 16 to 28 Pounds.

683. Four-ball Croquet Set, plain mallets, oiled balls and stakes varnished, ten arches, with book, in neat box with hinged cover...........$0.68
684. Same as No. 683, with 8 balls in dovetailed box with hinged cover............................. 1.10
685. Eight-ball Croquet Set, mallets of neat design, painted and striped, also balls, 2 large fancy stakes, heavy coppered arches. An excellent set at a low price (6)..................... 1.75
686. Eight-Ball Croquet Set, handsome maple, with fancy striped mallets, handles and balls, 2 elegant beaded steaks, heavy pointed arches painted, superior workmanship and materials in every part (7)................................. 2.20
686½. Eight Ball Croquet Set, shellac finish finish, 8 fancy striped 6 inch ebonized and bronzed malets, handles and balls beautifully finished, painted and striped, 2 elegantly beaded stakes heavy arches with sockets, an elegant set.... . 3.40

Base Balls.

At Manufacturers' prices.

687 Regular League Ball, warranted equal to the finest league balls. Dealers are authorized to refund the money or give new balls in every case where it fails to give satisfaction. Each ball wrapped in tin foil and packed in separate box and sealed. Each, **$1.00**; Per dozen, **$11.00.**
688 Amateur League, rubber center, with all wool core, wound with woolen yarn, horsehide cover; this ball will give satisfaction every time. Each, 65c. Per dozen, **$7.00.**
389 King of the Diamond Ball, horsehide cover; each ball in a box. Each, 40c. Per dozen, **$4.20.**
690 Boy's Favorite Ball, horsehide cover, regular make. Each, 25c. Per dozen, **$2.50.**

Sporting Goods Department.

ALL ORDERS for CARTRIDGES, LOADED and EMPTY SHOT SHELLS and AMMUNITION must be accompanied by cash in full.

ALL ORDERS for GUN IMPLEMENTS, TOOLS, SPORTING GOODS, ETC., must be accompanied by at least ONE-FOURTH of Catalogue price; if to be sent by express C. O. D.; if to be sent by freight cash in full must accompany order.

WE ALWAYS REFUND ALL MONEY if goods are not perfectly satisfactory.

Our base balls are the best in the market and are guaranteed regulation weight and size. Our League Association and Regulation balls are all warranted to stand a full game, which is all any maker claims for the very best balls that they make. Extra by mail, 5 to 7 cents.

691 Boys' Amateur ball, horsehide cover, regular make. Each, 15c. Per dozen, $1.25.

The above Nos., 690 and 691, are regulation weights and sizes, and no better balls made for the money.

Base Balls for Boys.

Cheap and well made, leather covered.

692. Ball, 8⅞ in; Boys' Lively, each, 9c; per doz., 87c.

693 Ball, 7½; Boss, each, 4c.; per doz., 45c.

Base Ball Bats.

We take pleasure in calling attention to our line of bats, which are made from improved models, and of the best selected timber, and are approved by the best players in the country.

Men's bats, 20 to 40 ounces, length 30 to 36 inches.

694 Men's Bat, best straight grain, second growth, white ash thoroughly seasoned; broad band on ends, antique finish and lathe polished, warranted equal in quality, style and finish to the best fancy named bats such as "Oriental, Wagon Tongue," etc. Each, 50c; per dozen, $5.49.

695 Men's Bats, best selected white ash, highly finished and lathe polished, broad band, regulation sizes, no better bat in the market for service. Each, 35c.; Per doz., $3.60.

696 Men's Bats, selected, first growth white ash, finished with best shellac and lathe polished, a good one. Each, 25c.; per doz., $2.50.

697 Men's Willow Bats, lathe polished, and finished with the best white shellac; the best light bat in the market. Each, 35c.; per doz., $3.60.

698 Men's Bat, best white ash, plain finish. Each, 15c., per doz., $1.30.

699 Boy's bat, best white ash. Each, 12c.; per doz., $1.30.

700 Boy's bat, best polished ask. Each, 15c.; per doz., $1.30.

701 Boy's bat, best polished rosewood finish. Each, 13c.; per doz., $1.30.

702 Canvas bat bags, heavy waterproof canvas, leather ends, to hold one dozen bats. Each, $3.80.

The higher priced bats are those commonly sold from 75 cents to $1.00.

Don't pay fancy prices for the dealer's name on a bat, when we sell the same article, minus the paint, for less than one-half the money. Sold in one-half dozen lots or over at dozen prices.

Base Ball Gloves.

703 Special baseman's glove, heavy oil tanned goat skin, extra heavy padded; full left hand, not tipped, right hand fingerless, hand sewed, warranted. Per pair, $1.50. Extra by mail, 15c.

Short Fingers.

704 Boy's Catcher's Gloves, full left hand, not tipped, best oil tanned goat skin,

703

full padded, a good article. Per pair, $1.00. Extra by mail, 5 cents.

705 Amateur Catcher's Gloves, oil-tanned goat skin, fingerless, open back, well padded, 65c.

706 Boys' Gloves, fingerless, open backs, padded, 20c. Extra by mail, 3 cents.

Base Ball Caps.

Made to order.

The Chicago Club or College cap, as represented in accompanying cut, is the most desirable and popular shape, having been adopted by nearly all the leading clubs. Extra by mail, 3 to 5 cents.

Base ball caps and clothing have to be made to order, consequently, in ordering allow as much time as possible.

707 Cap, white, red, royal blue, navy blue, black, brown, maroon, old gold, green and gray colors, with or without one or two stripes. Fine flannel, leather swert band; best quality, 65c.

708 Cap, white, red, royal blue, navy blue, black, light gray, medium gray, or dark gray, with one or two stripes. Good flannel, well made, leather sweat band, 55c.

709 Cap, same colors as No. 708, well made and durable, with one or two stripes or without stripes, 45c

710 Cap, all muslin, assorted colors, plain red, plain blue, plain white, no stripes or bands, all plain solid color, 12c.

Base Ball Suits.

711 Base ball suits, consisting of shirt, pants, cap, stockings and belt. $3.50, $5.00, $7.50, $10.00, $12.00.

Cash for full amount must accompany the order. Suit samples sent on application.

Safety Shoe Plates.

712 This is made of tempered steel; safe strong and tight, and is positively the best shoe plate made. They are nicely packed, each pair in envelope with suitable screws, all complete, one dozen pairs in a box. Extra by mail, 3c, per pair. Per pair, 15c.; per doz., $1.50.

713 Professional shoe plate, large size, per pair, 25c.; per dozen pair, $2.50.

714 Pitcher's toe plates, made of heavy brass, for right shoe, each, 45c.

Catcher's Masks.

Warranted the best mask made. It is made of the best material, well padded, and by an ingenious arrangement of the wires an unobstructed view is obtained. It is far superior to the old style of wire mask, or the heavy dangerous steel bar mask.

715 New neck protecting mask best wire, best padding, soft and pliable, $3.60.

716 Extra heavy special league masks, the very best made, warranted, each $2.97.

717 Regulation league masks, heavy wire and warranted first-class in every respect, each $2.50. Extra by mail, 30 cts.

718 Amateur Men's masks. We guarantee this mask to be equally as good as many dealers sell for the best league mask. Each, $1.50.

719 Amateur Boys' Masks. This mask is the same as the men's masks, only smaller, to fit a boy's face. Each, $1.35. Extra by mail, 20cts.

720 Youths' masks, without head or chin piece. Each, 80c.

721 Boys' masks, light wire, without head or chin piece. Each, 40c.

Sporting Goods Department

ALL ORDERS for CARTRIDGES, LOADED and EMPTY SHOT SHELLS and AMMU-NITION must be accompanied by cash in full.

ALL ORDERS for GUN IMPLEMENTS, TOOLS, SPORTING GOODS, ETC., must be accompanied by at least **ONE-FOURTH** of Catalogue price; if to be sent by express, C. O. D.; if to be sent by freight, cash in full must accompany order.

WE ALWAYS REFUND ALL MONEY if goods are not perfectly satisfactory.

Base Ball Belts.

Extra by mail 3 cents.

722. Cotton Web Belts. 2¼ in. wide, leather mounted, single strap and buckle, colors: red, blue, white, maroon, navy blue, red, white edge, blue, white edge, red, white and blue, red and white stripe, blue and white stripe, each 14c., per doz., $1.50.

723. Cotton Web Belts, 2¼ in. double strap, nickel buckle, (same colors as 722), each, 23c, per dozen, $2.30.

724. Worsted Web Belt, 2½ in., single leathered covered buckle, colors: Red, blue, navy brown, black, white, Maroon and old gold, each, 32c, per dozen, $3.40.

725. Worsted webb Belt, 2½ in., double leathered covered buckles, (same colors as 724.) each, 35c, per pozen, $3.60.

726. Special League Belt, worsted web, large nickel plated buckle, same colors as 725, each, 45c, per dozen, $4.70.

Spaulding's Base Ball Goods.

Base Balls.

Extra by mail, 10 cents each.

727. Spaulding's League Base Ball, per dozen, $13.90.

728. Spaulding's Double Seam Base Ball, per dozen, $14.50.

Sold in any quantity at the above prices.

Bats.

Weight 22 to 40 ounces.

729. Spaulding's Best Second Growth Ash Bat, wagon tongue, new rough handle, per doz., $11.95.

730. Spaulding's Second Growth Ash, Black Band League Bat, polished rough handle, special weight same price, per doz., $9.00.

731. Spaulding's Trade-Marked Black Band Willow Bat, per doz., $4.00.

Sold in any quantity at above prices.

Catchers' Mitts.

Throwing Glove.

Front.

732. Spaulding's Special League Mitt, finest quality drab buckskin, new model, laced, with patent short-fingered throwing-glove, each, $6.30.

733. Spaulding's League Mitt, Hogskin, with patent throwing glove, ea h, $4.25.

734. M. W. & Co's New League Mitt, best buckskin, fingerless throwing glove padded with extra thick felt, heavy rubber welt around front of fingers, fingers heavy leather tipped, as good as the best; once used you would have no other kind. As well padded and as good quality in every way as the best glove in the market; warranted, each, $4.85.

735. M. W. & Co's. Horsehide Back Locked Elastic Fastening League Mitt and throwing Glove, same make as No. 734. Made of good leather, soft and pliable, each, $3.00.

736. M. W. & Co's. Goatskin League Mitt and Throwing Glove, thick felt pad with welt around front of fingers. A good one, each, $2.30.

737. M. W. & Co's. Boys' League Mitt and Throwing Glove, laced fastening, heavy padded, fingers well protected, the best boys' mitt in the market, each, $2.25.

738. Men's Goatskin Mitt and Throwing Glove, well padded, each, $1.50.

739. Boys' Mitt and Throwing Glove, padded; good and strong, each, 50c.

Masks.

740. Spaulding's Sun-Protecting Base Ball Mask, each, $4.50.

741. Spaulding's New Patented Neck Protecting Mask, each $3.90.

742. Spaulding's Special League Musk, used by all the leading professional catchers, extra heavy wire, well padded with goat hair, padding faced with best imported dogskin, each, $3.45.

743. Spaulding's Regulation League, Mask, made of heavy wire, well padded and faced with horsehide, warranted first-class in ever___ pect. Weight 2¾ to 3½ lbs., each, $2.95.

Catchers' and Umpires' Breast Protectors.

Nicely made, and well padded and quilted, and are used by nearly all professional catchers and umpires.

744. Chamois and canvass, Wt. 1 lb., each, $2.90.

745. Spaulding's League Body Protector, inflated, $9.75.

746. Spaulding's Amateur Body Protector, $5.75.

Indian Clubs.

Sold in pairs only, and made of the best rock maple, and finely polished. Weight given is the weight on each club. If you order on pair 1 lb. clubs, you get two 1 lb. clubs, etc.

INDIAN CLUBS

No.	Weight		Per pair
747	1	lb.	$0.26
748	1½	lbs.	.30
749	2	lbs.	.35
750	3	lbs.	.50
751	4	lbs.	.66
752	5	lbs.	.80
753	6	lbs.	.90
754	7	lbs.	1.00
755	8	lbs.	1.20

Boxing Gloves.

757

Weight, 3 to 4 pounds, packed for shipment. Our Boxing Gloves are the latest designs and are the best gloves in the world for the money. Average weight, men's sizes, about 7 oz. each.

756. Boxing Gloves, the California patent, padded on end of fingers, side heel pads, dark buff color; weight, each glove, 8 oz.

Per set.................$6.00

728-31

758. Boxing Gloves, new style ends of fingers padded inside as well as out. very best quality with kid finish, $5.75.

759. Boxing Gloves, same style as 758 except black goat finish, quality not as good, but strong and durable, $3.70.

Sporting Goods Department

ALL ORDERS for CARTRIDGES, LOADED and EMPTY SHOT SHELLS and AMMUNITION must be accompanied by cash in full.

ALL ORDERS for GUN IMPLEMENTS, TOOLS, SPORTING GOODS, ETC., must be accompanied by at least ONE-FOURTH of Catalogue price; if to be sent by express, C. O. D.; if to be sent by freight cash in full must accompany order.

WE ALWAYS REFUND ALL MONEY if goods are not perfectly satisfactory.

760. Boxing Gloves, same style as 758 but not as good quality, color white. Per set **$1.95.**

761. Boxing Gloves, same style as No. 758, Better quality, Color black, Per set, **$2.40.**

732-40

762. Boys' sizes; well stuffed white kid, tan colored palms, good size, made of same material and just as well as the men's size. Per set of 4 gloves **$1.87.**

763. Men's sizes, same as 762. Per set of 4 gloves, well made and durable **$2.25.**

764. Men's sizes, well stuffed and extra tan leather, palms and wrists bound with fancy leather, per set, **$2.85.**

765. Men's sizes, same as No. 764, better quality, heel padded. Per set **$3.75.**

766. Same as 734, best quality, heel padded **$4.85.**

767. Kid Gloves, with best tan palms **$4.95.**

768. Finest Kid Gloves with ventilated palm, very best quality. Per set **$5.50.**

769. Same as 768, heel padded, **$5.75.**

770. Chandler's Professional kid Glove, for sparring exhibitions, being small and compactly stuffed, 6, 4 or 2 oz., **$5.50.**

We cannot furnish any better gloves than we quote above, as there are no better ones in the market at any price.

Dumb Bells.

Our Iron Dumb Bells are cast from pure gray iron, and are very much stronger and more durable than those ordinarily sold, which are usually made from scrap iron, tin etc., and are very brittle and break easily. We make them with weights as follows; 1 lb. 2, 3, 4, 5, 6, 8, 10, 12, 14, 15, 20, 25 pounds each. Sold by the pound. Price per lb.. 4c; 50 lbs., 5c; 75 lbs., 6c; 100 lbs., 6c. per lb.

771. Wood Dumb Bells, made of polished maple.

Weight	1 lb.	2 lb.	3 lb.	4 lb
Per pair	30c	40c	55c	70c

Foot Balls.

771½. The Association Foot Ball, genuine, made of best India rubber bladder, with fine leather outside case, hand sewed, laced, round. Postage, about 20c extra.

	Each.
22-inch circumference	$2.00
24-inch circumference	2.45
27-inch circumference	2.68
30-inch circumference	2.90
33-inch circumference	3.90

772. Rugby Foot Ball, oval shape, made of the best India rubber bladder, with outside leather case, hand sewed laced. Best quality.

	Each.
22-inch circumference	$2.00
24-inch circumference	2.50
27-inch circumference	2.65
30-inch circumference	2.93
33-inch circumference	3.90

773. Extra Foot Bladders for either Rugby or Association Foot Balls. In ordering state which kind is wanted.

	Each.
For 22-inch ball, weight 8 oz	$0.57
For 24-inch ball	.69
For 27-inch ball	.73
For 30-inch ball	.76
For 33-inch ball	.79

Rubber Foot Balls.

774. American Round Rubber Foot Ball. By mail, 7 to 12c extra.

No. 1, 6 in. diameter	$0.57
No. 2, 7 in. diameter	.68
No. 3, 8 in. diameter	.79
No. 4, 9 in. diameter	.90
No. 5, 10 in. diameter	1.00
No. 6, 11 in. diameter	1.15

775. Extra keys for foot ball, etc.. 10c.

776. Rubber Foot Ball Inflaters, nickeled tubes for filling up bladders. 40c.

Rubber Foot Balls, Rugby shape, made of heavy rubber, one size only, regulation, No. 5, each **$1.90.**

Foot Ball Inflators.

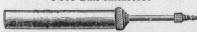

778. Foot Ball Inflaters, solid brass metal, new design and the best. Each 75c. By mail 6c extra.

Prices on Foot Ball Clothing will be furnished on application. Lowest prices guaranteed.

GYMNASIUM GOODS

Improved Striking Bags.

For Physical Culture.

Refines, elevates and ennobles; adds to our courage, zeal and health and thereby to our happiness.

The bag is intended to strengthen the arm, wrists, shoulders, back, loins, and particularly the muscles of the abdomen, and will teach the striker how to deal a blow. It is of inestimable value to everyone, especially to those whose business requires confinement.

779. Canvas Striking Bags, about 14 inches long with rubber bladder inside; good and durable. Each **$2.40.**

780. Leather Striking Bags with rubber bladder inside; good quality. Each **$2.88.**

781. Rubber Bladder for striking bags. Each **$1.40.**

782. Best Quality Striking Bags, leather cover, with rubber bladder inside, strong, durable, lace up tops. Each **$3.95.**

783. Rumsey's Patent Striking Air Bag with cords and screw eyes, complete, ready to set up, weight, 3 lbs. Each **$5.25.**

Horizontal Bars.

Weight, 4½ to 6 lbs.

Made of best quality second growth straight hickory, square ends.

	Each.
784. 4 ft. long	$0.50
4½ ft. long	.60
5 ft. long	.70
5½ ft. long	.95
6 ft. long	1.20

Trapeze Bars.

Weight, 2 to 3½ pounds.

Made of the best second growth hickory. Without ropes.

	Each.
785. 2 ft. Bar, without ropes	$0.45
2½ ft. Bar, without ropes	.48
3 ft. Bar, without ropes	.55
3½ ft. Bar, without ropes	.60
4 ft. Bar, without ropes	.70

We make any length of rope to order, 8 cents per foot.

═INDEX═

Guns, Revolvers and Sporting Goods.

Including all grades and makes of single and double barrel American and imported breech and muzzle loading **Shot Guns, All Standard American Made Rifles, Revolvers of all kinds and makes,** rifle sights, loaded and empty rifle and shot shells, ammunition of all kinds, gun implements and sporting goods of every description on pages **262 to 321**

TRIBUNE JOB PRINTING CO. MINNEAPOLIS, MINN.